# BARRON'S
## THE TRUSTED NAME IN TEST PREP

# AP®
# European History

## PREMIUM 14TH EDITION

Seth A. Roberts, M.A.

*AP Social Studies Teacher*
*Meade High School*
*Fort Meade, Maryland*

## Dedication

To those from whom I have learned the most, my students, my colleagues, my children, and my wife, Michelle.

—Seth A. Roberts

© Copyright 2025, 2024, 2023, 2022, 2020, 2018, 2016, 2014, 2012, 2010, 2008, 2003, 1998, 1994 by Kaplan North America, LLC d/b/a Barron's Educational Series

Published by Kaplan North America, LLC d/b/a Barron's Educational Series
1515 West Cypress Creek Road
Fort Lauderdale, Florida 33309
www.barronseduc.com

ISBN: 978-1-5062-9655-5

10 9 8 7 6 5 4 3 2 1

Kaplan North America, LLC d/b/a Barron's Educational Series print books are available at special quantity discounts to use for sales promotions, employee premiums, or educational purposes. For more information or to purchase books, please call the Simon & Schuster special sales department at 866-506-1949.

# About the Author

Seth Roberts is a fourth-generation educator who taught AP European History for 22 years at four schools. He also served for five years as the Secondary Social Studies Teacher Specialist for Frederick County where he oversaw more than 200 secondary social studies teachers from 2007–2011. He received a Master's in Community and Economic Development from Penn State and also holds an Administrator Certification from McDaniel College, which led to his leadership roles, including principal of a small international school in Taiwan and Director of Teaching and Learning at the International Bilingual School of Hsinchu. Mr. Roberts returned to the AP classroom in America at Meade High School in Fort Meade, Maryland, for the 2022–2023 school year. He was also the director of Model United Nations Operations for the UNESCO Center for Peace from 2004–2017. He has received many accolades for his teaching and coaching, including a distinguished teaching award from Stanford University and the World Scholar's Cup coach of the year in 2017.

Seth has been an adjunct professor of economics at both Frederick Community College and the University of Maryland Baltimore Campus (UMBC). He has two daughters and is devoted to his wife of 27+ years. His passions are economic history and disc golf.

Seth balances the two worlds that he loves, administration and teaching kids. In addition to AP European History, Seth has also taught AP Economics, AP World History, AP Psychology, IB History, and IB Theory of Knowledge as well as many other courses. He was invited to deliver professional development for the Federal Reserve and the Maryland Council for Economic Education as well as the Maryland Council for the Social Studies. He has served on accreditation teams in three nations, leading the International Bilingual School of Hsinchu Science Park and the Hsinchu County American School to full WASC accreditation. Seth also performed as an evaluator for Middle States accreditation visits.

Seth is a proud nerd. He has been the author of the Barron's *AP European History* since 2006. He is a lifelong learner devoted to educating the next generation so we can continue to make this small planet we share a little better to live on.

# Table of Contents

## PART 3: PRACTICE EXAMS

Visit Barron's Online Learning Hub for Time Period Practice Assessments plus more full-length practice tests

# How to Use This Book

This book is designed primarily to prepare you for the AP European History exam. It provides systematic methods for studying history; a guide to the AP European History exam; review chapters, including sample and practice questions on the various periods of European history; and two complete practice AP exams with answers plus three more online.

This book can be used as a supplement to classwork and study material. It can also be used as a review book to help you refresh your memory on what you learned throughout the year. However you choose to use the book, creating a study plan to suit your needs is simple and easy.

## Review and Practice

Beginning on page 3 with Systematic Methods for Studying History, you will first be introduced to the specific historical skills required by the AP European History Curriculum Framework. These include:

- How to analyze historical developments and processes
- How to analyze primary and secondary sources of historical evidence
- How to analyze claims, evidence, and reasoning within primary and secondary sources
- How to analyze the broader historical events, developments, or processes related to specific historical developments or processes
- How to analyze patterns and connections between and among historical developments and processes
- How to craft historical arguments and use historical evidence to support them

In addition, this book explains how to frame the big picture; how to read, take notes, and highlight; and how to connect events throughout history using the first four skill sets above and their subsets. These skills are all essential for helping you understand history, make sense of it, and retain and interconnect the most relevant bits of information needed to excel on the exam.

The next part of the book is "A Guide to the AP European History Exam" on page 14. Here the basics of the exam are explained. These include:

- The exam's duration (including the duration of each section)
- The number of questions and the types of questions in each section
- The subject matter
- The historical time span
- Sample questions
- Hints on how to approach questions

Knowing what to expect on test day will reduce any test anxiety you may have, thereby allowing you to perform your best.

Part two of this book consists of 12 chapters that review the major historical periods covered on the exam. It also includes sample multiple-choice questions and answers as well as practice thematic essays. The AP European History Curriculum Framework guides the organization of this book as it does the course. The course is divided into four time periods. These time periods reflect the themes of the course that are explained in the AP European History Curriculum Framework. This book is organized into nine units that are further divided into a total of 12 chapters that reflect the AP European History Curriculum Framework and thousands of years of historical inquiry. These chapters are organized into the four historical periods that are standard for the course. The historical periods are divided as follows:

Period 1: c. 1450 to c. 1648

Period 2: c. 1649 to c. 1815

Period 3: c. 1815 to c. 1914

Period 4: c. 1914 to the present

The AP European History course also revolves around seven themes that you are expected to explore as you gain an understanding of each period over the diverse geography of Europe:

1. Interaction of Europe and the World
2. Economic and Commercial Developments
3. Cultural and Intellectual Developments
4. States and Other Institutions of Power
5. Social Organization and Development
6. National and European Identity
7. Technological and Scientific Innovation

The themes are explored both within the text and through the sample multiple-choice and essay questions provided for each chapter and in the assessment created for each time period, which can be found on the Barron's Online Learning Hub.

## Practice Tests

Finally, part three of this book includes two practice AP exams with multiple-choice questions, thematic essays, and document-based questions with suggested answers. Take and score the practice tests in the book. Examine the questions you missed. Look for any connections that can tell you what areas you need to concentrate on when preparing for the AP exam.

## Online Practice

In addition to the two practice tests within this book, there are also three full-length online practice exams. You may take these exams in practice (untimed) mode or in timed mode. All questions include answer explanations.

## To the Teacher

This book can be used as a classroom aid. The various review chapters can be used as yearlong supplements to sum up or reinforce particular teaching units and homework assignments. The historical review section of each chapter will help your students make valid, well-supported historical arguments within and across the four time periods. The sample and practice long essay questions (LEQs), document-based questions (DBQs), short-answer questions (SAQs), and multiple-choice questions (MCQs) will reinforce the learning. Part two, the review section, can be used near the end of the year to pull the course work together and to prepare students for the AP exam. It's often helpful for students to study part one at the beginning of the course to help them study history and to give them an idea of what the AP exam will be like. Knowing what they will face is both a motivator and a method of organizing the course's information.

## To the Student

This book can be used independently of a course in European history. It can also be used along with assigned materials to sum up, pull together, clarify, and review. Start using this book at the beginning of the year and read part one right away. Reading part one will help you study better both in and out of class. It will also give you an idea of what's ahead if you decide to take the AP exam. Review the appropriate chapters in part two right before beginning each topic in class to "frame the picture" and to help fit everything into place. Instead, you can go to the appropriate chapter after studying that unit in class in order to pull together all the information. In order to use the book as review and practice for the exam, don't wait until late April or May to start. Instead of getting nervous and wasting energy on test anxiety, put time aside in late March or early April to study the review chapters and to do the sample questions on content you have already covered in class and in homework. Save the practice tests for late April or early May. Then use these tests to check your progress. Keep practicing the skills that will help you earn a 5 on test day.

# BARRON'S ESSENTIAL 5

As you review the content in this book to work toward earning that 5 on your AP European History Exam, here are five things that you MUST know above everything else:

**Know the important European dynasties and rulers, both autocratic and democratic.** This is a huge subject on the AP exam! Specific multiple-choice questions almost always ask about the most important rulers and ruling families and about how their power and decisions have reached through the ages to today.

- Know the Habsburgs, Romanovs, Valois, Bourbons, Hohenzollerns, Tudors, Stuarts, and Napoleon.

- Study England and the Netherlands as the first nations to move toward democratic principles.

- Compare revolutions and the rise of democracy in different nations.

- Examine the important rulers: monarchical, dictatorial, and democratic.

- Know the styles of each ruler and the external situations that affected how he or she ruled so that you can make connections within and across the four required time periods.

**Know the thematic learning objectives that are required by the College Board and tested on the AP exam.** You should consider seven themes while reading through this guide. Please consider each of the following themes separately and how they interact.

- Interaction of Europe and the world

- Economic and commercial development

- Cultural and intellectual development

- States and other institutions of power

- Social organizations and development

- National and European identity

- Technological and scientific innovation

- Examine this in more detail on pages 16–18

**3**

**Practice preparing for the document-based question (DBQ):** The DBQ is a hugely important factor in your success on the AP exam. In the weeks leading up to the test, practice at least a few complete DBQ responses. You won't know what the DBQ question is going to be. However, you will need to concentrate on the thoroughness of your response and on your ability to demonstrate point of view in the documents. You will also need to provide the amount of detail typical of high-scoring responses. Have your teacher or classmates help with this.

- Practice your point-of-view commentary on document authors.

- Show your understanding of the author's purpose, historical context, and audience.

- Remember to bring in outside information not given in the documents.

- Answer the question with a strong thesis and good support. Stay on track, and do not go off on a tangent.

---

**4**

**Be sure to know the important figures and movements in the 20th century.** This is essentially a modern-history course. Knowing the importance of many figures of the last century is key to success on the exam. Figures such as Kaiser Wilhelm II, Otto von Bismarck (not a 20th-century figure himself, but his machinations toward the end of the 19th century had a significant effect on the 20th century), Winston Churchill, Mohandas Gandhi, Margaret Thatcher, Adolf Hitler, Vladimir Lenin, and Mikhail Gorbachev should be known. Also, movements such as the peace movement, feminism, universal suffrage, fascism, communism, détente, decolonization, and *glasnost* should be evaluated.

- The exam is focusing more and more on recent history.

- The wars of the 20th century are great fodder for questions.

- The fights for minority rights are also a big topic for multiple-choice questions.

---

**5**

**Know the framework.** You need to be familiar with how you will be assessed on the exam. The College Board has created an AP European History Curriculum Framework explaining the course. It is available at *https:// apcentral.collegeboard.org/pdf/ap-european-history-course-and-exam-description-0.pdf?course=ap-european-history*. This framework has specific themes and, more importantly, specific learning objectives that are tied to every AP question. Read the framework to know what the College Board will ask.

# PART 1
# Introduction

# All About the Exam

## Systematic Methods for Studying History

What follows are some time-tested methods for studying history. These basic skills will aid you in becoming an involved student in any history course. These suggestions will help you with homework, supplementary reading, and preparation for the AP European History exam. After discussing the basic skills, this book examines the historical thinking skills expected of all AP history students.

## How to Recognize the Logical Order of History Materials

Most history readings, especially texts, are organized logically; some examples follow:

**FACTS SUPPORT A THEME:** The Magna Carta, the Puritan Revolution, and the personalities involved help one trace the development of constitutional government in England.

**GREAT EVENTS DEFINE AN ERA:** The French Revolution colored the political, social, cultural, and diplomatic life of Europe for over 100 years after it happened.

**CAUSE-EFFECT RELATIONSHIPS ARE ASCERTAINED:** The outbreak of the First World War in August 1914 was caused by long-term trends, such as militarism, nationalism, and imperialism, which stretched back decades into the 19th century.

**THE INFLUENCE OF INDIVIDUALS ON AN AGE IS IDENTIFIED:** The totalitarian dictatorships of Hitler and Stalin affected the entire planet before and long after the Second World War.

In reading history materials, the object is to focus on this inherent logical order. This can be done by *prereading* and by *framing the big picture*.

## How to Preread

Before tackling the text itself, be sure to skim the chapter by reading each of the following in order:

- The chapter heading
- The introductory paragraph
- Focus questions at the beginning of the chapter
- Subheadings
- The concluding paragraph
- Review questions at chapter's end
- **Bold** print or *italics* within the text

It is better to concentrate on reading at this point rather than on trying to take notes.

## How to Frame the Big Picture

During both the prereading and the reading of the text, pose the following questions as a natural way of keeping your mind's eye on the main story and on the logical order of the material:

- What is the theme of the chapter? (What is the chapter about? What is the author trying to prove? How does it fit into the themes elucidated by the *AP European History Curriculum Framework*?)
- What are the main events? (What happened, and what caused those events?)
- Who are the principal personalities? (Who did what, and why?)
- What are the important results? (Did new ideas, significant changes, and/or power shifts occur? Did one thing end and another begin?)

**Remember: Don't lose the forest for the trees.** These essays are often about putting pieces of little pictures together to make one bigger picture that fully answers the question.

## How to Read the Text

Once you have preread the material and framed the big picture, you are ready to attack the text itself. Difficult material deserves a "straight read" before you try to highlight, underline, or take notes. Most readings, though, allow you to do both simultaneously as long as you have preread the information.

## Sample Reading with Underlining, Accompanying Notes, Brief Outline

### Underlined Passage

Early 19th-century <u>industrialization</u> in England depended upon <u>steam</u> engines made of iron and fueled by coal. Steam-powered <u>textile mills</u> created a <u>factory economy</u> and a new <u>working</u> class. Steam-powered railway <u>trains</u> moved people and products speedily over great distances, <u>concentrating</u> <u>populations</u> into expanded cities and linking the sources of raw materials with the centers of manufacturing. Functional <u>new architectural</u> designs—using structural steel—reflected the practical needs of the new society. <u>Class</u> conflict, brought on by disparities of wealth, extremes of poverty, and the unexpected difficulties of industrialization, raged throughout most of the century.

### Notes

Industrialization, 19th-century England
Coal-fueled, iron steam engines powered textile mills = factory
    economy + new working class
Speedy steam-powered railroads = expanded cities; linked raw
    materials + factories
New steel architecture; class conflict because of income
    differences & effects of industrialization

### Brief Outline

19th-Century Industrialization in England
    I.   Steam power, the essential element
        A.   Iron engines fueled by coal
        B.   Textile factories, new working class
        C.   RRs move masses: people, products
   II.   Effects of industrialization
        A.   Expanded cities
        B.   New architecture
        C.   Class conflict: disparities of wealth

## SUMMARY FOR HOW TO READ HISTORY MATERIAL

1. *Preread:* Skim the chapter *heading, first and last paragraphs,* and *subheadings.*
2. *Focus* on the logical order of the reading—*themes, events, cause-effect relationships, personalities*—by *framing the big picture.*

   What is the chapter's theme?

   What are the main events, causes, personalities, results?
3. *Read* the text; highlight or take notes; outline.
4. Be able to answer the questions you posed while framing the big picture and any review questions in the text.

## Centuries and Chronology

A consistent problem in studying history is the failure to appreciate that significant trends are often concurrent, that influential people are sometimes contemporaries. For instance, the Reformation and the Age of Exploration shared the 16th century. The personification of absolutism, Louis XIV, reigned while the greatest scientist of the Enlightenment, Isaac Newton, formulated his theories of gravitation.

An excellent method for *connecting* events, trends, and personalities of history is to *identify their century or centuries.* History is not a series of separate strands but, rather, a fabric of causes, effects, and interwoven influences. Below is an abbreviated list of major figures and events of the centuries covered by the exam:

**15TH CENTURY (1401–1500)** The Renaissance; the fall of Constantinople to the Ottoman Turks; the voyages of Portuguese explorers and Columbus. Contemporaries: Leonardo da Vinci, Suleiman the Magnificent, Gutenberg, Henry the Navigator.

**16TH CENTURY (1501–1600)** The Reformation and Catholic and Counter-Reformations; the Age of Exploration; the growth of national monarchies. Contemporaries: Luther, Henry VIII, Loyola, Holy Roman Emperor Charles V, Copernicus, Elizabeth I, Magellan, Cabral, da Gama, Philip II.

**17TH CENTURY (1601–1700)** The Age of Colonization; the commercial revolution and the rise of capitalism; the rise of modern science; the Thirty Years' War; the Age of Absolutism and the rise of constitutionalism. Contemporaries: Descartes, Galileo, Newton, the Stuart kings and Cromwell, Locke, Richelieu, Drake, Mazarin, the Romanovs, Louis XIV.

**18TH CENTURY (1701–1800)** The growth of capitalism; the Age of Enlightenment and of Reason; the Age of Benevolent Despotism and of Revolution. Contemporaries: Adam Smith, Voltaire, Rousseau, Frederick the Great, Mary Wollstonecraft, Maria Theresa, Catherine the Great, Louis XVI, George III, Robespierre, George Washington.

**19TH CENTURY (1801–1900)** The Age of Napoleon; the Age of Metternich; the Age of Romanticism; the Age of Nationalism and Unification; the age of "-isms"; the Age of Imperialism; the Age of Progress; Women's Suffrage; Chartism. Contemporaries: Talleyrand, Metternich, Wordsworth, Goethe, Bismarck, Cavour, Marx, Darwin, Cecil Rhodes, Teddy Roosevelt, Gregor Mendel, Louis Pasteur.

**20TH CENTURY (1901–2000)** The Age of Violence; the Age of Technology; the Nuclear Age; the Age of Information; the Age of Anxiety; the Age of Totalitarianism; the Cold War; the European Union; the Age of Democracy. Contemporaries: Kaiser Wilhelm II, Clemenceau, Lenin, Wilson, Stalin, Hitler, Gandhi, Churchill, Freud, Einstein, Franklin Roosevelt, Hirohito, Mao, Adenauer, de Gaulle, Thatcher, Gorbachev, Reagan, Yeltsin, Walesa, Havel.

**TIP**

When studying a historical event, personality, or trend, do the following:

1. Determine its century (or centuries).
2. Make an open-ended chart of the centuries. Make a habit of placing pertinent events, people, and trends in the appropriate time frame on the chart.

# Historical Skills Used in All AP History Exams

The writers of the AP History exam came together and decided upon a common set of skills that all AP History students should possess. These skills come directly from the *AP European History Curriculum Framework*. These skills have been divided into two categories:

    I. AP historical thinking skills

    II. AP History reasoning processes

The first category, AP historical thinking skills, focuses more on the skills historians use to construct and test historical arguments. The second category of skills, AP History reasoning processes, focuses more on mental habits often referred to as "thinking historically." Within each skill type are subsets that you should master. These skills are in many ways similar to the skills required by the Social Studies C-3 framework that was adopted nationally for the subject area. These are in some ways an extension of the skills that all students should be practicing nationally. The skills are divided as follows:

    I. AP historical thinking skills

        1. Analyze historical developments and processes

        2. Analyze primary and secondary sources of historical evidence

        3. Analyze claims, evidence, and reasoning within primary and secondary sources

        4. Analyze the broader historical events, developments, or processes related to specific historical developments or processes

        5. Analyze patterns and connections between and among historical developments and processes

        6. Develop an argument

    II. Reasoning processes

        1. Contextualization (also seen in 4 and 5 in previous list)

        2. Comparison

        3. Causation

        4. Continuity and change over time (CCOT)

# AP History Disciplinary Practices

## Practice 1: Analyzing Historical Evidence

To develop and support an argument, you need to be able to examine multiple pieces of evidence in concert with each other, noting contradictions, corroborations, and other relationships among sources. It involves the capacity to extract useful information, make supportable inferences, and draw appropriate conclusions from historical evidence. Simultaneously, developing and supporting an argument also involves noting the context in which the evidence was produced and used, recognizing its limitations and assessing the points of view it reflects. This skill has been further divided into two categories:

    **1.** Analyzing primary sources

    **2.** Analyzing secondary sources

### Analyzing Primary Sources

This practice requires five specific traits. According to the College Board, you must be able to:

    **1.** Describe historically relevant information and/or arguments within a source.

    **2.** Explain how a source provides information about the broader historical setting within which it was created.

    **3.** Explain how a source's point of view, purpose, historical situation, and/or audience might affect that source's meaning.

4. Explain the historical significance of a source's point of view, purpose, historical situation, and/or audience.

5. Evaluate a primary source's credibility and/or limitations.

### Analyzing Secondary Sources

This practice requires six specific traits. According to the College Board, you must be able to do the following:

1. Describe the claim or argument of a secondary source as well as the evidence used.
2. Describe a pattern or trend in quantitative data in non-text-based sources.
3. Explain how a historian's claim or argument is supported with evidence.
4. Explain how a historian's context influences a claim or argument.
5. Analyze patterns and trends in quantitative data in non-text-based sources.
6. Evaluate the effectiveness of a historical claim or argument.

**REMEMBER** that using historical evidence properly shows many different historical skills in use at the same time. Almost none of the other skills will be demonstrated if you do not use evidence well.

**To master analyzing historical evidence, you must be able to do the following:**

- Evaluate evidence to explain its relevance to a claim or thesis, providing clear and consistent links between the evidence and the argument.
  - Show that you understand the background of historical evidence by paying special attention to bias in evidence due to the author's point of view or historical conditions.
  - Evaluate evidence used for validity and reliability.

- Relate diverse historical evidence in a cohesive way to illustrate contradiction, corroboration, qualification, and other types of historical relationships in developing an argument.
  - Show that you know what evidence is relevant by using it creatively and clearly to illustrate the support for or weakness of an argument and to find deeper relationships in historical events and outcomes.
  - This is related to argumentation in that you must use the evidence to make strong, thorough, clear, and concise arguments that are clearly and thoroughly supported with evidence.

## Practice 2: Argument Development

You need to be able to create an argument and support it using relevant historical evidence. Creating a historical argument includes defining and framing a question about the past and then formulating a claim or an argument about that question, often in the form of a thesis. A persuasive historical argument requires a precise and defensible thesis or claim supported by rigorous analysis of relevant and diverse historical evidence. The argument and evidence used should be framed around the application of a specific historical thinking skill (e.g., comparison, causation, or patterns of continuity and change over time). Additionally, argumentation involves the capacity to examine multiple pieces of evidence in concert with each other, noting contradictions, corroborations, and other relationships among sources to develop and support an argument.

This practice requires four specific traits. According to the College Board, you must be able to do the following:

1. Make a historically defensible claim in the form of an evaluative thesis.
2. Support an argument using specific and relevant evidence.
3. Use historical reasoning to explain relationships among pieces of historical evidence.
4. Consider ways that diverse or alternative evidence could be used to corroborate, qualify, or modify an argument.

**REMEMBER** that historical argumentation development is the primary skill for the long essay questions (LEQs), the short-answer questions (SAQs), and the document-based questions (DBQs). AP readers must look for sophisticated arguments that go beyond the traditional interpretations of evidence and show nuanced interpretations supported by specific facts.

**To master historical argument development, you must be able to do the following:**

- Articulate a defensible claim about the past in the form of a clear and compelling thesis that evaluates the relative importance of multiple factors and recognizes disparate, diverse, or contradictory evidence or perspectives.
  - Use the themes of the course to help structure arguments.
  - Write a strong thesis that *fully* answers the question and does not just rearrange the words in the question.
  - Get past traditional historical arguments and be able to argue various viewpoints about others' interpretations of history.
  - Use factual evidence cleverly and remember to interpret it for the reader.
  - Use multiple pieces of evidence (usually three or more) to prove a point.
  - Be able to explain why other interpretations of history have errors.
  - Use only relevant evidence to prevent tangents in your essays.

## Historical Thinking Skills

The College Board has further broken down the history disciplinary practices into six historical thinking skills. The sixth skill of argumentation has already been explained very well in the previous section, Practice 2: Argument Development. The other discrete skills can all be lumped into the disciplinary practice of analyzing historical evidence. The six discrete skills are the following:

1. Analyze historical developments and processes. Several types of questions refer to this skill:
   - Identify and describe a historical concept, development, or process.
   - Identify and describe a historical concept, development, or process illustrated by historical evidence.
   - Explain a historical concept, development, or process.
   - Explain a historical concept, development, or process illustrated by historical evidence.

2. Analyze primary and secondary sources of historical evidence (sourcing and situation). Several types of questions refer to this skill:
   - Identify and describe a source's point of view, purpose, historical situation, and/or audience.
   - Explain how primary source evidence provides information about the broader historical context within which that evidence was created.
   - Explain how the point of view, purpose, historical situation, and/or audience of a source might affect its interpretation.
   - Explain the relative historical significance of a source's point of view, purpose, historical situation, and/or audience.

3. Analyze claims, evidence, and reasoning within primary and secondary sources (source claims and evidence). Several types of questions refer to this skill:
   - Identify and describe a claim or an argument in a text-based or non-text-based source.
   - Identify the evidence used in a source to support an argument.
   - Describe a pattern or trend in quantitative data in a non-text-based source.
   - Compare the arguments or main ideas of two sources.
   - Identify claims or evidence that support, modify, or refute a source's argument.
   - Explain the limitations of a source's argument.

4. Analyze the broader historical events, developments, or processes related to historical developments or processes (contextualization). Several types of questions refer to this skill:

- Identify and describe a historical context for a specific historical development or process.
- Identify and describe a historical context for a specific historical development or process illustrated by historical evidence.
- Explain how a specific historical development or process is situated within a broader historical context.
- Explain how a specific historical development or process illustrated by historical evidence is situated within a broader historical context.

5. Analyze patterns and connections between and among historical developments and practices (making connections). Several types of questions refer to this skill:
   - Identify and describe patterns among or connections between historical developments and processes.
   - Identify and describe patterns among or connections between historical developments and processes illustrated in historical evidence.
   - Explain how a historical development or process relates to another historical development or process.
   - Explain how a historical development or process illustrated in historical evidence relates to another historical development or process.

6. Develop an argument (Disciplinary Practice 2). Several types of questions refer to this skill:
   - Make a historically defensible claim.
   - Support an argument using specific and relevant evidence.
   - Describe specific examples of historically relevant evidence.
   - Explain how specific examples of historically relevant evidence support an argument.
   - Use historical reasoning to explain relationships among pieces of historical evidence.
   - Corroborate, qualify, or modify an argument using diverse and alternative evidence in order to develop a complex argument.
   - Explain the nuance of an issue by analyzing multiple variables.
   - Explain relevant and insightful connections within and across periods.
   - Explain the relative historical significance of a source's credibility and limitations.
   - Explain how or why a historical claim or argument is or is not effective.

# AP History Reasoning Skills

## Historical Reasoning Skill 1: Contextualization

You must display the ability to connect historical events and processes to specific circumstances of time and place as well as broader regional, national, or global processes.

**To master contextualization, you must be able to do the following:**

- Describe an accurate historical context for a specific historical development or process.
- Explain how a relevant context influenced a specific historical development or process.
- Use context to explain the relative historical significance of a specific historical development or process.
  - When taken together, the above skills mean that you should situate historical events, developments, or processes within the broader regional, national, or global context in which they occurred in order to draw conclusions about their relative significance.
  - Contextualization relates to comparison because it allows you to place events in context.
    - One example would be asking you to explain two different accounts of *Kristallnacht* in Germany: one that was written by a Nazi at the time of the event and one that was written by a Jewish person in the 1970s.
  - Often contextualization is about finding the many ways a fact, figure, event, or movement fits into the other things going on at the time.

○ This is about repeating themes in history, such as prosperity and poverty, and being able to understand how the six themes of the *AP European History Curriculum Framework* interact to allow you to create a vivid picture of Europe in the past. These themes will be investigated in detail later, but they are:

- Interaction of Europe and the World
- Poverty and Prosperity
- Objective Knowledge and Subjective Visions
- States and Other Institutions of Power
- Individual and Society
- National and European Identity

## Historical Reasoning Skill 2: Comparison

You need to display the abilities to identify, compare, and evaluate multiple perspectives about a given historical event in order to draw conclusions about that event. You must also be able to describe, compare, and evaluate multiple historical developments within one society, one or more developments across or between different societies, and developments with various chronological and geographical contexts. Comparisons help historians understand which factors and characteristics are common and which are different when comparing events or conditions in different places or times. You also need the ability to identify, compare, and evaluate multiple perspectives on a given historical experience.

**To master comparison, you must be able to do the following:**

- Describe similarities and/or differences between different historical developments or processes.
- Explain relevant similarities and/or differences between specific historical developments and processes.
- Explain the relative historical significance of similarities and/or differences between specific historical developments and processes.
- Compare different historical individuals, events, developments, and/or processes, analyzing both similarities and differences in order to draw historically valid conclusions.
  ○ For example, what were the similarities and differences among the Dutch, English, and French experiences in gaining constitutional governments?
  ○ To accomplish this, you must cite specific facts that support your assertions and be sure to present nuanced arguments that show different levels of similarity and difference.
- Make comparisons across different time periods, across different geographical locations, and between different historical events or developments within the same time period and/or geographical location.
  ○ For example, how would a Marxist historian and a political historian differ in their perspectives about the French Revolution?
  ○ Much of studying history is about understanding different perspectives, such as how a peasant and a lord would view enclosure differently.

## Historical Reasoning Skill 3: Historical Causation

To be successful, you need to be able to identify, analyze, and evaluate the relationships among historical causes and effects, distinguishing between those that are long-term and those that are proximate. Historical thinking also involves the ability to distinguish between causation and correlation. (*This is very difficult; correlations are easier to prove than causations. It is best to examine relationships and any data fully to gather both empirical and anecdotal evidence when making claims of causation.*) Historical causation also involves an awareness of contingency, the way that historical events result from a complex variety of factors that come together in unpredictable ways and often have unanticipated consequences.

Debates among historians about the long-term causes of World War I and how the previous decades led to the war provide a good example of the problems of making claims of causation and supporting those claims with strong historical evidence.

**REMEMBER** that to get full credit for this skill, you can often do the following. State that a correlation is discovered but that not enough evidence is available to make a full claim of causation. Provided that you cite the correct facts, this is usually a sophisticated enough argument to earn full credit for this skill.

**To master causation, you must be able to do the following:**

- Explain long- and/or short-term causes and/or effects of a historical event, development, or process.
- Describe causes and/or effects of a specific historical development or process.
- Explain the relationship between causes and effects of a specific historical development or process.
- Explain the difference between primary and secondary causes and between long- and short-term effects.
- Evaluate the relative significance of different causes and/or effects on historical events or processes, distinguishing between causation and correlation and showing an awareness of historical contingency.
- Explain the relative historical significance of different causes and/or effects.

## Historical Reasoning Skill 4: Patterns of Continuity and Change Over Time

You must be able to recognize, analyze, and evaluate the dynamics of historical continuity and change over time periods of varying length. You must also have the ability to relate these patterns to larger historical processes or themes. The College Board *loves* this type of question and has for years. It is a great skill to be able to say that certain factors did not change while other factors did change over time in the following ways. The key to this skill is to acknowledge that most historical processes are uneven and affect different groups of the population at different rates based on class, gender, geography, and other factors.

**To master patterns of continuity and change over time, you must be able to do the following:**

- Identify patterns of continuity and change over time, and explain the significance of such patterns.
  - One example would be an explanation of parenting from the 18th to the 20th centuries. Much changed, such as parental involvement, patterns of work, and levels of education. However, much did not change, such as parents always being in charge. The changes affected how people interacted with each other at work and socially.
- Explain the relative historical significance of specific historical developments in relation to a larger pattern of continuity and/or change.
- Explain how patterns of continuity and change over time relate to larger historical processes or themes.
  - For example, changes in parental expectations in the 20th century coincided with improved standards of living and opportunities for higher education.

# Additional Skills Not Required by the College Board

The following skills are no longer required as discrete skills for the AP History courses, but they will add quite a lot to your writing. You are encouraged to understand and utilize these skills in order to master the AP exam.

## Additional Skill 1: Periodization

You must display the abilities to describe, analyze, and evaluate different ways that historians divide history into discrete and definable periods. Historians construct and debate different, sometimes competing, models of periodization. The choice of specific turning points or starting and ending dates might accord a higher value to one narrative, region, or group than to another. To accomplish this periodization, historians identify turning points, such as the Thirty Years' War or the invention of the steam engine. Historians also recognize that the choice of specific dates accords a higher value to one narrative, region, or group than to another narrative, region, or group. Therefore, historical thinking involves being aware of how the circumstances and contexts of a historian's work might shape that individual's choices about periodization.

**To master periodization, you must be able to do the following:**

- Explain ways that historical events and processes can be organized into discrete, different, and definable historical periods.
  - This is about finding turning points, which are best defined as moments when several significant changes occurred that had important long-term consequences or as key events that created periods.
  - One example would be the introduction of the steam engine, which revolutionized life in Europe as it spread through the Continent. The steam engine led to industrialization that caused drastic political, social, economic, and military changes.
  - Often this is about the terms used by historians to describe eras, such as the Age of Enlightenment, the Industrial Revolution, or the Age of Imperialism.
  - Students can always use centuries for periodization if they cannot think of any other way to divide a topic.
- Evaluate whether a particular event or date could or could not be a turning point between different, definable historical periods when considered in terms of particular historical evidence.
- Analyze and evaluate different and/or competing models of periodization.
  - Often you will be asked to argue for or against a particular perspective on history, such as whether World War II began in 1933 or 1937 rather than the traditional 1939.

## Additional Skill 2: Synthesis

To be successful using synthesis, you need to be able to develop an understanding of the past by making meaningful and persuasive historical and/or cross-disciplinary connections between a given historical issue and other historical contexts, periods, themes, or disciplines. Additionally, synthesis may involve applying insights about the past to other historical contexts or circumstances, including the present.

**REMEMBER** that synthesis is all about creating your own ideas. You need to show that you have the ability to take many different pieces of evidence learned throughout the course and put them together into a cohesive essay or short answer to display a full understanding of what was asked. The key is often to stay focused and prevent tangents.

**To master synthesis, you must be able to do the following:**

- Make connections between a given historical issue and related developments in a different historical context, geographical area, period, or era, including the present.
- Make connections between different course themes and/or approaches to history (such as political, economic, social, cultural, or intellectual) for a given historical issue.
- Apply insights about the past to other historical contexts or circumstances, including the present.
  - This is the highest level of historical analysis.
  - Draw conclusions, make claims, and support them with evidence that is clear and nuanced.

## Additional Skill 3: Interpretation

To be successful at interpretation, you need to be able to describe, analyze, and evaluate the different ways historians interpret the past. This includes understanding the various types of questions historians ask. It also requires you to consider how the circumstances and contexts in which individual historians work and write shape those historians' interpretations of past events and historical evidence. Historical interpretation requires analyzing evidence, reasoning, contexts, and points of view found in both primary and secondary sources.

**REMEMBER** that creating interpretation is somewhat open-ended *as long as* assertions are **SUPPORTED** with **SPECIFIC EVIDENCE**.

**To master historical interpretation, you must be able to do the following:**

- Analyze diverse historical interpretations.
  - This goes back to argumentation. Students must be able to look at multiple interpretations of the same events or period and analyze them for validity and relevance as well as for reliability.
  - Show a mastery of traditional historical arguments and be able to argue various viewpoints about others' interpretation of history.
- Analyze a historian's argument. Explain how the argument has been supported through the analysis of relevant historical evidence. Evaluate the argument's effectiveness.
  - Demonstrate an understanding of what historians believe changes over time and place; those historians also have biases that must be understood and interpreted as a part of their work.
  - This is about analyzing the evidence as support for the historical argument. So be certain to interpret the evidence clearly as it relates to the argument.

## Additional Skill 4: Analyzing Evidence Through Content and Sourcing

To be successful at this skill, you need to be able to describe, select, and evaluate relevant evidence about the past from diverse sources. These sources include written documents, works of art, archaeological artifacts, oral traditions, and other primary sources. You must also be able to draw conclusions about the relevance of this evidence to different historical issues. A historical analysis of sources focuses on the interplay between the content of a source and the authorship, point of view, purpose, audience, and format or medium of that source. This analysis assesses the usefulness, reliability, and limitations of the source as historical evidence. This is one of the tougher skills that the AP European History exam requires of you. It demands that you use higher-level thinking to evaluate the different levels of support for a thesis that each piece of evidence presented displays. The key is for you to illustrate the connections between evidence and the thesis to prove or disprove the thesis clearly.

**To master historical interpretation, you must be able to do the following:**

- Explain the relevance of the author's point of view, author's purpose, audience, format or medium, and/or historical context, as well as the interaction among these features, to demonstrate an understanding of the significance of a primary source.
  - This is the true work of the historian and, as such, it is the true test of a history student.
  - You will always display this skill on the DBQ as well as in other parts of the exam.
  - Point of view and audience are key factors in interpreting any source.
  - The trick here is to present the evidence and then evaluate it relative to the thesis. You must also avoid tangents.
  - Be sure to explain clearly how the evidence supports or contradicts the thesis.
- Evaluate the usefulness, reliability, and/or limitations of a primary source in answering particular historical questions.
  - You will always display this skill on the DBQ as well as in other parts of the exam.
  - Finding flaws in the reliability or limitations in the usefulness of a source is a good way to impress those who score the exam.

# A Guide to the AP European History Exam

## AP European History Goes Fully Digital

May of 2025 saw the AP European History transition into a digital exam format. It will be administered moving forward fully on the College Board Bluebook™ app. It must be installed on a school-owned device, and your teacher and AP coordinator should give you clear instructions on whether or not you need to bring a laptop to the exam on exam day.

Students can practice using the Bluebook app by going to *https://bluebook.collegeboard.org/students* and downloading the app to become familiar with it and how it functions. This will be very different for writing short-answer questions (SAQs), document-based questions (DBQs), and long essay questions (LEQs) than it has been to write them on paper. Students will need to practice viewing and marking both documents and questions of all types from multiple choice to the LEQ and DBQ in the Bluebook app.

The College Board is working to make the look of AP Classroom more consistent with Bluebook™, so please encourage your teacher to assign progress checks, quizzes, and all types of free-response questions via AP Classroom so that familiarizing yourself with the format of the digital test is not a part of what you are being assessed on when test day arrives. The College Board also created a great video with digital testing tips that may be a good idea to check out at *https://apcentral.collegeboard.org/exam-administration-ordering-scores/digital-ap-exams*.

While the format has become digital, the skills tested (other than typing), the types of questions asked, and the content that students are responsible for understanding remain unchanged.

**Section 1: 95 minutes**

**Part A**

- *Multiple-Choice Questions:* 50–55 questions are asked in groups of 2–5 questions based on a common stimulus.
  - 1 point per correct question is awarded for 55 points total
  - Analysis of primary and secondary texts, images, graphs, and maps
  - 55 minutes
  - 40% of the exam

**Part B**

- *Short-Answer Questions:* Three out of four questions with three tasks per question must be answered.
  - Answer two required questions, and choose between two other questions
  - 3 points per question
  - 40 minutes
  - 20% of the exam

**Section 2: 100 minutes (15-minute reading period included in the 100 minutes)**

**Part A**

- *Document-Based Question:* Used to assess your mastery of analyzing written, visual, and quantitative sources as historical evidence and using that evidence to develop an argument supported by that analysis.
  - Answer one question—55 minutes
  - Five to seven documents
  - Question covers years 1600–2001
  - 60 minutes
  - 25% of the exam

**Part B**

- *Long Essay Question:* You must develop an argument and support it with an analysis of specific, relevant historical evidence of your choosing.
- You choose **one** of three provided essay questions.
  - One choice from period 1, one from periods 2–3, and one from periods 3–4
  - 40 minutes
  - 15% of the exam

## Themes

As of 2020, this course has seven specific themes. These themes are required by the College Board and drive instruction throughout each of the four time periods also outlined in the *AP European History Curriculum Framework*. Each of these themes can be observed in each time period. The seven themes are as follows:

1. Interaction of Europe and the World
2. Economic and Commercial Developments
3. Cultural and Intellectual Developments
4. States and Other Institutions of Power
5. Social Organization and Development
6. National and European Identity
7. Technological and Scientific Innovation

**TIP**

The roles of women in history are significant because they relate to both economic-social and cultural-intellectual aspects of historical study. Therefore, exam questions are often related to this topic.

These themes were designed to foster your understanding of major historical issues and developments, helping you to recognize trends and processes that have emerged over centuries. Each theme is tied to specific learning objectives for each time period. Each theme has overarching questions that you should be able to tackle on exam day. To understand fully the specific learning objectives that *every* question on the AP exam is tied to, it is strongly recommended that you download and print the AP European History Course Outline and Exam Description available online at *https://apcentral.collegeboard.org/pdf/ap-european-history-course-and-exam-description-0.pdf?course=ap-european-history*.

The AP European History Course Outline and Exam Description contains the specific learning objectives for the course. It also includes some sample questions for the AP exam that show how each question is tied to both thematic and period-specific learning objectives. It explains each theme and time period in detail.

### Theme 1: Interaction of Europe and the World

This theme is about how Europe changed the world and how the world changed Europe. It traces the history of Europe's interactions starting with the Muslim influence in helping revive knowledge and beginning the Renaissance. This theme moves through the ages of exploration, imperialism, world wars, and decolonization and into the present. Major economic and cultural themes are expressed here as transatlantic and then global trade rapidly changed Europe and the world and eventually created a global economy, workforce, and cuisine.

**The overarching questions for this theme are the following:**

- Why have Europeans sought contact and interaction with other parts of the world?
- What political, technological, and intellectual developments enabled European contact and interaction with other parts of the world?
- How have encounters between Europe and the world shaped European culture, politics, and society?
- What effect has contact with Europe had on non-European societies?

### Theme 2: Economic and Commercial Developments

This theme is mostly economic and social history. However, it also includes many important political and military aspects. It examines how at the start of the time period covered in the course, around 1450, global wealth was fairly equally distributed geographically but how Europe came to dominate international trade until the Second World War. How this new commercial wealth eventually transformed Europe from a mostly agrarian, preindustrial feudal system into socialist democracies that emphasized the elimination of poverty and the equality of opportunity was an important trend to watch. The emergence of laissez-faire capitalism, Marxist communism, and socialism must be examined with an eye to business cycles and periods of prosperity, such as the 1890s, and periods of depression, such as the 1930s. How individuals and societies affected and were affected by these changes is the main thrust of this theme.

**The overarching questions for this theme are the following:**

- How has capitalism developed as an economic system?
- How has the organization of society changed as a result of or in response to the development and spread of capitalism?
- What were the causes and consequences of economic and social inequality?
- How did individuals, groups, and the state respond to economic and social inequality?

## Theme 3: Cultural and Intellectual Developments

This theme is about methods of acquiring knowledge and how those methods have changed from 1450 to the present. It examines the philosophical methods of the Renaissance and Reformation thinkers and how thinking evolved during the Enlightenment to include systematic methods of evaluation and inquiry. This theme investigates how knowledge claims gradually moved away from belief in absolute truths to increasingly subjective interpretations of reality. The relationship between the observations and the observer began to be investigated in the 19th century. Further developments created "big science" that dominated the 20th century in the fields of science and technology.

**The overarching questions for this theme are the following:**

- What roles have traditional sources of authority (church and classical antiquity) played in the creation and transmission of knowledge?
- How and why did Europeans come to rely on the scientific method and reason in place of traditional authorities?
- How and why did Europeans come to value subjective interpretations of reality?

## Theme 4: States and Other Institutions of Power

This theme is mostly political. As always, though, political and economic power are intrinsically linked in so many ways that Richelieu said "finances are the sinews of the state." The rise of states corresponds with the rise of state revenue in order to finance growing armies. The evolution of political power and the rise and fall of absolute monarchies are examined in this theme. The subsequent rise of parliamentary power, popular sovereignty, and the rule of law are also examined here. Balance of power diplomacy and the importance of alliances in aiding political power is a strong component of this theme. The rise and fall of totalitarian dictatorships and the tools of government for changing the lives of citizens in both positive and negative ways are examined. One example is the cycle of political history in France. The country was the model of absolutism under Louis XIV, had a bloody republican revolution from 1789–1795, then became the Napoleonic Empire at the start of the 19th century, and became a monarchy again in 1815. France went through five republics with periods of empire, occupation, and reestablishment of a republic.

**The overarching questions for this theme are the following:**

- What forms have European governments taken, and how have these forms changed over time?
- In what ways and why have European governments moved toward or reacted against representative and democratic principles and practices?
- How did civil institutions develop apart from governments, and what effect have civil institutions had on European states?
- How and why did changes in warfare affect diplomacy, the European state system, and the balance of power?
- How did the concept of a balance of power emerge, develop, and eventually become institutionalized?

## Theme 5: Social Organization and Development

This theme is mostly social, yet it pertains to all of the other economic, political, and technological factors that continually affect the lives of the people of Europe. This is an examination of the evolution of class structure, familial relations, gender roles, ethnic identities, and occupational roles. This theme also examines the rise of consumerism and the welfare state. Traditionally, exam questions rely heavily on this theme. If you can master this information, you can apply it to all other themes in order to get a strong historical picture of any event.

**The overarching questions for this theme are the following:**

- What forms have family, class, and social groups taken in European history, and how have they changed over time?
- How and why have tensions arisen between the individual and society over the course of European history?
- How and why has the status of specific groups within European society changed over time?

## Theme 6: National and European Identity

This theme's main focus is on how and why definitions and perceptions of regional, cultural, national, and European identity have developed and have been challenged over time. It examines the inception of nationality coming from early political units that varied in size from the tiny Italian city-states to regions such as Spain. The emergence of powerful monarchs, such as Louis XIV and Peter the Great, used common language and cultural identity to foster a sense of unity in their realms. The creation and dissemination of national symbols and stories are also a major thrust of this theme. The idea of European well-being that emerged from the Enlightenment is examined through this lens as well. The power of nationalism that emerged in the 19th century and how it affected the boundaries and stories of Europe and European nations are also paramount to this theme. The power of nation-states during the 20th century as well as the rise in European unity at the start of the 21st century are also major thrusts of this theme.

**The overarching questions for this theme are the following:**

- Where did national identity come from?
- How does national identity affect people's behavior?
- How did leaders use national identity?
- How and why did the concept of European identity emerge, and how did it affect Europe?
- How have people with minority national identities been treated by the majority?
- How did national and European identity affect both world wars and the Cold War and its aftermath?
- How and why does national identity affect European history?

## Theme 7: Technological and Scientific Innovation

This theme focuses on the emergence of new scientific discoveries and the creation of new technologies. The impacts of the development of new scientific ideas and of new technologies should be investigated under this theme. The pressures put on societies, economies, and governments by the creation of new technologies and the discovery of new ideas is also a major part of this theme. The methods of discovery, the development of new technologies, and how these discoveries are adopted by society are also very important.

**The overarching questions for this theme are the following:**

- How have both the intended and unintended consequences of scientific and technological innovations increased efficiency, improved daily life, and shaped human development and interactions?
- How have advances in technology contributed to the development of balance of power?
- How did the understanding of the natural world change and develop over time?
- How do innovations and advances in technology lead to social and economic changes?
- How did science and other intellectual disciplines develop and change over time?
- How have new technologies affected warfare?
- How have innovations and advances in technology influenced cultural and intellectual developments?

Note that a strong comprehension of and an ability to apply *economic* history can help you with each of the seven themes.

## Exam Organization

The scope of this course is the history of Europe from the Renaissance (1450) to contemporary times. All four time periods are covered equally on the exam.

**MULTIPLE-CHOICE QUESTIONS (55 QUESTIONS FOR 40% OF EXAM)** All multiple-choice questions are based on some sort of stimulus provided on the exam. There is a quote, a chart, a historian's argument, a map, an image, or a cartoon followed by a group of two to five questions based upon that stimulus. In general, the questions go from a lower reasoning level to a higher reasoning level within each group of questions.

**SHORT-ANSWER QUESTIONS (ANSWER THREE OF FOUR QUESTIONS FOR 20% OF THE EXAM)** Four questions directly address one or more of the thematic learning objectives for the course. *You must answer only three questions.* You are required to answer two questions from the period 1600–2001. You then choose to answer one of two questions (one from time periods 1–2 and one from time periods 3–4). Each question asks you to identify and analyze examples of historical evidence relevant to the source or question. There are three tasks in each question that are worth 1 point each.

**DOCUMENT-BASED QUESTION (ONE QUESTION FOR 25% OF THE EXAM)** This is where the readers want to see your skills with synthesis, analysis, periodization, causation, argumentation, and understanding of continuity and change. You must analyze the documents, including written materials, charts, graphs, and cartoons, and then use evidence from within those documents and evidence *not* contained in the documents to make a cogent, clear, concise argument that *completely answers all parts of the question.*

**LONG ESSAY QUESTION (ONE QUESTION FOR 15% OF THE EXAM)** You are given the choice between three different essay prompts that test the same historical skill, such as periodization or change and continuity over time. You must select one essay prompt and develop a strong thesis that addresses all parts of the question. You must further support that thesis with strong historical evidence that can come from both primary and secondary sources with which you are familiar.

| Section | Question Type | Number of Questions | Timing | Percentage of Total Exam Score |
|---------|---------------|---------------------|--------|-------------------------------|
| I | Part A: Multiple-choice questions | 55 questions | 55 minutes | 40% |
| | Part B: Short-answer questions | 4 questions Students are required to answer 2 questions from 1600–2001 and can choose to answer 1 of 2 questions (1 from time periods 1–2 and 1 from time periods 3–4) | 40 minutes | 20% |
| II | Part A: Document-based question (DBQ) | 1 question | 60 minutes includes a 15-minute reading period | 25% |
| | Part B: Long essay question (LEQ) | 1 question chosen from among 3 questions | 40 minutes | 15% |

## How the AP European History Exam Is Scored

The AP European History exam is composed of four parts grouped into two sections.

The multiple-choice part is scored with 1 point given for each correct answer. *There is no penalty for guessing as of May 2011*, so you should answer every question on the exam.

The long essay is given a score from 0 to 6, and the DBQ is scored from 0 to 7. Details about this are given later in this section and throughout the sample essays seen in the book.

To attain your final AP score, use the following method:

Multiple-Choice Score × 1.091 = _____

+

Short-Answer Score × 3.334 =    _____

+

DBQ Score × 5.357 =          _____

+

LEQ Score × 3.75 =          _____

**Total of all above scores is composite score = _____ (round your score)**

**To get a final score for the exam, compare your composite score to the chart below.**

### Composite Score Conversion Chart

| Score Range | AP Score |
|---|---|
| 104–150 | 5 |
| 91–103 | 4 |
| 79–91 | 3 |
| 69–78 | 2 |
| 0–69 | 1 |

### Scores

**5** Extremely well qualified; score is accepted by most colleges for either course credit or placement into a higher-level section.

**4** Well qualified; score is accepted by many colleges.

**3** Qualified; score is accepted by some colleges.

**2** Possibly qualified; score is rarely accepted for either course credit or placement.

**1** No recommendation; score is not accepted anywhere.

The previous Composite Score Conversion Chart is a sample chart. The score ranges change annually with each set of exam scores. However, this chart shows a good estimation of an average year's test score distribution.

You may choose to suppress a score on the AP exam once it has been reported to you. You may also cancel the test within a certain time after you have taken it but before the score has been reported.

Some colleges require additional documentation about course work.

## Multiple-Choice Questions (40% of the Exam)

The multiple-choice section is composed of approximately 55 questions organized into groups of two to five questions. You must assess and react to questions based on a common stimulus, such as a primary or secondary source, a historian's argument, or a historical problem. Each set of multiple-choice questions addresses one or more of the thematic and time period learning objectives for the course. These sets require you to have the skills outlined in the AP historical skills mentioned earlier. Although a set may focus on one particular period of European history, the individual questions within that set may ask you to make connections to thematically linked developments in other periods. These individual questions assess your abilities in the skill about change and continuity over time.

Multiple-choice questions evaluate your ability to analyze the stimulus material in tandem with your knowledge of the historical period being examined. The possible answers for a multiple-choice question reflect the level of detail present in the required historical developments found in the concept outline for the course. You should be prepared to utilize your knowledge of the forces in history to analyze specific information and situations cited in the stimuli provided.

## HINTS FOR TACKLING MULTIPLE-CHOICE QUESTIONS

1. Answer all questions. There is no penalty for incorrect answers.
2. The more incorrect answers you eliminate, the better your odds are for guessing the correct answer.
3. Be methodical. Even on questions you are sure of, put a line through *entire* incorrect answers as you eliminate them.
4. Circle the number of any question you are unsure of so you can return to it if you have the time.
5. Go with your intuition. Your first choice is usually correct, so change an answer only if you are absolutely certain.
6. Underline the key idea in each question.
7. Try reading the answer choices from D back to A.

### Types of Multiple-Choice Questions

- Analysis
- Quotation
- Interpretation of a picture, art object, cartoon, or photo
- Map study
- Graph or chart

### Sample Analysis Questions

*Analysis* lends itself to working out the answer with more general understandings or less specific information by considering cause-and-effect relationships or by sorting out the chronology.

**Questions 1–2 refer to the map below.**

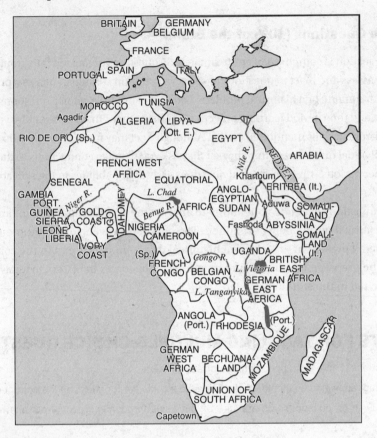

1. Which of the following is the best reason for the creation of the map above?

   (A) It was drawn to reflect the decolonization seen after the Second World War.
   (B) It was drawn to reflect colonial possessions on the eve of the First World War.
   (C) It was drawn to reflect the importance of rivers in the transport of African goods.
   (D) It was drawn to reflect the growing power of the French and the English in
       East Africa.

2. Which best describes the ways that Europeans used African ethnic divisions to guide them when creating the colonies and nations seen above?

   (A) Colonies and nations were created to keep ethnic groups united within Africa.
   (B) Colonies and nations were drawn that did not take any African ethnic divisions into account.
   (C) Colonies and nations were created to intentionally separate ethnic groups and create new colonies of
       disunited Africans.
   (D) Colonies and nations were created to meet the trade requirements of Europeans, and the sizes and
       boundaries of colonies and nations depended more upon how big the colonizing nation was.

## Answers

1. **B**
2. **C**

## Comments

*Analysis* questions let you eliminate some answers if you can figure out that one thing could not be a causation or result of another event or attitude. They make you use general knowledge in a specific way to reason out an answer. Knowing the general time frame of events and developments helps immeasurably. It is worth the trouble and time to try to figure out the answer to this type of question.

Question 1 is a classic *analyze the map to see the time period* question. If you can determine the sequence of events, you can eliminate certain choices. For example, German West Africa exists, so the time period is before 1918 and after 1905. However, Italy does not possess Eritrea or Somalia, so it must be before the 1930s. Additionally, the Belgian Congo still exists, so it must be before 1918. Now one must analyze *why* the map was drawn. It seems from the dates given that the only possible choice given was on the eve of the First World War, choice (B). All of the other answers are either before Germany had African colonies or after it lost them. Since the map shows nothing about transportation, and the French and English had little influence in East Africa other than in Egypt, which is not shown on the map, those choices can be easily eliminated.

Question 2 can be answered by determining the reasoning behind the drawing of colonial and, eventually, national borders in Africa. Here you must analyze which of the choices is *most* correct. Many responses have some truth to them. However, the best answer is the one that is most complete and that contains nothing inaccurate. In this case, the Europeans did have to take the internal relations of the Africans on the ground into account when drawing borders. The Europeans wanted to make the colonies easier to rule. So you must reason that because they were trying to rule the Africans, the Europeans would try to keep them disunited, thus eliminating choices (A) and (B). You must also look at the map and reason that the Belgian Congo would not be very big if choice (D) were correct, so that choice can be eliminated. Choice (C) is the correct answer because the Europeans intentionally divided the ethnic groups to keep the populations within each colony fighting with one another rather than with their colonizers.

## Sample Quotation Question

*Quotation* analysis, like most analysis questions, can be done with less specific information than identification requires. Again, chronology and cause-effect help in the process of elimination.

"Not only was he accused of imprisoning and torturing or murdering his enemies, but he set into place the whole apparatus of totalitarian repression. He denied basic human rights in pushing forward his policy of industrialization, and the human cost can be measured in the deaths of tens of millions of his own countrymen. His detractors also accuse him of governing according to a 'cult of personality.'"

1. The individual speaking above is describing the dictator of the Soviet Union through the Second World War and would most likely be which of the following?

    (A) An ardent Bolshevik who was a member of the Comintern under Stalin
    (B) An Enlightenment thinker who was looking for a better society
    (C) A Western writer or academic
    (D) A member of the cabinet of Leonid Brezhnev who tried to de-Stalinize the Soviet Union

Answer and Comments: **(C)**

Choice (A) is incorrect because leaders of the Communist Party under Stalin did not criticize him in any way.

Choice (B) is out because Stalin lived *after* the Age of Enlightenment. Thus, none of those great minds could comment on Stalin.

Choice (D) is out because Brezhnev actually re-Stalinized the Soviet Union after Khrushchev tried to reduce Cold War tensions there.

Choice (C) makes the most sense because during and even after the Cold War, "Western" (meaning pro-NATO) writers and academics were those most likely to criticize Stalin. This continues even up to today.

## Sample Interpretation Question

*Interpretation* can involve identifying the artist, style, subject, or period of a work of art; it may require interpretation of a cartoon, map, photo, or picture.

1.  From examining the map above, which of the following was the most important reason for the British to hold Egypt, which had built the Suez Canal?

    (A)  The British needed it to get goods from Africa to Asia.
    (B)  The British wanted to patrol the Red Sea to make certain that Somali pirates were defeated.
    (C)  The British wanted to secure trade routes from Asia to Europe to keep growing their trade empire.
    (D)  The British wanted to take over all French and German colonies in Africa.

Answer and Comments: **(C)**

You must analyze the map to see that the Suez Canal gave the British easy access from the Mediterranean to the Red Sea and, eventually, the Indian Ocean for trade with the entire empire.

*Map interpretation questions* require use of broad map skills and less general information to work out. They are worth the time and trouble to examine.

## Sample Graph or Chart Question

*Graphs and charts* frequently provide all the information necessary in order to answer the question correctly. Graphs are diagrams representing successive changes; charts are information sheets that employ tables or graphs.

**Populations of Cities (in Thousands)**

| Year | London | Paris | Antwerp | Berlin | Moscow |
|------|--------|-------|---------|--------|--------|
| 1800 | 960 | 600 | 60 | 170 | 250 |
| 1850 | 2,700 | 1,400 | 90 | 500 | 360 |
| 1900 | 6,500 | 3,700 | 280 | 2,700 | 1,000 |

1. Which would be the most likely explanation for the population change between 1800 and 1900 in the cities included on the chart above?

   (A) Malthusian "unbridled lust"
   (B) Foreign immigration
   (C) Population shift from other cities
   (D) Industrialization

Answer and Comments: **(D)**

The clue to the correct answer is in the early, nearly sevenfold increase of the population of London. The Industrial Revolution coincided with a mass movement from the countryside to the cities. This mass movement may also have been caused by the enclosure movement. Since the Industrial Revolution and the enclosure movement began in Britain and then caught on later in the rest of Europe, the answer is choice (D), industrialization.

## Written Section

This section requires you to write three types of responses, which include three short-answer questions and two essays total. One essay is a document-based question (DBQ) and one is a long essay question (LEQ). You must respond to the only DBQ prompt presented, but you choose among three LEQ essay choices that are similarly structured.

You are given 60 minutes to answer the DBQ, which includes a 15-minute reading section. You are then given 40 minutes to write the LEQ.

### Written Section Scoring (60% of the Exam)

Short-answer questions each have three specific tasks that can earn 1 point each. All LEQs are scored using the same rubric; each LEQ can earn a maximum of 6 points. All DBQs are scored using the same rubric; each DBQ can earn a maximum of 7 points. On LEQs, a score of 0–2 is pretty poor, a score of 3–4 is adequate, and a score of 5–6 is very good. For the DBQs, a score of 0–3 is pretty poor, a score of 4–5 is adequate, and a score of 6–7 is very good.

### Short-Answer Questions (20% of the Exam)

The short-answer section consists of four questions that require you to use historical thinking skills and content knowledge to respond to a stimulus with a direct, concise response. However, you must answer only three of the short-answer questions. You are required to answer two questions from 1600–2001 and can choose to answer one of two questions (one from time periods 1–2 and one from time periods 3–4). Just like in the multiple-choice section, stimulus material may include a primary or secondary source, including texts, images, charts, graphs, maps, etc. At least two of the four short-answer questions include stimulus material. Each short-answer question directly addresses one or more of the thematic learning objectives for the course and assesses one or more of the nine historical thinking skills. Each short-answer question asks you to analyze historical developments and/or processes using examples drawn from the concept outline or other examples explored in depth in classroom instruction. The short-answer questions may require you to take a position based on the stimulus material presented, identify a significant cause or effect, or account for differences and similarities in perspectives, historical developments, etc.

**Sample Short-Answer Question**

НЕГРАМОТНЫЙ тот-же СЛЕПОЙ
ВСЮДУ ЕГО ЖДУТ НЕУДАЧИ И НЕСЧАСТЬЯ ·

"The illiterate is a blind man: Everywhere pitfalls and
misfortunes await him." Soviet Poster, 1920.

(a)  Briefly analyze how the artwork above reflects artistic trends at the start of the twentieth century.

(b)  Based on the poster above and your knowledge of European history, explain TWO aspects of social life
    under Soviet rule.

This is both an art question and a social question. It is a common type of question on the AP exam. To understand
how to score the exam, examine the following scoring guide.

## Scoring Guide

**0–3 points (1 point for a and 2 points for b)**

(a) One point is given for analyzing how the poster is typical of the trends of the early 20th century. For example,
it is related to art nouveau or the Belle Epoch; it contains a master narrative; it espouses faith in a grand theory;
it supports hierarchy and order; it concentrates overall on improving society, mass marketing or mass media,
centralized knowledge, seriousness of intent and purpose, etc. This can also be juxtaposed with the Dada/surreal-
ist ideas going on contemporaneously.

   (b) One point is awarded (up to a total of two points) for each aspect of social life in the Soviet Union explained.
These aspects include lack of freedom, fear of the state, distrust of others, quotas at work, long lines for all goods,
lack of consumer goods, free medical care, free housing, guaranteed work, assumed equality, gender role relaxation, lack of religion, censored press and other media, governmental control of all aspects of life, etc.

Other types of questions include those that ask you to analyze arguments between historians; analyze a chart, map,
or graph; or respond to some historical generalization such as that the Enlightenment was not very enlightened for
most people.

## Interpreting the Essay Questions

In both the LEQs and the DBQs, you need to understand the way in which the answer must be presented. In order to do this, you must interpret the *key term or terms* in the question.

## Examples of Key Terms

1. **DEFEND OR REFUTE** (argue for or against a specific statement by framing an essay that uses *factual support*)

   Sample:

   "The Second World War was the inevitable result of a failure of the democracies to confront aggression by totalitarian dictatorships."

   *Defend or refute* this with factual evidence from the diplomatic history of the 1930s.

2. **ANALYZE** (examine in detail; determine relationships; explain)

   Sample:

   *Analyze* the ways in which the Protestant Reformation fostered both the growth of capitalism and the rise of modern science.

3. **EVALUATE** (judge the worth of; discuss advantages and disadvantages, pluses and minuses)

   Sample:

   *Evaluate* both the domestic policies and the foreign involvements of the government of France during the reign of Louis XIV.

4. **TO WHAT EXTENT AND IN WHAT WAYS** (how and how much?)

   Sample:

   *To what extent and in what ways* did Napoleon carry out the ideals of the French Revolution?

5. **ASSESS THE VALIDITY** (judge the value of; determine the truth)

   Sample:

   "The religious wars of the 16th and 17th centuries were more the result of the territorial ambitions of rival states and the economic interests of competing factions than of doctrinal differences."

   *Assess the validity* of this statement.

6. **CONTRAST AND COMPARE** (show differences and examine for similarities)

   Sample:

   *Contrast and compare* the art and architecture of the Renaissance with that of the Romantic period, and explain how each reflected the prevailing culture.

7. **EXPLAIN** (offer the meaning, the cause, the reason for; make clear; detail)

   Sample:

   *Explain* how the theories of Copernicus, Galileo, Kepler, and Newton affected the religious beliefs and intellectual trends of the 17th and 18th centuries.

8. **DISCUSS** (consider various points of view; write about; examine)

   Sample:

   *Discuss* the accomplishments of the various governments in France during the French Revolution.

9. **DESCRIBE** (tell about; offer an account or a word picture)

Sample:

*Describe* the lifestyle of noble women in Italy during the Italian Renaissance. Refer to family life, political status, and economic conditions.

Additional sample and practice short-answer and long essay questions appear in the review chapters and in the sample exams.

## The Long Essay Question (15% of the Exam)

You are given a choice among three comparable long essay options and must choose one. The long essay questions are designed to measure your use of historical thinking skills to explain and analyze one or more of the thematic learning objectives for the course. All essays require the development of a *thesis* or an argument supported by *analysis* of specific, relevant historical evidence. You must demonstrate in your responses that you have mastered a targeted skill, such as continuity and change over time, comparison, causation, or periodization.

All long essay questions on the exam target the same skill, which varies from year to year. The tasks required of you are very similar no matter which question you choose. The questions address different chronological periods and topics. Questions are limited to topics or examples specifically mentioned in the concept outline but framed to allow your answer to include in-depth examples, drawn either from the concept outline or from topics beyond the concept outline discussed in the classroom.

All long essay questions are scored using the long essay rubric found later in this section. You should study this rubric closely to know what is expected from your essay responses.

## How Does the College Board Score the Free-Response Question?

As Sun Tzu stated in *The Art of War*, "If you know your enemy and you know yourself, you cannot be defeated in one hundred battles." In the case of test preparation, the test and its graders are your "enemy," and understanding the rubrics for the DBQ and the LEQ will help you defeat them. Reading and understanding a sample rubric for the sample LEQ will help you know your enemy.

## AP European History Long Essay Question (LEQ) Rubric (6 Points)

| Category | Scoring Method | Helpful Hints |
|---|---|---|
| Thesis (0–1 points) | Responds to the question with an evaluative thesis/claim that makes a historically defensible claim that establishes a line of reasoning. (1 point) | To earn this point, the thesis must make a claim that responds to the prompt, rather than restating or rephrasing the prompt. The thesis must consist of one or more sentences located in one place, either in the introduction or the conclusion. |
| Contextualization (0–1 points) | Describe a broader historical context immediately relevant to the prompt. (1 point) | To earn this point, the response must describe broader historical events, developments, or processes that occur before, during, or continue after the time frame of the prompt that are relevant to the topic. This point is not awarded for merely a phrase or a reference. |
| Evidence (0–2 points) | Provides specific examples of at least 2 pieces of evidence related to the topic of the prompt. (1 point) OR To earn this point, student must **support an argument** in response to the prompt with **two** pieces of specific and relevant evidence. (2 points) | To earn one point, the response must identify specific historical examples of evidence relevant to the topic of the prompt. To earn two points, the response must use specific historical evidence to support an argument in response to the prompt. |

| Category | Scoring Method | Helpful Hints |
|---|---|---|
| Analysis and reasoning (0–2 points) | Uses historical reasoning (e.g., comparison, causation, CCOT) to frame or structure an argument that addresses the prompt.<br><br>(1 point)<br><br>OR<br><br>Demonstrates a complex understanding of the historical development that is the focus of the prompt, using evidence to corroborate, qualify, or modify an argument that addresses the question.<br><br>(2 points) | To earn the first point, the response must demonstrate the use of historical reasoning to frame or structure an argument, although the reasoning might be uneven or imbalanced or the evidence may be overly general or lacking specificity.<br><br>To earn the second point, the response must demonstrate a complex understanding through sophisticated argumentation relevant to the prompt. This can be accomplished in a variety of ways, such as:<br><br>■ Explaining multiple themes or perspectives to explore complexity or nuance; OR<br>■ Explaining multiple causes or effects, multiple similarities or differences, or multiple continuities or changes; OR<br>■ Explaining both cause and effect, both similarity and difference, or both continuity and change; OR<br>■ Explaining relevant and insightful connections within and across periods or geographical areas. These connections should clearly relate to an argument that responds to the prompt.<br><br>**A response may demonstrate a complex or nuanced understanding** through effective use of evidence relevant to an argument that addresses the prompt. This may be done in a variety of ways, such as:<br>■ Explaining how multiple pieces of specific and relevant evidence (at least four) support a nuanced or complex argument that responds to the prompt; OR<br>■ Using evidence effectively to demonstrate a sophisticated understanding of different perspectives relevant to the prompt.<br>■ This complex understanding must be part of the argument and may be demonstrated in any part of the response.<br>■ While it is not necessary for this complex understanding to be woven throughout the response, it must be more than merely a phrase or reference. |

## Interpreting the Long Essay Rubric

The rubric clearly shows what you must do to score well on the long essay. Here is a checklist to be sure the information is clear:

✔ The essay must have a thesis that responds to all parts of the question and makes a claim that can be defended with historical evidence and reasoning. (0–1 total points)

✔ The essay must place the historical argument from the thesis into a broader historical context and explain how that context influenced the topic that the question addresses. (0–1 total points)

✔ The essay must use specific historical examples to support the claim stated in the thesis and make use of historical reasoning skills to explain how the evidence cited interrelates. The essay must also use that evidence to qualify, moderate, or corroborate the argument from the thesis. (0–2 total points)

✔ The essay must use historical reasoning (e.g., comparison, causation, CCOT) to frame or structure an argument that addresses the prompt and demonstrates a complex understanding of the historical development that is the focus of the prompt, using evidence to corroborate, qualify, or modify an argument that addresses the question. (0–2 total points)

## General Advice for Writing Essays

Writing a good essay is like a good speech or a strong lesson in school. It generally requires three steps:

1. Tell them what you will tell them; include a THESIS.
2. Tell it to them; write the BODY AND SUPPORT.

Use evidence here to support your ideas. Your evidence can be factual or interpretive. However, using both is best. You must support your thesis with a plethora of evidence.

**3.** Tell them what you told them; write a CONCLUSION.

Summarize your main points. What was important? Why? Make your final points here.
The most important point to remember is to ANSWER THE ENTIRE QUESTION.

Other hints are found in the following box.

## HINTS FOR ANSWERING THE LONG ESSAY QUESTIONS

1. Read all three question choices before deciding on which one to answer.
2. Remember to choose the time period you are most comfortable with and knowledgeable of. The College Board chooses between historical developments or processes between 1450 and 1700, historical developments or processes between 1648 and 1914, and historical developments or processes between 1815 and 2001.
3. Underline each task in each question, and count the tasks. Try to take on the question that has the fewest tasks that can be fully answered.
4. Your primary consideration should be how much you know about the specific subject. This may seem obvious. However, it is easy to pass over a question if you are confused about what it asks. Read. Reread those questions that encompass areas you have focused on in class or in your studies.
5. Interpret the key terms. (See pages 27–28.)
6. Make your choice by mentally framing the argument of your essay. (The argument is the proof, the statement, the thesis, the core of your essay. You should follow your intuition since it flows from what you know most about.)
7. Read the question again, and jot down anything that comes to mind.
8. Organize your essay by outlining your argument. Don't fret over format; you are the only one who is going to see or use the outline.
9. Gather facts to support your argument. (If you are not certain of a fact—a date, an event, a cause, or a person—don't use it.)
10. Check for consistency. What seems like supporting evidence may actually contradict your assertions.
11. Be certain the thesis addresses all parts of the question and that the evidence is strong enough to support that thesis before beginning to write.
12. Now you are ready to write. Make a clear statement of the intent of your argument in the introduction, and include a clear summary of your argument in the conclusion.
13. Reread! Rewrite! Delete. Add. Remember—substance takes precedence over neatness. Don't be afraid to cross out words, sentences, whole paragraphs, and even whole pages.

## How to Write an Essay

Writing an essay is a lot easier than you think if you pick the right question, interpret the terms correctly, and follow a few simple procedures. The tricks to picking the right question and interpreting its terms are given in the preceding section.

What then are these "simple" procedures?

## The Essence of Your Essay Is the Body

It is in the body of the essay that you do your job of showing "to what extent and in what ways," of "assessing the validity," of "contrasting and comparing," of demonstrating "change and continuity over time," and so on. The introduction simply points out the direction your argument will take and presents a viable thesis that addresses all parts of the question. The conclusion simply summarizes your argument. The key to success in this task is to write a clear, convincing argument that clearly addresses the skill being assessed. That argument must clearly and repetitively tie the evidence to the thesis and explain how the evidence supports the thesis. The best essays also include counterarguments to the thesis or tie the response to additional time periods or movements than those being assessed by the question.

## The Simple Procedures

After determining whether the question assesses your skill at comparison, causation, or change and continuity over time, ask yourself the following questions:

- First, what does the question want to know?
- Second, what do you know about that topic?
- Third, how should you put the information into words?

> SAMPLE QUESTION:
> To what extent and in what ways did Napoleon's rule continue and expand the ideals of the Enlightenment and the French Revolution?

**First, what does the question want to know?**

How and how much did Napoleon, an autocrat, continue and expand the social, political, and economic aims of the Revolution and the pursuit of reason endemic to the Enlightenment? This is clearly a change and continuity over time essay and, therefore, must address the skills called for in that type of essay. The question also wants to know what the ideals of the Enlightenment and French Revolution were and then requires you to evaluate the extent to which Napoleon continued and expanded those ideals.

**Second, what do you know about that topic?**

Napoleon was a dictator and an emperor, and both are generally undemocratic roles. In contrast, the French Revolution was democratic in nature. Napoleon ignored the ideals of thinkers like Montesquieu and Rousseau who wanted the people to have a meaningful voice in government but followed the ideals of Voltaire who called for an enlightened despot.

Napoleon made domestic reforms in the law, education, and government that furthered democracy. He then spread his Napoleonic Code to the peoples of Europe whom he conquered. However, he was a conqueror, which went directly against the ideals of the Enlightenment. He carried some of the ideals of the Revolution—"liberty, equality, fraternity"—to other countries during his conquests. He had personal reasons for trying to change the *Ancien Régime*, or "Old Order." Napoleon enforced a meritocracy and rule of law, but he also enforced censorship and utilized secret police.

**Third, how should you put the information into words?**

Write about the historical irony: one of history's "bad guys" who was a dictator, conqueror, and vainglorious emperor actually helped to spread liberal ideals throughout Europe along with the rule of law through his Napoleonic Code. His conquest of Europe and creation of the German Confederation of the Rhine led to the emergence of the most radical of 19th-century European movements—nationalism.

There are two mainstream ways to structure this essay. You could write an introductory thesis paragraph, then one paragraph about the extent to which Napoleon carried out the ideals of the French Revolution, then one about the extent to which he carried out the ideals of the Enlightenment, and then another about how he spread these ideals across Europe. Alternatively, you could write a thesis and then one paragraph about each major ideal: liberty, equality, brotherhood, and Enlightenment ideals in general. Another advanced method could be to trace

Napoleon's narrative as those ideals were carried out chronologically and/or geographically, evaluating Napoleon's progress along the way with a strong thesis either at the start or the end. Preferably, *the thesis is stated at BOTH the beginning and end of every LEQ essay.*

Use the information in The Simple Procedures (page 31) to plan the body of every essay.

Use the Hints for Answering the Long Essay Questions (page 30) to do the actual writing.

Use the AP European History Long Essay Question (LEQ) Rubric (pages 28–29) to evaluate your response to every essay that you write for practice.

## The Document-Based Essay Question (25% of the Exam)

The document-based question (DBQ) is designed to test your ability to analyze documentary materials and use that analysis to support a thesis proposed by the prompt. In most years, *you can often earn almost one-half of the points needed to attain a score of 3 on the exam if you complete the DBQ properly.* This section is based on a skill that can be developed by using documents and the author's point of view in each of those documents to prove a historical point. Thus, this skill is worth practicing.

The document-based question emphasizes the ability to analyze and synthesize historical evidence, including textual, quantitative, or visual materials. The question also requires you to formulate a thesis and support it with relevant evidence. The five to seven documents accompanying the document-based question are not confined to a single format, may vary in length, and are chosen to illustrate interactions and complexities within the material. The diversity of materials, which may include charts, graphs, cartoons, and works of art alongside written documents, requires you to evaluate different kinds of documents and to utilize a broad spectrum of historical skills. Each DBQ focuses on one targeted skill (such as causation, continuity and change over time, or comparison) that varies from year to year.

The document-based question typically requires you to relate the documents to a historical period or theme and, thus, to focus on major periods and issues. The DBQ assesses your ability to incorporate *outside knowledge* related to the question but beyond the specifics of the documents. This ability to place the documents in the *historical context* in which they were produced is essential for your success.

The first key to success on the DBQ is to understand how the question is scored. The readers (people who score the exam) all must use a point-based rubric for grading the DBQ that, if understood, can be used to your advantage. An outline of that rubric follows.

## AP European History Document-Based Question (DBQ) Rubric (7 Points)

| Category | Scoring Method | Helpful Hints |
|---|---|---|
| Thesis/Claim (0–1 point) | Responds to the question with a thesis that makes a historically defensible claim/thesis that establishes a line of reasoning.<br><br>(1 point) | To earn this point, the thesis must make a claim that responds to the prompt rather than restating or rephrasing the prompt. The thesis must consist of one or more sentences located in one place, either in the introduction or the conclusion. |
| Contextualization (0–1 points) | Describes a broader historical context relevant to the question.<br><br>(1 point) | This point may be earned by relating the topic of the question to broader historical events, developments, or processes that occur before, during, or continue after the time frame of the question that are relevant to the topic. This point is NOT awarded for a phrase or reference. |

| Category | Scoring Method | Helpful Hints |
|---|---|---|
| Evidence (0–3 points) | Utilizes content of at least THREE documents to address the topic of the question.<br><br>(1 point)<br><br>OR<br><br>Utilizes the content of at least SIX documents to support an argument about the question.<br><br>(2 points)<br><br>OR<br><br>↓ | **To earn 1 point**, the response must accurately describe rather than simply quote the content from at least three of the documents.<br><br>**To earn 2 points**, the response must accurately describe rather than simply quote the content from at least six documents. In addition, the response must use the content of the documents to support an argument in response to the prompt. |
| Evidence beyond the documents (0–1 points) | Explains how at least one additional piece of specific evidence beyond those found in the documents relates to an argument about the question.<br><br>(1 point) | To earn this point, the response must describe the evidence and must use more than a phrase or reference. This additional piece of evidence must be different from the evidence used to earn the point for contextualization. |
| Analysis and reasoning (0–2 points) | **(0-1 Point)**<br>For at least **TWO** documents, explains how or why the document's point of view, purpose, historical situation, and/or audience is relevant to an argument. | To earn this point, the response must explain how or why (rather than simply identifying) the document's point of view, purpose, historical situation, or audience is relevant to an argument about the prompt for each of the two documents sourced. |
|  | **(0-1 Point)**<br>Demonstrates a complex understanding of the historical development that is the focus of the prompt, using evidence to corroborate, qualify, or modify an argument that addresses the question. | A response may demonstrate a complex understanding through sophisticated argumentation that is relevant to the prompt. This may be done in a variety of ways, such as:<br><br>■ Explaining multiple themes or perspectives to explore complexity or nuance; OR<br>■ Explaining multiple causes or effects, multiple similarities or differences, or multiple continuities or changes; OR<br>■ Explaining both cause and effect, both similarity and difference, or both continuity and change; OR<br>■ Explaining relevant and insightful connections within and across periods or geographical areas. These connections should clearly relate to an argument that responds to the prompt.<br><br>A response may demonstrate a complex understanding through effective use of evidence relevant to an argument that addresses the prompt. This may be done in a variety of ways, such as:<br><br>■ Effectively using seven documents to support an argument that responds to the prompt; OR<br>■ Explaining how the point of view, audience of at least four documents supports an argument that responds to the prompt; OR<br>■ Using documents and evidence beyond the documents effectively to demonstrate a sophisticated understanding of different perspectives relevant to the prompt.<br><br>This complex understanding must be part of the argument and may be demonstrated in any part of the response.<br><br>While it is not necessary for this complex understanding to be woven throughout the response, it must be more than merely a phrase or reference. |

**Scoring note:** If you can write an essay in 40 minutes that completes all of the elements described in the DBQ rubric, you will be very successful on the DBQ.

## Rules for Writing the DBQ

There are a few rules to writing a successful DBQ. If you follow these rules, your essay will be at the top of the scoring scale:

- **ANSWER THE QUESTION.** It is amazing how many students do not directly answer the question but, instead, go off on some tangent. Remember to check that the thesis addresses all parts of the question before proving the thesis.
- **READ THE DOCUMENTS** and write comments on them, including letters to indicate to what group each belongs. If groups are positive or negative reactions, use $\pm$.
- **CREATE AN OUTLINE** and check that you prove the thesis with it.
- **GROUP THE DOCUMENTS** to show you can understand and analyze them. There is usually some way to group the documents to show profession, nationality, class, or some other factor that affects the outlook of the document's author. This helps you gain the points for analysis of evidence.
- **INTEGRATE THE USE OF THE DOCUMENTS** smoothly into the overall reasoning of the essay. Do not make it a "laundry list" of documents and points of view. Do not accept all documents at face value. Instead, analyze each for *validity*, *origin*, and *purpose* of the author. Use the documents to answer the question and to show you understand and have the ability to use them as evidence.
- **STAY WITHIN THE TIME FRAME** of the question. The question usually gives a specific time frame—do not use anachronistic information.
  - Remember that you *can link* the documents or the question to a different time period in order to gain the synthesis point.
- **FOLLOW GRAMMATICAL CONVENTIONS.** Write an essay with good structure that *follows grammatical conventions*. Use the past tense. Avoid including clichés and terms like "the people," "history has taught us," "thing," "stuff," and overly simplistic generalizations such as good or bad. Always refer to authors and other historical figures by their last names or royal titles.
- **READ AND USE THE SOURCE CITATIONS.** The information given in those citations is critical to demonstrating point of view, audience, purpose, nationality, or historical context.
- **PRESENT POINT OF VIEW.** One strategy that helps in writing a successful DBQ response is to do a good job presenting *point of view*. Remember that the reader generally attributes persuasive document use, as well as expanded point of view use, to the writer who uses point of view well and often. In reference to the DBQ, point of view is best described as not just saying what an author wrote but *why* the author wrote it. The focus is on *why* the author chose to write in that particular tone or chose those specific words.
  - If you cannot get to the point of view of the author of the document, remember to assess at least six documents for point of view, author's purpose, historical context, and/or audience to be sure to earn the point for correct analysis of four documents in that area.
  - Apart from not directly answering the question asked, the most common error students make is not demonstrating clear point of view, audience, context, or purpose for the documents. If you show the various points of view of many authors, your DBQ response will likely be a success.

## Interpreting the DBQ Essay Rubric

The rubric clearly shows what you must do to score well on the long essay. Here is a checklist to be sure the information is clear:

- Your essay must have a strong thesis that makes a historically defensible claim and responds to all parts of the question. (1 point)
- Your essay must use evidence from at least *six* documents to support an argument that answers the question completely *and* explains the relationships between the evidence presented, including how the evidence modifies, qualifies, or corroborates the thesis. (1–3 total points)
- Your essay must explain how *either* the purpose, point of view, historical situation, and/or audience of the authors of at least *four* provided documents is relevant to the argument. (1 point)
- Your essay must place the answer you provide into a broader historical context that explains how the topic of the essay fits into the time period from which it comes. (1 point)
- Your essay must cite historical evidence related to the question that is not found in the documents provided in the question. (1 point)

## DBQ Organizer

The DBQ organizer that follows is provided to help you organize your thoughts. The organizer includes many boxes to help you think visually. It is strongly recommended that you copy this organizer and use it to practice organizing your DBQs as you work your way through this study guide. The organizer that follows was included to help you gather the evidence that you need to write your DBQ essay, so use it your first few times when writing. Once you get the hang of writing a DBQ essay, write without using the DBQ organizer because you will not have it with you on the day of the exam.

### Writing a DBQ

 **THESIS**

Your AP thesis statement should be *one to two sentences long*. The first sentence should explain your main argument or idea. *Example: Spanish intellectuals were justified in resisting authority when General Francisco Franco seized power because their lives were being threatened.*

Write thesis here:

**STEP 2**    **DEFEND YOUR THESIS**

Identify *three* more specific examples to back up your argument. These three examples help to prove that your first sentence is true. They also make your paper more specific and clear. *Example: More specifically, an illegal seizure of power, imposition of a one-party system, and the disappearance of over 100,000 political dissenters justified the actions of the intellectuals.*

Three examples here:

1.

2.

3.

**STEP 3**    **THREE TOPIC SENTENCES**

Write your topic sentences. Use the categories that you listed in step 2—defend your thesis—to create topic sentences. You do not need to answer all of the questions below (who, what, when, where, why) in your topic sentences. However, having some of that information in your topic sentences makes your thesis much clearer.

Category A: *(This should be one of the specific examples from your thesis.)*

Who:

What:

Where:

When:

Why this proves your thesis:

Combine the who, what, where, when, and why above into a topic sentence for your body paragraph:

<u>Category B</u>: *(This should be one of the specific examples from your thesis.)*

Who:

What:

Where:

When:

Why this proves your thesis:

Combine the who, what, where, when, and why above into a topic sentence for your body paragraph:

_____

_____

_____

<u>Category C</u>: *(This should be one of the specific examples from your thesis.)*

Who:

What:

Where:

When:

Why this proves your thesis:

Combine the who, what, where, when, and why above into a topic sentence for your body paragraph:

_____

_____

_____

**STEP 4**  **INTRODUCTION**

Turn your three-sentence thesis into a one-paragraph introduction.

You should design the introduction to attract the attention of the readers and give them an idea of the essay's focus. Remember that the readers are reading up to 400 essays daily. You want to attract their attention right away so that your essay is read more carefully. *Your thesis should be clear and as concise as possible to address all parts of the question, and it should hit the reader as soon as possible.*

1. Create a few sentences explaining your topic in general terms (some background information is usually helpful) that can lead the reader from your opening to your thesis statement. This should include historical context about what was happening in the world and in the specific country.

> Background Information:

2. Finish the paragraph with your thesis statement. Here you present your answer to the research question. Remember to include your main evidence at the end. *Your thesis should be clear and as concise as possible to address all parts of the question.*

> Thesis:

STEP 5  **BODY PARAGRAPHS**

List all evidence that you can think of that would support each category. *Example: British political policies might include the following.*

| DBQ Essay Facts and Analysis Chart | |
|---|---|
| A. Write topic sentence here: | 1. Evidence here: |
| | 2. Evidence here: |
| | 3. Evidence here: |
| | 4. Evidence here: |
| B. Write topic sentence here: | 1. Evidence here: |
| | 2. Evidence here: |
| | 3. Evidence here: |
| | 4. Evidence here: |

| DBQ Essay Facts and Analysis Chart | |
|---|---|
| C. Write topic sentence here: | 1. Evidence here: |
| | 2. Evidence here: |
| | 3. Evidence here: |
| | 4. Evidence here: |

**STEP 6**  **ANALYZE PRIMARY SOURCE DOCUMENTS**

Applying this analysis to each document helps you interpret it and can be done on the document itself.

**Historical Context**

- **Causation:** Can you bring connections between the document and historical facts into the open?
- **Chronology:** Can you place the primary source within its appropriate place in the historical narrative or timeline?
- **Prior knowledge:** What do you know that would help you further understand the primary source?

**Audience**

- For whom was the source created, and how might this affect the reliability or accuracy of the source?

**Purpose**

- *Why* or *for what reason* was the source produced at the time it was produced? What was the author's *goal*?

**Point of View**

- Can you identify an important aspect of *who* the author is and explain *how* this might have affected what the author wrote?
- Can you identify an influence that shaped the author or source and *explain how that influence* specifically affected the document's content?
- **The main idea:** What point is the author trying to convey?

Write one sentence that

- explains <u>why the source is important in relation to</u>—

-OR-

- explains <u>what the source has to do with the DBQ question.</u>

_____

_____

_____

_____

_____

_____

**STEP 7**  ADD PRIMARY SOURCE DOCUMENTS TO THE CORRESPONDING CATEGORIES ON YOUR EVIDENCE CHART IN STEP 5

**STEP 8**  WRITE BODY PARAGRAPHS USING I.Q.C. METHOD

For every document you mention in your essay, be sure to use I (introduction), Q (quote or paraphrase), and C (commentary analysis).

**I. Introduction for evidence #1:** Briefly explain where/when the source was created to help your reader understand the quotation you will use as evidence. You may want to include the author and date of the quote.

Author:

Date:

Now put it into one complete sentence. (Example: On August 1st, 1945, Hitler gave a speech about the war.)

**Q. Quotation or paraphrase—evidence #1:** Include a quote or fact that supports your topic sentence.

**C. Commentary analysis of evidence #1:** Explain how the quote supports your topic sentence and answers the research question. Your explanation should be at least two sentences long. Use the following commentary analysis words: *shows, explains, describes, demonstrates, elucidates, illuminates.*

This shows:



It is important because:


At the end of the analysis, you should put the document number in parentheses: (Doc 1).

**STEP 9    CONCLUSION**

The conclusion of a historical research paper is where you restate your thesis, make connections between your research and the larger world, and give your final thoughts or opinion on your topic.

**I. Restate or rephrase the thesis:** Remind your reader of your main argument and three supporting claims. Briefly explain how you have used evidence to support your argument successfully.



**II. Make a larger connection:** Make a connection between your historical evidence and another historical figure or era, current global or national events, another academic topic such as literature, or current events.

**III. Why do you care/final thoughts:** Here is where you leave your reader with your final ideas about your topic. You can share what you have learned, insights, reflections, and/or further questions that your analysis, research, and exploration have raised.

Now you are ready to write your essay. Remember to write a minimum of a five-paragraph essay with an introduction, at least three body paragraphs, and a conclusion.

## Sample DBQ

TIME:
15 MINUTES TO READ AND MARK DOCUMENTS
40 MINUTES TO WRITE ESSAY

---

**DIRECTIONS:** The following question is based on the accompanying Documents 1–7. This question is designed to test your ability to apply several historical-thinking skills simultaneously, including historical argumentation, use of relevant historical evidence, contextualization, and synthesis. Your response should be based on your analysis of the documents and your knowledge of the topic. The documents have been edited for the purpose of the exercise.

---

Question 1 is based on the accompanying documents.

In your response, you should do the following:

- Respond to the question with an evaluative thesis that makes a historically defensible claim.
- Use historical reasoning to explain relationships among the pieces of evidence provided in the response and how they corroborate, qualify, or modify an argument that addresses the entirety of the question.
- Explain how at least four documents' point of view, purpose, historical situation, and/or audience are relevant to the argument.
- Describe a broader historical context immediately relevant to the question.
- Explain how at least one additional piece of specific evidence beyond those found in the documents relates to an argument about the question.

The DBQ is designed to test your ability to read and interpret documents. Show your mastery of this skill by analyzing the content and the *point of view and validity of the source's author*. Answer the question fully by utilizing your analysis of the documents and the time period discussed to support a well-constructed essay.

1. Analyze how the various responses and reactions to the changes brought on by the advances in methods of production in Great Britain changed from the 1770s through the 1880s.

---

### DOCUMENT 1

Source: P. Bairoch International Industrialization Levels from 1750 to 1980 as published in the *Journal of European History,* fall of 1982.

**Industrialization Levels in Great Britain from 1750 to 1913**
**Level per Capita with 100 Being Equal to 1900 Production**

| Year | Production Level |
|------|------------------|
| 1750 | 10 |
| 1800 | 16 |
| 1830 | 25 |
| 1860 | 64 |
| 1880 | 87 |
| 1900 | 100 |
| 1913 | 115 |

## DOCUMENT 2

Source: Philosopher and economist Adam Smith, *An Inquiry into the Nature and Causes of the Wealth of Nations*, 1776.

To take an example, therefore, from a very trifling manufacture, but one in which the division of labour has been very often taken notice of, the trade of a pin-maker: a workman not educated to this business (which the division of labour has rendered a distinct trade), nor acquainted with the use of the machinery employed in it (to the invention of which the same division of labour has probably given occasion), could scarce, perhaps, with his utmost industry, make one pin in a day, and certainly could not make twenty. But in the way in which this business is now carried on, not only the whole work is a peculiar trade, but it is divided into a number of branches, of which the greater part are likewise peculiar trades. One man draws out the wire; another straights it; a third cuts it; a fourth points it; a fifth grinds it at the top for receiving the head; to make the head requires two or three distinct operations; to put it on is a peculiar business; to whiten the pins is another; it is even a trade by itself to put them into the paper; and the important business of making a pin is, in this manner, divided into about eighteen distinct operations, which, in some manufactories, are all performed by distinct hands, though in others the same man will sometimes perform two or three of them. I have seen a small manufactory of this kind, where ten men only were employed, and where some of them consequently performed two or three distinct operations. But though they were very poor, and therefore but indifferently accommodated with the necessary machinery, they could, when they exerted themselves, make among them about twelve pounds of pins in a day. There are in a pound upwards of four thousand pins of a middling size. Those ten persons, therefore, could make among them upwards of forty-eight thousand pins in a day. Each person, therefore, making a tenth part of forty-eight thousand pins, might be considered as making four thousand eight hundred pins in a day. But if they had all wrought separately and independently, and without any of them having been educated to this peculiar business, they certainly could not each of them have made twenty, perhaps not one pin in a day; that is, certainly, not the two hundred and fortieth, perhaps not the four thousand eight hundredth, part of what they are at present capable of performing, in consequence of a proper division and combination of their different operations.

**DOCUMENT 3**

Source: Letter from the Cloth Merchants of Leeds, England, advocating for the introduction of steam-powered looms, 1791.

If then by the Use of Machines, the Manufacture of Cotton, an Article which we import, and are supplied with from other Countries, and which can every where be procured on equal Terms, has met with such amazing Success, may not greater Advantages be reasonably expected from cultivating to the utmost the Manufacture of Wool, the Produce of our own Island, an Article in Demand in all Countries, almost the universal Clothing of Mankind?

In the Manufacture of Woollens, the Scribbling Mill, the Spinning Frame, and the Fly Shuttle, have reduced manual Labour nearly One third, and each of them at its-first Introduction carried an Alarm to the Work People, yet each has contributed to advance the Wages and to increase the Trade, so that if an Attempt was now made to deprive us of the Use of them, there is no Doubt, but every Person engaged in the Business, would exert himself to defend them.

From these Premises, we the undersigned Merchants, think it a Duty we owe to ourselves, to the Town of Leeds, and to the Nation at large, to declare that we will protect and support the free Use of the proposed Improvements in Cloth-Dressing, by every legal Means in our Power; and if after all, contrary to our Expectations, the Introduction of Machinery should for a Time occasion a Scarcity of Work in the Cloth Dressing Trade, we have unanimously agreed to give a Preference to such Workmen as are now settled Inhabitants of this Parish, and who give no Opposition to the present Scheme.

**DOCUMENT 4**

Source: *The People's Petition*, a petition circulated and sent to Parliament, 1838.

Humbly showeth:

That we, your petitioners, dwell in a land whose merchants are noted for their enterprise, whose manufacturers are very skillful, and whose workmen are proverbial for their industry. The land itself is goodly, the soil rich, and the temperature wholesome. It is abundantly furnished with the materials of commerce and trade. It has numerous and convenient harbors in facility of internal communication it exceeds all others. For three and twenty years we have enjoyed a profound peace. Yet with all the elements of national prosperity, and with every disposition and capacity to take advantage of them, we find ourselves overwhelmed with public and private suffering. We are bowed down under a load of taxes, which, notwithstanding, fall greatly short of the wants of our rulers. Our traders are trembling on the verge of bankruptcy, our workmen are starving. Capital brings no profit, and labor no remuneration. The home of the artificer is desolate, and the warehouse of the pawnbroker is full. The workhouse is crowded, and the manufactory is deserted. We have looked on every side; we have searched diligently in order to find out the causes of distress so sore and so long continued. We can discover none in nature or in Providence. ... The energies of a mighty kingdom have been wasted in building up the power of selfish and ignorant men, and its resources squandered for their aggrandizement. The few have governed for the interest of the few, while the interests of the many have been sottishly neglected, or insolently and tyrannically trampled upon. It was the fond expectation of the friends of the people that a remedy for the greater part, if not for the whole, of their grievances would be found in the Reform Act of 1832. They regarded that act as a wise means to a worthy end, as the machinery of an improved legislation, where the will of the masses would be at length potential. They have been bitterly and basely deceived. The fruit which looked so fair to the eye has turned to dust and ashes when gathered. The Reform Act has effected a transfer of power from one domineering faction to another, and left the people as helpless as before. Our slavery has been exchanged for an apprenticeship to liberty, which has aggravated the painful feelings of our social degradation by adding to them the sickening of still deferred hope. We come before your honorable house to tell you, with all humility, that this state of things must not be permitted to continue; that it cannot long continue, without very seriously endangering, the stability of the throne, and the peace of the Kingdom, and that if, by God's help, and all lawful and constitutional appliances, an end can be put to it, we are fully resolved that it shall speedily come to an end.

**WE DEMAND UNIVERSAL SUFFRAGE.**

The suffrage to be exempt from the corruption of the wealthy, and the violence of the powerful, must be secret.

**DOCUMENT 5**

Source: Philosopher and economist Karl Marx, *The Communist Manifesto*, 1848.

The bourgeois clap-trap about the family and education, about the hallowed co-relation of parents and child, becomes all the more disgusting, the more, by the action of Modern Industry, all the family ties among the proletarians are torn asunder, and their children transformed into simple articles of commerce and instruments of labour.

But you Communists would introduce community of women, screams the bourgeoisie in chorus.

The bourgeois sees his wife a mere instrument of production. He hears that the instruments of production are to be exploited in common, and, naturally, can come to no other conclusion that the lot of being common to all will likewise fall to the women.

He has not even a suspicion that the real point aimed at is to do away with the status of women as mere instruments of production.

For the rest, nothing is more ridiculous than the virtuous indignation of our bourgeois at the community of women which, they pretend, is to be openly and officially established by the Communists. The Communists have no need to introduce community of women; it has existed almost from time immemorial.

Our bourgeois, not content with having wives and daughters of their proletarians at their disposal, not to speak of common prostitutes, take the greatest pleasure in seducing each other's wives.

Bourgeois marriage is, in reality, a system of wives in common and thus, at the most, what the Communists might possibly be reproached with is that they desire to introduce, in substitution for a hypocritically concealed, an openly legalised community of women. For the rest, it is self-evident that the abolition of the present system of production must bring with it the abolition of the community of women springing from that system, i.e., of prostitution both public and private.

## DOCUMENT 6

Source: British illustration, 1860s.

## DOCUMENT 7

Source: Thomas Escott, Social and Political Historian, *England: Her People, Polity, and Pursuits*, 1885.

Before the eventful year 1832, most of the places under Government were in the hands of the great families. The Reform Bill admitted an entirely new element into political life; a host of applicants for Parliamentary position at once came forward, and as a consequence the social citadel was carried by persons who had nothing to do with the purely aristocratic section which had hitherto been paramount.

## Comments on the DBQ

It is amazing how many DBQ essays do not contain a thesis that directly answers all parts of the question.

The type of question in the sample DBQ is common because it asks you to describe the *reactions* and *responses* to some event or movement and how they changed over time. There are two tasks to this question. The first task is to identify the reactions and responses of Europeans to the rise of the Industrial Revolution. The second task is to illustrate how those reactions and responses changed over time. This question is clearly targeting the *continuity and change over time* skill. Different DBQs assess different skills. However, this skill is a common one as the type of question assesses the skills of determining and analyzing what has changed over time and what has remained constant.

Start the first task by reading the documents. Then analyze the documents and make notes on them. Then group them. Finally, use the documents to illustrate how Europeans reacted and responded to the new methods of production that were emblematic of the Industrial Revolution.

The second task is made easier because the documents are presented in chronological order. You can choose to have separate paragraphs, illustrating how the reactions and responses changed over time. Alternatively, you can write about a separate group of documents within each paragraph.

Do not forget to *demonstrate point of view*, purpose, audience, or at least historical context for many of the documents. This further helps to illustrate the reactions and possibly responses of Europeans to the onset of the Industrial Revolution.

Grouping documents is helpful for success, and there are many ways to group the documents presented in this DBQ. Possible groupings include those who viewed the Industrial Revolution in a positive light, those who viewed the Industrial Revolution in a negative light, the bourgeois bosses and their proponents, workers, and those who observed society, such as historians and artists.

Create a short outline. The structure that is easiest to write quickly includes a thesis that addresses both parts of the question and includes all of the groups you intend to use. The previous organizer was included to help you gather the evidence that you need to write your DBQ essay. So use it your first few times writing. Once you get the hang of writing a DBQ essay, write without using the organizer. Each group identified should have a separate paragraph, with a paragraph on change over time, followed by a concluding paragraph.

> **Tip**
>
> Before writing your essay, glance at the documents and their authors, and check the question to be certain that your thesis and your essay address all parts of the question!

## DBQ Sample Response

The evolution in the ways that goods were produced brought profound changes, first to Great Britain, and then to the rest of the world, during the Industrial Revolution, which increased Great Britain's production capabilities (document 1). Reactions and responses to these changes evolved as the era developed and can be understood through the eyes of those who observed society such as historians and artists (documents 2, 5, 6, 7), the bourgeois bosses and their proponents (documents 2&3), and the workers and their proponents (documents 4&5).

Historians and others who commented on society changed their views on the means of production as the methods and ethos of manufacturing evolved. Adam Smith, the father of economics, was very excited by the increases in productive capacity brought on by the introduction of the division of labor (document 2). As the first British student of economic conditions, he was naturally impressed by the gains made in that field. Karl Marx, the ultimate critic of capitalism, pointed out how this system of economy, and thus of production, exploits women by its very nature (document 5). He was likely to over exaggerate the flaws of a system that he was condemning to collapse. As the Industrial Revolution progressed, observers started to extol the virtues of the factory system again as can be seen in the drawing showing the general population's acknowledgement of the impressive nature of new machinery (document 6). The illustrator probably is representing modern technology in a positive light to satisfy the patrons of his/her work who are most likely wealthy industrialists who want their machines depicted. By the 1880s, historians like Escott were assessing the changes in the political climate (document 7). As a historian, Escott was trying to be unbiased, but was clearly influenced by the Victorian ideals of his times as well as the reform movement he studied. It appears that those who observed these changes professionally were at first in favor, then turned against these changes, and finally came to accept and study these changes.

One group that seemed to be universally in favor of the changes in production was the bourgeois bosses and their proponents. As time progressed, the bosses felt their power grow and demanded more control of their workers and their property. The Leeds wool manufacturers argued that their new methods of production were helping everyone in society, although they did note the fears of the workers (document 3). They were attempting to sway opinion in their direction to allow them to create steam-powered wool looms, so their facts were suspect due to their motives to increase output and thus profit. The community of businessmen continually favored changes in the modes of production over time. Governments and businesses teamed up in both world wars to improve and streamline modes of production and in fact in the First World War, production itself became a method of warfare.

Those who worked or who had worked in the factories seemed to think of the changes brought on by the Industrial Revolution in negative terms despite the fact that these changes had nearly doubled their standard of living by 1850. The People's Charter of 1838 demanded more rights for workers, such as voting, in order to help them address the ills of the factory system (document 4). This charter, which was signed by many workers and politicians of the day, became the basis for the workers' chartist movement that eventually did enlarge the franchise. The petition signers of the petition agreed that there should be a more equitable distribution of power to all citizens, a goal that Escott notes the results of in document 7. Karl Marx was in agreement with the People's Charter, but goes much further and intends to offend the bourgeois class by deriding their gender roles and equating them with class roles (document 5). Marx's forceful dissemination of his ideas would later be used as a justification for a revolution in Russia that attempted to skip the capitalist phase of society as Marx described it and go directly from monarchy to communism. This is clearly an impossible feat if one believes the majority of Marx's work, which describes an inevitable evolution of society that must go through a capitalist phase to achieve true control of the means of production and distribution by the proletariat. In many ways, the changing attitudes on industrialization and urbanization, including those of Karl Marx and others of the era such as Louis Blanc and Marcel Proust, led to the communist revolutions first in Russia, then in China, Vietnam, North Korea, and even Cuba.

The responses and reactions of the people living in Great Britain from 1770 through 1880 to the changes in production seem to be based upon their station in life with social observers changing their views to suit the times, employers being in favor of the changes, and workers being against them. However, it is clear that those best able to study those changes were at first in favor of them, became skeptical of them, and later decided to study the social and political effects of the evolution of the means of production from the 1770s through the 1880s.

## Comments on the Sample Answer to the DBQ

This is a top-notch answer that would receive a *score of 7*. This essay demonstrates insightful use of documents to prove a cogent *thesis that fully addresses all parts of the question*. More importantly, the essay clearly meets all parts of the DBQ rubric (found on pages 32–33) for the following reasons:

1. This essay is awarded *1 point* for an evaluative thesis that directly addresses all parts of the question and makes a historically defensible claim.
2. This essay is awarded *1 point* for *contextualization* because it situates the argument by explaining the broader historical events, developments, or processes immediately relevant to the question.
3. This essay is awarded *3 points* for *evidence* because it utilizes content from at least *six* documents and employs historical reasoning to explain relationships among the pieces of evidence provided in the response *and* how they corroborate, qualify, or modify an argument that addresses the entirety of the question. This includes *1 point* for *evidence beyond the documents* because it provides an example or additional piece of specific evidence beyond those found in the documents to support or qualify the argument.
4. This essay is awarded *1 point* for *document analysis* because it explains how more than *four* documents' point of view, purpose, historical situation, and/or audience are relevant to the argument.

The most important characteristic of this response is the creative use of point of view to demonstrate command of the skill of analyzing historical sources. The use of point of view in Document 5 was creative and historically supportable. The essay also had some panache without using clichés, which may set it apart from other essays the graders read.

For more information on scoring DBQ essays, turn to the AP European History Document-Based Question (DBQ) Rubric on pages 32–33.

# PART 2

# Review Section:
# Time Periods

For further explanation of the required objectives for this course, which occur both by theme and by time period as separate objectives, it is strongly recommended that you or the teacher reading this book read both the *AP European History Curriculum Framework* and the Course and Exam Description, both available at the AP European History College Board website.

# Examination of Periodization and Required Time Periods

The AP European History course has four time periods that are required for study. These time periods are important to understand. Many of the historical skills that are tested on the exam—such as periodization, patterns of continuity and change over time, contextualization, causation, and historical argumentation—utilize the periods that are required. The College Board has divided the course themes and key concepts into four chronological periods. These periods divide the years from c. 1450 to the present and provide a chronological framework for the course. *The instructional importance and assessment weighting for each period is equal.*

This does *not*, however, mean that each concept and set of events within each time period are equal. In fact, these are very broad time periods that need to be further divided. The four time periods are as follows:

Period 1: c. 1450 to c. 1648
Period 2: c. 1648 to c. 1815
Period 3: c. 1815 to c. 1914
Period 4: c. 1914 to the present

Each time period has a set of *key concepts* that are described before each section. The writers of the *AP European History Curriculum Framework* have delineated these time periods based upon major political events. The first time period begins at the start of the course in 1450 or so and ends with the Peace of Westphalia, which reshaped the balance of power in Europe. The second time period ends in 1815 with the defeat of Napoleon and the Congress of Vienna redesigning the map of Europe. The third time period ends with the advent of the First World War. The final time period is the most recent hundred years.

When combined with the themes in European history seen below, this delineation helps historians organize their ideas around some chronology. These themes, which are explained in detail in part one, are the following:

1. Interaction of Europe and the World
2. Economic and Commercial Developments
3. Cultural and Intellectual Developments
4. States and Other Institutions of Power
5. Social Organization and Development
6. National and European Identity
7. Technological and Scientific Innovation

The time periods were created to help organize the facts and movements in historical analysis and also to help you gain the skill of periodization. This skill requires you to describe, analyze, and evaluate different ways that historians divide history into discrete and definable periods. Historians construct and debate different, sometimes competing, models of periodization; the choice of specific turning points or starting and ending dates might attribute a higher value to one narrative, region, or group than to another. To help you understand that debate, periodization is discussed throughout this exam preparation guide. You should also note that the ability to test the periodization skill was a contributing factor in the decision to make the time periods so large; you are asked to undertake the task of correct periodization of evidence within and across the specified time periods.

The same is true for the creation of the nine units in European history. The nine units created by the College Board can be justified with historical thinking and evidence. However, arguments exist for dividing the course content in many different ways. For that reason, the nine units are covered in different ways in this book. Some units are covered in only one chapter while other units are covered in two or three chapters, depending on how much material is covered by each of the units created by the College Board.

This book also presents periodization that *mostly* agrees with the *AP European History Curriculum Framework* but *differs on two major points*: the Industrial Revolution and the English struggle for constitutionalism. Because of the timing of the period breaks—which makes so much sense from the perspective of a political historian—the history of those two important narratives of European history were bisected by the framework. This book deviates from the *AP European History Curriculum Framework* in that periodization in order to preserve those two narratives.

Because of the complexity of the material and because historians have traditionally broken European history into other periods that were shaped by the events of their own times, each time period and many units are broken into several chapters that fit more traditional historical periods, such as the Renaissance or the Reformation. The logic behind the longer, and more definitive, historical periods makes much sense. However, the traditional view is kept for its organizational value in order to preserve some historical narratives that may help with contextualization and periodization in the short-answer, DBQ, and LEQ tasks. It should also give you a strong basis of facts and historical interpretations to enable historical argumentation.

Each time period is broken into multiple chapters and units. Each chapter ends with 6 to 15 multiple-choice questions and answer explanations as well as some essay question answer possibilities with comments.

Each time period ends with an assessment section of about 15 multiple-choice questions, some short-answer questions, and two free-response question choices with essay and multiple-choice answer explanations.

# Time Period One: c. 1450 to c. 1648

## Learning Objectives

These are the Key Concepts for time period 1, according to the *AP European History Curriculum Framework*:

→ **KEY CONCEPT 1.1** The worldview of European intellectuals shifted from one based on ecclesiastical and classical authority to one based primarily on inquiry and observation of the natural world.

→ **KEY CONCEPT 1.2** The struggle for sovereignty within and among states resulted in varying degrees of political centralization.

→ **KEY CONCEPT 1.3** Religious pluralism challenged the concept of a unified Europe.

→ **KEY CONCEPT 1.4** Europeans explored and settled overseas territories, encountering and interacting with indigenous populations.

→ **KEY CONCEPT 1.5** European society and the experiences of everyday life were increasingly shaped by commercial and agricultural capitalism, notwithstanding the persistence of medieval social and economic structures.

## Time Period Overview

Time period 1 is about the birth of modern Europe. It examines the beginning of global trade, the acceptance of multiple religious truths, the conflict between divine right monarchy and parliamentary power, and the importance of the emergence of capitalism as Europe increasingly interacts with the rest of the world. This time period includes the traditional delineations of the following eras:

- The Renaissance
- The Reformation
- The Age of Exploration
- The Scientific Revolution

These traditional delineations do overlap in many ways. For example, Galileo, but not Newton, is included with the start of the Scientific Revolution. The themes within each delineation, as previously stated in the key concepts, can be seen woven through the first three chapters of this book.

# UNIT 1

# Renaissance and Exploration

## Unit 1 Overview: Renaissance and Exploration

**Unit description:** The first unit, Renaissance and Exploration, combines what have traditionally been two separate units into one. This combination makes a lot of sense as both were happening simultaneously. The Renaissance traditionally is taught as beginning in the 14th century and lasting through the 17th. The Age of Exploration is usually taught as occurring during the 15th through the 17th centuries. Both also focus on individualism, interaction of cultures and ideas, and the expansion of Europe intellectually, politically, and technologically. Both were driven by new ideas and new technology that allowed the separate but intertwined movements to occur.

This unit covers the events of the rise of the Renaissance and its spread throughout Europe. It also covers the causes, consequences, and events of the Age of Exploration. This unit should be examined through the lenses of six of the seven themes of the course, omitting only National and European Identity. Therefore, students should keep the other six themes in mind when studying this unit: Interaction of Europe and the World, Economic and Commercial Development, Cultural and Intellectual Developments, States and Other Institutions of Power, Social Organization and Development, and Technological and Scientific Innovation. The major topics of study in unit 1 include the following:

- Understanding context in Renaissance and Discovery

- Italian Renaissance

- Northern Renaissance

- Printing

- New monarchies

- Technological advances in the Age of Exploration

- Rivals on the world stage (Spain vs. Portugal vs. England vs. France)

- Colonial expansion and Columbian Exchange

- The slave trade

- The commercial revolution

- Causation in the Renaissance and Age of Discovery

# SPECIAL NOTE ON PERIODIZATION

Time period 1 contains three main topics that were taking place concurrently, the Renaissance (1300–1600s), the Age of Exploration (1492–1600s), and the Reformation and Counter-Reformation (1517–1648). Many history texts have decided to tackle these ideas individually. However, the College Board has decided to include Renaissance and Exploration together and yet separate the Reformation. Its choice in periodization gives some questions to consider:

- What are the differences/commonalities among the three topics?
- Why choose to divide them into two periods and place Exploration and Renaissance together?
- Were all three intellectual movements to some degree?
- Did all three impart social change?
- Did the wars of religion influence the spread of Renaissance ideas throughout Europe?
- Are the interactions between the natives and the Europeans influenced by the religion of the Europeans?
- What are the best ways to divide historical events into categories?

By determining answers to the questions above, you can really begin to think about the significant impact good reasoning in periodization can have on your test success. This impact varies from earning the contextualization point on free-response questions to showing deeper connections across time. Learning how historians create and question the creation of periods in history is a skill that separates the professionals from the amateurs.

Remember to look for links between and among different topics and units. If you do so, you will become a more adept historian. Finding unique ways to connect a diverse range of evidence into an analytic narrative that is compelling is a large factor in student success in this course.

**Note that all of unit 1 is contained in chapter 1.**

# 1

# The Renaissance and Age of Exploration

## Key Terms

- Renaissance
- City-states
- Elizabethan Age
- Secularism
- Christian humanism
- Humanism
- Individualism
- Mannerism
- Manorialism

- Open-field system
- Credit
- Interest
- Usury
- Mercantilism
- Deism
- Scientific Revolution
- Crop rotation
- Treaty of Tordesillas

- Triangle trade
- Columbian Exchange
- Potosi & Zacatecas
- Encomienda
- Fall of Constantinople
- Viceroyalty system
- Middle passage

## Key People

- Medici family
- Leonardo da Vinci
- Michelangelo Buonarroti
- Petrarch
- Boccaccio
- Niccolo Machiavelli
- Desiderius Erasmus
- Leon Battista Alberti
- Lorenzo Valla
- Thomas More
- Johann Gutenberg

- Albrecht Dürer
- Baldassare Castiglione
- Donatello
- Filippo Brunelleschi
- Raphael
- Fuggers
- Marsiglio Finicio
- Pico Della Mirandola
- Sir Francis Bacon
- René Descartes
- Nicolaus Copernicus

- Galileo Galilei
- Johannes Kepler
- Christopher Columbus
- Henry the Navigator
- Vasco da Gama
- Hernan Cortez
- Francisco Pizarro
- John Cabot
- Bartholomew Dias
- Ferdinand Magellan
- Sir Francis Drake

## Overview

The Renaissance and the Age of Exploration in many ways occurred because of each other. The revival of old ideas of the Greeks and Romans was supported by opening trade with the East as a result of the Crusades. The merchants of Genoa and Venice brought back ancient manuscripts as well as new ideas. More importantly, a market for goods from Asia was created, making travel there profitable. The ideas that they brought back spurred the greatest period of intellectual growth in European history from the Renaissance through the Scientific Revolution of the 17th century. The trade that was brought home created the motivation to sail west to find better trade routes to Asia. So exploration of the Near East during the Crusades led to the Renaissance. This created a market for new items and new ideas as well as sparked greater curiosity about the world, which led to the era of European exploration of the rest of the world.

Although the Renaissance was a period of artistic, cultural, and intellectual revival, the term *renaissance*, a rebirth, can be misleading. It implies that the 15th and 16th centuries marked a distinct awakening for Europeans from the "darkness" of the Middle Ages. Actually, the medieval period gave rise to the basic institutions of Europe: its laws, languages, and economics. The elite culture that developed during the 15th century in the city-states of the Italian peninsula not only borrowed from ancient Greece and Rome but also expressed a new conception of humankind, *individualism*, through innovative art and literature. It was in these independent domains, governed by a merchant class, by despots, or by republicans, that pure *secularism* (a belief that life was more than a preparation for the hereafter) first appeared in the modern world. The name *Renaissance* was not used until Jules Michelet employed it in the late 19th century. This explains why some historians may now see the delineation of the Renaissance as a separate era from the Reformation, the Age of Exploration, the Enlightenment, and the Scientific Revolution as arbitrary. The fall of Constantinople in 1453 to the Ottoman Turks caused many scholars of the Byzantine Empire to relocate in Italy, which helped usher in the Renaissance.

*Humanism* was a literary and educational movement. It was truly modern in that a class of nonclerical writers concerned themselves with secular issues but based their answers to current problems on the wisdom of the ancient Greeks and Romans. Humanism rose in Italy in the 14th and 15th centuries. With their special affinity for classical Greek and Roman culture, schools such as the Florentine Academy emerged. These schools studied classical authors such as Homer, Plato, Aristotle, and Cicero. In Northern Europe, the "pagan" humanism of the Italian Renaissance was rejected in favor of a blend of religion and classical literature. Christian humanists, such as Erasmus and Thomas More, tried to recapture the moral force of early Christianity by studying the Greek and Hebrew texts of the Bible and the writings of the Church Fathers.

Whether or not the Renaissance marked the beginning of the modern age, it provided a conception of the role and destiny of humankind that was vastly different from the ideas of the Middle Ages. In fact, its artistic achievements influenced the culture of all Europe.

Spurred by the curiosity of the Renaissance, desire for profit from trade, and the desire for individual glory that was now coming to individuals, many people began to increase Europe's interaction with the rest of the world through voyages of exploration. These voyages were often sponsored by *new monarchs* who had power and wealth beyond their predecessors. These voyages gave Europeans new perspectives, new products, new markets, and the beginning of a global economic community. They even found the Americas, which were previously unknown to them. Europeans also developed new ships and weapons that allowed them to dominate the peoples that they encountered and to impose unfair trade practices on many of those peoples. Europeans began to import enslaved Africans to the Americas and changed the ways of life of the natives almost everywhere they went. In order to improve navigation and also to increase the new focus on knowledge and inquiry from the Renaissance, a new type of analytical thought was developed that helped to discover ideas about how the universe worked; the Scientific Revolution began.

Since the Renaissance is defined less by specific events than by individual accomplishments and ideas, the following review focuses on significant personalities, achievements, and concepts. First, though, are a few words about the setting for one of the most creative periods in all of human history.

# The Italian Renaissance

## The Italian City-States

Italy was not so much a nation as an idea in the 15th century. It was an amalgamation of many distinct political entities known as city-states. By the 15th century, certain northern Italian towns that had been trade centers of the Roman Empire expanded into independent city-states that ruled wide areas of the surrounding countryside.

"Geography is destiny" proved true for the Italians of the 14th and 15th centuries. With their nation fragmented since the fall of Rome and their land becoming a battleground for the more unified peoples of Europe, Italians took advantage of their proximity to the sea. Italians applied the energy that springs from always being at the focus of a crisis to establish a sea-going trade with the peoples in the eastern Mediterranean. They became the "middlemen" of Europe.

## The Major City-States

- The Republic of Florence was considered the cultural center of the Italian Renaissance and is often compared to ancient Athens for its utter brilliance over a brief period.
- Republic of Genoa.
- Duchy of Milan.
- Rome, the Papal States.
- Naples, Kingdom of the Two Sicilies.
- Venice, Venetian Republic.
- Venice, Genoa, and Pisa (in the Republic of Florence) used their strategic locations on the Mediterranean Sea to control the European trade with the Middle East and Asia.
  - Florence, and to a lesser extent Rome, Naples, and Milan, thrived as manufacturing and market centers.
- Bankers from these prosperous cities made profitable loans to the people who shaped European life at the time.
  - Popes and monarchs of Europe financed successful commercial ventures.
    - The economic power of these city-states, combined with Rome as the center of Catholic power, made Italy a center of culture and luxury in Western Europe during the 14th and 15th centuries.
    - As a major cog in trade routes between Europe and Asia, Italian city-states helped to spread ideas from different cultures around the world throughout Europe.
  - The city-states shared Arab mathematics and technology as well as Asian ideas and products with the Continent (for a price and a hefty profit).
  - Ideas from many cultures, including the revival of ancient Greek and Roman ideas, were present.
    - Italians revived a sense of pride about their past.
    - These factors all contributed to creating a prosperous merchant-centered society that fostered the age of the Renaissance.
  - The powerful middle class of merchants and bankers controlled the governments of the city-states and served as patrons to the artistic geniuses of the times.
  - The newfound wealth of the middle class encouraged appreciation of earthly pleasures and diminished dedication to the pious traditions of the Middle Ages.
  - Most people were not irreligious. Rather, accidents of history and geography presented them with great wealth, far beyond any expectations of the subsistence feudal economy that had ruled Europe for a thousand years.
  - Money was meant to be spent. It just so happened that as more people spent money on the beautiful handiwork of the skilled artisans in their cities, more beautiful things were made to be bought.
- Thus, the Renaissance saw the beginning of the market economy in art, which drew the most talented geniuses to the field in search of profits and fame. This set the stage for other markets to emerge in labor and other resources.
  - Beauty for its own sake and art for art's sake—values absent from European culture since the end of the ancient world—replaced the medieval notion that art that is not dedicated to God is irreverent.
  - To these people, the world could be changed without the help of God. "Money is power" was becoming true regardless of one's status at birth.
  - Secularism, the concept of pursuing the pleasures in this life rather than the promises of the afterlife, was born. The rich nurtured it; the lower classes copied it.

## The Medici Family

The Medici family was the most famous dynasty of those merchants and bankers who used their vast wealth both to govern the city-states and to patronize illustrious creators in the arts.

- *Giovanni de' Medici* (d. 1429): Merchant and banker of Florence, founder of the dynasty.
  - He could be considered one of the world's first modern persons, an ultimate adapter who ignored the Church's prohibitions of lending for interest to provide the necessary funds for a changing world economy.
  - Although his son and great-grandson were the ones who brought glory to the family name by spending the fortune that he established, de' Medici's originality is reflected in his deeds rather than his ideas. He is one of the people of Europe whose restless genius molded the modern world.
- *Cosimo de' Medici* (1389–1464): Son of Giovanni who used the family fortune to fill the vacuum of power resulting from the lack of a national monarchy.
  - By forming alliances with other powerful families of Florence, he became the unofficial ruler of the republic.
- *Lorenzo the Magnificent* (1449–1492): Cosimo's grandson, not only the republic's ruler but a lavish patron of the arts.
  - He personified the Renaissance attitude of living life rather than waiting for its fulfillment after death.
  - Lorenzo's genius was his recognition and support of the creative talent in his city; his luck was to be surrounded by geniuses.

The Medici family ruled the Grand Duchy of Tuscany, of which Florence was the principal city, well into the 18th century. Two popes, many cardinals, and two queens of France belonged to the family.

## Individualism: A New Concept of Humankind

"Man is the measure of all things." A sense of human power replaced religious awe. Pleasure and accomplishment superseded the medieval dedication to the cloistered life of the clergy. Instead of the disdain for the concerns of this world that the piety of the Middle Ages had fostered, people now valued involvement, a life of activity.

*Virtu* literally means "the quality of being a man." It is possible for a woman to express but was expected among aggressive males, the movers and shakers of the day. Whatever a person's pursuit, in learning, in the arts, or even in war, *virtu* meant living up to one's highest potential and excelling in all endeavors. The Renaissance man was an all-around gentleman, as comfortable with the pen or the brush as with the sword—a lover, poet, painter, and conversationalist.

## The Arts as an Expression of Individualism

Before the Renaissance, the Church was the greatest patron of the arts. Painters and sculptors labored anonymously to fill the churches and cathedrals of the Middle Ages with figures of the saints—figures that lacked the proportions and animation of real human forms or faces. During the Renaissance, although the Church remained a major patron, the new commercial class and the governments of the city-states also supported the arts. Even though the work was religious in nature, the forms were anatomically proportional, the faces were filled with emotion, and the artists reveled in their individuality of style.

- Architecture adapted Greco-Roman symmetry, classical columns, arches, and domes.
  - Architects such as *Filippo Brunelleschi* (1377–1446), famous for Il Duomo (the first dome built since ancient times in Florence), and *Leon Battista Alberti* (1404–1472) studied ancient Roman buildings and used those buildings' principles of design to build cathedrals.
- Sculpture once again became freestanding, not designed to fit in niches of churches, and portrayed nude subjects in the Greek tradition in both religious and mythological representations.
  - *Lorenzo Ghiberti* (1378–1455): Sculpted a set of bronze doors for the Florentine baptistery with not only crowds of human figures but the illusion of depth.

- *Donatello*'s bronze *David* (c. 1440): The first freestanding nude sculpted since Roman times in Europe and a tribute to his teacher, Brunelleschi.

Painting was primarily religious in theme. However, it was radically different from medieval art because of the invention of oil paints and because of the illusion of three dimensions created by precise variation of size (perspective). Art was less symbolic and more representational. It depicted real people in recognizable settings and glorified the beauty of the corporeal world.

- *Giotto* (1267–1337): Painted on walls in Florentine buildings and created the illusions of depth and movement.
- *Masaccio* (1401–1428): Used light and shadow, linear perspective, nude figures, and the illusion of perspective.
- *Sandro Botticelli* (1444–1510): Painted themes from classical mythology, such as his *Birth of Venus.*
- *Raphael* (1483–1520): Considered one of the greatest painters of any era; his portraits and Madonnas epitomize the Renaissance style.

## The Greatest of the Great

- *Leonardo da Vinci* (1452–1519): Personification of the Renaissance man; painter, sculptor, architect, engineer, writer, scientist.
  - The versatility of his genius marks the last time that a single human could command virtually all the realms of knowledge and create masterworks in several areas of competence.
  - His *Mona Lisa* and his *Last Supper* rival any of the world's great paintings for the perfection of their execution and sheer beauty.
- *Michelangelo Buonarroti* (1475–1564): Primarily a sculptor whose *Pietá* (Mary mourning the body of Christ lying across her lap) is often considered the most perfect marble carving.
  - His awesome statues *Moses* and *David* are unrivaled masterpieces that reflect religiosity and real human emotion.
  - His paintings in the *Sistine Chapel* in Rome, over which he labored for four years, portray biblical and allegorical figures with power, grace, and human clarity.
  - Michelangelo glorified God by depicting the beauty of His earthly creations.

## Humanism

This was a literary and educational movement distinct from the writing of the late Middle Ages in both its subject matter and in its practitioners. The subject matter dealt with issues of politics and personal concern outside the realm of religion. The practitioners were laypeople who considered writing a profession rather than a pursuit of the clergy. They drew on antiquity, which ironically had been preserved by monks laboriously copying ancient manuscripts. They wrote in Italian rather than in Latin, and thereby created the first European vernacular literature.

- The works of the great poet *Dante* (1265–1321), especially his *Divine Comedy,* along with the speech patterns of Florence influenced the standard form of modern Italian.
- *Petrarch* (1304–1374): Considered the first "modern" writer, he wrote sonnets in Italian and other works in Latin. Petrarch used writing to contemplate the ebb and flow of his life and the human condition itself.
  - The irony is that he is most known as a modern writer. However, Petrarch's largest contribution to the era was popularizing the study of classical writers, such as Plato and Cicero.
- *Juan Luis Vives* (1493–1540): A humanist writer who outlined a theory of education based upon the classics that came to define humanism. He was also a strong influence on Montaigne.
- *Marsilio Ficino* (1433–1499): A Catholic priest and an influential philosopher of the Italian humanist movement; he was the first to translate Plato's works into Latin and was named by Cosimo de' Medici as the first heir to the revived Platonic Academy.

- *Boccaccio* (1313–1375): A contemporary of Petrarch and, like him, a Florentine.
  - His most famous work is the *Decameron*, which satirized society and the clergy with entertaining tales that reflected upon the human condition.
- *Leonardo Bruni* (1370–1444): A chancellor of the Republic of Florence in the late 14th century. He wrote perhaps the first modern history, an account of the development of Florence, by using narrative, drawing on authentic sources, and introducing new historical periods.
- *Baldassare Castiglione* (1478–1529): Offered a manual for the manners of the modern gentleman, *The Book of the Courtier*.
  - A gentleman is trained for polite company, poised and well dressed, skilled in arms and sports, capable of making music and conversation, a reader of the classics, a social mixer who is good humored, light-hearted, and considerate of others' feelings.
  - It was a civilized antidote to the crude social habits of the day, when even the wellborn spit on the floor, wiped their noses on their sleeves, ate without utensils, shrieked, and sulked.
- *Niccolò Machiavelli* (1469–1527): *The Prince* was the first meaningful treatise on political science, an observation of how governments actually rule without moral judgment or exhortation.
  - It is one of the most maligned and misinterpreted books of modern times, called both "cynical and ruthless" and the "handbook of dictators." It originated the concept of "the end justifies the means."
  - Machiavelli discovered that successful governments throughout history, whether Italian city-states or national monarchies, acted in their own political interests, making war or keeping the peace, true to their word or deceitful, and benevolent or brutal whenever useful.
    - Religion had virtually ceased to influence the process of governing as the rise of the nation-state became the ultimate goal.
  - *The Prince* (1513) offered keen insights and was meant as a guide to the survival of the independent city-states of Italy, which were vulnerable to the predatory powers in the North.
- *Laura Cereta* (1469–1499): A well-known humanist and early feminist, she probably taught moral philosophy at University of Padua, a center of Renaissance learning.
  - Her 1488 *Epistolae familiars* ("Familiar Letters") were widely condemned for her criticism of 15th-century gender bias.
  - When told by a man that intelligent women were unattractive, she retorted that so were unintelligent men.

## The Northern Renaissance

The Northern Renaissance was the spread of Renaissance ideals from Italy to Northern Europe, including what are modern-day Germany, England, Switzerland, France, Belgium, and Holland. This period saw the emergence of market economies in England and the Netherlands, bringing prosperity and artistic renewal to Northern Europe. The Northern Renaissance differed from the Italian Renaissance in that the Italian Renaissance was much more secular, whereas religion was emphasized in the North. Social reforms through Christian values and an emphasis on reforming all of society through better Christian living were the hallmarks of the Northern Renaissance. Pietism, encompassing more arduous religious devotion of the laity, emerged as an aspect of this line of reasoning.

- *Christian humanism* emerged as the thinkers and writers in the North adopted a Renaissance curiosity for knowledge but based their research on the Hebrew and Greek texts of the Bible. In contrast, the Italians applied their new zeal for knowledge to the earlier pagan texts of ancient Greece and Rome. Note that works from outside the Judeo-Christian ethic were referred to as pagan then and by historians now.
  - The Northern Renaissance originated in part because of cultural diffusion as northern students went to Italy to study and came back with new ideas and ideals.
  - The thirst for knowledge and the new artistic and engineering techniques of the Italian Renaissance were transferred to northwestern Europe, leading to a Renaissance that was strongest in the Germanic areas and the Low Countries (Holland and Belgium).

## Banking

One of the commonalities between the Italian Renaissance and the Northern Renaissance was the importance of rising economies and trade. This was typified by the Medici family in Italy as discussed earlier and the *Fugger* family in the German free imperial city of Augsburg, which peaked in banking power under *Jacob Fugger*. In many ways, the Renaissance was an upper-class movement that came about in no small part because of the growing wealth of merchants and bankers. While the Italians were the trendsetters in banking as early as the 1100s, the formalized systems that included banks with offices in multiple cities allowed merchants across Europe to travel without needing to carry gold. Now they could withdraw money from offices in many cities, making merchants less prone to robbery.

As the wealth of the common people grew, so did the banking industry. Christians began to compete with the Jewish money lenders when those Christians found ways around the *usury* ban in Christianity by requiring insurance for loans. As banking emerged into a field of finance, many bankers began to offer *credit* so that merchants could borrow money for purchasing wares to sell and then pay it back to the bankers with interest. Many stronger realms, such as the Ottoman Empire and France, even began to secure the services of a "court Jew" who could attain loans and make loans to citizens at interest to manage the finances of the state. Jewish people were not prevented from lending money by their religion, as Christians were. So that is why governments chose a Jewish person as their chief banker. These positions later evolved into the modern minister of finance.

The emergence of banking in Northern Europe and Italy coincided with the growth of the Renaissance and its spread of ideas. As merchants who were not nobility gained economic power, they also began to desire political power to match. In fact, much of the political developments of the Renaissance period were tied to the growth of banking.

## Germany

Much like Italy, Germany was a collection of principalities that would not be united into a single nation until the late 19th century. Often referred to in this text as the Germanic states, Germany consisted of over 300 individual political units during the 15th century. At the turn of the 16th century, on the eve of the Reformation, Germany was at the heart of European progress. Although politically diverse (the German-speaking world included most of central Europe, Switzerland, and parts of the Netherlands), its economy thrived anyway. Towns sprouted, grew, and traded. Banking expanded; the Fuggers and other German families controlled more capital than the Italian bankers and all other Europeans combined.

## Science and Technology

The *printing press* was popularized by *Johann Gutenberg* (c. 1400–1468), but Johann Faust and Peter Schoffer also used it around the same time as Gutenberg. The first printing press was actually invented in China. However, Gutenberg was the first to make *interchangeable movable type* from lead molds. The introduction of the printing press in Europe had a massive impact on society because spreading ideas, spreading propaganda, and stimulating education became easier. Books became cheaper, so more people read. This caused a *reading revolution* in society as reading became an individualized activity rather than one person reading aloud to a group. Now the Bible was printed in many vernacular languages for the laity to read for themselves, which had a significant social impact. This also helped lead to the advent of the Reformation as many in Europe did not need the Catholic priest to be God's intermediary, and worship became much more individualized.

- *Regiomontanus* (Johann Muller, 1436–1476) and *Nicholas of Cusa* (1401-1464) laid the foundations for modern mathematics and science in the 15th century.
- *Martin Behaim* (1459-1507) and *Johannes Schoner* (1477-1547) developed the era's most accurate maps.

- *Nicolaus Copernicus* (1473–1543) upset the time-honored *geocentric view* (that heavenly bodies revolved around the Earth) of astronomy with calculations that offered proof of a *heliocentric* (sun-centered) system.
  - This view contested the Aristotelian model adopted as the official Roman Catholic view of the solar system.
  - This contradiction is a *major milestone in the creation of a divide between religion and science* that began during the period of the Renaissance and continued as a theme throughout European history. It helped to mark the Renaissance as the start of the modern era.
- The notion that humankind could understand and control nature evolved from the work of these Germans.

## Mysticism

Mysticism involved the belief that an individual, alone, unaided by the Church or sacraments, could commune with God. The mystics, such as *Meister Eckhart* (1260–1328) and *Thomas à Kempis* (1380–1471), author of the inspirational *Imitation of Christ*, pursued religious depth rather than rebellion. They stayed true to the Church but sought to offer, to the few faithful who could understand, a substance that transcended traditional religiosity.

- *Gerard Groote* (1340–1384): A Dutch lay preacher, he organized the Brothers of the Common Life in the late 14th century; this was a religious organization that stressed the personal virtues of Christianity rather than doctrine. Its movement of *modern devotion* preached Christ-like love, tolerance, and humility.
- Both mysticism and the basic religious devotion of many laypeople contrasted, ominously, with the worldliness and smugness of the clergy.
- *Desiderius Erasmus* (1456–1536): "The Christian gentleman" personified Christian humanism in his philosophic stances known as "the philosophy of Christ."
  - A man of letters, he disdained the Middle Ages, ignored hard philosophy, admired antiquity, and wrote about humanist issues in purified Latin.
  - The ultimate moderate, he championed gradual reform, ridiculed hypocrisy among the powerful, distrusted the fickle opinions of common people, and abhorred violence.
  - He satirized the worldliness of the clergy and was critical of the Catholic emphasis on saints in *The Praise of Folly*.
  - He offered a model of practical Christian behavior in *Handbook of a Christian Knight*.
  - He translated new Greek and Latin editions of the Bible.
  - He was a confidant of kings and a critic of Church abuses.
  - His aim was gentle reform of the Church from within.
  - He was the most famous and influential intellectual individual of his times. Intellectuals used his writings and his example to preach peace, reason, tolerance, and loving reform.

## Artists

- *Albrecht Dürer* (1471–1528): One of the master artists of the era.
  - His self-portraits and woodblock prints, such as *The Four Horsemen of the Apocalypse*, are still revered today.
  - He was a mathematician who was painting landscapes and self-portraits at age 13.
- *Peter Brueghel the Elder* (1520–1569): Focused on lives of ordinary people and painted and made prints that depicted them at work and play. His work challenged the notion of the Italian Renaissance that art should be focused on only religious and aristocratic subjects.

## England

The Renaissance in England coincided with, and was fostered by, the reign of *Elizabeth I* (1558–1603). An era of intense nationalism produced by the resolution of dynastic rivalries and religious turmoil, it gave birth to perhaps the greatest vernacular literature of all time.

- An era of profound economic and cultural growth known as the *Elizabethan Age* prevailed under the reign of Elizabeth I.
- The dramatist *Christopher Marlowe* (1564–1593).
- Poet *Edmund Spenser* (1552–1599).
- Scientist *Francis Bacon* (1561–1626).
- The greatest writer in English, perhaps in any language, *William Shakespeare* (1564–1616) reflected the influence of the dramatists of the ancient world and also the writers of the Italian Renaissance.
  - He single-handedly set the standard for the English language.
- During the reign of Elizabeth's father, *Henry VIII* (1491–1547), a contemporary of Erasmus, *Sir Thomas More* (1478–1535), fostered the Erasmian spirit in his *Utopia*. This book criticized the correctable abuses of various institutions and offered a blueprint for a perfect society.
  - A devout Roman Catholic, Sir Thomas More was beheaded for not supporting the king against the Pope during the English Reformation.

## France

After the Hundred Years' War (1337–1453), the monarchy in France was strengthened by a renewal of commerce, which expanded and enriched the middle class. France was also realizing a wave of nationalism during the Renaissance era, possibly in part as a reaction to the Hundred Years' War. Government was centralized because the nobility had been weakened by a century of warfare, and the *bourgeoisie* (servant-keeping middle class) provided an ample source of revenue for the royal treasury. Through the late-15th and early-16th centuries, a succession of strong kings such as *Louis XI, Charles VIII,* and *Louis XII* reduced the power of the nobility, firmed up the structure of the modern nation-state, and brought the middle class into government as advisers.

- *Rabelais* (1494–1553), a priest and a classicist, attacked the failings of French society and the Church in his *Gargantua and Pantagruel* while advocating rational reform.
- *Montaigne* (1533–1592) invented the format of the essay, which is derived from the French term *essaier*, meaning "to test." His *Essays* preached open-mindedness and rational skepticism. They offered an urbane, modern view of life.

## Spain

Locked into Catholic orthodoxy by centuries of warfare against the Muslims (Moors), who had conquered much of the Iberian Peninsula, the Spanish reached the height of their expansion in the 16th century through exploration and overseas colonization.

Xenophobia and rigidity diluted the impact of Renaissance individualism and humanism in Spain. In 1492 (when Aragon and Castille united to form modern Spain), the Jews and Muslims, the core of the nation's educated middle class, were expelled. The expulsion of the Muslims (Moors) and Jewish people led to an intellectual and financial vacuum in Spain. The entire money-lending infrastructure in Spain had been run by the Jewish community. The loss of that community led to financial chaos for Spain in the late 1500s and into the 1600s. The lack of credit and financial acumen left Spain without a working financial system, which France's Cardinal Richelieu would later term "the sinews of the state." This factor combined with the outlet for Spanish entrepreneurs to settle newly "discovered" lands in the Americas left Spain without either a merchant class or financial expertise in the mother country.

The century from 1550 to 1650 marks the Golden Age of Spanish culture:

- *Miguel de Cervantes* (1547–1616) satirized his society's anachronistic glorification of chivalry and medieval institutions in one of the world's greatest novels, *Don Quixote*.
- *Lope de Vega* (1562–1635) wrote hundreds of dramas.
- *Bartolomé Estaban Murillo* (1617–1682) was one of the great Baroque painters.

- *Doménikos El Greco* (1541–1614) invented the mannerist painting style that was popular in Spain.
- *Diego Velázquez* (1599–1660) painted magnificent pictures on religious themes.
- *Francisco Suárez* (1548–1617) was a Jesuit priest who wrote widely admired works about philosophy and law.

## The Low Countries

Many societal and artistic achievements were made in the Low Countries, which became a center of banking and commerce. This wealthier society placed greater importance on knowledge and art, and thus produced some magnificent artists.

- *Jan van Eyck* (c. 1385–1441) was a Dutch painter of the 15th century who was known as one of the great masters.
    - He was famed for his excellent, and often highly symbolic, oil paintings with meticulous detail that focused on either religious or secular themes.
- *Hieronymus Bosch* (c. 1450–1516) was a Dutch painter of the era who used complex symbolism and explored themes of sin and moral failing.
    - His complex, imaginative, and prevalent use of symbolic figures and obscure iconography was undeniably original and may have been an inspiration for the surrealist movement of the early-20th century.
- *Rembrandt van Rijn* (1606–1669) was a Dutch master. He is generally considered one of the greatest painters and printmakers.
    - His use of chiaroscuro (dark and light) was powerful and manifested in his many self-portraits and paintings of stormy scenes.
    - He died very poor, as did many Northern Renaissance painters.

## Renaissance Views on Gender and Ethnicity

The Renaissance was a period of loss of status for upper-class and merchant women. The protections on their property and bodies that had been strong during the medieval era were rescinded. Whereas the penalty for rape in the medieval era had been castration, the penalty in the 15th century was a fine payable to the father or husband, whoever's "property" had been damaged. Women were banned from many guilds, preventing them from inheriting their husbands' businesses. Few women were allowed into institutions of higher learning, and women were not taken seriously as intellectuals. This makes women like Laura Cereta, Isabella d'Este, and Catherine de' Medici even more impressive.

- *Laura Cereta* was a prototype feminist and a lecturer at the most advanced university of the day, Padua.
- *Isabella d'Este* created a court at Mantua that became a center of arts and learning in her day.
- *Catherine de' Medici* was a power broker, queen, and regent of France as well as the mother of Louis XIII.
- The status of ordinary peasant women was not affected by the Renaissance.

This was also a time of renewed faith in many ways. Those who found that they disagreed with the Roman Catholic Church, which was the only official religion in Western Europe at the time, were often persecuted. Religious conflicts became more and more widespread in the 16th century. This era also saw the beginnings of racial bias against black African servants, who were simultaneously seen as exotic symbols of their masters' wealth and prestige due to their scarcity in Europe at the time and as evil because their dark skin was commonly believed to symbolize evil in the Bible. Consequently, black Africans were not afforded access to the higher levels of European society.

## Social Structure During the Renaissance

In much of Europe, there still existed the medieval social structure of *manorialism*, a system in which the nobility and monarchs held all political power and everyone else had power based upon only their income. Everyone owed some type of tribute to those above them on the social structure. Most areas that experienced the Renaissance had four distinct social classes, in descending order of power: nobility, merchants, tradesmen, and unskilled laborers. Remember that the Renaissance was mostly an urban phenomenon. The majority of people who lived in the countryside knew little of this phenomenon. The nobility was often not as well off economically as the merchant class that was beginning to grow in power at the time. The nobility lived on large estates outside the cities and, in most areas, acted as the military and as tax collectors. The nobility resented the growing power of the merchant class. The merchants were driven to gain increasing political power through multiple means, including marrying into noble families. To display this power, the merchants became patrons of the arts. The tradesmen were shop owners and craftsmen. Most of them belonged to *guilds* that regulated their area of trade and provided unity and support for guild members. The guilds set standards within each industry. They created rules for apprenticeship and for joining the guilds. They also limited competition in each productive industry. The unskilled laborers were by far the majority of society and also by far the lowest rung on the social ladder.

## Renaissance Points to Remember

- The Renaissance was focused on three ideals: humanism, secularism, and individualism.
- The Renaissance occurred primarily in cities because contact with other cultures happened there first.
- Secularism became more pervasive in the cities and in art, but the Renaissance *did not* abandon interest in religion. In fact, the greatest patron of the arts continued to be the Church.
- Intellectually, there was a focus on this world rather than the afterlife and on describing the world and universe rather than obeying a prescription to religious dogma.
- The use of the vernacular in literature revolutionized literature and helped national identities solidify.
- New intellectual ideals gained a following, especially in human experiences, manners, politics, and so on. These new subjects were known as *the humane letters*, from whence the term *humanism* is derived.
- For the first time, artists of all types, from painters to authors, became wealthy. The Renaissance was the birth of new professions that catered to wealthy patrons.
- The ideal of a "Renaissance man" emerged in the writings of Castiglione and Alberti as someone who is virtuous in every way and has many talents, such as the abilities to sing, compose poetry, dance, and engage in armed combat.
- Remember that the Renaissance was not a rebirth in law, government, or economic production. In most ways, Europe was still medieval.
- There was some difference in the way that the Renaissance was perceived in Northern and Southern Europe.
  - Southern Europe was wealthier due to increasing trade with the Arabs and the Byzantines, providing the luxury to spend on arts, learning, and public projects.
  - The fall of Constantinople left the Italians without any means to trade with the Arabs after the Ottoman Turks destroyed the Byzantine Empire.
  - Northern Europe focused more on practical learning, science, and technology. This is one reason why the Reformation began there—that and its distance from Rome, where the wealth and power of the Church were so prevalent. Northern Europeans created many institutions of higher learning, while the Italians and Spanish focused on art and religion, respectively. The North used the precepts of the Renaissance spirit of the individual and took it in a religious direction toward mysticism. This belief held that the individual soul can commune with God all by itself without the Church, other people, or sacraments.

# Exploration and Colonization: 1400s to 1600s

During the Crusades, soldiers were carried across the Mediterranean by Genoese and Venetian merchants. These merchants got wealthy off of their contracts to transport soldiers and off of the goods that they brought back from the Crusades in their empty ships after dropping the Crusaders near Jerusalem. The wealth that merchants gained from this trade and the ideas and texts that came from this trade helped to fuel the Renaissance. Additionally, the revival of ancient texts helped them to rediscover lost geography texts that aided Europeans in the Age of Exploration. At the same time (end of the 1200s), two separate but important European expeditions explored new lands. Marco Polo and his family explored China and the Far East for 17 years and brought the tales of different cultures and amazing goods back to Italy. This voyage of discovery to Asia cannot be ignored as his return also marked the start of the Renaissance. A few centuries before that, around 1000 C.E., the shores of North America were first colonized by Europeans called the Vikings. Erik the Red founded a colony in North America that recent historical investigation has confirmed. Although no exchange of trade was developed between the continents, which Columbus first exploited, the Vikings were clearly the first Europeans to "discover" the Americas.

Christianity was a stimulus for exploration as governments and religious authorities sought to spread the faith. For some, it served as a justification for the subjugation of indigenous civilizations. The three motivations generally attributed to the voyages of discovery were God, gold, and glory. This phrase meant that exploration was motivated by the desires to gain in wealth as well as to spread Christianity to the rest of the world. There was personal glory for the "discoverers" of "new lands."

The Portuguese, from the middle to the end of the 15th century, supported by their able leader, *Prince Henry the Navigator* (1394–1460), explored the South Atlantic. Explorers from several states on the Atlantic set out on their journeys of discovery. They were spurred by missionary zeal, personal gain, national pride, and Renaissance curiosity. These explorers were aided by the development of magnetic compasses, astrolabes, sextants, quadrants, cannons mounted on ships, and more seaworthy crafts such as the caravel, galleon, lateen, and carrack. These crafts gave Europeans the ability to sail more confidently across large bodies of water, far from shores.

European explorers also created maps called *portolani* that ship captains used as charts to find their way at sea. These advances in cartography, navigation, and military power allowed the Europeans to establish overseas colonies and empires in which they created trade networks through both coercion of and negotiation with the native peoples.

The Portuguese set up a vast trade network along the African coast, in South America, and in southern and eastern Asia. The Spanish set up an empire in the Americas, the Caribbean, and the Pacific that left them as the dominant state on the Continent. Shortly after the rise of Spain and Portugal through trade, the English, Dutch, and French began to expand their navigation and formed North American colonies to create their own trade networks.

The vast holdings of the Dutch, English, and French in the Caribbean led to significant boosts to the finances of the mother countries as well. The West Indies provided sugar to Europe at a tidy profit to those involved in its trade across the Atlantic Ocean. The distilled form of sugar that became rum also provided revenue streams for the colonial empires in the Caribbean. Additionally, the slave trade, both to the Caribbean Islands from Africa and later from the Caribbean Islands to America, also enriched the European mother countries. When the Dutch enlarged their trade routes to include Southeast Asia, they turned modern Indonesia into the *Dutch East Indies,* which was incredibly profitable and helped the Dutch create the strongest economy in Northern Europe at the time. These islands were also known as the Spice Islands. The Dutch became rich by bringing such spices as pepper, cinnamon, and anise from Asia to European tables.

- Expeditions led by *Diaz* (1450–1500), *da Gama* (c. 1460–1524), and *Cabral* (1467–1520) explored the coast of Africa and eventually established trading posts in India.
- *Christopher Columbus* (1451–1506), who sailed for the Spanish crown to find a direct route to Asia, encountered the Western Hemisphere, and reported its existence to other Europeans.

- ○ Despite opening the New World, Columbus laid the foundations for Europeans' oppression and exploitation of native peoples.
- ■ *Ferdinand Magellan* (1480–1521) circumnavigated the globe for Spain.
- ■ *Cortés* (1485–1547) and *Pizarro* (1475–1541), respectively, conquered the great American empires of the Aztecs and Incas.
  - ○ Gold and silver flowed from the New World mines into the coffers of the Spanish monarchs and to the merchants and manufacturers of the Netherlands.
- ■ These explorers opened up trade routes on three continents for new products that brought large profits to Europeans for centuries to come. The global exchange of goods, flora, fauna, cultural practices, and disease proved disastrous for the natives.
  - ○ This exchange of valuable goods and resources from each continent was known as the *Columbian Exchange.*
  - ○ This trade brought European manufactured goods and alcohol to Africa and the Americas. It also brought products such as lumber, fur, gold, sugar, peanuts, beans, potatoes, tobacco, chocolate, vanilla, and corn to Europe.
  - ○ This exchange was the largest redistribution of biological organisms among regions of the globe that the world had ever seen.
  - ○ This global exchange included diseases, people, and ideas as well as trade in goods and services.
  - ○ The Europeans introduced grains, such as wheat, rice, and barley, to the New World along with many other species, such as honeybees, cows, pigs, goats, horses, oxen, multiple types of trees and decorative plants, and many infectious diseases that they spread as they traveled.
  - ○ See the map below for more detail.

**The Columbian Exchange**

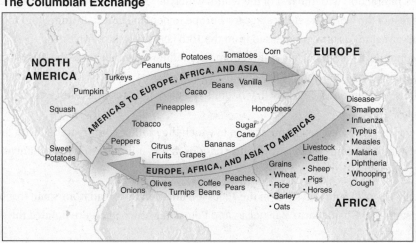

European rule in the Americas resulted in the Spanish and Portuguese raping the land and the people of all resources and wealth.

- ■ Within 50 years, 90 percent of all natives were killed by the germs, guns, steel weapons, and armor that Europeans brought with them.
- ■ Guns and gunpowder, along with horses and armor, gave the Europeans a huge advantage over the natives, who were slaughtered or else surrendered to the military superiority of the Europeans.
- ■ Old methods of agriculture, writing, and worship were forcibly changed; land was taken from natives and distributed to Europeans.
- ■ The slave trade from Africa expanded significantly as the Europeans brought enslaved people from Africa to work in the New World.

- Although Columbus thought he had sailed to India, explorer *Amerigo Vespucci* realized that Columbus had found two continents previously unknown to Europeans and dubbed them a *Mundus Novus*, or "New World."
  - These were later named the *Americas* after Vespucci. Spain reorganized territory in the New World into four viceroyalties:
    - New Spain
    - Peru
    - New Granada
    - La Plata
  - Justice in Spanish territories was enforced by an *audiencia*, a panel of 12 judges with the viceroy as head judge.
  - *Intendants* were local officials who received authority directly from the Crown to enforce laws and impose taxes.
  - The *quinto*, a tax on all precious metals found in the New World, was payable to the Spanish king.
    - This tax made up one-quarter of Spain's income during this era.
  - Local officials called *corregidores* enforced mercantilist laws banning trade between the Spanish colonies and other European powers.

The end result was a huge shift in power, both globally and within the European continent. Millions of indigenous peoples were deprived of life and property while those European nations on the Atlantic saw an unprecedented rise in wealth and power. The indigenous Americans, Africans, and Asians would be dominated by peoples of Western European ethnicities for over 400 years in ways that the other cultures of the world still have not fully recovered from. Many cultures were entirely wiped out. This was a major development in the history of Europe's interaction with the rest of the world, which left Europe with much power but did not endear Europeans to the rest of the world. It set the stage for Europe to become gradually more and more conciliatory with natives of other regions as time progressed from the 16th century to modern times.

Meanwhile, economic power in Europe shifted from the Mediterranean basin to the Atlantic coast. The result was competition among European nations for advantages in trade that often led to conflicts among nations over colonial possessions or aspirations. One way that nations engaged in this competition was through adopting mercantilist policies.

*Mercantilism* emerged as a new economic system in which the mother country traded with the colonies and the colonies were not allowed to trade directly with other nations. It was intended to lessen financial dependence on other European countries.

- The incredible influx of gold and silver in the 1500s led inflation to spread from Spain throughout Europe because the mines at Guanajuarto, Zacatecas, and Potosi in Mexico and Peru flooded the gold and silver markets.
  - The availability of gold in the New World lured many entrepreneurs there, damaging domestic industry in Spain.
  - Slavery, although it had existed since the dawn of time, increased and changed drastically in character—in large part because of exploration.
- Plantation agriculture was practiced by the conquering Europeans in the New World.
  - At first the Europeans exploited the natives, who died in the millions as a result of disease and harsh treatment.
  - Soon after, Europeans resorted to enslaving and importing African people. Race would be linked to slavery in the Americas from this point onward.
- Between 1453 and 1865, over 200 million Africans and their descendants were enslaved or killed in the slave trade.
- In 1790, Africans made up about 20 percent of the U.S. population.

- Enslavers dehumanized Africans, seeing them as beastly with potent sexuality.
- Many tried to justify slavery by stating that sub-Saharan Africans were subhuman and had no original culture of their own.

The *commercial revolution* (1500–1700) helped to bring about and intensify the Age of Discovery and Exploration. It had its roots in the invention of banking by the Medici in Florence and by the Fuggers in Antwerp and Amsterdam as well as in the tremendous population growth in Europe. These innovations in finance and banking led to the emergence of a commercial economy that eventually led to the creation of the market system.

- Most Europeans made their livings through agriculture during this period. They rotated their crops and left fields fallow to allow the soil to regenerate in some fields.
  - Most villagers oriented their lives around the seasons, the village, or the manor, although economic changes began to alter rural production and power.
  - The price revolution allowed agricultural workers to save money and begin to participate in a monetized economy. Once workers gained enough capital, a market economy emerged through the commercialization of agriculture.
  - The population returned to pre-plague levels after a few decades of surpluses in agricultural production.
- The huge profits from exploration and shipping, and the high risks associated with these endeavors, spurred the creation of the first joint-stock companies, such as the *Dutch East India Company* in 1602 and the *British East India Company* shortly thereafter.
  - Once companies could sell themselves to investors, stock markets were born. Stock markets began in the Netherlands and then spread.
  - New accounting methods, such as double-entry bookkeeping, allowed businesses and nations to assign revenues to specific expenses.
  - New banks, such as the Bank of Amsterdam, emerged as a result of the commercial revolution and the appearance of stock markets.
  - A new commercial elite class emerged that interacted with the traditional elite nobility in different ways and in different places.
  - As Western Europe moved toward a free peasantry and commercial agriculture, serfdom was codified in the East, where nobles continued to dominate economic life on large estates.
- From the late 16th century on, Europeans responded to economic and environmental challenges, such as the Little Ice Age, by delaying marriage and childbearing. This European marriage pattern restrained population growth and, ultimately, improved the economic condition of families.
- The emergence of banking and stock markets led to a rapid revolution in the way the economies of Western Europe worked.
  - Prices rose in part because of the influx of precious metals, rising populations, and enclosure but also because a new wealthy middle class began to emerge.
    - This is often called a *price revolution*.
  - Economies were further stimulated by the rise of the *putting-out industry*, sometimes known as the domestic system. In this system, people manufactured goods in their homes for sale to a capitalist who provided raw materials. Those with capital to invest found great opportunities for profits, and the new stock markets presented greater opportunities to invest.
  - The putting-out system also meant that more of the common people were paid in money. This led to them spending more and to the emergence of a market economy for the lower classes, which had not consistently existed in Europe before this time. The growth of consumer wealth at the bottom of the social pyramid led those higher up that pyramid to become entrepreneurial and create businesses to cater to the lower classes. However, hierarchy and status continued to define social power in both rural and urban settings.

- Most families continued to derive their livelihoods from agriculture. The seasons defined lives as did families' positions in their villages. Agriculture became commercialized during the commercial revolution, leading to massive social changes during the next two centuries.
- This combination of factors led to the beginning of the modern capitalist system that is now referred to as the *commercial revolution.*
- Merchants and bankers, which were a new elite class, were at the top of society in many towns.
- A new elite class emerged in Spain and its colonies, led by Spanish-speaking gentlemen termed *caballeros* and *hidalgos.*
- The *gentry*, or landed classes, in England emerged as the elites.
- In France, those who gained wealth could buy their way into the untaxed class of the nobility. Such people were termed the *nobility of the robe* as opposed to families that had been noble for centuries and were called the *nobility of the sword.*

## The Dutch, the Spanish, and Eastern Europe

Chafing under the oppressive rule of the Spanish Catholic *King Philip II* (r. 1556–1598), the Protestants of the prosperous Low Countries, whose leaders were Calvinist, revolted against Spanish rule in the years 1556–1587. The bitter and bloody conflict led to the division of the Low Countries into the mainly Catholic Spanish Netherlands in the south (which eventually became Belgium) and the mainly Protestant United Provinces of the Netherlands in the north (unofficially termed "Holland").

- The defeat in 1588 of Philip II's powerful *Spanish Armada* in its attempt to invade England, an ally of the Netherlands, marked the beginning of the decline of Spain's hegemony in Western Europe.
- The *Thirty Years' War* (1618–1648) began as a religious conflict, evolved into a national struggle for dominance of central Europe, and led to the destruction of vast areas in Germany and the decline of the regional hegemony of the Holy Roman Empire.
- The Austrian Habsburgs confronted the powerful Muslim Ottoman Turks who were attempting to expand their control of Eastern Europe.
- The 1683 attack on Austria by the forces of *Suleiman the Magnificent* was beaten back, and the Austrians eventually gained control of Bohemia, Hungary, and Transylvania.
- Russia and Western Europe experienced radically different paths of development until the 18th century.
  - For centuries, the princes of Moscow had been retainers of the Mongol conquerors. The *czars* (emperors) were able to use their influence with the Mongols to consolidate their power over the Russian people and to establish the hereditary role of czar.
  - Ivan the Terrible (r. 1547–1584) was an autocratic expansionist who limited the power of the nobles (*boyars*), expanded the realm, and solidified the role of czar.
  - A "time of troubles" ensued after Ivan's death, marked by civil war because of the lack of an heir.
  - The *Romanov* dynasty was established by the nobles in 1613. The family ruled with an iron hand, reinstituting serfdom and gaining virtual control over the Russian Orthodox Church.

## The Expansion of Europe

**(More information is found in chapter 4 because this enclosure movement actually crosses three time periods, beginning in the Netherlands and England in the 1600s and not starting in Russia until the 1900s.)**

- The *open-field system*, used during the Middle Ages, divided the arable land available to a farming community into narrow strips that were assigned to the individual families of the community. Because of a lack of effective fertilizers and ignorance about nitrogen-fixing crops, a large portion of the community's land lay fallow.

- A mini ice age hit Europe at the end of the medieval era. The advent of better weather led to more food and a population explosion, which then resulted in a cycle of famine and feast, depending upon harvests.
- For centuries, the need for fallow lands left most of Europe practicing subsistence agriculture by which they survived but created no surplus.
- New ideas, such as crop rotation to nitrogen-providing crops such as clover and turnips, allowed significantly higher output.
- A *price revolution* occurred as a result of the accumulation of capital, the expansion of the free-market economy, and the commercialization of agriculture, which enriched the landowners in Western Europe.
- The *enclosure movement*, which emerged first in the Low Countries of Belgium and the Netherlands and then emerged in England, occurred during the late-17th and the 18th centuries. It fenced off the open fields to enable large landowners to employ crop rotation.
  - Crop rotation was the planting of nitrogen-fixing crops, such as beans and certain grasses, in soil that had been used for other crops.
    - The idea spread with a two-crop rotation near the Mediterranean and a three-crop rotation in the North.
    - The soil remained fertile and little land lay fallow.
  - Many small or inefficient farmers were displaced, moving to the towns and cities. Ultimately, food production rose dramatically.
    - These small farmers were said to have free-hold tenure on their land.
    - Other farmers paid rent to landowners to farm their land or provided labor services in return for the right to farm on the land.
  - The village commons was closed, and villagers lost the ability to graze their own animals there.
  - Landlords' attempts to increase profits by abolishing the traditional rights of peasants led to revolts.
- A greater variety of foods and the introduction of foods from the New World, specifically the potato, improved general nutrition and contributed, along with the disappearance of the plague, to a dramatic increase in population.
  - Better sanitation, the introduction of quarantine methods, and the elimination of the black rat, whose fleas carried the plague microorganisms, eliminated the plague.
  - Except for the development of the smallpox vaccine in the late-18th century, the crude and often dangerous medical practices of the day contributed little to the health and longevity of the people.
  - *Mercantilism* was a system developed by various European states to guarantee a favorable balance of trade with other European nations or with their American colonies.
    - By creating an imbalance of exports over imports, the difference was made up in gold or silver payments.
    - European nations pursued policies to get precious metals from trading partners to pay for the costs of maintaining standing armies and government bureaucracies.
- Populations began to shift from a huge majority of people living and working in rural areas to many living in cities to pursue commerce and profit. This shift in populations put stress on the traditional political and social structures of those cities that were not prepared for that growth.
  - The shift in populations began during the recovery from the Black Plague during the 15th century. The inability of many to grow their own food led to a rapid rise in prices. The price revolution was far more favorable to the wealthy than to those less fortunate.
  - Cities faced many problems, including sanitation problems, higher unemployment, poverty, crime, and a loss of the guilds' ability to help govern the cities.
  - Many cities had to regulate public morals. Previously, religion and guilds had provided all regulation about morality.

- ○ In rural settings throughout Europe, morals were preserved through rituals such as the *charivari*. In these rituals, the community came together to give a mock serenade to adulterous couples or those who otherwise violated mores and norms, such as widows and widowers who remarried too soon. These serenades were boisterous, loud affairs meant to shame the violators back into following the norms. In England, the *skimmington* was similar, but it included a parade with effigies of the offenders.
- A new concept of the sovereign state emerged after the Peace of Westphalia in 1648. This new sovereign state as well as secular systems of law placed a new emphasis on creating new political institutions.
- The family remained the primary social and economic institution of 16th-century life. Most households, regardless of whether urban or rural, had clearly defined roles for each family member. The debates raised by the Renaissance and Reformation about women's roles is a theme that crosses all historical time periods in this course.
- Leisure activities and rituals of the time reflected persistent folk ideas. However, some leisure was seen as a challenge to communal norms. These challenges included blood sports, such as bear baiting or bull baiting, the huge Carnival festival that Mardi Gras is a remnant of, and other saints' days. When norms were violated, the violators would be disciplined by their church or town authorities. Punishments ranged from being put in the stocks, to public whipping, to the charivari, which encouraged a couple to wed.

## The Development of "Natural Philosophy" or Science

This part of the chapter is not a part of the unit plan from the College Board, but it fits into the narrative better here than elsewhere. Usually the development of science is taught with the Age of Absolutism or at the start of the Enlightenment. However, the events described here are clearly in time period 1 and were placed in this chapter as a result.

> **Note on Periodization**
>
> The Scientific Revolution took place mostly during time period 1. However, it is linked strongly to the Enlightenment in time period 2. Some of its important thinkers, such as Sir Isaac Newton, John Locke, and Robert Hooke lived during the start of period 2. This further illustrates the arbitrary nature of time periods created by historians.

The idea of studying the universe through scientific experimentation and observation emerged as the ultimate form of gathering knowledge. The great thinkers of the day turned away from their artistic pursuits, which had been so profitable, and began to try to explain the mysteries of the universe or even the multiverse. The term *science* would have to wait until the 19th century to be coined. For the time being, during the 16th and 17th centuries the study of natural phenomena was labeled "natural philosophy."

### The Philosophers of Modern Science

*Francis Bacon* (1561–1626) was an English thinker who advocated the *inductive* or *experimental method*: observation of natural phenomena, accumulating data, experimenting to refine the data, drawing conclusions, formulating principles that are subject to continuing observation, and experimentation. He is generally credited as an original empiricist.

*René Descartes* (1596–1650) was a French philosopher whose *Discourse on Method* (1637) argued that everything that is not validated by observation should be doubted but that his own existence was proven by the proposition "I think, therefore I am" (*cogito ergo sum*). God exists, Descartes argued, because a perfect being would have existence as part of its nature. *Cartesian dualism* divided all existence into the spiritual and the material—the former can be examined only through deductive reasoning; the latter is subject to the experimental method. His goal to reconcile religion with science was short-circuited by the very method of skepticism that subsequent philosophers inherited from his writings. Descartes is generally credited as an original rationalist.

## The Revolutionary Thinkers of Science

- *Nicolaus Copernicus* (1473–1543), a Polish astronomer, upset the comfortable assumptions of the *geocentric* (earth-centered) universe of *Ptolemy* (the second-century Egyptian) with his *heliocentric* (sun-centered) concept of the universe.
  - Although his work, *Concerning the Revolutions of the Heavenly Bodies*, was not published until after his death, his theories were proven by *Johannes Kepler* (1571–1630). Kepler was a German who plotted the elliptic orbits of the planets, thereby predicting their movements.
  - *Galileo Galilei* (1564–1642) made telescopic observations that validated Copernican theory. His spirited advocacy of Copernicus earned him condemnation by the Inquisition.
- The Copernican heliocentric view seemed to contradict the primacy of humanity in God's creation and thereby seemed to deny the teachings of the Church.
  - The heliocentric view was supported in Protestant Northern Europe, where the Reformation had questioned all orthodoxy.
  - The theory and the scientific method that had formulated it symbolized Europe's new intellectual freedom.
  - The Roman Catholic Church tried to suppress the Copernican revolution by banning writings of the charismatic Galileo and putting him under lifelong house arrest for possible heresy.
  - Galileo observed the moons of Jupiter as support for Copernicus, which earned him a lasting reputation for rigidity.
  - It took nearly 350 years for the papacy to exonerate Galileo.
- The field of medicine began to advance with the rising practice of human dissection, allowing medical knowledge to grow. New advances in anatomy, the study of human systems such as circulation, and toxicology occurred during this period. The practice of Rome's Greek-born physician and philosopher Galen, who had healed through adjusting bodily humors, was challenged on many fronts.
  - *Andreas Vasalius* (1514–1564) was the father of modern anatomy. His anatomy book *De Humani Corporis Fabrica* revolutionized the study of the human body. He is often credited with the discovery of the human skeletal, nervous, and other systems.
  - *Paracelsus* (1493–1541) was a German physician, botanist, and astronomer who invented toxicology. He rejected Galen and wanted to perform medical research based purely on observations in nature rather than by studying what others had previously written. He served as a physician in the Venetian wars.
  - *William Harvey* (1578–1657) explained the circulatory system in detail for the first time in his work *On the Motion of the Heart and Blood.*

## Results of the Scientific Revolution

- *Deism* emerged from the discovery of the natural sciences as the religious ideal in which God was a kind of cosmic clock maker who created a perfect universe in which He does not have to intervene.
- *Rationalism* resulted. It is the conviction that the laws of nature are fathomable by human reason and that humanity is perfectible—as an assumption and an achievable goal.
- The *Scientific Revolution* of the 16th and 17th centuries redefined astronomy and physics.
- Less dramatic but still-significant advances took place in *mathematics*, especially with the development of probability and calculus, and in *medicine* through advances in surgery, anatomy, and drug therapy and with the discovery of microorganisms.
- Learned societies dedicated to the advance of science, such as the *French Academy of Sciences* and the *Royal Society of London*, were created.
- The development of science transformed the intellectual life of Europe by convincing people that human reason could understand the secrets of the universe and transform life without the help of organized religion.

The 18th century marked the end of the *Age of Religion,* which had governed European thought for over a millennium. Skepticism and rationalism became offshoots of the development of science, which further encouraged the growth of secularism.

# The Renaissance Characters

The following charts each contain a brief description of people whose ideas began the modern era.

## Masters of the Arts

| | |
|---|---|
| Giotto di Bondone<br>1266–1337<br>Florence<br>Painter | ▪ Very influential pre-Renaissance painter and a friend of Dante<br>▪ Work notable for its use of realistic scenes from nature |
| Filippo Brunelleschi<br>1377–1446<br>Florence<br>Architect | ▪ Created *Il Duomo*, the first Italian freestanding dome since antiquity<br>▪ Credited with bringing perspective to Renaissance artists |
| Donatello<br>(Donato di Niccolò di Betto Bardi)<br>1386–1466<br>Florence<br>Sculptor | ▪ Created the first freestanding bronze statue of a human, *David*, in Europe since antiquity |
| Masaccio<br>(Tommaso di Ser Giovanni di Simone)<br>1401–1428<br>Florence<br>Painter | ▪ Often called the "Father of Modern Art," his *Expulsion* and *Holy Trinity* mark an advance from medieval to Renaissance painting because of the use of anatomy and perspective |
| Giovanni Bellini<br>1430–1516<br>Venice<br>Painter | ▪ A leading painter of the Venetian school, the master of Giorgione and Titian<br>▪ Known chiefly for his altarpieces and his Madonnas |
| Sandro Botticelli<br>1444–1510<br>Florence<br>Painter | ▪ Most famous for his *Birth of Venus*<br>▪ Assisted in decorating the Sistine Chapel<br>▪ A follower of Savonarola |
| Domenico Ghirlandiao<br>1449–1494<br>Florence<br>Painter | ▪ Founder of a school of painting and the teacher of Michelangelo |
| Leonardo da Vinci<br>1452–1519<br>Florence<br>Painter, sculptor, architect, engineer, and scientist | ▪ Painter of *The Last Supper, Mona Lisa,* and many other masterpieces<br>▪ An engineer who designed flying machines and tanks<br>▪ A rival of Michelangelo<br>▪ Patrons were Lorenzo the Magnificent and Lodovico Sforza |
| Michelangelo Buonarroti<br>1474–1564<br>Florence<br>Painter, sculptor, architect, and poet | ▪ His great sculptures: the *Pietá, David,* and *Moses*<br>▪ Famous for painting the ceiling of the Sistine Chapel for Pope Julius II<br>▪ The greatest sculptor of hands<br>▪ Part of the trinity of great 15th-century artists, including Leonardo da Vinci and Raphael |
| Raphael Sanzo<br>1483–1520<br>Urbino, Italy<br>Painter | ▪ Chief architect of St. Peter's Cathedral<br>▪ Master of oil painting in pieces such as *The School of Athens*<br>▪ Part of the trinity of great 15th-century artists, including Leonardo da Vinci and Michelangelo |

| Artemesia Gentileschi<br>1590–1642<br>Italian<br>Painter | ▪ Father was also a painter whose patrons included King Charles I of England<br>▪ Especially noted for her *Judith* paintings |
| --- | --- |

## Masters of Letters

| Dante<br>1265–1321<br>Florence | ▪ Author of *Divine Comedy* (about an imaginary journey through hell, purgatory, and heaven)<br>▪ In the *Divine Comedy*, helped define the *vernacular* of what is now the Italian language |
| --- | --- |
| Francesco Petrarch<br>1304–1374<br>Italian | ▪ The first great *humanist* thinker and a scholar of Latin<br>▪ Known as the "Father of Humanism"<br>▪ Major works: *Triumphs* and *On the Solitary Life* |
| Giovanni Boccaccio<br>1313–1375<br>Italian | ▪ Friend of Petrarch and a major contributor to the development of classic Italian prose<br>▪ Wrote *Decameron*, a classic bawdy tale of love in all its forms |
| Leonardo Bruni<br>1369–1444<br>Italian humanist | ▪ His history of Florence noted for a new sense of the need for authentic sources in examining history<br>▪ Translated Plutarch, Demosthenes, Aristotle, and Plato from Greek into Latin |
| Thomas à Kempis<br>1380–1471<br>German ecclesiastic and writer | ▪ German ecclesiastic and writer; early religious purist; wrote *Imitation of Christ*<br>▪ Taught that the individual soul could commune directly with God in perfect solitude, without sacraments, people, or the Church |
| Lorenzo Valla<br>1406–1457<br>Italian humanist | ▪ Leading Italian Renaissance humanist most famous for *On Pleasure*, about the Epicureans |
| Pico della Mirandola<br>1463–1494<br>Italian humanist | ▪ Leading humanist of the Italian Renaissance and author of *Oration on the Dignity of Man* |
| Erasmus of Rotterdam<br>1466–1536<br>Florence<br>Catholic author and scholar | ▪ Created new Greek and Latin translations of the New Testament<br>▪ Wrote *The Praise of Folly* and *Handbook of a Christian Knight*<br>▪ Enemy of Martin Luther<br>▪ Ally of Thomas More<br>▪ Wanted reform within the Catholic Church<br>▪ Leader in field of Renaissance learning in Northern Europe |
| Niccolò Machiavelli<br>1469–1527<br>Florence | ▪ Wrote *The Prince*, his application for employment with Lorenzo Medici, the most important work on political science for centuries |
| Baldassare Castiglione<br>1478–1529<br>Milan and Urbino | ▪ Author of *The Book of the Courtier*, the first book of etiquette for nobles |
| Thomas More<br>1478–1535<br>England | ▪ Author of *Utopia*<br>▪ As lord chancellor of England, opposed Henry VIII's break with the Catholic Church<br>▪ Beheaded for sticking to his principles |
| Benvenuto Cellini<br>1500–1571<br>Florence<br>Sculptor, goldsmith, and author | ▪ His *Autobiography* an excellent record of life in Renaissance Italy<br>▪ Illustrated why he was the prime exemplar of *virtu*<br>▪ Worked under Michelangelo<br>▪ Patronized by Pope Clement VII |
| François Rabelais<br>1494–1553<br>France | ▪ Priest who attacked the failings of the Church in *Gargantua and Pantagruel* |

| Michel de Montaigne<br>1533–1592<br>France | ▪ Invented the essay<br>▪ *Essay* derived from the French word for *test* |
|---|---|
| Miguel de Cervantes<br>1547–1616<br>Spain | ▪ Satirized the chivalry of the Spanish court and the medieval institutions of the state in his *Don Quixote* |

## Leaders of Religion

| Nicholas of Cusa<br>1401–1464<br>Rhineland (Germany)<br>Churchman | ▪ Roman Catholic prelate and philosopher<br>▪ Focused on mystical philosophy<br>▪ Anticipated Copernicus by his belief in Earth's rotation and its revolution around the sun |
|---|---|
| Pope Nicholas V<br>r. 1447–1455<br>Italian | ▪ A great patron of art and literature |
| Pope Innocent VIII<br>r. 1484–1492<br>Italian | ▪ Declared Henry VII lawful king of England and appointed Torquemada as Grand Inquisitor of Spain |
| Pope Alexander VI<br>r. 1492–1503<br>Spain | ▪ Bribed his way to the papacy<br>▪ Children were Cesare Borgia and Lucretia Borgia, often at the Vatican when young<br>▪ Gave papal land to his children<br>▪ A great patron of the arts, especially Bramante, Michelangelo, and Raphael<br>▪ Ordered execution of Savonarola<br>▪ Purportedly said, "God has given us the papacy. Now let us enjoy it!" |
| Pope Julius II<br>r. 1503–1513<br>Italian | ▪ Decided to rebuild St. Peter's Basilica<br>▪ Patronized Raphael, Michelangelo, Bramante, and others |
| Pope Leo X<br>r. 1513–1521<br>Italian | ▪ The second son of Lorenzo the Magnificent<br>▪ Most opulent lifestyle as pope; ate from gold plates and threw them away<br>▪ Failed to realize the importance of the Reformation<br>▪ Issued papal bull excommunicating Luther |
| Girolamo Savonarola<br>1452–1498<br>Ferrara, Italy<br>Dominican monk and church reformer | ▪ Gave vehement sermons about the corruption of secular life, the ruling class, and the worldliness of the clergy<br>▪ Led Romans to revolt<br>▪ Began the Bonfires of the Vanities into which Sandro Botticelli threw his paintings to be burned<br>▪ Drove Piero de' Medici from power in Florence<br>▪ Became virtual dictator of Florence, preaching a crusade for the establishment of an ideal Christian state<br>▪ Denounced by Pope Alexander VI; lost power in Florence to aristocrats<br>▪ Captured, tried for sedition and heresy, and then tortured, hanged, and burned |

## Scientific Minds

| Regiomontanus<br>1436–1476<br>Germany<br>Mathematician and scientist | ▪ Laid foundation for mathematical concept of universe |
|---|---|

| Nicholas Copernicus<br>1473–1543<br>Poland<br>Scientist | ▪ Revived idea of a heliocentric (sun-centered) solar system from the ancients<br>▪ Shocked Europe when *On the Revolutions of the Celestial Spheres* was published posthumously, but Galileo's support of his ideas later caused a bigger controversy |
| --- | --- |
| Johann Gutenberg<br>1398–1468<br>Germany | ▪ Often credited as the first to produce books with movable lead type, c. 1450 |

## Political Leaders

| Giovanni de' Medici<br>1360–1429<br>Florence | ▪ Merchant who became wealthy<br>▪ Supporter of smaller guilds and common people<br>▪ Virtual ruler of Florence, 1421–1429<br>▪ Began banking dynasty |
| --- | --- |
| Cosimo de' Medici<br>1389–1464<br>Florence | ▪ Son of Giovanni<br>▪ Banker, patron of the arts<br>▪ "Father of his country" |
| Lorenzo de' Medici<br>"The Magnificent"<br>1449–1492, grandson of Giovanni but not son of Cosimo<br>Florence | ▪ Major patron of the arts<br>▪ Father of a pope<br>▪ Allegedly immoral and tyrannical ruler |
| Cesare Borgia<br>1475–1507<br>Originally Spanish | ▪ Son of Pope Alexander VI<br>▪ Conquered much of central Italy, including Urbino<br>▪ Acted with cruelty and treachery<br>▪ Model for Machiavelli's prince |
| Isabelle d'Este<br>1474–1539<br>Marchioness of Mantua | ▪ Married to Giovanni Gonzaga<br>▪ Outstanding diplomat and patron of learning<br>▪ Turned Mantua into the center of learning and thought |

The Renaissance was *a significant artistic movement*, the first of many that occurred throughout European history.

For the AP European History exam, you should be aware of *all* artistic movements in Europe from the Renaissance through the modern era. The following chart summarizes the most notable ones.

# Important Artistic Movements in European History

## Italian Renaissance (1350–1550)

**Important artists:** Michelangelo, Raphael, Leonardo da Vinci, Botticelli, Brunelleschi, Giotto, Donatello, Titian
**Composers:** Palestrina
**Key writers:** Petrarch, Machiavelli
**Key ideas:**

- Individualism, humanism, secularism
- Perspective
- Use of triangles as architecture of art
- Individual portraiture
- Landscapes
- Freestanding human sculptures, nudes

## Northern Renaissance (1450–1700)

**Important artists:** Albrecht Dürer, Hans Holbein the Elder, Hieronymus Bosch, Pieter Bruegel the Elder, Jan van Eyck, Johannes Vermeer, Rembrandt van Rijn

**Composers:** Robert Cooper, John Milton, Cornelius Canis

**Writers:** Cervantes, Thomas More, William Shakespeare, Christopher Marlowe, Christine de Pizan

**Key ideas:**

- Centralization of power in nation-states
- Reformation
- Focus on common people in art
- More religious than Italian Renaissance

## Mannerism (1520–1600)

**Important artists:** Giorgione, Tintoretto, El Greco, Velazquez

**Composers:** Monteverdi

**Key ideas:**

- Transition between the end of the Renaissance and the beginning of the baroque era
- Art of the Reformation and Counter-Reformation focused on new ideas and how to express them

## Baroque (1550–1750)

Baroque was known for overornamentation, curved lines, and art that awed the viewer with impressive size and emotional reactions.

**Important artists:** Peter Paul Rubens, Nicholas Poussin

**Composers:** Johann Sebastian Bach, George Frideric Handel

**Writers:** Descartes, Nicolaus Copernicus, Kepler, Galileo, Newton, Hobbes, Locke, Vesalius, Harvey

**Key ideas:**

- The Scientific Revolution and divine right absolutism
- Emergence of classical ballet and theater
- English Civil War

## Rococo (1710–1790)

Rococo was typified as similar to baroque but more ornamental and less formal.

**Important artists:** Thomas Gainsborough, Jean-Honoré Fragonard, Antoine Watteau, Étienne Maurice Falconet

**Composers:** Wolfgang Amadeus Mozart, Franz Joseph Haydn

**Writers:** Jean Jacques Rousseau, Denis Diderot, Edmund Burke, Goethe, Montesquieu, Adam Smith, Voltaire

**Key ideas:**

- Enlightened despotism
- Enlightenment:
  - Salons
  - *Philosophes*, encyclopedia

## Neoclassicism (1790–1820s)

Neoclassicism was a revival of styles and the spirit of classic antiquity. It reflected the Age of Enlightenment and was initially a reaction against the excesses of the Rococo.

**Important artists:** Jacques Louis David, Francisco Goya, Jean-Auguste-Dominique Ingres, Jean-Antoine Houdon

**Composers:** Neoclassicism in music occurred at a later time, during the start of the 20th century. It had a very different meaning in music than it did in visual arts. In music, neoclassicism was an early-20th-century movement that reacted to the emotional music of the Romantic era by Replacing it with order and rhythm. Key composers were Igor Stravinsky, Sergei Prokofiev, and Nadia Boulanger.

**Key ideas:**

- French Revolution
- Napoleonic Empire
- Nationalism emerged

## Romanticism (1820s–1860s)

Romanticism evolved as a reaction to neoclassicism and the Industrial Revolution.

**Important artists:** Eugene Delacroix, John Constable, Joseph Turner, Théodore Géricault

**Composers:** Berlioz, Weber, Chopin, Mendelssohn, Liszt, Schumann, J. Strauss, Jr.

**Writers:** Lord Byron, Alexandre Dumas, Victor Hugo, William Wordsworth, Samuel Taylor Coleridge, John Keats, Mary Wollstonecraft Shelley, Percy Bysshe Shelley, Sir Walter Scott

**Key ideas:**

- Expression of emotional nationalism and heroism
- Glorified nature
- Glorified the past, peasants, and nationalist movements

## Realism (Late-1850s to 1870s)

Realism was an attempt to depict life as it really was. It was a reaction to the sentimentalism of Romanticism and showed the grittier side of life with a focus on the "common man."

**Important artists:** Camille Corot, Jean-François Millet, Honore Daumier, and the Barbizon School of landscape painters; some works by Edgar Degas and Edouard Manet

**Composers:** Wagner, Franck, Brahms, Bizet, Verdi, Puccini

**Writers:** Honore de Balzac, Charles Dickens, Gustave Flaubert, Guy de Maupassant, Henrik Ibsen, Friedrich Nietzsche, Marcel Proust, Emile Zola

**Key Ideas:**

- Focus on knowledge that can be known, or positivism
- Realpolitik, a turning away from emotion toward fact and a rejection of industrial progress
- Showed the ugliness of life for peasants
- Called pornography by critics

## Impressionism (1870s–1920s)

Impressionism was named for Claude Monet's painting *Impression of Sunrise*. It developed into the submovements of post-Impressionism and pointillism, which was made famous by Georges Seurat.

**Important artists:** Paul Cezanne, Mary Cassat, Edgar Degas, Paul Gauguin, Edouard Manet, Claude Monet, Camille Pissarro, Pierre-Auguste Renoir, Auguste Rodin, George Seurat, Henri de Toulouse-Lautrec, Vincent van Gogh

**Composers:** Claude Debussy, Gabriel Fauré, Gustav Mahler, Maurice Ravel

**Key ideas:**

- New subject matter and a new way of looking at the world
- Everyday life of the middle class became an acceptable subject for high art
- Painting in the outdoors gave new chances to study the play of light; identified with La Belle Epoque

## Modern Art and Postmodernism, Including Futurism, Surrealism, Dadaism, and Pop Art (20th Century)

During the 20th century, artists were strongly influenced by Sigmund Freud, Albert Einstein, the world wars, the coming of the atomic age, the rise of modern media, and the changes in the concept of identity. Art was less about sensual pleasure and more about making a statement.

**Important artists:** Constantin Brancusi, Georges Braque, Alexander Calder, Marc Chagall, Willem de Kooning, Roy Lichtenstein, Marcel DuChamp, Salvador Dali, Paul Giacometti, Rene Margritte, Henri Matisse, Joan Miro, Aristide Maillol, Henry Moore, Pablo Picasso, Jackson Pollack, Andy Warhol

**Composers:** Béla Bartók, Alban Berg, George Gershwin, Sergei Prokofiev, Richard Strauss, Igor Stravinsky

**Key ideas:**

- Expressionism (introspective into a world of emotional and psychological states)
- Abstractionism (detached examination of life distilling the essence of nature and sense experiences)
- Cubism: Picasso and Braque created angular impressions of the real world
- Futurism
  - Made fashionable by Fascists
- Surrealism (examined dream fantasies, memory images, and visual paradoxes)
- Dadaism (a revolt against previous classical artistic movements and a response to the horrors of World War I)
  - Nihilistic
  - Challenged polite society; was against order and reason

## Practice Questions

### Long Essay

These questions are samples of the various types of thematic essays on the exam. (See pages 27–28 for a detailed explanation of each type.) Check over the generic rubric (see pages 28-29) before you begin any of these essays, and use that rubric to score the essays you write.

### Question 1

To what extent and in what ways did the Italian Renaissance result from Italy's geographic advantage in the world trade of the 15th century?

### Comments on Question 1

"Geography is destiny," so it is said. And the strategic location of Italy, a peninsula jutting into the Mediterranean, gave it advantages in the world trade of the 15th century. This one is a *causation* question because it requires you to explain how much the Italian Renaissance was or was not caused by Italian geography. Remember to describe causes and/or effects of the Italian Renaissance.

You must explain the reasons for the causes and/or effects of the Italian Renaissance and Italian geography. "How and how much?" are the questions to answer. The clues are inherent in the geography. With what parts of the world did the Europeans carry on trade at this time? Why did Italy have an advantage? What were the rewards of that advantage? How were those rewards instrumental in fostering history's greatest brief period of creativity? What were the limits on the influence of geography?

To write a strong essay, you must point out how other influences, such as the importance of Crusaders departing from Rome on Venetian and Milanese ships or the independence of Padua, must also be examined to create a top-scoring essay.

## Question 2

"Although the term *renaissance* is misleading, the modern world began with Renaissance secularism and individualism." Assess the validity of this statement.

### Comments on Question 2

This question is about judging the truth or validity of the given statement. This question is a *change and continuity over time* (CCOT) question because it asks how the Renaissance marked a change in how the people lived, earned a living, were ruled, thought about their society, and thought about knowledge. You need to explain what remained the same after the Renaissance and what changed in all arenas of life, including social, political, intellectual, economic, religious, military, and artistic realms. You should explain how the Renaissance was different from and similar to the Middle Ages and how it was more or less similar to the periods following the Renaissance, such as the Enlightenment, the Age of Exploration, and so forth.

You must explain the extent to which the Italian Renaissance was different from and similar to developments that preceded and/or followed it. This question can be answered by taking either side, but you *must* choose a side and argue for it. The more conventional way would be to argue that individualism and secularism—as they relate to industrialization and the emergence of capitalism and democracy—support the generalization. You must support your answer by including citations from writers and thinkers from the Renaissance and Enlightenment who are more modern.

The other side could argue that terms like *modernity* and *renaissance* are not valid in this context and that citing any era as being caused by another is a dubious argument. Citing the emergence in the 19th century of the historical term *renaissance* may help here. Either way, the question requires careful thought and planning to answer it.

## Question 3

Explain why Machiavelli's *The Prince* is both the first modern treatise in political science and one of the most misinterpreted books of modern times.

### Comments on Question 3

This one seems to call for you to analyze *change and continuity over time* (CCOT) because you must analyze the extent to which *The Prince* was different from political thinking that came before it. You should analyze the extent to which Machiavelli's ideas were different from and similar to political thinking that came before *The Prince* was published. You must also provide a number of specific examples to support your analysis.

You must explain the extent to which *The Prince* was different from and similar to political science developments that preceded and/or followed the appearance of the book. You must examine in detail the ideas of Machiavelli and the development of political science. You must also determine the relationships between those ideas. Explain ways that the book has been misinterpreted. Remember, "explain" offers no choice. You must make clear, detail, and offer meanings, causes, and reasons for your analysis.

The essence of the book is in the phrase "The welfare of the state justifies everything." Is this equivalent to arguing that the end justifies the means? It is also important that Machiavelli says a prince must sometimes be bad in order to be a good prince. What was Machiavelli's purpose in writing the book? How did his methods of observation and his arguments make it the first modern treatise in political science? As stated, this essay must also address why and how *The Prince* has been misinterpreted. Would medieval philosophers have thought about the same issues as Machiavelli? If so, what would their arguments be based upon? Use the specific examples that Machiavelli used, and state that he used historical examples. Then cite other historical individuals who seem to use his ideas but could not have read his book, such as Henry VIII.

## Question 4

Compare the Italian Renaissance and the Northern Renaissance.

### Comments on Question 4

This is a *compare* skill question, so be sure to describe the similarities and differences between the Italian Renaissance and the Northern Renaissance. Account for or explain the similarities and differences by providing specific examples. Tie those examples to historical situations, such as the seat of Catholicism being in Rome, far from Northern Europe. In showing the differences, consider the following: how each Renaissance began, which one influenced the other, how their emphases differed, how they interpreted certain ideas differently, and how they expressed their differences. How did their art and literature differ? How did the personalities involved vary? Who was the "ideal Renaissance man" in Italy, in Northern Europe? What were the qualities of each?

In examining the similarities, consider the ideas the Italian and Northern Renaissances had in common, such as individualism and secularism. Look for similarities in their religious commitments, in their artistic and literary techniques and themes, and in their approaches to understanding human life.

## Question 5

Analyze how the Northern Renaissance gave rise to two diverse developments: religious mysticism and revival, and science and technology.

### Comments on Question 5

This one is a *causation* question because it requires you to decide how the Northern Renaissance brought about increased religious mysticism and a revival of science and technology at the same time. Remember to describe the causes and/or effects of the Northern Renaissance and explain the extent to which it can be credited (or blamed) for either development.

You must explain the causes and/or effects of the Northern Renaissance on intellectual movements. In this case, "analyze" primarily means to "determine the relationships" between the Northern Renaissance and two seemingly different approaches to the human condition: religion and science. How did the study of ancient texts—specifically Hebrew and Greek versions of the Bible and the writings of the early Church Fathers—revitalize religious devotion?

Consider how the concept of individualism could encourage the very personal religious experience of mysticism. How did individualism and skepticism give rise to modern science? Why did the revival of religion and the growth of mysticism occur primarily in Northern Europe? Was Italian religious devotion centered on the arts? Did the papacy have less sway in the North? Why did Northern Europe give birth to modern science? Was the desire to understand and control nature the northern counterpart to Italian *virtu*, or richness of the human spirit? Was it a tradition that began with the mathematician Regiomontanus and evolved into the Copernican formula for a heliocentric universe?

## Question 6

How did transatlantic trade and the Columbian Exchange change lives on both sides of the Atlantic?

## Comments on Question 6

This answer clearly calls for you to analyze *continuity and change over time* (CCOT) on both sides of the Atlantic. Be sure to describe the level of historical continuity and change. Analyze specific examples of what changed and what remained the same on both sides of the Atlantic Ocean. Analyze why things changed or stayed the same after the Columbian Exchange began, citing specific examples. The best approach to this question would involve explaining the time period politically, economically, socially, and religiously on both sides of the Atlantic before, during, and after the Age of Exploration and colonialism. The influx of gold and silver in Europe, the outlet for immigration, and cheap land, as well as the impact of new foods such as corn and potatoes in Europe, must be explored. The destruction of Native American cultures and the loss of their political, economic, and social power should be explained. The role of religion in exploration should be examined. The question is broad in scope but needs specific factual references to illustrate the main points.

## Question 7

Compare the contributions to the development of modern science of Bacon and Descartes with those of Copernicus and Galileo.

## Comments on Question 7

This task appears to be straightforward since, as the question implies, the roles of Bacon and Descartes in the rise of modern science are similar and they contrast with those of Copernicus and Galileo. This is a *compare* skill question, so be sure to describe similarities and differences. Account for or explain them by providing specific examples of how these men were similar and different. Tie that to historical developments such as the growth of modern science or technology. Bacon and Descartes were philosophers of science whose writings helped establish the methodology of science: skepticism, observation, generalization, and experimentation. Copernicus and Galileo, on the other hand, were genuine scientists whose theories or experimentation expanded the store of scientific knowledge. Additionally, both Galileo and Copernicus worked in the science of astronomy, and Newton claimed that he owed his accomplishments to the foundational work of Galileo.

The tricky part of this question is to apply the contrast and comparison rule to Bacon and Descartes and then apply it to Copernicus and Galileo. Did Bacon's writings contribute differently than Descartes's to the "scientific mind"? Were Copernicus's methods and findings different from those of Galileo? Also contrast and compare each pair to the other.

## Question 8

Explain how the replacement of the open-field system by the enclosure movement increased agricultural productivity in 18th-century Europe.

## Comments on Question 8

The enclosure movement should be explained as the most important and least-known revolution in European history. This one is also a *causation* question because it requires you to explain how one outcome increased agricultural output and resulted from a specific stimulus: the implementation of the enclosure movement. Remember to describe the causes and/or effects of increased agricultural productivity and to explain them through specific examples. The essay must explain the reasons for these causes and/or effects. For example, the ownership of land encouraged people to improve their land through fertilization and irrigation, which increased crop yields. You must describe how the enclosure movement caused increased agricultural productivity and analyze specific examples that illustrate how the enclosure movement did this. You must describe the open-field system and the concept of common lands, focusing on the limitations on land improvement and fallow lands. Explain how the enclosure movement made land improvement, such as irrigation, crop rotation, and fertilization, more practical and widespread. The best essays also examine how the enclosure movement led to the putting-out system that increased domestic production and disturbed the order of society by moving many farming families from their lands, causing them to find new means of employment.

## Short-Answer

1. Use the image below and your knowledge of European history to answer all parts of the question that follows.

By Raphael: *pintura.aut.org*, Public Domain, *The Small, Cowper Madonna*.

(a) Briefly explain TWO aspects of Renaissance art that are apparent in the image above.

(b) Briefly explain ONE aspect of medieval art evident in the image above.

2. Use the passage below and your knowledge of European history to answer all parts of the question that follows.

**Petrarch's Letter to Homer**

(Translated from Latin by James Harvey Robinson)

And now what shall I say about the matter of imitation? When you found yourself soaring so high on the wings of genius you ought to have foreseen that you would always have imitators. You should be glad that your endowments are such that many men long to be like you, although not many can succeed. Why not be glad, you who are sure of holding always the first place, when I, the least of mortals, am more than glad, am in fact puffed up with pride, because I have grown great enough for others—though I scarcely can believe that this is really true—to desire to imitate and copy me? In my case the pride and joy would only increase if among these imitators there should be found some few who were capable of surpassing me. I pray—not to your Apollo, but the true God of Intellect whom I worship, to crown the efforts of all who may deem it worth their while to follow after me, and to grant that they may find it an easy thing to come up with me, and outstrip me too. . . .

It was my intention to speak to you of Virgil, than whom, as Flaccus says, this earth has produced no soul more spotless; and to suggest to you, great master of us both, certain excuses for his conduct. . . . I admit the truth of everything that you say concerning him, but it does not necessarily follow that I lend a sympathetic ear to the charges that you base upon this failure of his to make anywhere any mention of your name, laden and bedecked though he is with your spoils,—mention, you remind me, such as Lucan made, remembering in grateful strains the honor due to Smyrna's bard.

(a) Briefly explain TWO aspects of Renaissance thought that are apparent in the letter above.

(b) Briefly explain ONE aspect of medieval thought evident in the letter above.

3. Answer all parts of the question based upon the passage and your knowledge of European history.

### Vasco da Gama: *Round Africa to India* (1497)

The inhabitants of this country are tawny-colored. Their food is confined to the flesh of seals, whales and gazelles, and the roots of herbs. They are dressed in skins, and wear sheaths over their virile members. They are armed with poles of olive wood to which a horn, browned in the fire, is attached. Their numerous dogs resemble those of Portugal, and bark like them. The birds of the country, likewise, are the same as in Portugal, and include cormorants, gulls, turtle doves, crested larks, and many others. The climate is healthy and temperate, and produces good herbage. On the day after we had cast anchor, that is to say on Thursday (November 9), we landed with the captain-major, and made captive one of the natives, who was small of stature like Sancho Mexia. This man had been gathering honey in the sandy waste, for in this country the bees deposit their honey at the foot of the mounds around the bushes. He was taken on board the captain-major's ship, and being placed at table he ate of all we ate. On the following day the captain-major had him well dressed and sent ashore.

On the following day (November 10) fourteen or fifteen natives came to where our ship lay. The captain-major landed and showed them a variety of merchandise, with the view of finding out whether such things were to be found in their country. This merchandise included cinnamon, cloves, seed-pearls, gold, and many other things, but it was evident that they had no knowledge whatever of such articles, and they were consequently given round bells and tin rings.

(a) Explain TWO results of European journeys like the one taken by Vasco da Gama and his crew during this period of time.

(b) Explain ONE motivation for journeys like the one taken by Vasco da Gama and his crew during this period of time.

4.  Please use the chart below and your knowledge of European history to answer all parts of the following question.

**Slave-Trading Nations**

The number of Africans who were transported to the "New World" between 1520 and 1867 is estimated at 10 million to 15 million persons with 4 million to 6 million additional people perishing on the journey.

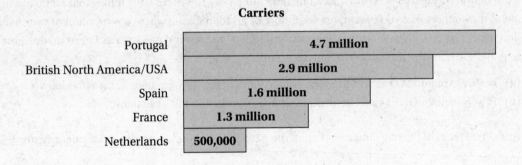

**Carriers**

| | |
|---|---|
| Portugal | 4.7 million |
| British North America/USA | 2.9 million |
| Spain | 1.6 million |
| France | 1.3 million |
| Netherlands | 500,000 |

(a)  Explain TWO results of the European slave trade from Africa to the Americas.

(b)  Explain ONE motivation for the European slave trade from Africa to the Americas.

## Multiple-Choice

**Questions 1–3 refer to the following quote from *The Myth of the Renaissance* by Dr. Jeremy Brotton.**

The term "Renaissance"—referring to the revolution in cultural and artistic life that took place in Europe in the 15th and 16th centuries—was first applied as late as the 19th century, when the French historian Jules Michelet used it in his *History of France* of 1855 . . .

Michelet's invention of the Renaissance was refined and established by the Swiss historian Jacob Burckhardt, in his book *The Civilization of the Renaissance in Italy* (1860). Like Michelet, Burckhardt believed that the cultural achievements of the period heralded a "rebirth" (the French "renaissance") of the classical Greek and Roman values of literary purity and aesthetic beauty . . .

Until very recently, this invention of the European Renaissance has remained a powerful and seductive myth, which has ignored much of what was truly revolutionary about this extraordinary period in European history. The problem with the approach of both Michelet and Burckhardt to the Renaissance is that it reflected their own 19th century world, characterized by European imperialism, industrial expansion, the decline of the church, and a romantic vision of the role of the artist in society. Neither of these writers explored how trade, finance, science and exchange with other cultures decisively shaped what they saw as the cultural flowering of the European Renaissance.

1. What is Dr. Brotton's primary argument against the traditional view of the Renaissance as proposed by Michelet and Burckhardt?

   (A) The work of the earlier historians was flawed because they were too focused upon economic causes and effects of the era.
   (B) The work of the earlier historians was flawed because they ignored the importance of trade, finance, science, and cultural exchange in their analysis of the era.
   (C) The work of the earlier historians was flawed because they were living in the nineteenth century.
   (D) The work of the earlier historians was flawed because they ignored the impact of the arts on the growth of math and sciences.

2. Which of the following was more likely to be emphasized by Burckhardt and Michelet than by Brotton?

   (A) The role of the Roman Catholic Church in promoting the Renaissance and its values
   (B) The importance of the invention of double-entry bookkeeping
   (C) The role of the Fuggers and Medici in creating a commercial environment favorable to the Renaissance
   (D) The role of foreign trade in supporting the cultural diffusion needed for the Renaissance to bloom

3. The Renaissance was a time known for educational and intellectual breakthroughs often attributed to which of the following educational systems?

   (A) The secular system taught at universities in Italy, which ignored all religious traditions
   (B) The individualism taught by artists and their patrons
   (C) The navigational methods of the school of Henry the Navigator
   (D) The focus on Greek and Roman classics required by humanism

**Questions 4–6 refer to the image below.**

*David* by Michelangelo Buonarroti (1501–1504).

4. Michelangelo's *David* displays which of the following thematic innovations of Renaissance artists?

   (A) The depiction of religious personages
   (B) Accurate human anatomy
   (C) The use of marble as a material
   (D) The portrayal of enigmatic expressions

5. The sculpture of David was placed in front of the new Republic's town hall, the Palazzo della Signoria, in Florence, facing Rome and the pope as a warning against the former power of which of the following families?

   (A) The Habsburg family, who dominated politics on the Italian Peninsula and throughout Europe for over a century
   (B) The Valois family, who dominated Italy and Germany as a part of their dominance of religious and political life in the 1400s
   (C) The Medici family, who dominated Italy through banking
   (D) The Fugger family, to whom the pope owed huge amounts of money, which eventually led to selling of indulgences

6. Which of the following would explain why the city of Florence commissioned a statue of David rather than another biblical or classical hero?

   (A) The story of the righteous underdog who defeated a giant had resonance in the young republic, which wanted to preserve its freedom.
   (B) The city of Florence had named David its patron saint and wanted to celebrate him.
   (C) The thousands of Florentine Jewish people combined their wealth to sponsor the creation of an Old Testament hero for their city to recognize.
   (D) David's purity of actions and thought throughout his story in the Bible made him the perfect representative of the most artistic city of the Italian Renaissance.

**Questions 7–9 refer to the following chart.**

### Spanish Gold Exports from the Americas to Seville

| Year | Gold Exported (kg) | Silver Exported (kg) |
|---|---|---|
| 1501–1505 | 517 | 0 |
| 1536–1540 | 2,039 | 12,148 |
| 1551–1555 | 4,707 | 33,497 |
| 1581–1585 | 1,336 | 232,208 |
| 1611–1615 | 795 | 196,820 |
| 1641–1645 | 167 | 196,820 |

7. Which of the following can be proven by the chart above?

    (A) Silver imported to Seville slowly built up but peaked near the end of the 16th century.
    (B) The value of the silver imported was greater than that of the gold.
    (C) The Spanish purchased many imported goods with this gold and silver.
    (D) The value of the silver leaving Seville was greater than that of the gold.

8. Which of the following shows the short-term, medium-term, and long-term results of the influx of precious metals seen in the chart above, listed in the correct chronological order?

    (A) Inflation, wealth generation, consumer economy
    (B) Wealth generation, market economy, consumer economy
    (C) Wealth generation, consumer economy, market economy
    (D) Market economy, wealth generation, inflation

9. Which of the following was the most important change brought on by the opening and expansion of transatlantic trade?

    (A) The drastic increase of wealth of the Europeans occurred at the expense of the rest of the world.
    (B) The increased political power of Europeans allowed them to dominate the entire world within a century.
    (C) The biological exchange between continents changed life globally.
    (D) The improvements in naval technology allowed Europeans to dominate world commerce and politics.

# Answers and Explanations

## Short-Answer Explanations

1. **0–3 points (2 points for a and 1 point for b)**

   (a) 1 point will be given for *each* of *two* explanations of *how* the painting is representative of Renaissance art. These may include the realistic depiction of anatomy, use of perspective, use of light and/or color, nature depicted in the background, portraiture based upon triangles, attention to details of the face and hands, proportion, or prevalence of nature.

   (b) 1 point will be given for an explanation of *how* the image is still representative of medieval art. The main thrust here should be that it is still religious art depicting Madonna and child, the most important image in Christendom. The use of blue for the Madonna or the idea that the most important parts of the image are the largest could also be cited for credit.

2. **0–3 points (2 points for a and 1 point for b)**

   (a) 1 point will be given for *each* of *two* explanations of *how* the passage is representative of Renaissance thought. These may include individualism, revival of Greco-Roman ideas and ideals, focus on intellectualism, pursuit of excellence, the imitation of the styles of other masters, or support of secularism.

   (b) 1 point will be given for an explanation of *how* the passage is still representative of medieval thought. The main thrust here should be that it is still written in Latin and that it focuses on the ideals supported by the Roman Catholic Church. The nod to the "God of Intellect" can also be used to show that it supports monotheism.

3. (a) A good response includes *two* of the results of the era of exploration. They can be social, economic, political, military, or religious results. Social results include the decimation of the peoples of the Americas; the Columbian Exchange; African slavery in the Americas; the European dominance over the rest of the world for four centuries; the

disappearance of many indigenous traditions, languages, legal systems, and lifestyles; European racism against the other peoples of the world; the European diaspora to the Americas and Asia; the intermixing of ethnic groups; and the spread of European languages, laws, and traditions. Political results could include the rise of European colonies around the world, the growing power of non-noble Europeans as their wealth increased, the loss of indigenous control over their own lands, European conflicts over overseas possessions, the rise and fall of Spanish power, and European-style governments emerging all over the world. Religious results may include the spread of Christianity, the growing European awareness of other religious beliefs, the rise of missionaries and missions, and reduced threats to Europe from Islam. The economic results may include rising European wealth, a higher standard of living in Europe, more social mobility for Europeans, loss of wealth for the other peoples of the world, the availability of more goods in Europe, a growing slave trade, merchants rising in status, and growing flows of income into Europe.

   (b) A good explanation looks at *one* of the reasons that Europeans explored the world. These may include the pursuit of wealth, curiosity about the rest of the world, Europeans' belief in their superiority over all other peoples of the world, the desire to spread Christianity, the desire for freedom from European rigid class structures and legal codes, and the desire for adventure.

4. (a) A good response includes *two* of the results of the European slave trade. They can be social, economic, or political results. Social results include the mixing of Africans with Native Americans and Europeans to create offspring of mixed race, the plantation culture emerging in the Americas, the belief that wealthy people in the Americas did not need to do

any manual labor, the end of slavery of the indigenous peoples of the Americas, rising racism, religious opposition to slavery, and the long history of subjugating the descendants of Africans in the Americas. Political results could include the rising European influence on African politics, the rising power of Europe globally, wars for trade in the Atlantic and Caribbean, and the emergence of race-based laws. The economic results may include rising European wealth, a higher standard of living in Europe, a growing slave trade, merchants rising in status, the rising importance of African trade, the emergence of *triangle trade*, and flows of income growing in Europe.

(b) A good explanation explains *one* reason that Europeans brought enslaved Africans to the Americas. Reasons may include the pursuit of wealth, Europeans' belief in their superiority over all other peoples of the world, the writings from people like Bartolomé de las Casas against enslaving Native Americans, the massive dying off of the Native Americans (90 percent within 50 years of Columbus's first voyage), the African resistance to European diseases, African knowledge of European style agriculture, and European racism.

## Practice Multiple-Choice Questions

1. (A) is wrong because a big part of Brotton's argument was that the earlier historians ignored the economic growth of the era.

   **(B) is CORRECT. Brotton says the work of the earlier historians was flawed because they ignored the importance of trade, finance, science, and cultural exchange.**

   (C) is wrong because (B) is a clearer summation of why they were wrong even though Brotton does mention the 19th century; (B) is a much better answer.

   (D) is wrong because the impact of the arts on the growth of math and science was not large enough to be a major historical factor.

2. **(A) is CORRECT because of the factors listed; this matches best with Michelet and Burckhardt, who ignored economics in large part.**

   (B) is wrong because Michelet and Burckhardt ignored economics and finance in large part, and double-entry bookkeeping is a form of finance.

   (C) is wrong because Michelet and Burckhardt ignored economics and finance in large part, and the Medici and Fuggers were banking families.

   (D) is wrong because Michelet and Burckhardt ignored the importance of foreign trade and cultural diffusion into Europe.

3. (A) is wrong because humanism was the educational system of the Renaissance, and universities at the time neither were secular nor ignored traditions.

   (B) is wrong because humanism was the educational system of the Renaissance. Although individualism was an important part of modern identity, it was not an educational system.

   (C) is wrong because humanism was the educational system of the Renaissance. Although navigational methods taught at Prince Henry's school were important, they were not the educational system for most wealthy youth.

   **(D) is CORRECT because the educational system of the Renaissance was humanism, which focused on the classical ideas and works of Greece and Rome.**

4. (A) is wrong because, although David was a person mentioned in the Bible, biblical stories were the dominant theme of art in Europe for the past 700 years or more.

   **(B) is CORRECT because accurate and proportionate representations of anatomy were Renaissance "innovations" reintroduced from classical sculpture.**

   (C) is wrong because, by the year 1500, marble had been used as a material of artists for thousands of years.

   (D) is wrong because enigmatic expressions were not a theme of the Renaissance, so (B) is a better answer.

5. (A) is wrong because, although the Habsburgs did dominate Italy, the new Republic of Florence was more fearful of its former rulers, the Medici, whose family included the current pope.

(B) is wrong because, although the Valois did dominate Italy, the new Republic of Florence was more fearful of its former rulers, the Medici, whose family included the current pope.

**(C) is CORRECT because the new Republic of Florence was fearful of its former rulers, the Medici, whose family included the current pope.**

(D) is wrong because the Fuggers, who dominated Northern European banking, were not involved in internal Italian politics.

6. **(A) is CORRECT because David was placed in front of the Palazzo della Signoria facing Rome to celebrate the heroism of the new republic's expulsion of the Medici and as a warning that it takes heroism to preserve freedom.**

(B) is wrong because David was not the patron saint of Florence.

(C) is wrong because David was commissioned by Catholics, and Judaism had nothing to do with its commission or creation.

(D) is wrong because David did not live a pure life according to the Bible but, instead, sent a man (Uriah the Hittite) to his death in order to marry the man's wife (Bathsheba).

7. **(A) is CORRECT because it is the only answer choice that the data given can support without other evidence.**

(B) is wrong because it requires you to know the relative values of silver and gold, which are not given.

(C) is wrong because it requires you to know what the Spanish did with all of that gold, which is not given in the chart.

(D) is wrong because it requires you to know the relative values of silver and gold, which are not given.

8. (A) is wrong because inflation occurred after wealth generation, not before it.

**(B) is CORRECT because first wealth was generated, creating a market economy, which eventually led the masses to use money and be paid in money. This was a factor that led to a consumer economy along with the desire to emulate the upper classes.**

(C) is wrong because a society cannot develop a consumer economy without first creating a market economy.

(D) is wrong because wealth must be present in order to create a market economy.

9. (A) is wrong because, although the rise in European wealth and power changed the world a lot, of the choices given the biological exchange of foods, diseases, textiles, and even medicines has had the greatest impact on the daily lives of all peoples of the world.

(B) is wrong because, although the rise in European wealth and power changed the world a lot, of the choices given the biological exchange of foods, diseases, textiles, and even medicines has had the greatest impact on the daily lives of all peoples of the world.

**(C) is CORRECT because the biological exchange of foods, diseases, textiles, and even medicines has had the greatest impact—of perhaps any event in modern world history—on the daily lives of all peoples of the world.**

(D) is wrong because, although the rise in European naval power changed the world a lot, of the choices given the biological exchange of foods, diseases, textiles, and even medicines has had the greatest impact on the daily lives of all peoples.

# UNIT 2
# Age of Reformation

## Unit 2 Overview: Age of Reformation

**Unit description:** The second unit, the Age of Reformation, is focused on three themes: Cultural and Intellectual Developments, States and Other Institutions of Power, and Social Organization and Development. These themes are seen throughout the unit. This unit is mostly about the condition of the Roman Catholic Church and its split with Protestantism. The social, political, cultural, and intellectual movements of this era were related to this divide. So students must understand how the destruction of Roman Catholic unity in Western Europe brought on these political, intellectual, and cultural changes.

This unit covers the events of the Protestant Reformation, the creation of new churches, the wars of religion, the Catholic Reformation, and the Counter-Reformation. These events should be analyzed for continuity and change over time as well as to see how the impact of the changes regarding religion were reflected in cultural, intellectual, political, and economic changes in Western Europe. The major topics of study for this unit are the following:

- Contextualizing 16th- and 17th-century challenges and developments
- Luther and the Protestant Reformation
- Protestant reform continues
- Wars of religion
- Catholic Reformation
- 16th-century society and politics
- Art of the 16th century: mannerism and baroque art
- Causation in the Age of Reformation and the wars of religion

The final part of this chapter explaining causation in this era is very important to your study. The entire unit is contained in chapter 2.

# 2

# Protestant Reformation, Catholic and Counter-Reformations, Wars of Religion (1517–1648)

---

### Key Terms

- Reformation
- Peace of Augsburg
- Indulgences
- The Diet of Worms

- Spanish Inquisition
- Huguenots
- Council of Trent
- Jesuits

- Index of Prohibited Books
- The Thirty Years' War
- War of Three Henrys
- Edict of Nantes

### Key People

- Sir Thomas More
- Martin Luther
- John Calvin

- Ignatius of Loyola
- Cardinal Richelieu

- Charles V of Spain and Austria
- Philip II of Spain

---

## Overview

This chapter fits 100 percent within the first time period for the course. Historians generally agree that the Protestant Reformation was one of the markers of the beginning of modern Europe and was a crucial part in the transformation of Western civilization. What began as an attempt to reform the Roman Catholic Church was co-opted by political forces. It resulted in the destruction of the religious unity of Western Europe and the outbreak of bitter wars of religion. The Protestant and Catholic reformations fundamentally changed theology, religious institutions, culture, and attitudes toward wealth and prosperity. The Protestant faiths looked much more kindly on profit and wealth than Catholicism did.

The conflicts among different religious groups overlapped with political and economic competition among states. This was manifested in the fact that religious reforms both strengthened some states and acted as a justification for challenging royal authority in others.

Protestantism was adopted by the growing nation-states of the North as they were about to replace Italy and Spain as leaders of modern Europe; the Inquisition enforced orthodoxy. The Inquisition in Spain was designed to encourage a sense of national unity based on Catholicism. The Muslim Moors and the Jews who had been the educated groups in Spanish society were either driven into exile or forcibly converted. The Inquisition was later adapted in Spain and in Spanish territories to combat Protestantism, and it was imported to Italy for the same purpose. Protestantism, though, dominated most of Northern Europe. The Continent suffered devastating disruptions during the wars of the 16th and 17th centuries.

## Causes of the Reformation

1. The Roman Catholic Church showed much corruption during the Renaissance, including the sale of church offices (simony), the sale of indulgences, nepotism, absenteeism, and the decline of morality among the clergy.
2. The impact of Renaissance *humanism* questioned Church traditions. Humanism emphasized the glorification of humanity.

- Humanism contradicted the Church's emphasis on salvation.
- The educational system of humanism opened people's minds to multiple perspectives that competed with the Church's monopoly on knowledge of the universe.

3. Prosperity brought the "virtue of poverty" into disrepute. The Church lost the "spirit" of Christ's message and was out of touch with the mass of believers. The rising consumerism of the age left the people ready to welcome a faith that justified their newfound prosperity. As states became more prosperous, their populations urbanized, leading to migration to cities from the rural areas. This shift in populations often caused strains on the cities and their governments as well as on traditional political and social structures.

4. The prestige of the papacy was declining:

- The *Babylonian Captivity* of the Church in the 14th century occurred when popes, subservient to the French king, took up residence in Avignon and lost prestige in the rest of Christendom.
- The *Great Schism* began in 1378 when French and anti-French cardinals elected two popes, one of whom lived in Rome and the other in Avignon. This schism lasted over 40 years.
- The *moral decline* of the Renaissance popes bred cynicism. Papal involvement in secular politics fostered contempt.

5. The influence of religious reformers, such as John Wycliffe (c. 1330–1384) and Jan Huss (c. 1372–1415), stressed personal communion with God. This had two effects:

- It diminished the importance of the sacraments.
- It weakened the influence of the clergy.

6. The resentment of secular rulers over the power of the popes and clergy had several effects:

- Monarchs of growing nation-states resisted papal supremacy over national churches.
- Secular rulers resented the vast landholdings of the Church within national boundaries.

7. Resistance to the power of the Holy Roman Emperor, Charles V, caused the following:

- The princes of the Germanic lands resented the new Holy Roman Emperor.
- Charles V (r. 1519–1558), who at age 19 took the throne along with his vast Habsburg holdings, proclaimed at his coronation, "The empire from of old has had not many masters, but one, and it is our intention to be that master."
- The Holy Roman Emperor was a symbolic title, and his desire to make it more actual caused resistance to the power of Charles V.
- Protestantism helped Germanic princes resist the power of the Holy Roman Emperor.

8. The invention of the *printing press* allowed dissenters to spread their ideas throughout Europe and made the Bible available to the common people. It also meant that a person's ideas and influence in the world would live on long after that person died. This became more important as new sects of Christianity challenged the Roman Catholic Church. Those sects were not easily silenced once the ideas of their leaders were recorded. This was in stark contrast to how they had been in the days of Jan Huss.

## Chronological Overview of Events, Personalities, and Ideas

### 1517

*Johann Tetzel* (c. 1465–1519), a wandering friar, was authorized by *Pope Leo X* to sell *indulgences* (which guaranteed the remission of sins), the proceeds of which would be used to rebuild St. Peter's Church in Rome and to provide funds to local dioceses.

*Martin Luther* (1483–1546), a Roman Catholic priest, Augustinian monk, and theologian at the University of Wittenburg in Germany, condemned the sales of indulgences as impious expediencies. Tormented by obsessions of his own damnation despite a life dedicated to holy service, he came to believe that the traditional means of attaining salvation (good works, such as the sacraments, prayer, and fasting) were inadequate. He supposedly nailed his *95 Theses* to the door of the Wittenburg church (his day's equivalent of calling a press conference). Luther listed the points of his opposition to the indulgences and invited debate. It is important to note that the use of the *printing press* to spread Luther's ideas helped to propagate them and gain acceptance for their ideas.

## 1519–1520

When an appeal to Pope Leo X (r. 1513–1521) for reform of this abuse went unanswered, Luther began to formulate the tenets of his beliefs, ideas that he had been mulling over for nearly a decade.

The following shows the tenets of Lutheranism as published in a series of tracts:

- *Salvation by faith alone:* Good works (the sacraments) cannot guarantee salvation but, rather, are an outward manifestation of the faith that a loving God will grant that salvation. This concept was inspired by Luther's reading, many years earlier, of a passage from Romans 1:17, in which St. Paul says, "The just shall live by faith."
- *The Bible is the ultimate authority:* Neither the Pope nor church councils can define Christian doctrine. Every believer should read and interpret the Bible, and the faithful will be divinely guided.
- *The grace of God brings absolution:* Neither indulgences nor confession can bring forgiveness of sins. The individual is freed of sin only by the grace of God. Pilgrimages, veneration of saints, fasts, and worship of relics are useless.
- *Baptism and communion are the only valid sacraments:* The Roman Catholic Church regarded seven sacraments (baptism; confirmation; Eucharist or communion; matrimony; penance; extreme unction, last rites, or anointing of the sick; and holy orders) as outward signs of inner grace. Luther rejected all but baptism and communion. Luther also rejected the Roman Catholic doctrine of *transubstantiation*. This is the belief that while the bread and wine of the Mass maintain their appearance, they are transformed into the body and blood of Christ. In its place, Luther offered the doctrine of *consubstantiation*. This is the doctrine that the transformation of the bread and wine was not literal but that God was actually present in more than a symbolic way.
- *The clergy is not superior to the laity:* Marriage is permitted; Christianity is a "priesthood of all believers"; monasticism should be abolished.
- *The Church should be subordinate to the state:* In the appointment of Church officials, the matter of taxing Church lands, the organization of the Church, and all matters other than the theological, the state is supreme. This appealed to the monarchs and to the German princes who resented papal authority and who coveted the vast landholdings and wealth of the Roman Catholic Church. It would have ramifications for Lutheranism in Germany well into the 20th century.

## 1520

Luther publicly burned a *papal bull*, an official proclamation that demanded his recantation, and he was excommunicated by *Pope Leo X*. Holy Roman Emperor *Charles V*, instead of arresting Luther and suppressing Lutheranism, which had a growing appeal in Germany and Scandinavia, honored a political debt to Frederick the Wise, Elector of Saxony, by refusing to outlaw Luther without a hearing.

## 1521

Luther was called to the Rhineland in Germany to appear before *The Diet of Worms*, a tribunal of the Holy Roman Empire with the power to outlaw, which means to condemn Luther to being burned at the stake. Confronted by the sharpest theological debaters of the Roman Catholic Church, Luther contended that only the Bible or reason would convince him. "I neither can nor will I recant anything, since it is neither right nor safe to act against conscience." The Diet outlawed him. "Kidnapped" to safety in Wittenberg by Frederick the Wise, Luther organized his reformed church and translated the Bible into the vernacular, profoundly influencing the development of the modern German language.

- The support of Frederick the Wise illustrated the growing control the state had over religion and how it was used (in this case by Frederick the Wise) to challenge the authority of political rulers like Charles V.
- This support also displayed the overlap of religious change with political and economic competition within and among the states.
- Religious conflicts such as this or the Thirty Years' War became the basis for eventually challenging the control of religious institutions.

## 1520s

Lutheranism spread. Preoccupied with wars against the Ottoman Turks and the French, *Charles V*, the Holy Roman Emperor, was unable to suppress the growth of Protestantism in Northern Europe. In addition to northern Germany, Denmark and its province of Norway, Sweden and its holdings in Finland, and the Eastern Baltic all embraced Lutheranism.

## 1521

A group of *Anabaptists*, who preached adult baptism and the equality of all Christians, began to spread their ideas in Germanic states. Their religious movement began to gain ground.

## 1522

A league of knights, under the leadership of *Franz von Sickengen*, converted to Lutheranism and attacked the Catholic princes of the Rhineland. They were suppressed, but this clash encouraged most of the German princes to convert. One motive for von Sickengen's followers and the later conversions was the financial gain brought by confiscating Roman Catholic lands.

## 1524–1526

Luther's theological dissent inspired a variety of radical religious sects to form and to demand social reform based on the early Christian model. Demanding abolition of *manorialism*, the economic and social order of medieval feudalism, German peasants rebelled against the landowners; Germany was wracked by the *Peasants' War*. Luther supported the princes by publishing *Against the Murderous, Thieving Hordes of Peasants*.

The Anabaptists supported the revolt, and Luther targeted them in some of his most specific chidings. He was appalled by these extremists and others who, he believed, took his ideas too far. The Anabaptists preached adult total-immersion baptism, and the Millenarians expected the imminent return of Christ. He condemned the rebels as "filthy swine" and encouraged the princes to exterminate them.

The radical revolt influenced Luther to demand that his followers obey constituted authority and that, while they read the Bible themselves, they leave its interpretation to knowledgeable ministers. His social and economic conservatism helped check the spread of Lutheranism in southern Germany and elsewhere in Europe. This event is further evidence of how religious conflicts became a basis for challenging the monarch's control of society.

## 1529

*The Diet of Speyer* refused to recognize the right of the German princes to determine the religion of their subjects.

## 1531

The *League of Schmalkalden* was formed by newly Protestant princes to defend themselves against the emperor. Charles V appealed to the Pope to call a church council that could compromise with the Lutherans and regain their allegiance to the Roman Catholic Church. The Pope, fearing the papacy's loss of power, refused and lost a potential opportunity to reunite western Christendom.

## 1530s

The Reformation spread beyond Germany.

## 1531

In Switzerland, *Huldrych Zwingli* (1484–1531), who established Protestantism in Switzerland, was killed in a nationwide religious civil war. Although his followers accepted most of Luther's reforms, they argued that God's presence during communion is only symbolic. *The Peace of Cappel* allowed each Swiss canton to determine its own religion.

## 1534

*Pope Paul III* (r. 1534–1549) assumed office as the first of the "reform popes."

## 1534

In England, Parliament passed the *Act of Supremacy*, which made *Henry VIII* (r. 1509–1547) and his successors the head of the Anglican Church and its clergy.

- In 1521, when Luther was outlawed by the Holy Roman Empire, Henry VIII had been awarded the title "defender of the faith" by Pope Leo X for Henry's tract "Defense of the Seven Sacraments."
- By 1529 and partly because of Henry's influence, Parliament declared the English Church independent of Rome.
  - Parliament cut off revenues to the papacy.
  - Henry, eager to divorce *Catherine of Aragon* in order to marry *Anne Boleyn*, was denied an annulment by the Pope for political reasons.
- Catherine was the aunt of Charles V, Holy Roman Emperor.
  - Henry appointed *Thomas Cranmer* as Archbishop of Canterbury in 1533, was granted a divorce by him, and was excommunicated by the Pope.

## 1534–1539

The English Parliament abolished Roman Catholic monasteries and nunneries, confiscated their lands, and redistributed them to nobles and gentry who supported the newly formed Anglican Church.

## 1536

In Switzerland, *John Calvin* (1509–1564) published his *Institutes of the Christian Religion* in the Swiss city of Basel. Like Zwingli, he accepted most of Luther's ideas but differed on the role of the state in church affairs:

1. *Predestination:* Calvin argued (from an idea of St. Augustine [354–430]) that since God knows even before birth whether a person is saved or damned, there is nothing anyone can do to win salvation. *The Elect* or *saints* are a select few saved only by God's love from corrupt humanity and given indications of their status by *conversion* (a mystical encounter with God) or by material prosperity. The latter gave rise to the *Puritan* or *Protestant ethic,* an incentive to avoid poverty as a sign of damnation, and served to justify the rise of capitalism.

2. *Church government:* Calvin replaced the Catholic hierarchy with a democratic system whereby each individual congregation elected its minister and governed its policies. He disagreed with Luther's claim that the church should be subordinate to the state and argued that it should actually be a moral force in the affairs of secular government. This stand encouraged *theocracy,* whereby Calvinism became the official religion and intolerant of dissent not only in parts of Switzerland but later in England and the Massachusetts Bay Colony in North America. This demonstrates one instance of the Protestant Reformation increasing governmental power over its people.

3. Calvin and some others such as the Anabaptists refused to recognize that the church should be subordinate to the state. They created theocracies and believed that the state was inferior to religion. This idea that religion should control the government has reemerged with the Iranian Ayatollahs, the Taliban, and ISIS in the 20th and 21st centuries.

4. John Calvin also made good use of the *printing press* and publishing to create books like the *Institutes of Christian Religion*, which helped to spread his ideas and allowed them to gain acceptance.

## 1539

In England, Parliament approved the *Statute of the Six Articles*:

1. The seven sacraments were upheld.
2. Catholic theology was maintained against the tenets of both Lutheranism and Calvinism.
3. The authority of the monarch replaced the authority of the pope.

Despite attempts by *Mary I of England* (1516–1558, Henry VIII's daughter by Catherine of Aragon) to reinstitute Catholicism and the *Puritan Revolution* of the following century, the Six Articles helped define the Anglican Church through modern times.

## 1540s

Calvinism spread. In Scotland the *Presbyterian Church* and in France the *Huguenots* were emerging based upon the ideas of Calvin as his religion spread through the wealthy merchant elite throughout Northern Europe. The Counter-Reformation began. The Presbyterians and Huguenots were religions that justified personal wealth rather than criticized it. They spread like wildfire during the commercial revolution.

## 1540

The *Catholic Reformation* began as the Roman Catholic Church began to reform itself and fight the corruption from within the Church through the creation of new orders like the Jesuits and through reforms like the *Council of Trent*. A similar and parallel *Counter-Reformation* was also undertaken by the Church to win back lost followers and stop the spread of the Protestant Reformation.

*Ignatius of Loyola* (1491–1556) established the *Jesuits* (Society of Jesus). It was a holy order that was organized in a military fashion and required of its members blind obedience and absolute faith.

The Jesuits swore to suppress Protestantism:

1. Jesuits served as advisers to Catholic kings.
2. They suppressed heresy through the Inquisition (clerical courts that tried and convicted religious dissenters who were subject to deportation, torture, or death).
3. Jesuits established schools in Catholic nations to indoctrinate the young.
4. They sent missionaries to the far corners of the Earth to convert "the heathen."
5. The *Society of Jesus* (Jesuits) became the militant arm of the Counter-Reformation.

## 1541

1. Calvin set up a model theocracy in the Swiss city of Geneva.
2. The Scottish Calvinists (*Presbyterians*) established a national church.
3. The French Calvinists (*Huguenots*) made dramatic gains but were brutally suppressed by the Catholic majority.
4. The English Calvinists (Puritans and Pilgrims—a separatist minority) failed in their revolution in the 1600s but established a colony in New England.

## 1542

The Jesuits were given control of the Spanish and Italian *Inquisitions.*

- Perhaps tens of thousands were executed on even the suspicion of heresy.
- The *Index of Prohibited Books* was instituted in Catholic countries to keep heretical reading material out of the hands of the faithful.

## 1545–1563

*The Council of Trent* responded to the challenge of Protestantism by defining Catholic dogma. The following lists its main pronouncements:

1. Salvation is by both *good works* (such as the veneration of saints and fasts) and *grace.*
2. The seven sacraments are valid, and transubstantiation is reaffirmed.
3. The sources of religious authority are the Bible, the traditions of the Church, and the writings of the Church Fathers. Individuals cannot interpret the Bible without the guidance of the Church. The only valid version of the Bible is the Vulgate, which is St. Jerome's Latin translation.
4. Monasticism, with celibacy of the clergy, and the existence of purgatory are reaffirmed.
5. Attempts were made to reform abuses. The principle of indulgences was upheld while its abuses were corrected. Bishops were given greater power over clergy in their dioceses. Seminaries were established in each diocese for the training of priests.

## 1555

The *Peace of Augsburg*, after over two decades of religious strife, allowed the German princes to choose the religion of their subjects although the choice was limited to either Lutheranism or Catholicism. *Cuius regio, eius religio*: "Whose the region, his the religion."

## Results of the Protestant Reformation

1. Northern Europe (Scandinavia, England, much of Germany, parts of France, Switzerland, and Scotland) adopted Protestantism.
2. The unity of western Christianity was shattered.
3. Religious wars broke out in Europe for well over a century.
4. The Protestant spirit of individualism encouraged democracy, science, and capitalism.
5. Protestantism, specifically Lutheranism, justified nationalism by making the church subordinate to the state in all but theological matters.

## The War of the Three Henrys (1587–1589)

The War of the Three Henrys was partially a religious war and partially a dynastic war. The weak king, Henry III of France, was counseled to root out the Protestant Huguenot nobility by Henry of Guise.

- The Huguenots in France gained power among about 10 percent of the nobility.

- When Henry of Navarre (a Huguenot politique) married Margaret of Valois, the king's sister, a massacre of Huguenot friends of Henry of Navarre by Roman Catholics known as the St. Bartholomew's Day Massacre erupted, initiating this war.
    - Henry of Navarre won the war but converted back to Catholicism to rule as Henry IV of France.
    - He issued the *Edict of Nantes*, allowing Huguenots religious freedom in strongholds.
    - He was know as a *politique*, which is a term for people who practiced realpolitik in France. This occurred at the time due to his willingness to change religion in order to rule France.
    - He is reported to have said, "Paris is well worth a mass," before converting back to Catholicism.

## The Thirty Years' War (1618–1648)

1. The Thirty Years' War was the first continent-wide war in modern history and was fought mostly in Germany. It involved the major European powers.
2. It was the culmination of the religious wars of the 16th century between Catholics and Protestants.
3. Politically, German princes sought autonomy from the Holy Roman Empire; France sought to limit the power of the Habsburgs who sought to extend power in Germany; Sweden and Denmark hoped to strengthen their hold over the Baltic region.

## The Four Phases of the Thirty Years' War

1. *The Bohemian Phase (1618–1625):*

    - The Czechs, also called Bohemians, who together with the Slovaks formed the modern nation of Czecho-slovakia after World War I, were largely Calvinist.
    - Fearful that their Catholic king, *Matthias,* would deny their religious preferences, they *defenestrated* (used the old custom of registering dissent by throwing officials out a window) the king's representatives and briefly installed as king a Calvinist, *Frederick V of the Palatinate*, or Elector Palatine.
    - After Matthias's death, *Ferdinand II* became Holy Roman Emperor and King of Bohemia.
        - Ferdinand II was supported by troops of the Spanish Habsburgs. He defeated the Bohemians at the *Battle of White Mountain* in 1620.
        - Ferdinand II gave away the lands of the Protestant nobles to Catholics who supported him.
        - He enabled the Spanish to consolidate power along the Rhine River.

2. *The Danish Phase (1625–1630):*

    - *Christian IV of Denmark* (r. 1588–1648), a Lutheran, entered the war to bolster the weakened Protestant position in Germany and to annex German lands for his son.
    - Holy Roman Emperor Ferdinand II (r. 1619–1637) countered by commissioning Albert of Wallenstein to raise a mercenary army, which pillaged and plundered Germany and which defeated the Danes in 1626.
    - In 1629, the emperor issued *The Edict of Restitution*, which restored all the land to the Roman Catholic Church in states in Germany that had left the Church before the Peace of Augsburg in 1555.
    - When Wallenstein disapproved, Ferdinand dismissed him.

3. *The Swedish Phase (1625–1630):*

    - *Cardinal Richelieu*, Roman Catholic regent of France, was concerned with the gains made by the Holy Roman Emperor Ferdinand II in Germany.
    - France decided to pursue nationalist interests rather than religious ones as a matter of state policy under *Cardinal Richelieu.*
        - It was good policy to keep the Germanic states divided as France's neighbor.
        - France wanted to weaken the Habsburgs, the ruling house of the Holy Roman Empire.
        - France gained prestige.

- ○ Richelieu offered subsidies to encourage the capable Swedish king *Gustavus Adolphus* (r. 1611–1632) to enter the war.
  - ▪ Adolphus, a Lutheran, was eager to help the Protestant cause.
  - ▪ After decisive victories over the Habsburg forces, Adolphus was killed.
  - ▪ Wallenstein was assassinated for contemplating disloyalty to the emperor.
  - ▪ The Protestant states of Germany made a separate peace with the emperor.
- ▪ *The Peace of Prague* revoked the Edict of Restitution.
- ▪ The Swedes were defeated, but Richelieu was determined to undermine Habsburg power in Germany.

**4.** *The French-International Phase (1635–1648):*

- ○ France, Holland, and Savoy entered the war in 1635 on the Swedish side.
- ○ Spain continued to support the Austrian Habsburgs.
- ○ After a series of victories and reversals on both sides, *Henri Turenne*, a French general, decisively defeated the Spanish at Rocroi.
- ○ In 1644, peace talks began in Westphalia, Germany.

## The Peace of Westphalia, 1648

- ▪ The Peace of Augsburg was reinstated, but Calvinism was added as acceptable for Germany.
- ▪ The Edict of Restitution was revoked, guaranteeing the possession of former Church states to their Protestant holders.
- ▪ Switzerland and Holland were made independent states and freed from the Habsburg dominions.
- ▪ France, Sweden, and Brandenburg (the future Prussia) received various territories.
- ▪ The German princes were made sovereign rulers, severely limiting the power of the Holy Roman Emperor and the influence of the Austrian and Spanish Habsburgs. With over 300 separate rulers in Germany, national unification was ignored until well into the 19th century.
- ▪ Perhaps most importantly, the concept of *Westphalian Sovereignty* was born. This new type of diplomacy focused on nations as representatives of an ethnic group that could determine the codes of behavior for their citizens. This led to the modern concept of national sovereignty, which supports almost all treaties today.

## Effects of the Thirty Years' War

- ▪ Germanic states were devastated; the population was reduced in some parts by well over a third. Once cultural and political leaders in Europe, the Germanic states stagnated, helping to prevent their establishment as a sovereign, united nation for more than two centuries and complicating their relations with the rest of the world into the 20th century.
- ▪ The age of religious wars ended; the modern age of sovereign states began in Europe. *Balance of Power* politics prevailed in Europe, whereby nation-states and dynasties went to war to prevent any one power from dominating the Continent.
- ▪ The Habsburgs were weakened. The Austrian monarchy lost most of its influence over Germany, ending the possibility of a Europe united under the family. Habsburg Spain was left a second-rate power.
- ▪ The Counter-Reformation was slowed; Protestantism was firmly established in its European strongholds.
- ▪ The Holy Roman Empire ceased to be a viable political structure, and the Germanic states would not be unified again until 1871.
- ▪ *Westphalian Sovereignty* emerged as the current theory about national powers and limitations on those powers.
- ▪ Calvinism gained acceptance throughout Protestant Europe.
- ▪ Anabaptists were persecuted and disappeared as a religion.

# Gender and Ethnicity During the Reformation

- The previously established hierarchies of class, religion, and gender continued to define status and social position in both rural and urban settings. This included the church hierarchy, governing systems, guilds, and separate but intertwined roles for men and women of this era.
- The Renaissance was primarily a male upper-class movement. However, the Reformation saw a small rise in the status of women in many areas.
- The Renaissance and Reformation raised debates about the education of females and the roles of women in the church, family, and society.
- Women received mixed blessings from this era.
- Women did rise in status.
  - Luther and the Protestants preached that there was merit in all work in the eyes of the Eternal, including the household work of women.
    - Ministers were allowed to marry, which considerably raised the status of the women who had previously been their lovers but who now married them.
    - Women could have more official roles in Protestant religious life than in that of the Roman Catholic Church.
    - Some women became preachers.
    - Women were encouraged to read the Bible themselves, increasing female literacy and intellectual roles in general.
  - On the other hand, there was still considerable misogyny evident in this society.
    - Witch trials were prevalent at this time.
    - Mostly women were accused of practicing witchcraft. Many were burned at the stake after confessions were extracted through torture or even simply without evidence.
    - Nunneries closed in Protestant areas, leaving few options other than marriage or prostitution open to women.
    - Many former nuns were forced into marriage.
    - Women were still denied access to university education.
- This was an age in which minority religion was finding its power.
  - This was also an era of zealotry.
- City and local governments were responsible for regulating the moral behavior of their residents.
  - Social norms were enforced through public humiliation rituals, such as the backward donkey ride during Lent for adulterers.
  - Witchcraft trials spread through Northern Europe.
  - Leisure activities were still arranged around the religious and agricultural calendars and remained communal activities during this era.
- Practitioners of many religions were intolerant of those who practiced other faiths.
  - This resulted in the many religious wars of the era.
  - The Anabaptists were exterminated.
- Europeans enslaved and mistreated people of African descent in larger numbers both in Europe and in the colonies.
  - In the colonies, European migrants mistreated, abused, and forced conversion onto native peoples.
  - The European conquistadors and settlers killed tens of millions of Native Americans.
  - Spain and other European powers became rich from the natural bounty of those lands.
  - Slavery and genocide of Africans and indigenous Americans is part of the legacy of this age.

# The Baroque Period of Art

The visual arts began to flourish and become more awe inspiring; thus, baroque art was born. The general intent of the *baroque period* was to create a unity where all forms of art in a single expressive purpose could converge toward a single aim: to engage the viewer physically and emotionally. This art was meant to overpower the viewer and make the viewer feel small in comparison to the art and its subject matter. The term *baroque* derives from a Portuguese word jewelers used to denote an irregularity in a misshapen or irregular pearl. Baroque therefore literally meant imperfect, grotesque, or absurd. The baroque era began in the late-16th century in Italy and ended in some areas around the early-19th century.

- The term *baroque* also refers to the 17th century as a whole. It is sometimes used as a general term indicating eccentric or fanciful modes of paintings, architecture, sculpture, dress, or behavior in any period.
- Baroque art spread throughout Western Europe and into Russia and other places in Europe influenced by the court of Louis XIV.
- Baroque art was also found in Latin America, the English colonies, and Northern Europe.
  - Never had the Western world known such active international exchange in the intellectual field.
  - The internationalism was not checked by differences in religious beliefs.
    - For example, Peter Paul Rubens (1577–1640), a Flemish painter, worked in Italy, France, Spain, and England.
    - Rubens was considered a "European" painter, whereas Jacques-Louis David (1748–1825), a Neoclassical French painter, worked only in France for most of his life.
- Baroque art was an instrument of the *Counter-Reformation*, which took place from 1545 until the end of the Thirty Years' War in 1648.
  - The Catholic Church was losing its followers in rapid numbers due to the rise of Protestantism.
    - The *Council of Trent* was created to set about renovating the Catholic Church.
    - Society at this time was generally illiterate.
  - Knowing this, the Catholic Church decided to bring back wayward Catholics through art.
    - Baroque artists frequently capitalized on the immediacy of their viewers' emotional reactions, and spiritual art became an art of sensation.
    - The effect of baroque art was not to elevate the spirit but to stagger and overpower the senses.
- Baroque art was larger than life, escaping boundaries and overpowering the viewer.
- It is important to contrast the baroque style with that of the Calvinist painters of the Dutch Golden Age who concentrated on realistic details in portraits and the interiors of buildings. These artists included Vermeer, Rembrandt, and Hals. The works of Calvinist painters were much smaller and more detailed; they attempted to shine insights into slices of life and individual personalities.
  - *Rembrandt Van Rijn* (1606–1669) created innovative portraits and was known for his use of light.
  - *Johannes Vermeer* (1632–1675) created clear domestic scenes.
  - *Franz Hals* (c. 1582–1666) made portraits of wealthy citizens of Antwerp and Amsterdam.

Some examples of baroque painters and their defining characteristics include the following:

- *Peter Paul Rubens* (1577–1640) painted fleshy nudes and overwhelming biblical scenes.
- *Michelangelo Merisi da Caravaggio* (1571–1610) contrasted light and dark in his work.
- *Artemisia Gentileschi* (1593–1652) created paintings of dramatic tension and suffering.
- *Gian Lorenzo Bernini* (1598–1650) was the greatest sculptor of the era.

In the musical world, the following are some of the greatest baroque composers:

- *Johann Sebastian Bach* (1685–1750) was the ultimate baroque composer.
- *Claudio Monteverdi* (1547–1643) wrote the oldest opera still performed, *Orfeo*.
- *Antonio Vivaldi* (1678–1741) composed *The Four Seasons*.
- *George F. Handel* (1685–1759) wrote *Messiah*, which has become a classic.

Eventually, the baroque style led to the *rococo* style of art, which was characterized by elegance, pleasantness, and frivolity. It greatly contrasted the emotional grandeur of the baroque.

## Many Faiths Chart

This chart may be helpful in remembering the differences among the many new Christian faiths that emerged from the Protestant Reformation.

### The Many Faiths of the Protestant Reformation

| | Catholic | Anglican | Lutheran | Calvinism | Zurich Protestant | Presbyterian | Anabaptist |
|---|---|---|---|---|---|---|---|
| Leadership | Pope and religious hierarchy | King and religious hierarchy | Luther | Ministerial government divinely ordained | Zwingli | Knox | No head |
| Sacraments | Seven | Began with communion, baptism, and penance; then became just communion and baptism | Communion, baptism | Communion, baptism | Communion, baptism | Communion, baptism | Lord's supper and baptism |
| Clergy | Priests: Only clergy may interpret scripture | Married priests | Ministers and priesthood of all believers | Ministers, elders, deacons, congregants | Ministers | Ministers | Ministers, including women |
| How is salvation achieved? | Faith and works | Faith and works | Faith: When one is justified, one is forgiven; therefore, one can repent fully and do good works | Faith: Good works may or may not be evidence of justification, but wealth is | Faith: Justification is God's endorsement of the morals of the individual | Faith | Faith |
| Role of state | The Pope is the Catholic leader of sovereigns | The sovereign controls the church | Religious choices are up to the individual, who owes obedience to the lawful ruler | Religious organization dominates the state, and in fact is the state; for example, Geneva | Religion controls the state | | Separation of church and state |
| Where | Italy, parts of Germany, Ireland, Poland, France, Spain | England | Parts of Germany, Sweden, Norway, Denmark | Holland, France, and Geneva, Switzerland | Zurich, Switzerland | Scotland | Switzerland and Northwest Germany (Munster) and Netherlands |
| Eucharist | Transubstantiation | | Consubstantiation | Eucharist is just a symbol, not a divine action | Eucharist is a memorial, not a sacrifice | | |
| Other | Indulgences, purgatory, and abuses: simony, nepotism, pluralism, absenteeism | | | Predestination, "Protestant ethic and the spirit of capitalism"—19th century historian Max Weber "The Elect" | Focused on rebuilding the community, not the individual | | |

# Practice Questions

## Long Essay

The questions that follow are samples of the various types of thematic essays that appear on the AP exam. See pages 27–28 for a detailed explanation of each type. Check over the generic rubric (see pages 28–29) before you begin any of these essays, and use that rubric to score your essay if you write one.

## Question 1

"Calvin's doctrines were a radical departure from those of both the Roman Catholic Church and Lutheranism." Evaluate this statement.

### Comments on Question 1

This one seems to call for you to analyze *change and continuity over time* (CCOT) because you must explain the relative historical significance of Calvin's doctrines in relation to the overall Protestant Reformation as well as the overall pattern of European religious history. You should analyze the extent to which Calvin's ideas were different from and similar to the beliefs of Luther and of the Roman Catholic Church. You must provide multiple specific examples to support the analysis. To get the second point, the essay must analyze the extent to which the ideas and doctrines of Calvin were different from and similar to developments that preceded and/or followed the emergence of Calvinism. This question leaves some room for choice. In evaluating the statement, you may choose to compare the doctrines on *salvation* of each of these Christian sects. In his stand against indulgences, Luther departed from Roman Catholic doctrine and from Church tradition. Calvin argued still another view. The question could be approached through this issue alone.

Another way to attack the question would be through the differing relations of each of these sects to the issues of religion and the state and of Church government. A clear contrast can be shown among the three.

## Question 2

To what extent was the Reformation caused by long-term political, social, and economic developments?

### Comments on Question 2

This essay question requires that you take a stand on the statement and decide if the Reformation was indeed caused by social, political, and economic developments. This one is a *causation* question because it requires you to decide how the Reformation was caused by the other developments. Remember to describe causes and/or effects of the Reformation and to state how much each specific development caused the Reformation and how it did not. The essay must explain the reasons for the social, political, and economic causes and/or effects of the Protestant Reformation. In this particular question, the crucial term is "caused." Any great historical event is brought about by multiple and complex developments. These are the long-term causes. For instance, corruption among Church officials and the influence of Renaissance ideas are long-term causes of the Reformation. However, people and their distinct personalities are often at the center of immediate causation. Immediate causes are actions that precipitate great events. Tetzel's sale of indulgences provoked Luther to issue his *95 Theses*.

## Question 3

To what extent was the Protestant emphasis on one's personal relationship with God a logical outgrowth of the Renaissance?

## Comments on Question 3

This one is another *causation* question because it requires you to explain to what extent and how the Renaissance caused the Protestant emphasis on a personal relationship with God. Remember to describe the causes and effects of an increased personal relationship with God, indicating the degree to which it was caused by the Renaissance. The essay must explain the reasons for the causes and/or effects of the Protestant emphasis on a personal relationship with God. The pivotal concept in this statement is "logical outgrowth." Consider its implications before choosing an approach. Does it mean a necessary effect? Or was it the result of one influence among many? In order to answer this, you must be familiar with the Renaissance ideas that emphasized individuality as well as how they differed with notions of the preceding age (the medieval period). These ideas must then be linked as influences for various Protestant theological or social concepts that differed from Roman Catholic views. This is a tough question! It would be easy to fall into the trap of oversimplifying by jumping to conclusions based on a superficial knowledge of complex ideas and doctrines.

## Short-Answer

1.  Use the map below and your knowledge of European history to answer all parts of the following question.

**Protestantism in Europe**

(a)  Briefly explain TWO effects on European politics of the spread of Protestantism during the second half of the 16th century as seen in the map above.

(b)  Briefly explain ONE effect on the economies of Europe of the spread of Protestantism during the second half of the 16th century as seen in the map above.

2.  Use the passage below and your knowledge of European history to answer all parts of the following question.

**Martin Luther's Address to German Nobility (ca. 1520)**

The grace and might of God be with you, Most Serene Majesty, most gracious, well-beloved gentlemen!

It is not out of mere arrogance and perversity that I, an individual poor man, have taken upon me to address your lordships. The distress and misery that oppress all the Christian estates, more especially in Germany, have led not only myself, but everyone else, to cry aloud and to ask for help, and have now forced me too to cry out and to ask if God would give His Spirit to anyone to reach a hand to His wretched people. Councils have often put forward some remedy, but it has adroitly been frustrated, and the evils have become worse, through the cunning of certain men. Their malice and wickedness I will now, by the help of God, expose, so that, being known, they may henceforth cease to be so obstructive and injurious. God has given us a young and noble sovereign, and by this has roused great hopes in many hearts; now it is right that we too should do what we can, and make good use of time and grace.

(a)  Briefly explain ONE cause of the conflict referenced by Luther in the above excerpt.

(b)  Briefly explain ONE result of the conflict referenced by Luther in the above excerpt.

(c)  Briefly identify and describe how ONE country in early modern Europe other than the Germanic states experienced this conflict.

## Multiple-Choice

**Questions 1–4 refer to the print depicting the Saint Bartholomew's Day Massacre below.**

*An Account of the Saint Bartholomew's Day Massacre* by François Dubois, a Huguenot painter born in northern France. From the Musée Des Beaux-Arts, Lausanne, Switzerland. The Granger Collection, New York.

1. The picture on page 113 depicts which two groups engaged in battle?

    (A) The French Huguenots and Catholics
    (B) French and Austrian Soldiers
    (C) Catholics and Anabaptists
    (D) Peasants and nobles

2. The use of propaganda through writing and imagery such as that seen above proliferated during the era of religious conflict in Europe, making which of the following a crucial reason for the success of the Protestant Reformation?

    (A) The widespread use of ballads as a way to share information between towns and villages
    (B) The implementation and proliferation of the printing press
    (C) The political conflict between the Catholic Church and the Germanic princes
    (D) The greatly improved travel network in the Holy Roman Empire

3. The clash depicted on page 113 sparked a greater conflict sometimes characterized by historians as a civil war that was ended by which of the following movements toward religious toleration?

    (A) Elizabeth I issued her Elizabethan Settlement, allowing private worship.
    (B) Louis XIV issued the Edict of Fontainebleau, allowing many Protestants to worship as they pleased in fortified towns.
    (C) Henry of Navarre converted back to Catholicism, became Henry IV of France, and issued the Edict of Nantes, allowing many Protestants to worship as they pleased in fortified towns.
    (D) The Peace of Westphalia in 1648 allowed Calvinism to be practiced by people in principalities whose leaders chose to follow that religion and its offshoots.

4. Which of the following factors most influenced the image on page 113 depicting opposing groups regulating public morals?

    (A) The spread of Anabaptist ideas and ideals from Muenster to France, causing armed insurrection
    (B) The spread of Austrian nationalism throughout the Germanic states and Italy
    (C) The spread of Calvinist ideas and ideals from Geneva into France, causing religious conflict
    (D) The spread of Anglicanism from England, causing religious conflict

**Questions 5–9 refer to the reading below.**

How violently the restless Jesuits and their followers are exerting themselves to undo, by their absurd interpretations and preposterous attacks, the precious and solemnly ratified Religious Peace [of Augsburg] which was drawn up long years ago for many weighty reasons by his Roman Imperial Majesty and all the estates of the empire, is but too clear. Nay, they would completely abolish it and then do away altogether with our true Christian religion, in which we were born and brought up and in which we would live and die. All this is sufficiently proved by the innumerable, violent, and poisonous books which they issue throughout the Roman Empire, directed against the said Religious Peace and its clear provisions, declaring it to be no more than ad interim, a temporary concession of toleration, designed to last only until the conclusion of the Council of Trent; even going so far as to imply that his Imperial Majesty of happy memory had no authority to arrange the peace among the estates of the empire without the consent of the pope . . .

. . . Moreover, since the nature and character of the Jesuits and their followers are as notorious among Catholics as among Protestants, and since what they have been up to in Sweden, Poland, France, the Netherlands, and, recently, in Italy, is well known, they should be estimated accordingly and precautions taken against their dangerous plots.

—Letter from Protestant Elector of Saxony, 1618

5. The document on page 114 was most likely written at the start of which of the following dynastic and religious conflicts?

    (A) The War of the Three Henrys
    (B) The Habsburg-Valois Wars
    (C) The Thirty Years' War
    (D) The Dutch Revolt

6. "[H]is Roman Imperial Majesty" in the document on page 114 refers to the Holy Roman Emperor, whose role after the conflict that succeeded the document can best be described in which of the following ways?

    (A) The Holy Roman Emperor consolidated his control over the Germanic states and ruled them as one single province.
    (B) The Holy Roman Emperor lost power and prestige as the Peace of Westphalia reduced his influence and importance significantly.
    (C) The title of Holy Roman Emperor was abolished at the end of this conflict, never to emerge again.
    (D) The Holy Roman Emperor consolidated his control over the Germanic states but was banned from ever being a Habsburg again.

7. Ignatius of Loyola, who founded the Society of Jesus, or the Jesuit order mentioned on page 114, would most likely agree with which of the following statements?

    (A) The Bible is the word of God, and its authority is more important than that of the Pope.
    (B) The Pope is the ultimate authority on Christianity but must be protected from the immorality that infects all humans.
    (C) The Pope is pure perfection, and if he tells me that the white I see before me is black, then I will agree that what I see is black.
    (D) A nonbeliever or pagan is much worse than a Protestant.

8. The conflict that the Elector of Saxony describes in his letter resulted in which of the following?

    (A) The establishment of several religiously pluralistic and tolerant states within the German-speaking regions
    (B) The weakening of the Holy Roman Empire and the strengthening of smaller sovereign states within its boundaries
    (C) The virtual extinction of all Christian denominations except Lutheranism and Roman Catholicism within the German-speaking regions
    (D) The political unification of most of the German-speaking regions under a Protestant, rather than a Catholic, monarch

9. Which of the following can be safely inferred about the Elector's religious affiliation solely based upon the passage?

    (A) He was an ardent Calvinist.
    (B) He was a somewhat devout Lutheran.
    (C) He was not Roman Catholic.
    (D) He was not a practicing Christian.

# Answers and Explanations

## Short-Answer Explanations

1. **0–3 points (2 points for a and 1 point for b)**

   (a) 1 point will be given for *each* of *two* explanations of how the politics of Europe changed due to the spread of Protestantism. The explanations can include the Thirty Years' War, the monarchy of Henry VIII and his descendants, the Protestant Union, the emergence of Sweden as a European power, the Counter-Reformation, the conquest of Belgium by the Habsburgs, the rise of Dutch power, the loss of power and unity caused by the decline of the Catholic Church, or the War of the Three Henrys.

   (b) 1 point will be given for an explanation of how the European economy changed, including the rise of England and the Netherlands as seafaring powers; the rise of wealth for the common man; the emergence of joint-stock companies and/or stock markets; the enclosure movement; and/or the loss of financial power for the Roman Catholic Church.

2. **0–3 points (1 point for a, 1 point for b, and 1 point for c)**

   (a) A good response would describe one of several possible causes of the Protestant Reformation. These include immorality/corruption of the Roman Catholic Church, the selling of indulgences, the Great Schism and the Babylonian Captivity, increased literacy and access to the Bible through the printing press, political frustration with the Holy Roman Emperor, the increased wealth of the non-nobility, the rising middle class, the rise of scientific thought that contradicted Roman Catholic teachings, high Church taxes (the tithe), and the ability to spread ideas more easily through printed materials.

   (b) A good response would describe one of several possible results of the Protestant Reformation. These include the loss of European religious unity, religious wars such as the Thirty Years' War or the War of the Three Henrys, religion used as a tool to undermine monarchs, removal of the ban on money lending by Christians, the pursuit of wealth being considered permissible by Christianity, and the emergence of new religions such as Lutheranism, Calvinism, and Anglicanism.

   (c) A good response would describe how Protestantism came to other countries in Europe. England's Anglican Church founded by Henry VIII, the French Huguenots' struggle in the War of the Three Henrys, Scotland's adoption of Presbyterianism, and Sweden's adoption of Calvinism are the best examples. The rise of Calvinism and Zwingli's emergence in Zurich may also be considered non-Germanic by some, so these may be included.

## Practice Multiple-Choice Questions

1. **(A) is CORRECT because the St. Bartholomew's Day Massacre was between French Catholics and Huguenots that started the War of the Three Henrys in France.**

   (B) is wrong because soldiers of neither nation are depicted in the image.

   (C) is wrong because the Anabaptists were in Muenster, not France, and are thus not seen being massacred in this print.

   (D) is wrong because those depicted in battle in this print are not engaged in a peasant revolt against either nobility or its suppression.

2. (A) is wrong because ballads had been used for years and did not help reformers before Luther such as Hus or Kempis.

   **(B) is CORRECT because the printing press allowed the spread of propaganda and the Bible itself as well as a proliferation of religious texts on both sides.**

   (C) is wrong because propaganda was less of an issue in the political battle than the religious one.

   (D) is wrong because the roads in the Holy Roman Empire were terrible at the time and not a factor in Luther's success.

3. (A) is wrong because Elizabeth ruled England rather than France where this was depicted.

   (B) is wrong because the *Edict of Fontainebleau* actually revoked the *Edict of Nantes*, which had allowed religious toleration under Henry IV.

   **(C) is CORRECT because the *Edict of Nantes*, which had allowed religious toleration under Henry IV, was passed after he converted and became king.**

   (D) is wrong because this image is about France rather than Germany and is thus not related to the *Peace of Westphalia*.

4. (A) is wrong because the Anabaptists were destroyed by other religious groups. Although their ideas later inspired groups such as Quakers, the ideas of the Anabaptists did not spread into France. Additionally, the Anabaptists were pacifists who would not attack others.

   (B) is wrong because Austrian nationalism did not spread to Germans and Italians, who resented Austrian rule. Additionally, the depiction is of Huguenots being attacked by Catholics in France.

   **(C) is CORRECT because the Calvinist ideas came to France where the Huguenots, who were attacked, adopted most of their ideas and ideals from Calvinism.**

   (D) is wrong because Anglicanism never spread to France in any important way.

5. (A) is wrong because this letter was written in 1618, which is when the Thirty Years' War began. In addition, because it was written by a Germanic prince whose focus would be on the Thirty Years' War rather than on the French War of the Three Henrys.

   (B) is wrong because this letter was written in 1618, which is when the Thirty Years' War began. In addition, the letter cites the Peace of Augsburg, which ended the Habsburg-Valois Wars in Germany in 1555.

   **(C) is CORRECT because this letter was written in 1618, which is when the Thirty Years' War began. In addition, it was written by a Germanic prince whose focus would be on the Thirty Years' War.**

   (D) is wrong because the Dutch revolt was not of importance to the Germanic kingdoms other than as a way to keep Catholic Counter-Reformation forces busy and out of their hair.

6. (A) is wrong because the Thirty Years' War ended in the Peace of Westphalia of 1648 that reduced the power of the Holy Roman Emperor to mostly ceremonial status, allowing France to intervene in Germanic affairs at will. However, the title did not disappear until Napoleon conquered the region in 1806.

   **(B) is CORRECT because the Thirty Years' War ended in the Peace of Westphalia of 1648 that reduced the power of the Holy Roman Emperor to mostly ceremonial status, allowing France to intervene in Germanic affairs at will.**

   (C) is wrong because the Thirty Years' War ended in the Peace of Westphalia of 1648 that reduced the power of the Holy Roman Emperor to mostly ceremonial status, allowing France to intervene in Germanic affairs at will. However, the title did not disappear until Napoleon conquered the region in 1806.

   (D) is wrong because the Thirty Years' War ended in the Peace of Westphalia of 1648 that reduced the power of the Holy Roman Emperor to mostly ceremonial status, allowing France to intervene in Germanic affairs at will. However, the title did not disappear until Napoleon conquered the region in 1806.

7. (A) is wrong because St. Ignatius of Loyola, who started the Jesuits, based his order upon fanatical dedication to the Pope and saw him as the ultimate authority in everything.

   (B) is wrong because St. Ignatius of Loyola, who started the Jesuits, based his order upon fanatical dedication to the Pope and saw him as infallible and thus not in need of protection from immorality.

   **(C) is CORRECT because St. Ignatius of Loyola, who started the Jesuits, based his order upon fanatical dedication to the Pope and saw him as the ultimate authority in everything. In fact, St. Ignatius of Loyola actually said something very close to choice (C).**

(D) is wrong because St. Ignatius of Loyola, who started the Jesuits, saw Protestants as the worst abomination against God for perverting Catholicism and pagans as simple people who did not know better but needed to be educated.

8.  (A) is wrong because the Thirty Years' War did not result in the creation of pluralistic and religiously tolerant states in Germany but, instead, in religiously stringent and combative areas.

    **(B) is CORRECT because the Thirty Years' War resulted in the decline of the Holy Roman Empire and the rise of the power of Germanic states dominated by France.**

    (C) is wrong because the Peace of Westphalia, which ended the Thirty Years' War, did not result in the removal of all non-Lutheran Christian sects as had the Peace of Augsburg before it.

    (D) is wrong because the Thirty Years' War did not result in the unification of the Germanic states at all but in their disunity, much to the benefit of France.

9.  (A) is wrong because the specific religious affiliation of the Elector is not given or inferred other than Protestant. The only thing that the passage makes certain is that he is *not* a Roman Catholic.

    (B) is wrong because the specific religious affiliation of the Elector is not given or inferred other than Protestant. The only thing that the passage makes certain is that he is *not* a Roman Catholic.

    **(C) is CORRECT because the only thing that the passage makes certain is that the Elector is *not* a Roman Catholic.**

    (D) is wrong because the passage makes it clear that the Elector is a Protestant of some type.

---

Visit Barron's Online Learning Hub to take the Time Period One (1450–1648) Practice Assessment

# Time Period Two:
# c. 1649 to c. 1815

## Learning Objectives

These are the Key Concepts for time period 2, according to the *AP European History Curriculum Framework*:

→ **KEY CONCEPT 2.1** Different models of political sovereignty affected the relationship among states and between states and individuals.

→ **KEY CONCEPT 2.2** The expansion of European commerce accelerated the growth of a worldwide economic network.

→ **KEY CONCEPT 2.3** The popularization and dissemination of the Scientific Revolution and the application of its methods to political, social, and ethical issues led to an increased, although not unchallenged, emphasis on reason in European culture.

→ **KEY CONCEPT 2.4** The experiences of everyday life were shaped by demographic, environmental, medical, and technological changes.

## Time Period Overview

This time period examines the further growth of Europe's institutions, power, intellectual progress, and economy as Europe was on the verge of becoming the dominant continent in the world. It examines the expansion of global trade, multiple religious truths being accepted, the conflict between divine right monarchy and parliamentary power, and the importance of the emergence of capitalism as Europe increasingly interacted with the rest of the world. This time period includes the traditional delineations of the following eras:

- The Age of Absolutism
- The Enlightenment
- Mercantilism and the rise of capitalism
- The American and French Revolutions
- Napoleonic Europe and the Congress of Vienna
- The emergence of proto-industrialization and urbanization

These traditional delineations do overlap in many ways. The themes within them as stated in the key concepts can be seen woven between the next two chapters of this book. Major challenges to periodization in this time period include the emergence of proto-industrialization or the "putting-out" system and the proliferation of the enclosure movement. Although the enclosure movement began in period 1 and had its impacts fully felt in the time periods 3 and 4, the College Board has placed this unit in period 2. The conditions that led to industrialization, and are thus a large part of the narrative of this historical phenomenon, began in this time period with James Watt's invention of the condensing chamber steam engine around 1775. However, the Industrial Revolution has its most significant impact on society, economies, and politics during the third time period. As a result, *industrialization*, which crosses time periods, is covered entirely in period 3. However, industrialization began with the putting-out system in the 1600s and had effects felt all the way to the 20th century. The constitutional struggles in

England and the rise of powerful monarchs like Louis XIV began in period 1 but reached their apogee during the second time period. The slow and erratic natures of the spread of the enclosure movement, proto-industrialization, the evolution of monarchical power, and true industrialization pose significant challenges to comprehending competing models of periodization during this second time period.

## SPECIAL NOTE ON PERIODIZATION

The third chapter of this section presents a problem to the historian. Much of the groundwork for *New Monarchs* was laid during the first time period as monarchs began to consolidate power. The *AP European History Curriculum Framework* presents a split in time periods in 1815. This makes a lot of sense for political history as that is the date of the fall of Napoleon and the rise of the alliance system first put in place by Metternich and that was later altered by Bismarck. However, *the Industrial Revolution does not fit nicely into that division*. While war was raging across the Continent, the British were undergoing the start of an industrial revolution that enabled them to gain political and economic power. This revolution continued to occur throughout the 19th century. In fact, many of its impacts were felt in the decades following 1815.

For that reason, this book presents the Industrial Revolution in one chapter in order to preserve the narrative of the historical movement and to encourage you to examine periodization more critically. Historians construct and debate different, sometimes competing, models of periodization. The choice of specific turning points or starting and ending dates might accord a higher value to one narrative, region, or group than to another. If you are to master this skill, then you need to see competing models of periodization. To preserve the continuity of the subject, the Industrial Revolution is covered entirely in chapter 6, although some of the content covered is included in period 2 by the College Board. The chapter makes clear delineations of which material belongs in which time period to help you with the skill of periodization.

Additionally, because the College Board prepares questions on the exam that use one prompt but come from different time periods, this section will also help you prepare for that better.

# UNIT 3
# Absolutism and Constitutionalism

## Unit 3 Overview: Absolutism and Constitutionalism

**Unit description:** The third unit, Absolutism and Constitutionalism, is focused on three themes of the course: Economic and Commercial Developments, States and Other Institutions of Power, and Technological and Scientific Innovation. These themes are woven throughout the content of the course to allow students to assess the political, economic, and technological impacts of the rise of absolute monarchs and constitutional governments. This unit covers the rise of the monarchies of Europe that dominated the politics of the 17th through the 19th centuries. It also covers the rise of constitutionalism in the Netherlands, England, and elsewhere. The main dynastic families to watch are the Stuarts of England (with Oliver Cromwell ruling for a time), the Bourbon family of France, the Habsburgs of Spain and Austria, the Hohenzollerns of Prussia, and the Romanovs of Russia. The main topics of study for this unit are as follows:

- Contextualizing state building
- The English Civil War and Glorious Revolution
- Continuities and changes to economic practice and development
- Economic development and mercantilism
- Dutch Golden Age
- Balance of power
- Absolutist approaches to power
- Comparison in the Age of Absolutism and Constitutionalism

This chapter provides a narrative of the rise of absolutism, the development of constitutionalism, the rise and fall of mercantilism, and the emergence of balance of power politics. The final goal is that students be able to compare and contrast absolutism and constitutionalism.

This unit has some material covered in period 1 and some from period 3, but most of it lies within period 2.

# 3

# Absolutism and Constitutionalism

---

## Key Terms

- Concordat of Bologna
- Edict of Nantes
- Divine right theory of rule

- Commercial revolution/ price revolution
- The Glorious Revolution
- Crop rotation

- Roundheads
- Cavaliers
- Baroque art

## Key People

- Peter the Great
- Frederick William I of Prussia
- Francis I
- Catherine de' Medici
- Henry II

- Henry IV
- Cardinal Richelieu
- Louis XIV
- Jean-Baptiste Colbert
- Henry VIII
- Elizabeth I

- John Locke
- James I
- Charles I
- Oliver Cromwell
- Charles II

---

## Overview

By the start of the 16th century, centralization of governments had led to the rise of powerful nation-states, to concomitant European exploration of the globe, and to regional wars on the Continent. Spain, following the Portuguese lead, explored the Atlantic and soon surpassed its Iberian neighbor in colonies, wealth, and military power. Gold and silver from the New World helped shift the balance of power from the Mediterranean basin to the Atlantic coast of Europe. The search for wealth helped to usher in an age of scientific discovery that began to reshape European thinking. The wealth from mines in the Spanish colonies created a financial and commercial center in the Netherlands, brought about rampant inflation in Europe, and eventually led to the decline of Spain as a major power. Much of this was already explained in chapter 1.

Feudalism died gradually. The Hundred Years' War (1337–1453), which devastated France and exhausted its nobility, indirectly led to a strong monarchy. Peace encouraged commerce, which gave rise to a taxable middle class that could support a national army independent of the nobility. From the middle of the 15th century to the second decade of the 16th, the monarchs of France centralized the state, recruited bourgeois administrators into government, and strengthened the army. Through most of the 16th century, the foreign adventures of two strong kings and the upheaval caused by the Reformation weakened monarchy in general. Under the intelligent guidance of Cardinal Richelieu (1585–1642), who was prime minister to Louis XIII (r. 1601–1643), the central government brought peace, prosperity, and stability to the realm during the first half of the 17th century.

The strong government that developed in France contrasted with the constitutional system that evolved in England. The powers of the English kings had been checked by the nobility as far back as the 13th century with the *Magna Carta*. The Tudors took the English throne in the 15th century as a compromise among the claimants who battled over it in the Wars of the Roses (1455–1487). Having only a tenuous hereditary right to the monarchy, the Tudors were forced to work through Parliament, which gradually represented a greater and greater portion of English society and, therefore, avoided the class distinctions that divided France. The Reformation had its effects on English government. The independence of the Anglican Church from the papacy strengthened the monarchy and Parliament. In addition, the Puritan Revolution established the supremacy of Parliament over the king and nurtured the tradition of constitutionalism.

A strong tradition of absolutism developed in Eastern Europe, especially in the rising states of Russia, Prussia, and Austria. Conflicts between the Ottoman Empire and the Austrians emerged over control of southeastern Europe because of Austrian territorial expansion. Social reform was sporadic and largely ineffectual; serfdom was widespread in the region. The baroque style of architecture was favored by the absolute monarchs of these states as a manifestation of the power and glory of their reigns.

## SPECIAL NOTE ON PERIODIZATION

Unlike in the first two chapters of this book, the concepts taught in this chapter do not neatly fit into the time period (1648–1815). For example, the struggle for constitutional rule in England ran from 1640 until at least 1689, when the *Glorious Revolution* resulted in the English Bill of Rights and in William and Mary on the throne. Another prime example is the problem of examining the rise of absolutism without being able to study the crowning glory of Louis XIV and his imitators, such as Peter I of Russia. The Golden Age of France was during the reign of the Sun King, Louis XIV (r. 1643–1715). His absolutist monarchy dominated all classes in Europe's wealthiest and most populous country, upset the balance of power on the Continent, and claimed the "divine right" of rule. Additionally, you are compelled to examine the scientific contributions of very early thinkers such as Copernicus, Kepler, Descartes, and Galileo (from chapter 1) without being able to examine the ideas of Newton or the great Enlightenment thinkers. The Industrial Revolution, which is covered in this book in period 3, also has strong roots in time period 2. During period 2, James Watt invented his steam engine, which brought on the era of industrialization. You should recognize, in some ways, the arbitrary nature of periodization. Should we stop at the Glorious Revolution of 1689 or perhaps the defeat of Louis XIV in the War of the Spanish Succession in 1713? Those students who truly examine history well apply this idea of questioning periodization in their essays.

## The Development of Absolutism in France

- *Francis I* (r. 1515–1547), a Valois rival of Holy Roman Emperor Charles V, battled unsuccessfully to weaken the Habsburgs as Europe's most powerful family.
  - He managed to consolidate absolutism in France by instituting the *taille* (a direct tax on land and property).
  - With the *Concordat of Bologna,* he granted the Pope the right to collect *annates* (the first year's revenue from Church offices) in return for the power to nominate high officials in the French Church.
  - Francis I effectively nationalized the Church in France and increased the power of the monarchy.

- His successor, *Henry II* (r. 1547–1559), expanded the policies of Francis I and actively persecuted the *Huguenots* (French Calvinists).
- Continued persecution under *Francis II* and *Charles IX* provoked civil war, which was halted by an *edict of toleration* issued by *Catherine de' Medici*, mother of and regent for Charles IX.
- The *Massacre of St. Bartholomew's Day* renewed the brutal civil war when Catholic mobs slaughtered Huguenot leaders who had gathered in Paris to celebrate a royal wedding.
  - During the *War of the Three Henrys*, King Henry III was murdered. Henry of Guise, the Catholic leader, was later assassinated.
  - Although the Huguenots were never more than 10 percent of the French population, they wielded great influence since they came from the nobility and the bourgeoisie.
- Persecution, civil war, and dynastic rivalry left *Henry of Navarre*, a Huguenot, as the only legitimate claimant to the French throne.
  - He ascended, after an expedient conversion to Catholicism ("Paris is worth a mass"), as *Henry IV* (r. 1589–1610).

- ○ Henry IV was known as a *politique* for his willingness to put the practical matters of ruling a nation above religious obligations.
- ○ He issued the *Edict of Nantes*, a remarkable expression of religious tolerance that guaranteed civil and religious freedom to the Huguenot minority.
- ○ The finance minister, the *Duke of Sully*, reformed the tax collection system to make it more equitable and efficient, improved transportation, stimulated trade and industry, and fostered prosperity.
- ○ These changes resulted in an increase in the prestige and power of the monarchy.
- ○ The divine right to rule theory gained ground under the support of philosopher and jurist *Jean Bodin*, who wrote in support of indivisible power in the hands of the monarch.
- ■ After the death of Henry IV, the government suffered from corruption and mismanagement during the regency of *Louis XIII*.
  - ○ In 1624, Louis XIII appointed *Cardinal Richelieu* as prime minister, a post Richelieu held from 1624–1642.
  - ○ Richelieu further centralized the government.
    - ■ He encouraged the commerce and industry that increased the tax base.
    - ■ He strengthened the military.
    - ■ Richelieu instituted the *intendant system*, in which bourgeois officials were answerable only to the king who supervised the provinces. This system diminished the power of the nobility.
    - ■ Richelieu's domestic polices strengthened absolutism in France and prepared the way for its supreme embodiment in the *Sun King, Louis XIV*.

> **NOTE**
>
> All of the material up to this point about France occurred during period 1, but the development of absolutism is key to understanding period 2. Louis XIV is the first ruler of France in period 2.

- ■ *Louis XIV* (r. 1643–1715) was age four when he ascended the throne of France.
  - ○ His mother was his regent.
  - ○ She chose the Italian *Cardinal Mazarin* (1602–1661) as prime minister.
  - ○ Louis XIV was scared by the *Fronde* revolt as a youth.
  - ○ His finance minister, *Jean-Baptiste Colbert*, extended the administrative, financial, military, and religious control of the central state over the French population.
  - ○ Like Richelieu, Cardinal Mazarin was a capable administrator but not a religious man. In fact, Mazarin was not even a priest when he was made a cardinal.
  - ○ Louis XIV became the model monarch for all of Europe.
  - ○ He built *Versailles* as a "pleasure palace" for the nobility and required them all to live there for a part of the year.
  - ○ Responded to most inquiries with "*je verrai*," which means "we shall see."
  - ○ Was also known to have said "*l'état, c'est moi*," or "I am the state."
  - ○ France was such an important hub of European development at the time that it was said that "when Louis XIV sneezed, all of Europe caught cold."
  - ○ Louis XIV was at war for more than half of his reign in the following four wars: the War of Devolution (1667–1668), the Dutch War (1672–1678), the War of the League of Augsburg (1688–1697), and the War of Spanish Succession (1702–1713).
  - ○ His final thought on his death bed was "I have gone to war too often and pursued it for vanity's sake."

## The Development of Constitutionalism in England

*Henry VII* (r. 1485–1509), the first of the *Tudor* monarchs, established a strong central government even though many regarded the family as usurpers, invited to the throne as an expedient compromise to end the Wars of the Roses. By regulating trade and internal commerce through monopolies, charters, and licenses, Henry raised revenue from the prosperous middle class. This money enabled him to finance a standing army and keep the nobility in check. The *Court of the Star Chamber* administered central justice and further subdued rebellious nobles. Since the Tudors were beholden to Parliament for inviting them to the throne, Henry and his successors, including his son *Henry VIII* (r. 1509–1547), consulted Parliament on significant issues.

- Unlike his father Henry VII, who was levelheaded and tightfisted, *Henry VIII* was an impetuous, extravagant, and passionate man whose temper, ambitions, and appetites were legendary.
  - The need to maintain legitimacy by having a male heir led Henry VIII to make the decisions, with Parliament's support, that led to the *English Reformation*.
- *Edward VI* (r. 1547–1553) assumed the throne upon the death of his father, Henry VIII.
  - Since Edward VI was only 10 years old and of fragile health, the government was headed by a regent, the *Duke of Somerset*.
  - The basic tenets of the English Reformation were restated, and the *Anglican Book of Common Prayer* was made the basis for all church services.
  - Edward died at the young age of 16.
- *Mary I of England* (r. 1553–1558), the daughter of Henry VIII by his first wife, the Catholic Catherine of Aragon, became queen when Edward VI died.
  - Mary I was unpopular not only because she was Roman Catholic but because she was married to *Philip II* of Spain.
  - Mary I had to suppress a rebellion against her rule and her alliance with Spain.
  - She earned the nickname "Bloody Mary" when she burned hundreds of Protestants at the stake for dissenting against her attempt to reinstitute Catholicism in England.
  - When she died, Mary I was succeeded by her half-sister, *Elizabeth I*, Henry's daughter by his second wife, Anne Boleyn.
- *Elizabeth I* (r. 1558–1603) was the last and the greatest of the Tudor monarchs.
  - Elizabeth I reigned when the combined population of England and Wales was between 3 and 4 million while that of France was over 16 million and that of Spain nearly 9 million.
  - Enriched by its conquests and colonies in the New World, Spain was the predominant power of Europe during Elizabeth's reign.
  - England, which is part of the British Isles, was at the geographic and political fringe of numerous powerful nations. England was vying for respect from the major powers, such as France, Russia, and Austria.
    - The Church of England was independent from Rome, but its teachings were close to Roman Catholic theology.
    - Elizabeth's government balanced power between the monarchy and Parliament.
    - England's wealth came from rich, arable land and an energetic populace that excelled in commerce and trade.
    - England's social system was unique.
  - The gentry, lesser nobles whose original wealth came from ownership of land, expanded their wealth by entering the world of commerce and by intermarrying with the middle class.
  - There were no glaring distinctions between the upper and middle classes in England, as there were on the Continent. The interests of nobles, gentry, and bourgeoisie were represented in Parliament.
  - Since the Tudors had been invited to the throne of England to settle the rival claims of the Houses of York and Lancaster during the Wars of the Roses, Elizabeth, her charismatic father, and her capable grandfather all lived under the shadow of being considered *dynastic pretenders*.
    - Elizabeth I was the child of Anne Boleyn, whose marriage to Henry VIII was considered scandalous.
    - Elizabeth I was given the nickname the *Virgin Queen*. (This was a euphemism for Elizabeth's having never married even though she had notorious love affairs.) She had to prove her mettle in the face of the prejudices against her line, her parentage, and her gender.

- Her natural intelligence had been honed by substantial education; her powerful personality had been toughened by living as a family outcast at the courts of her father, half-brother, and half-sister.
- Elizabeth I was adored by her people and feared by her enemies, both at home and abroad.
- She reigned for nearly a half-century as one of Europe's greatest monarchs and one of the world's greatest women.

# The Elizabethan Age

## Religion

Upon assuming the throne, Elizabeth I repealed Mary's pro-Catholic legislation and reinstated the Acts of Supremacy and Uniformity that had established the English Reformation during her father's reign.

*The Thirty-Nine Articles* (1563) followed Protestant doctrine and were vague enough to accommodate the majority of the English population, except the *Puritans* (English Calvinists). Puritans believed that the *liturgy* (prescribed ritual) and the *hierarchy* (the order of rank within the organization) needed "purification" from Catholic influence. Militant Puritans challenged royal authority. Although the Puritans were suppressed for a time, they grew stronger during the reigns of Elizabeth's successors and later influenced the development of constitutionalism.

## Diplomacy

When the Netherlands, a Habsburg possession that had adopted Protestantism, revolted against Spanish rule, Elizabeth entered into an alliance with the Dutch in 1577. Both England and the Netherlands had strong traditions of democracy and a Protestant majority among their populations. This alliance protected England because the country previously feared that Holland would provide a base from which Spain could invade England. Both England and Holland sent *privateers* to prey on the Spanish treasure ships from her colonies in the New World. (Privateers were warships not commissioned by the state but covertly supported by the government. Privateers were also the individuals, sometimes called "pirates with papers," on those ships.)

- Outraged by the alliance, *Philip II*, the Spanish king and Holy Roman Emperor, conspired with English Catholics to overthrow Elizabeth I and put her cousin, the Catholic Mary Stuart, queen of the Scots, onto the throne.
- In 1587, Elizabeth ordered the execution of Mary for treason, and Philip II declared war on England.
- *La Grande y Felicísima Armada*, or "great and most fortunate fleet," of 132 heavily armed warships loaded with troops was defeated in 1588 by the superior naval tactics of the smaller, more maneuverable English fleet led by *Sir Francis Drake* (1540–1596) and by bad weather.
- The superior navigational skills and tactics of the English were aided by winds that drove the Spanish Armada into the North Sea. Severe storms eventually sank many Spanish ships.
- The failure of the Spanish Armada marked the beginning of the decline of Spanish naval dominance and the rise of the British.

## Culture

This was the Golden Age of English literature, the era of Shakespeare, Spenser, Donne, Marlowe, More, and Francis Bacon. During this age, brilliant national literature was written that instilled pride in the uniqueness of English culture.

## The Stuart Kings and Parliament (1603–1688)

### SPECIAL NOTE ON PERIODIZATION

This topic does not fit neatly into either period 1 (c. 1450 to c. 1648) or period 2 (c. 1648 to c. 1815). However, it is presented to you here to help weave the narrative of English history and because the first time period ends in the midst of the English Civil War. Remember as you read about the Stuart kings and Parliament that although the section goes from 1603 until 1690, the second time period begins in 1648.

*James I* (r. 1603–1625), king of Scotland and son of Mary, Queen of Scots, took the English throne upon Elizabeth's death since she had no direct heirs. A believer in the divine right of kings, James failed to understand the importance of Parliament in governing England. A conference at *Hampton Court* in 1604 failed to reconcile the Puritans, who opposed the Anglican hierarchy as the Church of England. The *Gunpowder Plot*, in 1605, was uncovered before disgruntled Catholics (led by Guy Fawkes), who objected to James's enforcement of laws that required participation in Anglican services, could blow up the king and Parliament. The years 1610–1611 saw Parliament enmeshed in the issue of its role in financing government.

- The *Addled Parliament* met in 1614, so-called by James because it spent its entire session arguing that taxes could be levied only with its consent and that rule was by king and Parliament in conjunction.
  - James I dissolved Parliament. He tried to rule without it until England's involvement in the Thirty Years' War necessitated his reconvening Parliament.
  - In 1621, after a rancorous session in which Parliament criticized James's foreign policy, Parliament passed the *Great Protestation*, claiming free speech and authority in conducting governmental affairs. James dissolved the body a second time and arrested its leaders. He then had the remainder of Parliament call for new elections if it wanted to remain a body.
- *Charles I* (r. 1625–1649) was, like his father James I, devoted to the divine right theory and, unlike his father, woefully inept at dealing with Parliament.
  - While embroiled in wars on the Continent, Charles I called for Parliament to vote for funds to carry England through those wars.
  - Parliament refused to do so until Charles signed the *Petition of Right*.
  - The Petition of Right guaranteed the following:
    - Parliament alone can levy taxes.
    - Martial law cannot be declared in peacetime.
    - Soldiers may not be quartered in private homes.
    - Imprisonment required a specific charge.
  - The Bishops' War of 1639–1640, after Archbishop Laud persecuted Puritans and tried to force Anglican worship upon the Presbyterian Scots, led Charles I to reconvene Parliament in order to pay war debts from his loss.
  - The *Long Parliament* (1640–1660) demanded the following in return for paying for Charles's defeat:
    - Impeach his top advisers.
    - Allow Parliament to meet every three years without his summons.
    - Promise not to dissolve Parliament without its consent.
  - When Charles attempted, in early 1642, to arrest opposition members, Parliament seized control of the army.
    - Charles gathered his forces.
    - The *English Civil War* (1642–1649) began.

▪ The English Civil War was a conflict between Parliament, the monarchy, and other power elites over their roles in the political structure. This conflict exemplified the struggle between monarchs and other elites for power in the era of absolutism and constitutionalism.

## The Course of the Conflict

The civil war in England was caused by a conflict between the king and the Parliament about where sovereignty lies and what its limits are. In the end, the hostilities left Parliament as the sovereign power of England, with the monarch reduced to more of a ceremonial role from the 1650s onward. The rising middle class, many of whom were members of Parliament, wanted to gain political power. So this civil war is often viewed by economic historians as a conflict between the monarchy and nobility on one side and the bourgeoisie on the other. The middle class, the merchants, the major cities, and a small segment of the nobility supported Parliament and were called *Roundheads*. The Anglican clergy, the majority of the nobility, and the peasants backed the king and were referred to as *Royalists* or *Cavaliers*.

### 1643

The Roundheads allied with Presbyterian Scotland, promising to impose Presbyterianism on England in exchange for military assistance. Charles I called on Irish Catholics for help.

### 1644

*Oliver Cromwell* (1599–1658), a Puritan leader of Parliament, led his *New Model Army* of Puritans against the Cavaliers at *Marston Moor* and defeated them decisively.

### 1645

Charles I surrendered to the Scots.

### 1647

The Scots turned Charles I over to Parliament, which was led by Cromwell's *Independents*, who favored religious toleration. The Scots turned about and allied with Charles, who promised that he would impose Presbyterianism on the English.

### 1648

Cromwell defeated the Scots at the *Battle of Preston* and helped purge the Presbyterians from Parliament. He thereby created the *Rump Parliament*, which voted to behead Charles for treason.

> Period 2 begins in 1648. All of the material about England before this box was included to build the background and give students insights into the development of constitutionalism in England over time. All of the material about England after this box belongs to period 2.

### 1649

With the execution of Charles I, England became a republic, called the *Commonwealth*. Cromwell and his army wielded power. In suppressing Irish supporters of the Crown, the Puritans committed terrible atrocities and imposed injustices that would exacerbate the *Irish Question* for centuries.

**1653–1660**

Cromwell was designated *Lord Protector* by a puppet Parliament and ruled with its support until his death in 1658. His son Richard, a far less capable ruler, was deposed in 1660. Then *Charles II* (r. 1661–1685) was proclaimed king.

## The Stuart Restoration (1660–1688)

The *Cavalier Parliament* (1660–1679) marked the development of the first political parties, the Tory and Whig parties.

- The *Tories,* made up of nobles, gentry, and the Anglicans, were Conservatives who supported the monarchy over Parliament and who wanted Anglicanism to be the state religion.
- The *Whigs,* mainly middle class and Puritan, favored Parliament and religious toleration.
    - Since the Tories prevailed in the Cavalier Parliament, Anglicanism was restored by a series of laws that forbade dissenters to worship publicly, required government officials and military personnel to practice Anglicanism, and discriminated against other faiths.
    - The *Whig Parliament*, elected in 1679, was suspicious of Charles II's absolutist and pro-Catholic tendencies. It enacted the *Habeas Corpus Act*, which limited royal power by doing the following:
        - Enabling judges to demand that prisoners be in court
        - Requiring just cause for continued imprisonment
        - Providing for speedy trials
        - Forbidding *double jeopardy* (being charged again for a crime that one had already been acquitted of)

## The Glorious Revolution

The *Glorious Revolution* was actually the culmination of an evolutionary process over centuries that increased the power of Parliament over the monarchy through historical accident, outright conflict, and painstaking design. *James II* (r. 1685–1688) was unpopular from the moment he took the throne. A devout Roman Catholic, he appointed Catholic ministers to important posts and gave the appearance of trying to impose Catholicism upon the English.

- In 1688, important nobles invited *William of Orange*, a Hollander, and Mary, the wife of James's oldest child, to rule England conditional upon their granting a bill of rights.
- When *William and Mary* (r. 1688–1704) arrived in England, James II fled to exile in France.
- The new monarchs accepted from Parliament, as a condition of their reign, the *Declaration of Rights* (enacted into law as the *Bill of Rights* in 1689).
- The *Habeas Corpus Act*, the *Petition of Right*, and the Bill of Rights have all become part of the *English Constitution,* which is a *common law* constitution rather than a written one.
- In the centuries that followed, monarchs in England came to reign while Parliament came to rule.

Although, at the time of the Glorious Revolution Parliament served the interests of the wellborn or the wealthy, it came to represent "the people" as government came to be viewed as existing and functioning according to *John Locke's* Enlightenment concept of *consent of the governed.* The English, and those who inherited their political traditions, would guarantee individual rights and would create modern democracy.

In the end, the Glorious Revolution *protected the rights of the gentry and aristocracy from absolute monarchs* through the assertion of the power of Parliament. The common people later (mostly in the 1800s) gained political power as they sporadically gained the right to vote across Europe.

# The Dutch Revolt and the Golden Age of the Netherlands

## The Dutch Revolt

When the Spanish under King Philip II tried to consolidate power in the Low Countries (the 17 provinces of the Netherlands, today's Belgium and the Netherlands), they met stiff resistance. Here, Philip II ignored two of Machiavelli's basic instructions: do not change the religion of newly conquered people and do not raise their taxes. His policies and the policies of his representatives in the Low Countries united both religious and economic powers against his rule.

- The Netherlands was the commercial hub of the developing capitalist world at the time.
  - The people had known a significant degree of self-governance.
  - Philip II tried to tighten the reins by sending his sister, Margaret, who had been personally educated by *Ignatius of Loyola*, there to rule.
    - She introduced the Dutch Inquisition and raised taxes.
    - The Protestants (Calvinists) united with those who resisted the tax hikes and with peasants who suffered from high prices for grain.
    - Protestants began to smash Catholic churches all over Antwerp and the surrounding area.
    - This was mostly a middle-class revolt.
    - The Netherlands had the largest middle class by percentage of population in all of Europe.
  - Philip sent the *Duke of Alva* with 20,000 troops to pacify the rebellion in 1567.
    - The Duke of Alva established the *Council of Blood*.
    - He ruthlessly "purified" the Netherlands of Protestant opposition.
    - The Duke of Alva added a 10 percent tax to all transactions, crippling the best economy in Europe and under Spain's dominion.
    - Margaret resigned her regency after the Duke of Alva killed 1,500 people on one day in 1568.
- Prince William ("The Silent") of Orange united the 17 provinces against the rule of Spain in 1576.
  - *Alexander Farnese, the Duke of Parma*, was sent by Philip II to put down the rebellion in 1578 once and for all.
  - Farnese was a good general with a great plan:
    - He laid siege to one city at a time and avoided pitched battles.
    - Farnese slowly took the 10 lower (southernmost) provinces and forced the Protestant forces out of those areas.
- The repercussions of this war affected the political and military events in Europe over the next few decades:
  - The 10 lower provinces became the Spanish Netherlands and, later, Belgium.
  - The seven northern provinces of the Netherlands formed the Union of Utrecht and declared their independence from Spain (1581) as the United Provinces of the Netherlands.
    - The Dutch dikes were broken to flood the area as a way to repel invaders. This occurred so many times that the tactic hurt the economy by destroying agricultural production.
    - The Dutch kept their land free.
    - English support of the Dutch Protestants led in part to the Spanish Armada campaign, which the Dutch helped to win with successful early engagements against Spanish forces along their own coast.
    - The United Provinces of the Netherlands developed as a commercial powerhouse because of the following:
    - Independence
    - Religious tolerance
    - The Protestant work ethic

## The Golden Age of the Netherlands

The United Provinces of the Netherlands saw a Golden Age during the 17th century. The Netherlands was a confederation of seven provinces. Each province was autonomous and had its own leader, a *stadtholder*, who was a representative to a ruling council that ran the confederation. The United Provinces of the Netherlands was the wealthiest and most economically, educationally, scientifically, and artistically advanced country in Europe, ruled by an oligarchy of merchants called *regents*.

- It was the model for Europe of a republican form of government based on economic prosperity.
- Religious tolerance and trading with all religions (always buying and selling in bulk) led to massive profits and prosperity.
  - Amsterdam became the regional center of commerce, replacing Antwerp.
  - Industry shifted from fishing to shipping.
  - The *Dutch East India Company* was formed in 1602.
    - The Dutch were able to corner the maritime shipping market by charging the lowest rates in Europe.
  - They perfected the joint-stock company and created the first stock markets where stocks, or ownership of a part of a company, could be traded.
  - Society was able to share in the profits.
  - In 1630, stock in the East India Company was returning a 35 percent profit annually.
  - Holland had accidentally created the investment industry.
    - Holland became the center of a bustling new industry.
  - Because of its thriving economy, the Netherlands became *an island of plenty in a sea of want* as the rest of Europe still saw crippling poverty among many of its citizens.
- The *enclosure movement* came to the Netherlands early, and it led to a significant rise in agricultural output per hectare.
  - Enclosure led to a more monetized system of exchange and greater wealth for agricultural workers with land (the majority of society).
  - The new monetized system of exchange led to a *commercial revolution* in which the average citizens began to get paid in money rather than produce and land rights for their labor, thus creating conditions needed for a market economy to emerge.
  - As land was enclosed, many peasants lost their rights to farm the land. Many moved to do work from their homes in various industries but especially the textile industry. As a result, the *putting-out system* or the *domestic system* was created.
  - Enclosure also led to improving the land by draining swamps, fertilizing the fields, *rotating the crops* grown on each field, and building irrigation systems.
  - As the first to adopt this new economic model, the Dutch found incredible prosperity for their small nation as a result of shifting more toward a market economic system.
- Dutch economic prosperity brought on a Golden Age of Dutch art that may still be unrivaled to this day.
- Superb artists revolutionized the visual arts by painting detailed domestic interiors, focusing on the lives of commoners, and providing amazing detail in their work. Some of these great Dutch artists include the following:
  - *Rembrandt van Rijn*
  - *Johannes Vermeer*
  - *Jan van Eyck*
  - *Albrecht Dürer*
- Their art captured the emotion and milieu of the lives of the people who lived in the Netherlands as opposed to the overawing prosperity and power of the patron communicated by such baroque artists as *Peter Paul Rubens*.

## ART ANALYSIS TIP

The Roman Catholic Church and monarchs patronized mostly baroque art, while mainly Protestant merchants and princelings patronized the art of the *Dutch Masters*. This explains the different subject matter, the emotional content, and even why the baroque pieces were much larger than most of the works of the Dutch Masters.

# Women During the Age of Absolutism

There were a few female monarchs, such as Elizabeth I and Catherine de' Medici, who showed by example how powerful a woman could be. When Elizabeth I visited her troops who were gathered for an expected land battle during the Spanish Armada campaign, her speech was a rousing testament to what a woman can accomplish. Her rule was perhaps one of the greatest periods in the history of her nation and laid the foundation for the creation of the British Empire. Catherine ruled France as regent with the aid of Cardinal Richelieu and used Machiavellian tactics to empower her son and his successors to rule France.

The *Pragmatic Sanction* of 1717 in Austria allowed Maria Theresa to inherit the Austrian Habsburg holdings intact even though she was female. This also set a new standard for how females in monarchical families could inherit the throne.

# Absolutism in the Ottoman Empire

Although Suleiman the Magnificent's push into central Europe came to a halt in Austria in 1529, he was still able to capture Belgrade (Serbia) and nearly half of Eastern Europe, including the Balkan territories, most of Hungary, and part of southern Russia. He collected enslaved people instead of taxes from the conquered territories.

- Many young enslaved males collected from the Christian areas were converted to Islam and trained as soldiers loyal to the sultan. These soldiers were called *janissaries*.
- The Ottoman Empire practiced some religious toleration and formed communities of non-Muslims called *millets*. These communities each contained people of the same religious minority, such as Christian or Jewish.
  - These communities were similar to the ghettos that Europeans forced their religious minorities, such as Jews or Muslims, to live in until the 19th and 20th centuries.

- After Suleiman the Magnificent's death in 1566, the Ottoman Empire ceased major expansion and historians have often noted this point as the start of Ottoman decline, while others argue if that characterization is over simplified.
- During the late 1600s, there was a strong revival of Ottoman power.
  - The Ottomans laid siege to Vienna in 1683.
  - Vienna was saved from the Turkish attackers by Habsburg and Polish troops.
  - Russians and Venetians attacked during the retreat of the Turks.
  - The Ottoman Empire's territorial designs on Eastern Europe began to decline again and deteriorated until the late 1800s.
  - The Ottoman conflicts with Russia over these areas led the Ottoman Empire to side with the Central Powers in the First World War.

# Absolute Monarchs of the Late-17th and Early-18th Centuries

### Louis XIV: The Ideal Monarch Who Domesticated the Nobility

*Louis XIV* (r. 1643–1715) was four years old when he ascended to the throne of France. His mother was his regent, and she chose Italian *Cardinal Mazarin* (1602–1661) as prime minister.

- Like Richelieu, Mazarin was a capable administrator. He protected Louis's claim to the throne during the tumultuous *Wars of the Fronde*, which reached their height from 1650–1652.
- The *Frondeurs* were nobles who sought to limit the powers of the monarch and to decentralize the government in order to extend their own influence. With the support of the bourgeoisie and the peasants, who had little to gain in a return to the feudal order, Mazarin was able to subdue the *Frondeurs* and their ally, Spain.
- When Mazarin died in 1661, Louis declared himself as his own prime minister.
  - *L'état, c'est moi* ("I am the state") became the credo of this most absolutist monarch during the Age of Absolutism.
  - *Bishop Jacques Bossuet* (1607–1704) provided the philosophical justification for the *divine right theory of rule*.
  - Bossuet claimed that Louis, like any absolutist monarch, was placed on the throne by God and therefore owed his authority to no person or group.
- According to feudal tradition, French society was divided into three *estates,* made up of the various classes.
  - The *First Estate* was the clergy, which contained up to 1 percent of the population.
  - The *Second Estate* was the nobility and comprised 3–4 percent of the population.
  - The *Third Estate* included the great bulk of the population: the bourgeoisie or middle classes, the *artisans* and *urban workers*, and the *peasants*.
  - Since France was, as were all European nations at this time, predominantly *agrarian,* 90 percent of the French population lived on farms in the countryside.
- Louis XIV reigned over the Golden Age of French culture and influence.
  - With a population of 17 million (about 20 percent of Europe's total), France was the strongest nation on the Continent.
  - French industry and agriculture surpassed that of any other European country.
  - *Jean Baptiste Colbert* (1619–1683), called the father of French mercantilism, revitalized trade as Louis's finance minister by abolishing internal tariffs and creating a free-trade zone in most of France.
    - He stimulated industry by subsidizing vital manufacturing and by building up the military.
    - He hoped to make France self-sufficient by building a large fleet that would rival that of the English and Dutch and enable the French to acquire an overseas empire.
    - Since even France could not afford both a powerful army and navy, Louis opted for the army.
- The result was the global supremacy of the British, whose navy ruled the seas of the world for over a century over an empire so large that the sun literally did not set on it.
- French became the *universal tongue*, spoken by diplomats and in the royal courts of all Europe.
  - Louis patronized artists and especially writers, such as *Corneille, Racine* (1639–1699), *Molière* (1622–1673), *de Sévigné, de Saint-Simon* (1607–1693), *La Fontaine*, and *de La Rochefoucauld* (1621–1695).
  - French literature and style (in dress, furniture, and architecture) became standards by which all Europeans measured their sophistication.
- France developed Europe's first modern army.
  - The military revolution begun by France during the Habsburg-Valois Wars continued.
  - Artillery, usually supplied by civilian private contractors, was made a part of the army.
  - The government—instead of officers—recruited, trained, equipped, and garrisoned troops.
  - A chain of command was established, and the army was increased from 100,000 to 400,000, becoming the largest in Europe.

## War Was an Instrument of Louis's Foreign Policy

For two-thirds of Louis's reign, France was at war.

- *The War of the Devolution* (1667–1668): This was France's unsuccessful attempt to seize the Spanish Netherlands (Belgium) as part of a feudal claim.

- *The Dutch War* (1672–1678): This was revenge for the Dutch role in defeating France in the War of Devolution and an attempt to seek France's "natural boundary in the west," the Rhine River. The Dutch War was largely unsuccessful for France.

- *The Nine Years' War* (1688–1697): This was also called the War of the Grand Alliance or the War of the League of Augsburg. It was a major war of the late-17th century.
  - France was opposed by a European-wide coalition, the Grand Alliance. The Nine Years' War was fought primarily on mainland Europe and its surrounding waters.
  - A campaign in colonial North America between French and English settlers and their respective indigenous allies, called *King William's War* by the English colonists, was a part of this war.
  - Although France retained Luxembourg, most of Louis's ambitions were frustrated.

- *The War of the Spanish Succession* (1702–1714): Louis threatened to upset the balance of power (the theory that no single state should be predominant on the Continent) in Europe by laying claim to the Spanish throne for his grandson.
  - The Grand Alliance, which included the major states of Western Europe, fought to prevent this union of the French and Spanish thrones.
  - The *Treaty of Utrecht* (1713–1714) restored the balance of power by allowing Philip V, Louis's grandson, to remain on the Spanish throne as long as France and Spain were never ruled by the same monarch.
    - Also awarded to the victors were various European and overseas possessions of the Spanish Empire.

## Summary of Louis XIV's Reign

Although his reign solidified the central government and marked the high point of absolutism in France, Louis's many wars exhausted the treasury. This left the bourgeoisie and the peasantry with an enormous tax burden since the clergy and nobility were exempted from paying most taxes. His personal extravagances aggravated the situation. The royal palace at *Versailles* cost over $2.3 billion in 2015 U.S. dollars to build. Added to that price was the money spent on his elaborate entertainments for the "captive nobility" at court. Louis defanged the nobles by making participation in court life a social requirement. He suppressed religious dissent, outlawing *Jansenism* (a form of Catholic Calvinism); revoked the *Edict of Nantes*, which had guaranteed toleration for the Huguenots; and made Catholicism mandatory.

Louis XIV did have several accomplishments:

- The central government that developed in France since the era of the religious wars made Louis's reign more efficient.
- The power of the nobles was weakened.
- Tax collection was systematized.
- Royal edicts were enforced.
- The bourgeoisie were given a role in the administration.
  - The economic system was successful.
  - Agriculture and trade were stimulated.
  - The seeds for revolution were sown in the national debt that had to be paid off by the Third Estate, which bore many responsibilities and enjoyed few privileges.

## Prussia

Prussia was an army before it was a nation. Its origin was as an outpost of the Holy Roman Empire. Its *Hohenzollern* rulers cultivated a superbly trained and well-equipped army drawn from all areas of their domain. Local loyalties were transferred to the army, which then served as the focal point for Prussian nationalism. Brandenburg, an electorate of the Holy Roman Empire, was able to gain a degree of independence as a result of the weakening of the Habsburg rule during the Thirty Years' War.

- The Hohenzollern ruler, *Frederick William I* (r. 1713–1740), solidified autocratic rule over Brandenburg, Prussia, and the Rhine territories with a strong army, an efficient bureaucracy, and a policy of weakening the nobles (Junkers) and suppressing the peasants. The Junkers served as elite officers in the army, and absolutist rule was established in Prussia.
- *Frederick William, Elector of Brandenburg* (r. 1640–1688) and his son and grandson, *Frederick I* (r. 1688–1713) and *Frederick William I* (r. 1713–1740) of Prussia, respectively, centralized the government and encouraged industry in order to support the state's relatively large standing army.

## Russia

Russia became a state in the 15th century when the *Duchy of Muscovy*, under *Ivan the Great* (r. 1462–1505), overcame subjugation by the Central Asian *Tartars.* After the *Fall of Constantinople* to the Ottoman Turks in 1453, Russia became not only the inheritor of Byzantine culture and the center of the Orthodox Church but also an empire. Moscow was "the third Rome" and had a *czar* (Caesar) or *tsar* on the throne.

- Under *Basil (Vasily) III* (r. 1505–1533) and the much maligned but very capable *Ivan the Terrible* (1533–1584), expansion and consolidation of the new empire continued in a sporadic fashion with some advances and some reversals.
  - In order to attain soldiers, the empire gave aristocratic landowners, the *boyars,* control over their peasants. These peasants gradually fell into *serfdom,* a condition of being bound to the land (serfdom had ended in virtually all of Western Europe).
  - The boyars influenced government policy through a council, the *Duma.*
- A theme common in most nations with a monarchy, there was a continuing battle for supremacy between a strong central government and a powerful aristocracy.
- *Peter the Great* (r. 1689–1725), a Romanov and a contemporary of Louis XIV of France, gained vast territories ranging from the Baltic Sea in the north, to the Black Sea in the south, and eastward toward the Pacific Ocean. Probably his greatest contribution was the *westernization of Russia.*
  - Peter the Great expanded the power of the state and of the czars by establishing a powerful standing army, a civil service, and an educational system to train technicians in the skills developed by Western science and technology. He imposed economic burdens, Western ideas, and social restrictions on the peasants to further his power. He erected the planned city of St. Petersburg on the Baltic and built magnificent, ornate baroque palaces, churches, and public buildings to glorify his reign. Russia became one of the major powers of Europe during this period.
  - Although Peter the Great could not be considered an enlightened despot, he recruited hundreds of Western artisans, built a new capital on the Gulf of Finland called *St. Petersburg* (his "window to the West"), reformed the government bureaucracy and the Russian Orthodox Church, reorganized and equipped the army with modern weapons, and encouraged commerce and industry.

## A Guide to Monarchs and Their Families

Many students throughout the years have had trouble keeping historical rulers straight. This chart of national monarchical history is intended to help you with that task.

Rulers in **bold** mean STOP, memorize their names, and know why they are important. These people will very likely be on the AP test.

Rulers in *italics* mean PAUSE, and be familiar with these people. They may be on the test and rate some attention.

Rulers in regular text mean KEEP GOING. Sure, one might be on the test every 10 years or so as a distraction in one of the last multiple-choice questions, but that is a chance you should be willing to take. These names are included mainly for continuity's sake. However, most history professors do not know who these individuals are, and you do not need to know either.

Insofar as dates go, keep a ballpark figure of when people reigned, lived, and so on. However, memorizing the exact dates is frustrating and not necessary.

## Austria

In 1276, Rudolf I of Habsburg became the Duke of Austria. This might be significant, but the test does not start until 1450. So, instead, the following table will begin with Maximilian, the first Habsburg Holy Roman Emperor. In the left column is the ruler's given name and, sometimes, the anglicized version beneath the name. An important adviser is listed in parentheses on his own line below the ruler he served.

| Name (Anglicized) | Reign | Notes |
| --- | --- | --- |
| *Maximilian I* | *1493–1519* | |
| **Charles V** | **1519–1556** | **Divided up the Habsburg lands** |
| Ferdinand I | 1556–1564 | |
| Maximilian II | 1564–1576 | |
| Rudolf II | 1576–1612 | |
| Matthias | 1612–1619 | |
| **Ferdinand II** | **1619–1637** | **Started the Thirty Years' War** |
| Ferdinand III | 1637–1657 | |
| Leopold I | 1658–1705 | |
| Joseph I | 1705–1711 | |
| *Charles VI* | *1711–1740* | *Pragmatic sanction* |
| **Maria Theresa** | **1740–1780** | |
| *Joseph II* | *1780–1790* | *Initiated enlightened reforms* |
| *Leopold II* | *1790–1792* | *Reversed the reforms of his brother* |
| Franz I (Francis) | 1792–1835 | Declared Emperor of Austria in 1806 |
| **(Klemens von Metternich; Foreign Minister of Austria)** | **1819–1848** | **Congress system** |
| Ferdinand I | 1835–1848 | |
| *Franz Josef I (Francis Joseph)* | *1848–1916* | |
| Karl (Charles) | 1916–1918 | |

## Great Britain

The first nation in which a king agreed that his power was limited was also the first country to have the legislative branch legally execute the monarch. By the 16th century, the English monarchy was as much about negotiating between powerful parties and religious factions as it was about pomp and circumstance.

| Name | Reign | Notes |
| --- | --- | --- |
| *Henry VII* | *1485–1509* | *Tudor* |
| **Henry VIII** | **1509–1547** | **Tudor** |
| *Edward VI* | *1547–1553* | *Tudor* |
| *Mary I* | *1553–1558* | *Tudor; "Bloody Mary"* |
| **Elizabeth I** | **1558–1603** | **Tudor; "The Virgin Queen"** |

| Name | Reign | Notes |
|---|---|---|
| *James I* | *1603–1625* | *Stuart; also called James VI of Scotland* |
| **Charles I** | **1625–1649** | **Stuart; civil war 1642–1649** |
| **Oliver Cromwell** | **1649–1658** | **"Lord Protector" (Dictator)** |
| Richard Cromwell | 1658–1660 | |
| Charles II | 1660–1685 | Stuart |
| James II | 1685–1688 | Stuart |
| **Mary II/William III** | **1689–1702** | **Stuart/Orange; Glorious Revolution** |
| Anne | 1702–1714 | Stuart |
| *George I* | *1714–1727* | *Hanoverian* |
| George II | 1727–1760 | Hanoverian |
| **George III** | **1760–1820** | **Hanoverian** |
| George IV | 1820–1830 | Hanoverian |
| William IV | 1830–1837 | Hanoverian |
| **Victoria** | **1837–1901** | **Saxe-Coburg-Gotha; niece of William IV** |
| Edward VII | 1901–1910 | Saxe-Coburg-Gotha |
| George V | 1910–1936 | Windsor |
| *Edward VIII* | *1936* | *Windsor; abdicated to marry a divorcée* |
| George VI | 1936–1952 | Windsor |
| *Elizabeth II* | *1952–2022* | *Windsor* |
| *Charles III* | *2022–* | |

## France

France was the model of absolutism under Louis XIV. This nation was once ruled by Louis's grandfather, who changed religion three times and, in the final conversion before taking the throne, declared, "Paris is worth a mass." Important advisers are listed in parentheses on their own lines below the ruler they served.

| Name | Reign | Notes |
|---|---|---|
| *Charles VII* | *1422–1461* | *Valois* |
| *Louis XI* | *1461–1483* | *Valois; "Spider King"* |
| Charles VIII | 1483–1498 | Valois |
| Louis XII | 1498–1515 | Valois-Orléans; "Father of the People" |
| Francis I | 1515–1547 | Valois-Angoulême |
| Henry II | 1547–1559 | Valois-Angoulême |
| Francis II | 1559–1560 | Valois-Angoulême |
| Charles IX | 1560–1574 | Valois-Angoulême |
| *Henry III* | *1574–1589* | *Valois-Angoulême* |
| **Henry IV of Navarre** | **1589–1610** | **Bourbon** |
| *Louis XIII* | *1610–1643* | *Bourbon* |
| **(Cardinal Richelieu; Chief Minister and Regent of France)** | **1624–1642** | |

| Name | Reign | Notes |
|---|---|---|
| **Louis XIV** | **1643–1715** | **Bourbon; "The Sun King"** |
| Louis XV | 1715–1774 | Bourbon |
| (René de Maupeou; Chancellor) | 1770–1774 | |
| *Louis XVI* | *1774–1792* | *Bourbon; executed* |
| Louis XVII | 1793–1795 | Bourbon; jailed throughout his "reign" |
| **Legislatures** | **1789–1795** | **The First Republic** |
| **National Assembly** | **1789–1791** | |
| **Legislative Assembly** | **1791–1792** | |
| **National Convention** | **1792–1795** | **Committee on Public Safety (1793–1794)** |
| **Directory (Directoire)** | **1795–1799** | **The First Republic** |
| **Napoléon Bonaparte** | **1799–1815** | **Bonaparte; First Consul until 1804** |
| *Louis XVIII* | *1814–1824* | *Bourbon; monarchy restored* |
| Charles X | 1824–1830 | Bourbon |
| *Louis Philippe* | *1830–1848* | *Bourbon-Orléans; "Citizen King"* |
| *(François Guizot; Chief Minister)* | *1840–1848* | |
| **Louis Napoléon** | **1848–1852** | **Second Republic (President)** |
| **Napoléon III (Louis Napoléon)** | **1852–1870** | **Second Empire (Emperor)** |

## Germany

Germany was formed in 1871 as a combination of many different German states, kingdoms, cities, and so on that were dominated by the ruler of Prussia, Wilhelm I of the House of Hohenzollern. Wilhelm traced his lineage from Brandenburg's prince-electors (those who formally approved the successor to the Habsburg throne). The Hohenzollern lineage is outlined in this table. An important adviser is listed in parentheses on his own line below the ruler he served.

| Name (Anglicized) | Reign | Notes |
|---|---|---|
| **Friedrich Wilhelm (Frederick William)** | **1640–1688** | **"The Great Elector"** |
| *Friedrich I (Frederick)* | *1688–1713* | *Crowned King of Prussia in 1701* |
| **Friedrich Wilhelm I** | **1713–1740** | **"The Soldier King"** |
| **Friedrich II** | **1740–1786** | **"Frederick the Great"** |
| Friedrich Wilhelm II | 1786–1797 | |
| Friedrich Wilhelm III | 1797–1840 | |
| Friedrich Wilhelm IV | 1840–1861 | |
| *Wilhelm I (William)* | *1861–1888* | *Kaiser of the Second Reich* |
| **(Otto von Bismarck; Chancellor)** | **1862–1890** | |
| Friedrich III | 1888 | |
| **Wilhelm II** | **1888–1918** | **Kaiser during WWI** |

## Russia

Though there were princes of Muscovy before the czar, he is the one credited for forming the modern nation of Russia and, more importantly, the earliest czar the test makers would consider putting on the test. Important advisers are listed in parentheses on their own lines below the ruler they served.

| Name | Reign | Notes |
|---|---|---|
| **Ivan III** | **1440–1505** | **"Ivan the Great"** |
| Vasily III | 1505–1533 | |
| **Ivan IV** | **1533–1584** | **"Ivan the Terrible"** |
| Theodore I | 1584–1598 | |
| **Disputed Line of Succession** | **1598–1613** | **"Time of Troubles"** |
| *Michael* | *1613–1645* | *Romanov* |
| Alexis I | 1645–1676 | Romanov |
| Theodore III | 1676–1682 | Romanov |
| Ivan V | 1682–1689 | Romanov |
| **Peter I** | **1682–1725** | **Romanov; "Peter the Great"** |
| Catherine I | 1725–1727 | Romanov |
| Peter II | 1727–1730 | Romanov |
| Anna | 1730–1740 | Romanov |
| Ivan VI | 1740–1741 | Romanov |
| Elizabeth | 1741–1762 | Romanov |
| Peter III | 1762 | Romanov |
| **Catherine II** | **1762–1796** | **Romanov; "Catherine the Great"** |
| Paul I | 1796–1801 | Romanov |
| *Alexander I* | *1801–1825* | *Romanov* |
| Nicholas I | 1825–1855 | Romanov |
| *Alexander II* | *1855–1881* | *Romanov; reformer* |
| Alexander III | 1881–1894 | Romanov |
| *Nicholas II* | *1894–1917* | *Romanov; killed by Bolsheviks along with his entire family* |
| *(Sergei Witte; Minister of Finance)* | *1892–1903* | |
| *(Peter Stolypin; Chief Minister)* | *1906–1911* | |

## Spain

Ferdinand and Isabella were the first king and queen of a unified Spain; hence, we start with them. Each "ruled" their own kingdom, although after 1506 Ferdinand became the regent of Castile as well.

| Name | Reign | Notes |
|---|---|---|
| **Ferdinand** | **1474–1516** | **King of Aragon; joint rule** |
| **Isabella** | **1474–1504** | **Queen of Castile; joint rule** |
| Joanna and Philip I | 1504–1506 | Rulers of Castile |
| **Ferdinand** | **1506–1516** | **Regent of Castile; King of Aragon** |
| **Charles I** | **1516–1556** | **Habsburg also called Charles V of Austria** |
| **Philip II** | **1556–1598** | **Habsburg** |
| Philip III | 1598–1621 | Habsburg |
| Philip IV | 1621–1665 | Habsburg |
| Charles II | 1665–1700 | Habsburg |
| *Philip V* | *1700–1746* | *Bourbon; great-grandson of Philip IV* |
| Ferdinand VI | 1746–1759 | Bourbon |
| Charles III | 1759–1788 | Bourbon |

| Charles IV | 1788–1808 | Bourbon |
| Ferdinand VII | 1808 | Bourbon |
| Joseph Bonaparte | 1808–1813 | Bonaparte |
| Ferdinand VII | 1813–1833 | Bourbon (restored) |
| Isabella II | 1833–1868 | Bourbon |
| Francisco Serrano y Domínguez | 1869–1870 | Elected regent |
| Amadeus | 1870–1873 | Elected regent |
| Estanislao Figueras | 1873 | First Republic; President |
| Francisco Pi y Margall | 1873 | First Republic; President |
| Nicolás Salmerón y Alonso | 1873 | First Republic; President |
| Emilio Castelar y Ripoll | 1873–1874 | First Republic; Prime Minister |
| Alfonso XII | 1874–1885 | Bourbon; King |
| Alfonso XIII | 1886–1931 | Bourbon; King |
| Niceta Alcalá Zamora | 1931–1936 | Second Republic; President |
| Manuel Azaña | 1936–1939 | Second Republic; President |
| *Francisco Franco* | *1939–1975* | *Nationalist Government; Chief of State* |
| Juan Carlos I | 1975–2014 | Bourbon; constitutional monarch |
| Felipe VI | 2024– | Bourbon; constitutional monarch |

# Practice Questions

## Long Essay

These questions are samples of the various types of thematic essays on the AP exam. See pages 27–28 for a detailed explanation of each type. Check over the generic rubric (see pages 28–29) before you begin any of these essays, and use that rubric to score your essay if you write one.

## Question 1

Compare the development of the nation-state in France and in England from the early-16th to the end of the 17th centuries.

## Comments on Question 1

This is clearly a *compare* skill question. So be sure to describe the similarities and differences between English and French development as nation-states. Account for or explain why they were so different by providing specific examples of how monarchical power was used differently in each nation. The contrast is glaring in that during this period, the French developed *absolutism* to its pinnacle while England continued the evolution of *constitutionalism*. Who did what, when, where, and how is a convenient formula for tracing the separate developments. Be careful not to get lost in the details. The large scope of the question requires a big-picture perspective.

Comparing the development of these two very different styles of government is more difficult. *Comparing* means measuring for similarities and differences. Were there similarities? Did the monarchs of these two diverse nations have similar traits of personality and/or similar methods for consolidating power? Were there similar obstacles to overcome, such as the vested interests of the nobility or the need for governmental revenue? Despite the differences between absolutism and constitutionalism, were there common goals: consolidation, centralization of authority, and modernization? Be sure not just to describe the commonalities and differences but also to analyze the reasons for those similarities and differences, or at least evaluate the historical significance of the emergence of constitutionalism.

## Question 2

Analyze the development of absolutism in France (1500–1715).

### Comments on Question 2

This one tests the *change and continuity over time* (CCOT) skill. Be sure to describe the level of historical continuity and change. For historical continuity, you can write about what did not change in political and social life in France from 1500–1715. When writing about change, you can include what did change in political and social life in France from 1500–1715. Explain the reasons for these changes, citing specific examples of what changed and what parts of French society and political power changed compared to the parts that did not, such as the preservation of the *Ancien Régime* and the monarchy. Examine the roles of the early Valois monarchs in centralizing authority, taking into consideration the religious wars of the 16th century. Also examine the role of Henry IV in restoring national order and royal esteem. Examine the profound accomplishments of Richelieu (one of Hollywood's favorite villains), and discuss the reign of Louis XIV. Be sure to describe both what remained unchanged and what did change. Use specific examples to illustrate and analyze those changes over time.

## Question 3

To what extent, and in what ways, did the Puritan Revolution contribute to the supremacy of the English Parliament in 1689?

### Comments on Question 3

This is a difficult question because it requires that you demonstrate how, and how much, a complex set of events contributed to a complex development. This one is a *causation* question because it requires you to decide to what extent the Puritan Revolution contributed to (caused) the rise to supremacy of Parliament in England in 1689. Remember to describe, by using specific examples, the causes and/or effects of the emergence of parliamentary power. Explain the reasons for these changes, citing specific examples of what changed and what parts of English political power changed compared to the parts that did not, such as the preservation of the aristocracy and the continuation of the monarchy. An effective approach would be to divide the bigger issue into smaller questions: What was the Puritan Revolution? How did it increase the power of Parliament? How did the Restoration affect Parliament's role? How was the monarchy weakened by the Puritan Revolution? How supreme was the monarchy? Did Puritans do anything that reduced its supremacy? How and why did the Glorious Revolution occur?

## Question 4

To what extent did the Tudors bring England into the modern era?

### Comments on Question 4

This one is a *causation* question because it requires you to decide to what extent the Tudors brought England into the modern era, or caused England to become modern. Describe the causes and/or effects of England becoming more modern through specific examples. Be sure to explain the reasons for these changes. Cite specific examples of what changed. Describe what parts of English society, economy, political power, military power, and prestige changed under the Tudors compared to the parts that did not. To evaluate this question, the essay must clarify what is meant by "the modern era." Examine the Tudor reign, specifically that of Henry VII, Henry VIII, and Elizabeth I. Demonstrate whether or not the Tudors accomplished a transformation. Be careful about dismissing Henry VIII because of "bad press." Despite his glaring personal failings, abused wives, and gluttony among the most prominent, he strengthened the monarchy and initiated the English Reformation. Elizabeth I may be famous for standing up to the superpower of her day, Spain, but the Golden Age of English culture also occurred during her reign, as did the birth of the commercial revolution and overseas colonization. Her reign set the stage for future British Empire building.

## Question 5

Explain how the Glorious Revolution of 1688 established a constitutional government in England.

### Comments on Question 5

This one is also a *causation* question because it requires you to explain how one event, the Glorious Revolution, resulted in a specific outcome: constitutional government in England. Remember to describe the causes and/or effects of the Glorious Revolution and to explain them through specific examples. The essay must explain the reasons for the causes and/or effects of the Glorious Revolution, such as how the rise of the power of Parliament that resulted in the Glorious Revolution occurred. Remember that those in Parliament were gaining economic power and wanted political power to match. Although this requires you have specific knowledge of events, laws, and effects, the essay should make clear how the abdication of James II, the invitation for William and Mary to take the throne, and the conditions set for this by Parliament laid the foundation for a modern democratic state. How was Parliament's power solidified? How did the Bill of Rights establish rule of law? How did the supremacy of Parliament and those basic rights limit the monarchy?

## Short-Answer

> **DIRECTIONS:** In your responses, be sure to address all parts of the questions you answer. Use complete sentences; an outline or a bulleted list is not acceptable.

1. John Locke, *Second Treatise of Civil Government* (1690)

### The Extent of the Legislative Power

The great end of men's entering into society being the enjoyment of their properties in peace and safety, and the great instrument and means of that being the laws established in that society: the first and fundamental positive law of all commonwealths is the establishing of the legislative power. . . .

Though the legislative . . . be the supreme power in every commonwealth, yet . . . it is not, nor can possibly be, absolutely arbitrary over the lives and fortunes of the people. For it being but the joint power of every member of the society given up to that person, or assembly, which is legislator, it can be no more than those persons had in a state of nature before they entered into society, and gave it up to the community. . . .

The supreme power cannot take from any man any part of his property without his own consent. . . .

These are the bounds [limits] which . . . society, and the law of God and Nature, have set to the legislative power of every commonwealth, in all forms of government:

First, they are to govern by . . . established laws, not to be varied in particular cases, but to have one rule for rich and poor, for the favorite at court and the countryman at plow.

Secondly, these laws also ought to be designed for no other end ultimately but the good of the people.

Thirdly, they must not raise taxes on the property of the people without the consent of the people.

Answer all parts of the question based upon the passage and your knowledge of European history.

(a) Explain how the work shown was written to justify a specific event in English history.

(b) Identify the trend in government that was accelerated by this piece of writing, and explain how John Locke's work helped accelerate the trend.

(c)  Identify the political ideology that is identified with this work by Locke and how that political ideology affected the evolution of governments from 1690–1815.

2.  **Letter from Louis XIV to the Town Officers and People of Marseilles**

Considering how advantageous it would be to this realm to reestablish its foreign and domestic commerce, . . .we have resolved to establish a council particularly devoted to commerce, to be held every fortnight in our presence, in which all the interests of merchants and the means conducive to the revival of commerce shall be considered and determined upon, as well as all that which concerns manufactures.

We desire, in this present letter, not only to inform you concerning all these things, but to require you, as soon as you have received it, to cause to be assembled all the merchants and traders of your town of Marseilles, and explain to them very particularly our intentions in all matters mentioned above, in order that, being informed of the favorable treatment which we desire to give them, they may be the more desirous of applying themselves to commerce. Let them understand that for everything that concerns the welfare and advantage of the same they are to address themselves to monsieur Colbert . . .

—Louis XIV

Please use the excerpt from the letter and your knowledge of European history to answer all parts of the following question.

(a)  Briefly identify and describe the economic policy for improving the nation's wealth that Louis XIV is promoting in this letter.
(b)  Briefly identify and describe ONE positive aspect of the impact of the rule of Louis XIV on France.
(c)  Briefly identify and describe how the policy Louis XIV supported was discredited less than a century after his rule.

## Multiple-Choice

**Questions 1–3 refer to the following passage.**

Moreover, that no one may assume that the Israelites were peculiar in having kings over them who were established by God, note what is said in Ecclesiasticus: "God has given to every people its ruler, and Israel is manifestly reserved to him." He therefore governs all peoples and gives them their kings, although he governed Israel in a more intimate and obvious manner.

It appears from all this that the person of the king is sacred, and that to attack him in any way is sacrilege . . .

But kings, although their power comes from on high, as has been said, should not regard themselves as masters of that power to use it at their pleasure; . . . they must employ it with fear and self-restraint, as a thing coming from God and of which God will demand an account. "Hear, O kings, and take heed, understand, judges of the earth, lend your ears, ye who hold the peoples under your sway, and delight to see the multitude that surround you. It is God who gives you the power. Your strength comes from the Most High, who will question your works and penetrate the depths of your . . . For God fears not the power of any one, because he made both great and small and he has care for both."

Kings should tremble then as they use the power God has granted them; and let them think how horrible is the sacrilege if they use for evil a power which comes from God.

—Bishop Jacques Benigne Bossuet (1627–1704)
passage from *Politics Derived from Holy Writ*

1. Bishop Jacques Bossuet, in the passage above, laid out the theoretical foundation for which of the following forms of sovereignty?

   (A) Theocratic aristocracy
   (B) Divine right of kings
   (C) Constitutional monarchy
   (D) Totalitarian control

2. Which of the following political philosophers would be most likely to agree with Bossuet about the proper power structure for a nation's government?

   (A) Jean-Jacques Rousseau, who wrote *The Social Contract*
   (B) Baron Montesquieu, who wrote *The Spirit of the Laws*
   (C) Thomas Hobbes, who wrote *Leviathan*
   (D) John Locke, who wrote *Two Treatises on Civil Government*

3. The most important governmental innovation of Cardinal Richelieu in France, who was an adherent of the ideas of Bishop Bossuet, was which of the following?

   (A) The intendant system used to undermine noble power
   (B) The creation of Versailles as a pleasure palace for the nobility
   (C) The implementation of the *taille* on all French citizens
   (D) The requirement that all French nobility study abroad for at least three years

**Questions 4–6 refer to the following print.**

*Estates General in Palais Bourbon, Paris.* By unidentified artist
after a 17th-century print. Published in *Magasin Pittoresque*, Paris, 1840.

4. Which of the following was most likely the topic of discussion at the meeting depicted above?

   (A)  The doctrines of the Roman Catholic Church within France
   (B)  The proper weapon to be used when fighting against the English
   (C)  The regulations for which classes can wear which type of clothing and furs
   (D)  Changing the levels of taxation and laws within France

5. The meeting depicted in the print included members of all three estates of the *Ancien Régime* in France. In the 17th century, though, French political power was beginning to change in which of the following ways?

   (A) New monarchies laid the foundation for the centralized modern state, which witnessed monarchs taking power from the nobility and creating state bureaucracies.

   (B) New monarchies laid the foundation for the centralized modern state, which witnessed new monarchs giving greater power to their nobility to control the peasants in France.

   (C) New monarchies laid the foundation for the centralized modern state, which witnessed the rise of parliamentary power and the decline of the divine right of monarchs.

   (D) New monarchies laid the foundation for the centralized modern state, which witnessed the rise of popular sovereignty.

6. Which of the following paintings would a political historian be most likely to use to contrast this meeting with the famous meetings of the Estates General in 1789?

   (A) *Liberty Leading the People* by Eugene Delacroix
   (B) *The Tennis Court Oath* by Jacques-Louis David
   (C) *The Storming of the Bastille* by Joseph Delaunay
   (D) *The Consecration of the Emperor Napoleon and the Coronation of the Empress Josephine by Pope Pius VII* by Jacques-Louis David

# Answers and Explanations

## Short-Answer Explanations

1. (a) A good response explains how the Glorious Revolution of 1689 had just occurred and that Locke was creating a philosophical justification for removing one king, James II, and replacing him with another, William of Orange. The response should clearly state that the document was written to provide a moral ground for the removal of a king who was not fulfilling the social contract with his subjects.

   (b) A good response explains how the "Second Treatise of Civil Government" began a trend in Europe toward more representation of the people's will in government. Once the Parliament offered the crown to William and Mary, the trend of rising citizen power and the rise of legislative power began to emerge. This trend eventually led to most of Europe being ruled by legislative bodies. Students can identify either the rise of legislative power or the rising political power of the citizens to improve their social contract with the rulers.

   (c) Students should identify the political ideology as liberalism and explain that its spread led to wider and wider representation of the people in government. They should say that liberalism was focused on the idea that society could be improved with enlightened leadership. The concept of rising political power of legislatures and citizens was a part of liberalism, as was the concept of laissez-faire economics. Both could be seen to expand after the work of John Locke.

2. (a) Students must identify either mercantilism or bullionism as the economic policies of Louis XIV and Colbert. Students must describe them as policies in which the nation hoped to buy goods and services only from itself, its colonies, and other possessions in order to increase the wealth held within the nation.

   (b) Students may explain any of the following: the rise of French prestige internationally, the growing wealth of the French upper classes, the conquest of the nobility by the intendant system and Versailles, the growth of French military might, France becoming the center of European culture, and the emergence of the Enlightenment after his death.

   (c) Students must identify mercantilism and explain how Adam Smith's *Wealth of Nations* argued against mercantilism and favored free trade in a movement that has remained strong to this day around the world. Students should explain how Smith proved that the removal of trade barriers was better for consumers, who make up the bulk of society. They should also explain that the rise of free market economics governed by supply and demand emerged as a counterargument to mercantilism.

## Practice Multiple-Choice Questions

1. (A) is wrong because Bossuet was arguing for a strong king who answers to God, not a government run by religion.

   **(B) is CORRECT because Bossuet laid the foundations for the divine right of kings theory of government that new monarchs used to consolidate all power within their realms.**

   (C) is wrong because Bossuet did not support any control other than God on the monarch.

   (D) is wrong because Bossuet did not support a form of government that would not appear for another almost 400 years when he wrote the passage.

2. (A) is wrong because Rousseau completely disagreed with Bossuet, as Rousseau supported rule by a legislature elected by the general will of the people.

   (B) is wrong because Montesquieu advocated dividing government into three branches, while Bossuet preferred all power in the hands of a monarch guided by God.

   **(C) is CORRECT because Hobbes and Bossuet agreed that the alternative to a strong monarch is anarchy.**

   (D) is wrong because Locke believed in overthrowing tyrants if they did not preserve the natural rights of citizens.

3. **(A) is CORRECT because the French intendant system of tax collectors, army recruiters, and other government bureaucrats took the governing power from the nobility and consolidated it in the hands of the king, just as Bossuet advised.**

   (B) is wrong because, although Louis XIV's use of Versailles increased his power, Versailles was not created by Richelieu and did not have nearly the impact on true power as did the intendants.

   (C) is wrong because Richelieu did not reintroduce the *taille* on everyone because members of the first and second estates were exempt from taxation.

   (D) is wrong because there was no requirement for French nobility to study abroad.

4. (A) is wrong because the Estates General was a French parliament that addressed the taxes and laws of the nation and stayed out of Church affairs.

   (B) is wrong because the Estates General was a French parliament that addressed the taxes and laws of the nation and avoided making decisions about weaponry and the military.

   (C) is wrong because the Estates General was a French parliament that addressed the taxes and laws of the nation; clothing regulations were mostly local and were becoming less prevalent at the time of the meeting shown in the print.

   **(D) is CORRECT because the print shows a meeting of the Estates General, which was the French parliament that approved laws and taxes.**

5. **(A) is CORRECT because new monarchs were associated with consolidating their own power by undercutting the nobility and building state bureaucracies.**

   (B) is wrong because, during this era, new monarchs took power from their nobility rather than gave power to them.

   (C) is wrong because, during the era of new monarchs, parliaments lost power.

   (D) is wrong because popular sovereignty did not gain power on a grand stage in Europe until after WWI.

6. (A) is wrong because *Liberty Leading the People* is about the revolutions of 1830 rather than the 1789 revolution, and it is not as political and therefore is not as good a match as is *The Tennis Court Oath*.

   **(B) is CORRECT because the analogy of *The Tennis Court Oath* as compared to the staid meeting of the Estates General discussed in the question makes a great political statement about the differences between the times depicted.**

   (C) is wrong because *The Storming of the Bastille* is not about a political meeting and therefore is not as good a match as is *The Tennis Court Oath*.

   (D) is wrong because *The Consecration of the Emperor Napoleon and the Coronation of the Empress Josephine by Pope Pius VII* is about a coronation rather than a political meeting and therefore is not as good a match as is *The Tennis Court Oath*.

# UNIT 4

# Scientific, Philosophical, and Political Developments (1648–1789)

## Unit 4 Overview: Scientific, Philosophical, and Political Developments

**Unit description:** This unit covers the greatest revolution in thought in the history of Western civilization: the Enlightenment. This time period challenged previously held beliefs in almost all areas of knowledge. New ways of knowing things were developed as were new tools that allowed people to gather more information about the universe and analyze that information better. This unit focuses on four themes of the course that are interwoven throughout the unit: Cultural and Intellectual Developments, Social Organization and Development, National and European Identity, and Technological and Scientific Innovation. This is the unit most focused on technological and scientific innovation. It covers the birth of science as a discrete field of knowledge and begins to see that field broken into many smaller fields, such as anatomy, physics, chemistry, philosophy, etc. This unit also covers many developments in social science, politics, and law. The foundational documents that support the concept of popular sovereignty were written during this era by such towering figures as John Locke, Baron Montesquieu, Jean-Jacques Rousseau, Thomas Paine, and others. The study of humanity and the idea that humans could improve their society and world gave birth to the political idea of *liberalism*, which emerged during this era as an ideology that would support the concept that society could progress and evolve beneficially. The main topics of study for this unit are as follows:

- Contextualizing the Scientific Revolution and Enlightenment
- Scientific Revolution (this was mostly covered in unit 1 as it takes place in time period 1)
- Enlightenment
- 18th-century society and demographics
- 18th-century culture and arts
- Enlightened and other approaches to power
- Causation in the Age of Scientific Revolution and Enlightenment

Most of the material in this chapter takes place during time period 2. The Scientific Revolution is the outlier, occurring mostly during time period 1.

# 4

# Scientific, Philosophical, and Political Developments (1648–1789)

## Key Terms

- Mercantilism
- *Discourse on Method*
- Seven Years' War
- Capitalism

- Deism
- Scientific Revolution
- The Enlightenment
- Physiocrats

- War of Spanish Succession
- Nine Years' War

## Key People

- Adam Smith
- René Descartes
- Nicolaus Copernicus
- Galileo Galilei
- Isaac Newton
- Johannes Kepler
- Madame Geoffrin

- Voltaire
- Jean-Jacques Rousseau
- Baron de Montesquieu
- Denis Diderot
- François Quesnay
- Mary Wollstonecraft
- Louis XIV

- Frederick II (the Great)
- Joseph II
- Philip II
- Peter I (the Great)
- Maria Theresa
- Frederick William I
- Catherine II (the Great)

## Overview

An agricultural revolution took place during the later years of the 17th century and through the 18th century. The traditional open-field system, which was an utterly inefficient method of agricultural production, was replaced by enclosures. Despite the social cost, productivity increased dramatically. New foods and a disappearance of the plague fostered rapid population growth. An Atlantic economy, built on trade between Europe (primarily England, France, and Holland) and the Americas benefited both Europe and the colonies economically and socially. A series of conflicts over imperial possessions broke out among the leading European competitors during the 18th century, culminating in the French and Indian War in North America (the Seven Years' War on the Continent) and the American Revolution.

From the end of the 15th century to the beginning of the 18th, the newly formed interactions between Europe and the New World and the opening of the Atlantic to exploration and colonization changed the economy of Europe. Mercantilism became the prevailing economic system of the growing nation-states. Inflation, brought about by the stores of gold and silver expropriated from the New World, led to an increase in trade and manufacturing that encouraged the growth of early capitalism. As economic activity shifted from the Mediterranean to the Atlantic, the Italian city-states declined as trading middlemen between Europe and both the Near and Far East that they had controlled through their interaction with the Byzantine Empire and later the Ottomans. Portugal and Spain became the major powers of the 16th century—the Netherlands, France, and England in the 17th century.

The impact of science on the modern world was immeasurable. If the "Greeks had said it all" two thousand years earlier, the Renaissance Europeans rediscovered, evaluated, and either elaborated or contradicted the ideas of Aristotle, Ptolemy, and other thinkers. Observation took precedence over tradition. To find out how many teeth a horse had, medieval academics scoured ancient texts to appeal to authority; modern thinkers just opened the horse's mouth.

The 16th and 17th centuries saw the fruition of Renaissance individualism in religion and thought. Luther and the Protestants questioned the traditions of the Catholic Church and rebelled. Copernicus, Galileo, and Newton subjected the theories of Aristotle and Ptolemy to the inductive method and redefined the natural world. The habit of skepticism, which the Renaissance had reintroduced and the Reformation had strengthened, was science's driving force. The printing press and the salons of enlightened aristocrats fomented the dissemination of the ideas of this era more easily than in past eras.

This skepticism gave rise to *rationalism*, the concept that human reason could uncover the natural laws that govern the universe and humankind itself. Inspired by the revolutionary theories of 16th- and 17th-century astronomy and physics, European thinkers ceased to be swayed by medieval superstition, by a belief in miracles, and by blind acceptance of tradition. Rationalism gave rise to the 18th-century Enlightenment, whose philosophers or *philosophes* argued that humans could discover the immutable laws of the universe through the light of reason and, therefore, that human progress was inevitable. As critics of the status quo, these philosophers commented on the political, economic, and social ills of society and offered designs for the betterment of humanity. Their optimism and impatience aroused the forces for change and contributed to the French Revolution.

## The Expansion of Europe

**(An abbreviated version of this information is also found in chapter 1.)**

During the 17th century, small landholdings, low-productivity agricultural practices, poor transportation, and adverse weather limited and disrupted the food supply, causing periodic famines. By the 18th century, the balance between population and the food supply stabilized, resulting in steady population growth. The *open-field system*, used during the Middle Ages (400 C.E.–1450 C.E.), divided the arable land available to a farming community into narrow strips, which were designated to the individual families of the community. Due to a lack of chemical fertilizers and ignorance about nitrogen-fixing crops, a large portion of the community's land lay fallow.

- The *enclosure movement* in England, during the late-17th and the 18th centuries, fenced off the open fields to enable large landowners to employ crop rotation.
  - By planting nitrogen-fixing crops, such as beans and certain grasses, in soil that had been used for other crops, the soil remained fertile and little land lay fallow.
  - Many small or inefficient farmers were displaced to the towns and cities, but ultimately, food production rose dramatically.
- This *Agricultural Revolution* included selective breeding of animals, utilizing of fertilizer, rotating of crops, and generally improving the land for farming.
  - It resulted in huge crop yields and surpluses of food, which freed up labor and allowed populations to increase.
- A greater variety of foods and the introduction of foods from the New World, specifically the potato, improved general nutrition and contributed, along with the disappearance of the plague, to a dramatic increase in populations.
- Except for the development of the smallpox vaccine in the late-18th century, the crude and often dangerous medical practices of the day contributed little to the health and longevity of the people.
- The disappearance of the plague, combined with better food production, encouraged the emergence of consumerism and leisure activities for the masses, such as coffeehouses and the theater.
- The enclosure movement and increased agricultural production led many to move to cities to look for economic advancement. This started the trend of *urbanization* that continued to build into the 20th century.
  - This increased urbanization changed marriage patterns and led to more illegitimate births toward the end of the 18th century.

- ○ As people became more crowded, they developed a new sense of privacy and built homes and read books that reinforced those ideas.
- ■ Cities offered economic opportunities. These opportunities attracted increasing migration from rural areas, transforming urban life and creating challenges for the new urbanites and their families.
  - ○ The Agricultural Revolution produced more food using fewer workers; as a result, people migrated from rural areas to the cities in search of work.
  - ○ The growth of cities eroded traditional communal values, and city governments strained to provide protection and a healthy environment.
  - ○ The concentration of poorer people in cities led to a greater awareness of poverty, crime, and prostitution as social problems and also prompted increased efforts to police marginalized groups.
- ■ Labor and trade in commodities were increasingly freed from traditional restrictions imposed by governments and corporate entities through the advent of market-driven wages and prices.
- ■ By the middle of the 18th century, higher agricultural productivity and improved transportation increased the food supply, allowing populations to grow and reducing the number of demographic crises (a process known as the Agricultural Revolution).
- ■ *Mercantilism* was a system developed by various European states to guarantee a favorable balance of trade with other European nations or with their American colonies.
  - ○ By creating an imbalance of exports over imports, the difference was made up in gold or silver payments.
  - ○ Mercantilism was pursued as an attempt to get precious metals from indigenous peoples to pay for the costs of maintaining standing armies and government bureaucracies.
- ■ Competition for colonies and for hegemony on the Continent culminated in the *Seven Years' War* (1756–1763) fought by Britain and its allies against France and its allies.
  - ○ The Seven Years' War was the first war that the Europeans fought on multiple continents; battles occurred in North America, Europe, and Asia.
  - ○ The British won a decisive battle against the French in India at the *Battle of Plassey* in 1757, which led to British dominance of India until after World War II.
  - ○ The war resulted in the loss of France's North American possessions and in the growing independence of the British North American colonies.
- ■ Mercantilism was largely discredited by the economic liberalism of *Adam Smith*, who argued that free competition, limited government regulation, and individual self-interest expressed through a supply-and-demand market system would foster economic growth.

# Mercantilism and the Rise of Capitalism

## The Commercial Revolution

For over 150 years after Columbus "discovered" the Americas for the Europeans, thousands of tons of silver and nearly 200 tons of gold came to Spain from the riches of the conquered Native Americans and from the mines established by the Spanish colonials. *Inflation*, "too much money chasing too few goods," resulted because while the money supply had vastly increased, productivity had remained stable, giving money reduced purchasing power.

- ■ *Inflation stimulated production* because craftsmen, merchants, and manufacturers could get good prices for their products. The middle class, also called the bourgeoisie, acquired much of this wealth by trading and manufacturing. Their political influence and social status also increased.
- ■ The consumer revolution of the 18th century was shaped by a new concern for privacy, encouraged the purchase of new goods for homes, and created new venues for leisure activities.

- Peasant farmers benefited when their surplus yields could be turned into *cash crops*. The nobility, whose income was based on feudal rents and fees, actually suffered a diminishing standard of living in this inflationary economy.
- The rise in population and the flight of entrepreneurs and industrious people to the New World further exacerbated this inflation as industry in Spain declined and new opportunities for the middle classes to make money emerged.
- The transatlantic *slave-labor system* expanded in the 17th and 18th centuries as demand for New World products increased.
  - Examples of this system include the *triangle trade, the Middle Passage*, and the *plantation system* developed by Europeans in their colonies.
  - The *Middle Passage* was the brutal journey by ship from Africa to the New World that killed as many as 50 percent of the enslaved people on board, who were dehumanized and treated like cargo.

## The Rise of Capitalism

*Capital* is another term for money used as an investment; instead of investing labor, an individual invests capital in some venture in order to make a profit. The bourgeoisie, having accumulated more money than was needed to maintain a subsistence standard of living in 17th- and 18th-century society, used money to make money.

- They invested in *chartered companies* that were given a monopoly on trading rights within a certain area by nations such as Britain and the Netherlands.
- *Joint-stock companies* (forerunners of modern corporations), which sold shares of stock publicly in order to raise large amounts for various ventures, provided *limited liability* to the shareholders and offered a profitable return for the original investment.
- In the *bourse,* a kind of stock exchange, profit made from investment enabled more investment.
- Private banks were able to turn private savings into venture capital that allowed investment in overseas trade and other capitalist ventures such as the first factories.
- New definitions of property rights, such as limited liability for owners of stocks and protections against the confiscation of property due to bad stock investments, encouraged greater investment.
- Insurance companies emerged to make overseas trade less risky.
- The Bank of England was founded to provide venture capital for English firms.
- The expansion of money created prosperity, advanced science and technology, and supported the growth of the nation-state.
- As infant and child mortality decreased and as commercial wealth increased, families dedicated more space and resources to children and child rearing as well as to private life and comfort.
- The rise in wealth led first to the emergence of a market economy, then to the emergence of a consumer economy, and finally to a consumer society after World War II.
  - Overseas products, such as silk, sugar, tea, tobacco, rum, and coffee, led to the emergence of a consumer culture.

## Mercantilism

The monarchs of the early modern period needed money to maintain the *standing armies* that dominated the powerful nobles of the realm and protected the state against foreign enemies. The commercial revolution and the growth of capitalism enriched a sizable segment of the population; personal riches translated into good tax revenues.

*Mercantilism* prevailed in the 17th century and well into the 18th century as an economic policy, because it seemed to offer a way for the monarchs of Europe to consolidate their centralized authority.

### The Theory

- A nation's wealth was measured by the amount of precious metals it had accumulated (*bullionism*) rather than by its productivity.
- Idea is often credited to Jean Baptiste Colbert, the finance minister of Louis XIV.
- A *favorable balance of trade* (exports exceed imports) increased the flow of gold and silver into the national economy and therefore increased the store of precious metals.
- Overseas colonies supplied the *mother country* with essential raw materials for manufacture and trade.
- Essential industries, such as manufacturing for the national defense or making a product unique to the nation and valuable in trade, were encouraged through subsidies and tax credits.
- The goal of mercantilism was national economic self-sufficiency.

*Overseas colonization* (old imperialism) was encouraged by the policy of mercantilism.

- Spain and Portugal, following up on the momentum of their early explorations to Asia around the African continent and to the Americas across the Atlantic, monopolized colonization in the 16th century.
- By the 17th century, the balance had shifted to the Dutch, French, and British, whose internal disorders of the previous century had stabilized and whose inroads in Asia and North America overcame the supremacy of the Spanish and Portuguese.
- The colonialism fostered by the British Empire far surpassed that of any other European nation because British colonies attracted proportionately more of its subjects for settlement.
  - Later, a number of British colonies became powerful independent states: the United States, India, Canada, Australia, and a number of other nations in Asia and Africa. For a time, though, all of those modern nations were a part of the British Empire.

The variety and volume of printed material grew enormously during this period in spite of state and Church censorship. The literate reading public grew exponentially as well, which helped lead to the development of public opinion. Coffeehouses, salons, lending libraries, and new academies of learning helped develop this new reading audience. Some of what people read included *almanacs*, newspapers, other periodicals, pamphlets, and, of course, Denis Diderot's *Encyclopédie*.

## The Enlightenment

The towering giant of the Scientific Revolution was an Englishman named *Isaac Newton* (1642–1727). He wrote, "If I have seen further it is by standing on the shoulders of giants," when referring to Galileo (1564–1642). The work of Galileo made Newton's scientific investigation into astral physics possible. If Copernicus (1473–1543) shook the medieval conception of Christianity to its foundations, the work of Isaac Newton not only tested the notion of God's intervention in human affairs but also established the ascendancy of science in the modern world.

> **NOTE**
>
> Please see chapter 1 for the section "The Development of 'Natural Philosophy' or Science." All important figures of the Scientific Revolution are explained in detail there.

- Newton demonstrated that natural laws of motion account for the movement of heavenly bodies and earthly objects.
  - These laws are unchangeable and predictable.
  - God's active participation is not needed to explain the operations of the forces of nature—a repudiation of medieval belief.
  - Newton went on to chair the *Royal Society of London*, where his status as the preeminent thinker of his day made England the center of scientific thought for a short while.

- Newton's work in astronomy and physics convinced European thinkers that human reason, unaided by the tenets and rituals of religion, could uncover the immutable laws of nature.

- An Englishman named Isaac Newton inspired the Enlightenment; a group of Frenchmen called the *philosophes* shaped it.

  - The *philosophes*, who were actually literary figures more than academic philosophers, argued that once the natural laws that governed nature and human existence were discovered, society could be organized in accordance with them and progress would be inevitable.

  - This idea that society could progress and become better was the fundamental belief behind the ideology of *liberalism* that emerged as a part of the Enlightenment.

  - As leaders of French culture, which dominated Europe, the *philosophes* lauded Newton, borrowed from John Locke, and flooded Europe with radically optimistic notions about how people should live and govern themselves.

  - Ideas were created that would shake the "old order" to pieces and build in its place the democratic, pluralistic, humanistic Western world.

- While Newton's theories served as the inspiration for the natural law philosophy of the Enlightenment, *John Locke's* political writings translated the natural law assumption into a conception of government.

  - Locke (1632–1704), an Englishman, provided a philosophical apology for the supremacy of Parliament during the Glorious Revolution with his *Two Treatises on Civil Government*:

    - In the *state of nature*, before governments existed, humans lacked protection.

    - Governments, once instituted, replace individual action with the rule of law.

    - However, governments rest upon the consent of the governed.

    - The *social contract*, the agreement between a fair government and responsible individuals, is not unconditional.

    - If government oversteps its role in protecting the life, liberty, and property of its citizens, the people have the right to abolish and replace that government.

  - These conceptions of the *consent of the governed*, the *social contract*, and the *right of revolution* spearheaded the *philosophes's* criticism of the absolutist *Ancien Régime,* or "Old Order."

## The *Philosophes*

*Voltaire* (1694–1778) personified the Age of Reason. Born *François Marie Arouet* in Paris at the height of Louis XIV's reign, he lived until two years after the American Declaration of Independence. Although Voltaire was more writer than philosopher, he wrote in many formats. As a poet, an essayist, a dramatist, and, most importantly, a satirist, his genius for social criticism helped ignite a desire for change and set the stage for the Age of Revolution.

- Voltaire preached against injustice and bigotry and preached for human rights and science.

- *"Ecrasez l'infame"* ("Crush the infamous") was his rallying cry against religious zealotry, governmental abuse, and vestiges of medievalism.

- Imprisoned briefly in the Bastille, he visited England and lived in the court of *Frederick the Great* (r. 1740–1786), the *Enlightened Despot* of Prussia.

- Like most of the Enlightenment thinkers, Voltaire was raised as a Christian but came to reject organized religion as corrupt in its leadership and remote from the urgent message of Jesus.

- He was a staunch advocate of *deism,* the theological offshoot of natural law theory.

  - Voltaire believed that prayer and miracles violated the perfect natural order God had created and that the world's evils were caused by people straying from the natural law.

  - The social reforms that Voltaire called for fit the deist notion that human reasoning alone could uncover the natural law and guide humans to comply with it.

*Jean-Jacques Rousseau* (1712–1778) is often considered a *philosophe*, a man of the Enlightenment. He is more accurately called the founder of the Romantic movement. After the excesses of the French Revolution, the Enlightenment's emphasis on the *rule of reason* gave way to a glorification of emotion.

- Despising, intellectually and personally, the rigid and inequitable class structure of the *Ancien Régime,* Rousseau developed the idea of the *noble savage*: that civilization corrupted humankind and that life in the *state of nature* was purer, freer, and more virtuous than "civilized" man.
- The goal of the individual, he argued in his many writings, was to attain full expression of natural instincts by stripping away the artificial restraints of society and returning as far as possible to nature.
- Rousseau believed that the goal of a people was to achieve self-determination.
  ○ A call to the nationalism that the French Revolution awakened all over Europe
- In *The Social Contract*, he wrote, "Man is born free, and everywhere he is in chains." Rousseau meant that property, when regarded as more important than people, causes social injustice.
- Rousseau thought that the *general will*, a kind of consensus of the majority, should control a nation. This was intended to support a democratic view of government. Because it does not recognize minority viewpoints and since it has no clear way to show itself, the general will could be used to rationalize extreme nationalism and repression.
- Whatever the flaws in his philosophy, Rousseau is considered one the most influential thinkers of his day.
- His distrust of *civilization* and its institutions led him to criticize rigid educational practices and the strict discipline of children.
  ○ In his treatise *Emile*, Rousseau argued that children have to be understood as individuals and that they need caring from their teachers as well as from their parents.
  ○ He and other Enlightenment critics helped to change the educational and child-rearing practices of 18th-century Europe.

*Baron de Montesquieu* (1689–1755) in his work *The Spirit of the Laws* argued that the powers of government (legislative, executive, and judicial) must be separated in order to avoid despotism. When these functions are divided among various groups or individuals, he claimed, each *checks and balances* the powers of the others. His theories served as a blueprint for the governmental structure outlined in the U.S. Constitution. Montesquieu is often remembered for his statement that the powers of "the sword and the purse" should be separated into different branches of government.

*Cesare Beccaria* (1738–1794) published his *On Crimes and Punishments* in 1764, which added to Montesquieu's ideas by outlining proportions between crimes and punishments and by arguing against torture. He focused on deterring people from committing crimes.

*Denis Diderot* (1713–1784) published the writings and popularized the ideas of many of the *philosophes* in his *Encyclopédie,* a collection of political and social critiques rather than a compilation of facts.

*François Quesnay* (1694–1774) led the *physiocrats,* whose motto was *laissez-faire.* They believed that government should remove all restraints to free trade, such as tariffs, so that the natural laws of economics were free to operate for the good of society.

*Adam Smith* (1727–1790), a Scotsman, refined and expanded the laissez-faire philosophy of the *physiocrats* in his *An Inquiry into the Nature and Causes of the Wealth of Nations.* Published in 1776, the year of the Declaration of Independence, it is the book that defined capitalism. In it, Smith stated that the economy is governed by natural laws, such as *supply and demand*; in a free economy, competition will induce producers to manufacture most efficiently in order to sell higher quality, lower-cost goods than competitors; and government regulation only interferes with this natural self-governing operation. He also railed against mercantilism as the embodiment of foul government intervention in the economy.

It is important to remember that these new ideas existed alongside the traditional ideas that Europeans had held dear for centuries. Alchemy and astrology continued to appeal to elites and some natural philosophers, in part because they shared with the new science the notion of a predictable and knowable universe. Most peasants and urban folk continued to believe that the cosmos was governed by both divine and demonic forces.

*Salons* were the sites for meetings of the great minds of the day in the houses of the prominent women of the day, such as *Madame Geoffrin* (1699–1777) or *Madame Stael* (1766–1817). The salons supported a discourse of ideas without the *censorship* that was so prevalent in the writings of the day and that Voltaire rebelled against so strongly. They also functioned as a means for women to attain an education on the cutting edge of knowledge and thought of the time.

The *coffeehouses* of France and much of Europe served as further meeting places for conversation. Some have theorized that the advent of tea and coffee was a factor that led to the Enlightenment. Caffeine had recently replaced alcohol in daily beverages. As a result, people thought with much more clarity and had more energy for thoughtful discourse.

During the Enlightenment, the rational analysis of religious practices led to natural religion and the demand for religious tolerance. Intellectuals, including Voltaire and Diderot, developed new philosophies of deism, skepticism, and atheism. *Baron d' Holbach* (1723–1789) was the primary proponent of an atheistic world at the time. He disrupted the salons of the day by his insistence on publicly and ardently advocating his belief that God was just an illusion in salons. Religion became increasingly a private rather than a public concern. By 1800, most forms of Christianity were tolerated by most European governments, who also gave civil equality to Jewish people in many cases. The ideas of the *philosophes* were spread through the new media of the printing press and through salons, resulting in the emergence of an international intellectual community.

The new field of science emerged based upon observations and mathematics, which challenged the classical views of everything from the cosmos to the human body and everything in between. However, traditional views of the universe continued to be supported by many more traditional thinkers. The conflict between traditional thinking and the enlightened approach to knowledge based on observations and mathematics continued throughout the history of Europe as the pendulum of conservatism and liberalism swung back and forth over the ages.

## Gender and Ethnicity During the Enlightenment

This era saw the emergence of feminist ideas for the first time in earnest. Women like *Mary Wollstonecraft* (1759–1797) and Madame Geoffrin made it clear to society that women could do anything intellectually that men could do. The first women graduated from many European universities, and intellectuals discussed openly the idea that women should be equal before the law. The Enlightenment ideals of natural rights and just laws made people reexamine their preconceived notions of gender roles, and women's rights made some grudging progress despite the protests of many men in the field.

The same Enlightenment ideals that made men such as Rousseau and Voltaire question how they treated women had these men examine how they treated enslaved people and the peoples of other nations, too. White men would still be the prominent power in Western society and the other societies of the world that they dominated. However, these men began to examine the morality and the consequences of their perspectives during this era due to the works of people such as Rousseau (in his novel *Emile*) and others such as Olympe de Gouges (1748–1793). Reform came slowly. England outlawed slavery in all British holdings first. France and the United States eventually followed the European trend. Religious intolerance also began to be reduced, leading to more social harmony.

## Enlightened Despotism

The ideal enlightened despot was a ruler who aimed for the advancement of society by fostering education, aiding the economy, and promoting social justice. Since Voltaire and most of the *philosophes,* and certainly most of Europe's monarchs, believed that the mass of people were incapable of self-government, enlightened despots stayed in power while promoting the good of their people.

In the 17th century, Russia and Prussia rose as powerful states, challenging Poland, the ancient Habsburg *state of Austria*, and the declining empire of the Ottomans. In Prussia and, ironically, in Russia (whose culture often lagged decades, even centuries, behind that of the West), enlightened despotism held sway during important periods of the 18th century. Such rule helped slow the decline of Austria, whose monarchs still held the title of Holy Roman Emperor. In Western Europe, enlightened despotism manifested itself in Sweden, Spain, and Portugal but shone most brilliantly in the East such as in Prussia, Russia, and Austria.

## Prussia

Prussian enlightened despotism reached fruition during the rule of Frederick I's grandson, *Frederick II* or *Frederick the Great* (r. 1740–1786). "First servant of the state," as he called himself, Frederick the Great was a military genius who made Prussia a major power in Europe. He was an urbane and educated man who patronized the great Voltaire. Frederick the Great was also a domestic reformer who improved education, codified laws, fostered industry, invited immigration, and extended religious tolerance. Twenty years after he died, although Napoleon was able to defeat his army on the battlefield, it remained the strongest institution within the state. The remnants of the Junker (landowning aristocracy) officer corps rebuilt the army and fostered German nationalism to create a strong German state.

## Russia

*Catherine the Great* (r. 1762–1796), a German who succeeded to the throne after the murder of her husband *Czar Peter III* (r. 1762), was a patron of many of the French *philosophes* and considered herself an enlightened despot. When a rebellion of the Cossacks, the *Pugachev Rebellion*, gained some ground with the peasantry, Catherine at first tried to dismiss the rebellion. Later, she took it much more seriously and ended her enlightened reforms. She did continue Peter the Great's work of territorial expansion by annexing both Polish and Ottoman land.

## Austria

In Austria during the 18th century, *Maria Theresa* (r. 1740–1780) and her son *Joseph II* (r. 1780–1790) qualified as genuine enlightened despots. *The War of the Austrian Succession* (1740–1748) was fought over the issue of whether or not Maria Theresa could inherit her kingdom and also gave Silesia to Prussia. The *Habsburg Dynasty* had been weakened by the time Maria Theresa inherited the throne under a cloud of counterclaims. She was determined to strengthen the realm by centralizing the government, promoting commerce, and limiting the power of the nobles. Joseph furthered his mother's reforms by guaranteeing freedom of the press and of religion, by reforming the judicial system toward greater equality for all classes, by making German the official language for the empire's many ethnic minorities in order to foster centralization, and especially by *abolishing serfdom*.

# Great Thinkers of the Scientific Revolution and Enlightenment

This section has two purposes. First, it is designed to help you comprehend the ideas that may be tested. Second, it contains specific items that you may use as evidence when writing essays about the era.

## Copernicus (1473–1534), Poland/East Prussia

He was responsible for spreading the heliocentric (sun-centered) theory of the solar system throughout Europe. His *On the Revolutions of the Heavenly Spheres* was published posthumously.

## Anton van Leeuwenhoek (1632–1723), Netherlands

He invented and used microscopes to create a basis for modern biological science; his drawings of blood corpuscles, sperm, and bacteria began the science of microbiology.

## Michel de Montaigne (1533–1592), France

He was a skeptic and inventor of the essay. He stated that he knew nothing decades before Descartes wrote, "*Cogito ergo sum*" ("I think, therefore I am").

## Francis Bacon (1561–1626), England

He is often cited as the codifier of the inductive method. He believed that "knowledge is power" and that knowledge should be put to practical use.

## René Descartes (1596–1650), France

He was an ardent advocate for the deductive method. His *Discourse on Method* defined two kinds of matter: thinking substance (everything within the mind) and extended substance (the objective world or everything outside the mind). This division of reality is known as Cartesian dualism. He invented analytical geometry and wrote the eternal line, "*Cogito ergo sum*" ("I think, therefore I am").

## Tycho Brahe (1546–1601), Denmark

This eccentric astronomer collected vast amounts of data and hired a mathematically gifted assistant named Johannes Kepler.

## Johannes Kepler (1571–1630), Germany

He was Brahe's assistant. Kepler discovered three laws of planetary motion that helped Newton later understand gravity. He also proved that the orbits of planets are ellipses.

## Galileo Galilei (1571–1642), Italy

Perhaps the best example of the Enlightenment emerging from the Renaissance, Galileo was a master of many sciences and tried to know everything he could. His astronomical observations of the moons of Jupiter proved that Earth was not the center of the universe, which caused him to be put under house arrest by the Roman Catholic Church. His experiments with inertia proved that objects of different weights fall at the same rate.

## Vesalius (1514–1564), Belgium

His anatomical drawings based on dissected corpses were the first detailed anatomical maps of the human body.

## William Harvey (1578–1657), England

He was the author of *On the Movement of the Heart and Blood*, which explained the circulation of the blood through arteries and veins.

## Isaac Newton (1642–1727), England

He synthesized Kepler's and Galileo's ideas together in his laws of motion. Newton's definition of physics defined what scientists knew about the universe until Einstein conceived of relativity. Newton developed calculus to measure and predict curves and trajectories. He also explained the laws of universal gravitation. He said he "stood on the shoulders of giants" in deference to Galileo.

## Leibniz (1646–1716), Germany

He invented calculus simultaneously with Newton.

# *Philosophes* of the Enlightenment

### Bernard de Fontenelle

He was influential in bringing scientific matters to educated people who were not scientists themselves. He also was among the first to think that science contradicted religion and caused people to think about the nature of religious truth.

**Major work:** *Conversations on the Plurality of Worlds* was a truly liberal book because it focused on the concept that humans can make progress and marveled at the progress already made. This book also made scientific progress up to that point in history available to many people and presented it on their level of understanding.

### Pierre Bayle

A leading skeptic, his conclusion foreshadowed that of Heisenberg and stated that there is basis for doubt in absolutely everything.

**Major work:** *Historical and Critical Dictionary*, published in 1697, discussed past religion and persecution.

### Baruch Spinoza

He equated God and nature, and he believed in an impersonal mechanical universe. Spinoza also denied free will. He was Jewish by birth but became one of the first ardent atheists.

**Major works:** *Ethics, Tractatus Theologico-Politicus,* and *Tractatus Politicus*

### Denis Diderot

He is best known as the editor of the first European *Encyclopédie*, which was supported by Voltaire and Catherine II (the Great) of Russia. He was a writer and member of prominent salons in Paris.

**Major work:** *Encyclopédie*, or *A Systematic Dictionary of the Sciences, Arts and Crafts*

### Jean-Baptiste le Rond d'Alembert

He was a famous philosopher, physicist, mathematician, scientist, and writer. He co-edited the *Encyclopédie* with Diderot.

**Major work:** *Encyclopédie,* or *A Systematic Dictionary of the Sciences, Arts and Crafts*

### Baron de Montesquieu (Charles-Louis de Secondat)

He defined the theory of separation of powers of the three branches of government. He outlined a system of checks and balances by which a government could be controlled. Montesquieu also discussed what conditions were favorable to liberty and greatly admired the English balance of power. He satirized European society as well in *The Persian Letters*. His work helped design most of the governmental systems in the world today.

**Major works:** *The Spirit of the Laws* and *The Persian Letters*

### Voltaire (Francois-Marie Arouet)

- He was jailed, and many of the books he wrote were censored. However, he wrote over 70 books.
- Voltaire was vehemently tolerant of all religions but was a deist.

- A biographer summarized Voltaire's ideas by saying, "I disagree with what you say but would defend to the death your right to say it."
- He was a minister to Frederick the Great of Prussia.
- He did his best work while living with *Madame du Châtelet,* who translated Newton's *Principia Mathematica* and cared for Voltaire with her husband's tacit approval.
- In 1745, Voltaire was appointed the Royal Historiographer of France. Voltaire believed that monarchy was the best form of government because he did not trust people to rule themselves.

**Major works:** *Candide, Zadig, The Maid of Orleans,* and *The Age of Louis XIV*

## Thomas Paine

He advocated deism and progress, the idea of an improved society through natural laws. He moved to the British Colonies in America and advocated for American independence.

**Major works:** *The Age of Reason* and *Common Sense*

## Marquis de Condorcet (Marie Jean Caritat)

He was the chairman of the French Academy of Sciences. He stated that human progress would eventually lead to its perfection. He claimed there are ten stages of the mind—nine have occurred and the tenth will lead to perfection. He was against gradual, hard-won progress and wanted catastrophic change, much as Karl Marx later would. He committed suicide to avoid the guillotine of the French Revolution.

**Major works:** *Progress of the Human Mind* and *Essay on the Application of Analysis to the Probability of Majority Decisions*

## Baron Paul d'Holbach (Paul-Henri Thiry)

He was a staunch atheist who refused to compromise on anything. He was known for giving financial support to Diderot and Rousseau.

- He claimed that people were machines controlled by outside forces.
- He stated that free will, God, and immortality were myths.
- He was seen as dogmatic and intolerant due to rigid atheism. It broke the unity of the Enlightenment by dividing thinkers.

**Major works:** *The System of Nature* was one of his major works. He also contributed to the *Encyclopédie.*

## David Hume

He was a Scotsman who emphasized limitations of human reasoning and stated that the human mind is nothing but a bundle of impressions. Later, he became a dogmatic skeptic who undermined the Enlightenment. He was the best friend of Adam Smith.

**Major works:** *A Treatise of Human Nature* and *Dialogues Concerning Natural Religion*

## Jean-Jacques Rousseau

- He believed rationalism and civilization were destroying rather than liberating the individual.
- He emphasized nature and passion, and he influenced the early Romantic movement.
- He was surly and paranoid in his later years and had a bowel problem.
- He was against the culture of the Enlightenment.
- He believed that the *general will* reflects public opinion, and the people (as assessed by the majority of the legislature) should displace the monarch as the holder of sovereign power.

- His work *Emile* called for showing greater love and tenderness toward children, for not using wet nurses, and for not swaddling babies. He claimed these ideas showed the growth of humanitarianism and potential from the Enlightenment.

**Major works:** *The Social Contract* and *Emile*

## Immanuel Kant

He argued in 1784 that freedom of the press would result in Enlightenment. He separated science and morality into distinct branches of knowledge. He believed that science could describe natural phenomena of the material world but could not provide a guide for morality.

**Major works:** *Critique of Practical Reason, The Metaphysics of Morals,* and *Critique of Judgment*

## Mary Wollstonecraft

She was the first true feminist. She was a defender of the *Declaration of the Rights of Man*. Her daughter was Mary Shelley. She believed marriage was legalized prostitution. She engaged in a public debate with Edmund Burke about the French Revolution and in a private debate with Rousseau on the rights of women.

**Major works:** *A Vindication of the Rights of Man, A Vindication of the Rights of Woman,* and *Thoughts on the Education of Daughters*

## Olympe de Gouges

Another early feminist, she was the daughter of a baker and rose to run her own salon. She was an abolitionist. She was executed during the Reign of Terror.

**Major work:** *Declaration of the Rights of Woman and the Female Citizen*

## Adam Smith

He wrote the original statement of capitalist views. He basically created modern economics.

- His writings stated that mercantilism was stifling and that government regulations and granted privileges made the marketplace not only unfair but also inefficient.
- He thought free trade would limit government to three duties—defense, civil order, and public institutions.
- He believed that individual competition in the market led to balance.
- He believed in the invisible hand of supply and demand to control the marketplace and to keep competition free and fair.
- He was a professor in Scotland, traveled to France with a student, and met Quesnay, the first economist there.
- He explained how division of labor makes work more efficient.
- He thought profit was stolen from the laborer.

**Major works:** *An Inquiry into the Nature and Causes of the Wealth of Nations (1776)* and *Theory of Moral Sentiments*

## Madame Geoffrin (Marie Thérèse Rodet Geoffrin)

She was one of the leading Enlightenment personalities. She used her husband's money to host the liveliest salon in France at the time. Her guests included most of the people mentioned above. Other prominent salonnières include Louise de Warens and Julia de Lespinasse. Women were only treated like thinking people in the salons; they were the only place for a woman to learn about the world and the issues of the day. According to gender theory, women played an important role in organizing salons. Geoffrin created an independent setting free from censorship where diverse, educated people could form their public opinions.

**Major work:** Supported the publishing of the *Encyclopédie*

Artistic movements and literature of the era began to reflect the outlook and values of the emerging commercial and bourgeois society as well as new Enlightenment ideals of political power and citizenship. This can be seen in the paintings of the Dutch masters—such as Jan Vermeer, Rembrandt van Rijn, and Frans Hals—who depicted mostly the leaders and servants of bourgeois society in all their glory. The writings of Goethe, Henry Fielding, Jane Austen, and Daniel Defoe also captured similar ideas and ideals of the time.

## The Evolution of Political Thought of Hobbes, Locke, and Rousseau

This chart is designed to compare the ideas of the great political thinkers of the 16th, 17th, and 18th centuries.

| | Thomas Hobbes (1588–1679) English | John Locke (1632–1704) English | Jean-Jacques Rousseau (1712–1778) French |
|---|---|---|---|
| State of nature: What is life like for the uncivilized? | "Life is nasty, brutish and short." Hobbes believed that in a state of nature, might makes right and that we agree to be governed to protect ourselves from living in a state of nature. | People are born good and corrupted by society. People are created equal not in ability but in rights. All people have the rights to life, liberty, and property. | People are inherently unequal in ability, but this inequality matters only for the corrupted "civilized" man who deviated from the nobility of "savagery." |
| Natural law: Defines what the basic human rights are in all societies | The natural law that Hobbes focused on is survival. He stated that in nature every being is so concerned with survival, that any idea of rights includes only what one can physically protect. | All humans are endowed at creation with rights to life, liberty, and property. These are the basic rights that all people have. | Rousseau described the state of nature as noble. He explained that we only deviate from natural law, in which the needs of each individual are met by the group, because the corrupting force of civilization induces us to do so. |
| Social contract | People give up some of their rights in order to gain some protection provided by the government. | People give up some of their rights in order to gain some protection provided by the government. However, if the government does not do its job, the people must change the government. | The social contract is between the people, not between the people and the government. Each person gives up all rights to the "general will," which then incorporates every individual through the legislature. |
| Role of the state | The state prevents people from taking each other's property and from killing each other. | The state protects a person's right to life, freedom, and property. | The state enacts the "general will" of the people as expressed through the legislature. |
| Property | Hobbes saw property as a limited resource for which people compete. | Ownership of property is among everyone's natural rights. | Property is one of the worst inventions of society; it is used to manipulate the masses. |
| Religion | Hobbes believed that the state must have only one religion for unity. | Locke believed in religious toleration by the state. | Rousseau abhorred organized religion, especially Christianity, but did not reject God. |
| Favored form of government | Hobbes favored an absolute monarchy. | Locke favored any representative government: constitutional monarchy, democracy, or republic. | Rousseau favored a complete consensus based on dictatorship of the "general will." |

| | Thomas Hobbes (1588–1679) English | John Locke (1632–1704) English | Jean-Jacques Rousseau (1712–1778) French |
|---|---|---|---|
| What was his essential question? | How can society prevent chaos and violence? | How can government protect the citizen and his or her possessions? | How can society combat inequality? |

# Practice Questions

## Long Essay

These questions are samples of the various types of thematic essays on the AP exam. See pages 27–28 for a detailed explanation of each type. Check over the generic rubric (see pages 28–29) before you begin any of these essays, and use that rubric to score your essay if you write one.

## Question 1

Evaluate the extent to which Newton inspired the Enlightenment, Locke provided the blueprint, and the *philosophes* shaped it.

## Comments on Question 1

This is a *causation* question because it requires you to decide if Newton inspired the Enlightenment, if Locke guided it, and if the *philosophes* shaped it. Remember to describe causes and/or effects of the Enlightenment, and support your analysis of those causes with specific examples. Explain the reasons for those causes and effects with supporting evidence. Remember that assessing the validity of a statement usually means a causation skill is being tested. The goal here is to ascertain how Newtonian physics and astronomy gave rise to natural law theory, how Locke applied that theory to the relationship between the individual and government, and then how the *philosophes* used Newtonian natural law and Lockean political theory to shape the Age of Reason. Be careful to define natural law, to spell out Locke's applications of it in his theory of government, to characterize the Enlightenment that dominated the intellectual life of 18th-century Europe, and to show how important *philosophes* such as Voltaire, Montesquieu, Rousseau, Smith, Wollstonecraft, and others influenced the movement. This type of question has at least four parts (Newton's inspiration, Locke's blueprint, shaping by *philosophes*, and the validity of each). You need to remember to complete all parts of the question.

## Question 2

Compare Locke's and Rousseau's concepts of the social contract.

## Comments on Question 2

The chart on the evolution of political thought from this chapter can help you develop an outline for this essay. This is a *compare* skill question, so be sure to describe similarities and differences between Locke's and Rousseau's concepts of the social contract. Account for or explain the reasons for the similarities and differences by providing specific examples of how they are similar and different. Then tie that to historical developments, such as the rise of constitutionalism and democracy. Locke, who lived before the Enlightenment, influenced Rousseau. Rousseau, who dominated the Enlightenment's push for social reform, has been called more of a Romantic than a *philosophe* insofar as he departed from Locke's political theory. The way to show differences would be first to examine similarities in the men's concepts of the state of nature and the social contract, then to show how Locke's ideas influenced

Rousseau's, and finally to examine how Rousseau departed from Locke. Although this question is straightforward, it requires a thorough understanding of the abstract theories involved.

## Question 3

Were the enlightened despots more despotic than enlightened?

### Comments on Question 3

According to the democratic biases of our age, an enlightened despot is a contradiction in terms. For the world of the 18th century, which was mired in the excesses of absolutism, the enlightened despots were products of the Age of Reason. This is a *compare* skill question. So be sure to explain what makes each example despotic or enlightened as well as account for or explain why some enlightened despots were more enlightened than others. Provide specific examples of how the rulers were both despotic and enlightened and different and tie that to historical developments such as the Pugachev Rebellion, or the emancipation of serfs eventually. The essay must explain the reasons for the similarities and differences between an enlightened ruler and a despot. This requires you to include specific references and evaluations of the various monarchs who claimed to be, or have been labeled by history as, enlightened despots. Make reference to three or four. Measure their reigns for genuine reform. Did the reforms change the lives of the people? Did the reforms last? Decide whether to defend or refute.

## Question 4

Explain how the replacement of the open-field system by the enclosure movement increased agricultural productivity in 18th-century Europe.

### Comments on Question 4

This is a *causation* question because it requires you to explain how one event, the replacement of the open-field system by the enclosure movement, resulted in a specific outcome: increased agricultural productivity in 18th-century Europe. Remember to describe the causes and/or effects of enclosure and the Agricultural Revolution and to support your analysis of those causes by including specific examples. The essay must explain with specific evidence the reasons why the enclosure movement increased agricultural activity. The enclosure movement should be explained as the most important and least-known revolution in European history. Describe the open-field system and the concept of common lands, focusing on the limitations on land improvement and fallow lands. Explain how the enclosure movement made land improvement, such as irrigation, crop rotation, and fertilization, more practical and widespread. The best essays also examine how the enclosure movement led to the putting-out system that increased domestic production and disturbed the order of society by moving many farming families from their lands, causing them to find new means of employment.

## Question 5

Why did the population of Europe increase dramatically in the 1700s?

### Comments on Question 5

This is a *causation* question because it requires you to explain the causes of the dramatic population increase of the 1700s. Remember to describe the causes and/or effects of the population increases and to support your analysis of those causes through specific examples. The essay must explain the reasons why the population rose at that time; include specific evidence as support. Explain the roles of food production, new foods, and the disappearance of the plague. Emphasize that the medical practices of the day played little part in the increase. An increase in the overall standard of living for many of the people in rural Europe at the time due to the emergence of domestic industry may also be mentioned.

**Short-Answer**

1. Answer all parts of the following question based upon the image below and your knowledge of European history.

Frontispiece of: "Tabulae Rudolphinae: quibus astronomicae . . ." by Johannes Kepler.

(a) Briefly analyze how the artwork above reflects the artistic trends in the first half of the 17th century.

(b) Based on the print and your knowledge of European history, briefly analyze TWO aspects of change that affected Europeans' perceptions during the Enlightenment period.

2. Use the excerpt from the letter below and your knowledge of European history to answer all parts of the following question.

### Letter from Louis XIV to the Town Officers and People of Marseilles

Considering how advantageous it would be to this realm to reestablish its foreign and domestic commerce, . . .we have resolved to establish a council particularly devoted to commerce, to be held every fortnight in our presence, in which all the interests of merchants and the means conducive to the revival of commerce shall be considered and determined upon, as well as all that which concerns manufactures.

We desire, in this present letter, not only to inform you concerning all these things, but to require you, as soon as you have received it, to cause to be assembled all the merchants and traders of your town of Marseilles, and explain to them very particularly our intentions in all matters mentioned above, in order that, being informed of the favorable treatment which we desire to give them, they may be the more desirous of applying themselves to commerce. Let them understand that for everything that concerns the welfare and advantage of the same they are to address themselves to Sieur Colbert. . . .

—Louis XIV

(a) Briefly identify and describe the economic policy for improving the nation's wealth that Louis XIV is promoting in this letter.

(b) Briefly identify and describe ONE positive aspect of the impact of the rule of Louis XIV on France.

(c) Briefly identify and describe how the policy Louis XIV supported was discredited less than a century after his rule.

## Multiple-Choice

Questions 1–4 refer to the image of a French stamp from the 1970s below.

1. Which of the following is the best explanation of the popular nickname for Louis XIV as alluded to in the postage stamp above?

    (A) *L'état c'est moi* because Louis XIV was the state of France

    (B) *The Sun King* because all of Europe revolved around Louis XIV

    (C) *The Sun King* because all light in Europe came from Louis XIV

    (D) *The Wig King* because Louis XIV began a trend of wigs being worn across Europe

2. The Palace of Versailles seen in the background of the stamp was used by Louis XIV in which of the following ways?

    (A) It was a pleasure palace that the nobility flocked to voluntarily to enjoy the grand court of Louis XIV.

    (B) It was built to display the wealth and power of Louis XIV in order to overawe foreign diplomats and officials of the Roman Catholic Church.

    (C) It was a state building constructed to glorify France and to build the pride of the French people.

    (D) It was built as a pleasure prison to control the nobility by requiring their attendance there annually.

3. Which of the following was the greatest weakness of Louis XIV according to many historians and his probable dying declaration?

    (A) Louis XIV was too focused on controlling his own nobility.

    (B) Louis XIV was a notorious womanizer who ruined many women's lives.

    (C) Louis XIV spent over two-thirds of his reign at war, and much of it was fruitless.

    (D) Louis XIV was too attached to secular pleasures and was not religious.

4. All of the following are reasons why the French government would choose to issue the stamp above during the 1970s EXCEPT which one?

    (A) French nationalism needed rebuilding after defeats in Algeria and French Indochina.

    (B) The recent death of Charles de Gaulle left the French in need of a hero.

    (C) The social movement in France in the 1970s was building to restore a constitutional monarch.

    (D) Nostalgia was building for better times when France was central to world politics.

**Questions 5–8 refer to the painting below.**

Oil by Lemonnier of Madame Geoffrin (1699–1777)
in her salon at Hotel de Rambouillet in Paris.

5. The painting above is a gathering of notable writers and thinkers in order to do which of the following?

   (A) Plan a new constitution for their country
   (B) Evaluate different paintings being exhibited
   (C) Observe the latest fashions in clothing
   (D) Discuss important philosophical issues and points of knowledge

6. Which of the following was a direct result of many meetings in France such as the one depicted above?

   (A) The general population of France latched onto these ideas and called for democracy after attending such meetings.
   (B) The control of the Roman Catholic Church was challenged over the creation and dissemination of knowledge.
   (C) The control of France by the nobility was challenged by these gatherings of mostly bourgeois activists who wanted to destroy the social order.
   (D) The economy of France was mended, putting off a financial crisis until the final years of Louis XVI.

7. Which of the following statements was most likely to be agreed upon by everyone at a meeting like the one depicted above?

   (A) The best form of government is a constitutional monarchy.
   (B) The best form of government is a republic with universal suffrage.
   (C) Society can be improved through the use of reason.
   (D) This is the best of all possible worlds.

8. Madame Geoffrin and her assembled guests were largely responsible for which of the following projects?

   (A) The rewriting of the French constitution
   (B) The creation of the first European encyclopedia
   (C) Writing a satire that examined Dutch society
   (D) Creating a collection to match the Library of Alexandria

# Answers and Explanations

## Short-Answer Explanations

1. (a)  1 point is given for an analysis of how the image represents the art of the Northern Renaissance. The factors used to support this can include the theme that is secular and scientific, the detailed linear perspective, the appeal to Greco-Roman classicism, scientific and rational understanding of the world, the emergence of copper engraving as an art form, the rise of book illustrations, and detailed realism.

   (b)  2 points are awarded, 1 *each*, for an analysis of change that affected European thought during the period of the Scientific Revolution and Enlightenment. A change must be more than just mentioned but should be explored for causes and effects to be awarded a point for this question. Some changes to analyze include but are not limited to: gaining faith in reason and science or in religion to solve problems, increasing scientific knowledge alongside increasing moral knowledge, the growth and spread of printed books, the rise of astronomy as an area of study, the decline of religious control of thought, the emerging conflict between religion and science, the rise of deism, the increase in precision of measurement, the fascination with learning the rules of the universe, and the focus on gaining knowledge and applying it to social issues.

2. (a)  The student must identify mercantilism or bullionism as the economic policies of Louis XIV and Colbert. The essay must describe them as policies in which the nation hoped to buy goods and services only from itself, its colonies, and other possessions in order to increase the wealth held within the nation.

   (b)  The student may explain any of the following: the rise of French prestige internationally, the growing wealth of the French upper classes, the conquest of the nobility by the intendant system and Versailles, the growth of French military might, France becoming the center of European culture, and the emergence of the Enlightenment after the death of Louis XIV.

   (c)  The student must explain how Adam Smith's *The Wealth of Nations* argued against mercantilism and favored free trade in a movement that has remained strong to this day around the world. The rise of free-market economics governed by supply and demand should also be covered.

## Practice Multiple-Choice Questions

1. (A)  is wrong because Louis XIV was the Sun King around whom all of Europe revolved, but he did declare that he was the state and is known for the quote given in choice (A).

   **(B)  is CORRECT because Louis XIV was the Sun King around whom all of Europe revolved.**

   (C)  is wrong because Louis XIV was the Sun King around whom all of Europe revolved, not the source of all light.

   (D)  is wrong because, although Louis XIV did prefer and spread his preference for wigs, Louis XIV was the Sun King around whom all of Europe revolved.

2. (A)  is wrong because the nobility was forced to come to Versailles by Louis while his government officials called *intendants* administered to governmental affairs throughout the country, reducing the power of the nobility.

   (B)  is wrong because, although Versailles was used to overpower diplomats, its primary use was to control the nobility there while his government officials called *intendants* administered to governmental affairs throughout the country, reducing the power of the nobility.

   (C)  is wrong because Versailles was built to glorify the monarch, not the state, and because the people resented it rather than took pride in it.

   **(D)  is CORRECT because the nobility was forced to come to Versailles by Louis while his government officials called *intendants* administered to governmental affairs throughout the country, reducing the power of the nobility.**

3. (A) is wrong because, although Louis XIV did subjugate his nobility, that was a benefit to his rule. Louis's biggest flaw was his pursuit of war for two-thirds of his reign. His dying declaration is often cited as "I have gone to war too lightly, and pursued it for vanity's sake."

(B) is wrong because, although Louis XIV did have many mistresses, Louis's biggest flaw was his pursuit of war for two-thirds of his reign. His dying declaration is often cited as "I have gone to war too lightly, and pursued it for vanity's sake."

**(C) is CORRECT because Louis XIV's biggest flaw was his pursuit of war for two-thirds of his reign. His dying declaration is often cited as "I have gone to war too lightly, and pursued it for vanity's sake."**

(D) is wrong because, although Louis XIV was engaged in the pursuit of pleasure, he was very religious.

4. (A) is wrong because French nationalism did need rebuilding after these defeats.

(B) is wrong because the French people did need to remember a great French hero without a current one present in their nation.

**(C) is CORRECT because there was no popular movement to restore a monarchy in France in the 1970s.**

(D) is wrong because there was a building nostalgia in France for a time when France mattered more internationally as the Cold War progressed during the 1970s.

5. (A) is wrong because this meeting is a salon in which the enlightened thinkers, or *philosophes*, would discuss the important issues of the day rather than plan a constitutional convention.

(B) is wrong because this meeting is a salon in which the enlightened thinkers, or *philosophes*, would discuss the important issues of the day rather than evaluate an art exhibit.

(C) is wrong because this meeting is a salon in which the enlightened thinkers, or *philosophes*, would discuss the important issues of the day rather than observe a fashion show.

**(D) is CORRECT because this meeting is a salon in which the enlightened thinkers, or *philosophes*, would discuss the important issues of the day.**

6. (A) is wrong because salons did not affect the general population at all; they were merely for the social elite to discuss important issues without government or religious censorship.

**(B) is CORRECT because the social elites meeting at the salons were able to avoid religious and governmental censorship by speaking their ideas rather than publishing them, and thus were able to shift the control of knowledge and thought away from the Church.**

(C) is wrong because salons did not challenge the social order and because the nobility had already been subjugated in France a century earlier.

(D) is wrong because the economy of France was not fixed at this time, and these meetings had nothing to do with economic planning for France.

7. (A) is wrong because, although there would be many constitutional monarchists at a salon, many would disagree with that idea. In contrast, they would all agree that reason could be used to improve society.

(B) is wrong because, although there would be many republicans at a salon, none would have supported universal suffrage.

**(C) is CORRECT because most people at a salon would agree that reason could be used to improve society.**

(D) is wrong because many would disagree with Pangloss's assertion in *Candide* because they saw so much that could be done to improve society.

8. (A) is wrong because the salons were discussion groups; the participants did not try to rewrite the constitution.

**(B) is CORRECT because Madame Geoffrin was a major supporter of the *Encyclopédie* created by Denis Diderot, and her guests often wrote articles for it.**

(C) is wrong because the salon was not engaged in writing a satire about the Dutch.

(D) is wrong because, although they were trying to collect knowledge, the participants wanted to write their own books rather than collect others.

# UNIT 5

# Conflict, Crisis, and Reaction in the Late 18th Century

## Unit 5 Overview: The French Revolution, Napoleon, and the Congress of Vienna

**Unit description:** This unit covers the causes and consequences of the most glorified political uprising in European history, the French Revolution. This revolution and its aftermath, including the rise and fall of Napoleon Bonaparte, had significant political and social impacts across the Continent. This is the final unit in the second period because the fall of Napoleon was such a significant event in the history of Europe that the College Board decided to end the period with it. This unit is central to understanding the political and social movements that took place afterward. It also marks a turning point toward the power of the masses increasing. This unit expects students to incorporate five of the seven themes of European history into their understanding of the period: *Cultural and Intellectual Developments, Social Organization and Development, National and European Identity, States and Other Institutions of Power,* and *Technological and Scientific Innovation.*

This unit is mostly focused on the development of political power. However, it does delve into warfare, including tactics and weapons, changing social structures, new scientific and technological innovations, and the power of finances to influence all other outcomes. This unit begins with a good look at Europe before the conflict, and then explores the causes and consequences of the conflict. The rise and fall of Napoleon along with the Congress of Vienna should be put into context. Finally, the entire era is examined through both artistic and political lenses by examining Romanticism and the evolution of political thought from 1450 to the present.  The topics of study for this unit are as follows:

- Contextualizing 18th-century states
- Rise of global markets
- Britain's ascendancy
- French Revolution
- Effects of the French Revolution
- Napoleon's rise, dominance, and defeat
- Congress of Vienna

- Romanticism
- Political developments 1789–1815

Most of the unit is covered in chapter 5, except for the rise of global markets, which already was covered in chapter 4 to preserve the narrative of economic development. The entire unit occurs during time period 2.

# 5

# The French Revolution, Napoleon, and the Congress of Vienna

## Key Terms

- Estate system or *Ancien Régime*
- National Assembly
- Constitution of 1791
- *Declaration of the Rights of Man and of the Citizen*
- *Declaration of the Rights of Woman*
- March on Versailles

- Declaration of Pillnitz
- Bastille
- Civil Constitution of the Clergy
- Liberal phase
- Radical phase
- Code Napoleon
- Concordat of 1801

- Abolition of provinces and division of France into departments
- Secret police
- Nepotism
- Bourbons
- Congress of Vienna
- Women's role in the French Revolution
- Haitian Revolution

## Key People

- Robespierre
- Marat

- Danton
- Jacobins

- Girondins
- Napoleon

## Overview

In 1789, France had a population of about 25 million, a productive economy, rich farmlands, and a culture that dominated the Continent. French was not only the language of diplomacy, but it was also the tongue spoken in most of the courts of Europe. France was the center of the 18th-century Enlightenment. Despite its wealth and influence, France's government was corrupt, inefficient, and in debt; its class structure was archaic and unjust; and its institutions were encrusted with medieval traditionalism. Smoldering class resentments stoked by the ideals and illusions of the Enlightenment, by financial turmoil, and finally, by *famines brought on by bad harvests*, erupted in revolution. The French Revolution began as a moderate attempt at reform, degenerated into radical bloodletting, and then swung back to authoritarianism and a short flirtation with an empire in search of order. Impelled by the ideals of *liberty, equality, fraternity* and by military power, the French Revolution became an international movement that overthrew the feudal structures of the old regime in France and shook the foundations of the political and social order throughout all of Europe.

Napoleon defined an age, 1799–1815. His genius for military success created, in less than a decade, a French empire that stretched across the Continent. His gift for administration and reform implemented the ideals of the Revolution. Ambition, growing nationalism throughout Europe, and unexpected events led to Napoleon's downfall. He lost the cream of his magnificent army in the wasteland of the Russian winter; his campaigns arrayed most of Europe against him when his victories in the field awakened nationalism in the rest of Europe. After his fall in 1815, the old order tried to restore itself at the Congress of Vienna. A balance of power maintained relative peace for a century. However, Europe had entered the age of "-isms," and powerful new social, economic, and political forces redefined the Western world. The rise of the power of the masses had begun.

# The French Revolution

## The Old Regime

A class structure left over from the Middle Ages determined the political and social order of France.

*The First Estate* (<1 percent) consisted of the clergy. Despite comprising a tiny fraction of the population, the Roman Catholic Church of France (Gallican Church) owned 20 percent of the land. The clergy and the Church were exempt from paying taxes. The king also belonged to the First Estate.

*The Second Estate* (2–4 percent) consisted of the nobles, who owned about 20 percent of the land. The nobles were also exempt from taxes.

*The Third Estate* (95–97 percent) consisted of the middle class, urban artisans, and peasants. Although France had developed a significant commercial or middle class, called the *bourgeoisie*, the mass of the people were peasants who lived off of the land.

The Third Estate, especially the peasantry, was subjected to a variety of oppressive taxes:

- *Taille*, a land tax
- Tithe, a Church tax equivalent to 10 percent of annual income
- Income tax
- Poll tax
- Salt tax
- Local duties paid to the feudal lord

Personal freedom was jeopardized by the *lettre de cachet* by which the government could imprison anyone without charges or trial. The bourgeoisie was disenchanted by its lack of influence in a system that it disproportionately supported financially. This restriction of personal freedom went directly against the Enlightenment ideals that supported the public expression of emotions and feelings.

Burdened by debts run up by the wars and extravagances of *Louis XIV* (r. 1643–1715), by the corruption and inefficiency of the administration of his successors, and by France's support of the American Revolution, the government of *Louis XVI* (r. 1774–1792) attempted to tax the previously exempt clergy and nobility. A high court of France, the *Parlement of Paris*, ruled that new taxes could not be levied unless approved by the *Estates-General*, the legislative body equivalent to a parliament representing the three estates mentioned above but that had not met in 175 years.

## European International Relations Before the French Revolution

The commercial revolution and the expansion of international trade set the stage for European rivalries over trade and the balance of power among European nations. States competed with each other as the system of mercantilism spread, and nations tried to increase the gold in their national coffers at the expense of their rivals. Many trade wars erupted between the British and the Dutch over rights to trade in different areas. This also manifested as a battle over naval superiority among the British, Dutch, Spanish, and French over who would control the Atlantic economy. The rivalry between the French and the British intensified until the *Seven Years' War* established British dominance of trade with India and both North American and Dutch control over the East Indies.

## The Seven Years' War

From 1756–1763, the major European powers of Britain, Prussia, Portugal, and some smaller Germanic states allied against France, Austria, Spain, Russia, and Sweden in a war that was the first truly global conflict. It was fought in Europe, the Americas, Africa, and Asia. The war resulted in British dominance of international trade with North America and India. The Dutch, who remained neutral throughout the war, retained control over the Dutch East Indies. This war left France with huge war debts that would be increased by French spending on the American

Revolution in support of the colonial rebels. At the conclusion of the Seven Years' War, Britain emerged as the dominant power in Europe, taking the place that France formerly held.

## Timeline: The First or Liberal Stage of the Revolution (1789–1792)

**MAY 5, 1789:** The Estates-General met at Versailles for the first time in 175 years. Each estate had traditionally received one vote for the whole estate, and disputes about how voting should be counted erupted. There were more members of the Third Estate at the meeting than the other two estates combined. So members of the Third Estate wanted each member to have one vote rather than each estate having only one vote.

**JUNE 13, 1789:** Supported by a few members of the First Estate, the Third Estate broke a voting deadlock in the Estates-General by declaring itself the *National Assembly*.

**JUNE 20, 1789:** After being locked out of their meeting place by the king's troops, members of the National Assembly went to the tennis court in Versailles and swore the *Tennis Court Oath* not to disband until they had written a new constitution for France.

**JULY 14, 1789:** After food riots in the cities, peasant rebellions in the countryside, and the inaction of Louis and his ministers, a Parisian mob stormed the *Bastille*, which was a fortress that symbolized royal injustice. It was a prison and an armory that gave the mob access to weapons. The mob also freed the prisoners, one of whom ironically was a noble who had been imprisoned for abusing peasants.

**AUGUST 4, 1789:** The decrees of this date mark when the National Assembly *abolished feudalism and manorialism*. They marked an end to the feudal system of obligations and land rights that dated back to the fall of the Roman Empire. This was a fundamental challenge to the existing political and social order.

**AUGUST 26, 1789:** The *Declaration of the Rights of Man and of the Citizen* was passed. Freedom of speech, thought, and religion were guaranteed, as was due process of law; taxes could be imposed only by consent of the governed; the right to rule was said to belong not just to the king but to the whole nation.

**AUGUST 1789–1790:** The *Great Fear* swept through the countryside as the Third Estate rose up against the nobility and destroyed feudal records and noble residences. This movement lent strength to the movement to end feudalism.

**OCTOBER 1789:** A Paris mob, mostly of women, was incited by Jean Paul Marat to *march on Versailles* and force the king to relocate to the *Tuileries*, the royal residence in Paris. The National Assembly also went to Paris and was intimidated by the Parisians.

**NOVEMBER 2, 1789:** The National Assembly *seized Church and monastery lands* for revenue.

**1790:** *The Civil Constitution of the Clergy* was drafted. Convents and monasteries were abolished; all clergymen were to be paid by the state and elected by all citizens; the clergy was forbidden to accept the authority of the Pope. Alienated by this decree, half of the priests of the Gallican Church refused to accept it.

**1791:** The National (Constituent) Assembly drafted a new constitution that instituted an *elected Legislative Assembly*, which made the king chief executive officer and largely responsible to the assembly. The National (Constituent) Assembly also established voting qualifications for male citizens.

**JUNE 14, 1791:** The *Le Chapalier Law* was passed banning guilds and the right to strike, which enraged the *sans-culottes*, who were the poorest people in the city.

**JUNE 21, 1791:** The *Flight to Varennes* of the royal family in order to raise a counter-revolutionary army was stopped, and the king and queen became prisoners of the Parisian mob.

**AUGUST 1791:** The *Declaration of Pillnitz* by the king of Austria threatened military action to restore order in France and encouraged the radical revolutionaries who wanted to overthrow the monarchy in defiance of the declaration from foreign aristocrats.

**SEPTEMBER 5, 1791:** The *Declaration of the Rights of Woman and the Female Citizen* was written by Olympe de Gouges. This document reflected the lack of rights of females in the *Declaration of the Rights of Man and of the Citizen* written by the National Assembly. She tried to rally people for gender equality but was accused of treason and executed for it. Nevertheless, although the document did not influence the French Revolution very much, it did make a mark for feminist history.

## Timeline: The Second or Radical Stage of the Revolution (1792–1795)

**APRIL 20, 1792:** The Legislative Assembly, the legislature under the new constitution, *declared war on Austria* in response to an ultimatum. The international *Wars of the French Revolution* began.

**JULY 25, 1792:** The commander of a Prussian army, who was about to invade France, issued the *Brunswick Manifesto*, threatening the people of Paris if harm came to the king. *Jacobin* (radical republican) leaders aroused the Paris mobs.

**AUGUST 10, 1792:** The *Tuileries were stormed*, and the king was taken prisoner; the mobs slaughtered over a thousand priests, bourgeoisie, and aristocrats who opposed the radicals' ambitions.

**SEPTEMBER 21, 1792:** *France was proclaimed a republic*, the first of *five* to come.

**1793:** An appeal to nationalism inspired the French people to drive back invaders. The *First Coalition*, an alliance of Austria, Great Britain, Netherlands, Prussia, and Spain, was organized to combat any French advance. Revolutionary armies, raised by mass conscription, sought to bring the changes initiated in France to the rest of Europe. *This popular support for the revolution against the old order of Europe represented how revolution and war were expressions of the emotional power of mass politics and nationalism.*

The *Jacobins*, supported by the Paris mobs, and the *Girondins*, supported by the peasants in the rural areas, battled for control of the *National Convention*, which was the new assembly under the republic.

One of the most important legacies of the French Revolution was the development of the political spectrum. The concepts of left being liberal and right being conservative have their birth in the fact that the Jacobins sat on the left in the National Assembly and the Girondins sat on the right. The debate between the more radical Jacobins and the more conservative Girondins led to the liberal-conservative battles of the modern era. The political spectrum that most social scientists follow emerged out of the situation in the National Assembly and can be seen below.

## POLITICAL SPECTRUM

RADICAL   LIBERAL   MODERATE   CONSERVATIVE   REACTIONARY

This continuum shows the generally accepted
political spectrum developed from the French Revolution.

*Maximilien Robespierre* (1758–1794), leader of the Jacobins, pushed for execution of the king. Both Louis XVI and his queen, *Marie Antoinette* (1755–1793), were guillotined in January 1793.

**SUMMER 1793:** A dictatorial *Committee of Public Safety* launched the *Reign of Terror*. Over 20,000 people (nearly 75 percent of them working class and peasants) were executed from the summer of 1793 to that of 1794.

**LATE 1793:** The *Republic of Virtue* was proclaimed by the Committee of Public Safety in an attempt to de-Christianize France; it largely alienated the Catholic majority of the nation.

**1794:** When public opinion turned against the excesses of the Reign of Terror, both *Danton* (1759–1794), who was an original Jacobin, and Robespierre, who was leader of the Republic of Virtue, were executed by the National Convention.

## Timeline: The Final or Reactionary Stage of the Revolution (1795–1799)

The *Thermidorian Reaction*, which was the execution of Robespierre, took place during the month of Thermidor (August 18–September 16) on the new non-Christian calendar and returned the moderate bourgeois reformers to power.

**1795–1799:** The *Directory*, a five-member executive committee, was established by the National Convention to run the government. When a Paris mob threatened the new government, *Napoleon Bonaparte* (r. 1799–1815), a young general who by chance was in Paris at the time, put down the riot and was rewarded with command of the French armies fighting the Austrians in Italy.

## Reaction to the French Revolution

While many were inspired by the Revolution's emphasis on equality and human rights, others such as Edmund Burke condemned its violence and disregard for traditional authority.

- Burke's *Reflections on the Revolution in France*, 1793, set the stage for the emergence of conservatism as practiced by *Klemens von Metternich* after Napoleon's reign.
- Mary Wollstonecraft and others in Great Britain and France rejected Burke's thinking, as exemplified by Wollstonecraft's *Vindication of the Rights of Man*, which she wrote in reaction to Burke.
- Enslaved people in Haiti held a revolt and took over their country. To date, this was the first successful revolt of formerly enslaved people in history. This revolt was a direct result of the French Revolution as Haiti was a French colony whose citizens wanted the same freedoms as the French people. *Toussaint L'Ouverture* led this revolt and also defeated Napoleon's soldiers who came to quell the revolt.

# Women's Role in the French Revolution

Women played a major role in the French Revolution. In October of 1789, the revolution was at a turning point. In the midst of a continuing shortage of bread, rumors of counterrevolution spread among the guards and royalty at Versailles. In response, many women (and some men dressed as women) gathered in Paris to march to the royal palace at Versailles to demand an accounting from the king. They marched 12 miles in the rain and were joined by thousands of men. The next day, the crowd became rowdy and eventually broke into the royal apartments, killing two of the king's bodyguards. To prevent further bloodshed, Louis agreed to move his family back to Paris.

Women's participation was not confined to rioting and demonstrating. Women started to participate in meetings of political clubs, and a guarantee of women's rights became a topic of discussion during the revolution. In July of 1790, the Marquis de Condorcet published a newspaper article in support of full political rights for women, which increased the importance of the discussion. He argued that France's women should enjoy equal political rights with men. His ideas were supported by the publication of the *Declaration of the Rights of Woman* by Olympe de Gouges and the subsequent defense, *Vindication of the Rights of Woman*, by Mary Wollstonecraft in 1791. In the end, the women of France would have to wait until after the First World War to gain legal rights that approached those of men because the French Republic and the Napoleonic Code gave women a lower legal status than men.

# Cause-and-Effect Chart for the French Revolution

If you can understand and retain the information on this chart, then you are ready for any question that the AP exam asks about the French Revolution.

---

**1. The Estates-General met for the first time in 175 years**
**Cause:** The French nation had seen famine and economic collapse. The Estates-General had not met in 175 years but was convened in order to raise taxes after the Parliament of Paris refused to do so.
**Effect:** The meeting unified the nobility with the Third Estate. They took the Tennis Court Oath, promising not to leave until they had created a constitution for France.

**2. *Declaration of the Rights of Man***
**Cause:** The monarchy consolidated power through the intendant system; both the crops and the economy failed. These woes, along with the ideas of the Enlightenment and the American Revolution, led to the demand for a French constitution at the Storming of the Bastille, which helped to create such a constitution.
**Effect:** The French Revolution began in earnest with the Great Fear, and the path was cleared for the creation of the National Assembly.

**3. The Great Fear**
**Cause:** The pent-up aggression of the Third Estate was unleashed as a reaction to the *Declaration of the Rights of Man.*
**Effect:** A chasm developed between the nobility and the peasantry. Factions formed in France about what the new government should look like and how it should act.

**4. Formation of the National Assembly**
**Cause:** The disintegration of order in France and the *Declaration of the Rights of Man* led to the formation of the National Assembly, or Constituent Assembly, in order to make a constitution and rule the country.
**Effect:** The National Assembly created a constitution that allowed for election of a legislative assembly with the king at the helm. The king then tried to escape with his family.

**5. Attempted escape of Louis XVI and family**
**Cause:** The revolutionary mood in France made the king and his family fear more for their lives than for their titles and possessions.
**Effect:** This further cemented national sentiment against the royal family and was a factor in their later execution.

**6. The Legislative Assembly declared war on Austria**
**Cause:** The Declaration of Pillnitz saw Austria try to intervene in French affairs by pursuing military action to protect the monarchy.
**Effect:** The *sans-culottes* and the radicals came together with support building all over France against foreign invasion.

**7. Radicals and *sans-culottes* gain power**

**Cause:** The pendulum of change had been held to the right for so long that it swung far in the other direction. Pent-up aggression from the Third Estate led to the most demagogical leaders gaining power: *Marat, Danton*, and *Robespierre*.

**Effect:** Revolutionary zeal swept the common people of France. Society was turned upside down, and the Reign of Terror eventually resulted.

**8. The National Convention was formed**

**Cause:** The new constitution, which created the First Republic, called for a National Assembly to be formed.

**Effect:** This body was very politically biased with the radical Jacobin Party in power. The modern-day terms *right* for conservative and *left* for liberal came from the seating arrangement in this body.

**9. The Jacobin Club gained prominence**

**Cause:** The radical mood of Paris and the overwhelming support of the poor and the peasants led the radical Jacobin Party to gain power. The powerful demagogues mentioned in box 7 and France's military needs also contributed.

**Effect:** The revolution went through a second stage that was more radical and is sometimes known as the *Reign of Terror*.

**10. Execution of King Louis XVI**

**Cause:** This was the radical turn of the revolution. The king's alliance with Austria and his life of excess and poor national management led to his execution.

**Effect:** The other nations of Europe condemned France. The revolution turned more radical as it became clear that no one who opposed the revolution was safe in France.

**11. Committee of Public Safety oversaw the Reign of Terror**

**Cause:** The radical mood of Paris, the rise of radicals, and the execution of the king combined to lead the Third Estate to kill over 20,000, most of whom were in the Third Estate. Anyone associated with nobility was in danger, and many innocents were executed at the guillotine.

**Effect:** Many abroad opposed the revolution, and the Reign of Terror soon convinced many French that the revolution had gone too far.

**12. End of the Reign of Terror and rise of the Directory**

**Cause:** The leadership of the Committee of Public Safety turned on each other. By 1794, Marat, Robespierre, and Danton were dead, the last two killed as enemies of the revolution. The radical phase had run its course, and the people wanted stability.

**Effect:** France was ruled by moderates, and many of the *sans-culottes* felt abandoned by the revolution.

**13. Napoleon rose to power**

**Cause:** There was definitely a power vacuum. The nation was looking for a strong leader to emerge, which Napoleon did in style. He was a brilliant general and a lesser noble who was not a part of the establishment but who understood power very well.

**Effect:** Napoleon took over France and conquered most of Europe. He instituted reforms of the law and instituted freedom of religion across the Continent. He also unified Italy for the first time in centuries and unified Germany for the first time ever. His legacy was a reorganization of European power at the Congress of Vienna after his defeat.

## Summary of Social Change During the French Revolution

In many ways, the onslaught of the French Revolution was an example of Europeans attempting to use rational and empirical thought to challenge traditional values and ideals. It was a spread of the ideas on constitutionalism of John Locke from Great Britain to the Continent. At the same time, religion was becoming increasingly a matter of private rather than public concern. The increased population made possible by the Agricultural Revolution caused strains on social and political norms. The disappearance of the plague and the introduction of a smallpox vaccine significantly reduced death rates as well. The consumer revolution explained in the previous chapter led to higher expectations of political freedom as well. New consumer goods from abroad, such as porcelain, tobacco, sugar, and tea, also changed society. Other consumer goods, such as mirrors, printed art, and linens, also became more abundant as consumer society emerged.

# Napoleon

In 1799, after spectacular victories against the Austrians and later against British armies in Egypt, Napoleon overthrew the Directory in a coup d'état and formed a new government, the *Consulate*. The Consulate was made up of three consuls, with Napoleon as head consul.

## Napoleon's Domestic Reforms

Even as emperor, Napoleon was committed to many of the ideals of the French Revolution. He was an outsider to Paris, raised on Corsica (which had only recently become French), and without wealth or connections, which makes his meteoric rise even more noteworthy. Napoleon reached the heights he did because the French Revolution opened society to men of ability. His reforms assured the dissolution of the *old regime* by establishing egalitarianism in government, before the law, and in educational opportunity for men.

- In *The Concordat of 1801*, the papacy renounced claims over Church property seized during the French Revolution. Napoleon was also allowed to nominate bishops.
  - In return, those priests who had resisted the Civil Constitutions of the clergy replaced those who had sworn an oath to the state.
  - Since the Pope gave up claims to Church lands, those citizens who had acquired the lands pledged loyalty to Napoleon's government.
- With the *Code Napoleon*, 1804, Napoleon replaced varied and inequitable medieval law with a uniform legal system.
  - This became a model for codes of law in many European countries.
- In 1808, Napoleon instituted a *state-supported educational system* with rigorous standards and made it available to the masses.
- He created a *merit system* to recruit and reward those in government, despite the fact that Napoleon practiced flagrant *nepotism* by placing his relatives onto the thrones of nations he conquered.
- He lowered the taxes on farmers.
- Napoleon guaranteed that the redistributed Church lands remained in the hands of their new owners, who were mostly peasant farmers.
- He created an *independent peasantry* that became the backbone of French democracy.

## Napoleon's Conquests and Defeats

Napoleon's aim was to unite Europe under France's leadership. In a decade, he was able to conquer vastly more territory and to influence the destinies of more nations than the Sun King, Louis XIV, had during his 72-year reign. Napoleon's very success convinced the peoples he conquered or battled with that their future lied in national unity. The force of nationalism eventually led to his downfall and shaped the destiny of Europe well into the 20th century. Napoleon's *new military tactics* allowed him to exert direct or indirect control over much of the European continent, spreading the ideals of the French Revolution across Europe. These tactics included the use of "light" artillery, forcing a pitched battle from the front and then sending a cavalry charge from behind, and the use of professional ambulance corps and a professional supply system.

Napoleon had the largest army that Europe had ever seen. In some battles of the wars to defend France after the revolution, more than one million soldiers were on the field for France at once. This large revolutionary army was infused with patriotism for France and the ideals of the French Revolution to promote liberty, equality, and fraternity. The soldiers in this army were conscripted and forced to join the army. As Napoleon brought them across Europe during his conquests, the soldiers themselves wanted to promote changes to conquered areas that matched their revolutionary ideals. The export of the Napoleonic Code to the conquered territories exemplified this spreading of revolutionary ideals.

*Italy:* In 1797, Napoleon's victories led to a northern Italian republic, the *Cisalpine*, and to several satellites in central and southern Italy under French control.

- By 1809, Napoleon controlled virtually all of Italy, abolishing feudalism and reforming the social, political, and economic structures.
- He practiced nepotism by placing family members onto many European thrones.
- Revolutionary ideals inspired a slave revolt led by *Toussaint l'Overture* in the French colony of Saint Domingue, which became the independent nation of Haiti in 1804 despite Napoleon sending troops to put down the rebellion. This was Napoleon's first defeat.
- He decided against *national* unity for the Italians, who had been divided into competing city-states and kingdoms during the Middle Ages, because unity might pose a threat to French dominance of the region.

*Germany:* After soundly defeating the two most powerful and influential German states, Austria and Prussia, Napoleon reorganized Germany.

- He consolidated many of the nearly 300 independent political entities (among these consolidations was the *Confederation of the Rhine*).
- Napoleon abolished feudalism and carried out reforms.
- He awakened German nationalism.

## The Continental System

Through a series of shifting alliances, the British consistently opposed the upset of the European balance of power brought about by French victories on the Continent. So Napoleon decided to engage in economic warfare rather than launch an actual invasion of the island. This economic warfare was called the *Continental System*.

- Since he was unable to overcome British supremacy at sea and invade, Napoleon decided to starve Britain out by closing the ports of the Continent to British commerce.
- He coerced Russia, which was then a temporary ally of the French, defeated enemy Prussia, neutral Denmark, neutral Portugal, and French satellite Spain all to adhere to the boycott.
- This policy was a complete failure and caused inflation and dissent in his empire, contributing to Napoleon's downfall.

*Spain:* When Napoleon tried to tighten his control over Spain by replacing the Spanish king with one of his own brothers, the Spanish waged a costly *guerrilla war* that was aided by the British under one of their most able commanders, the *Duke of Wellington* (1769–1852).

*Russia:* Napoleon *invaded Russia* in June of 1812 when the Russians withdrew from the Continental System. That system was preventing Russia from trading with Great Britain and was causing Russian economic hardship.

- Napoleon assembled more than 600,000 of his best soldiers and marched into Russia, only to be met by *scorched-earth* tactics rather than pitched battle.
  - The Russians destroyed all materials that could be foraged for Napoleon's army and attacked in skirmishes only at strategically advantageous points.
- Napoleon's army took Moscow. Due to the city being burned, his stretched supply lines, and the oncoming winter, he retreated.
- He returned from Russia with only about 22,000 soldiers.
- This devastated Napoleon's army and diminished his image.

## The Collapse of the Napoleonic Empire

Napoleon's empire was in disarray after his defeat in Russia. The other powers he had defeated saw his vulnerability and unified to attack him.

- Napoleon lost 500,000 of his 600,000-man Grand Army in Russia.
- Riots occurred in Italy against his rule.
- The British invaded southern France using Wellington's army.
- Napoleon was defeated by the combined forces of Russia, Prussia, and Austria in October 1813 at the *Battle of Leipzig*, also known as the *Battle of Nations*.
  - *Napoleon abdicated* as emperor on April 4, 1814.
  - The *Bourbons* were restored to the throne of France in the person of *Louis XVIII* (r. 1814–1824).
  - Napoleon was exiled to the island of *Elba* in the Mediterranean.
  - France surrendered all territory gained since the international wars of the French Revolution began in 1792.
  - King Louis created a legislature that represented only the upper classes.
  - The restoration, however, maintained most of Napoleon's reforms such as the Code Napoleon, the concordat with the Pope, and the abolition of feudalism.

## Romanticism Emerges

At the end of the Enlightenment, Jean-Jacques Rousseau began to question the cold logic of that era and shot off the opening salvo in a debate that still rages today about emotional ways of knowing things. Rousseau and the Romantic artists, writers, and composers who emerged after him argued for the importance of emotion and sentimentality. In some ways, the Romantic era of art is a rejection of both the Enlightenment logic and the changes to society brought on by industrialization and urbanization. Romanticism will be covered in much greater detail in chapter 8 and will explain many of the creative minds of the era. Romanticism also witnessed a religious revival as demonstrated by the success of *John Wesley*'s campaign to spread his *Methodist* religion with a new message of hope that all could achieve salvation regardless of wealth or past deeds. The French Revolution also demonstrated the power of mass politics for the first time, which played into the messages of personal participation in bettering oneself, one's nation, and the world found in the Romantic movement. In many ways, Napoleon's conquest of Europe spread Romanticism across the Continent, with nationalism being a key component of the Romantic philosophy.

## The Congress of Vienna (September 1814–June 1815)

Representatives of the major powers of Europe, including France, met to redraw territorial lines and to restore, as far as was possible, the social and political order that existed before the French Revolution and Napoleon. The *rule of legitimacy* was one primary goal: to return the "rightful" rulers of Europe to their thrones. A return to a balance of power that would guarantee peace was the other goal.

The August assemblage consisted of *Klemens von Metternich* (1773–1859), chancellor of Austria; Viscount *Castlereagh* (1769–1822), foreign minister of Great Britain; *Czar Alexander of Russia* (r. 1801–1825); *Prince Hardenberg* of Prussia; and *Charles Maurice de Talleyrand* (1754–1838), foreign minister of France. Metternich, Castlereagh, and Talleyrand constituted the first "Big 3" in European history.

## The Settlement

To prevent her future expansion, France was surrounded by a number of strong states:

- A newly united Holland and Belgium, called the Kingdom of the Netherlands
- A Prussian satellite area on the Rhine
- Austrian buffer states in Northern Italy

In Germany, Napoleon's reorganization remained. The 300 originally independent states were reduced to 39. The Habsburg Holy Roman Empire was not reestablished.

## The Hundred Days

*The Hundred Days* began on March 1, 1815, when Napoleon managed to escape from his exile in Elba and made it to the south of France with a small honor guard of less than 100 men, marching, to popular acclaim, into Paris.

- Napoleon raised an army.
- He defeated a Prussian army in Belgium.
- He was defeated on June 18 at *Waterloo*, in Belgium, by the Duke of Wellington and Prussian General Gebhard von Blücher.
- Napoleon was imprisoned on the island of *St. Helena* in the South Atlantic and died there on May 5, 1821.

*The Concert of Europe* was created in November 1815 by a coalition known as the *Quadruple Alliance*: Great Britain, Prussia, Russia, and Austria.

- Its aim was to maintain the status quo that the Congress of Vienna had established, upholding the territorial boundaries and shoring up the monarchies of Europe against the spread of revolutionary ideas, such as *republicanism* (that the people should elect their rulers).
- The *Holy Alliance* of Austria, Prussia, and Russia was formed to prevent dual economic and political revolutions from occurring anywhere in Europe.
- In effect, the members of this alliance pledged to send their armies to any area intent on destroying monarchies and the status quo. The Holy Alliance, the Concert of Europe, and the Quadruple Alliance were effective in the short term at preventing republican and economic revolutions in Poland, Italy, and Spain. They also contributed to the failure of the Decembrists in Russia.
- Belgium did gain independence in 1830.
- In 1848, all bets were off when most of Europe erupted into short-lived revolution, and Metternich fled to England.

Even though the Quadruple Alliance did not last for long, the balance of power created by the Congress of Vienna prevented a general war for a hundred years.

## Criticism of Napoleon

Napoleon was criticized by his contemporaries and by historians for many of his practices. He curtailed the freedoms of his own people through *police censorship*, *limitation of women's rights*, and his use of *secret police* to spy on his own people. He also used nepotism to appoint family members to positions of rule and ignited nationalism across the Continent in reaction to his conquests. He was egotistical to the point that he designed his own tomb so that those who wished to view him must bow to him.

# Practice Questions

## Long Essay

These questions are samples of the various types of thematic essays on the AP exam. See pages 27–28 for a detailed explanation of each type. Check over the generic rubric (see pages 28–29) before you begin any of these essays, and use that rubric to score your essay if you write one.

## Question 1

Compare the stages of the French Revolution.

### Comments on Question 1

This is a *compare* skill question. So be sure to describe the similarities and differences between each stage of the French Revolution (moderate, radical, and reactionary). You must also account for or explain the reasons for the similarities and differences between each phase by providing specific examples of how they were similar and different and by tying that to the overall course of the French Revolution or the bigger fight for individual rights and sovereignty through specific evidence. The "differences" part of this question is easy since the various stages of the Revolution have significant differences: the groups, personalities, and methods are glaringly different in each. The tough part of this question is to detail what the stages had in common, what their similarities were. Each had a form of government, a type of leadership, a constitution, a legislative body, and its own goals. Sort them out and stress their similarities.

## Question 2

Analyze the way the attempt of Louis XVI to raise taxes to pay off the debts of his government precipitated the French Revolution.

### Comments on Question 2

This is a *causation* question because it requires you to explain how one factor, Louis's attempt to raise taxes, resulted in a specific outcome, the French Revolution. Remember to describe the causes and/or effects of the French Revolution and to support your analysis of those causes with specific details. The essay must explain the reasons why Louis's attempts to pay off his huge debts resulted in the French Revolution—citing specific evidence as support. To answer this question, the essay must apply all the meanings of the term "analyze." It must determine the relationship between the revolution and Louis's attempt to raise taxes. The assembling of the Estates-General for the first time in almost 175 years started the chain of events. You must examine the sequence of events in detail. Class factionalism in the Estates-General led to the creation of the National Assembly. You must also explain why this particular attempt to raise taxes was significantly different from previous attempts. Louis wanted to tax the First and Second Estates, which had been exempt from paying taxes since the Middle Ages.

## Question 3

To what extent did Napoleon's successes in battle awaken the nationalistic forces that defeated him?

### Comments on Question 3

This is a *causation* question because it requires you to explain how one factor, Napoleon's successes in battle, resulted in a specific outcome, awakening nationalistic forces that defeated him. Remember to describe the causes and/or effects of Napoleon's defeat, supporting your analysis of those causes with specific details. To get the second point, your essay must explain the reasons for Napoleon's military success awakening the forces that defeated him—citing specific evidence as support. The strategy is simple; show how his victories over specific states led to increased nationalism both there and back in France. Napoleon's installation of relatives as heads of state, his weakening of Habsburg power, and his addiction to winning victories should also be mentioned. Perhaps the most important factor to cite is that Napoleon united Germany and Italy, a feat that the Germans and Italians themselves had failed to accomplish.

## Question 4

To what extent and in what ways did the Congress of Vienna restore the old order in Europe?

### Comments on Question 4

This question clearly calls for you to analyze *continuity and change over time* (CCOT). Be sure to describe the level of historical continuity and change. When discussing historical continuity, explain what did not change from the old order after the Congress of Vienna redrew the map of Europe. When discussing change, explain how national security, international diplomacy, and national character changed as a result of Napoleon's defeat. Explain the reasons why European diplomacy and the balance of power were altered—citing specific evidence as support. Here the essay must examine in detail as well as determine relationships. How and how much did the Congress of Vienna restore the old order? What had the old order been? How did the French Revolution and Napoleon's campaigning change it? What provisions of the Congress of Vienna dealt with the old order? What was the overall result, both immediately and in the long term?

## Short-Answer

1. Use the passages below and your knowledge of European history to answer all parts of the following question.

### Source 1

Napoleon was synonymous with the history of Europe for almost two decades. His influence on events was so immense that he was adored and feared by the people he ruled and those whom he conquered. He brought a set of legal codes with him to all of the territory he controlled. His reach was immense, as was his desire for order and logic. France under Napoleon was at its zenith of international power and has declined ever since his fall. Also, Napoleon is indirectly responsible for the emergence of many of the current nations of Europe, such as Germany and the Czech Republic. He was a figure so grand and so spectacular that King Louis Philippe brought his remains back from St. Helena, where he died, to be entombed at Les Invalides, where the tradition of bowing to the tomb is a homage that onlookers must perform to see the tomb, a perfect epitaph.

—Historian Burke Arielle

**Source 2**

Napoleon may have been a dominating figure in European history, but he was a flash in the pan compared to the reigns of figures like Otto von Bismarck or Louis XIV. He had to work to ensure his own legacy after his imprisonment on St. Helena by writing about his own posterity. He may have been good for France for a short while, but his actions led to the creation of European nationalism and sowed the seeds for France's greatest defeats. He himself designed his own tomb so that all viewers would have to bow down to him in order to see his grave.

—Historian Jessica Gillespie

(a)  Based on source 1, briefly analyze the positive aspects of the reign of Napoleon for the European continent.

(b)  Based on source 2, briefly analyze the negative aspects of the reign of Napoleon for the European continent.

(c)  What role did international trade play in the rise and fall of Napoleon?

2.  Use the following legislation and your knowledge of European history to answer all parts of the question that follows.

ARTICLE I. The National Assembly hereby completely abolishes the feudal system. It decrees that, among the existing rights and dues, both feudal and *censuel*, all those originating in or representing real or personal serfdom shall be abolished without indemnification. All other dues are declared redeemable, the terms and mode of redemption to be fixed by the National Assembly. Those of the said dues which are not extinguished by this decree shall continue to be collected until indemnification shall take place.

II. The exclusive right to maintain pigeon houses and dovecotes is abolished. The pigeons shall be confined during the seasons fixed by the community. During such periods they shall be looked upon as game, and every one shall have the right to kill them upon his own land.

III. The exclusive right to hunt and to maintain uninclosed warrens is likewise abolished, and every land-owner shall have the right to kill, or to have destroyed on his own land, all kinds of game, observing, however, such police regulations as may be established with a view to the safety of the public.

—National Assembly

(a)  Briefly explain ONE economic development that led to the changes asked for in the piece of legislation above.

(b)  Briefly explain ONE political result of the ideas in the legislative document above.

(c)  Briefly explain ONE social change brought on as a result of the ideas in the legislation above.

## Multiple-Choice

**Questions 1–3 refer to the following excerpt from *"What is the Third Estate?"* by Emmanuel Joseph Sieyès in 1789.**

Who then shall dare to say that the Third Estate has not within itself all that is necessary for the formation of a complete nation? It is the strong and robust man who has one arm still shackled. If the privileged order should be abolished, the nation would be nothing less, but something more. Therefore, what is the Third Estate? Everything;

but an everything shackled and oppressed. What would it be without the privileged order? Everything, but an everything free and flourishing. Nothing can succeed without it; everything would be infinitely better without the others.

It is not sufficient to show that privileged persons, far from being useful to the nation, cannot but enfeeble and injure it; it is necessary to prove further that the noble order does not enter at all into the social organization; that it may indeed be a burden upon the nation.

1. The assertion made by Sieyès above—that the Third Estate is everything—is best supported by which of the following?

   (A) The Third Estate included over 95 percent of the French population.
   (B) The Third Estate was the most powerful political body in France at the start of 1789.
   (C) The Third Estate was unified and equal within its own estate.
   (D) The Third Estate was supporting a foreign invasion of France.

2. Which of the following best describes the role of *"What is the Third Estate?"* in the French Revolution?

   (A) It was a rallying cry for the nobility, who used it to get foreign aid.
   (B) It steadied the soldiers as they prepared to meet the Austrians in battle.
   (C) It was a catalyst that helped get the people of France ready to revolt against their king.
   (D) It refuted the logic of the Enlightenment and embraced raw emotion instead.

3. The reform of the French Revolution that was most consistent from the French Revolution onward was which of the following?

   (A) The people had increased participation in shaping the direction of France.
   (B) The Roman Catholic Church lost all power within France.
   (C) A constitutional monarchy was created.
   (D) The hereditary privileges of the nobility were abolished.

**Questions 4–6 refer to the following chart of the deaths during the Reign of Terror in France from March 1793 to August 1794.**

| Social Class | Number Killed | Percentage of People in That Estate of All Executed | Percentage of Population |
|---|---|---|---|
| None given | | 1% | |
| Clergy (First Estate) | 920 | 7% | 0.5% |
| Nobility (Second Estate) | 1,158 | 8% | 1.5% |
| Middle class | 3,452 | 25% | 4% |
| Working class | 4,399 | 31% | 8% |
| Peasants/farmers | 3,961 | 28% | 86% |
| **Total** | 13,890 | 100% | 100% |

4. Which of the following groups saw the highest percentage of its members executed during the Reign of Terror?

(A) The working class

(B) The middle class

(C) The clergy

(D) The nobility

5. Who or which of the following did NOT help control governmental power in France during the Reign of Terror?

(A) Napoleon Bonaparte

(B) Maximillian Robespierre

(C) Georges Danton

(D) The Committee of Public Safety

6. The immediate cause of the outbreak of revolution in 1789 was which of the following?

(A) Grinding poverty among all classes of society

(B) Government oppression

(C) The ideas of the *philosophes*

(D) The government's financial crisis

## Answers and Explanations

### Short-Answer Explanations

1. (a) You should explain the unity Napoleon brought to Europe as well as the freedoms he guaranteed to the peoples of Europe in his *Napoleonic Code*. The rise of France to controlling most of Europe should also be noted. Other aspects that may be taken into account include his military genius; his ability, through charisma, to make people believe in him; his saving of many ideals of the French Revolution; his keen political mind; and the patriotism he expanded in France and later throughout the Continent as a reaction to his conquest of the Continent.

(b) You should begin with his huge ego and shortsightedness. You may then explain how Napoleon's legacy was bad for France by citing how his legacy led to many tragedies for France and for Europe, including the Franco-Prussian War, the two world wars, the growth of nationalism as a force, the continued subjugation of women, nepotism, and trade wars.

(c) This part must examine the Continental System and how Napoleon attempted to prevent the rest of Europe from trading with Britain. It should also explain that Napoleon invaded Russia, his costliest and most foolish military maneuver, to enforce the Continental System when Russia began to trade with Britain. Partial credit can be given for an explanation of the Battle of Trafalgar and how the British exerted their dominance of the sea after that point in history for over a century, enriching Great Britain at the expense of the rest of the Continent.

2. (a) You should explain the conditions under the *Ancien Régime* that divided France into three estates with privileges based upon the family into which one was born. The growth of the commercial revolution and economic prosperity for some should be examined as a cause for the people wanting more political freedom. The bankruptcy of France and the famine of 1787–1789 within the country could also be used as economic explanations of the worsening conditions for the emerging middle and lower classes in France.

(b) You should explain one of the political results of the French Revolution. These results range from the rise of Robespierre, to the rise of Napoleon, to the creation of the National Convention, to the battle for power between the Girondins and Jacobins, to the Great Panic, and to the Reign of Terror. The rise of France as an international military power again may also be mentioned as a political result.

(c) You should discuss the complete transformation of French society, for example with former street urchins such as the *sans-culottes* gaining power. You can discuss the death of over 20,000 in the Reign of Terror, revolutionary colors becoming fashionable, adults calling each other "citizen," the long tradition from 1789 to the present of French people engaging in protests against their governments or other institutions, the rise of the middle class, and/or the ideals of equality, brotherhood, and freedom being adopted (liberty, equality, and fraternity).

## Practice Multiple-Choice Questions

1. **(A) is CORRECT because the fact that the Third Estate was 95 percent of France supports the idea that the Third Estate was everything and would have been better without the nobility and the clergy.**

   (B) is wrong because the Third Estate had very little political power in 1789 until the French Revolution began in July.

   (C) is wrong because the Third Estate was stratified and divided between many social levels of people.

   (D) is wrong because the Third Estate never supported foreign invasion of France.

2. (A) is wrong because the nobility were not helped in any way by this document and did not use it to get aid.

   (B) is wrong because this document was written before the French Revolution to incite the people to revolt against an unfair feudal system. It did nothing to help soldiers prepare to meet Austrians in battle.

   **(C) is CORRECT because this document was written before the French Revolution to incite the people to revolt against an unfair feudal system.**

   (D) is wrong because this document relied on the logic of the Enlightenment to argue that France needed a new social structure.

3. (A) is wrong because the participation of the people in politics increased and decreased over the next century, depending on who was ruling France.

   (B) is wrong because the Roman Catholic Church in France did lose influence, then regained it, and then lost it again.

   (C) is wrong because the constitutional monarchy in France appeared, then disappeared, then reappeared, and then disappeared.

   **(D) is CORRECT because, after feudal privileges were suspended, they were never reinstated.**

4. (A) is wrong because the clergy at just ½ of 1 percent of the population made up 7 percent of the executed, making their death rate 14 percent of the total per 1 percent of population, while the working class saw a death rate of about 4 percent per 1 percent of population.

   (B) is wrong because the clergy at just ½ of 1 percent of the population made up 7 percent of the executed, making their death rate 14 percent of the total per 1 percent of population, while the middle class saw a death rate of about 6.25 percent per 1 percent of population.

   **(C) is CORRECT because the clergy at just ½ of 1 percent of the population made up 7 percent of the executed, making their death rate 14 percent of the total per 1 percent of population.**

   (D) is wrong because the clergy, at just ½ of 1 percent of the population, made up 7 percent of the executed, making their death rate 14 percent of the total per 1 percent of population, while the nobility saw a death rate of about 5.3 percent per 1 percent of population.

5.  **(A)  is CORRECT because Napoleon did not hold power until after overthrowing the Directory in a coup d'état in 1799.**

    (B)  is wrong because Robespierre did hold political power during the Reign of Terror.

    (C)  is wrong because Danton did hold political power during the Reign of Terror.

    (D)  is wrong because the Committee of Public Safety was the sole holder of all political power during the Reign of Terror.

6.  (A)  is wrong because, although there was poverty, there always had been poverty in France; so poverty was nothing new.

    (B)  is wrong because government oppression, although present, did not lead directly to the revolution.

    (C)  is wrong because, although the ideas of the *philosophes* were long-term causes of the revolution, the meeting of the Estates-General and the events that followed were directly caused by a financial crisis in France.

    **(D)  is CORRECT because the meeting of the Estates-General and the events that followed were directly caused by a financial crisis in France.**

---

Visit Barron's Online Learning Hub to take the Time Period Two (1649–1815) Practice Assessment

# Time Period Three: c. 1815 to c. 1914

## Learning Objectives

These are the Key Concepts for time period 3, according to the *AP European History Curriculum Framework*:

→ **KEY CONCEPT 3.1** The Industrial Revolution spread from Great Britain to the Continent, where the state played a greater role in promoting industry.

→ **KEY CONCEPT 3.2** The experiences of everyday life were shaped by industrialization, depending on the level of industrial development in a particular location.

→ **KEY CONCEPT 3.3** Political revolutions and the complications resulting from industrialization triggered a range of ideological, governmental, and collective responses.

→ **KEY CONCEPT 3.4** European states struggled to maintain international stability in an age of nationalism and revolutions.

→ **KEY CONCEPT 3.5** A variety of motives and methods led to the intensification of European global control and increased tensions among the Great Powers.

→ **KEY CONCEPT 3.6** European ideas and culture expressed a tension between objectivity and scientific realism on one hand, and subjectivity and individual expression on the other.

## Time Period Overview

This time period is about the industrialization of Continental Europe; the growth of nationalism, modernization, and urbanization; the spread of imperialism; conflicts between competing economic and political theories; the birth of existentialism; and the struggles to replace absolute monarchies with constitutional governments that gave citizens a voice in politics across the Continent. This time period examines how the industrialization of Europe led to urbanization and social problems. These, in turn, led to changes in government and in people's expectations of their governments. The fragile stability of the European balance of power is examined in detail through the assessment of many alliance systems of the era. The European dominance of the rest of the world is assessed from many perspectives. This time period includes the traditional delineations of the following eras:

- The Industrial Revolution
- The Age of Metternich (1815–1848)
- Nationalism
- Imperialism

These traditional delineations do overlap in many ways. The themes within them, as stated above in the key concepts, can be seen woven through the next three chapters of this book. The College Board has created two units to cover the time period. There is one unit called Industrialization and Its Effects, which also discusses the Age of Metternich. There is another unit that combines nationalism and imperialism into one unit entitled 19th-Century

Perspectives and Political Developments. Each unit is comprised of two chapters for this time period. The first unit (unit 6) consists of chapters 6 and 7, which discuss industrialization and the Age of Metternich, respectively. The second unit (unit 7) consists of chapters 8 and 9, which discuss nationalism and imperialism, respectively.

## SPECIAL NOTE ON PERIODIZATION

As stated in the preface to time period 2, the subject of the Industrial Revolution was split between time periods by the framework for European history. To preserve the continuity of the subject, the Industrial Revolution is covered entirely in chapter 6, which is contained in the period 3 section of this book.

In many ways, the delineation chosen by the College Board for this period makes a lot of sense. One unit examines industrialization and its effects. The other unit looks at the more political and economic side of the same time period through the lenses of nationalism, imperialism, and European cultural dominance of the world. However, it can be challenged because conservatism, communism, socialism, and liberalism are addressed in unit 6 while nationalism, paternalism, imperialism, and social Darwinism are addressed in unit 7, dismissing the relationship between the new economic ideas in unit 6 and the political and economic events of unit 7. This further underscores the problem of *periodization* in European history. The publishers of this book grouped chapters 8 and 9 on nationalism and imperialism, respectively, into the unit on 19th-Century Perspectives and Political Developments while covering Industrialization and Its Effects and the Age of Metternich in chapters 6 and 7. This format is the best compromise to help the student understand the delineations of the College Board but also to be literate in European history and be able to discuss it with other experts.

# UNIT 6
# Industrialization and Its Effects

## Unit 6 Overview: The Industrial Revolution Reshapes Europe

**Unit description:** This unit explains the greatest revolution in scientific and technological innovation that Europe saw. The fact that Europe industrialized before the rest of the world gave the Europeans a huge advantage in dominating the rest of the world. Industrialization made Europe the center of world production, beginning with England. At one point in the early-19th century, England produced almost one-half of the world's output. In 1750, before the Industrial Revolution began, incomes were generally similar all over the world and world wealth was centered in Asia. By 1970, a person in Europe or the United States was, on average, earning 25 times what a person in Asia, Africa, or Latin America was earning. Wealth was centered in the United States and Europe, with Westerners in general owning over 20 times what others did. Europe exploited its advantage in production and weaponry to dominate the rest of the world. The Industrial Revolution was slow and erratic in its spread, beginning in the late-18th century in England and spreading slowly to the rest of the world. In fact, places like Myanmar and Indonesia are just having their Industrial Revolutions now.

Industrialization also brought many changes to society, the economy, and government. The social, economic, and political repercussions of the industrialization of society were immense, with the entire order of society being turned asunder. Everything from gender roles, to political power, to the way people ate and found leisure, to where people lived changed as a result of industrialization. This unit focuses on five of the seven themes of the course that are interwoven throughout the unit: Economic and Commercial Developments, Cultural and Intellectual Developments, States and Other Institutions of Power, Social Organization and Development, and Technological and Scientific Innovation. Like the unit on the Enlightenment, this unit has its main focus on scientific and technological innovation. However, these changes in technology also caused massive changes to society, politics, everyday lives, gender roles, states, and all other kinds of institutions of power, such as the Church. The main topics of study for this unit are the following:

- Contextualizing industrialization using its origins and effects
- The spread of industry throughout Europe
- Second-wave industrialization and its effects
- Social effects of industrialization
- Triumph of conservatism
- Reactions and revolutions
- Ideologies of change and reform movements
- Effects of the "-isms"
- Institutional responses to reform
- Causation in the Age of Industrialization

Most of this information is covered in chapter 6. However, some of the ideologies, "-isms," nationalism, and conservatism are expanded in chapters 7 and 8 on the Age of Metternich and the ideologies of the 19th century, respectively. This is the first unit that affects multiple chapters. This was done to preserve the traditional structure of the study of history that has generally divided this unit into discrete topics of nationalism, conservatism, and industrialization. All topics discussed in this unit took place during time period 3.

# 6

# Industrialization Reshapes Europe

## Key Terms

- Capitalism
- Industrial Revolution
- Medieval common lands
- Proletariat

- Child labor laws
- Factory Act of 1833
- Mines Act of 1842
- Ten Hours Act of 1847

- Bourgeoisie
- Class consciousness
- Utilitarianism
- Socialism

## Key People

- Jeremy Bentham
- John Stuart Mill
- Thomas Malthus

- David Ricardo
- Comte de Saint-Simon
- Karl Marx

- James Watt
- Adam Smith

## SPECIAL NOTE ON PERIODIZATION

Periodization is done based upon many different markers in history. One historian may use political markers such as the Peace of Westphalia, while another may choose economic markers, such as the opening of transatlantic trade and the Columbian Exchange. The *AP European History Curriculum Framework* uses the political markers of the Peace of Westphalia, the Congress of Vienna, and the outbreak of World War One. Unfortunately, social and economic movements do not always fit into the same delineations as political history. The largest problem for the traditional historian in periodization posed by the framework is contained in this chapter. The author believes that it is more important to preserve the narrative of industrialization than to alter the narrative to fit the framework. Therefore, special attention will be given to the periodization outlined in the *AP European History Curriculum Framework* in this chapter to help avoid confusion and to give you ideas about how to display the skill of periodization in your essay. The *AP European History Curriculum Framework* was written to emphasize the use of historical thinking rather than the memorization of facts. The author believes that by offering an alternate sense of periodization compared to that framework, your understanding of that skill and of the many different markers that can be used with periodization will be enhanced.

Great Britain had begun industrialization by the 1790s. It saw industrial output soar and demographics change mightily before the end of the Napoleonic Wars in 1815, when period 2 ended according to the *AP European History Curriculum Framework*. However, in 1815 the Industrial Revolution was just getting into full swing. As yet, parts of Europe had not even seen enclosure or an agricultural revolution, much less an industrial one. So the slow cultural diffusion of enclosure and then industrialization, as well as the fact that its implementation came with bursts and lulls, make fitting this chapter into the framework a challenge. The issues of *urbanization* and the growth of *consumerism* are of particular concern as they occur over both time periods. This chapter addresses the following Key Concepts from the *AP European History Curriculum Framework*.

## Learning Objectives

→ **KEY CONCEPT 2.4** The experiences of everyday life were shaped by demographic, environmental, medical, and technological changes.

→ **KEY CONCEPT 3.1** The Industrial Revolution spread from Great Britain to the Continent, where the state played a greater role in promoting industry.

→ **KEY CONCEPT 3.2** The experiences of everyday life were shaped by industrialization, depending on the level of industrial development in a particular location.

→ **KEY CONCEPT 3.3** Political revolutions and the complications resulting from industrialization triggered a range of ideological, governmental, and collective responses.

## Overview

The Industrial Revolution fostered into existence by the growth of commerce, the development of capitalism, the introduction of improved technology, and the unique political climate in Britain during the 18th century changed life in Western Europe in the 1800s more profoundly than had the French Revolution. The landowning aristocracy, which had its origins in the early Middle Ages and whose decline had begun with the growth of a commercial and professional middle class, lost more wealth and political power with the inception of a spectacularly wealthy capitalist class. The lives of the mass of Europeans shifted from the farm to the factory, from the predictable rhythms of a rural existence to the grinding and impersonal poverty of the industrial cities. Along with the capitalists, a new *proletariat*, or working class, was created. A whole new set of social and economic doctrines sought to explain the rights of the working class and better their lives. The family was reshaped, concepts of time were changed, and trade unions and other organizations promoting social welfare were created. The European balance of power was shifted multiple times by industrial production as first the United Kingdom and then Germany dominated industrial output and thus gained international power. Because industrialization also created the capability to reshape the world, industrialization became a national project with ramifications for those who advanced the slowest or the most quickly. Added to the "-isms" that grew out of the French Revolution—such as republicanism, conservatism, and nationalism—were *socialism* and *Marxism*. By the last third of the 19th century, an Age of Progress, which was a technological revolution, had altered the Western world and led the way into the woes and wonders of the 20th century.

## The Industrial Revolution

Industrialization was never really a revolution or a violent, drastic change. Instead, industrialization has been a continuous and usually gradual process throughout human existence, from the use of the first stone tools to the development of high technology. The so-called *Industrial Revolution* in Europe was a period of rapid development, roughly between *1780 and 1850*, during which new forms of energy from coal and other fossil fuels powered machines rather than muscles, water, or wind. The advent of the steam engine allowed massive amounts of energy to be exerted by machinery, such as the water frame and power looms, that appeared in large factories, where most textile workers began to work. This contrasted markedly with preindustrial society where textiles were made in cottages from thread spun on wheels and fabric was woven on human-powered looms.

Industrialization began in Britain in the second half of the 18th century. It moved to France, Holland, Belgium, and the United States in the second decade of the 19th century. It began in Germany, Austria, and Italy in the middle of the 19th century. Industrialization then arrived in Eastern Europe and Russia at the end of the 19th century and in parts of Asia and Africa well into the 20th century. It carries on today as new technologies continue to reshape society.

## The Agricultural Revolution in Britain

After the Glorious Revolution of 1688, British landowning aristocrats dominated Parliament and passed the *Enclosure Acts*, which fenced off the *medieval common lands*. The *enclosure movement* is the least understood and possibly most important change that happened to legal rights in Europe during its history. The movement took centuries to complete and radically changed the relationships people had with the land, production, and each other.

- The enclosure movement put into place the last of the four needed ingredients for capitalism: land, labor, capital, and markets (entrepreneurs and technology).
- It allowed the struggle for money to be based on factors other than just birth and luck.
- Opportunities for advancement were now there for anyone who had a profitable idea and a work ethic.
- The modern economy began.
- The struggle between capital and labor became a true battle.

## Results of the Enclosure Movement

- Large landowners became prosperous; they invested in technology, which meant machinery, breeding, and improved planting methods. Crop yields and livestock production soared.
- Surplus production enabled agriculture to support a larger population in the cities.
- The population of Britain doubled during the 18th century.
- Small farmers who were displaced by the enclosure movement moved to the cities and made up the growing force of factory workers (the *industrial proletariat*).

## Demographic Changes Altered Lifestyles

The population explosion of the 16th century resulted in both food shortages and food gluts throughout Europe during the 17th and 18th centuries, resulting in mortality disasters. The European marriage pattern, which limited family size, became the most important check on population levels, although some couples also adopted birth control practices to limit family size. By the middle of the 1750s, better weather, improvements in transportation, new crops and agricultural practices, less epidemic disease, and advances in medicine and hygiene meant a reduction of, or end of, the cycle of feast and famine. By the start of the 19th century, reductions in child mortality and increases in life expectancy led to the emergence of new attitudes toward children and families.

- Economic motivations for marriage, while still important for all classes, diminished as the middle-class notion of companionate marriage began to be adopted by the working classes.
- This demographic revolution, along with the rise in prosperity, produced advances in the general standard of living that allowed cultural and intellectual growth for the masses.
  - Greater prosperity was associated with increasing literacy, increasing education, and richer cultural lives. This included the following:
    - The growth of publishing and libraries
    - The founding of schools
    - The establishment of orchestras, theaters, and museums
  - As the 19th century began, it was clear that a large percentage of Europeans were better fed and healthier, lived longer, and were more secure and comfortable in their material well-being than at any previous time in history.
  - This relative prosperity was offset by increasing numbers of the poor throughout Europe.
    - The poor depended upon charitable resources.
    - Their existence distressed government officials and local communities.

- A *consumer revolution* changed the lives of the European people as it spread from the Dutch and British, first to Western Europe and then more slowly southward and toward the East.
  - Consumers demanded new items, such as porcelain, mirrors, manufactured cotton goods, and even printed art.
  - New leisure venues, such as taverns and opera houses, attracted these emerging consumers.
  - Blood sports and betting were also common entertainments for the working classes.
- Family patterns and ideas about privacy began to change.
  - The number of illegitimate births exploded between 1750 and 1850 throughout Europe.
    - Labor became more mobile, and social punishments for moral infractions were no longer easy to enforce.
    - Infant and child mortality decreased, and commercial wealth increased. Families could dedicate more space and resources to children and child rearing as well as to private life and comfort.

## Urbanization

Perhaps the most important change that took place during the 19th century era of industrialization was the huge migration from the rural village to the relative anonymity and fast pace of the cities. A trend that took centuries to spread throughout Europe and one that is still occurring in parts of the world today, *urbanization* is a change that has reshaped human existence.

- Communal values were eroded when families that did not know each other migrated from villages to the big cities.
- Reforms transformed unhealthy and overcrowded cities by modernizing infrastructure, regulating public health, reforming prisons, and establishing modern police forces. The reforms were enacted by governments motivated by such forces as public opinion, prominent individuals, and charity organizations.
- At first, certain areas in cities had large concentrations of many poor people, which led to a greater awareness of poverty, crime, prostitution, and other social problems. This caused many to want better policing of those living on the margins of society.
- Cities experienced overcrowding and filthy living conditions.
- Rural areas suffered labor shortages and weakened communities.
- Social activists brought the problems of the poor to light.
- Cities were redesigned with urban planning and zoning.
- Labor unions were established.
- Governments responded to the problems of urbanization.
- Reformers promoted compulsory public education to advance the goals of public order, nationalism, and economic growth.
- Many nongovernmental organizations were formed, many of which were religious, to assist the poor and end serfdom and slavery.
  - Sunday schools were created by churches to help build moral character.
  - The temperance movement emerged to fight against the evils alcohol caused in society.
  - The British abolitionist movement advocated for ending slavery.

## Technological Advances

Inventions of new machines and the improvement of production processes throughout the 18th century made large-scale production possible in *textile manufacturing* and *coal mining*. The *steam engine* revolutionized transportation.

## The Scarcity of Energy

By the 18th century, most of Britain's forests were gone, and its supply of wood for fuel was nearly depleted. The British were importing wood from Russia. *Coal*, plentiful but traditionally shunned as a fuel because it polluted the air, gradually replaced wood as both a fuel and for industrial processes. Most British coal was mined near the coasts.

- Coal was the most profitable energy source humans had yet found. It produced a calorie extraction ratio to yield results that varied from 1:27 to 1:200.
  - This meant that for every calorie invested in mining, 27–200 calories of energy were extracted.
  - Fossil fuels became the way for Europe to power a way to reshape the world.
- Mines kept filling with water, so pumps were needed to empty them.
  - The early steam engines, such as Thomas Newcomen's clumsy contraption that was a maze of rods and leather straps, used heat from burning coal to boil water that made steam power to set the engine in motion. These early steam engines were employed as pumps in mines.
  - *James Watt* in 1763 saw the problems of the earlier engines, such as those of Newcomen and Thomas Savery. He realized that their machines lacked a condensing chamber. So Watt created an improved steam engine that became a great success in Britain.
    - Watt's steam engine revolutionized every mode of production and transportation, starting with mining, then moving to the textile industry, and culminating in the railroad industry.

The mastery of coal, then oil, and then natural gas gave Western Europeans the power to dominate the world and to improve the lives of workers. European workers could now accomplish much more with machines powered by fuel than by using animals, water, and wind. In many ways, the mastery of coal and then electricity led to the beginning of the end of slavery that humans had practiced for thousands of years.

The increased work that machines were able to do at a much cheaper price than slave labor made slavery economically less advantageous than building a large factory with many machines and paying laborers wages.

## Textiles

The story of the textile industry mirrors that of industrialization. In many ways, the textile industry was the first to be industrialized, so it is often tied to the teaching of this unit. Second, everyone needs clothes. So making clothes more quickly and less expensively allowed for huge profits and generated a consumer market and a feeling of consumerism. What follows is a list of important events in the development of the textile industry that are often asked about on the AP exam:

- The *fly shuttle* (John Kay, 1733) cut manpower needs on the looms in half.
- The *spinning jenny* (James Hargreaves, 1764) mechanized the spinning wheel.
- The *water frame* (Richard Arkwright, 1769) improved thread spinning.
- Use of the *steam engine* (Richard Arkwright, 1780s) powered the looms and required factory production of textiles instead of domestic industry.
- The *cotton gin* (Eli Whitney, American, 1793) separated seed from raw cotton fiber and increased the supply of cotton, which was spun into thread and then woven into cloth.

## Coal

- The *steam pump* (Thomas Newcomen, 1702) rid coal mines of water seepage.
- The *condensing chamber steam engine* (James Watt, 1763) was created.
- Plentiful coal boosted iron production and gave rise to *heavy industry* (the manufacture of machinery and materials used in production).

- The use of coal and steam power led to the creation of huge factories and ended the *putting-out system* in which families worked from their homes in the production of textiles and other products.
- The better forms of energy and the new factories that were created for paid laborers indirectly brought about an end to slavery as hiring workers in a factory and paying them became more economically efficient than buying enslaved people and housing and feeding them. Slavery became a less efficient means of production, so it ended.

### Transportation and Communication

New efficient methods of transportation and other innovations created new industries, improved the distribution of goods, increased consumerism, and enhanced the quality of life:

- The *steamboat* (Robert Fulton, American, 1807) was built.
- The *railroad steam locomotive* (George Stephenson's *Rocket*, 1829) was built.
  - Both the *steamboat* and *steam locomotive* enhanced an already-efficient system of river transportation that had been expanded in the 18th century by a network of canals.
  - The canals meant that transportation was cheap and easy for most of the nation, leading to trade networks and higher demand for goods as well as for higher transportability of resources.
  - Together the steamboat and steam locomotive opened new sources of raw materials and new markets for manufactured goods. They also made it possible to locate factories in population centers.
  - The railroad building boom, from 1830–1850, brought about massive social and economic changes in Britain's largely agrarian economy.
  - The ease of transport encouraged rural workers to move to the cities.
  - The lower costs of shipping goods in bulk fostered expanding markets.
  - The railroad was a culminating invention of the Industrial Revolution because it utilized steel and a steam engine. The railroad was so massive that it encouraged many workers to learn the skills needed for an industrial society.
  - The railroad also allowed the creation of *mass marketing* through the use of catalogs.
  - Refrigerated railcars added much to the ability to feed the world cheaply.
  - The railroad and steamboat led to the ability to gather raw materials more easily.
  - The railroad and steamboat led to the advent of trolleys, streetcars, and eventually subways, which opened the cities to new designs.
- New technologies and means of communication and transportation—including railroads—resulted in more fully integrated national economies, a higher level of urbanization, and a truly global economic network.
  - Streetcars and trolleys revolutionized cities and allowed their redesign.
  - Bicycles allowed the common person some freedom of transportation at an affordable price.
  - Automobiles, and eventually airplanes, completed the transportation network by the advent of the First World War in 1914.
- Communication advanced notably with the invention of the telegraph, then the radio, and then the telephone.

### Oil

By the end of the 19th century, the refinement of petroleum allowed its use as a fuel for the newly developed *internal combustion engines* that propelled automobiles, locomotives, and even ships. Oil was also was used for heating and industrial processes.

## Britain Was First in Industrialization

Great Britain was the first nation to industrialize for many reasons, not the least of which was the availability of coal, the energy source that powered the first Industrial Revolution. The Continent did not see industrialization until after the end of the Napoleonic Wars, which ravaged the Continent for the first 15 years of the 19th century. Why was Britain the first nation to industrialize?

- Stable governments and government institutions supported business.
- Britain's ready supplies of coal, iron ore, and other essential raw materials promoted industrial growth. In addition, Britain ran out of wood for charcoal, which forced it to turn to coal as a fuel source.
- Great Britain established its industrial dominance through the mechanization of textile production, iron and steel production, and new transportation systems in conjunction with uniquely favorable political and social climates.
- Economic institutions and human capital such as engineers, inventors, and capitalists helped Britain lead the process of industrialization, largely through private initiative.
- The population of Britain had high levels of economic freedom.
- Economic institutions and human capital were available in Britain.
- No wars were fought on British soil.
- Enclosure made land, labor, markets, and entrepreneurship available.
- Britain's parliamentary government promoted commercial and industrial interests because those interests were represented in Parliament. The British government supported industrialization with financial rewards for inventors.
- Britain already had a strong network of canals and roads.
- Private businessmen created many of the inventions and networks needed to industrialize.

After the British industrialized, they tried to keep their methods of production a secret and banned engineers from foreign travel. However, after the defeat of Napoleon, industrialization spread to Europe through people such as *Fritz Harkort*, who made steam engines in Germany. The Continent slowly caught up to Britain after she invited the world to see her wonders at the Great Exposition of 1851, held in the *Crystal Palace*, London, an exhibition venue built for the exposition. The British gave financial awards to inventors and did everything possible to promote industry within the British realm.

## The Nations on the Continent Followed Later

**PRUSSIA:** The state became a leader of a unified Germany, which rapidly industrialized with strong government leadership and some industrial leaders. Industrialization in Prussia allowed that state to become the leader of a unified Germany, which subsequently underwent rapid industrialization under government sponsorship.

- The *Zollverein*, or the Prussian-led trade union of German states, allowed the German states to unify their efforts at industrialization.
- *Friedrich List* was a writer and philosopher who did the following:
  - He believed manufacturing was the primary means of increasing people's well-being and relieving poverty; hence he felt it was the duty of the government to improve industry.
  - He wrote *National System of Political Economy*.
  - He conceived of and advocated for the *Zollverein*, or German customs union, which was created in 1834.

- For the first time, goods were allowed to move within German states without tariffs.
- Protective tariffs on foreign goods (from outside the *Zollverein*) were still high.
- Industrialization helped to develop growing German nationalism.

- *Fritz Harkort* got ideas for machinery from Britain:
  - Known as the "Watt of Germany," he borrowed materials and hired foreign workers to build steam engines in Germany.
  - The roads were too bad to deliver the machinery fully assembled.

**FRANCE:** The state experienced slower industrialization with less dislocation of traditional methods of production in order to try to prevent societal upheaval. The strong guilds that resisted changes to production brought on by industrialization and the Napoleonic Wars delayed the Industrial Revolution's emergence in France. The government supported banks, canals, and a national railroad.

**SOUTHERN AND EASTERN EUROPE:** A combination of factors, including lack of resources, feudal traditions, geography, the persistence of serfdom in some areas, and the lack of government sponsorship, accounted for Eastern and Southern Europe's lag in industrial development.

## Results of the Industrial Revolution

- The most significant result was the *increased production and availability of manufactured goods.*
  - Material prosperity increased because cheaper, high-quality goods were available.
  - Increased consumption led to more jobs.
- Factory workers lived in poverty on low wages.
  - Housing was in dismal tenements.
  - For the first half of the 19th century, entire families, including children from age five and up, worked 14 hours a day under unsafe and unhealthy conditions.
  - Crowded slums were worsened by the absence of public services in cities that had expanded too rapidly.
  - Although these living conditions did not differ much from those under which people had lived for centuries on farms, the *concentration of the population* made them more unhealthy.
  - This visibility of poverty in the cities led thinkers to ponder the causes of poverty and prompted the institutions of society to push for its alleviation.
    - The *Sadler Commission* in Great Britain helped initiate legislation to improve working conditions in factories.
- *Urbanization* was one of the Industrial Revolution's most important socioeconomic effects.
  - Working-class injustices, gender exploitation, and standard-of-living issues became the 19th century's great social and political dilemmas.
  - Literally tens of millions of people moved from the countryside to the city as the factory system replaced the domestic system.
  - The family structure changed greatly in that productive work was taken out of the home and moved to the factory, causing children to be separated from their families and from rural settings.
  - Gender roles changed.
    - Women's work was seen as less valuable and was increasingly associated with domestic duties.
    - Men were separated from their wives and children; they left home to go to work or worked in different factories than other members of their family.
- By the end of the century, wages and the quality of life for the working class improved because of laws restricting the labor of children and women, creating social welfare programs, and promoting improved diet and the use of birth control.
  - The many reform laws that restricted the labor of women and children included the following:
    - The Factory Act of 1833
    - The Mines Act of 1842
    - The Ten Hours Act of 1847

- The Industrial Revolution may have prevented a large-scale human tragedy by increasing production. However, the filthy conditions of crowded city life and the grinding poverty of the cities led many reformers, such as *Edwin Chadwick*, to call for changes.
- Because of the continued existence of more primitive agricultural practices and land-owning patterns, some areas of Europe lagged in industrialization while facing famine, debt, and land shortages.

## Effects on Class and Gender

Two new overall classes developed as a result of the Industrial Revolution: *industrialists/capitalists* and *factory workers*. However, the reality was that there were many levels of class distinction within each of these overall classifications. Thus, class distinctions became more important at the time.

- There was a huge divide between the *bourgeoisie*, which was the servant-keeping middle class, and the *proletariat*, which was the working class.
- Bourgeois families became focused on the nuclear family and the cult of domesticity, with distinct gender roles for men and women.
- Class identity developed and was reinforced through participation in philanthropic, political, and social associations among the middle classes and through mutual aid societies and trade unions among the working classes.
- The division of labor by gender was much more pronounced among the upper classes, where women were homemakers, than in the lower classes, where women often had to work outside the home.
- The gap between wealthy and working classes remained enormous.
  - 5 percent of British households received 33 percent of all income.
  - 20 percent of households made 50–60 percent of British income.
  - 80 percent of the British population shared 40 percent of the income.
  - The competitive nature of the markets led many of the factory owners to offer low wages for long hours, to create poor and unsafe working conditions, and to employ child labor.
  - The rigid discipline of factory work contrasted with the rural pace of farmwork to which most of the laborers had been accustomed.
  - Not until the mid-19th century did the standard of living improve for the average industrial worker.
  - *Child labor laws* were enacted after the first three decades of the 19th century to limit the number of hours children could be required to work.
- Feminists began to advocate for legal, economic, and political rights for women.
  - Flora Tristan, a French/Peruvian woman, wrote about the link between rights for women and for the working classes.
  - The British Women's Social and Political Union advocated for female suffrage.
  - Emmeline Pankhurst and her family were good examples of female suffragists.
- Gender division of labor split males and females into separate working spheres.
  - Men became the main breadwinners, while married women tended to stay home to raise the children.
  - It was considered a terrible situation if both parents had to work outside of the home.
  - Jobs available to women were "dead-end" and paid poorly.
  - The early attempts of workers to organize were met with hostility from industrialists and anti-union regulations from governments; these attempts had very limited success.
- Class diversity was remarkable, even within the traditional classes.
  - The upper class was created when the newly wealthy industrialists intermarried with the fading nobility to create a new top notch in European society.
  - The middle class, or *bourgeoisie*, saw huge diversity:
    - They tended to their own homes.

- They usually made about $10,000/year while the poor made $400/year.
- They spent 25 percent of their money on food and 25 percent on servants.
- Victorian behavior patterns emerged as the norm.
- Workers formed workers' unions and political parties to create social and political reforms.
  - The Liberal and Conservative parties emerged in Great Britain.
    - In France, Socialist and Conservative parties emerged.
    - The German Social Democratic Party, the British Labour Party, and the Russian Social Democrats or Kadets were all parties that represented the interests of the masses in creating social and political reforms.
- The *Chartist Movement* advocated for voting rights for all adult males.
- Drinking, gambling, and sex were condemned as vices.
- These same vices were hypocritically ignored in private.
- This age became one of the most sexually repressed yet privately perverted ages in history.
  - Included industrialists, bankers, white-collar workers, bureaucrats, shopkeepers, business owners, and technical workers.
  - The lower class or *proletariat,* which also had huge diversity, totaled about 80 percent of the population.
    - The top of the lower classes tried to emulate the upper classes' Victorian behavior.
    - There were many different levels of lower classes. Labor aristocracy or those who could hire and fire were at the top.
    - Skilled workers, such as plumbers or masons, were the next level of lower classes.
    - Semiskilled laborers, such as carpenter's assistants, were the next level.
    - The next level down were day laborers, who did jobs for a day's pay, such as loading ships.
    - Domestic servants were low on the level of working-class workers but were relatively well paid. In fact, many young women spent time as domestic servants.
- By the end of the century, higher wages, laws restricting the labor of children and women, social welfare programs, improved diet, and increased access to birth control affected the quality of life for the working class.

## Leisure Time

Leisure time centered increasingly on the family or small groups, concurrent with the development of activities and spaces to use that time. Some of the activities included the following:

- Enjoying the parks
- Attending sporting events
- Going to the beach
- Shopping in department stores
- Visiting museums
- Attending operas and the theater

## Reforms Began in the Cities

The rapid growth of cities during the Industrial Revolution necessitated urban reforms to improve conditions that had existed for centuries: poor sanitation and other services, overcrowded housing, and inadequate transportation. Influenced by *Jeremy Bentham* (1748–1832), whose philosophy of *utilitarianism* emphasized "the greatest good for the greatest number," city planners and urban reformers redesigned many European cities and initiated a public health movement to improve urban life for all classes.

- The Chadwick Report of 1842 indicated that British citizens were living in filthy, unsanitary conditions that were spreading disease.
  - The report calculated that installing sewage and water systems in British cities would be less expensive than exporting the filth by other means.
  - A cholera epidemic broke out after the report's release, supporting its conclusions.
  - The cholera outbreak showed the need to create the Public Health Act of 1848.
- Paris was redesigned between 1853 and 1870 by *Georges Haussmann*.
  - This was the first urban planning in Europe.
  - Slums were destroyed.
  - Public transportation was created.
  - Zoning laws were passed.
    - Shopping districts were placed at street level with housing above.
    - Large townhomes were built.
    - Many large roundabouts were built.
    - Parks and open spaces were added.
  - Sewage and water systems were added.
  - Soon followed by electricity.
  - Broad avenues were built to prevent revolutionary barricades.
  - Other cities, such as Vienna, followed the French example.
- The standard of living improved for most Europeans from the middle of the 19th century and into the early-20th century.
- Disparities in wealth between the classes led to conflict between them.
  - This disparity encouraged the growth of political radicalism.
  - Hierarchies of wealth and status existed among both the middle and working classes.
- The relegation of women to menial jobs or to child raising fostered a women's rights movement.
  - A first wave of *feminism* emerged.
  - Goals of the movement included gender equality in opportunity and both legal and voting rights.

## Theories of Economics

The competing economic theories below mostly emerged during period 2 but were hotly contested during period 3. So you must be familiar with all of the theories and theorists listed below. In reality, all of them, except for the *Comte de Saint-Simon*, Louis Blanc, and Karl Marx, did most of their work during period 2. The volatile business cycles in the last quarter of the 19th century led corporations and governments to try to manage the market through a variety of methods, including monopolies, banking practices, government management of the economy, and tariffs.

- *Adam Smith* (see page 165) can be considered the first modern economist.
  - His *Wealth of Nations* has been called the "Bible of capitalism" and is the foundation for *classical* or laissez-faire economics. It opposed the regulations imposed by mercantilism by arguing that certain natural laws, such as *supply and demand,* govern an economy and be free to operate.
  - He claimed that people follow their own enlightened self-interest without the interference of government in the economy.
  - This private initiative, Smith believed, would result in benefits to all in society.
- *Thomas Malthus* (1766–1834) was the first of the classical economists to try to explain why the mass of people did not benefit from the operation of the natural laws of economics.
  - Poverty existed, he said, because the *population increased at a geometric rate while the food supply increased arithmetically.*

- ○ He believed that poverty was a divine punishment for humankind's lust.
- ■ *David Ricardo* (1772–1823) introduced the *Iron Law of Wages*: the natural wage is that which maintains a worker's subsistence.
  - ○ When labor is in demand, Ricardo believed, the wage will increase, the worker will prosper, the size of families will increase, and the general population will grow.
  - ○ He stated that the result will be more workers competing for fewer jobs and inevitable starvation.
  - ○ Ricardo believed government attempts to change this only led to greater suffering.
- ■ *Utopian socialists* rejected the *dismal science* of the classical economists and sought solutions to the plight of the masses.
  - ○ *Robert Owen* (1771–1858) was a Scottish textile manufacturer. His humane working conditions—shorter workday, decent housing, and free education—served as a model for capitalists who wanted to make a profit without exploiting workers.
  - ○ The *Comte de Saint-Simon* (1760–1825) was one of the early French founders of *socialism*.
    - ■ He helped define the movement by advocating *public ownership of factories*.
    - ■ He wanted a professional managerial corps to run factories: the *technocrats*.
    - ■ He coined the slogan "From each according to his ability, to each according to his need," which was an idealistic but vague proposal for a *planned economy*.
  - ○ *John Stuart Mill* was one of the most important thinkers of the 19th century. He was called the most influential English speaking philosopher of his day.
    - ■ Mill wrote against the *tyranny of the majority*.
    - ■ He wrote *On Liberty* in which he explained freedom better than anyone before him.
    - ■ Although he was originally a liberal and proponent of *utilitarianism*, Mill debated against liberalism at times when he thought it too dogmatic.
  - ○ *Louis Blanc* (1811–1882) had a more practical approach than did other early French utopian socialists.
    - ■ Blanc urged workers to fight for universal suffrage and to overthrow the state peacefully.
    - ■ He believed the government should set up workshops and factories to guarantee full employment.
    - ■ His ideas had an opportunity to be tested when he briefly became a leader of France after the Revolution of 1848.
  - ○ Socialists called for the redistribution of society's resources and wealth; they evolved from a utopian to a Marxist scientific critique of capitalism.
- ■ *Karl Marx* (1818–1883) was the primary proponent of the *class struggle* model of history.
  - ○ His *Communist Manifesto,* written with *Friedrich Engels* (1820–1895) during the revolutions of 1848, called for radical solutions to the dilemma of mass poverty in the industrialized world.
  - ○ Marx also wrote *Das Kapital,* the first volume of which was published in 1867. In it, he offered a complete analysis of capitalism and an explanation of communism.
  - ○ Marx's scientific socialism provided a systematic critique of capitalism and a deterministic analysis of society and historical evolution.

## Marx's Theories

Karl Marx was a proponent of several different theories.

*Hegelian dialectic* (so named after the German philosopher Georg Hegel): The Hegelian dialectic stated that in every historical period a prevailing ideal, called a *thesis*, conflicted with an opposing ideal, called an *antithesis*, and resulted in a new ideal, called a *synthesis*. This synthesis became the thesis of the next period and the process continued. See the "Chart of Hegelian Dialectic."

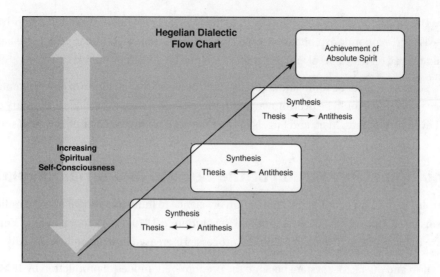

Chart of Hegelian dialectic.

*Dialectical materialism:* Marx adapted the Hegelian dialectic to argue that society was a reflection of economics. He claimed that history progressed from agrarian communalism to slave-holding, feudalism, bourgeois commercialism, capitalism, socialism, and, finally, to *communism* (a classless society in which the workers owned the means of production and government is unnecessary). Marx saw this as an inevitable process, and that led him to believe more strongly in his predictions.

The chart "Dialectical Materialism Flow Chart" and the explanation below it should help you understand Marx's theories on capitalism, communism, and the coming revolution.

*Class struggle:* Marx believed that the *dominant class* in every society, whether it consisted of slaveholders, feudal lords, or capitalists, is a thesis with an antithesis, such as enslaved people, serfs, or workers, respectively. Marx claimed that the antithesis will overthrow the old order.

*Inevitable revolution:* This was the result of the capitalists' increasing profits gained by lowering the workers' wages for labor to the point that the proletariat cannot afford to consume the products of manufacture (*surplus-value theory*). Marx believed that economic depression would occur and would be a hardship on the working class until that same working class carried out a revolution. A *dictatorship of the proletariat* would establish a socialist government to wipe out capitalism, Marx believed.

## Dialectical Materialism Flow Chart

Thesis: Feudal Lords — Antithesis: Serfs and Peasants

Synthesis: New Thesis: Medieval Town Life — Antithesis: Guilds

Synthesis: New Thesis: Entrepreneurs (Bourgeoisie)

Antithesis: Proletariat

Synthesis: New Thesis: Classless Communism

*Communism:* The *"withering away of the state"* would follow, Marx explained. He stated that private property would cease to exist and economic exploitation would stop, ending crime, vice, and injustice. He believed that democracy would prevail on a local level and that a *utopia* (a perfect society) would result.

- *Anarchists*, such as Mikhail Bakunin and Georges Sorel, asserted that all forms of governmental authority were unnecessary and should be overthrown and replaced with a society based on voluntary cooperation. They went even further than Marx and Engels in their message about the corrupt nature of society.

## The Technological Revolution or the Second Industrial Revolution

Around the last third of the 19th century, the application of science to industry brought about a radical change in the way Europeans lived. During the Second Industrial Revolution (c. 1870–1914), more areas of Europe experienced an increase in industrial activity, and industrial processes increased in scale and complexity.

- Mechanization and the factory system became the predominant modes of production by 1914.
- *Mass production* lowered the cost of goods and made them available to the general public; consumer goods became part of the mass market.
- Smaller companies merged and consolidated until whole industries were dominated by *big businesses*.
- High wages in the cities caused a *population shift* from the countryside.
- Electricity and the internal combustion engine not only increased productivity but also improved the quality of life.
- New industries emerged, adding to the new consumerism of the era:
  - The chemical industry
  - The electricity industry
  - Leisure travel
  - Professional sports
  - The automobile industry
- New means of communication, such as the telegraph and telephone, changed business and culture.
- New forms of transportation changed everything from business to migration patterns to marriage patterns.
- Industrialization and mass marketing increased both the production and the demand for a new range of consumer goods— including clothing, processed foods, and labor-saving devices—and created more leisure opportunities.
- Increased consumerism changed leisure and home life, including the spread of the following:
  - Advertising
  - Department stores
  - Catalogs

## Inventors of the Industrial Revolution

| 1708 | Jethro Tull's mechanical seed drill made cultivation in rows widespread as it was more efficient than manual work and allowed easier weeding. |
| --- | --- |
| 1712 | Thomas Newcomen built the first commercially successful steam engine. It kept deep coal mines clear of water. It was the first significant industrial use of fossil fuels. It marked the first major power source invented since wind, water, and animal power were used. |
| 1733 | John Kay invented the flying shuttle, which improved weaving significantly. |

| 1761 | James Brindley's Bridgewater Canal opened. Barges carried coal from Worsley to Manchester. |
|---|---|
| 1765 | James Hargreaves invented the spinning jenny, automating thread spinning for the first time. |
| 1769 | Richard Arkwright's water frame allowed much more efficient spinning of thread. |
| 1775 | James Watt created the first efficient steam engine with a condensing chamber. |
| 1779 | The first steam-powered mill used Crompton's "mule" and Hargreaves's and Arkwright's machines, fully automating the weaving process. |
| 1787 | Cartwright built a power loom. |
| 1792 | William Murdock (James Watt's assistant) lit his home with coal gas. |
| 1793 | Eli Whitney developed the cotton gin, increasing the efficiency of cotton as a source of raw material for textiles. |
| 1801 | Robert Trevithick demonstrated his steam locomotive. |
| 1807 | Robert Fulton built the *Clermont,* the first successful steamboat. |
| 1826–1842 | Marc Brunel built the first underwater tunnel—under the Thames. |
| 1830 | The Liverpool and Manchester Railway began the first regular commercial rail service. |
| 1831 | Michael Faraday discovered electromagnetic current, making possible generators and electric engines. |
| 1834 | Charles Babbage created the analytic engine, the first ancestor of the computer. |
| 1837 | Samuel F. B. Morse developed the telegraph and Morse Code. |
| 1838 | Daguerre perfected the daguerrotype, an early form of photography. |
| 1849 | Joseph Monier developed reinforced concrete. |
| 1850 | Gasoline was refined for the first time. |
| 1851 | Singer invented the first practical sewing machine. |
| 1854 | Henry Bessemer invented the steel converter, which revolutionized the production of steel. |
| 1858 | First transatlantic cable completed. Cathode rays discovered. |
| 1867 | Alfred Nobel created dynamite, the first high explosive that could be safely handled. |
| 1876 | Alexander Graham Bell invented the telephone. |
| 1877 | Thomas Alva Edison invented the phonograph. |
| 1879 | Edison invented the incandescent lamp. |
| 1883 | The first skyscraper (10 stories tall) was built (in Chicago). The Brooklyn Bridge opened; this large suspension bridge was a triumph of engineering. |
| 1884 | Hiram Maxim invented the machine gun, making possible mass slaughter and beginning the mechanization of warfare. |
| 1885 | Karl Benz developed the first internal-combustion automobile engine. |
| 1889 | The Eiffel Tower was built for the World Exposition in Paris. |
| 1896 | Guglielmo Marconi patented the wireless telegraph. |
| 1901 | Guglielmo Marconi transmitted the first transatlantic radio message (from Cape Cod, Massachusetts). |

# Practice Questions

## Long Essay

These questions are samples of the various types of thematic essays on the AP exam. See pages 27–28 for a detailed explanation of each type. Check over the generic rubric (see pages 28–29) before you begin any of these essays, and use that rubric to score your essay if you write one.

## Question 1

Analyze how the opening of Atlantic commerce sparked the rise of capitalism.

### Comments on Question 1

This question is testing the *causation* skill because it wants to know how one factor, the opening of Atlantic trade, sparked another outcome, the rise of capitalism. Remember to describe the causes and/or effects of the rise of capitalism and to support your analysis of those causes and effects by including specific examples. Explain the reasons why the opening of Atlantic trade sparked the rise of capitalism with specific evidence to support claims made. The essay must clearly indicate multiple ways that capitalism's rise was caused by the opening of transatlantic trade. This question requires all the applications of analysis: examining in detail, determining relationships, and explaining. A special emphasis should be on determining the relationships between the new intercontinental trade and the growth of capitalism. How could the Atlantic discoveries and colonization of the New World have encouraged the growth of capitalism in Europe? Strong and complex relationships formed between the colonization of the New World and the growth of capitalism, including the development of international banking, stock markets, and nationally chartered companies as well as the taking of risk to make profits. New markets, new products (such as tobacco, vanilla, and cocoa), new territories, and new opportunities spurred the entrepreneurship seen in men like Cortez, Pizarro, and those who accompanied them. Abundant resources from the New World, including precious metals, led to exploitation by merchants, giving them huge profits. Along with the resulting creation of the first merchant class and the development of surplus wealth, capitalism developed through these methods. The emergence of mercantilism and Adam Smith's theory of *laissez-faire capitalism* as an antidote to mercantilism should also be discussed. The essay could also focus on inflation caused by the gold flow into Europe and the emigration of skilled entrepreneurial artisans and merchants to the New World. A lot of supporting evidence can be used in this essay.

## Question 2

Analyze the extent to which industrialization changed human interaction with the environment and other people.

### Comments on Question 2

This question is asking you to use the *change and continuity over time* (CCOT) skill because you must analyze the extent to which the Industrial Revolution changed the interactions of people with each other and with the environment. This question is asking what changed and what remained the same. Remember to explain the European economy in 1750 and in 1850. Provide specific examples of how things changed after the opening of transatlantic trade. Your essay must explain the extent to which human interaction with the environment and with other people was changed after industrialization began. This essay is asking you to decide how much industrialization changed life on many levels.

Approach this by first considering what life was like both before and after industrialization. The list of things that were similar among most people before industrialization should be a long list: where people lived, people's relationships to time/seasons, family life and structure, types of jobs done, standard of living, education, political representation, and more. In contrast, the list of things that were similar among people after industrialization should be a short list: class distinctions still existing, difficulty in rising up in class, war, taxes, and differences between city and rural life. Then write a thesis that offers specific answers to the question by using items from your lists. Support your answer with many facts. Be certain to explain why human interaction was different from what came before or why it was the same. Be clear, and assume nothing about what the readers will link together on their own.

## Question 3

Explain why it was no accident that the Industrial Revolution started in late 18th-century Britain.

### Comments on Question 3

This is a *causation* question because it requires you to explain how one environment—18th-century Britain—resulted in a specific outcome, the Industrial Revolution. Describe the causes and/or effects of the Industrial Revolution occurring in Britain. Support your analysis of those causes and effects with specific examples. The essay must explain the reasons that the environment of Britain fostered the advent of the Industrial Revolution. You must examine why fertile farm fields nurtured the development of industrialization in Britain from 1780–1830. You must identify the links in the causal chain: the supremacy of Parliament after 1688, the enclosure movement, the Agricultural Revolution, the growth of towns, the improvement of technology, available capital and land, stable government, lack of foreign invasion, transportation networks, existing cottage industry, and the abundance of coal.

## Question 4

To what extent did the Industrial Revolution diminish the quality of life of the common person in Europe?

### Comments on Question 4

This question is testing the *causation* skill because it requires you to evaluate the extent to which one thing, the Industrial Revolution, resulted in a specific outcome, the diminished quality of life of the common person in Europe. Remember to describe the causes and/or effects of the Industrial Revolution on the lives of common Europeans. Support your analysis of those causes and effects with specific examples. The essay must explain the reasons for the changes in the quality of life at the time. Use facts to argue for or against. This essay question is very open-ended. The appropriate response is to write an essay that says both, depending on the era under discussion. The quality of life for the average Briton was clearly reduced from 1750–1850. However, the quality of life for the British and for the entire world began to improve after 1850 and continues to do so today, mostly due to the wonders of industrialization. Therefore, the miserable labor and living conditions of the early-19th century, as well as the reforms of the later part of that century and how living improved, each deserve a paragraph. A strong thesis needs to explain why the statement is both supported and refuted, depending upon what vantage point one uses.

## Short-Answer

1. Answer all parts of the question that follows based on your knowledge of European history. Historians have argued that urbanization changed the age-old relations between families, the land, production, and the government.

    (a) Identify TWO pieces of evidence that support this argument and explain HOW that evidence supports the argument.

    (b) Identify TWO pieces of evidence that refute this argument and explain HOW that evidence supports the argument.

2. Use the image and passage below and your knowledge of European history to answer all parts of the question that follows.

**Source 1**

By Andrew Ure, Peter Lund Simmonds, H. G. Bohn, 1861.

**Source 2**

The number of Scribbling-Machines extending about seventeen miles south-west of LEEDS, exceed all belief, being no less than one hundred and seventy! and as each machine will do as much work in twelve hours, as ten men can in that time do by hand, (speaking within bounds) and they working night-and day, one machine will do as much work in one day as would otherwise employ twenty men.

As we do not mean to assert anything but what we can prove to be true, we allow four men to be employed at each machine twelve hours, working night and day, will take eight men in twenty-four hours; so that, upon a moderate computation twelve men are thrown out of employ for every single machine used in scribbling; and as it may be supposed the number of machines in all the other quarters together, nearly equal those in the South-West, a full four thousand men are left to shift for a living how they can, and must of course fall to the Parish, if not timely relieved. Allowing one boy to be a bound apprentice from each family out of work, eight thousand hands are deprived of the opportunity of getting a livelihood.

—Leeds Woollen Workers Petition, 1786

(a) Briefly explain ONE social change brought about by changes in the textile industry between 1770 and 1815.

(b) Briefly explain ONE reason that creating more woolen cloth with less labor became important after 1750.

(c) Briefly explain ONE political change brought on by the increase in textile production in England.

## Multiple-Choice

**Questions 1–3 refer to the chart below.**

| Population Estimates in the Millions | | |
|---|---|---|
| Selected Nations in Europe | 1800 | 1900 |
| BRITAIN | 9 | 33 |
| GERMANY | 25 | 56 |
| ITALY | 17 | 34 |
| FRANCE | 27 | 39 |

1. The chart provides population estimates for selected European countries in the years 1800 and 1900. Which of the following is the most valid interpretation of the statistics?

   (A) The population doubled in each of the countries identified.
   (B) The population of Italy and Germany doubled because of national unification.
   (C) The population growth reflects the degree to which each of the nations industrialized.
   (D) The population of Britain grew at a faster rate than any of the other nations identified.

2. Which of the following played the LEAST significant role in creating the demographic change noted in the chart?

   (A) Transatlantic trade brought many immigrants from the Americas, Asia, and Africa.
   (B) The Agricultural Revolution increased food production.
   (C) The Black Plague disappeared, and a vaccination for smallpox was developed.
   (D) Transatlantic trade brought many new foods to all parts of the world, increasing output and thus population.

3. Scholarly statistical studies of the condition of the British working class indicate that during the 19th century, which of the following was true?

   (A) Their standard of living improved from the beginning of industrialization.
   (B) Incidences of infanticide increased throughout the 19th century.
   (C) Improvement in the standard of living did not come until the period after 1830.
   (D) Only skilled workers enjoyed improvements in their standard of living.

**Questions 4–6 refer to the print below.**

A woodcut print of the Krupp steelworks in Essen, Germany.

4. The illustration shows the industrialization of Germany, including the bucolic surrounding area, indicating that this piece belongs in which of the following artistic movements?

   (A) Naturalism
   (B) Romanticism
   (C) Neoclassicism
   (D) Impressionism

5. The mass production of this woodblock print was most likely done for which of the following reasons?

   (A) The owner of the factory wanted a copy to put into his office.
   (B) The capitalists who built factories wanted pictures of their competitors' factories.
   (C) The workers at the factories could now afford to put art into their houses.
   (D) The town council required it of the artist if he wanted to live there.

6. The greatest change workers faced with the shift from cottage industry to factory work, as depicted in the print, was which of the following?

   (A) A new tempo and discipline
   (B) Harder work
   (C) The destruction of family unit labor
   (D) Lower wages

# Answers and Explanations

## Short-Answer Explanations

1. (a) You may cite many trends of change, from growing illegitimacy to wage workers, loss of agricultural jobs, putting-out changing to factory work, new regulations on the poor, foundling homes, changing gender roles, increasing literacy, increased political activity of the lower classes, reductions in church attendance, tenement living, increased pollution and sewage problems, increased education, new laws regulating work hours and conditions, and the Chartist Movement. Explain how each piece of evidence was a change from life previous to the start of the 19th century.

   (b) You may cite many pieces of information, from the poor still having a small political voice to many one-wage families, the remaining rural workers, the ongoing importance of agriculture, the class system that was not very different from manorialism, and the rise of conservative ideas. Explain how each piece of evidence proves that life was similar to life previous to the start of the 19th century.

2. (a) You should *fully explain* one of the following: changes in gender roles, less interaction between the genders, creation of factories, changing family lives due to work outside of the home, changes in class identity, the emergence of the capitalist class, destruction of guilds, the end of domestic industry, increased urbanization, drop in the price of clothes leading to fashion emerging, or landholders gaining wealth.

   (b) This answer revolves around the enclosure movement coming to full fruition around 1700 in England. The increase in wool from the sheep that replaced peasants on many estates meant that the wool had to be turned into cloth. Another approach would be to explain the domestic industry in wool and how the weavers of cloth needed many spinners before the spinning jenny. You could

also explain that the increased production led England to be a dominant force in international trade as it had a ready export to sell.

   (c) You should *fully explain* one of the following: the rise of England on the international stage as trade increased in importance, the new regulations affecting child labor and women at work, the Chartist Movement, the Poor Laws, or the banning of unions.

## Practice Multiple-Choice Questions

1. (A) is wrong because the population of France did not double.

   (B) is wrong because the chart does not indicate why the population increased. The increase may be due to an agricultural revolution there.

   (C) is wrong because France industrialized more than Italy during this period but did not see its population grow as much as that of Italy.

   **(D) is CORRECT because the chart clearly shows the population of Britain grew faster than that of any other nation shown on the chart.**

2. **(A) is CORRECT because migration into Europe did not affect the population growth nearly as much as the other factors listed.**

   (B) is wrong because migration into Europe did not affect the population growth nearly as much as the surplus of food created by the Agricultural Revolution did.

   (C) is wrong because migration into Europe did not affect the population growth nearly as much as the conquest of these diseases did.

   (D) is wrong because migration into Europe did not affect the population growth nearly as much as the surplus of food created by the new foods such as corn and the potato did.

3. (A) is wrong because the standard of living for workers actually worsened at the start of the Industrial Revolution but improved after about 1830.

(B)  is wrong because infanticide started to rise at the start of the century but was reduced as the century came to a close.

**(C)  is CORRECT because the standard of living for workers actually worsened at the start of the Industrial Revolution but improved after about 1830 or 1850, depending on which statistics are used.**

(D)  is wrong because the standard of living for all workers actually improved after about 1830.

4. (A)  is wrong because the print does not show the depiction of nature as supreme as the naturalists sought.

**(B)  is CORRECT because the portrayal of industry as polluting pristine nature is a hallmark of romantic art of all genres.**

(C)  is wrong because there is no reference to Greco-Roman themes or architecture seen in neoclassical works.

(D)  is wrong because the details are too clear to be impressionist.

5. (A)  is wrong because, if the owner wanted just one copy, a painting would have been commissioned.

(B)  is wrong because the print has none of the details that a capitalist would need to spy on a rival.

**(C)  is CORRECT because the new consumer market meant that the artist could create and sell many copies of his work.**

(D)  is wrong because there is no record of town councils requiring such tasks of citizens without payment.

6. **(A)  is CORRECT because adjusting to the tempo set by the company clock rather than that set by nature, as well as the discipline of the boss in a factory rather than the freedom of putting-out work or farming, was very challenging.**

(B)  is wrong because the work was in many ways easier but also more tedious in many cases.

(C)  is wrong because, at first, families came to work together in factories. Then the tempo and discipline in factories required them to leave.

(D)  is wrong because factory workers earned higher wages than cottage workers.

# 7

# The Growth and Suppression of Democracy: From the Age of Metternich to the First World War (1815–1914)

## Overview

The period from the fall of Napoleon in 1815 to the Revolutions of 1848 is often referred to by historians as the Age of Metternich. Klemens von Metternich (1773–1859) personified the spirit of reaction that followed a quarter century of revolution and war. Chancellor of Habsburg Austria and one of the chief participants at the Congress of Vienna, Metternich and others who shared his desire to preserve monarchy and the status quo designed a continental balance of power all over Europe that would, for the most part, preserve the peace for a century (until the First World War). However, this balance was challenged in 1848 and seemed it would burst at the seams. Metternich was a tall, handsome man whose charm worked equally well on his fellow diplomats and on the elegant ladies of Vienna. He was the prototype of conservatism in leadership style for European ministers. He spoke five languages fluently, thought of himself as a European and not as a citizen of any single country, and once said, "Europe has for a long time held for me the significance of a fatherland." Early in his career, Metternich linked himself to the Habsburgs and became Austria's foreign minister, an office he held for 39 years. Because of his immense influence on European politics, those years are often called the *Age of Metternich*. He felt liberals were imposing their views on society, mostly motivated by their nationalist self-determination ideals—a position that threatened Austria because of its diverse and large population.

During the Age of Metternich, two great nations developed the basis for modern constitutional democracy. Britain continued its democratization through the perpetuation of the unique and stabilizing evolutionary process that represented the interests in government of more and more of its populace. France, on the other hand, experienced destabilizing seesaw battles between reaction and radicalism. Volatile business cycles in the last quarter of the 19th century led corporations and governments to try to manage the market through monopolies, banking practices, and tariffs. The processes continued through the 19th century and into the early-20th century until the British and the Germans (along with brave examples set by the Scandinavian nations) established the foundations for modern welfare states by the 1930s.

Three nations that played important roles in the 19th and early-20th centuries—Germany, Austria, and Russia—suppressed the democratic urges of significant elements of their populations. In Germany, the move toward unification of the varied and independent states fell out of the hands of the constitutionalists and into those of Prussian militarists. In Austria, the Germanic Habsburg rulers continued to suppress the move toward autonomy of the polyglot nationalities that made up the empire. In Russia, sporadic attempts at reform and modernization were consumed by the ruling class's obsession with "autocracy, orthodoxy, and nationalism."

# The Growth of Democracy

## Britain

The ideals and promises of the French Revolution and a growing but poverty-stricken working class shook the foundations of stability in Europe's greatest emerging democracy. Parliament, after the end of the Napoleonic Wars in 1815, represented the interests of aristocrats and the wealthy.

- The *Corn Laws of 1815* effectively raised prices at a time when Europe was war-torn because importation of foreign grain was prohibited until the price rose above 80 shillings per quarter-ton, benefiting the landowners who ran Parliament.
  - This resulted in many riots and political unrest as food prices rose for the poor.
  - The Corn Laws were repealed in 1846 in large part because of the actions of the Anti-Corn Law League, which convinced Prime Minister Robert Peel and some of his Tory party (the Conservative Party) members to do what was "right for Britain rather than their personal interests." Free import of grain was again allowed.
  - By the 1820s, though, new and younger leaders of the Tories implemented reforms such as restructuring the penal code, providing for a modern police force, allowing membership in labor unions, and granting Catholics basic civil rights.
- Workers established labor unions and movements promoting social and economic reforms that also developed into political parties.
- By 1830, when abortive revolutions had broken out all over the Continent, the *House of Commons*, which is the lower chamber of Parliament, had not been reapportioned since 1688.
  - Many of the boroughs that elected representatives to Parliament in fact no longer existed, while large and growing industrial cities had no representation at all.
  - The *Great Reform Bill*, 1832, abolished the *rotten boroughs,* expanded the electorate, and empowered the industrial middle class.
- The *Chartist Movement*, which represented demands by radical working-class activists, sought an array of reforms from 1838 into the late 1840s.
  - It advocated universal male suffrage, a secret voting ballot, "one man, one vote" representation in Parliament, abolition of property qualifications for public office, and public education for all classes.
  - Although its program failed during the decade of its existence, all of its features were eventually incorporated into British society.
- When the discontent of the working class on the Continent exploded during the *Revolutions of 1848,* the British proletariat was able to trust in its government's capacity to make gradual reforms.
- In 1866, *Whig* (liberal party) prime minister *William E. Gladstone* (1807–1898) attempted to expand voter eligibility but was defeated in Parliament.
- A new government under Tory (Conservative) *Benjamin Disraeli* (1804–1881) turned the tables on the Whig reformers by getting the *Second Reform Bill*, 1867, through Parliament.
  - The bill not only doubled the size of the electorate but gave the vote to many industrial workers.
  - When Disraeli's party lost the general election in 1868 (the head of the party that wins the most seats in a

parliamentary election forms a government and becomes prime minister), Gladstone returned to power and enacted sweeping reforms.

- *Labor unions were legalized*; the *secret ballot* was introduced.
- *Free public education* was offered to working-class children.
- The Third Reform Bill of 1885 largely granted universal male suffrage.
- Feminists pressed for legal, economic, and political rights for women as well as for improved working conditions.
- In the decade immediately before the start of the First World War, Britain laid the foundations for its *social welfare state*: government institutions and laws that guaranteed all citizens a decent standard of living.
  - The right of unions to strike was put into law.
  - Government insurance was provided for those injured on the job.
  - Unemployment insurance and old-age pensions were enacted.
  - A compulsory school attendance law went into effect.
  - Women received the right to vote and other rights as time progressed.

## France

The *Age of Metternich* was the period of reaction after the 1815 Congress of Vienna and ended with the Continent-wide Revolutions of 1848. During the Age of Metternich, France was ruled by Bourbon reactionaries and a "bourgeois" king whose watered-down constitutions excluded the expanding proletariat from representation. After the upheavals of 1848, a self-styled emperor, who was a relative of Napoleon, took the French throne.

- When Bourbon *Louis XVIII* (r. 1814–1824), a brother of the guillotined Louis XVI, was restored to the throne in 1814, he issued a constitution but gave power to only a small class of landowners and rich bourgeoisie.
- Absolutist pretenses were continued with Louis XVIII's successor and younger brother, *Charles X* (r. 1824–1830). Charles's repressive measures led to rioting in Paris and his abdication in the summer of 1830, a year when abortive insurrections broke out all over Europe.
  - Charles's abdication caused a rift between radicals, who wanted to establish a republic, and bourgeoisie, who wanted the stability of a monarchy.
  - Through the intercession of the Marquis de Lafayette, hero of the American Revolution, Louis Philippe (r. 1830–1848), an aristocrat, became the *"bourgeois" king* by agreeing to honor the Constitution of 1814. His reign empowered the bourgeoisie but left the proletariat unrepresented.
  - Known as the *July Revolution*, this insurrection in 1830 included the Three Glorious Days of July 27–29 in which students were massacred and the "bourgeois" king was placed upon the throne, resulting in no gains for the movement. This vain revolution was glorified in great French works such as *Liberty Leading the People* by Eugene Delacroix.
- Rampant corruption in the government of Louis Philippe incited republican and socialist protests. These protests erupted in violence and led to his abdication in February 1848, another year that saw mostly abortive insurrections all over Europe.
  - The *Chamber of Deputies,* the lower house of the two-chamber French legislature that was created in 1814 by Louis XVIII's constitution, was pressured by Parisian mobs to *proclaim a republic* and to name a provisional government that would rule temporarily until a Constituent Assembly could be elected to draft a new constitution.
  - When the provinces—the countryside outside the large cities—elected a largely conservative Constituent Assembly, conflicts among the government, socialists, and radical workers erupted into bloody class battles on the streets of Paris by early summer 1848.
- The June Days Uprising was an uprising staged by the workers of France in response to plans to close the National Workshops, created by the Second Republic to provide work and a source of income for the

unemployed. The National Guard, led by General Louis Eugène Cavaignac, was called out to quell the protests. Over 10,000 people were either killed or injured, while 4,000 more were deported to Algeria.

- Frightened by the threat of a radical takeover, the Constituent Assembly brutally suppressed the riots. Then it established the *single-chambered Legislative Assembly* and *a strong president,* both to be elected by *universal male suffrage.*

- *Louis Napoleon Bonaparte* (r. 1848–1870), Napoleon's nephew, was elected president of the *Second Republic.* (The First Republic was established in 1792, during the French Revolution.)
  - He dedicated his presidency to law and order, to the eradication of socialism and radicalism, and to the interests of the conservative classes: the Church, the army, property owners, and businesses.
  - Through a political ploy, he was able to discredit many members of the Legislative Assembly, win a landslide reelection, and proclaim himself in 1852 as Emperor *Napoleon III* of the *Second French Empire.* (His uncle, Napoleon Bonaparte, had crowned himself emperor in 1804.)
  - Although the Second Empire was not an absolutist government, it was an autocracy.
  - Napoleon III controlled finances and initiated legislation.
  - He was immensely popular in the early years of his reign because of his internal improvements, such as highway, canal, and railroad construction, and because of his subsidies to industry and his stimulation of the economy.
  - The bourgeoisie were grateful for the general prosperity; the proletariats were appreciative of employment and the right to organize unions.
  - During the *Liberal Empire* (1860–1870), Napoleon III eased censorship and granted amnesty to political prisoners.
  - Foreign affairs were his downfall.

- The *Crimean War* (1853–1856), in which the French and British were allies and went to war to prevent the Russians from establishing dominance over the Black Sea possessions of the Ottomans, was costly on all sides.

- The *Franco-Prussian War*, which helped unify Germany, was a disaster for the French and Napoleon III. The Germans crushed the French and laid siege to Paris, forcing a humiliating defeat upon the French that contributed to the destabilization of Western Europe during the 20th century.

- The French defeat in the Franco-Prussian War ended the Second Empire and began the Third Republic. Controlled by monarchists and the bourgeoisie, the new National Assembly brutally suppressed a radical socialist countergovernment, the *Paris Commune.*

- In 1875, the assembly voted to set up a *Chamber of Deputies*, which was elected by universal male suffrage; a *Senate*, which was indirectly elected; a ceremonial president, who was elected by the whole legislature; and a premier, who was directly responsible to the Chamber of Deputies.

- From the establishment of the Third Republic in 1871 to the beginning of the First World War in 1914, *the French government fell dozens of times.* The governments were inherently unstable because there were so many political parties. France had a *multiparty system*, unlike the British or American two-party systems. So no party could win a clear majority in the Legislative Assembly, and the coalitions fell apart during many a crisis.

- The *Dreyfus Affair* (1894–1906), in which a Jewish army captain was falsely accused of spying by anti-republican conservatives, was one instance of the political infighting that often paralyzed the government.

- The multiparty system of France seemed to carry democracy to excess. By the First World War, though, France had universal male suffrage and had instituted a *social welfare system* similar to that in Britain.

By the early part of the 20th century, Britain and France had evolved into two of the world's three most powerful democracies, the United States being the third. The old liberalism of laissez-faire government had been replaced by a new liberalism that supported the extension of suffrage and the improvement of living conditions for all citizens.

# The Suppression of Democracy

## The Concert of Europe

After the Congress of Vienna, the Concert of Europe acted like an early form of the United Nations. It ended in failure when the British pulled out in 1823. However, it was originally created as a venue for the powerful nations of Europe to join together in first the Quadruple Alliance and then the Quintuple Alliance to pursue international policies to preserve the status quo. Metternich was the architect and leader of the Concert of Europe. In many ways the Concert of Europe was the earliest predecessor to the United Nations. Thus, its creation marked a beginning of a move toward more internationalism in Europe, however short-lived it was.

## The Holy Alliance, the Quadruple Alliance, and the Quintuple Alliance

The most conservative of the European nations came together at the Congress of Vienna to form the *Holy Alliance*, which was dedicated to preserving autocracy, religious orthodoxy, and the status quo in all things. Russia's Czar Alexander I proposed the Holy Alliance to the other powers at the Congress of Vienna. This alliance relied on the personal obligations of the monarchs to preserve monarchy in Europe. The Holy Alliance was led by Metternich of Austria but also included Russia and Prussia. They joined the United Kingdom in forming the *Quadruple Alliance* to protect the balance of power in Europe and to prevent France from disturbing that balance again.

The Quadruple Alliance was created as a means of preserving the balance of power set up at the Congress of Vienna. It required all four nations to preserve the conditions of the treaty ending the Congress of Vienna. It required the great powers to meet at regular intervals to address issues that could disturb the balance of power in Europe. All four nations pledged to fight against any revolutions against monarchies. The Greek independence movement was the death knell for this alliance in the 1820s.

The *Quintuple Alliance* was the addition of France to the Quadruple Alliance after enough time had passed since the defeat of Napoleon. All three of these alliances—the Holy Alliance, the Quadruple Alliance, and the Quintuple Alliance—were very conservative in nature. They all supported preservation of the political and economic status quo in Europe.

## Germany Through the Age of Metternich (1815–1848)

The Congress of Vienna set up a *Germanic Confederation* of the 39 independent German states that existed after the fall of Napoleon, which destroyed the Holy Roman Empire once and for all. *Klemens von Metternich*, the chancellor of Austria, was the leading force promoting conservatism on the Continent as a means to preserve the unity and power of his multiethnic empire.

- Radical student organizations, *Burschenschafts*, which were dedicated to the creation of a unified Germany that would be governed by constitutional principles, organized a national convention in 1817. In 1819, these organizations attempted the assassination of reactionary politicians.
- In 1819, Metternich issued the infamous Carlsbad Decrees, which were antisubversive laws designed to get the liberals out of Austria, the Austrian press, and Austrian universities.
  - Metternich had a state secret police. He attempted to control what was published and what was discussed at universities. The Carlsbad Decrees drove liberalism and nationalism underground.
- Although the reactionary forces in Germany quickly put down the *Revolutions of 1830*, Prussia set up an economic union of 17 German states, the *Zollverein*, that eliminated internal tariffs and set the tone for greater union.

## Liberalism vs. Conservatism

Metternich was the leader of a conservative movement that had emerged as a reaction to the French Revolution across Europe. *Edmund Burke*, an Englishman who condemned the French Revolution, is also one of the earliest conservative thinkers in European history.  In many ways, the emergence of the conservative ideology as a response to the spread of liberalism supported the Hegelian perspective of history. In this perspective, an idea emerged and was fostered by society, then an antithesis was proposed and was adopted by society, finally the two ideas merged to create a synthesis of a new worldview. If conservatism emerged as a reaction to liberalism, what were both ideas about?

- Liberalism was centered on the concept that society could be improved by civic-minded, enlightened leaders. Liberals generally believed in the following:
  - They believed in popular sovereignty.
  - Liberalism shifted from laissez-faire to interventionist economic and social policies in response to the challenges of industrialization.
  - Liberals believed in individual rights.
  - They pursued enlightened self-interest.
  - Not all agreed on the extent to which all groups in society should participate in its governance.
  - Liberal thinkers included *Jeremy Bentham, John Stuart Mill*, and *Montesquieu.*
- Conservatism was based upon the idea that societal change is dangerous and that the status quo should be protected.  Conservatives generally believed in the following:
  - They believed in traditional religious authority.
  - Conservatives wanted to maintain the status quo in society.
  - They believed that human nature is not perfectible.
  - Conservatives believed that the *Concert of Europe* could preserve the status quo.
  - They suppressed movements for change.
  - Some famous conservatives included *Klemens von Metternich, Joseph de Maistre*, and *Edmund Burke.*
- The clash between these two ideologies—liberalism and conservatism—created a social and political conflict between members of society that still rages today.
- These ideologies were adopted by politicians who propagandized their views to the public in elections and in the press.
- Both ideologies were found on the political spectrum that emerged after the French Revolution.
- Europe passed through periods in which governments were primarily liberal or primarily conservative, marking a political cycle of popular opinion regarding these ideologies.
- *Do not confuse the concepts of "liberal" and "conservative" from European history with the claims of modern American liberals and conservatives. These terms mean different things in European history than they do in contemporary American politics.*

## Greece Won Independence from the Ottoman Empire

In 1825, the Greek nationalists organized a national revolt against their Ottoman rulers. Metternich of Austria was, as expected, in favor of preserving the status quo. However, the British and the Russians both had compelling cultural, political, and economic reasons for supporting the Greeks in their fight for independence. With Russian military and British naval support, the Greeks won their war and established the nation of Greece in 1828. This was an anomaly during the Age of Metternich as most revolutions of this era, such as the ones in France and Italy, were brutally suppressed.

- Greeks were supported by Russia, the United Kingdom, and France.
- Ottomans were supported by Egypt and North African vassal states.

- The Egyptian fleet was defeated at the Battle of Navarino.
- Greece was recognized as a sovereign state in 1830.

## Poland's Revolt Suppressed by Russia

In 1830 in reaction to a Russian plan to use Polish soldiers to help quell the July Revolution in France, the Polish army revolted against their Russian overlords. Poland had been partitioned in the Congress of Vienna among Prussia, Russia, and Austria, so it disappeared from the map as an independent nation. When the Polish nationalists in the army started to revolt, they received some assistance from Lithuanians, Belorussians, and Ukrainians who were also ethnic minorities in the Russian Empire. The Russians reestablished the ideals of the Holy Alliance that they had previously ignored in Greece due to their other obligation to protect all those of the Eastern Orthodox faith. The Russians once again stood against changes to the status quo politically when their own empire was threatened by nationalism. The Polish forces were easily defeated by 1831. The Polish people would have to wait until after the First World War to put their nation back on the map. The suppression of this nationalist uprising became a romantic cause for those in favor of ethnic self-determination all over the world.

## The Age of Metternich Ended in the Revolutions of 1848

- Every nation in Europe save the most advanced, Britain, and the least advanced, Russia, experienced revolutions.
- This year saw Metternich flee Austria during the Continent-wide uprisings.
- These revolutions proved what Mary Wollstonecraft had said in reference to the oppression of women, "The bow that is bent twice as far snaps back twice as hard."
- The revolutions ended in failure for the most part because the political conditions after the revolutions were unchanged from what they had been before the revolutions.
- The Prussian king, Frederick William IV (r. 1840–1861), reacted to the *Revolutions of 1848* by calling a nominal Legislative Assembly rather than using military force.
  - In 1850, he granted a constitution that established a House of Representatives elected by universal male suffrage but controlled by the wealthiest classes.
  - The Frankfurt Assembly, an extralegal convention not to be confused with the king's Legislative Assembly, met from May 1848 to May 1849 and *established the nature of the future union of Germany.*
  - Frederick William advocated a *Greater Germany* (*Grossdeutsch*). He wanted to include Austria and to have a Habsburg emperor rule over the union.
  - Supporters of a *Lesser Germany* (*Kleindeutsch*) wanted to exclude Austria and to have Prussia lead the union.
- The debate was resolved when Austria backed away from the proposed union. When the Frankfurt Assembly offered Frederick William the crown of a united Germany with Austria excluded, he declined by saying that he would accept it only from the German princes themselves.
- The failure of the Frankfurt Assembly to implement its design for a democratic union (it had framed a kind of bill of rights) left the job of German unification to Prussian militarism and *Bismarck's policy of "blood and iron."* (German politics until the First World War are considered in a later chapter.)

# The Revolutions of 1848

## France

| Causes | Length of Time | Protagonists | Events | Results |
|---|---|---|---|---|
| The economic changes in Britain as well as the expansion of the franchise there led to social pressures in France. Political demonstration was outlawed, so people held political banquets instead, which were outlawed. The oppression of Louis Napoleon and his repressive minister, Guizot, pushed the people to the breaking point because of censorship and restriction of freedoms when 52 demonstrators were killed by soldiers. | 1847–1848 | Louis Blanc, Pierre Proudhon, Louis Cavaignac, Alphonse de Lamartine, and Napoleon III | Louis Philippe fled to Britain, and Guizot resigned as barricades emerged across Paris. The Second Republic was formed in 1848 based on universal male suffrage. A class struggle ensued between rich and poor, rural and urban. The urban workers tried a Marxist experiment that failed. | Napoleon III reigned after winning elections in landslides. Napoleon III dismissed the National Assembly and ruled with more power and control than Louis Philippe had held. |

## German States

| Causes | Length of Time | Protagonists | Events | Results |
|---|---|---|---|---|
| The news of the revolutions in France spread throughout Europe, and the people of the 39 Germanic states began to demand rights. | February 1848– May 1848 | The French leaders and the bourgeoisie of Germany and Richard Wagner | The people of Baden demanded the first German Bill of Rights in February of 1848. Soon a crowd threatened the palace in Berlin. After an incident in which demonstrators were killed, King William Frederick IV demonstrated support for the revolutionaries and promised to reorganize his government. King Ludwig abdicated in Bavaria, and Saxony also saw calls for reform. | The king still reigned. Otto von Bismarck would soon come to power with Wilhelm I. They would unite the western German states into modern Germany through almost dictatorial rule. |

## Habsburg Empire

| Causes | Length of Time | Protagonists | Events | Results |
|---|---|---|---|---|
| This multiethnic empire was held together with force by Metternich's political machinations. | February 1848– August 1849 | Many listed in other columns. | The empire burst into separate parts. | The Habsburg Empire was returned to its former state of a multiethnic empire. |
| In 1848, Continental Europe was mostly France, Germany, Russia, and either the Habsburg Empire or former Habsburg Empire. | | | Austria, with the help of archconservative Russian Czar Nicholas I, was able to reassemble a weakened empire. | Croats, Slovaks, Germans, Austrians, Poles, Magyars, Serbs, Ruthenians, Italians, and Czechs all advocated for the right to their own nations representing their ethnic groups. |

| Causes | Length of Time | Protagonists | Events | Results |
|---|---|---|---|---|
| The Habsburg Empire was in decline and was not held together well. | | | | The Habsburg Empire returned to its former state of a multiethnic empire. |
| The different ethnic groups all attempted to gain autonomy in 1848 as the idea of nationalism seemed to sweep the Continent. | | | | The central authority was further weakened, and the empire lasted only until 1918. |
| In this year the Communist Manifesto was published in German. | | | | |

## Hungary

| Causes | Length of Time | Protagonists | Events | Results |
|---|---|---|---|---|
| Ethnic oppression by the Austrian Habsburgs burst the Austrian Empire into separate parts in 1848. The Hungarian parliament was called in 1825 to address financial matters. A bloodless revolution occurred in March of 1848, led by a governor and a prime minister. | March 1848– October 1849 | Louis Kossuth and Louis Bathyany | The Hungarians took advantage of the general revolutions throughout the Habsburg Empire and got Austria to grant them autonomy. Once Austria beat down the other revolutions, the new emperor, Franz Josef I, decided to crush Hungary. With help from Russia, the Hungarians were defeated in a failed war for independence. | The Habsburg Empire was returned to its former state of a multiethnic empire of Croats, Slovaks, Germans, Austrians, Poles, Magyars, Serbs, Ruthenians, Italians, and Czechs. The Hungarians practiced passive resistance against the Habsburgs. |

## Italian States

| Causes | Length of Time | Protagonists | Events | Results |
|---|---|---|---|---|
| Giuseppe Mazzini | March 1848– May 1849 | Giuseppe Mazzini and Giuseppe Garibaldi | The revolutions resulted in Venetian and Roman republics. The Austrians marched through Piedmont and southward into Italy, conquering most of Italy by May of 1849. | Almost 1,000 people were killed by the Austrians as they regained power throughout the peninsula. |

## Poland

| Causes | Length of Time | Protagonists | Events | Results |
|---|---|---|---|---|
| The Prussians armed Polish prisoners and encouraged them to return to Poland with revolutionary and anti-Russian motives. | March 1848– June 1848 | Jerzy Zdrada, Frederick William IV, Natalis Sulerzyski, and Seweryn Elzanowski | The Prussians supported a Polish revolution to weaken the Russians. The Poles did not trust the Prussians but needed them. The Poles and Prussians ended up in armed conflict, which the Prussians won. | The Poles learned that they could not bargain with the Germanic states to gain statehood. The Poles focused on economic growth rather than on political growth. |

## Reflections on the Revolutions of 1848

Although all of the revolutions ended in failure, they set the stage for the next great political movements in Europe, the unification of Italy and Germany. The lesson learned from the revolutions as a whole is that it is much easier to unite the people against the current government than it is to get them to agree on a better form of government for the future. Most of the revolutions fell apart due to conflicts between the rebels about what they should do after gaining power. Their lack of a unified plan to rule allowed the former governments, for the most part, to return to power. The failure of the revolutions was also an indicator of how factionalism can be an impediment to popular sovereignty as the factions within the revolutionary groups were largely responsible for the failures of the Revolutions of 1848.

## Austria from the Age of Metternich to the First World War (1815–1914)

The Revolutions of 1830 hardly touched the reactionary government of Austria under Metternich. However, the ethnic mix that made up the Austrian Empire—Germans, Hungarians, Slavs, Czechs, Italians, Serbs, Croats, and many others—helped bring about revolution in 1848.

- When Paris erupted in rebellion in March of 1848, *Louis Kossuth*, a Hungarian nationalist, aroused separatist sentiment in the *Hungarian Diet* (a national assembly legal in the empire).
  - Rioting broke out in Vienna.
  - Prince Metternich, then chancellor, fled the country. The Hungarians, the Czechs, and three northern Italian provinces of the empire declared autonomy.
  - The empire collapsed temporarily.
  - The Prague Conference was called by the Czechs in response to the all-German Frankfurt Conference.
- Austria developed the notion of Austroslavism, by which the Slavic groups within the empire would remain part of the empire.
- Austria set up autonomous national governments in ethnic regions.
  - Before the idea could be adopted, a series of victories by Austrian armies restored Habsburg authority over the various nationalities that had declared independence.
- *Franz Joseph* (r. 1848–1916) replaced *Emperor Ferdinand I,* and conservative forces within the government centralized power and suppressed all opposition.
  - The Revolutions of 1848 failed in Austria largely because the empire's ethnic minorities squabbled among themselves instead of making a united front against imperial Habsburg forces.
- The defeat of Austria in the Austro-Prussian War of 1866 (which is considered in a subsequent chapter) led to some governmental reform.
- The Compromise of 1867 set up a constitutional government with limited suffrage, granted the Hungarians internal autonomy, and created a *dual monarchy*, called the *Austro-Hungarian Empire*.
  - Exclusion of the Slavic minorities from a voice in government encouraged the *Pan-Slavic movement* to seek independence for ethnic minorities.
  - The Compromise of 1867 was an important cause of the First World War.

## Russia from the End of the Napoleonic Wars to the First World War (1815–1914)

*Alexander I* (r. 1801–1825) began his reign by extending the reforms of Catherine the Great, by modernizing the functioning of his government, and by offering greater freedom to Jews within his empire. Napoleon's invasion of Russia in 1812 turned this disposition about until, by 1820, Alexander had ordered statewide censorship and the adherence of all his subjects to the Russian Orthodox Church.

- When Alexander died, a confusion in succession (his two brothers, *Constantine* and *Nicholas,* were both in line) led to the *Decembrist Revolt* of army officers in December 1825 in the capital of St. Petersburg.

- The army officers supported the candidacy of Constantine, who they believed would modernize the nation and offer a constitution.
- *Nicholas I* (r. 1825–1855) attained the throne after crushing the revolt, and his reign continued Alexander's autocratic policies.
  - Nicholas was creator of the infamous *Third Section*, the secret police who prevented the spread of revolutionary or Western ideas. *Orthodoxy, autocracy, nationality* was the rallying cry against these ideas.
  - Intellectuals in Russia developed two opposing camps during this period:
    - *Slavophiles* believed that Russian village (the mir) culture was superior to that of the West.
    - *Westernizers* wanted to extend the *genius of Russian culture* by industrializing and setting up a constitutional government.
- *Alexander II* (r. 1855–1881) began his reign as a reformer and ended it as a conservative.
  - His *Emancipation Proclamation* of 1861 *ended serfdom*, the medieval institution largely abolished in the rest of Europe. Under serfdom, peasants were bound to the land and were virtually owned by the aristocratic landowners.
  - His murder at the hands of a militant faction of the *Narodniks,* a socialist group that wanted Russia to return to some mythical ideal of village life, increased repression under his successors, who turned to autocracy, orthodoxy, and nationality.
- By the 1890s, Russia had undertaken *industrialization* in order to remain a world power.
  - *Sergei Witte*, the greatest economic thinker in imperial Russian history, led the drive for economic change as the Minister of Finance. He planned the industrialization of Russia and invited foreign companies to build factories in Russia.
  - At the beginning of the First World War, 25 million of the Russian population of 140 million were city dwellers.
  - The *Trans-Siberian Railroad* linked European and Asiatic Russia.
  - The members of the growing proletariat were largely employed in state-owned factories that exploited and abused them.

## Practice Questions

### Long Essay

These questions are samples of the various types of thematic essays on the AP exam. See pages 27–28 for a detailed explanation of each type. Check over the generic rubric (see pages 28–29) before you begin any of these essays, and use that rubric to score your essay if you write one.

### Question 1

To what extent and in what ways did the failure of the German constitutionalists lead to the Prussian militarists unifying Germany?

### Comments on Question 1

This is a *causation* question because it requires you to explain how one event, the failure of the constitutionalists to unify Germany, resulted in a specific outcome, the Prussian militarists dominating German unification. Remember to describe the causes and/or effects of German unification. Support your analysis of those causes and effects with specific evidence. The essay must also explain how the failure of the constitutionalists led Germany to be united later by Bismarck and the Prussian militarists. Cite specific evidence as support. There is little room for choice in this question since it requires that you show how and how much of German unification was the result of a failure of the forces of democracy to take the lead, thereby leaving it to the militarists in Prussia. Refer to specifics in the breakdown of the leadership of constitutional forces, in the assumption of leadership by Prussia, and in the militaristic nature of Prussian leadership.

## Question 2

To what extent did Austria's suppression of Slavic autonomy within the empire create more dissolution than unity?

### Comments on Question 2

This is a *causation* question because it requires you to explain to what extent one factor, Austrian suppression of a Slavic minority within the empire, resulted in a specific outcome, the dissolution of unity within the empire. Remember to describe the causes and/or effects of the dissolution of the Austrian Empire. Support your analysis of those causes and effects with specific evidence. The essay must explain the reasons that suppression of the Slavic minority did or did not result in the dissolution of the empire. In this case—because of the crucial phrase "more dissolution than unity"—the argument must show that one or the other was true.

   As is often the case, the question itself shows the direction of the best possible argument: that dissolution was the result of Austria's policy toward its Slavic minorities. Back this up with both previous and future actions and evaluations of the strength of the Austrian Empire over time. Then tie the result to the causation, which was the attempt to suppress the Slavs, and decide to what extent that attempt was the cause of the weakening of the empire.

## Question 3

Compare the growth and suppression of democracy in 19th-century Europe.

### Comments on Question 3

This is a *compare* skill question. Be sure to describe the similarities and differences between how democracy simultaneously grew and was crushed during the era. You must also account for or explain those similarities or differences by providing specific examples of how they could suppress democracy. Tie the trends in political voices being heard to historical developments, such as the rise of conservatism. This has a double effort: to show differences and to examine similarities. Democracy did not grow easily in the states where it was ultimately successful, nor did it flounder completely in those where it was suppressed. This is a broad question that requires more than a comparison of only two states.

## Short-Answer

1. Answer all parts of the question that follows based on your knowledge of European history. Historians have often referred to the period of European history between 1815 and 1848 as the Age of Metternich.

   (a) Provide TWO pieces of information that support this characterization of the period and explain how they support it.

   (b) Provide ONE piece of information that refutes this characterization of the period and explain how the information refutes it.

2.  Use the image and the passage below to answer all parts of the following question.

### Source 1

The reception of Queen Victoria by Napoleon III at St. Cloud, August 18, 1855.

### Source 2

#### James Russell Lowell, *On Democracy*

But is it democracies alone that fall into these errors? I, who have seen it proposed to erect a statue to Hudson, the railway king, and have heard Louis Napoleon hailed as the savior of society by men who certainly had no democratic associations or leanings, am not ready to think so. But democracies have likewise their finer instincts. I have also seen the wisest statesman and most pregnant speaker of our generation, a man of humble birth and ungainly manners, of little culture beyond what his own genius supplied, become more absolute in power than any monarch of modern times through the reverence of his countrymen for his honesty, his wisdom, his sincerity, his faith in God and man, and the nobly humane simplicity of his character.

(a)  Explain one accomplishment of Louis Napoleon.

(b)  Assess the form of government in France when Louis Napoleon took power in 1848.

(c)  Assess the form of government used by Louis Napoleon by the end of his reign in 1870.

## Multiple-Choice

**Questions 1–4 refer to the writing of historian Jonathan Sperber in his *The European Revolutions 1848–1851* below.**

Rather darker is another version of the 1848 revolutions that views them primarily as farce, a revolution made by the revolutionaries who were at best incompetent dilettantes, and at worst cowards and blowhards who stole away from the scene when going got rough. This version features the story of the Parisian revolutionary observing from his window a demonstrating crowd go by, springing up from his chair, and rushing out, proclaiming 'I am their leader; I must follow them.' Another typical victim of the retrospective contempt is the Frankfurt National Assembly, the all-German parliament.

The third and probably most substantial of the historians' versions of 1848 directs attention to the failure of the revolutions of that year to establish new regimes, pointing out that after a shorter or longer interval, usually shorter, the authorities overthrown at the onset of the revolutions were returned to power.

1. Which of the following viewpoints is Sperber most likely to support according to the excerpt above?

    (A) The Revolutions of 1848 had no impact on European political evolution.
    (B) The Revolutions of 1848 were failures mostly because of poor leadership.
    (C) The Revolutions of 1848 ended with mostly the same people in power as when they had begun.
    (D) The Revolutions of 1848 changed Eastern Europe more than Western Europe.

2. Which of the following was destroyed as a result of the Revolutions of 1848?

    (A) The Concert of Europe
    (B) The European alliance system
    (C) The belief that liberal republics could be formed
    (D) The legacy of Klemens von Metternich

3. Which of the following countries did NOT experience a revolution in 1848 for the reason given in the answer?

    (A) Britain, because it was already experiencing an industrial revolution
    (B) Britain, because it had already become a mostly capitalist democracy
    (C) France, because the French Revolution made the French less likely to revolt in the future
    (D) Italy, because the independent states began to work together to eliminate poverty there

4. Which of the following utopian socialists got the opportunity to test out his ideas in France during the Revolutions of 1848?

    (A) Henri de Saint-Simon
    (B) Louis Blanc
    (C) Charles Fourier
    (D) Louis Kossuth

**Questions 5–7 refer to the image below.**

Troops storming a barricade in the Donesgasse in Frankfurt,
Germany, in 1848. The Granger Collection.

5. The Revolutions of 1848 were most often led by which of the following?

   (A) Aristocrats tired of losing their privileges
   (B) Military leaders fed up with inefficient leaders
   (C) Liberal bourgeois gentlemen dedicated to romantic ideals
   (D) The poorest citizens who had nothing to lose

6. Which of the following was the original goal of the Frankfurt Assembly (1848–1849)?

   (A) Design and implement a constitutional government for a unified Germany
   (B) Consolidate Germany under Austrian Habsburg leadership
   (C) Unify the northern states of Germany under Prussia
   (D) Create a united Germany for Germans only

7. The overall results of the Revolutions of 1848 can best be described as which of the following?

   (A) Overthrew the governments of France, Germany, and Russia
   (B) Dissipated the nationalistic urges of the peoples of Eastern Europe
   (C) Marked the decline of the political influence of the proletariat
   (D) Gave rise to communism and realpolitik

# Answers and Explanations

## Short-Answer Explanations

1. (a) You should cite *two* of the following and *explain how* each supports the characterization of the time period as the Age of Metternich: rise of conservatism, Austria's central role in European politics at the time, Metternich's redesign of Europe after the Congress of Vienna to create the Concert of Europe, Metternich's role at the Congress of Vienna, the Holy Alliance, and/or Austria's dominance over the other Germanic states.

   (b) You should cite *one* of the following and *explain how* it refutes the characterization of the period as the Age of Metternich: the rise of the United Kingdom as a European power, the collapse of the Concert of Europe, the Revolutions of 1830 and 1848, the decline of the Austrian Empire, the lack of Austrian international trade, the concurrent rise of democracy in much of Europe (U.K. and France), and/or Metternich fleeing to London in 1848.

2. (a) You may fully explain any one of the following: eradication of radicalism in France, banning socialism in France, creating the Second French Empire, improving France's infrastructure, AND bringing prosperity to the French bourgeoisie.

   (b) You must indicate that Louis Napoleon was elected by popular vote and ran a democratic state when he was first elected president.

   (c) You must explain the rise of the Second French Empire and the fact that Napoleon III was an emperor by the end of his rule in 1870. You should also mention that this was an autocratic government and that Napoleon III was able to hold most power by himself.

## Practice Multiple-Choice Questions

1. (A) is wrong because the Revolutions of 1848 changed European society and awakened a desire for popular sovereignty.

   (B) is wrong because Sperber was arguing that the most substantial version is the one that returned old leaders to their original posts, not the view that poor leaders ruined it.

   **(C) is CORRECT because Sperber was arguing that the most substantial version is the one that returned old leaders to their original posts.**

   (D) is wrong because 1848 affected Western Europe much more than Eastern Europe, which was controlled mostly by Russia, Austria, and the Ottomans.

2. **(A) is CORRECT because the Concert of Europe disintegrated when Metternich fled in 1848.**

   (B) is wrong because the European alliance system was revived by Bismarck and played a large role in Europe through the First World War.

   (C) is wrong because many still believed in liberal republics after 1848, but those republics would not become a reality in most of Europe until after the First World War.

   (D) is wrong because Metternich's legacy as the prototype conservative lived on after 1848.

3. (A) is wrong because most of Europe was in the middle of an industrial revolution when it had revolts in 1848, so that does not explain why Britain was spared.

   **(B) is CORRECT; Britain was spared a revolution because it was already politically and economically more advanced than the rest of Europe.**

   (C) is wrong because the Revolutions of 1848 began in France.

   (D) is wrong because Italy did experience revolutions in 1848.

4. (A) is wrong because Saint-Simon was already dead in 1848 (he died in 1825).

   **(B) is CORRECT because Louis Blanc was helping rule France for a short time in 1848 and tried National Workshops and other socialist methods to try to help France recover.**

(C) is wrong because Fourier was already dead by 1848 (he died in 1837).

(D) is wrong because Louis Kossuth was a Hungarian leader in 1848 and had little to do with France.

5. (A) is wrong because the aristocracy was not taking to the streets to try to regain privileges they had lost, as the time of their authority had passed.

(B) is wrong because the military leaders were in the minority in the revolts that were mostly led by romantically minded liberal bourgeois young men who thought they could fix the world.

**(C) is CORRECT because the revolutions were led mostly by romantically minded liberal bourgeois young men who thought they could fix the world.**

(D) is wrong because the poor citizens were followers rather than leaders.

6. **(A) is CORRECT because the Frankfurt Assembly was created to design and implement a German constitution for all Germanic states. The assembly offered the crown to Wilhelm of Prussia, but he refused.**

(B) is wrong because there was never a plan to unify Austria and Prussia at the Frankfurt Assembly.

(C) is wrong because the plan was to unify all German states.

(D) is wrong because Germans did not take part in ethnic cleansing in the 1800s.

7. (A) is wrong because Russia did not have an uprising in 1848.

(B) is wrong because nationalism remained strong in Eastern Europe after 1848 and would be an immediate cause of the First World War.

(C) is wrong because the proletariat would continue to gain strength well into the 20th century.

**(D) is CORRECT because the ideas of realpolitik and communism were continually used after 1848 to change European society.**

# UNIT 7

# 19th-Century Perspectives and Political Developments

## Unit 7 Overview: Nationalism, Imperialism, and Progress into Modernity

**Unit description:** This unit covers several chapters. It discusses much of the progress of Europe from the beginning of the Industrial Revolution to the creation of modern Europe in political, social, and economic institutions. The unit also covers cultural and artistic trends during the era from 1830–1914. The European domination of the rest of the world through imperialism and the movement toward creating the modern map of Europe with the unification of Italy and Germany are the major focus of this unit. The interaction between European nations and the rest of the world as well as European interactions among themselves as new unified nations emerged provides most of the narrative for the unit. The changing cultural, intellectual, and artistic trends of the 19th century are also examined in this unit. This unit is very important when setting the stage for the global conflicts of the two world wars and setting up the societies and economic forces that would create the modern world. Five of the seven themes of AP European history are interwoven throughout the unit: Interaction of Europe and the World, Cultural and Intellectual Developments, States and Other Institutions of Power, National and European Identity, and Technological and Scientific Innovation.

This unit is focused on the changing relationships between Europe and the rest of the world and the emergence of nationalism as a social and political force in Europe. Topics of study include: Contextualizing 19th-Century Perspectives and Political Developments, Nationalism, National Unification and Diplomatic Tensions, Darwinism and Social Darwinism, The Age of Progress and Modernity, New Imperialism: Motivations and Methods, Imperialism's Global Effects, 19th-Century Culture and Arts, and Causation in 19th-Century Perspectives and Political Developments.

This unit is comprised of chapters 8 and 9, in which all events occur during time period 3.

# 8

# The Ideologies of the 19th Century: Liberalism, Conservatism, Nationalism, and Culture

## Key Terms

- Unification
- Austro-Prussian (Seven Weeks' War)
- Franco-Prussian War
- Dreyfus Affair
- Realpolitik

- Breach loading rifle/ needle gun
- Congress of Berlin
- Liberalism
- Pan-Slavism
- Socialism
- Romanticism

- Meiji Restoration
- Realism
- Impressionism
- Germ theory
- Antiseptics
- Anesthesia

## Key People

- Otto von Bismarck
- Kaiser Wilhelm I
- Guiseppe Mazzini
- Louis Napoleon/ Napoleon III
- Guiseppe Garibaldi
- Camillo di Cavour

- Victor Emmanuel II
- Theodore Herzl
- Sergei Witte
- Peter Stolypin
- Pablo Picasso
- Max Planck
- Marie Curie

- Friedrich Nietzsche
- Louis Pasteur
- Georges Sorel
- Henri Bergson

## Overview

The period following the French Revolution and the Napoleonic Wars, known as the Age of Metternich, saw the rise of powerful ideologies. Some were legacies of the French Revolution, and some were responses to the political, economic, and social upheavals of the previous decades. Nationalism was both the most promising and the most destructive of these. Nationalism was the prime motive for the unification of Italy and of Germany. It was a force that redefined political boundaries and loyalties and that encouraged claims of national or racial superiority.

Liberalism, socialism, and romanticism profoundly influenced the politics, economics, and culture of the first half of the 19th century. European ideas and culture expressed a tension between objectivity and scientific realism on one hand and subjectivity and individual expression on the other.

*Realism* defined the literature of the latter half of the century. *Impressionism* brought the artist's personal visual experience to painting. *Social Darwinism* and positivism provided scientific models for politics and the arts.

One decade, 1861–1871, saw the triumph of the large nation-state as Europe's primary political unit. Italy and Germany consolidated; Austria and Hungary formed autonomous but united states; Russia centralized governmental control.

The nation-state was founded upon a sense of nationalism: a common identity; a specific geographic area; and a common language, history, destiny, culture, ethnicity, or religion. It was a consciousness of belonging and of the differences between one's own people and all others on this planet.

The French Revolution and Napoleon's military successes inspired the drive to national unity throughout Europe. Nationalism promised power, the mystical connection that the Romantic movement glorified, and autonomy from the remote leadership of amorphous, arbitrarily controlled and administered multinational empires. France and England were the two most powerful nation-states before 1861. Italy became united as a kingdom in 1861. Germany formed a new empire in 1871. War played a crucial role in the unification of both Italy and Germany.

The idealism of the Revolutions of 1848 failed to realize the nationalist aspirations of the Italians or the Germans. If the Italian and German peoples, traditionally separated into small independent states, were ready for unification, it still took the "power politics" (*realpolitik*) of two determined men to bring about unity. These men were Camillo di Cavour, who was Sardinian prime minister, and Otto von Bismarck, who was Prussian chancellor. They used the might and prestige of their states to bring smaller independent entities together to create the modern nation-states of Italy and Germany. After 1871, the balance of power in Europe was changed in a way that would last well into the 20th century.

## The Age of Nationalism

After 1848, nationalism became more prevalent in Europe and around the world. A new breed of conservative leaders—including Napoleon III, Cavour, and Bismarck—co-opted the agenda of nationalists for the purposes of creating or strengthening the state. The supremacy of the nation-state was gaining ground in organizing the political, social, economic, and cultural activities of a group. Ethnic identities were central to the development of nationalism, which should not be confused with patriotism or with the level of support for a nation-state.

- *Napoleon III* (also known as *Louis Napoleon*) was the nephew of *the Napoleon* (Napoleon I) who, despite defeat, exile, and death, was considered by the French to be one of their greatest leaders.
  - Louis Napoleon was elected president of France by a landslide in 1848, largely because of his illustrious name.
  - Between 1852, when he had proclaimed a Second Empire, and 1870, after France's ignominious defeat in the Franco-Prussian War, Napoleon III made many improvements:
    - He restored the economy.
    - He laid the foundations for democratic reforms.
    - He renewed the national pride of the French people.
- The creation of the dual monarchy of Austria-Hungary, which recognized the political power of the largest ethnic minority, was an attempt to stabilize the state of Austria into the Austro-Hungarian Empire by reconfiguring national unity.
- The Civil War (1861–1865) in the United States resulted in a more solid union and in a more powerful federal government, setting an example for Europe.
- After defeat at the hands of the French and English in the *Crimean War* (1853–1856), Russia modernized and industrialized. It initiated a program of limited reforms to solidify czarist control over the multinational peoples of Russia's vast reaches.
  - The Crimean War demonstrated the weakness of the Ottoman Empire and contributed to the breakdown of the Concert of Europe.
  - As a result, the conditions in which Italy and Germany could be unified arrived after centuries of fragmentation.
- In Russia, autocratic leaders pushed through a program of reform and modernization. This gave rise to revolutionary movements (and eventually to the Revolution of 1905) and included: the economic reforms of Czar Alexander II, who emancipated the serfs in 1861; *Sergei Witte*'s economic reforms and attempted industrialization; and the attempted but failed agricultural reforms of *Peter Stolypin*.
- Japan, in response to Western incursions in the 1850s and 1860s, developed a modern military, an industrial

economy, and a centralized government under Emperor Meiji, whose ancestors had been mere figureheads, in what became known as the *Meiji Restoration*.

- Many nations were formed in Europe between 1860 and 1914.
- *Pan-Slavism* emerged as a force calling for Russia to protect other majority Slavic nations.
- Anti-Semitism emerged as a form of nationalist hatred against Jewish neighbors within their nation.
  - As a result, *Theodore Herzl* conceived of the idea of *Zionism*, or establishing a Jewish homeland in Israel. This concept picked up energy through the 19th century and became a reality after the end of the Second World War and the *Holocaust*.

# The Unification of Italy

## Italy Before Unification

### Four Separate States

- *The Kingdom of Naples* (Two Sicilies) was made up of the island of Sicily and the southern half of the Italian Peninsula.
- The *Papal States* comprised the middle of the peninsula.
- *Lombardy-Venetia*, industrialized provinces in the North, were ruled by Austria, as were Tuscany, Lucca, Modena, and Parma.
- *The Kingdom of Sardinia* (Piedmont-Sardinia) was made up of the island of Sardinia and the northwestern provinces of Nice, Savoy, and Piedmont.
  - Sardinia was a constitutional monarchy ruled by *Victor Emmanuel II* (r. 1849–1878).
  - Sardinia was the only independent state in Italy.
  - *Camillo di Cavour* (1810–1861) became prime minister of the parliament instituted during the Revolutions of 1848.
    - He rejected the romantic nationalism of *Giuseppe Mazzini* (1805–1872), who had argued in his *Duties of Man* that the nation was a divine device and an extended family.
    - Cavour decided that Italy could be unified only through force and that Sardinia would have to lead the battle.
    - In order to gain the support of liberals throughout Italy, Cavour reformed the government of his state by doing the following:
    - Weakening the influence of the papacy
    - Investing in public works, such as railroads and harbor improvements
    - Abolishing internal tariffs
    - Encouraging the growth of industry
    - Emancipating the peasantry from the vestiges of manorialism
    - Making the Sardinian government a model of progressive constitutionalism

## Cavour's "Power Politics"

After the Crimean War ended in 1856, Cavour, who had brought Sardinia into the war on the side of France in order to attain the favor of France in future situations, petitioned Emperor Napoleon III to support Sardinia in a projected war with Austria, which controlled many Italian provinces.

- In 1858, Cavour persuaded Napoleon III to send a supporting army into Italy in the event that Sardinia could maneuver Austria into a war. This was called the Plombières Agreement.
- Napoleon, who wanted to weaken the Austrians, was promised the French-speaking provinces of Nice and Savoy in return for allowing the Sardinians to annex Northern Italy.
- In April 1859, *Austria declared war on Sardinia* and the French came to Cavour's aid.

- After a series of victories by the combined Sardinian-French forces, Napoleon suddenly pulled out of the war because of criticisms at home and threats from the Prussians.
- The Austrians kept Venice.
- Lombardy went to the Sardinians.
- Several of the northern duchies under Austrian domination declared independence and carried out plebiscites for union with Sardinia by 1860.
- *Giuseppe Garibaldi* (1807–1882), an ardent nationalist, invaded Sicily in 1860 with the encouragement of Cavour.
  - His thousand-man *Red Shirts* used popular support to defeat a Bourbon ruler's force that was 10 times that number.
  - Within months, Garibaldi had subdued Sicily and Naples.
  - The Two Sicilies (Kingdom of Naples) joined Sardinia. In March 1861, *the Kingdom of Italy was proclaimed*, with Victor Emmanuel II on the throne.

## Final Unification

By 1870, the last holdouts of the kingdom of Lombardy-Venetia and the Papal States, despite opposition from the Pope, were incorporated into the growing nation of Italy. *Italia irredenta*, meaning "Italy unredeemed" or Italian areas still under Austrian control, remained "unliberated." However, Italy had been united and was a constitutional monarchy. Democracy was diluted by the small percentage of the male population that had suffrage and by the dominance, in southern Italy, of the landowners. There was a divide between the wealthier and more industrialized northern Italy and the more agrarian and less prosperous southern Italy.

# The Unification of Germany

## Germany Before Unification

In the two decades or so before German unification took place, the population, productivity, and wealth of the German states increased many times over. The *Zollverein* (customs union) had opened most of the states to a mutually advantageous trade, and Germany became a single economic unit. Prussia, with its booming industry, powerful army, militaristic Junkers (land-owning aristocrats), and expansionist ambitions led the states of northern Germany in a face-off with Austria. The Habsburgs of Austria were rulers of a multinational empire held together by tradition and raw power and were also the prime influence among the divided states of Germany. The Habsburgs long feared a Germany united by the Hohenzollerns of Prussia. After the Frankfurt Assembly failed to unify the independent German states in 1848, however, the Prussian *Hohenzollern* kings determined to achieve it by force.

## Bismarck's Realpolitik

When the Prussian parliament refused to approve military expenditures in 1862, *King Wilhelm I* (r. 1861–1888) appointed Otto von Bismarck (1815–1898), a prominent and conservative Junker, as chancellor. Bismarck trampled the parliament by collecting illegal taxes, ignoring its protests, enlarging the army, and in the process, killing democracy in Prussia. His ability to adopt the welfare system that his people wanted even though he did not want it as a way to get the support of the masses is a perfect example of his policy of *realpolitik*. This concept is all about a leader being pragmatic rather than ideological in matters of state. In many ways, realpolitik is a form of *Machiavellianism*.

- *"Blood and iron,"* Bismarck insisted, would solve the issues of his day and unite Germany.
- Bismarck achieved German unification after Prussia won three wars:
  - *The War Against Denmark,* 1864, allied Prussia, Austria, and the other German states in an *all-German war* against Denmark, which had hoped to annex the neighboring province of *Schleswig*.
    - Denmark was quickly defeated. After some prodding by Bismarck, Prussia and Austria fell out over who should get the spoils of war.
  - The *Austro-Prussian War* (*Seven Weeks' War*), 1866, broke out when the issues of the war with Denmark remained unresolved.
  - Although the Austrians enlisted the help of most of the other German states, the superior arms, training, and leadership of the Prussian army defeated Austria in seven weeks, which is why this is sometimes called the Seven Weeks' War.
    - Hoping to gain Austria's support in the inevitable struggle with France, which had become alarmed by Prussia's swift victories, Bismarck made the surrender terms lenient.
- Bismarck established the *North German Confederation* in 1867 to replace the loose union of the *German Confederation* that Napoleon had set up and that the Congress of Vienna had confirmed.
  - Under the leadership of the Prussian king, Wilhelm I, 21 Germanic states of Northern Europe united and created a two-house legislature:
    - The *Reichstag*, or lower house, represented all the people. Its members were to be elected by universal male suffrage.
    - The *Bundesrat*, or upper house, was created to represent the former nobility.
- The *Franco-Prussian War* of 1870 broke out after a dynastic dispute over the Spanish throne led to a flurry of diplomatic exchanges between Prussia and France.
  - Bismarck deliberately altered the wording of the *Ems Dispatch*, an account of the German king's meeting with the French ambassador over the issue. Bismarck then made the inflammatory revision public.
  - Napoleon III, bowing to public opinion and bad advice, declared war on Prussia in July 1870.
  - By September, the Prussian army defeated the French in battle, took the emperor prisoner, and began a four-month siege of Paris.
  - The *Treaty of Frankfurt,* May 1871, gave *Alsace-Lorraine* to Germany and imposed a punishing *indemnity*, both of which the defeated French people were to resent for generations to come.
    - This treaty's harshness led the French to demand punishing terms for Germany in the *Treaty of Versailles* after the First World War.
    - Alsace-Lorraine would go back to France after the First World War.

## Unification

Four southern German states—Baden, Bavaria, Hesse, and Württemberg—that did not already belong to the North German Confederation joined after the flush of Prussian victory. As a result, *the German Empire was born* in January 1871. The Prussian king, Wilhelm I, became emperor, or *kaiser*.

- After 1871, Otto von Bismarck became the hinge upon which the political fate of Europe rested. His attempts to reestablish an alliance system to create a new balance of power that included Germany lasted from 1871–1914, when the First World War broke out and long after Bismarck had been dismissed from office by the foolhardy Wilhelm II. The Bismarckian Alliance System as it was known, however, is also often cited as one of the causes of the First World War.
  - Bismarck convinced Russia and Austria-Hungary to join the *Three Emperors League* from 1873–1878 in which the three autocrats united against Ottoman pressures from the east. It was restarted for two years in 1881, but Russia wanted out.
  - The *Triple Alliance* was an alliance of Germany, Austria-Hungary, and Italy for mutual assistance if any of them were attacked by a foreign power. It existed from 1882–1915.

- ○ Bismarck was concerned about Russia to his east, so he created a Reinsurance Treaty with Russia to agree not to invade each other. The kaiser did not like this, and it led to Bismarck's final dismissal.
- ○ The Russians, French, and British formed their own alliance, the *Triple Entente*, to protect themselves against the Germans, Austrians, and Italians.

## The Empire Under Kaiser Wilhelm II and Bismarck

Although the lower house of the imperial legislature, the *Reichstag*, was elected by universal male suffrage, it had little real power because the chancellor and his ministers were responsible to the kaiser rather than to the legislature.

- Democracy in Germany took a backseat to autocracy.
- Bismarck's *Kulturkampf* (cultural struggle) was his repression of the so-called subversive elements in the empire, such as the Roman Catholic Church and socialists.
- Reversing his original attacks on the Catholic Center Party by the late 1870s, Bismarck turned to the socialist "menace," represented by the growing Social Democratic Party.
- When his official measures backfired and the Social Democratic Party grew even more popular, Bismarck pulled the rug out from under it by *sponsoring a series of social reforms*.
  - ○ He established workmen's compensation, old-age pensions, and medical protection, creating one of the world's most advanced social welfare systems.
  - ○ He took away any reason for the liberals to complain and thereby consolidated his power.
- When *Kaiser Wilhelm II* (r. 1888–1918) assumed the throne in 1888, he brought with him the archaic notion of *divine right* of rule and a deep resentment of Bismarck's personal power.
  - ○ In 1890, Wilhelm II *dismissed Bismarck*. Up until his abdication at the close of the First World War in 1918, he dominated his chancellors.
  - ○ His dismissal of Bismarck led the Bismarckian Alliance System to become a system of mutually antagonistic alliances that heightened international tensions and led to the First World War.
  - ○ Wilhelm II's arrogance, ambition, and ineptitude in the early 1900s upset the balance of power and drove Europe toward world war.

# Results of Nationalism

Nationalism became a very important force in both world and European politics during the last half of the 19th century. It became one of the major causes of the First World War. The unification of Italy and of Germany changed the balance of power in Europe. That disturbance of the balance of power and the new power of nationalism led to two devastating global conflicts that utilized the tactic of total war. They also led to popular sovereignty in most of Europe as most nationalist movements came with democratic reforms. National identities became increasingly important. National autonomy for each ethnic group, in the form of national self-determination, became an ardent desire for many historically oppressed ethnic groups, just as it became an important justification for the unification of Italy and of Germany. The identity of a "we versus them," discussed by Johan Gottfried Herder as part of his concept of the *volk* (folk of one nation), also explains much of the war and hardship of the 20th century. Many of the worst conflicts in the world today still focus on this concept of one nation or ethnic group supposedly being better than or having more right to a particular land than any other nation or group.

## Nationalism and the Balkan Peninsula

Both the Austrian Empire and the Ottomans claimed the Balkan Peninsula for centuries. The peninsula kept going back and forth between them. When Austria became the Austro-Hungarian Empire after 1848, the Balkans also had some uprisings. The Serbians wanted to expand Serbia to gain access to the sea and include all Serb peoples. The buildup of pressure in the Balkan Peninsula was the flash point that sparked the start of the First World War. So nationalism in this region should be explored in more detail. Bismarck famously said that the next big war would "be about some damn thing in the Balkans."

- In 1878, Bismarck hosted the six great powers of Europe at the *Congress of Berlin* to determine sovereignty in the region. Serbia, Montenegro, and Romania were given full sovereignty. Austria got Bosnia-Herzegovina, which was populated mostly with Serbs and had access to the sea.
- Russia saw herself as a defender of the Russian Orthodox faith (which Serbians believed in) and thus supported Serbia to gain power.
- The *First Bosnian Crisis* or the *Annexation Crisis* happened in 1908 when Bulgaria declared independence from the Ottomans at the same time that the Austro-Hungarians claimed full rights to Bosnia-Herzegovina.
- The *First Balkan War* began when the Balkan League of Serbia, Greece, Montenegro, and Bulgaria declared war on the Ottomans and tried to expand their territories in 1912. The Balkan League pushed the Ottomans off of the European continent for the most part.
- The *Second Balkan War* was in 1913 when Bulgaria, which had done a lot of the fighting in the First Balkan War, did not get what it wanted from the peace treaty. So Bulgaria attacked Serbia and Greece. This was mostly a fight over Macedonia.
- The Third Balkan War became the First World War.

## Modern Leaders of Assorted European Countries, or "Musical Chairs"

Starting in the early 1800s, the parliamentary system began to come into vogue across the Continent, although in a lurching manner. When a country adopted a parliamentary system, it usually had several parties and coalition governments. Rarely would one party gain enough votes to form its own government. This led to the creation of coalition governments composed of several parties with different agendas. Party loyalties shifted frequently and sometimes without an apparent cause. When one party decided to withdraw from the government (often for personal and seemingly ridiculous reasons), new elections would have to be held. Thus, you need to keep track of the many changes in European leadership. The following tables show the leadership in the parliamentary governments of several countries. When reading the tables, be aware of the following:

- Rulers in **bold** mean STOP, memorize their names, and know why they are important. These individuals will very likely be on the AP test.
- Rulers in *italics* mean PAUSE, and be familiar with who these people are. They may be on the test and rate some attention.
- Rulers in regular text mean KEEP GOING. Sure, one might be on the test every 10 years as a distraction in one of the last multiple-choice questions, but that is a chance you should be willing to take. These names are included mainly for continuity's sake. However, most history professors do not know who these individuals are, and you do not need to know either.
- Insofar as dates go, keep a ballpark figure of when people reigned, lived, and so on. However, memorizing the exact dates is frustrating and not necessary.

### France

The French have changed rulers as often as some people change clothes. The variety of rulers has been mostly unimportant, but a few French leaders after 1871 may indeed pop up on the AP exam.

| Name | Duration in Office | Which Government? |
| --- | --- | --- |
| *Louis Adolphe Thiers* | *1871–1873* | *Third Republic (President)* |
| Marie E. P. M. de MacMahon | 1873–1879 | Third Republic (President) |
| François P. J. Grévy | 1879–1887 | Third Republic (President) |
| Sadi Carnot | 1887–1894 | Third Republic (President) |
| Jean Casimir-Périer | 1894–1895 | Third Republic (President) |
| François Félix Faure | 1895–1899 | Third Republic (President) |
| Émile Loubet | 1899–1906 | Third Republic (President) |
| Clement Armand Fallières | 1906–1913 | Third Republic (President) |
| **Raymond Poincaré** | **1913–1920** | **Third Republic (President)** |
| Paul E. L. Deschanel | 1920–1920 | Third Republic (President) |
| Alexandre Millerand | 1920–1924 | Third Republic (President) |
| Gaston Doumergue | 1924–1931 | Third Republic (President) |
| Paul Doumer | 1931–1932 | Third Republic (President; assassinated) |
| Albert Lebrun | 1932–1940 | Third Republic (President) |
| *Henri Philippe Pétain* | *1940–1944* | *Vichy Government (Chief of State)* |
| **Charles de Gaulle** | **1944–1946** | **Provisional Government (President)** |
| Félix Gouin | 1946 | Provisional Government (President) |
| Georges Bidaul | 1946–1947 | Provisional Government (President) |
| Vincent Auriol | 1947–1954 | Fourth Republic (President) |
| René Coty | 1954–1959 | Fourth Republic (President) |
| **Charles de Gaulle** | **1959–1969** | **Fifth Republic (President)** |
| Georges Pompidou | 1969–1974 | Fifth Republic (President) |
| Valéry Giscard d'Estaing | 1974–1981 | Fifth Republic (President) |
| François Mitterrand | 1981–1995 | Fifth Republic (President) |
| *Jacques Chirac* | *1995–2007* | *Fifth Republic (President)* |
| Nicolas Sarkozy | 2007–2012 | Fifth Republic (President) |
| François Hollande | 2012–2017 | Fifth Republic (President) |
| Emmanuel Macron | 2017– | Fifth Republic (President) |

## Germany

The German nation came into existence in 1871 but did not gain democratic rule until after World War I. This table contains a list of German chancellors and the governments they represented.

| Name | Duration in Office | Which Government? |
| --- | --- | --- |
| Friedrich Ebert | 1919–1925 | Weimar Republic |
| Paul von Hindenburg | 1925–1934 | Weimar Republic |
| **Adolf Hitler** | **1934–1945** | **Third Reich** |
| Karl Doenitz | 1945–1945 | Third Reich |
| **Konrad Adenauer** | **1949–1963** | **West Germany** |
| Ludwig Erhard | 1963–1966 | West Germany |
| Kurt Georg Kiesinger | 1966–1969 | West Germany |

| Name | Duration in Office | Which Government? |
|---|---|---|
| **Willy Brandt** | **1969–1974** | **West Germany** |
| Helmut Schmidt | 1974–1982 | West Germany |
| **Helmut Kohl** | **1982–1990** | **West Germany** |
| Wilhelm Pieck | 1949–1960 | East Germany |
| Walter Ulbricht | 1960–1973 | East Germany |
| Willi Stoph | 1973–1976 | East Germany |
| *Erich Honecker* | *1976–1989* | *East Germany* |
| Egon Krenz | 1989 | East Germany |
| Manfred Gerlach | 1989–1990 | East Germany |
| Sabine Bergman-Pohl | 1990 | East Germany |
| *Helmut Kohl* | *1991–1998* | *Germany* |
| Gerhard Schröder | 1998–2005 | Germany |
| **Angela Merkel** | **2005–2021** | **Germany** |
| Olaf Scholz | 2021– | Germany |

## United Kingdom

Although the cabinet system was begun under Charles II in the mid-1600s, the position of a prime minister answerable to Parliament did not really develop until Robert Walpole in the early 1700s.

The British party system developed around the time of the American Revolution. The *Tories* were the *conservative* party, while the *Whigs* were the more *progressive* party. Eventually these evolved, respectively, into the Conservative (old Tory) and Liberal (old Whig) parties. The Liberal Party went on to become the Labour Party. During times of national emergencies (the First World War, the Second World War, and the Falkland Islands War), the two parties would overcome their differences and form coalition governments, which usually broke apart once peace was in sight.

The table lists all of the British prime ministers since Walpole.

| Name | Duration in Office | Notes |
|---|---|---|
| *William Pitt the Younger* | *1783–1801* | *Tory* |
| Henry Addington | 1801–1804 | Tory (Later, Viscount Sidmouth) |
| *William Pitt the Younger* | *1804–1806* | *Tory* |
| *Baron Grenville* | *1806–1807* | *Whig* |
| Duke of Portland | 1807–1809 | Tory |
| Spencer Perceval | 1809–1812 | Tory |
| Earl of Liverpool | 1812–1827 | Tory |
| George Canning | 1827 | Tory |
| Viscount Goderich | 1827–1828 | Tory (Later, Earl of Ripon) |
| *Duke of Wellington* | *1828–1830* | *Tory (Led British troops in defeat of Napoleon at Waterloo)* |
| Earl Grey | 1830–1834 | Whig |
| Viscount Melbourne | 1834 | Whig |
| *Sir Robert Peel* | *1834–1835* | *Tory* |
| Viscount Melbourne | 1835–1841 | Whig |

| Name | Duration in Office | Notes |
| --- | --- | --- |
| *Sir Robert Peel* | *1841–1846* | *Conservative* |
| Lord John Russell | 1846–1852 | Whig (Later, Earl of Russell) |
| Earl of Derby | 1852 | Conservative |
| Earl of Aberdeen | 1852–1855 | Liberal/Conservative |
| *Viscount Palmerston* | *1855–1858* | *Liberal* |
| Earl of Derby | 1858–1859 | Conservative |
| *Viscount Palmerston* | *1859–1865* | *Liberal* |
| Earl Russell | 1865–1866 | Liberal |
| Earl of Derby | 1866–1868 | Conservative |
| **Benjamin Disraeli** | **1868** | **Conservative** |
| **William Gladstone** | **1868–1874** | **Liberal** |
| **Benjamin Disraeli** | **1874–1880** | **Conservative** |
| **William Gladstone** | **1880–1885** | **Liberal** |
| Marquess of Salisbury | 1885–1886 | Conservative |
| **William Gladstone** | **1886** | **Liberal** |
| Marquess of Salisbury | 1886–1892 | Conservative |
| **William Gladstone** | **1892–1894** | **Liberal** |
| Earl of Rosebery | 1894–1895 | Liberal |
| Marquess of Salisbury | 1895–1902 | Conservative |
| *Arthur Balfour* | *1902–1905* | *Conservative* |
| Sir Henry Campbell-Bannerman | 1905–1908 | Liberal |
| *Herbert Asquith* | *1908–1916* | *Liberal* |
| **David Lloyd George** | **1916–1922** | **Coalition** |
| Andrew Bonar Law | 1922–1923 | Conservative |
| *Stanley Baldwin* | *1923–1924* | *Conservative* |
| *Ramsay MacDonald* | *1924* | *Labour* |
| *Stanley Baldwin* | *1924–1929* | *Conservative* |
| *Ramsay MacDonald* | *1929–1931* | *Labour* |
| *Ramsay MacDonald* | *1931–1935* | *National* |
| *Stanley Baldwin* | *1935–1937* | *National* |
| **Neville Chamberlain** | **1937–1940** | **National** |
| **Winston Churchill** | **1940–1945** | **Coalition** |
| **Clement Attlee** | **1945–1951** | **Labour** |
| **Sir Winston Churchill** | **1951–1955** | **Conservative** |
| *Sir Anthony Eden* | *1955–1957* | *Conservative* |
| Harold Macmillan | 1957–1963 | Conservative |
| Sir Alec Douglas-Home | 1963–1964 | Conservative |
| Harold Wilson | 1964–1970 | Conservative |
| Edward Heath | 1970–1974 | Conservative |
| Harold Wilson | 1974–1976 | Labour |

| Name | Duration in Office | Notes |
|---|---|---|
| James Callaghan | 1976–1979 | Labour |
| **Margaret Thatcher** | **1979–1990** | **Conservative** |
| John Major | 1990–1997 | Conservative |
| Tony Blair | 1997–2007 | Labour |
| Gordon Brown | 2007–2010 | Labour |
| David Cameron | 2010–2016 | Conservative |
| Theresa May | 2016–2019 | Conservative |
| Boris Johnson | 2019–2022 | Conservative |
| Liz Truss | 2022–2022 | Conservative |
| Rishi Sunak | 2022–2024 | Conservative |
| Keir Starmer | 2024– | Labour |

## Russia

Russian "democracy" was born out of the Russian Revolution of 1905. It has seen a series of either ineffectual or oppressive rulers hold the top elected post in the nation since that time.

| Name (Anglicized) | Reign | Notes |
|---|---|---|
| Prince Georgi Lvov | 1917 | Provisional Government |
| *Alexander Kerensky* | *1917* | *Provisional Government* |
| **Vladimir Ilyich Lenin** | **1917–1924** | **Union of Soviet Socialist Republics** |
| **Joseph Stalin** | **1924–1953** | **Union of Soviet Socialist Republics** |
| Georgi M. Malenkov | 1953–1955 | Union of Soviet Socialist Republics |
| Nikolai A. Bulganin | 1955–1958 | Union of Soviet Socialist Republics |
| **Nikita S. Khrushchev** | **1958–1964** | **Union of Soviet Socialist Republics** |
| *Leonid I. Brezhnev* | *1964–1982* | *Union of Soviet Socialist Republics* |
| Yuri V. Andropov | 1982–1984 | Union of Soviet Socialist Republics |
| Konstantin U. Chernenko | 1984–1985 | Union of Soviet Socialist Republics |
| **Mikhail S. Gorbachev** | **1985–1991** | **Union of Soviet Socialist Republics** |
| *Boris Yeltsin* | *1991–1999* | *President of Russian Republic* |
| Vladimir Putin | 2000–2008 | President of Russian Republic |
| Alexander Medvedev | 2008–2011 | President of Russian Republic |
| *Vladimir Putin* | *2011–* | *President of Russian Republic* |

## NOTE

You may have noticed that Austria has been omitted. There is a simple reason for this. After 1917 (and some would argue after 1848), the country ceased to be important to international politics.

# Unification of Italy and of Germany Chart

| Year | Italy | Germany |
|---|---|---|
| 1848 | ▪ Revolutions erupted throughout Europe after the French Revolt.<br>▪ Each revolt was unsuccessful and was quickly put down.<br>▪ *Giuseppe Garibaldi* fled back to Uruguay with other expatriates.<br>▪ Victor Emmanuel ruled Piedmont–Sardinia after the Austrians repressed the revolts. | ▪ Frederick William IV refused to accept the crown of a united Germany "from the gutter" when the Frankfurt Assembly offered it to him.<br>▪ The revolutions in Germany led to Frederick William IV reorganizing the government and promising to be more attuned to the people. |
| 1852 | ▪ *Count Camillo Benso di Cavour* became prime minister of Piedmont–Sardinia. | |
| 1859 | ▪ The French saved Piedmont–Sardinia from Austrian invasion.<br>▪ The French then betrayed them in a separate peace, which infuriated many Italians.<br>▪ Tuscany, Modena, Parma, and Romagna all voted to join Piedmont–Sardinia. | |
| 1860 | ▪ *Giuseppe Garibaldi* and his 1,000 *Red Shirts* invaded Sicily and started to move northward up the peninsula.<br>▪ Garibaldi wanted to establish a *republic*.<br>▪ Victor Emmanuel and Cavour wanted a monarchy.<br>▪ Garibaldi was met with overwhelming support from the people who joined his forces.<br>▪ Garibaldi met Cavour outside the Papal States, and a deal was made to create a *constitutional monarchy* in Italy. | |
| 1861 | ▪ All of Italy, except Rome and Venice, became part of a unified Italian Peninsula with a parliament. | ▪ Wilhelm I became the King of Prussia.<br>▪ Wilhelm I named **Otto von Bismarck** as his chief minister. |
| 1864 | | ▪ Prussia defeated Denmark in the battle of Schleswig-Holstein. |
| 1861–1866 | | ▪ Bismarck engaged in a constitutional struggle with the Prussian parliament.<br>▪ He utilized his *gap strategy* to ensure monarchical privilege. |
| 1866 | ▪ Venice joined Italy in 1866 after Austria's defeat in the *Seven Weeks' War*. | ▪ Prussia defeated Austria in the *Seven Weeks' War*.<br>▪ The war demonstrated that Prussia was the most powerful Germanic military. |
| 1867 | | ▪ Bismarck organized the North German Confederation of the 21 northern, mostly Protestant, German states. |
| 1870 | ▪ Rome was added to Italy when French troops left during the Franco-Prussian War.<br>▪ The entire Italian Peninsula was united into one nation for the first time since the fall of Rome. | ▪ Bismarck manufactured causes for a war with France as a means of uniting the German states against a common enemy.<br>▪ The Franco-Prussian War was a rout in which the Parisians were besieged and shelled.<br>▪ All of the German states united behind Wilhelm I and Bismarck. |
| 1871 | | ▪ Wilhelm I was declared the first *kaiser* of Germany at Versailles, and Bismarck was named chancellor. |

# Ideology and Culture

## Liberalism

Classical *liberalism*, an offshoot of the ideals of liberty and equality of the French Revolution, set as its political goals legal equality, freedom of the press, nationalism, freedom of assembly and of speech, and above all, representative government. Reacting to monarchical absolutism and to reactionary repression, the liberalism of the early-19th century generally opposed government intervention. (Note that reactionary repression can be represented by the policies of Austria's Prince Metternich, whose conservative attempt to roll back the ideals of the French Revolution amounted to a crusade against liberalism.)

- *Laissez-faire,* a form of economic liberalism and a principle espoused most convincingly by Adam Smith, argued for a free market system unfettered by government regulations.
    - Although this concept fostered economic growth, the theories of economists Thomas Malthus and David Ricardo (see chapter 6) were often used to back up the predatory business practices of early capitalists and industrialists, which could be supported by Smith as well.
- After the first few decades of the 19th century, liberalism was espoused mostly by the middle class and tended to ignore the rights and aspirations of the working class.

## Socialism

Early *socialism* was a reaction to the gross inequities created by the Industrial Revolution. The exploitation of workers by the early capitalists convinced the *utopian socialists* (see chapter 6) that one of the best remedies for this was to have governments intervene in the economy.

- Socialists wanted programs of government control of property, economic equality for all, and government economic planning.
    - *Charles Fourier* (1772–1837), a Frenchman, described a scheme for a utopian community based on a socialist idea.
    - His countryman, *Louis Blanc,* pushed the democratic takeover of the state by workers to guarantee full employment.
- The impracticality of their programs relegated the early *utopian socialists* to a minor political role, and modern socialism was largely shaped by the theories of Karl Marx (see chapter 6).

## Anarchists

Anarchists stated that all forms of government were oppressive and, therefore, the best government was none at all. They ignored the ideas of Thomas Hobbes and went even further than Marx against the current forms of government. They believed that society should be based upon voluntary associations of people.

- Anarchy was popular in Russia.
- Its main proponents were Mikhail Bakunin and Georges Sorel.

## Romanticism

*Romanticism*, a glorification of the emotional component of human nature, was a reaction to the rationalism and restraint of the Enlightenment. The excesses of the French Revolution and the destructiveness of the Napoleonic Wars eroded faith in the "inevitable perfectibility" of humankind through reason.

- Romantic artists, composers, and writers shared a worldview.
    - They had a willingness to express the deepest and most turbulent emotions.

- They fervently believed in personal freedom.
- They were in awe of nature.
- They had great reverence for history.

## Some Representative Figures

*William Wordsworth* (1770-1850) was an English poet who glorified the beauty and solemnity of nature.

*Victor Hugo* (1802-1885) was a French poet and dramatist best remembered for his vibrant novels, such as *The Hunchback of Notre Dame*, which explored the darker side of the human experience.

*Johann Wolfgang von Goethe* (1749-1832) was a German writer, dramatist, and scientist (botanist) who was an early proponent of the storm and stress movement. He is considered one of the greatest German thinkers of all time.

*John Constable* (1776-1837) was an English painter who said, "Nature is spirit visible." He painted bucolic scenes that attempted to cast rural life in an idyllic fashion, typifying the emotional examination of nature and history seen in this artistic movement.

*J. M. W. Turner* (1775-1851) was a Romantic painter famous for his portraits of storms and ships, epitomizing the *Sturm und Drang* or storm and stress characteristic of Romantic-era works.

*George Sand* (1804-1876) was a French countess who took a man's name as her pen name. She wrote modern, autobiographical, emotionally revealing novels about unconventional love.

*Eugene Delacroix* (1798-1863) was a French painter who epitomized the visual arts of this time period by creating powerful, large paintings of national pride such as *Liberty Leading the People*.

*Percy Shelley* (1792-1822) was a famous English Romantic poet known for writing odes and for appreciating nature. He also was married to *Mary Shelley*, the author of *Frankenstein*.

*Ludwig van Beethoven* (1770-1827) was German. His musical genius was expressed in virtually every musical form of his day, from songs to symphonies, and his evolution as a Romantic was evident in the course of his composing. The symphonic music of his later period made full use of the expanded orchestra, a Romantic innovation that added three times as many instruments as the classical orchestra known to Mozart and expressed the profound emotionality of Romantic music.

*Frédéric François Chopin* (1810-1849) was a Polish composer who was also known as the greatest pianist of his day. He was close with Liszt and resided in Paris for most of his career.

*Richard Wagner* (1813-1883) was a German composer of the era who wrote very long operas that glorified the history of Germany such as *The Valkyrie*. He would later become Adolf Hitler's favorite composer.

*Pyotr Ilyich Tchaikovsky* (1840-1893) was a Russian Romantic composer who created the *The Nutcracker* and the *1812 Overture*.

## Realism

Realist and materialist themes and attitudes influenced art and literature as painters and writers depicted the lives of ordinary people and drew attention to social problems. *Realism*, the literary movement that had replaced literary romanticism by the middle of the 19th century, portrayed a kind of *determinism*. This is the belief that human nature and human destiny are formed by heredity and environment and that human behavior is governed by natural laws that preclude free will.

- Realist writers devoted their work to a depiction of everyday life, especially of the working class and especially of its more unsavory aspects.
- Realism was focused on the here and now.
- Realist writers often shocked readers with their objective depictions of life in the cities, the slums, and the factories.
  - Frenchmen *Emile Zola* (1840-1902), *Honoré de Balzac* (1799-1850), and *Gustave Flaubert* (1821-1880) were all realist writers.

- ○ Englishwoman *George Eliot* (Mary Ann Evans) (1819–1880) was a realist writer.
- ○ Russians *Fyodor Dostoyevsky* (1821–1881) and *Leo Tolstoy* (1828–1910) were realists.
- ○ The popular *Charles Dickens* (1812–1870) was also a well-known realist author in England as was *Thomas Hardy* (1840–1928).
- ○ These writers spurned the Romantic obsession with distant times and distant places.

## Impressionism

The popularization of photography in the 19th century encouraged a group of artists, the *impressionists,* to avoid realistic depiction, which was better served by photography. Instead, the impressionists captured the transitory feeling of a scene, the personal "impression."

- ■ Impressionism was most famous in France but spread like the Renaissance around the world.
- ■ The following were some of most famous impressionists:
  - ○ *Pierre-Auguste Renoir* (1841–1919)
  - ○ *Claude Monet* (1840–1926)
  - ○ *Edouard Manet (1832–1883)*
  - ○ *Edgar Degas* (1834–1917)
  - ○ *Mary Cassatt* (1844–1926)

## Post-Impressionism, Cubism, and the Birth of Modern Art

After the impressionist movement, new ideas in visual arts emerged that were much more representational and emotional. This movement was not concerned with accurately depicting reality, which was a further reaction artistically to the spread of photography. Famous artists of this era include the following:

- ■ *Vincent van Gogh* was the most important post-impressionist. His work went beyond impressionism but was not distorted to the point of cubism. His most famous works were *Starry Night* and *Sunflowers*, which were a series of paintings.
- ■ *Pablo Picasso* was the father of cubism. It depicted people and scenes in geometric abstract forms that represented and deformed the subject of the painting. *Georges Braque* was another important cubist; he worked with Picasso.
- ■ *Henri Matisse* helped redefine what art was at the start of the 20th century. He was known for his intense colors and as one of the *Fauves* (wild beasts), which was a group of artists. Matisse emphasized flattened forms and decorative patterns.

## Feminism

Feminists, such as Flora Tristan, began to push for women's political rights, economic rights, and better working conditions.

- ■ In 1858, Barbara Bodichon set up the *English Woman's Journal.*
  - ○ This journal was an organ for discussing employment and equality issues directly concerning women and for discussing the reform of laws pertaining to the genders.
- ■ The Women's Social and Political Union (WSPU) was founded in Manchester in October 1903 by Emmeline Pankhurst.
  - ○ Her sister, Christabel, once disrupted a speech by Winston Churchill in order to make a statement about women's lack of rights.
- ■ Women fought for suffrage and other citizenship rights that they did not get until after the First World War.

## Science

After the first few decades of the 19th century and directly as a result of the technological requirements of the Industrial Revolution, "pure" scientific discoveries found application in explaining how the machinery and techniques of industrial processes worked.

- *Positivism,* or the philosophy that science alone provides knowledge, emerged to emphasize the rational scientific analysis of human affairs.
- Physicists were able to formulate principles of *thermodynamics* applicable to a variety of technological systems, such as the operation of engines, which convert heat into motion.
- *Max Planck* founded the science of particle physics with his new quantum theory.
- *Marie and Pierre Curie* experimented with radioactivity, further supporting quantum theory.
- The theories of biology were used by researchers, such as *Louis Pasteur* (1822–1895), to preserve food and to improve medical procedures.
- A burgeoning chemical industry provided a variety of new products ranging from medicines to synthetic dyes.
- The generation of electricity created whole new industries in transportation and lighting.
- *Charles Darwin* (1809–1882) was not the first theorist to formulate the concept of evolution. However, his meticulous research and voluminous specimens added weight to his idea that life evolved in its myriad forms from a common ancestor through the process of a *struggle for survival.*
  - The mechanism that aided this was the development of anomalies in a given species, which would actually aid in the survival of that species.
  - His insight predated the development of the science of *genetics.*
  - For instance, Darwin claimed that when the only foliage available for grazing was on high trees, the mutant long-neck giraffe would outlive and out-propagate its short-neck cousins; thus, its characteristics would be more successfully passed on to later generations.
  - Darwin's theory had a powerful effect on the intellectual life of Europe.
  - It was used by skeptics to attack the biblical account of creation and religion itself.
  - *Herbert Spencer* (1820–1903) used Darwin's theories to argue that history and human society reflect a struggle for supremacy resulting in the *survival of the fittest.*
    - Spencer claimed that the rich, the rulers, and the powerful nations were "fit." He also believed that the poor, the downtrodden masses, and the world's colonies were "weak."
    - This *social Darwinism* appealed to those in power and to racists and imperialists of every stripe.
- Philosophy largely moved away from rational interpretations of nature and human society toward an emphasis on irrationality and impulse, a view that contributed to the belief that conflict and struggle led to progress.
- *Friedrich Nietzsche* (1844–1900), a German philosopher and contemporary of Darwin, argued that Christianity presented a "slave morality" that fettered the creativity of great individuals, the *übermensch* (superman), who must free themselves from conventionality and redefine life and morality.
- *Henri Bergson* (1859–1941) believed that immediate experiences and intuition were more important to people as reasons for actions than was abstract rationalism.
- *Freudian psychology* proffered a new account of human nature that emphasized the role of the irrational and the struggle between the conscious and unconscious.

# Practice Questions

## Long Essay

These questions are samples of the various types of thematic essays on the AP exam. See pages 27–28 for a detailed explanation of each type. Check over the generic rubric (see pages 28–29) before you begin any of these essays, and use that rubric to score your essay if you write one.

### Question 1

To what extent was Italian unification the result of the strong personal wills and tenacity of Mazzini, Cavour, and Garibaldi?

### Comments on Question 1

This question is testing the *causation* skill because it requires you to evaluate whether two things—the personal wills and tenacity of Garibaldi, Cavour, and Mazzini—resulted in a specific outcome: the unification of Italy. Remember to describe the causes and/or effects of the Italian unification. Support your analysis of those causes and effects with specific evidence. The essay must explain how these three men brought about Italian unification— be sure to support those claims with specific evidence. Mazzini has been called the "heart" of Italian unification, Cavour the "brain," and Garibaldi the "sword." How and how much did Mazzini's proselytizing of the glories of mystical union prepare the Italian people and the world for the realpolitik of Cavour? How and how much did Garibaldi's flamboyant appeal and adventures in the Two Sicilies enable Cavour to complete unification? What compromises and other events led to complete unification of the Italian Peninsula?

### Question 2

Explain how nationalism was a liberal ideal during the Napoleonic era and the Age of Metternich but became a conservative ideal by the time the First World War broke out in 1914.

### Comments on Question 2

This question is asking you to use the *change and continuity over time* (CCOT) skill. You must analyze how the view of nationalism changed over time from a force that leaders had to contend with to a force that leaders used to build national unity and identity. Be sure to describe the extent to which the view of nationalism in 1814 was different from, and similar to, the way it was viewed in 1914. Provide multiple specific examples to support the analysis. Your essay must explain the extent to which nationalism changed from a liberal idea to a conservative one, with specific supporting evidence. Your essay must first examine the nationalist reactions to Napoleon's domination of Europe, perhaps focusing on Spain and the Confederation of the Rhine but also on Russia and Austria. The multiethnic nature of many European empires, such as the Russian and the Austrian, especially must be addressed as must the conservatism of Metternich. The revolutions of the 1820s, 1830, and 1848 must also be addressed as liberal nationalist movements that mostly failed (except for Greece). You must explain how Cavour, Bismarck, and others co-opted nationalism as a conservative tool to unite nations through "blood and iron." Discussing later uses of nationalism, such as the Berlin Conference, will add a lot to this essay. Overall, the essay needs to explain how nationalism was at first a change favored by liberals and that the idea was used by conservatives to unify new nations and hold older empires together until the First World War.

### Question 3

To what extent did Bismarck's use of war result in German unification?

## Comments on Question 3

This question is testing the *causation* skill because it requires you to evaluate whether one factor, Bismarck's use of war, resulted in a specific outcome, the unification of Germany. Remember to describe the causes and/or effects of German unification. Support your analysis of those causes and effects with specific evidence. This essay should explain the reasons that Bismarck's use of war resulted in the unification of Germany, citing specific evidence as support. Examine in detail how the war for Schleswig-Holstein (the all-German war), the Seven Weeks' War, and the Franco-Prussian War were used by Bismarck to effect unification. This was a process of distinct stages. War with Denmark aroused a sense of German nationalism and set Austria up for the fall. The Seven Weeks' War aligned most Germanic states with the loser, Austria, and against the winner, Prussia. Generous terms achieved the establishment of the North German Confederation. Finally, victory over France, which had historically dominated the Germanic states, inspired a patriotic yearning for union that created the German Empire.

## Question 4

What were the differences between the political situations in Italy from 1820–1850 and from the 1850s through 1871 that allowed Piedmont-Sardinia to take the lead in Italian unification?

## Comments on Question 4

This is a *compare* skill question. So be sure to describe the similarities and differences between the political situations in Italy during the specified periods. Account for or explain them by providing specific examples of how they were similar and different; tie that to historical developments. The Revolutions of 1848 were the kinds of failures that whetted the appetite for greater success and that pointed the way toward unification led from above rather than from the masses. Power politics grew out of the frustrations of the erstwhile reformers. Piedmont was the logical leader of unification because it was the only independent state in Italy with any economic prosperity. Most of the North was under the yoke of Austria. Central Italy was controlled by the traditionalistic politics of the papacy. The South was underdeveloped and under the sway of anachronistic manorialism. When Cavour reformed and strengthened Piedmont, he was making the most of its opportunities. The lack of a strong state in Italy that could have led a unification movement in the earlier part of the century was part of the reason for the failure of the revolutions of the 1820s and 1848. The disunity of the plans and leaders calling for Italian leadership before 1850, such as Garibaldi, Mazzini, and Gioberti, also contributed to the failure of this political movement until Cavour's leadership emerged.

## Short-Answer

1.  Use the excerpt below and your knowledge of European history to answer all parts of the question that follows.

### Liberalism Evaluated

The social problem of the future we considered to be, how to unite the greatest individual liberty of action, with a common ownership in the raw material of the globe, and an equal participation of all in the benefits of combined labor. We had not the presumption to suppose that we could already foresee by what precise form of institutions these objects could most effectually be attained, or at how near or how distant a period they would become practicable. We saw clearly that to render any such social transformation either possible or desirable, an equivalent change of character must take place both in the uncultivated herd who now compose the laboring masses, and in the immense majority of their employers. Both these classes must learn by practice to labor and combine for generous, or at all events for public and social purposes, and not, as hitherto, solely for narrowly interested ones. But the capacity to do this has always existed in mankind, and is not, nor is ever likely to be, extinct. Education, habit, and the cultivation of the sentiments, will make a common man dig or weave for his country, as readily as fight for his country.

—John Stuart Mill, 1873

(a) Briefly explain TWO of the social changes that European society was going through as liberalism emerged.

(b) Briefly explain the political philosophy that emerged to counteract liberalism in the late 19th century.

2. Use the image below and your knowledge of European history to answer all parts of the following question.

**Water Lilies and Japanese Bridge**

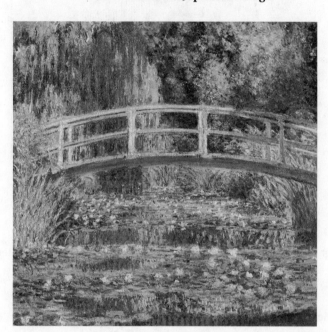

Claude Monet, 1897–1899.

(a) Briefly analyze how the artwork above reflects artistic trends of the late-19th century.

(b) Briefly analyze TWO aspects of change that affected Europeans' perceptions during the late-19th century.

## Multiple-Choice

**Questions 1–4 refer to the map of Italian city-states below.**

Map showing the unification of Italy.

1. Which of the Italian city-states on the map above was the dominant power in a united Italy after 1861?

    (A)  Modena
    (B)  Parma
    (C)  Piedmont-Sardinia
    (D)  Kingdom of the Two Sicilies

2. Which of the following gave up his dream of a united republic of Italy in order to preserve the movement for Italian unification?

    (A)  Count Camillo Benso di Cavour
    (B)  Giuseppe Garibaldi
    (C)  Giuseppe Mazzini
    (D)  Victor Emmanuel II

3. Which province shown on the map was gained by the Kingdom of Italy in return for its support of Prussia in the Seven Weeks' War against Austria?

    (A)  Parma
    (B)  The states of the Church
    (C)  The Papal States
    (D)  Venetia

4. The new nations of Italy and Germany disrupted which of the following the most?

   (A) Balance of power
   (B) Social changes
   (C) Global commerce
   (D) The industrialization of the world

**Questions 5–7 refer to the following passage by Prussian Chancellor Otto von Bismarck.**

We had to avoid wounding Austria too severely; we had to avoid leaving behind in her any unnecessary bitterness of feeling or desire for revenge; we ought rather to reserve the possibility of becoming friends again with our adversary of the moment, and in any case to regard the Austrian state as a piece on the European chessboard and the renewal of friendly relations as a move open to us. If Austria were severely injured, she would become the ally of France and of every other opponent of ours; she would even sacrifice her anti-Russian interests for the sake of revenge on Prussia.

   On the other hand, I could not see any guarantee for us in the future of the countries constituting the Austrian monarchy, in case the latter were split up by risings of the Hungarians and Slavs or made permanently dependent on those peoples. What would be substituted for that portion of Europe which the Austrian state had hitherto occupied from Tyrol to Bukowina?

—Otto von Bismarck, *Memoirs*

5. Which of the following changes in the nationalist movement was documented by the passage above?

   (A) Nationalism was supported by liberals and radicals.
   (B) Nationalism was most supported by conservatives.
   (C) The nationalist agenda was co-opted for the purposes of creating or strengthening the state.
   (D) Prussian leaders arrested nationalists who threatened their monopoly on control.

6. Which of the following tactics was NOT employed by Bismarck in his attempt to unify Germany?

   (A) Industrialized warfare and weaponry
   (B) Motorized infantry
   (C) Diplomatic negotiations
   (D) Manipulation of foreign affairs

7. What was the clearest Prussian goal in Bismarck's alliance system?

   (A) To create a fully inclusive German confederation
   (B) To isolate France from the rest of Europe
   (C) To control Russian trade and expansion
   (D) To defeat the British navy

# Answers and Explanations

## Short-Answer Explanations

1. (a)   You should look at the changes brought on by the Industrial Revolution and enclosure movement that tore European society asunder by the mid-19th century. You may include any TWO of the following: increased urbanization, changing gender roles, changing work schedules, the emergence of laissez-faire capitalism, the redesign of cities, the sanitation movement, the rise of public education, changing leisure activities, the decline in illegitimacy rates in the 19th century, increased personal liberties, the loss of communal lands and therefore communal life, and/or the end of the putting-out system.

   (b)   You should identify *conservatism* as the response to *liberalism*. Explain the characteristics and impact of conservatism, including: rising governmental power, rising nationalism, rebounding of religious devotion, supporting the bourgeoisie over the workers, growing militarism, and the reemergence of traditional family roles.

2. (a)   You should identify the artistic trend as *impressionism* and identify how it is a reflection of that movement. You should identify Monet as the man who coined the term *impressionism* and explain the style as one that moved away from a realistic depiction of the world to a more blurred impression of a scene in action. Impressionism should be noted as a momentous break from tradition in European painting. You should identify the change in the look of these paintings as brought about by a change in methodology: applying paint in small touches of pure color rather than broader strokes and painting out of doors to catch a fleeting impression of color and light. You should explain that impressionist art is a style in which the artists capture the image of an object as someone would see it if they just caught a glimpse of it and that the artists capture their images without detail but with bold colors.

   (b)   You should discuss the rise of science and technology, including the invention of the camera, as motivations to create this new style of art. You should also look at the emergence of Romanticism as a change in the sentiment of society that harkened to the simpler life before industrialization. Other aspects you may explore as changes that brought on impressionism were the changing gender roles, class divisions, the uses of leisure time, changing professions, changing modes of production, changing political ideologies from liberalism to conservatism, and a general blurring of roles and expectations in the early modern world.

## Practice Multiple-Choice Questions

1. (A)   is wrong because Modena was a small, weak state, while Piedmont-Sardinia dominated the new Italian state, which was ruled by the king of Piedmont-Sardinia, Victor Emmanuel II.

   (B)   is wrong because Parma was a small, weak state while Piedmont-Sardinia dominated the new Italian state that was ruled by the king of Piedmont-Sardinia, Victor Emmanuel II.

   **(C)   is CORRECT because Piedmont-Sardinia dominated the new Italian state that was ruled by the king of Piedmont-Sardinia, Victor Emmanuel II.**

   (D)   is wrong because the Kingdom of the Two Sicilies was a poorer, more agrarian area that was dominated by Piedmont-Sardinia, and Italy was ruled by the king of Piedmont-Sardinia, Victor Emmanuel II.

2. (A)   is wrong because Cavour realized his dream of a united Italy under his king, Victor Emmanuel II.

   **(B)   is CORRECT because Garibaldi and his Red Shirts invaded Sicily, then southern Italy, and fought all the way to the Papal States, where Garibaldi agreed to give up an Italian republic in order to attain a united nation with a constitutional monarchy.**

(C) is wrong because Mazzini was gone from Italy by 1860 and played only an inspirational role in the unification of Italy.

(D) is wrong because Victor Emmanuel gave up very little and became the first king of a united Italy.

3. (A) is wrong because the Seven Weeks' War ended in 1866 when Venice was given to Italy; Parma was already allied with Piedmont-Sardinia.

(B) is wrong because the states of the Church were fictional.

(C) is wrong because the Papal States were the last to join Italy in 1871, well after the Seven Weeks' War.

**(D) is CORRECT because Venetia was ceded to Italy as a reward for its support of Prussia during the Seven Weeks' War.**

4. (A) **is CORRECT because the entire global balance of power was disrupted by the unification of Italy and of Germany.**

(B) is wrong because the balance of power was disrupted significantly while the changes to society continued to mount.

(C) is wrong because the balance of power was hurt by this change, but global trade was not.

(D) is wrong because the balance of power was disrupted more than the industrialization of the world as a result of these new nations being formed.

5. (A) is wrong because liberals and radicals were always the main supporters of nationalism; what changed was that the conservative Prussian leaders co-opted nationalism for their own purposes.

(B) is wrong because the passage makes it clear that conservative Austria would be ruined by nationalism.

**(C) is CORRECT because what changed was that the conservative Prussian leaders co-opted nationalism for their own purposes.**

(D) is wrong because Prussia was the most friendly regime to nationalism in Western Europe since 1848.

6. (A) is wrong because Bismarck relied heavily upon industrialized warfare and weaponry, such as the first cartridge rifles, to fight the three wars that unified Germany.

**(B) is CORRECT because motorized infantry did not exist during the end of the 19th century but was introduced during the First World War.**

(C) is wrong because Bismarck relied heavily upon diplomatic negotiations to unify Germany.

(D) is wrong because Bismarck relied heavily upon manipulation of foreign affairs, such as the Ems Telegram incident, to unify Germany.

7. (A) is wrong because Bismarck did not rely heavily upon the alliances to unify his nation. He really became a player in the alliance system after Germany unified. However, he used his alliances to attempt to isolate France, particularly from Great Britain.

**(B) is CORRECT because Bismarck used his alliances to attempt to isolate France, particularly from Great Britain.**

(C) is wrong because Bismarck did not interfere with Russian trade in any major way.

(D) is wrong because Bismarck knew better than to try to take on the British navy.

# 9

# Imperialism and the Causes of the First World War (1870–1914)

## Key Terms

- Surplus capital
- "White Man's Burden"
- Social Darwinism
- Sepoy Mutiny
- Open Door Policy
- Suez Canal
- The Boxer Rebellion
- Meiji Restoration

- Zulu resistance
- Opium Wars
- Russo-Japanese War
- Colonialism
- Berlin Conference
- French-Algerian War
- British East India Company
- Dutch East India Company

- Quinine
- Algeciras Conference
- Militarism
- Pan-Slavism
- Balkan Wars
- Balkan Crisis
- Moroccan Crisis

## Key People

- Mohandas K. Gandhi

## Overview

A contemporary definition of imperialism is any instance of a more-powerful nation or group of nations acting, or being perceived to be acting, at the expense of a lesser power, usually when the more powerful nation dominates militarily or economically. Imperialism is therefore used not only to describe overt empire-building policies—such as those of the Roman Empire, the Spanish, or the British—but was also used controversially and/or disparagingly. For example, most of Europe referred to Napoleon's actions as imperialistic. The colonial power may rule the colony politically, exploit it economically, or impose its culture on the colony. During the so-called old imperialism of the 16th through 18th centuries, the Europeans did not acquire overseas territories. (The exception was the Americas, where the death of 90 percent of the native population allowed the establishment of European colonies). Instead, the Europeans primarily set up trading stations. They largely respected and frequently cooperated with the local rulers in India, China, Japan, Spice Islands (Indonesia), and the other geographic areas where a flourishing trade developed between locals and European coastal trading centers.

The new imperialism that began in the 1870s colonized Asia and Africa by using military force to take control of local governments, by exploiting the local economies for the raw materials required by Europe's growing industry, and by imposing Western values on the colonies. Most of Asia's rich and ancient cultures were either carved up into economic "spheres of influence" or colonized outright, virtually all of Africa was taken over by only six European nations, and Latin America was dominated by the United States.

## Causes of Imperialism

### The Search for Markets and for Raw Materials

The rapidly industrializing and competing nations of Europe produced more manufactured goods than their own populations could consume. Since a favorable balance of trade was not possible for all European nations, colonies promised potential markets.

- In the long run, since the non-Europeans lacked purchasing power, the promise of markets far outweighed the reality.
- Studies of foreign trade from 1870–1914 show that the best consumers of manufactured goods were other industrialized nations rather than less econimically developed colonies.
- As the income level of Western workers rose, so did the profitability of investing surplus capital into domestic ventures.
- Colonies were needed as sources of raw materials to supply newly industrialized Western society.
- They argued that unless their more advanced technologies and business methods were applied to the mining and processing of these materials, not enough would be supplied to the voracious factories.
- They claimed that they had to set up colonies in order to maintain the stability that would protect their investments.

## Missionaries

A burst of religious revivalism during the mid-19th century in Western Europe and the United States led to development of worldwide missions to convert the people of Asia and Africa to Christianity.

- On rare occasions, missionaries were attacked or endangered by locals.
- Religion was used as an excuse to erase cultures and take wealth and power.
- Many medical and technological improvements were made in some colonies (mostly British colonies).

## Military Bases

Once trade developed, the home (or mother) countries felt compelled to establish a chain of naval bases to protect their overseas interests and to form military outposts to stake claims and maintain order. European national rivalries and strategic concerns fostered imperial expansion and competition for colonies.

- This process tended to feed on itself since a competition to acquire colonies developed among the industrialized nations.
- They claimed to want to maintain the international balance of power.
- This was more about international prestige.
- This led to increased tensions when the "haves" (like the British Empire, which had acquired colonies for two or more centuries) clashed with the "have-nots" (like the Germans and Italians, whose late-blooming national unity gave them a slow start in the race).

## Ideology

Europeans justified imperialism through an ideology of cultural and racial superiority. The so-called *White Man's Burden* was a form of racist paternalism that preached that the "superior" Westerners had an obligation to bring their culture to "uncivilized" peoples in other parts of the world.

- *Social Darwinism*, a half-baked philosophical application of Darwin's theory of natural selection, bolstered the idea that some races or peoples were more fit for survival than others and therefore designed by nature for rule.
- Imperial adventures appealed to the masses in the industrialized countries, who felt part of some great crusade to improve people whose lot, they were led to believe, was even worse than theirs.
- Imperialism won votes; politicians coddled the voters.

## Industrial and Technological Developments

Industrial and technological developments (the Second Industrial Revolution) facilitated European control of global empires.

- Advanced weaponry, such as the machine gun, the breech-loading rifle, and other gunpowder weapons, allowed the Europeans to dominate the natives of all regions and conquer them quickly.
- Advances in communication, such as the radio, telegraph, and telephone, allowed Europeans to coordinate their efforts to dominate the rest of the world.
- Advances in medicine, such as *quinine, anesthesia, antiseptics, public health projects*, and *Louis Pasteur's germ theory*, supported European control of Africa and Asia by preserving European lives.

# Regions

## Africa

- After winning autonomy within the Ottoman Empire in the mid-19th century, Egypt became a British protectorate in the 1880s.
- The British invested in the Suez Canal, a vital link to India and Asia. To maintain stability in the region, they helped Egypt take control of the Sudan and set up an Anglo-Egyptian administration for both areas.
- Wealthy industrialist Cecil Rhodes planned to build a railroad that crossed the African continent, but he did not build it.
- South Africa became an important colony to the British, who fought the Afrikaners in the two *Boer Wars*. Superior British weaponry helped defeat the Afrikaners and also the Zulus.
- The Zulu Wars were one of the best examples of organized African resistance to imperialism.
- The DeBeers family profited by taking natural resources from the north and south of the continent, but they did little to develop any sustainable industry or improve the lives of people.

Algeria, Tunisia, and most of Morocco fell into French hands right before the First World War. Libya, once part of the decrepit Ottoman Empire, was taken by the Italians.

- Africa *south of the Sahara* was terra incognita until the 1870s, when Belgian, German, and French explorers began to lay claims.
- Scottish medical missionary David Livingstone was the first white man to do humanitarian and religious work in South and Central Africa.
- Livingstone had been writing a regular column for London papers and failed to report; his worried readers thought he must be dead.
- In 1871, after six years of no word from Livingstone, American journalist Henry M. Stanley found him in a remote part of East Africa. Stanley's newspaper reports created greater European interest in Africa.
- *King Leopold II of Belgium* sought the aid of Stanley to dominate the Congo region. Leopold ruled the Congo in a brutal and exploitative fashion. He became an example of a cruel imperialist master, ruling with whips and threats.
  - The Belgian Congo—previously called the Congo Free State—was over 70 times the size of Belgium and was ruled privately by King Leopold until 1908.
  - Reports of abuses in the Belgian Congo resulted in it being taken over by a Belgian administration, dominated by the Roman Catholic Church, until it won independence in 1960.

The Berlin Conference of 1885, sponsored by Bismarck to prevent disputes among the imperialists, set up rules that diminished squabbles and encouraged partitioning of the entire African continent among the major European powers.

## Asia

In 1857, the *Sepoy Mutiny* in India became the best-known aspect of a wider rebellion of native troops against their British and Indian commanders. The Hindu and Muslim troops objected to disrespectful treatment and to their bullets being wrapped in animal fat, which was offensive to their faiths.

- The Sepoy Rebellion was put down. However, the British East India Company was relieved of its rule over India, and British government administration of the Indian subcontinent began.
- Over the next 90 or more years, the Indian people struggled with British rule until the British finally left after the Second World War.

By the mid-1880s the British also took control of Burma, the Malay Peninsula, and North Borneo.

- The British did not interfere with the basic social structure in the colonies of Burma, the Malay Peninsula, and North Borneo.
- The British introduced educational reforms and technological advances, especially to India, that smoothed the way for eventual independence.
- Of all the colonial powers, the British proved to be most "enlightened."

## Other Colonial Holdings

- The Dutch expanded their hold over the *Dutch East Indies* (the islands of Indonesia).
- The French seized Indochina (Vietnam, Cambodia, and Laos).
- The Germans had small African holdings and occupied islands in the Pacific.
- The Russians set up a sphere of influence (an area under the economic and military control of one imperial power) in Persia (Iran).

China, with its teeming population, vast land area, and incredibly rich and ancient culture, was carved up into spheres of influence by the Western powers after the Opium Wars of the 1840s and 1850s.

- Extraterritoriality made Westerners in China subject to their home country's laws rather than China's.
- In China, exclusive trading rights and limited governing powers were given to Western nations.
- The Chinese were forced to cede outlying regions of historical Chinese influence, such as Siberia, part of Manchuria, and Korea to the Russians and the Japanese, by the late 1800s.
- The Taiping Rebellion from 1850–1864 cost 15–20 million lives and resulted in the Qing dynasty being further weakened when it sought American and British help to end the rebellion.
- The Open Door Policy, implemented by the United States in 1899 in order to open Chinese commerce to imperial latecomers like itself, urged the Europeans to allow free trade within China while respecting China's territorial integrity.
- The *Boxer Rebellion*, a patriotic uprising by Chinese nationalists against Western encroachment, was put down by the imperial powers in 1900.
  - Since the Dowager Empress, who had seized control of the government, supported the Boxers, the Manchu dynasty fell into decline until it was overthrown in 1911.
- Sun Yat-sen set up a republic dedicated to modernizing China through three principles: nationalism, democracy, and livelihood.

Japan was the only major Asian power to resist being swallowed up by the imperialists.

- In the mid-16th century, Portuguese traders opened the insular Japanese to commerce and Christianity, both of which were suppressed by the shogun (medieval military ruler).
- U.S. warships, under the command of Commodore Matthew Perry, reopened the islands in 1853. Unlike China and India, the Japanese rapidly modernized.
- The rule of the shogun in Japan was replaced by that of a powerful emperor, Meiji.

- Japanese feudalism was abolished. Industry was fostered. A central government was installed. Education and the military were reformed.
- Japan engaged in a modernization movement in which it sent people abroad to learn from other cultures. These individuals came back and rebuilt Japan rapidly, which is known as the *Meiji Restoration*.
- Japan became so westernized, while maintaining its basic social structure, that it jumped on the imperialist bandwagon by going to war with China in 1898 and winning Korea.
- Japan shocked the West by decisively defeating the Russians in 1905 during the *Russo-Japanese War*.

The Philippines were taken over by the United States following the *Spanish-American War* of 1898, which America ostensibly fought to "liberate" the colonies of Spain from the yoke of their colonizers.

- The United States was victorious in the Spanish-American War; it gained control of Cuba, Puerto Rico, Guam, and the Philippines.
  - When the United States claimed the Philippines as an American territory in January 1899, a revolt of the Filipino people followed within a month.
  - The rebellion was brutally suppressed but lasted several years, with the deaths of 35,000 Filipino fighters and as many as 200,000 civilians.
  - The United States turned from champion of the oppressed to oppressor within a few months.
- Due to its actions in Japan, China, and Hawaii and the possessions it gained from the Spanish-American War, the United States had entered its own era of being an imperialist power.

## The End of Colonialism

### SPECIAL NOTE ON PERIODIZATION

Much of this information is included, although it is part of period 4, in order to preserve the narrative of imperialism and to help you see the connections across periods. This will help you understand how to apply the skill of periodization on the exam.

Traditional imperialist acquisitions ended before the First World War when virtually the entire non-Western world was divided among the Western powers.

*Colonialism* was the control of overseas colonies by imperialist powers. It was based on the idea that Europeans and Americans were superior in culture to the rest of the world and therefore were helping to "civilize" the peoples they conquered while making a tidy profit. Colonialism was shaken by the First World War and collapsed in the decades following World War II.

- The long-term causes for colonialism's fall were many. They included the hypocrisy of people who wanted to rule themselves with liberty and democracy but who still ruled colonies whose citizens had no voice in government. Also, the economic and political realities of a post–World War II world helped cause the end of official colonialism for the following reasons:
  - *Westernized educational systems* preached the ideals of democracy and awakened nationalistic yearnings among the colonials.
  - The concept of *self-determination* was espoused by the Allies after the First World War.
  - The example and ideals of the *Russian Revolution* and the anti-imperialist *dogma of communism* appealed to many who lived in colonies.
  - Europe declined in the decades after the Second World War.
  - Japan set an example of resistance to Western domination after the Meiji Restoration.

## The British Empire

- India, the "jewel in the crown" of the British Empire, attained independence in 1948.
  - Decades of *nonviolent resistance*, led by *Mohandas K. Gandhi*, known as Mahatma, helped prepare the populace for self-rule.
  - Bloody clashes between Hindus and Muslims marred the move to independence.
  - The Indian subcontinent was partitioned by mutual agreement of the British and leaders of India into mainly Hindu India and mainly Muslim Pakistan.
- Britain's colonies in Southeast Asia—Ceylon (Sri Lanka), Burma (Myanmar), and Malaya (Malaysia)—and its colonies in Africa attained independence in the two decades after the Second World War.
- Most former colonies joined the British *Commonwealth of Nations*, a loose political grouping that offered economic advantages.
- When the former British mandate, Palestine, was created as a Jewish state in 1948, long-standing rivalries between westernized Jewish settlers and Muslim Arabs developed into a volatile and ongoing conflict.
  - Wars between Israel and neighboring Arab countries broke out in 1948, 1956, 1967, and 1973.
  - Nationalization of the Suez Canal, a waterway vital to British trade, by charismatic Egyptian leader Gamal Abdel Nasser provoked war in 1956 between Egypt and allies Britain, France, and Israel.
  - The area continues to be one of the world's most unstable.

## The Dutch Empire

Early in the Second World War, the Japanese drove the Dutch out of the *Dutch East Indies*. This area was originally called the *Spice Islands* by the Europeans but was called *Indonesia* after independence.

- When the Dutch tried to resume control of the Dutch East Indies after the war, nationalists under the leadership of *Sukarno* (an eventual dictator until his overthrow in 1966) fought a bloody war of resistance and attained total independence in 1954.

## The French Empire

After the Second World War, the French colonies in Indochina (Vietnam, Cambodia, and Laos) tried, like the Dutch in Indonesia, to take back the possessions they had been driven from by the Japanese.

- After a costly seven-year guerrilla war, nationalists under Communist *Ho Chi Minh* (1890–1969) attained independence from France in 1954.
  - The Geneva Accords recognized the independence of Vietnam, Cambodia, and Laos. The agreement provisionally partitioned Vietnam into northern and southern sectors until nationwide elections could determine leadership.
  - The agreement broke down into full-scale civil war between the Communist-led North Vietnam and the pro-capitalist South Vietnam.
  - By the mid-1960s, the United States had sent massive military forces to aid South Vietnam.
- In North Africa, Morocco and Tunisia were granted independence by the French in 1956.
- *Algeria*, considered by many French to be an integral part of France, was not granted independence.
  - The bitter *French-Algerian War* led to independence in 1962 and the mass exodus of French settlers.
  - This war drained the French of resources and of their belief in the ability of their forces to win any major conflict in the developing world.

## African Independence

In sub-Saharan Africa, independence came suddenly from the late 1950s through the 1960s.

- The process was painful and costly in some places.
- In the former Belgian Congo (Democratic Republic of the Congo), a legacy of violence and corruption was left by the Belgians who made few infrastructure improvements to their colony.
  - A horrific genocide between the ethnic groups in Rwanda and Burundi (Tutsi and Hutu) occurred as a direct result of Belgian racial policies that enabled the minority Tutsis to rule the majority Hutus.
- Because the Europeans had ignored tribal loyalties when drawing imperial boundaries, the newly independent states in Africa often lacked a unified heritage.
- Former British colonies were best prepared for self-rule since the British had gradually transferred administration to locals and had built the best infrastructure, such as roads, railroads, and telecommunication lines.

## Impact of the End of Imperialism

The collapse of the European colonial empires was one of the modern world's most revolutionary and sudden developments.

- Within two decades after the Second World War, the European colonies, encompassing more than 25 percent of Earth's population, had disappeared.
- Most of the newly independent states, though, still do not enjoy genuine freedom and democratic rule.
- Although those newly independent states often started out with democratic institutions, poverty, ethnic conflicts, and inexperience in self-rule often led to military dictatorship or to one-party rule.
- Freedom from foreign rule did not guarantee political freedom.
- Many new nations became pawns of the United States and the Soviet Union during the Cold War.
- The end of imperialism and its messy outcome still cause problems in the world today, such as the conflicts in Sudan and Syria as well as the conflict in the Middle East.
- Although imperialism exploited and abused its colonial peoples, it provided them with the technological, industrial, and cultural achievements of the West and linked all the world's peoples.

## Modern Thought and Art Emerge

Imperial encounters with non-European peoples influenced the styles and subject matter of artists and writers. These encounters also provoked debate over the acquisition of colonies. A new relativism in values and the loss of confidence in the objectivity of knowledge led to modernism in intellectual and cultural life. Philosophy, science, the arts, and literature contributed to this crisis of confidence and conscience. However, they also offered new models to explain and portray humanity.

### Philosophy

- *Friedrich Nietzsche* (1844-1900), a German, attributed the decline of Western civilization to the *slave morality* of Christian ethics.
- *Henri Bergson* (1859-1941), a French thinker, argued that intuition and experience are just as powerful as science and reason for understanding the human condition.
- *Soren Kierkegaard* (1813-1855), a Dane, established the foundations of *existentialism,* a philosophical school popularized by *Jean-Paul Sartre* after the Second World War that emphasized individual responsibility and the capability for giving meaning to a meaningless universe.

### Psychology

- *Sigmund Freud* (1850-1939), an Austrian, portrayed human behavior as the interplay of powerful irrational and *unconscious* forces.
  - The *id* was the driving force of the personality, a reservoir of sexual and aggressive drives.

- The *ego* attempted to satisfy the desires of the id rationally and negotiated between the id and the superego.
- The *superego*, in the unconscious mind like the id, presented conflicting parental and social values that clashed with the selfish drives of the id.
- Freud claimed that individual lives and civilization itself were fragile balancing acts to keep these unconscious and potentially destructive forces in balance.

## Physics

- The work of *Max Planck* (1858–1947), a German, demonstrated that atoms were not the basic building blocks of the universe.
- *Marie Curie*, a Pole, and her husband *Pierre Curie*, a Frenchman, discovered radioactivity, and that proved that atoms were made of yet smaller particles.
- The work of *Albert Einstein*, a German, revolutionized physics in his "miracle year" of 1905, in which he published four papers on the photoelectric effect, Brownian motion, special relativity, and the equivalence of mass and energy. These papers vaulted him to the center of the academic debates in physics.
  - Einstein further disrupted the comfortable assumptions of an orderly, rationally discoverable universe that Newton's 17th-century physics had supported. Einstein encouraged relativism in ethics, politics, and worldviews. Thus, the new field of quantum physics emerged.

## Art

- Imperial encounters with non-European peoples influenced the styles and subject matter of artists and writers. These encounters provoked debate over the acquisition of colonies.
  - Jules Verne's different voyages of discovery from *Around the World in Eighty Days* to *Journey to the Center of the Earth* and others epitomized Europeans' new fascination with different cultures and cultural relativism.
  - The Japanese prints that inspired Vincent van Gogh displayed the influence of outside cultural forces on European visual arts.
  - Joseph Conrad's *Heart of Darkness* and Rudyard Kipling's *The Jungle Book* displayed different European reactions to imperialism and different philosophies on how Europeans should interact with natives.
  - Paul Gauguin and Pablo Picasso developed a style of *primitivism* that was influenced by art from other cultures. Their works and the name of the style itself display European views of residents of other places on the planet.
- *Expressionism,* abstract and nonrepresentational, replaced *impressionism*. Expressionism was pioneered by *Vincent van Gogh* (1853–1890), *Paul Cézanne* (1839–1906), and *Paul Gauguin* (1848–1903), who painted with bold colors and images to focus on emotions and imagination.
- *Pablo Picasso* (1881–1973), a Spaniard, invented *cubism,* the depiction of mood through the use of geometric angles, planes, and clashing lines. His *primitivism* stage was influenced by European attitudes toward other peoples of the world.
- Architecture exemplified functionalism, buildings designed with practicality and clean lines instead of ornamentation.

## Literature

- Joseph Conrad's *Heart of Darkness* portrayed Africa as a dark continent made darker by the imperialism of Europeans and the horrors brought with it.
- *Vladimir Lenin* wrote strongly against imperialism in his *Imperialism, the Highest Stage of Capitalism* as did J. A. Hobson in *Imperialism: A Study*.
- British writer Rudyard Kipling wrote *The White Man's Burden* and *The Jungle Book* to portray the superiority of Western thought over that of the "less civilized" peoples of the world.

# Timeline of Imperialism

| Year | Event |
|---|---|
| 1839–1842; 1856–1860 | The *First Opium War* (1839–1842) and the *Second Opium War* (1856–1860) occurred in China. The British gained the rights of extraterritoriality, to sell opium, to stay in China all year, and to trade without the Cohong, which was a guild of Chinese merchants. |
| 1854 | Commodore Matthew Perry used gunboat diplomacy to open up Japan for trade with the Western world. |
| 1854–1856 | In the Crimean War, Russia lost to the Western nations and Turkey, ending Russia's imperialist aims. |
| 1857–1858 | ■ The *Sepoy Mutiny* in India was led by Hindu and Muslim soldiers who believed that their ammunition was exposing them to pig and cow fat, contrary to their religious beliefs.<br>■ The sepoys were the 300,000 South Asian soldiers in the British East India Company army. |
| 1869 | The Suez Canal was completed with French investment. |
| 1871 | Diamonds were discovered near Cape Town, South Africa, in what became the Kimberley diamond mines. |
| 1871 | Germany united into one nation. |
| 1872 | Henry Stanley met David Livingstone in the African jungle. |
| 1873 | The League of the Three Emperors formed: Germany, Austria-Hungary, Russia. |
| 1877 | Queen Victoria of Great Britain was crowned Empress of India. |
| 1877–1878 | ■ The Russo-Turkish War over Romania and Bulgaria was fought. Russia defeated the Ottoman Empire and gained access to warm-water ports in Bulgaria and elsewhere on the Balkan Peninsula.<br>■ The *Congress of Berlin of 1878* was held by Bismarck to host the great powers. The purpose was to avoid problems in the Balkan region after the Russo-Turkish War of 1878 and to establish peace between all powers regarding that region, which was divided among Austria-Hungary, the Ottoman Empire, and the four Balkan states (Greece, Serbia, Romania, and Montenegro). |
| 1879 | The British were defeated by the Zulus at the Battle of Isandlwana. |
| 1879 | The Dual Alliance between Austria-Hungary and Germany was established. |
| 1881 | Italy joined the Dual Alliance, forming the Triple Alliance. |
| 1884–1885 | Egypt was declared a British protectorate. |
| 1885 | ■ The *Berlin Conference* divided Africa among the European nations, but this division occurred only on a map.<br>■ The European nations did not hold the African lands they claimed at this point. Africans who were living on those lands believed that they ruled themselves. |
| 1888–1895 | Britain and Germany created East, Central, and South African trading companies. |
| 1896–1897 | The Sino-Japanese War occurred in which Japan went from being imperialized in 1854 to being imperialist itself just 42 years later. |
| 1898 | The Battle of Omdurman occurred in which the British led by General Kitchener killed 10,000 Ansar warriors and injured 13,000 more while losing only 48 men. |
| 1898 | Ethiopia repelled an attempted Italian invasion. |
| 1898 | The *Fashoda Incident* occurred in which Kitchener went south "up the Nile," defeated the Muslims, and met the French at *Fashoda*.<br>■ The French backed down and recalled their general, Marchand.<br>■ A crisis was averted. |
| 1899 | Rudyard Kipling wrote *The White Man's Burden* to encourage the United States to get into the imperialism business. |

| Year | Event |
|---|---|
| 1899–1902 | ▪ The Spanish-American War was fought in which the Americans helped win independence for Cuba.<br>▪ The U.S. also gained control of Puerto Rico and the Philippines.<br>▪ Spain was no longer a colonial power.<br>▪ The Filipinos revolted against the Americans, resulting in a brutal suppression that killed between 100,000 and 500,000 Filipinos. |
| 1901 | ▪ The Second Boer War was fought in South Africa, in which the British signed up in large numbers to fight for the right to "civilize" the people of Africa.<br>▪ This was a turning point in world opinion toward imperialism. The brutal tactics used to suppress the Afrikaners were reported, and Europeans lost some of their zeal for imperialism.<br>▪ This was also the first war of the new century; the 1900s began with war and saw the most brutal wars ever fought. |
| 1904–1905 | The Russo-Japanese War was fought; Japan defeated the Russian navy completely and demonstrated that an Asian nation could defeat a European nation. |
| 1905 | The *Moroccan Crisis* occurred in which Germany attempted to prevent France from attaining the colony of Morocco.<br>▪ This crisis was settled by the Algeciras Conference in 1906 in which the Germans tried to bully France into again turning against Britain. This brought Britain and France closer together. The conference resulted in hostile attention from Britain, France, Russia, and the United States toward Germany. This was Wilhelm II getting a wake-up call that he ignored. |
| 1911 | The Serbian "Black Hand" nationalist group formed; one of its members assassinated Archduke Ferdinand in 1914. |
| 1911 | The *Moroccan Crisis of 1911* saw a German gunboat sent to Morocco to protest French occupation of the city of Fez. Britain supported France again, and Germany backed down in return for minor concessions in equatorial Africa. |
| 1914 | The Panama Canal opened, reducing the shipping miles from Asia to Europe. |
| 1916 | Mohandas K. Gandhi returned from South Africa to India, where he tirelessly fought for Indian independence through *passive resistance* and the *Indian Congress Party* until India won its independence in 1947. |

## The Imperialism Debate

There was debate between the intelligentia about the benefits and costs as well as the morality of imperialism. This debate really began with Adam Smith in his *Wealth of Nations*, but it raged on during this period of time. Some defended imperialism as the moral and beneficial choice, as did Kipling with *The White Man's Burden*. Others criticized it as inefficient and benefiting only a few in society at the cost of the many, as seen in J. A. Hobson's critique of imperialism. Others, such as Vladimir Lenin, characterized imperialism as theft and oppression by the capitalist class of developed nations against the developing nations of the rest of the world. The debate is still going on today with it focusing more on what power national influence should have on trade and commerce.

## Long-Term Causes of the First World War

There were four MAIN causes of the First World War: *militarism* (M), *alliances* (A), *imperialism* (I), and *nationalism* (N). These four forces converged at a time and place that could only result in war and revolution across Europe.

It is also important to look at two factors *not* covered by the acronym MAIN: *socialism* and *industrialization*. The rise of socialism was a factor because governments in Europe were being led by conservative leaders who wanted to use the war to distract the frustrated working classes (who wanted social changes) by making patriotic calls for unity against their enemies. Further, the *industrialization* of Europe gave countries the ability to conduct massive military buildups as never before. Overconfident military leaders were eager to use their new weapons and tactics to wage war on an industrial scale. Additionally, this war was fought over natural resources needed for industry for the combatant nations.

## Militarism

Militarism emerged as a powerful force at the beginning of the 20th century. A warship-building race emerged between Great Britain and Germany, with Germany constructing a navy intended to rival the British navy. A massive buildup of arms and weapons—including modern artillery and explosives, machine guns, and rifles—increased pressure for war in Europe.

## Alliances

Alliances held Europe in a balance of power from the time of Charlemagne through Machiavelli and onward. The complex alliances in place during this period constitute what is referred to as *Bismarck's Alliance System*. In this system, no one declared war because they knew the alliances would make war too costly.

- The League of Three Emperors of 1873 failed when Russia and the Ottomans battled over the Balkans, and Russia was too near to Austria for its liking. Bismarck alienated Russia at the Congress of Vienna (Austria acquired Bosnia-Herzegovina), but he wanted peace and unity in Eastern Europe.
- The *Congress of Berlin of 1878* was held by Bismarck to host the great powers and avoid problems in the Balkan Peninsula after the Russo-Turkish War of 1878. Bismarck intended to establish peace among all powers regarding that region, which was divided between Austria, the Ottoman Empire, and the four Balkan states (Greece, Serbia, Romania, and Montenegro).
- He then created the *Dual Alliance* between Germany and Austria-Hungary, which lasted from 1879–1918.
- He pressed Russia and Austria-Hungary into the League of the Three Emperors in 1881.
  - A mutual defense pact against the Ottomans in the Balkans and France in the West was signed.
  - Russia refused to renew its membership in 1887.
- In the Triple Alliance (1882–1915), Bismarck tried to tilt the balance of power in his favor at the Congress of Berlin.
  - He arranged a defensive alliance among Italy, Austria-Hungary, and Germany.
  - Italy withdrew in 1915 because Germany and Austria-Hungary had gone on the offensive.
- Russia exited the League of Three Emperors in 1887.
  - Germany, in an attempt to keep peace with Russia, arranged the *Russian German Reinsurance Treaty* in which both countries promised neutrality if the other was attacked.
  - Kaiser William II did not like this friendly attitude toward Russia and dismissed Bismarck as a result.
  - Refused to renew the policy.
  - France and Russia then became allies.

In 1902, the two imperialist island nations that industrialized first on their respective continents, Britain and Japan, formed an alliance.

- Britain and Japan were firmly committed in the Anglo-Japanese Alliance (1902–1915).
  - The United States was its usual noncommittal self but followed loyally at Britain's side.
- Anglo-French Entente seemed like a good idea to both sides by 1904.
- Britain was the only great power (splendid isolation) that remained uncommitted to any other country during this time.
- After the *Boer War*, some countries began to feel threatened and considered an alliance among Austria-Hungary, France, Germany, and Russia against Britain.
  - Britain tried to resolve this problem and remain on good terms with the other countries.
  - France's prime minister, Theophile Déclassé, also wanted better relations with Britain and France; he arranged the Anglo-French Entente.
- The Anglo-French Entente settled any outstanding disputes between Britain and France.
- France gave support to Britain if the other countries decided to form an alliance against it.

- At the *Algeciras Conference* in 1906, the Germans tried to persuade France to turn against Britain.
  - This brought Britain and France closer together. The conference resulted in hostile attention from Britain, France, Russia, and the United States toward Germany.
  - This conference was Wilhelm II getting a wake-up call that he ignored.
- In 1907, the Russians, whose fleet was recently destroyed in battle against the Japanese, asked the British to join an alliance.
  - The Anglo-Russo Alliance began.
  - The *Triple Entente* would finally emerge with Russia, Britain, and France in 1914.
  - Britain, France, and Russia, along with the United States, would be known as the *Allied Powers* during the First World War.

## Imperialism

Imperialism was also a major factor leading up to the First World War. Throughout the 19th century, each major European country's population pressure, desire for wealth, and pride urged it to gain overseas possessions regardless of the desires of its people. Imperialism was also vital to a capitalist economy, encouraging that economy to expand.

The following are some examples of how imperialism increased international tensions:

- The *Berlin Conference* in 1885 marked Germany's late arrival to imperialism, which led Bismarck to spearhead the movement to establish rules for carving up Africa.
- The *Kruger Telegram* in 1902 roused British ire at Germany for congratulating the Boers on their victories over British troops in South Africa.
- The *Moroccan Crisis* of 1911 saw a German gunboat sent to Morocco to protest French occupation of the city of Fez.
  - Britain supported France, and Germany backed down in return for minor concessions in equatorial Africa.

## Nationalism

Nationalism caused leaders and countries to do strange things for national pride. Wilhelm II of Germany was building up his navy to attempt to rival the British navy. This forced Britain to build its navy rather than focus on David Lloyd George's *People's Budget*.

- German nationalism was looking for another great military victory to bring glory and colonies to Germany.
- Nationalism was tearing apart the dual monarchy of Austria-Hungary.
- A good example of nationalism is the Balkan Wars.
  - In the *First Balkan Crisis* (1874–1878), Bosnia and Herzegovina rebelled against Ottoman rule, leading to Serbia declaring war on the Ottoman Empire in June 1876.
  - Russia, which was a largely Slavic country like Serbia, had a policy of *pan-Slavism*, or protecting all Slavic people, and declared war on the Ottoman Empire.
  - Britain, concerned with protecting its Mediterranean interests against Russian movements, supported Turkish Sultan Hamid I.
  - In 1878, Turkey sought peace.
- Greece and Bulgaria took Macedonia, leading to the *Second Balkan Crisis* (1885), a conflict between Bulgaria and Serbia over territory.
  - Russia warned it was ready to occupy Bulgaria if it did not yield to Serbian demands over Macedonia.
  - Austria-Hungary supported Bulgaria, and Germany supported Austria-Hungary.
  - This nationalist pressure ended the League of the Three Emperors.

- In the *Third Balkan Crisis* (1912–1913), Italy was in conflict with the Ottoman Empire over holdings along the Adriatic Sea.
- In the *First Balkan War*, Serbia took Macedonia in 1912.
- In the *Second Balkan War* (1913), Serbia attacked Bulgaria in hopes of gaining a seaport.
  - Russia, with its policy of pan-Slavism, supported Serbia, while Austria-Hungary still supported Bulgaria.
  - Britain and Germany urged peace.
  - Serbs were enraged at Austria-Hungary for its support of Bulgaria and its occupation of Bosnia-Herzegovina.
  - In the end, nationalism directly led to the *Third Balkan War*, which turned into the First World War.

## Practice Questions

### Long Essay

The questions that follow are samples of the various types of thematic essays on the AP exam. See pages 27–28 for a detailed explanation of each type. Check over the generic rubric (see pages 28–29) before you begin any of these essays, and use that rubric to score your essay if you write one.

### Question 1

Compare the European colonial policies before 1815 with those of the later-19th and early-20th centuries.

### Comments on Question 1

This is a *compare* skill question. So be sure to describe the similarities and differences between the "European colonial policies before 1815" and the "European colonial policies of the later-19th and early-20th centuries." Account for, or explain, these similarities and differences by providing specific examples. Tie those similarities and differences to historical developments, such as the growth of technology, economic ambitions, nationalistic tensions, and political ideas. Sometimes called colonialism, the European colonial policies before 1815 followed the Age of Exploration of the mid-15th to the early-19th centuries. It was characterized by commercial ventures, control of seaports for the seagoing trade, and trade with the local peoples. There was little attempt, except in the New World, to encourage immigration to the colonies; there was very little attempt to impose the European social, political, or economic structures on the local population.

In contrast, the "new imperialism" of the late-19th century took over the governing of its colonies. It exploited native labor and natural resources. It judged local behavior according to European mores. It also forced religious conversion.

The two forms of imperialism were similar in that the Europeans rarely attempted to absorb the culture of their colonies nor did they encourage colonial immigration to the mother country.

### Question 2

By the end of the 19th century, to what extent had European nations divided the rest of the world among themselves?

### Comments on Question 2

This question tests the *change and continuity over time* (CCOT) skill. Be sure to describe the level of historical continuity and change. Analyze specific examples of what changed, what parts of the world were divided by Europe, and what remained the same in the colonies, such as religions, traditions, and class structure. Explain why things changed or stayed the same as European imperialism evolved. The essay must explain how Europe conquered most of the world during the 19th century and must support assertions with specific evidence.

Consider the various regions that were targets of imperialism in the 19th century. The scramble for Africa left only two independent nations: Liberia and Ethiopia. In Asia, coastal China and some inland regions were divided into spheres of influence that left a disintegrating monarchy, but one that was Chinese. Japan maintained its independence. When it was forced to open up to Western trade, Japan rapidly industrialized. Within 50 years, Japan defeated Russia in a land and naval conflict to become the only Asian nation to win a war against a European power. In the Western Hemisphere, the United States regarded Latin America as its sphere of influence.

## Question 3

Compare the responses of China and Japan to Western encroachment.

### Comments on Question 3

This is a *compare* skill question. So be sure to describe the similarities and differences between the Japanese and Chinese reactions to European imperialism. Account for or explain them by providing specific examples of how they are similar and different. Tie those similarities and differences to historical developments, such as the use of Western ideas and technology.

The contrast was glaring. China resisted westernization, and parts of the country became regions dominated by foreign influence. In contrast, Japan modernized and kept its autonomy. Why and how did this happen? Detail the Chinese response to Western imperialism from the Earl of McCartney to the Opium Wars to the Boxer Rebellion to the establishment of Sun Yat-sen's republic. Trace the Japanese response from the "opening" by Commodore Perry to the Russo-Japanese War. Compare the similarities by explaining that both nations managed to hold onto their rich and ancient cultures: one did so by stubbornly sticking to tradition, the other by blending the best of the West with its own unique ways.

### Short-Answer

1.  Use the excerpt below and your knowledge of European history to answer all parts of the question that follows.

**Imperialism, the Highest Stage of Capitalism**

Precisely the parasitism and decay of capitalism, which are characteristic of its highest historical stage of development, i.e., imperialism. As is proved in this pamphlet, capitalism has now singled out a handful (less than one-tenth of the inhabitants of the globe; less than one-fifth at a most "generous" and liberal calculation) of exceptionally rich and powerful states which plunder the whole world simply by "clipping coupons." Capital exports yield an income of eight to ten billion francs per annum, at prewar prices and according to prewar bourgeois statistics. Now, of course, they yield much more.

Obviously, out of such enormous superprofits (since they are obtained over and above the profits which capitalists squeeze out of the workers of their "own" country) it is possible to bribe the labor leaders and the upper stratum of the labor aristocracy. And the capitalists of the "advanced" countries are bribing them; they bribe them in a thousand different ways, direct and indirect, overt and covert.

—Vladimir Ilyich Lenin, 1916

(a) Briefly explain why the author of the document would believe and assert that imperialism is "the highest stage of capitalism."

(b) Cite ONE piece of evidence that supports Lenin's assertion and explain why it supports the assertion.

(c) Cite ONE piece of evidence that refutes Lenin's claim and explain why it refutes that claim.

2.  Use the excerpt of the treaty below and your knowledge of European history to answer all parts of the question that follows.

### The Dual Alliance Between Austria-Hungary and Germany—October 7, 1879

ARTICLE 1.

Should, contrary to their hope, and against the loyal desire of the two High Contracting Parties, one of the two Empires be attacked by Russia the High Contracting Parties are bound to come to the assistance the other with the whole war strength of their Empires, and accordingly only to conclude peace together and upon mutual agreement.

ARTICLE 2.

Should one of the High Contracting Parties be attacked by another Power, the other High Contracting Party binds itself hereby, not only not to support the aggressor against its High Ally, but to observe at least a benevolent neutral attitude towards its fellow Contracting Party.

ARTICLE 4.

This Treaty shall, in conformity with its peaceful character, and to avoid any misinterpretation, be kept secret by the two High Contracting Parties, and only communicated to a third Power upon a joint understanding between the two Parties, and according to the terms of a special Agreement.

(a)  How did the treaty help cause the First World War?
(b)  Briefly explain each of the four main causes of the First World War that historians usually cite.
(c)  Briefly explain why many historians do not see the First World War as the first truly global conflict.

## Multiple-Choice

**Questions 1–3 refer to the image below.**

The Sepoy Mutiny, 1857–1858: contemporary illustration by an
unknown native artist. The Granger Collection.

1. The picture is of a rebellion against the British in 1857 in which of the following areas where the British had gained dominance?

   (A) Egypt
   (B) China
   (C) India
   (D) Ceylon

2. Which of the following is the most likely reason that the British were successful in putting down the rebellion depicted in the image?

   (A) The natives were poorly trained fighters.
   (B) The British had superior weapons.
   (C) The British outnumbered the natives.
   (D) The natives were not dedicated to their rebellion.

3. Which of the following was a contributing cause in the rebellion depicted in the image?

   (A) The sepoys were fierce warriors who could not be trusted by the British.
   (B) The sepoys were tired of long hours and low pay.
   (C) The British belief in their own superiority led them to ignore native traditions.
   (D) The British banned all native people from first-class travel within the empire.

**Questions 4–7 refer to the poem written by Rudyard Kipling in 1899 below.**

**The White Man's Burden**
Take up the White Man's burden—
Send forth the best ye breed—
Go, bind your sons to exile
To serve your captives' need;
To wait, in heavy harness,
On fluttered folk and wild—
Your new-caught sullen peoples,
Half devil and half child.

Take up the White Man's burden—
In patience to abide,
To veil the threat of terror
And check the show of pride;
By open speech and simple,
An hundred times made plain,
To seek another's profit
And work another's gain.

Take up the White Man's burden—
The savage wars of peace—
Fill full the mouth of Famine,
And bid the sickness cease;
And when your goal is nearest
(The end for others sought)
Watch sloth and heathen folly
Bring all your hope to naught.

4. This poem is associated with which of the following concepts that shaped Europe's interaction with the rest of the world in the late-19th century?

   (A) Ethnic self-determination
   (B) Social Darwinism
   (C) Cultural nihilism
   (D) The Golden Rule

5. Which of the following is the best description of the impact of this poem and the philosophy it represents?

   (A) It created a mass political movement that shook monarchies.
   (B) It was used to discourage nations from engaging in imperialist actions.
   (C) It was used to encourage native populations who had been imperialized to revolt.
   (D) It was used to justify European conquest of overseas territories.

6. By 1914, which of the following countries reaped the greatest benefits from adopting and exporting the philosophy supported by the poem?

   (A) Japan
   (B) China
   (C) India
   (D) Egypt

7. Which of the following is the best description of European overseas empires from 1750-1914?

   (A) European empires were steadily growing in a consistent manner throughout the period cited.
   (B) The same nations that started with large colonial empires continued to be the largest empires as they all built on their strong starts.
   (C) The focus of European empires shifted from Asia to the Americas due to rising profits there as the period progressed.
   (D) The colonies in the Americas broke free from Europe, and Europe began to colonize Africa and Asia as the period progressed.

# Answers and Explanations

## Short-Answer Explanations

1. (a) You should explain that Lenin, as the founder of the U.S.S.R., was pointing out the evils and oppression caused by capitalism as part of his communist viewpoint. He wanted to gain support for his communist ideas and to get the Russians to reject capitalism in favor of communism. You should further explain that Communists call for all workers to seize power together to wrest it from the hands of the elite wealthy classes so that there can be a more equitable distribution of wealth and output. You should also explain that the evils done in the name of imperialism, from the genocide of the Native Americans to the destruction of the Congo, gave Lenin a platform from which he could claim that communism had the higher moral ground.

   (b) You could note any ONE of the following and explain why it supports Lenin's assertion: vast wealth going from the rest of the world to Europe, military and political dominance of most of the world enriched Europe, Europeans' concept of the "White Man's Burden," the few Europeans who gained wealth from imperialism while the costs were spread among all taxpayers, or exporting capitalism to imperialized nations.

   (c) To refute the claim, you should note and explain why any ONE of the following refutes the claim that imperialism is the highest level of capitalism: government involvement in imperialism; some foreigners became wealthy, too; improvements to infrastructure in imperialized nations; the Japanese reaction to imperialism, going from isolation to imperial power in 50 years; or the improved standard of living for most citizens of imperialized nations due to European intervention.

2. (a) You should explain that the secret treaty between Austria and Germany forced both to go to war if either were attacked or if either got into a conflict with Russia. You could also explain that the overall system of alliances turned a local conflict into a European war with all powers getting involved and that imperialism also brought the distant regions Europeans had colonized into the conflict as well. You may include that Russia did not have a plan to mobilize troops against either Germany or Austria.

   (b) You should cite militarism, alliances, imperialism (or industrialization), and nationalism—the MAIN causes of the First World War—and briefly explain how they each led to war. Militarism could simply be the military buildup of the European powers at the start of the 20th century or the competition between Germany and the United Kingdom for naval dominance. Alliances should be blamed for igniting a local conflict in the Balkans into a full-fledged world war because of nations' obligations to each other. Imperialism could point to the competition for the best colonies as a cause of the war. Others may cite the Fashoda Incident or other actions taken by the Germans and the British and French leading up to the war.

   (c) You should cite other conflicts that were fought on multiple continents. The one most often cited is the Seven Years' War, which was fought in Asia, the Americas (called the French and Indian War by the British colonists in North America), Europe, and the coast of Africa. Another possible example would be the Crimean War, if all combatants are accounted for.

## Practice Multiple-Choice Questions

1. (A) is wrong because the Sepoy Mutiny was in India.
   (B) is wrong because the Sepoy Mutiny was in India.
   **(C) is CORRECT because the Sepoy Mutiny was in India.**
   (D) is wrong because the Sepoy Mutiny was in India.

2. (A) is wrong because the sepoys were soldiers trained by the British.

   **(B) is CORRECT because the British (and all European imperialists) relied heavily on the superiority of their weapons to control native populations many times larger than the British occupying force.**

   (C) is wrong because the natives were far more numerous than the British.

   (D) is wrong because natives were dedicated but could not defeat the superior weapons and technology of the British.

3. (A) is wrong because the British used the sepoys as their soldiers before the rebellion.

   (B) is wrong because the sepoys received better pay and hours from the British than they did working for Indian rulers.

   **(C) is CORRECT because the British forced the sepoys to use bullets coated with cow and pig fat, which was against the religious beliefs of the sepoys; this was a cause of the rebellion.**

   (D) is wrong because the British did not ban all natives from first-class travel.

4. (A) is wrong because the poem supports Western domination, not ethnic self-determination.

   **(B) is CORRECT because the idea of social Darwinism is associated with the poem and the concept of *The White Man's Burden*.**

   (C) is wrong because cultural nihilism means a lack of culture, which is not evident here.

   (D) is wrong because the Golden Rule is a biblical concept of "treat others how one wishes to be treated," which is certainly not evident here.

5. (A) is wrong because the poem and social Darwinism did not lead to massive social movement in Europe.

   (B) is wrong because the poem and the philosophy it represents encouraged, not discouraged, imperialism.

   (C) is wrong because the poem and the philosophy it represents was in favor of the conquest, not the revolt, of the natives in Africa and Asia.

   **(D) is CORRECT because *The White Man's Burden* was used as a support for social Darwinism, which was a justification for the European conquest of natives around the world.**

6. **(A) is CORRECT because Japan used the help of the West to modernize and, by 1905, defeated Russia, a European power, in war.**

   (B) is wrong because China's best coastal cities were controlled by foreign powers at the end of the Qing dynasty, and the country is just now recovering from the 19th century.

   (C) is wrong because India was controlled by the British until after the Second World War.

   (D) is wrong because Egypt was mostly controlled by the British after 1882.

7. (A) is wrong because Spain lost its empire and the British lost the United States during this period.

   (B) is wrong because Spain was in full decline by 1914.

   (C) is wrong because the Europeans were focused on building colonies in Africa and Asia, not on trade with the Americas.

   **(D) is CORRECT because, as the American colonies broke free, European countries turned to Asia and Africa for new sources of markets and raw materials.**

Visit Barron's Online Learning Hub to take the Time Period Three (1815–1914) Practice Assessment

# Time Period Four: c. 1914 to Present

## Learning Objectives

These are the Key Concepts for time period 4, according to the *AP European History Curriculum Framework*:

→ **KEY CONCEPT 4.1** Total war and political instability in the first half of the 20th century gave way to a polarized state order during the Cold War and eventually to efforts at transnational union.

→ **KEY CONCEPT 4.2** The stresses of economic collapse and total war engendered internal conflicts within European states and created conflicting conceptions of the relationship between the individual and the state, as demonstrated in the ideological battle between liberal democracy, communism, and fascism.

→ **KEY CONCEPT 4.3** During the 20th century, diverse intellectual and cultural movements questioned the existence of objective knowledge, the ability of reason to arrive at truth, and the role of religion in determining moral standards.

→ **KEY CONCEPT 4.4** Demographic changes, economic growth, total war, disruptions of traditional social patterns, and competing definitions of freedom and justice altered the experiences of everyday life.

## Time Period Overview

This time period encompasses the 20th century and the early-21st century. It was defined by the total-war military policy of the First and Second World Wars as well as by the efforts toward diplomacy and European unity that followed the Cold War. The 20th century was characterized by large-scale suffering brought on by warfare and genocide, but there also were tremendous improvements in the standard of living. The rise and fall of communism in Europe is examined in this unit, from the Russian Revolution through the fall of the Berlin Wall and until the conflicts in Ukraine in 2014 and 2015, including the effects of the rise and fall of the Soviet Union, which weigh heavily on European history. Likewise, the rise and fall of other ideologies of the 20th century, such as fascism, must be examined to understand the era. The primacy of economic life in Europe becomes apparent in this time period, with the Great Depression and many European responses to it creating the true modern welfare state. The peak of imperialism in the years just before the First World War and then its decline after the Second World War are also important forces to be examined. The marginalization of minorities and then their recognition after the Second World War is also of note. The ideological conflict known as the Cold War was a central theme of this period and must be examined in detail. Crucial to understanding this time period are the movements both toward and away from unity within Europe, culminating in the creation of the Eurozone. This time period includes the traditional delineations of the following:

- The First World War
- The Russian Revolution
- The age of anxiety, or interwar years
- The Second World War
- Decolonization, recovery, and Cold War
- Modern Europe

These traditional delineations do overlap in many ways. The themes within them, as stated in the key concepts, can be seen woven through the next three chapters of this book. The College Board has divided the time period into two units: 20th Century Global Conflicts and Cold War and Contemporary Europe. This book groups chapters 10 and 11 into the unit on 20th-Century Global Conflicts, and the final unit is covered in the final chapter alone. Some of the events of this time period related to decolonization were included in chapter 9 to preserve the narrative of imperialism and to organize in one place the information related to the rest of the world.

# UNIT 8

# 20th-Century Global Conflicts

## Unit 8 Overview: The First World War, the Age of Anxiety, and World War II

**Unit description:** This unit covers two chapters and sets the stage for the contemporary world. The two terrible world wars drastically changed society, political relationships, economic interactions, gender roles, standards of living, and almost every other aspect of life. Some of this was brought on by increased industrialization and the spread of consumer society. The 20th century was characterized by large-scale suffering brought on by warfare and genocide but also characterized by tremendous improvements in the standard of living.

Governments gained increasing control over their citizens during this period in much of Europe. The final part of this unit is dedicated to the conflict between totalitarian governments and popular democracies on both sides of the conflict. Governments began to make total claims on the thoughts and actions of their populations; state propaganda rose in prominence as a way of controlling the masses. The stresses of economic collapse and total war engendered internal conflicts within European states and created conflicting conceptions of the relationship between the individual and the state, as demonstrated in the ideological battle among democracy, communism, and fascism.

The industrialization of warfare allowed warfare on an unprecedented scale. The utilization of all of the resources for a society led to the spread of the tactic of *total war* in Western Europe and *war communism* in the Soviet Union. New weapons of war, from tanks to atomic weapons and bombers, were created and used to kill humans on an industrial scale. Nationalism and ideology were used by governments to convince their citizens to kill each other. Additionally, demographic changes, economic growth, total war, disruptions of traditional social patterns, and competing definitions of freedom and justice altered the experiences of everyday life.

After World War II, the world came together to form the United Nations and promote ethnic self-determination. The pursuant decolonization of former European colonies helped create the conflicts of the late-20th and early-21st centuries. This unit utilizes six of the seven of the themes in European history: Interaction of Europe and the World, Economic and Commercial Developments, Cultural and Intellectual Developments, States and Other Institutions of Power, National and European Identity, and Technological and Scientific Innovation.

This unit is focused on the world wars, the rise of dictatorships, and changes to culture between the wars. The major topics of study are the following:

- Contextualizing 20th-Century Global Conflicts
- World War I
- The Russian Revolution and Its Effects
- Versailles Conference and Peace Settlement
- Global Economic Crisis
- Fascism and Totalitarianism
- Europe During the Interwar Period
- World War II
- The Holocaust
- 20th-Century Cultural, Intellectual, and Artistic Developments
- Continuity and Changes in an Age of Global Conflict

This unit is comprised of chapters 10 and 11. It takes place entirely during period 4.

# 10

# The First World War, Russian Revolution, and U.S.S.R. Until 1939

## Overview

The beginning of the First World War marked the height of European power on this planet; its ending marked the beginning of the decline. Great empires fell in this war: the Russian, Austro-Hungarian, German, and Ottoman. Others (Britain and France), which had reached the zenith of imperialist expansion by 1914, saw their economies all but extinguished by 1918. A generation of young European men was decimated in the trenches of France, on the plains of Eastern Europe, and on other global battlefronts.

It was the first *total war*. The First World War involved mass civilian populations in a war effort that required rationing, employed both sexes in war plants, and pumped up popular fervor with distorted propaganda.

Narrow nationalism flourished with the fall of the old, ethnically diverse empires when dominant ethnic groups formed the basis for smaller nation-states, such as Yugoslavia, Czechoslovakia, Austria, and Hungary. The triumph of communism in Russia was a direct result of the war. Fascism in Italy and Nazism in Germany were indirect results. The drain of Europe's resources made the United States the world's leading creditor and greatest producer. The unresolved issues of the vindictive and haphazard peace process led inevitably to the Second World War.

Meanwhile, czarist Russia had been in decline for some time. Defeats in foreign wars tended to lead to domestic reform in Russia. The Russian losses in Crimea in 1856 and against Japan in 1905 led to massive change, such as the slow emancipation of the serfs and the creation of the Duma, a Russian legislature. The brutal exploitation of rural peasants under feudal serfdom changed to the oppression of industrial workers in factories, which led many to call for another way.

The Russian Revolution of 1917 began as an attempt at reform by the middle class and some enlightened nobles. When the moderates maintained Russia's unpopular involvement in the war, the radical Marxist Bolsheviks seized power and established the Communist regime that changed the politics of the 20th century.

## Events Leading to the First World War

The events leading to the First World War were outlined at the end of chapter 9. The four MAIN causes of the war—militarism, alliance, imperialism, and nationalism—along with the increasing industrialization and technological innovation were examined along with the events at the end of period 3. Specifically, the Balkan Wars at the start of the 20th century, including the *First Balkan War* of 1912 and the *Second Balkan War* of 1913, were precipitous events that led to the outbreak of global conflict. However the "spark" that ignited the Balkan crisis into a global conflict was the assassination of the heir to the Austro-Hungarian throne by Serbian nationalists.

*June 28, 1914:* Archduke Franz Ferdinand, heir to the Austrian throne, was assassinated along with his wife in Sarajevo, capital of the Austrian province of Bosnia and Herzogovina.

- When evidence was uncovered that high Serbian officials had plotted the murder, Austria sought German support to crush Serbia.
- Kaiser Wilhelm II issued the infamous *blank check*, promising backing for any action Austria might take.
- Serbia turned to "big brother" Slav, Russia, which in turn got a guarantee of French support against Germany and Austria in a similar *blank check*.

*July 23, 1914:* Austria presented an ultimatum to Serbia that made Serbia a virtual protectorate of Austria.

*July 28, 1914:* Austria declared war on Serbia after pronouncing the Serbian response inadequate. Russia mobilized.

*August 1, 1914:* Germany declared war on Russia.

*August 3, 1914:* France declared war on Germany.

*August 4, 1914:* Britain declared war on Germany after German forces violated Belgium's neutrality in the German campaign to invade France.

## The First World War

### The Combatants

*The Allies* had the following members:

- Britain, which was part of the Triple Entente, entered the war in 1914.
- France, which was part of the Triple Entente, entered the war in 1914.
- Russia, which was part of the Triple Entente, entered the war in 1914 and exited in 1917.
- Italy entered the war in 1915.
- The United States entered the war in 1917.

*The Central Powers* consisted of the following:

- Germany
- Austria-Hungary
- Ottoman Empire
- Bulgaria

### The Western Front

In August–September 1914, Germany's *Schlieffen Plan* for a rapid invasion of France failed. Since a *war of attrition* (wearing down of the resources and morale of the enemy) was to Germany's disadvantage because of the superior land mass, resources, and population of its enemies, Germany aimed for a quick victory.

### The Strategy of the Schlieffen Plan

1. Defeat France in six weeks, as in the Franco-Prussian War.
2. Hold off Russia, which the German high command estimated would take six months to mobilize fully.
3. Invade France through neutral Belgium, by being granted access, in order to outflank the French armies and seize Paris.

### Why the Schlieffen Plan Failed

1. The Belgians protested and put up unexpectedly stiff resistance.
2. The Russians mobilized with great speed, drawing German forces to the Eastern Front to bolster the Austrians in the field.
3. The French counterattacked heroically at the *Battle of the Marne* (September 5, 1914) to stop the German drive to Paris.

### The Western Front Stalemated into Trench Warfare

1. The trench lines extended from the coast of the North Sea to the border of Switzerland in the south.
2. The bloody, costly fighting, after the Battle of the Marne, achieved no significant breakthrough for either side.
3. Technological developments in weaponry were far in advance of the infantry tactics. These developments include the following:

   - Machine guns
   - Poison gas
   - Submarines
   - Barbed wire
   - Mass artillery
   - Tanks
   - Aerial strafing
   - Bombing from aircraft

4. The result was the slaughter of a generation of young Western Europeans in the trenches of France and Flanders (a region of northern France and parts of Belgium).
5. The *Battle of the Somme*, July–November 1916, typified this stalemate. It was one of the bloodiest battles in world history, with over 1,200,000 soldiers killed or wounded. The *Battle of Verdun* lasted through most of 1916 and is another example where fixed fortifications failed at a cost of 700,000 casualties. The fortifications at Verdun were supposedly impenetrable. However, the Germans annihilated the fortress and the surrounding area, proving the futility of fixed fortifications in the modern era.
   - The Battle of the Somme lasted from July until November 1916 and saw changes of territory amounting to only 125 square miles.

## The Eastern Front Remained a Mobile War

In 1914, the following occurred:

- German forces under *Paul von Hindenburg* (1847–1934) and Erich Ludendorff won important victories over the Russians. (Paul von Hindenburg later became a president of the postwar Weimar Republic.)
- The Russians pushed the Austrians out of Galicia (western Poland).

The year 1915 was a year of success for the Central Powers:

- Combined German-Austrian forces pushed the Russian forces out of Poland and inflicted awesome casualties.
- Bulgaria entered the war on Germany's side. (Germany and its allies became known as the Central Powers.)
- The Germans overran the Balkans.
- The British launched the *Gallipoli Campaign* to knock the Ottoman Empire (Turkey), which had joined the Central Powers, out of the war. The British landed at the Dardanelles, a vital control point for access between the Aegean and Black Seas.

○ This campaign failed as the Ottomans drove back the combined British, Indian, and Australian troops and held the straits.

In 1916, the Germans pushed deep into Russian territory.

- Czar Nicholas II went to the front to take personal command of the troops in a conflict in which Russia was being outfought and outproduced.
  ○ The Russians were still using single-shot rifles that had to be reloaded after each shot, while the Germans were using machine guns.
  ○ Millions of Russians—soldiers and civilians—were slaughtered or starved in this war.
  ○ Nicholas was no help. He was now personally responsible for the ongoing defeat of his army by the Germans, who continued to advance.
  ○ The people of Russia wanted peace and food.

- The Gallipoli Campaign failed. Its planner, future British Prime Minister Winston Churchill (1874–1965), resigned his post as First Lord of the Admiralty in charge of the navy.

In 1917, the Russians retreated and the war spread.

- The Russian czar abdicated in March; the provincial government under Alexander Kerensky (1881–1970) continued the war.
- The Bolsheviks seized power in November and eventually pulled Russia out of the war.
- The Russian withdrawal from the war was exactly what the Allies did not want.
- This left Germany with only one front on which to fight. However, the United States had joined the Allies just before Russia pulled out of the war, somewhat balancing the loss of Russia as an ally.
- If Russia had stayed in the war, the Central Powers could have been defeated sooner.
- The Japanese, who had joined the Allies, attacked parts of China in a bid for colonial territory and natural resources.
- Near the end of the war, Turkish forces slaughtered around a million Armenian civilians in what is becoming widely termed the *Armenian Genocide*.
  ○ Difficult to rule a multiethnic empire.
  ○ Accusations of disloyalty during the First World War added to this slaughter.

## Waging the War

The First World War was the 20th century's first *total war*, whereby the entire civilian populations of the belligerent nations were mobilized for winning the war.

- Propaganda lionized the men at the front and dehumanized the enemy.
- News was censored.
- Economic production was focused on the war effort.
  ○ Women replaced male factory workers who were now in uniform.
  ○ Rationing of food and scarce commodities was instituted.
  ○ People financed the war by buying bonds.
  ○ Each side tried to starve out the enemy by cutting off vital supplies to the civilian population.
- The war in Europe quickly spread to non-European theaters, transforming the war into a global conflict.
  ○ The *Arab Revolt* against the Turks in 1916 was exploited by the British, specifically by their agent T. E. Lawrence, who fought with the Arabs against the Turks from within the Ottoman Empire. This eventually led to British claims on the mandate of Palestine.
  ○ The Japanese used the war as an excuse for imperialism on the Chinese mainland and elsewhere in the Pacific.
  ○ Hundreds of thousands of colonial soldiers from Africa and Asia were used by both sides during this war.

## Naval Blockades

- Britain used its superior fleet and sea mines to cut off the Central Powers from overseas trade.
- Germany employed *unrestricted submarine warfare* to prevent the British from getting vital materials from their colonies and war supplies from the United States.
  - The sinking of the British passenger ship *Lusitania* in May 1915, with many American passengers onboard, helped turn U.S. public opinion against Germany.
  - Note that there is strong evidence to suggest that the *Lusitania* was carrying contraband munitions as the Germans claimed.

## Diplomacy

In 1915, neutral Italy entered the war against the Central Powers (its former allies) with the promise of being given *Italia irredenta* (unredeemed Italy) and some German colonies and Ottoman territories.

In 1917, the infamous *Zimmermann Note* promised Mexico some of its former American holdings if it entered the war on Germany's side against the United States.

- Arabs and Jews in Palestine were promised autonomy if they joined the Allies.
- Eastern Europeans were promised ethnic control in return for support of the Allies.

## The End of the War

Although the United States had only a small standing army when the war began, it was able to field nine divisions in France by the summer of 1918. This was in time to help halt the last major offensive of the exhausted German army. The effects of military stalemate and *total war* induced the citizens, both military and civilian, to protest and turn to insurrection in the belligerent nations. This eventually led to revolutions that changed the international balance of power.

By the fall of 1918, Bulgaria and Turkey had sued for peace, Austria-Hungary had collapsed, and Germany was wracked with revolution. The Kaiser abdicated and fled to neutral Holland. A provisional German government requested negotiations on the basis of U.S. President Woodrow Wilson's *Fourteen Points peace plan*.

On the 11th hour of the 11th day of the 11th month of 1918, an *armistice* ended the First World War.

### NOTE

More people died in the influenza epidemic, called the Spanish Flu, that followed the war than died in the war itself—10 million died in combat and nearly 20 million died from the disease. Yet the First World War, called the Great War at the time, was still the bloodiest war the world had ever seen.

## The Peace Settlements

The *Fourteen Points* was U.S. President Woodrow Wilson's peace plan. It was never implemented because of the secret treaties and diplomatic maneuvering that had taken place among the Allies before the United States entered the war. The following are some of the points in that peace plan:

1. End to secret treaties
2. Freedom of the seas
3. Free trade

**4.** Arms reduction

**5.** Just settlement of colonial claims

**6–13.** Evacuation of occupied territories *and* national self-determination

**14.** Establishment of a League of Nations: an international political organization to settle disputes

---

**NOTE**

Ironically, even though the League of Nations was Wilson's creation, the United States never joined the league. The League of Nations was largely ineffectual, for this and other reasons, in dealing with the aggressive dictatorships of the 1930s.

---

## The Paris Peace Conference, January 1919

*The Big Three—Woodrow Wilson* of the United States, *David Lloyd George* (1863–1945) of Britain, and *Georges Clemenceau* (1841–1929) of France—made all the decisions at the Paris Peace Conference. *Italian Vittorio Orlando* was also a leader of the conference at its beginning. However, he left, upset that Italy was not getting the gains he had hoped for when his country joined the war on the Allied side. The competing goals of the negotiators pitted the diplomatic idealism of Woodrow Wilson's Fourteen Points against the desire of the French and others to punish Germany and promote their national security. During the Paris Peace Conference, the following occurred:

- The Central Powers were excluded.
- The Fourteen Points were compromised.
- Nationality lines in Central and Eastern Europe were blurred.

The *Treaty of Versailles* ended the war with Germany. However, it *never settled* the explosive issues that had led to war in the first place. *Many of its provisions provided grist for Nazi propaganda mills in the 1920s and 1930s.*

### Provisions of the Treaty of Versailles

**1.** Certain German territories were ceded to the Allies, such as Alsace to France, Schleswig to Denmark, West Prussia to Poland, control of the mineral-rich Saar region to France. German overseas colonies were distributed among the Allies.

**2.** Poland was re-created as a sovereign nation and was granted a large territory with access to the sea.

**3.** New nations of Hungary, Yugoslavia, and Czechoslovakia were created to divide former Ottoman and Austrian holdings in Europe.

**4.** Germany was blamed for starting the war in the infamous *War Guilt Clause*, article 231.

**5.** The German army and navy were severely cut back to 100,000 servicemen.

**6.** The Rhineland (the vital strip between France and Germany) was to be demilitarized and occupied by Allied troops.

**7.** The *League of Nations* was created to intervene in international disputes and prevent future wars. It was a weak organization, and the United States never joined.

**8.** Germany had to pay *indemnities* for the civilian damage done in the war, totaling $33 billion. That is over $500 billion when adjusted for inflation to 2014 dollars. This hindered the German *Weimar Republic*'s ability to establish a stable legitimate government.

**9.** The *mandate system* redistributed former German and Ottoman possessions to the British Empire and the French. This altered the balance of power and set up conflicts over oil resources in the Middle East. Countries that were members of the British mandate system included the following:

- Palestine

- Syria
- Iraq
- Lebanon

In the end, the Treaty of Versailles satisfied few. The general dissatisfaction with the treaty led the great powers to be lax in the treaty's enforcement later, which allowed Germany to rearm and prepare for the worst global conflict so far, World War II.

This dissatisfaction with the Treaty of Versailles is exemplified by the reaction of John Maynard Keynes, who was a British negotiator at the conference. He walked out of the conference, declaring that the treaty would cause the economic destruction for all of Europe. Keynes wrote *Economic Consequences of the Peace* to protest the treaty. Then he wrote the *General Theory of Employment, Interest, and Money* to create a new economic theory to be ready to combat the coming Great Depression that he predicted. Thus, *Keynesian economics* was born.

## The Causes, Events, and Results of the First World War

### Causes of the First World War

- Historians generally agree that the German military buildup and the personal will of Kaiser Wilhelm II to use his new military, especially his navy, helped cause the First World War.
  - Wilhelm's offer to Austria to pay any war reparations if Austria was defeated also helps historians perceive the immediate causes of the war in this light.
- Events leading to the war included the Balkan Wars, the assassination of Archduke Franz Ferdinand and his wife, and increased conflict and bickering over colonial holdings, such as the *Fashoda Incident* and the *Boer War*.
- Sidney Bradshaw Fay and Henry Elmer Barnes stated that the First World War was inevitable and that blame rested on all the involved nations equally.
- Fay and Barnes blamed Austria-Hungary and Serbian nationalism (Gavrilo Princip's assassination of Archduke Franz Ferdinand and his wife) as short-term causes.
- They saw the long-term causes as militarism (arms races and economic rivalry), the alliance system, imperialism, and nationalism (MAIN).
- This view was accepted and led to the Treaty of Versailles not being fully enforced against Germany, which may have helped lead to the Second World War.
- In 1961, German historian *Franz Fischer* refuted the now-classic view stated above by using German secret documents as evidence. "He believed that Germany did not will and covet the Austro-Serbian war."
- Fischer said Germany was worried about Russia. He stated that Germany's growing ambitions for colonies and more territory in Europe, and its attempt to distract the socialists at home, all led to the First World War.

### Events of the First World War

- The war quickly became a global conflict, with the colonial empires of all belligerent nations becoming involved to some degree or another.

  - The Ottomans engaged in the attempted genocide of the Armenian people as a part of the First World War. This foreshadowed many other events of *ethnic cleansing* in the 20th century, ranging from the Nazi Holocaust to the conflict in Serbia in the 1990s.
  - The Battle of Gallipoli saw Australian troops defeated at the straits of the Dardanelles, resulting in terrible losses.
  - T. E. Lawrence was a British archaeologist who worked during the war to lead an Arab independence movement from the Ottoman Turks. The results of this struggle led to the division of the Middle East into most of the current countries in the region.

- The Japanese took over many German possessions in the Pacific, helped support the British against the threat of an Indian soldier mutiny, and invaded China during the First World War.
- This war was fought by people who lived on six continents.
- The Germans quickly advanced on Paris, but the *Battle of the Marne* stopped them before they could take the French capital.
- Both sides built miles of parallel trenches, leading to a stalemate in which battle after battle saw each side attempt to break through the enemies' lines.
- At the *Battle of Verdun*, the Germans again tried to break through, leading to over 700,000 killed and wounded.
- The *Battle of the Somme* was the Allied counterattack, costing over 1,200,000 casualties (killed, wounded, and missing) for no clear gain.
- The Eastern Front saw Germany destroy the Russian army. That loss led to the abdication of the czar and the eventual Russian Revolution.
- The First World War led to the Russian Revolution.
- In the only major naval engagement, the *Battle of Jutland*, the German navy failed to break through the British naval blockade and from then on resorted to submarine warfare, which drew in the United States.
- American involvement decided the outcome of the war due to the productive capacity of the United States, which escaped warfare at home.
- Revolutions overthrew monarchies in Russia, Germany, Austria, and the Ottoman Empire, resulting in each one pulling out of the war or calling for an armistice.

## Results of the War

- The war cost over $300 billion. That is over $4.5 trillion in 2014 dollars when adjusted for inflation.
- The Russian, German, Austrian, and Ottoman Empires ended.
- The war strained the resources of all the belligerents as they experimented with command economies.
- National unity was reinforced for a time but also caused great hardship due to lack of supplies, disruption, and dislocation.
- The war contributed greatly to the increased involvement of the government in society, leading to increased propaganda.
- The war also contributed to women's suffrage.
- Many social customs faded out, and society became more open (at least for a time).
- There was also a rapid development of new technology.
- The economy was greatly hurt by the war as world trade was totally disrupted, changed to a wartime economy, and then had to transition back.
- The Russian Revolution put the world's first Communist country on the map.
- A patchwork of weak, ethnically mixed states was created for political conveniences in Central and Eastern Europe.
  - New nations, such as *Poland, Czechoslovakia, Hungary*, and *Yugoslavia*, were created in Europe as a result of the *Treaty of Versailles*.
- The German and Ottoman colonial possessions were divided up between France and Great Britain, and the *British mandate system* was imposed in the areas Britain controlled.
  - This mandate system disturbed the balance of power.
  - It remains a factor today in the unrest in the Middle East, where the bulk of these territories were located.
  - Stability in the Middle East was made worse by the discovery of oil there and by historical Western support for dictatorial regimes there.
- Turkey modernized, and Kamal Ataturk created a secular democracy in Turkey that endured for over a century. Turkey has been literally and figuratively a bridge between Europe and Asia.

- ○ In the 1990s, a suspension bridge between the continents was built in Istanbul. One can now travel from Asia to Europe and back without leaving Turkey.
- Over 25 million people died as a result of the war. Another 21 million soldiers were wounded, leaving a generation grieving after losing many of their best leaders.

*The Second World War broke out in Europe 20 years after the signing of the Treaty of Versailles.*

## The Russian Revolution and the Soviet Union Until 1939

### Chronology

### 1881–1894

*Czar Alexander III* (r. 1881–1894), reacting to the assassination of his predecessor by radical socialists, instituted a reactionary policy of "Russification, orthodoxy, and autocracy."

### 1890s

Russia industrialized. However, the great majority of its population was still made up of rural peasants whose quality of life was comparable to that of farmers in the West during the Middle Ages.

- Since the French were eager for Russian support against the Germans, they granted loans and credits that enabled the Russians to build factories, import Western technology, and expand the railroad system.
- The *Trans-Siberian Railroad* linked European and Asiatic Russia.
- A commercial middle class grew in influence.
- A proletariat of exploited workers also grew.
- Political parties were formed to meet the demands of these new elements.
  - ○ *Constitutional Democrats (Kadets)* reflected the aims of the new middle class and some liberal landowners for parliamentary government and gradual reform.
  - ○ *Social Revolutionaries (Narodniks)* stressed the glories of Slav culture (Slavophiles) and sought to keep Russia agrarian.
  - ○ *Marxists* urged radical revolution.

### 1903

A meeting of the Russian Marxist Congress resulted in a split in the party when *Vladimir I. Lenin* (1870–1924) favored a party of elite revolutionaries instead of an open democratic organization.

- When most of the attendees walked out in protest, Lenin convinced those remaining to endorse his ideas.
- Although his supporters made up a minority of the party, he called them *Bolsheviks* (majority) and referred to the actual party majority as Mensheviks (minority).

### 1904–1905

In the *Russo-Japanese War*, Russia and newly modernized Japan came to blows. They were competing over Manchuria, which was a mineral-rich province of China.

- What the czar hoped would be a "short, glorious war" to divert unrest in his realm was a devastating defeat, the first in modern times of a European power by a nation outside of Europe.
  - ○ A surprise attack on the Russian fleet at Port Arthur in Manchuria, a defeat at the Battle of Mukden on Manchurian soil, and the sinking of the Russian European fleet in the Tsushima Straits brought a peace mediated by President *Theodore Roosevelt.*
  - ○ The Treaty of Portsmouth granted Japan Russia's railroad rights in Manchuria, half of the Sakhalin Islands off Russia's Pacific Coast, and a guarantee of Japan's protectorate in Korea.

- A humiliated Russia suffered from the Revolution of 1905 before the Russo-Japanese War was even over.
- The *Revolution of 1905:* Faced with the growing unrest of the working class, *Czar Nicholas II* (r. 1894–1918) commissioned a Russian Orthodox priest, *Father Gapon*, to organize a conservative union to counteract the radical Marxists.
  - Gapon, horrified by the conditions in St. Petersburg (the czarist capital), led a peaceful protest march of tens of thousands of workers and their families on Sunday, January 22, 1905.
  - Troops fired on the crowd, killing hundreds. This *Bloody Sunday* provoked general strikes, peasant uprisings, and the formation of workers' revolutionary councils, called *soviets*.
  - In the *Zemstvos*, the liberals demanded reforms. (The Zemstvos were the provincial councils elected by landowners and peasants. They were set up in 1864 by Czar Alexander II (1818–1881) as part of his great reforms.)
  - After a general strike was called by the Soviet of St. Petersburg, Nicholas II issued a promise for reform, called the *October Manifesto*.
- Its major provisions were a constitution, civil liberties, and a Duma (legislature) to represent all classes.

## 1906

A Duma (Russian assembly) was elected. However, it did not include the Marxists, who boycotted the elections because they mistrusted the czar's motives.

- Nicholas dissolved the Duma anyway because it demanded that his ministers be answerable to it.
- Reforms were instituted, including the strengthening of the Zemstvos, abolishing the peasant debt for the emancipation of serfs in the 1860s, and thereby creating a wealthy peasant class. These wealthy peasants were called the *kulaks*. They farmed large tracts of land and hired workers.

## 1914

With the outbreak of the First World War, the government suspended the Duma so that political bickering would not compromise the war effort.

- A national union of Zemstvos, made up of the various local elective districts, was organized to increase productivity.
- *Rasputin* (1869–1916), called "the mad monk," began to influence *Czarina Alexandra* after he claimed to have cured the czar's only son of hemophiliac episodes.

## 1915

Horrific losses at the front provoked the national union of Zemstvos and the middle class to demand that the Duma be reconvened to initiate reforms.

## 1916

The Duma met for the first time since its disbanding and, with support of its dominant conservatives, criticized the czar's government.

- Rasputin, whose sway over Czarina Alexandra had poisoned her advice to her easily influenced husband, was murdered by a band of young noblemen.
- The czar attempted to suppress any reform.

## 1917

The *March Revolution* occurred. Food riots broke out in Petrograd (St. Petersburg). When the czar ordered the Duma to dissolve and troops to suppress the disorder, neither obeyed.

- Workers and soldiers in Petrograd organized the radical legislative bodies called soviets.
  - Rebellion spread throughout the country and to the troops at the front.
  - Soldiers deserted by tens of thousands.
- On March 14, the Duma formed a provisional government under *Prince Georgii Lvov* (1861–1925).
- *Alexander Kerensky* (1881–1970), a moderate member of the soviet, played a major role in running the *provisional government.*
- On March 15, the czar abdicated.
- On March 17, Russia was proclaimed a republic.
- *Lenin* and other *Bolshevik* leaders came back from exile to Petrograd in April.
  - They made several demands of the provisional government:
    1. Russia must withdraw from the war.
    2. The Petrograd Soviet must run the government.
    3. Land was to be distributed to the peasants, and factories were to be controlled by the workers' committees (soviets).
- After an abortive coup in July, Lenin and the Bolshevik leaders fled to Finland.
- Prince Lvov turned over the provisional government to Kerensky.

The *October Revolution* began in November 1917 of the Western calendar.

- Kerensky's government failed to win the support of the people because of continued shortages and because it stayed in the war against the Central Powers.
- Lenin returned to Petrograd with the rallying cry of "peace, land, and bread."
- According to orthodox Marxism, a social revolution is possible only in highly developed capitalist countries, such as those in the West during this period.
  - Since Russia was virtually a feudal society and primarily agrarian, some Bolsheviks argued for a coalition with the middle classes until Russia had developed sufficiently.
  - Lenin argued that since Western Europe was ripe for revolution, a Marxist seizure of Russia would precipitate such takeovers elsewhere. These, in turn, would help Russia to bypass the capitalist stage. This was called *Leninist doctrine.*
  - Lenin won the support of Leon Trotsky (1870–1940), Joseph Stalin (1878–1953), and most of the Bolshevik leaders.
- On *October 6–7*, the Bolsheviks stormed the *Winter Palace*, headquarters of Kerensky's government, and seized other key centers in Petrograd.
  - Kerensky's provisional government fled.
  - The Congress of Soviets, representing the local soviets, formed all over Russia.
  - A Council of People's Commissars was established.
- A new government was formed with Lenin as head, Trotsky as foreign minister, and Stalin as nationalities minister.
  - Within months, the government abolished the freely elected legislative assembly and established a secret police organization, the Cheka, also variously known later as the OGPU, NKVD, MVD, and KGB.

## 1918

The *dictatorship of the proletariat* was proclaimed, in tune with Leninist doctrine; the Bolsheviks renamed their party the *Communist Party*.

- Important industries were nationalized.
- Russian Orthodox Church lands were seized.
- Russia pulled out of World War I, surrendering Latvia, Lithuania, Estonia, Poland, and the Ukraine to Germany in the *Treaty of Brest-Litovsk*.

### 1918–1922

The *Russian Civil War* was fought for control of the remainder of the Russian Empire.

- Opposed by czarists, the middle class, many peasants, and socialist factions, the Communists were able to win because their enemies could not unite.
- Despite the intervention of many Allied nations, including the United States, which feared the spread of communism, the Red Army under Trotsky conquered European Russia by the end of 1920 and Siberia and Central Asia by 1922.
- The Communist International (Comintern), to organize communism worldwide, was organized in 1919.
  - Lenin also began to institute policies designed to improve economic conditions in the new Soviet Union and to rebuild the damage caused by the First World War and the Russian Civil War.
    - The plan was called Lenin's *New Economic Policy* (NEP).
- Lenin allowed peasants some autonomy in selling their own goods.
- The state controlled all banks, foreign trade, and large industrial projects.
- Private ownership of some small enterprises was allowed.

### 1922

*Nationalities reform* occurred. What remained of the Russian Empire was reorganized into the Union of Soviet Socialist Republics (U.S.S.R.), uniting the various nation groups into a federal entity of major republics and smaller autonomous regions. Cultural identity was encouraged, and toleration of various ethnic groups became official policy.

### 1924

The Constitution of the Soviet Union was written. It stated the following:

1. Only workers and peasants were allowed to vote for local soviets.
2. Local soviets elected provincial or district soviets that, in turn, chose a republic soviet for each autonomous republic.
3. The *Congress of Soviets* represented all the republics and elected a *Council of People's Commissars*, which was similar to a government cabinet.

Lenin died at the age of 54, never fully recovering from an assassination attempt in 1920.

- Trotsky was at a disadvantage in becoming Lenin's successor both because he was a Jew in an anti-Semitic society and because he was considered an intellectual by the rank and file.
- As secretary of the Communist Party, Stalin garnered loyalty within the party by making many key appointments.
- Policy differences between Lenin and Trotsky further alienated the men from each other.
  - Trotsky pushed for a worldwide revolution.
  - Stalin argued for a strengthening of the U.S.S.R. by industrialization before it undertook the promotion of worldwide revolution.
    - Stalin adopted a theory that called for "building socialism in one country."

### 1927

- Stalin won the support of the Communist Party.
- Trotsky fled the country.
  - He was murdered in 1940 by a Stalinist agent.

### 1928

The first *five-year plan* promoted rapid industrialization by centralized planning.

- Coal and steel production were accelerated.
- A modern transportation system was developed, using the domestic resources of the U.S.S.R. since foreign nations were hostile to the new government.

### Early 1930s

- *Farm collectivization* consolidated small farms into *communes*, modernizing agriculture but displacing many peasants, some of whom resisted the process.
- The *kulaks*, who had been the most successful peasant farmers, were destroyed as a class.
  - Between 5 and 12 million people perished by murder and famine.
  - Most deaths occurred in the Ukraine.

### 1933

A second five-year plan was begun.

- The plan increased production of steel and heavy industry.
- It modernized Soviet factories.
- The plan created a boom in the U.S.S.R. when the West was in the depths of the *Great Depression*.
  - It made the Soviet Union into a leading industrial power.

### 1936–1937

Stalin's paranoid tendencies convinced him of plots within the party and the government to unseat him. Many original Bolsheviks, who were instrumental in carrying out the revolution, as well as high military officers (some of the most competent) were tried on trumped-up charges. Their trials were called the *purge trials*.

- As many as one million were executed.
- Approximately five to seven million were sent to the gulags (Siberian labor camps), where many died.
- Stalin strengthened his hold over the party, the government, and the nation.
- Stalin became one of the century's most powerful dictators.

## Figures and Events of the Russian Revolution

| Figure/Event | When | Important Facts |
|---|---|---|
| Czar Alexander II | 1861 | <ul><li>He emancipated the serfs because of the following:<ul><li>He felt pressure from below.</li><li>It was his personal will.</li><li>He needed to react to the loss of the Crimean War.</li></ul></li><li>He began the process of emancipation in 1861.</li><li>His assassination in 1881 moved Russia to the right.</li></ul> |
| Czar Nicholas II | 1894–1917 | <ul><li>The last czar of Russia, he was a better family man than he was a ruler.</li><li>His major weaknesses were the following:<ul><li>His devotion to his German wife, Alexandra, and their children</li><li>His lack of interest in affairs of state from an early age</li><li>His familial responsibilities to his cousins, George V, who ruled England, and Wilhelm II, who ruled Germany</li></ul></li></ul> |

| Figure/Event | When | Important Facts |
|---|---|---|
| Russo-Japanese War | 1904–1905 | ■ Russia was humiliated when its attempt to take parts of China was foiled by Japan, which defeated the Russian navy twice and left her without a functioning fleet.<br>■ This led to the Revolution of 1905 and the creation of the Duma, Russia's legislative body. |
| Father Gapon/ *Bloody Sunday* | 1905 | ■ He was a priest who was state appointed to help emancipated serfs adjust to their new lives; he circulated a workers' petition to the czar that was considered revolutionary.<br>■ Over 200,000 people marched on the Winter Palace in St. Petersburg to present the petition to the czar, but troops opened fire, killing many. |
| Peter Stolypin | 1905–1911 | ■ He oversaw the creation of the Duma as prime minister to Czar Nicholas II.<br>■ His agrarian reforms were very unpopular, and he was assassinated in 1911. |
| Gregori Rasputin | 1905–1916 | ■ He was a peasant-born mystic healer whom Alexandra believed helped keep her sickly son Alexei alive.<br>■ His debauchery was legendary, and rumors of his influence on the Romanov family helped lead to its downfall. |
| First World War | 1914–1918 | ■ Russia entered the First World War in 1914 to play its traditional role as protector of the Eastern Orthodox faith, this time in defense of Serbia.<br>■ Russia was not industrialized enough to be prepared for this war, for which Germany and England had been arming.<br>■ Russia was decimated by the Germans. Even though Czar Nicholas II took personal control of the army, Russia still lost, leading to his abdication in 1917.<br>■ The provisional government was committed to staying in the war. Lenin used that commitment to help overthrow the provisional government in the October Revolution. |
| Alexander Kerensky | 1917 | ■ He was the leader of the provisional government formed in March 1917 when Czar Nicholas II abdicated.<br>■ He and his popular Kadet (Social Democrat) Party fought for land reform while he kept the war going as a middle ground. This was in contrast to the Bolsheviks, who wanted to end the war immediately. |
| General Kornilov | 1914–1918 | ■ He was an important First World War general who stayed loyal to Kerensky as his commander in chief.<br>■ Kornilov was described as having the "heart of a lion and the brains of a sheep."<br>■ He led the White Army during the Russian Civil War in which he was captured and killed. |
| Vladimir Ilyich Lenin | 1917–1924 | ■ Lenin was the Father of the Russian Revolution.<br>■ He was the Russian Bolshevik leader who was banished in 1903 and who convinced the Germans to allow him back into the country in 1917.<br>■ He promised the people "peace, land, and bread" and won them over to his side.<br>■ He used the soviets in each town and the educated elite to foment revolution among the masses.<br>■ This new take on Marxism led to a successful revolution, placing him in power over the world's first Communist nation, the Union of Soviet Socialist Republics (U.S.S.R.), after a brutal civil war. |

| Figure/Event | When | Important Facts |
|---|---|---|
| Leon Trotsky | 1917–1924 | ■ He was Lenin's co-conspirator in the revolution.<br>■ He helped issue *Army Order Number 1* in which companies voted whether or not to follow commands.<br>■ He took over the military and the train stations during the October Revolution that placed Lenin in power.<br>■ He was pushed out by Joseph Stalin, who created a completely totalitarian regime in the U.S.S.R. and eventually had Trotsky killed in Mexico. |
| Joseph Stalin | 1924–1953 | ■ He ruled the U.S.S.R. with an iron fist.<br>■ He instituted *five-year plans* to modernize and industrialize while purging his nation of supposed enemies.<br>■ Between ruining the agricultural output, causing starvation, and authorizing political imprisonment and killings, it is estimated that Stalin killed more than 50 million of his citizens.<br>■ He did, however, rally his people to defeat the German invasion during the Second World War.<br>■ His actions and lack of trust with Franklin Roosevelt and Winston Churchill led directly to the Cold War. |

## Practice Questions

### Long Essay

These questions are samples of the various types of thematic essays on the AP exam. See pages 27–28 for a detailed explanation of each type. Check over the generic rubric (see pages 28–29) before you begin any of these essays, and use that rubric to score your essay if you write one.

### Question 1

To what extent was each of the belligerents in Europe responsible for the outbreak of the First World War?

### Comments on Question 1

This is a *caustion* question because it requires you to explain how each of the belligerent nations caused a specific outcome: the outbreak of the First World War. Remember to describe the causes of the First World War, indicating which was caused by which belligerent nation. Support your analysis of the causes and effects of that war with specific facts. The essay must also explain how each nation was or was not responsible, citing specific evidence. Many Americans, influenced to this day by creative Allied propaganda and by German aggression in the Second World War, believe that Germany alone was responsible for starting the First World War. Certainly the kaiser's prewar arrogance was one of the friction points. However, England, France, and Russia each carried out policies that aggravated the tension. In framing your answer, consider the following: the network of alliances that France and Germany engineered after the Franco-Prussian War, economic rivalry between Germany and Britain, the roles of Britain as well as Germany in the naval arms race, the mentalities of both "have" and "have-not" nations in the race for colonies, Russian support for pan-Slavism in Austria-Hungary, and the volatile Balkan situation.

### Question 2

Explain why the First World War ended the Russian, Austro-Hungarian, Ottoman, and German Empires.

## Comments on Question 2

This is another *causation* question because it requires you to explain how the collapse of each of the empires listed—Russian, German, Austro-Hungarian, and Ottoman—was caused by a specific stimulus, the First World War. Remember to describe the causes of the decline of each empire. Indicate the degree to which each one's downfall was caused by the First World War, using specific evidence to prove the cause of the decline of these empires. "Explain" in this context means to offer the causes and reasons for the collapse of those great empires. The scope of the issue is very broad, so a detailed accounting of each issue is not practical. Look for causes common to all three: the strains of a war of attrition, shortages, casualties, political instabilities, nationalist pressures, weakness of colonial holdings, and defeats in battle. Emphasize the different characters of each empire's problems: the Bolshevik movement in Russia, ethnic rivalries in Austria-Hungary, Arab nationalism within the Ottoman Empire, and democratic and socialist opposition movements in Germany.

## Question 3

Compare the Fourteen Points with the peace settlements in Paris.

### Comments on Question 3

This is clearly a *compare* skill question. Be sure to describe the similarities and differences between Woodrow Wilson's Fourteen Points peace plan and the reality of the Treaty of Versailles. Also account for or explain why they were so different by providing specific examples of how the plans for peace went awry. It is also important to tie the events of the peace conference to other historical trends politically, militarily, socially, economically, or scientifically.

Had President Woodrow Wilson's idealistic plan for peace been implemented, the grievances that led to the Second World War might have been settled. The main provisions of the Fourteen Points were no secret treaties, freedom of the seas, free trade, arms reduction, settlement of colonial claims, national autonomy and adjustment of borders, and establishment of a League of Nations. The Big Four Allied leaders met in Paris and drew up three treaties to end the war without the involvement of representatives from any of the Central Powers. It is not necessary to show the differences or to ascertain similarities between the Fourteen Points and each of these treaties. In general terms, show what Wilson gave up during the negotiations in order to attain his prime goal, the League of Nations.

## Question 4

To what extent and in what ways did the failure of reform and the abortive Russian Revolution of 1905 lead to the Russian Revolution of 1917?

### Comments on Question 4

This is another *causation* question because it requires you to explain to what extent and how the failure of reforms in Russia and the weak Revolution of 1905 caused the Russian Revolution of 1917. Support your analysis by citing specific evidence. Remember to describe the causes and effects of the Russian Revolution, indicating the degree to which the revolution was caused by failed reforms and the abortive Revolution of 1905. Support your explanation of the causes and effects of the revolutions with specific facts. "To what extent and in what ways" did attempts to make the government better, improve the economy, and modernize the institutions of Russia cause the open rebellion of the people against the government and the social structure? "To what extent and in what ways" did the failed Revolution of 1905 contribute? What were the attempts at reform? When did Russia modernize its economy, and how did this lead to greater discontent among the people? Why was the Duma reconvened, and how did it precipitate events? How did the Russo-Japanese War cause discontent? What was Bloody Sunday? What reforms were aimed at by the marchers? What was the October Manifesto? What were Stolypin's reforms? What were the implications of his death?

## Question 5

Evaluate the modernization of the Soviet Union under Lenin and Stalin.

### Comments on Question 5

This question tests the *change and continuity over time* (CCOT) skill. Be sure to describe the level of historical continuity and of change. Historical continuity means what did not change and how the Soviet Union did not progress. Change means how the Soviet Union increased industrial production and urbanization. Then analyze specific examples of what changed and what parts of Soviet society advanced compared to the parts that did not, such as the agricultural disaster created by collectivization and the gulags. The use of the Cheka and other secret police after them can be seen as one part of continuity, while victory in the Second World War must be seen as evidence of huge industrial advancement. The impulse is to claim that starting soviet totalitarianism was not worth the cost, which was over 30 million lives. It is easy to overlook the modernization and industrialization of a feudal society on the face of the facts alone and without reverting to ideological biases. The first step in answering this question is to define "modernization." Is it economic? Social? Some indefinable movement forward? One can get lost in trying to measure the improvement of the human condition from one age to another. Do the drudgery and social stagnancy of feudalism compare to the alienation and confusion of modernity?

Stick to the tangible. Write about the New Economic Policy and the five-year plans. Did they improve life for the Soviet people, and at what cost? Did the Russian people have a better standard of living under communism or under the czar? Was Communist tyranny worse than czarist despotism?

Remember, whether you defend or refute, it is the case you make that counts.

## Question 6

Compare the methods of governing the Soviet Union under Lenin and Stalin.

### Comments on Question 6

This is clearly a *compare* skill question. So be sure to describe the similarities and differences between Lenin's methods of governing the Soviet Union and the way Stalin did it. Also account for or explain why these methods were so different by providing specific examples of how the two men differed in experiences, style, outlook, and mental health. It is also important to tie the events of Lenin's and Stalin's lives to other historical trends politically, militarily, socially, economically, or scientifically.

The contrast is glaring. Lenin established the basic institutions of Soviet communism; Stalin evolved them into a grotesque parody of their original aims. Lenin ruled for about 7 years; Stalin ruled for over 30. Lenin believed that the end justifies the means; Stalin's paranoia distorted even this precept. Lenin designed the blueprint for modernization and reform; Stalin built the edifice into one of the world's worst totalitarian regimes.

The similarities are in their usurpation of power to gain their ends, their use of dictatorship, and their methods of suppressing dissent.

This is a difficult question that requires broad statements backed by selective facts.

An examination of both of their relationships with Trotsky may add light to this subject as well.

## Short-Answer

1.  Use the diary excerpt and your knowledge of European history to answer all parts of the question that follows.

### Selections from My Daily Journal, 1915–1916

We notice our rations are increased but there is no variety—tea, bread, hard biscuits, butter, jam, bacon, bully-beef, maconochie, fresh meat, cheese, rice, dried vegetables. These are the supplies but they are not of daily occurrence. It may be tinned food one day and fresh meat the next and so on. It is general knowledge that rations are increased when we go into the line. The rum we heard so much about came up tonight. We are given a tot—a few teaspoons full either at night or early morning. It is much appreciated as it helps the circulation which gets very slow these cold nights for want of movement. . . . The way our old soldiers, physical drill instructors, bayonet fighting instructors disappeared under the stress of battle to realms of easier work was a great disappointment to us. . . .

   Before being relieved the enemy had taken its toll. Tom Smith going to the assistance of a wounded man was sniped at receiving an explosive bullet in the arm and shattering it completely, returning to Calgary several months later, an amputation case. Blackie Sayce had his arm almost torn off and is disabled for life. Hannan was also wounded and both bombing officers were casualties. L/Cpl. Dalziel, 6 ft. 2 ins. of humanity, finally came out of the shambles, leading the remaining bombers with an enhanced reputation.

—Private Donald Fraser, Canadian Expeditionary Force

(a) Briefly explain ONE economic change that the Allied powers implemented to ensure that the troops received the food and other materials they needed to fight the Central Powers during the First World War.

(b) Briefly explain ONE way that the social structure in Europe was changed after the First World War as a reaction to life in the trenches as described in the excerpt.

(c) Briefly explain how the technology from the Industrial Revolution impacted the way that the First World War was fought.

2. Use the image and the excerpt below and your knowledge of European history to answer all parts of the following question.

## Source 1

### Soviet Poster, 1922

Caption reads: "We Don't Want to Fight, but We'll Defend the Soviets."

## Source 2

### DECLARATION OF THE RIGHTS OF THE TOILING AND EXPLOITED PEOPLES, 1918

The Constituent Assembly sets for itself as a fundamental task the suppression of all forms of exploitation of man by man and the complete abolition of class distinctions in society. It aims to crush unmercifully the exploiter, to reorganize society on a socialistic basis, and to bring about the triumph of Socialism throughout the world. It further resolves:

1. In order to bring about the socialization of land, private ownership of land is abolished. The entire land fund is declared the property of the nation and turned over free of cost to the toilers on the basis of equal right to its use. All forests, subsoil resources, and waters of national importance as well as all live stock and machinery, model farms, and agricultural enterprises are declared to be national property.

2. As a first step to the complete transfer of the factories, shops, mines, railways, and other means of production and transportation to the Soviet Republic of Workers and Peasants, and in order to ensure the supremacy of the toiling masses over the exploiters, the Constituent Assembly ratifies the Soviet law on workers' control and that on the Supreme Council of National Economy.

3. The Constituent Assembly ratifies the transfer of all banks to the ownership of the workers' and peasants' government as one of the conditions for the emancipation of the toiling masses from the yoke of capitalism.

4. In order to do away with the parasitic classes of society and organize the economic life of the country, universal labor duty is introduced.

(a) Please explain ONE way in which the messages of Source 1 and Source 2 are consistent with each other.

(b) Please explain TWO ways that Source 2 changed Russian (Soviet) society.

## Multiple-Choice

**Questions 1–3 refer to the propaganda poster from the First World War below.**

1. This poster depicts the sinking of the ocean liner *Lusitania,* which the poster seems to use to encourage which of the following?

   (A) Putting women on the front lines
   (B) Men joining the war effort
   (C) Submarine warfare
   (D) Women's suffrage

2. Which of the following nations gained the most power and international influence as a result of the First World War?

   (A) Great Britain
   (B) France
   (C) Germany
   (D) The United States

3. Which of the following artistic styles should the poster be considered an example of?

   (A) Art deco
   (B) Impressionism
   (C) Art nouveau
   (D) Surrealism

**Questions 4–7 refer to the photograph below of the Russian soldiers taking the oath of allegiance to the October Revolution in 1917.**

Russian army officers take the oath of allegiance to the October Revolution. 1917.
Soldiers gathered in the square of the Winter Palace.

4.  To which of the following Russian governments were the soldiers loyal immediately before the October Revolution in 1917?

    (A) The royal government of Czar Nicholas II
    (B) The provisional government led by General Kornilov
    (C) The provisional government led by Kerensky
    (D) The Bolshevik government under Trotsky

5.  Which of the following was something like a shadow government in Russia from February 1917 until October 1917 and helped plan the October Revolution and win workers' support for governmental actions?

    (A) The Petrograd Soviet
    (B) The provisional government
    (C) The Bolshevik Party
    (D) The Menshevik Party

6.  Which of the following was V. I. Lenin's plan to improve the Soviet Union's production and distribution of goods and services?

    (A) The five-year plans
    (B) The New Economic Policy
    (C) The New Deal
    (D) The act of collectivization

7.  Lenin and Trotsky needed the allegiance of the army, seen in the photograph, for which of the following?

    (A) To defeat Germany in the First World War
    (B) To defeat the invading capitalist corporations that wanted to stop the Russian Revolution
    (C) To win a territorial war with Poland
    (D) To win the Russian Civil War

# Answers and Explanations

## Short-Answer Explanations

1. (a) You should identify either the rationing on the home front or the government agencies such as the War Raw Materials Board in Germany that took control of the economy as a part of the total war effort. You should go on to explain how the transition to a mostly command economy was a huge and temporary change to the mostly market economies seen in Europe before the First World War.

   (b) You should explain the growing equity in society after the First World War that resulted from the indiscriminate way that enlisted men and officers died without regard to their positions in civilian life. You should cite more equal voting rights, more government programs to promote equity and alleviate poverty, and the rise of social welfare and employment programs.

   (c) You should explain how war became much more mechanized and much more deadly as a result of the Industrial Revolution. You should cite support from among the following facts: artillery became much more prevalent and larger; trains were used to move troops, weapons, and supplies; poison gas was used; total war meant that all of industry supported the war efforts in Europe; machines were used to build trenches; and there were new weapons such as machine guns, grenades, tanks, airplanes, and submarines.

2. (a) You should note that the most prevalent consistency between the sources is that people must sacrifice and give up what they have (peace in Source 1 and possessions in Source 2) to support the Soviet government. For this point, you should further explain that both sources are uses of propaganda for credit.

   (b) You must explain TWO of the following to receive credit: The class structure was completely turned asunder; private property was abolished, which changed the distribution of wealth; the idea of class was abolished; banks were abolished, which destroyed the entire upper class; all Soviet citizens were required to work for the state; workers gained power over their former masters; the peasant classes were more equalized; mismanagement of the resources of the state led to famine; increased militarism made military service among the best jobs in the nation; collectivization of agriculture changed the social structure of peasants; the capitalist and entrepreneurial class was abolished; and many wealthy and noble Russians emigrated to save their lives and/or what wealth that they could take with them.

## Practice Multiple-Choice Questions

1. (A) is wrong because women were not allowed on the front lines in the United Kingdom until the 21st century.

   **(B) is CORRECT because the *Lusitania*'s sinking was used to get men (and the United States) to join the war effort.**

   (C) is wrong because the poster is actually against unrestricted submarine warfare.

   (D) is wrong because this poster does not support women's suffrage in any way.

2. (A) is wrong because Great Britain did gain power after winning the First World War but not nearly as much as did the United States.

   (B) is wrong because, although France did gain power after winning the First World War, it did not gain nearly as much as did the United States.

   (C) is wrong because Germany lost power and prestige after losing the First World War.

   **(D) is CORRECT because the United States went from being a nonfactor in world issues to becoming the only undamaged economy in the Western world. It gained financial and military respect as a result of the war and both the Dawes and Young Plans after the war.**

3. (A) is wrong because this poster is too flowing and decorated to be art deco, which is very geometric and clean.

(B) is wrong because the image is far too clear to be an impressionist piece.

**(C) is CORRECT because the emotionality of the subject, the flowing and curvilinear designs, and the propagandist message all point to the art nouveau period.**

(D) is wrong because the image is too realistic to be surrealist.

4. (A) is wrong because the czar had abdicated in the February Revolution, months earlier, and both the provisional government and the Petrograd Soviet ran the country until the October Revolution.

(B) is wrong because General Kornilov was not the ruler of the provisional government; Kerensky was.

**(C) is CORRECT because the government overthrown in the October Revolution was the provisional government of Kerensky.**

(D) is wrong because the Bolshevik government is who the soldiers are swearing allegiance to in the photograph.

5. **(A) is CORRECT because the Petrograd Soviet was a workers' council that met in St. Petersburg right next to the Duma, and this soviet approved the decisions of the Duma for the workers.**

(B) is wrong because the provisional government of Kerensky was the one being overthrown in the photograph.

(C) is wrong because the Bolshevik Party, although powerful, did not have full control of the Petrograd Soviet and used the Mensheviks to help them plan.

(D) is wrong because the Menshevik Party did not have control of the Petrograd Soviet and instead shared power in the Petrograd Soviet with the Bolsheviks.

6. (A) is wrong because the five-year plans were Stalin's plans for economic progress after Lenin died.

**(B) is CORRECT because Lenin's plan for economic growth in the U.S.S.R. was called his New Economic Policy.**

(C) is wrong because the New Deal was Roosevelt's plan to help the American economy recover.

(D) is wrong because "collectivization" was done by Stalin rather than Lenin.

7. (A) is wrong because Russia surrendered to Germany with the treaty of Brest-Litovsk as soon as Lenin took power.

(B) is wrong because capitalist corporations did not invade the Soviet Union.

(C) is wrong because there was no war with Poland since Poland did not exist as a separate nation until after the First World War.

**(D) is CORRECT because the Soviets needed to defeat the White Army in the Russian Civil War and required the army to succeed.**

# 11

# Democracy, Depression, Dictatorship, World War and Its Aftermath (1919–1945)

## Key Terms

- Isolationism
- Great Depression
- Age of anxiety
- Stream of consciousness
- Tariff policies
- Keynesianism
- Surrealism
- Stock market crash
- German Weimar Republic
- Fascist

- Weimar Constitution
- National Socialist German Workers' Party (Nazis)
- *Mein Kampf*
- Nuremberg Laws
- Holocaust
- League of Nations
- Axis powers
- *Blitzkrieg*

- British mandate system
- Nonaggression Pact
- Atlantic Charter
- United Nations
- Armenian Genocide
- New technology of warfare
- Superpowers
- Iron Curtain
- Cold War
- Marshall Plan

## Key People

- James Joyce
- Franz Kafka
- Jean-Paul Sartre

- Erich Remarque
- Virginia Woolf
- Werner Heisenberg

- Benito Mussolini
- Adolf Hitler
- Joseph Stalin

## Overview

The First World War saw states increase the degree and scope of their authority over their economies, societies, and cultures. Total war required the centralization of power and the regimentation of the lives of citizens. During the war, governments sought to control information and used propaganda to create stronger emotional ties to the nation and its war effort. Ironically, these measures also produced distrust of traditional authorities. The fall of four great empires after the First World War—Russian, German, Ottoman, and Austro-Hungarian—not only created a Central Europe comprised of smaller nations but left a political vacuum among peoples without a tradition of democracy.

Weak economies and ethnic tensions compounded the problem of a lack of democratic traditions, making progress in these newly created nations difficult. These factors also pushed citizens to accept more extreme viewpoints and solutions to perceived national problems. In the two decades between the world wars, totalitarian dictatorships were established in Russia (the Stalinist regime in the U.S.S.R.), Italy, Spain, and Germany. For the first time in history, governments of great nations were dedicated to the total control of every area of human life, and individuals were expected to subordinate themselves to the needs of the state as defined by the single party in control. Soviet communism, despite its idealistic goal of the withering away of the state, imposed brutal repression to enforce the *dictatorship of the proletariat*. Italian fascism and German Nazism shared a common ideology of racist nationalism and the glorification of war. Fascism promised to solve economic problems through state direction, although not ownership, of production. These movements also promised to counteract the provisions of the Treaty of Versailles by rearming and by territorial expansion. The efforts of Fascist governments to revise the Treaty of Versailles led to the most violent and destructive conflict in human history (the Second World War), a clash between Fascist states and liberal democracies that were temporarily allied with Communist Russia.

The Western democracies of England, France, and the United States came out of the First World War with their heritage of democracy intact. In the 1930s, their tradition of dissent and their democratic institutions were sorely tested both by economic collapse and by the aggressions of the dictatorships. Ten years after the end of the First World War, the worst depression in modern history began and lasted for over a decade. The human misery brought each of these nations close to the point of collapse and encouraged extremist movements, both on the left and the right, to offer simple solutions that would have destroyed democracy.

Wracked by weakness and dissent, the democracies were unwilling to respond to the aggressions of the European dictators and the Japanese militarists. The policy of appeasement, which sought to placate the aggressors with concessions, only whetted the dictators' appetites and eventually led to worldwide war.

During the 20th century, European thought and culture generally moved from an optimistic view that modern science and technology could solve the problems of humankind to the formation of eclectic and sometimes skeptical movements that doubted the possibility of objective knowledge and of progress. Existentialism, postmodernism, and renewed religiosity challenged the supremacy of science as an epistemological method. While European society became increasingly secular, religion continued to play a role in the lives of many Europeans.

As many as 70 million people perished in the Second World War. For the first time in history, tens of millions of the casualties were noncombatants. Saturation bombing of cities, widespread starvation caused by war damage and displacement of people, and state-sponsored murder to exterminate a people (genocide) contributed to the terrible losses.

The war was fought on three continents by combatants from six continents. It was global in scale and was made up of separate conflicts, each with an identifiable beginning and end. World War II was a series of strategic improvisations rather than the result of carefully laid plans. It began at various times, as early as 1931 for the Manchurians and Japanese and as late as 1941 for the Americans.

The Second World War began over issues never resolved after the First World War: the failure of the Treaty of Versailles to settle the problems of nationalistic yearnings for autonomy, of economic security, and of blame for the First World War. The nations without large colonial holdings (Germany, Italy, and Japan) fell under the rule of repressive dictatorships and sought to redress what they saw as the inequities of the peace settlements after the First World War. The imperialist nations, the United States, France, and England, were absorbed in dealing with economic depression and with avoiding another costly war. When the Western democracies' policy of appeasement failed to stop the aggressions of the formative Axis powers, war resulted. War was officially declared in Europe in September 1939 after Germany's invasion of Poland. It ended with the unconditional surrender of Nazi Germany to the Russians, British, Americans, and French in May of 1945 and with the surrender of Japan in September 1945.

World War II not only changed the balance of power in Europe with an international balance of terror created by nuclear weapons, but it gave rise to a nonmilitary conflict between the world's two new superpowers: the Cold War.

## The Western Democracies After the First World War

The conflicting goals of the First World War peace negotiators in Paris pitted diplomatic idealism against the desire to punish Germany, producing a settlement that satisfied few. The war created a *lost generation*, fostered disillusionment and cynicism, transformed the lives of women, and democratized societies. Wilsonian idealism clashed with postwar realities in both the victorious and the defeated states. During the 20th century, diverse intellectual and cultural movements questioned the existence of objective knowledge, the ability of reason to arrive at truth, and the role of religion in determining moral standards. Democratic successor states, such as Poland, Czechoslovakia, Hungary, and Yugoslavia, emerged from former empires and eventually succumbed to significant political, economic, and diplomatic crises. The *League of Nations*, created to prevent future wars, was weakened from the outset by the nonparticipation of major powers, including the United States, Germany, and the Soviet Union. The Treaty of Versailles, particularly its provisions on the assignment of guilt and reparations for the war, hindered the *German Weimar Republic*'s ability to establish a stable and legitimate political and economic system. The relationship of Europe to the world shifted significantly with the globalization of the conflict, the emergence of the United States as a world power, and the overthrow of European empires.

## 1920s in England

England did not recover, during the 1920s, from the economic losses suffered during the First World War. Its merchant fleet was decimated by German submarines, and its foreign trade declined disastrously. International competition from worldwide industrialization; the proliferation of tariffs; rival shipping nations; defaulted loans by investors, business owners, and homeowners; and war relief programs further eroded a British economy already saddled by war debts.

### Politics

- The Liberal Party, headed by David Lloyd George, fell into decline.
- It was replaced by the Conservatives (Tory Party), who favored high tariffs and welfare payments to the growing numbers of unemployed.
- The Labour Party, whose program included a gradual nationalization of major industries, took power briefly.
- By 1929 and the start of the Depression, an alliance of Labourites and Conservatives led by *Ramsay MacDonald* (1866–1937), then *Stanley Baldwin* (1867–1947), and finally *Neville Chamberlain* (1869–1940) ran the government until the start of the Second World War.
  - Chamberlain's black umbrella became a symbol for the policy of *appeasement* (the willingness to give in to the demands of aggressive dictatorships).

### Foreign Policy

- The League of Nations distributed former German and Ottoman possessions to France and Great Britain through the mandate system, thereby altering the imperial balance of power and creating strategic interest in the Middle East states and their oil.
  - Middle East mandates included *Lebanon, Syria, Iraq*, and *Palestine*.
- British foreign policy during this period was consumed by the *Irish Question*, the granting of eventual independence to southern Ireland after failure to suppress rebellion.
- The ending of the *British protectorate* in *Egypt*, although control of the Suez Canal was continued, was another major issue.
- The Statute of Westminster formally recognized the equality of the British dominions such as Canada and Australia.
  - It set up a Commonwealth of Nations, which enjoyed special trading privileges.

## 1920s in France

The death, devastation, and debt of the First World War created economic chaos and political unrest in France. When the Germans defaulted on their reparation payments to France, which was to get 52 percent of the German reparations of $33 billion (valued at $510 billion in 2014 dollars), the French economy nearly collapsed.

### Politics

- Throughout the 1920s, the French government (a multiparty system requiring coalitions to function) was dominated by the parties on the right—which supported the status quo and had the backing of business, the military, the Church, and the wealthy upper classes.

### Germany and Reparations

- In 1922 when Germany managed to pay only part of that year's reparation bill, French Prime Minister Raymond Poincaré (1860–1934) sent troops to occupy the mineral-rich Ruhr Valley in western Germany.
- The Versailles settlement, particularly its provisions on the assignment of guilt and reparations for the war, hindered the German Weimar Republic's ability to establish a stable and legitimate political and economic system.
- The Dawes Plan, the Young Plan, and the Lausanne Settlement each, in turn, pared down German payments and diminished the ability of the French to collect.
- Tax and spending reforms by Poincaré's government, though, led to a temporary resurgence of prosperity in France until the worldwide depression hit.

### French Foreign Policy

- It was aimed at neutralizing Germany in the event of a resurgence of militarism there.
- A series of alliances with buffer states, such as Belgium and Poland, surrounded Germany with French allies.
- The *Locarno Pact* of 1925 attempted to settle French-German border disputes.
- The *Kellogg-Briand Pact* of 1928 aimed at outlawing war and was championed as the high point of post–First World War diplomacy, despite its futility in reality.

## 1920s in the United States

### Foreign Policy

- Disillusionment with the *Treaty of Versailles* resulted in the Senate's rejection of U.S. membership in the League of Nations.
- Despite nostalgia for traditional *isolationism*, the United States participated in a series of naval disarmament conferences that agreed to limit the building of new battleships and fix the size of the major powers' navies.
- Despite an economic boom in the United States, international trade was thwarted by a series of shortsighted *tariffs* (taxes on imports) that contributed to the *Great Depression* by diminishing foreign markets and limiting the ability of the Europeans to pay off their war debts to the United States.
- Immigration quotas, which favored Northern Europeans over those from the South and East, ended the *age of immigration* that peaked at the turn of the century.

# The Age of Anxiety

The carnage and disruption of the First World War and the collapse of the old order that had defined European politics and diplomacy for nearly a century resulted in what commentators have called an *age of anxiety*. The traditional assumption of the perfectibility of humankind through reason collapsed under the weight of events and new ideas.

Philosophy, science, the arts, and literature contributed to this crisis of confidence and conscience. However, they also offered new models to explain and portray humanity.

## The Lost Generation

After the First World War, Ernest Hemingway popularized Gertrude Stein's term, the *Lost Generation*, to describe those who came of age during the war. It included the thinkers listed below who rejected the belief in reason and technology to solve the problems of humanity.

## Philosophy

*Edmund Husserl* and *Martin Heidegger* (1889–1976), both Germans, extended the work of Nietzsche and *Soren Kierkegaard* (1813–1855) to establish the foundations of *existentialism*. This was a philosophical school, popularized by *Jean-Paul Sartre* after the Second World War, that emphasized individual responsibility and the capability for giving meaning to a meaningless universe.

## Physics

*Werner Heisenberg* (1901–1976) developed the *uncertainty principle* that stated that a particle's velocity or position (but not both at the same time) could be calculated.

- This fundamental uncertainty about the nature of matter is endemic of the *age of anxiety*.
- The theories of *relativity* of *Albert Einstein* (1879–1955), another German, further disrupted the comfortable assumptions of an orderly, rationally discoverable universe that Newton's 17th-century physics had supported and encouraged: *relativism* in ethics, politics, and worldviews.
- *Niels Bohr* explained the fundamental ideas of chemistry and quantum physics by explaining the arrangement of electron shells around the nucleus of an atom.
- *Enrico Fermi*, an Italian, worked on inducing radioactivity and eventually built the first nuclear reactor in Chicago.
- *Erwin Schrödinger* created a wave-particle theory that shook up quantum physics.

## Literature

Throughout the 20th century, a number of writers challenged traditional literary conventions, questioned Western values, and addressed controversial social and political issues. The aftermath of the war and intellectual trends, such as Freudianism, influenced writers to emphasize the irrational aspects of the human condition.

- *Stream of consciousness*, which is the portrayal of an individual's random thoughts and feelings, was a style perfected by Irish novelist *James Joyce* (1882–1941) and by English fiction writer *Virginia Woolf* (1882–1941).
  - Stream of consciousness reflected the prevailing view of human life as alienated, irrational, and chaotic.
- The horrors of the First World War were examined by *Erich Remarque* in *All Quiet on the Western Front*, which found meaninglessness in war. This novel was subsequently banned by the Nazi government.
- *Franz Kafka* explored the overreaching power of the state in *The Trial* and *Metamorphosis*, which explored themes of alienation, brutality (both physical and psychological), bureaucratic labyrinths of futility, and parent-child conflicts.

## Visual Art

*Expressionism*—abstract and nonrepresentational—replaced impressionism and was pioneered by Vincent van Gogh (1853–1890), Paul Cézanne (1839–1906), and Paul Gauguin (1848–1903), who painted with bold colors and images to focus on emotions and imagination.

- Pablo Picasso (1881–1973), a Spaniard, invented cubism, which is the depiction of mood through the use of geometric angles, planes, and clashing lines.
- Dadaism and surrealism were among the abstract styles created by artists of many nationalities, most of whom did their experimentation in postwar France.
- Architecture exemplified *functionalism*—buildings designed with practicality and clean lines instead of ornamentation.

## Architecture

The Bauhaus movement considered form and function to be united and saw excessive ornamentation as a crime. Clean-lined steel and glass buildings were created as well as modernist furniture to go into these buildings.

- A house was seen as a machine in which to live.
- Bauhaus encouraged design that was minimalist and spartan in nature.
- It was the foundation of the modernist artistic movement.
- Walter Gropius was a leader of this movement.

## Music

Some music of the era challenged existing aesthetic standards, explored subconscious and subjective states, and satirized Western society and its values.

- Igor Stravinsky revolutionized classical music with his *Rites of Spring* and other works. He eventually adopted the 12-tone technique of composition of Arnold Schoenberg, another revolutionary composer of the era.
- The tone poems of Richard Strauss were also a new way to look at music.

## Medicine

Medical theories and technologies extended life but posed social and moral questions that eluded consensus and crossed religious, political, and philosophical perspectives. The following are some of the most controversial theories and technologies:

- *Eugenics* was the idea of breeding the best people and sterilizing or killing the undesirables; eugenics was utilized by Hitler.
- *Birth control* revolutionized reproductive freedom, but many religious and moral objections abounded.
- Abortion became legal throughout much of Europe and remains controversial to this day.
- Fertility treatments were developed to allow those with conception problems to become parents, but they are very expensive and the world is overpopulated.
- Genetic engineering is now approaching the point where we can clone and engineer humans. Should we?

## Media

Film and radio became major means for entertainment, information, and propaganda in the 1920s and 1930s. National broadcasting networks were set up by every major European power. Radio was employed by Adolf Hitler and other European dictators for propaganda and indoctrination.

- Movies became a prime medium for mass entertainment and also were employed to produce powerful propaganda.
- The modern cult of celebrity or the (ironic) glorification of the personalities who portrayed people other than themselves was born with the advent of movies.

# The Great Depression (1929–1939)

The Great Depression, caused by weaknesses in international trade and monetary theories and practices, undermined Western European democracies and fomented radical political responses throughout the Continent.

- First World War debt, nationalistic tariff policies, overproduction, depreciated currencies, disrupted trade patterns, and speculation all created weaknesses in economies worldwide.
- Dependence on post–First World War American investment capital led to financial collapse when, following the 1929 stock market crash, the United States cut off capital flows to Europe.

- Despite attempts to rethink economic theories and policies and to forge political alliances, Western democracies failed to overcome the Great Depression and were weakened by extremist movements.

## United States

The *economic boom* of the Roaring Twenties masked a deep-seated malaise. Farm prices dropped disastrously after the selling peak during wartime. Sizable segments of the population were poor. Buying on credit encouraged exorbitant personal debt. Once the market for radios, autos, and refrigerators had been saturated, a dearth of new products discouraged business investment.

- The *stock market crash* of October 1929 was more a symptom than a cause of the economic depression that seized America and most of the industrialized world for the next decade.
- There were many contributing factors to the Great Depression:
  - Buying stocks on large margins.
  - A stock bubble that was not sustainable.
  - Adjustment from a wartime economy to a peacetime economy.
  - Increased mechanization creating structural unemployment.
  - Changes in international patterns of trade.
  - Declines in consumption caused by the aftermath of the First World War.
- The Federal Reserve also exacerbated a weak economy by tightening the money supply when it needed to be loosened.
  - This created deflation, which further devastated a weakened world economy.
  - The world was using the dollar more than any other single currency.
- *American and European economies were interdependent through extensive investments and war debts owed to the United States.*
- The failure of the U.S. economy led to a global breakdown.
  - The *command economy* of the U.S.S.R. managed to maintain, and even surpass, earlier productivity.
  - By 1932, nearly 15 million Americans were unemployed, about one-quarter of the workforce.
  - Herbert Hoover's stubborn insistence that the Great Depression was a normal fluctuation of the economy that would run its course brought the Roosevelt Democrats into the White House with a *New Deal*.
  - Franklin Delano Roosevelt (FDR) (1882–1945) and the New Deal may not have ended the Great Depression in America, but they helped preserve capitalism and democracy in the United States.
    - The New Deal used the deficit-spending theories of economist *John Maynard Keynes* (1883–1946), who had predicted the Great Depression.
- Roosevelt established a theory that justified profound involvement of the federal government in the economy.
- The New Deal created the idea of economic stimulus and restraint.
- Although the Great Depression ended in the United States only when it began to rearm (1940–1941), the New Deal created a social *welfare state* with the obligation to relieve economic hardship while preserving a modified and revitalized American capitalism.

## Great Britain

During the 1930s under the *National Party* (the coalition of Labourites and Conservatives), the British tried to alleviate the Great Depression by reorganizing industry, abandoning free trade, reforming finances, and cutting government spending.

- Britain utilized the ideas of Keynes to help alleviate the worst parts of the Great Depression.
  - Great Britain was able to create a strong recovery and, by 1937, advanced output to 20 percent above that of 1929.

- Conservative governments paid generous unemployment benefits.
- The British government focused more on the domestic market than on exports.
- Low interest rates brought on a housing boom.
- New industries like appliances and automobiles helped spur consumption.
- The north stayed depressed while the south expanded and renovated.
- Like the United States, Britain came out of the Great Depression only through arming for the coming world war.

## France

The Great Depression increased class tensions and gave birth to a radical right that supported government reorganization along Fascist lines.

- After a financial scandal that involved high government officials in 1934, pro-Fascist riots broke out all over France.
- A coalition of Socialists, Republicans, labor unionists, and Communists responded by organizing the *Popular Front*, which opposed fascism, supported reform, and upheld the republic.
    - In 1936, socialist *Leon Blum* (1872–1950) became prime minister under the Popular Front banner.
    - He instituted a *French New Deal*, which offered labor and agricultural reforms similar to those in the United States. Blum's measures, though, were ineffective in ending the Great Depression in France.
    - Opposed by the conservative bloc in the Senate, the program failed to hold together the Popular Front coalition. Blum resigned in 1937 and was replaced by conservative Edouard Daladier (1884–1970), who overturned the Blum reforms and practiced a policy of *appeasement* of Hitler's aggressions.

## Scandinavia

In answer to the Great Depression, the Social Democrat Party in Norway and Sweden developed a unique brand of socialism.

- It included strong worker and peasant reforms.
- The Scandinavian tradition of cooperative community action was used to create a flexible, nonrevolutionary socialism.
- Agricultural cooperatives joined together to form organizations that benefited all.
- Labor leaders and capitalists worked together.
- Deficit spending was encouraged to stimulate the economy.
- Higher taxes were instituted.
- The socialism in Norway and Sweden was like the New Deal but was more intense with greater spending and taxation of the wealthy.
- This worked and was seen as a middle way between capitalism and communism.
- This plan created the model for the *modern welfare state.*
- This unique brand of socialism is still in practice in most of Europe today.

# Dictatorships

## What Is Fascism: A Brief on Fascist Ideology

Fascism is the belief in a strong state allied with corporations to organize and control a "willing" population and glorify the state. It is one-party *totalitarianism* that limits the political power of the individual and sees people as mere cells in the organism of the state. It is extremely nationalist in nature and is led by a charismatic dictator with unlimited power, usually a military leader. Fascists favor private ownership of property, and Fascist governments ally with big businesses to weaken or eliminate labor unions and Communists. It is important to note that fascism was a negative response to communism and that the two ideologies were opposed to each other. However, *both* fascism and communism were created in this era as *totalitarian* systems of rule by only one party. The unique aspect of totalitarian regimes is that they make total claims on the actions and thoughts of the populations ruled by them. Fascist dictatorships used modern technology and propaganda that rejected democratic institutions, promoted charismatic leaders, and glorified war and nationalism to attract the disillusioned. The following Venn diagram shows the similarities and differences between the two ideologies as they existed in Europe during the first half of the 20th century.

**Communism:**
- Class differences disappear
- International brotherhood
- Destruction of middle and upper classes
- Private property nationalized
- Rapid industrialization
- Collective agriculture

- Promised workers better lives with less confusion
- Used force to destroy all opposition

**Fascism:**
- National community
- Often racist
- Glorified war and military
- Destroyed workers' movements
- Pro big business through corporative state

*Nazism* was a special case of fascism in which race was the primary factor for determining one's role in the state in Germany. Nazis believed that Germans were the "master race," meant to be served by the Slavic peoples of Europe, who would be enslaved as workers. Other ethnic groups, such as Jews and the Roma, were to be eliminated to make more room for the "superior" Germanic people.

## Fascism in Italy

The peace settlements that ended the First World War were extremely disappointing to Italian nationalists. None of the Austrian and Ottoman territories and German colonies in Africa that had been promised to Italy were received. To add to Italian discontent, a depression hit in 1919 and provoked nationwide strikes and class antagonisms. Terrified of a Communist revolution, the propertied classes looked hopefully for a strong leader to restore order.

*Benito Mussolini* (1883–1945), editor of a socialist newspaper and, paradoxically, an ardent nationalist, organized the Fascist Party, a combination of socialism and nationalism. The party was named after *fasces*, which were the rods carried by Imperial Roman officials as symbols of power.

- His *squadristi*, or paramilitary *Blackshirts*, attacked Communists, socialists, and other enemies of his program.
- Promising to protect private property, Mussolini won the support of the conservative classes and quickly abandoned his socialist programs.
- The Fascist *March on Rome*, October 1922, caused the government to collapse and won Mussolini the right to organize a new government. King Victor Emmanuel III granted him dictatorial powers for one year to end the nation's social unrest.
- The *corporate state* was the economic core of Italian fascism. "Labor unions" run by the Fascist Party managed and controlled industry.
  - Those unions set the national political agenda.

- Unlike socialist corporate states, where workers make decisions, authority flowed from the top.
- The Fascists consolidated power through the 1920s by rigging elections and both intimidating and terrorizing opponents.
  - By 1928, all independent labor unions were organized into government-controlled syndicates, the right to vote was severely limited, and all candidates for the Italian parliament were selected by the Fascist Party.
  - Through the 1930s, an organization of corporations, headed by Mussolini, effectively replaced parliamentary government.
  - Democracy was suppressed; the totalitarian state was created in Italy.

## Fascist Accomplishments in Italy

- Internal improvements were made, such as electrification and road building.
- Municipal governing was more efficient.
- Suppression of the Mafia occurred.
- Improvements were made to the justice system (except for *enemies of the state*).
- Reconciliation with the papacy occurred through the *Lateran Pact* of 1929, which gave the papacy $92 million for seized church lands in return for Pope Pius XII's recognition of the legitimacy of the Italian state.
- The notoriously undependable trains in Italy finally ran on schedule.

## Fascist Failings in Italy

- Italian democracy was destroyed.
- The press was censored.
- People did not have the right to strike.
- All forms of dissent were denied.
- Suffrage was destroyed.
- Terrorism became a state policy.
- Poor industrial growth was seen due to militarism and colonialism.
- Attempt to recapture the imperialistic glories of ancient Rome led to disastrous involvements in war.

# The Rise of Nazism in Germany

## The Weimar Republic

In November 1918, a provisional government in Germany that was both socialist and democratic was organized to negotiate a peace with the Allies. Although this government had very little input in the decisions made at the Paris Peace Conference, it did sign the Treaty of Versailles. This government was then held responsible by conservative factions in Germany for the pact's inequities.

- The *Weimar Constitution*, drafted in July 1919, set up Germany's first modern democracy, called the *Weimar Republic*.
  - The constitution provided for a directly elected president.
  - It also provided for a directly elected parliament (the *Reichstag*).
  - A senate (the *Reichsrat*) would represent the German states.
  - The constitution provided for a chancellor (prime minister), who represented the majority party of the Reichstag, and for a cabinet to run the government.
- After the *inflation of 1923*, Germany defaulted on its reparations to France, the French seized the Ruhr Valley, and German workers there went on a general strike.
- To pay these workers, the Weimar government printed paper currency and the prevalent inflation in the country became runaway.

- When debtors rushed to pay off their creditors with this worthless currency, the middle class was financially wiped out.

## The Munich Beer Hall Putsch

The Weimar government's economic disasters in 1923 encouraged *Adolf Hitler* (1889–1945) and his Nazi *Brownshirts* to attempt to seize power from the government of Bavaria, a state of southern Germany. Hitler, who was Austrian by birth, had fled poverty in his native land and joined the German army at the start of the First World War. He helped organize the *National Socialist German Workers' Party (Nazis)* after the war.

- Racist, paranoid, sociopathic, and megalomaniacal, Hitler was a brilliant orator and political strategist who played on popular discontent with the Weimar government.
  - He blamed democracy, communism, and the Jewish people for Germany's ills.
- He and *Erich Ludendorff* (1865–1937), a distinguished general who had led German troops to victory on the Eastern Front during the First World War, led an attempted coup in Munich at the end of 1923. This coup was called the Munich Beer Hall Putsch.
  - The coup was suppressed, and Hitler was sentenced to five years in jail.
  - He served only about a year of his already-lenient term.
  - Many higher-ups in the justice system sympathized with Hitler's narrow nationalistic goals.
  - While in prison, he wrote his blueprint for domination of Germany and eventually Europe, called *Mein Kampf (My Struggle)*.
    - It was a rambling, irrational, but convincing work.
    - In *Mein Kampf*, Hitler argued that Germany was never defeated in the First World War but was betrayed from within by Jews and Socialists.
    - He claimed the Treaty of Versailles was a humiliation.
    - *Mein Kampf* propagated the idea that Germans were a master race destined to expand into Eastern Europe to obtain *Lebensraum* (living space) and to rule or exterminate "inferior" races, such as Jews and Slavs.

## Germany 1923–1933

After the *Dawes Plan* stabilized Germany's economy in 1924, the Nazi Party's membership fell off. By 1928, the Nazis won only 12 seats in the Reichstag.

- For a short while after the Munich Beer Hall Putsch, conditions were hopeful in Germany and in Europe as a whole.
- Gustav Stresemann, the chancellor and then foreign minister of the Weimar Republic, oversaw a short period of prosperity from 1925–1929, known as the Weimar Golden Age.
  - Stresemann was one of the authors of the *Locarno Treaties* of 1925 in which all European nations agreed to respect the borders drawn after the First World War.
  - Stresemann was also a signatory to the 1928 *Kellogg-Briand Pact*, condemning warfare.
  - The Weimar Golden Age was a culturally vibrant and politically idealistic brief flicker in the otherwise dismal Germany of the early-20th century.
  - The German legislature was bicameral with the Reichstag as the lower house and the Bundesrat the upper house.
  - The Weimar Golden Age can be used to contrast the political and cultural conservatism that dominated the rest of the period.
- When the Great Depression hit Germany in 1930, the Nazis won 107 seats and the Communists 77 in the Reichstag.
  - Center parties, the Socialists and Christian Democrats, were unable to maintain a ruling coalition.

- Many conservatives, including large landowners, industrialists, and army officers, threw their support toward Hitler to avoid a Communist takeover.
  - In January 1933, after a series of machinations, Hitler was invited by the aging president of the Weimar Republic, *Paul von Hindenburg* (1847–1934), who was another renowned general of the First World War, to form a government as chancellor.
  - Hitler entered government legally, according to the constitution that he was publicly dedicated to destroy.

## The Nazi Revolution

The week before the elections of March 1933, which Hitler ordered, were to give him a clear majority in the Reichstag, the *Reichstag building was destroyed by arson.*

- Although Nazis are believed to have started the fire, Hitler used it as a pretext to declare emergency powers for the government.
- The election that followed was influenced by suspension of freedom of the press and of speech and by outright terrorizing of political opponents.
- After gaining a majority coalition in the Reichstag, the Nazis granted dictatorial powers to Hitler for four years with the *Enabling Act.*
- Within six months, all political parties but the Nazis were outlawed in Germany.
- When President Hindenburg died in 1934, Hitler merged his office of chancellor with that of president with 90 percent of the German voters approving.

## The Nazis Consolidated Power

- *Dachau*, the first concentration camp, was opened in March 1933.
  - Although the camps did not become death factories for mass extermination until 1941, they were brutal centers for punishing political opponents of the Nazis.
- During the *Night of the Long Knives*, in June 1934, Hitler purged the party. He executed left-wing Nazis who had pushed for the socialist programs that Hitler had promised. He also executed leaders of the Brownshirts who had maintained autonomy within the party.
  - The black-uniformed elite guard, the infamous *SS* (*Schutzstaffel* or "Protection Squadron") became the party's and the nation's enforcers.
  - The *Gestapo* was the secret police force of the SS.
    - A rigorous selection and training process was set up for the SS.
    - The Gestapo became the overseers of the death camps.
- Labor unions were replaced, as in Fascist Italy, by a Nazi-led labor organization.
  - Strikes were outlawed.
  - Factories were put under the management of local Nazi officials who had dictatorial powers over the workers.
- Full employment resumed with military production that thrived despite its prohibition under the terms of the Treaty of Versailles.
- A policy of *autarky*, economic self-sufficiency, was developed to make Germany independent of imports and foreign markets.
- The *Nuremberg Laws* of 1935 stripped Germany's half-million Jews of their rights as citizens.
  - When Nazi mobs wrecked Jewish shops and synagogues throughout Germany during *Kristallnacht* ("Night of the Broken Glass") in 1938, it was the beginning of the *Holocaust*—the systematic extermination of Jews in Germany and eventually throughout Europe.
  - About 200,000 German Jews managed to escape from Germany.
  - Of those Jews who remained in Germany, over 90 percent were murdered.

- The Holocaust was used to eliminate all of Hitler's enemies:
  - Many ethnic groups.
  - Those politically opposed to him.
  - Those who Hitler's theories stated were weakening the German state.
  - Communists, Catholics, Jewish people, Jehovah's Witnesses, Roma, LGBTQ+ people, and people with disabilities were systematically imprisoned, enslaved, and eliminated.
  - In the end, over 6 million Jews and 7 million others were killed, with millions more enslaved or imprisoned.

## The Spanish Civil War and the Rise of Fascism in Spain

In 1931, the king of Spain, Alfonso XIII, offered his people a chance to choose their type of government. They chose a liberal republic led by a coalition of moderates and leftists including Communists. A coalition of nationalist right-wing parties came together to lead a military revolt against the republican government. *General Francisco Franco* used the new media form of radio to address Spain. He asked the mostly right-leaning military officers and soldiers to revolt against their republican government. A civil war erupted in 1936 between the *republicans* on the left and the *nationalists* on the right.

- The war lasted from 1936–1939 and ended with a Fascist dictatorship with General Francisco Franco in power.
- Fascist Germany provided air support, and Italy provided troops to help the nationalist forces take the country.
  - Germany was not prepared for a world war yet and was still rearming, so it sent cautious air support for Franco's troops.
  - Mussolini was emboldened by his conquest of Libya and sent troops to help his Fascist nationalist brethren.
  - Germany saw this as a testing ground for new military technology and techniques like air cover.
- Communist Russia provided the only supplies of arms to the republicans.
- Europeans and Americans came to fight in this war on both sides, fighting over the ideologies that they held dear.
- After setting siege to Madrid, Franco took power and brutally suppressed all opposition with purges and mass killings of republican loyalists.
- In republican-held areas, atrocities against nationalist supporters were also reported.
- Spain employed its own type of fascism from 1939–1975 and avoided participation in World War II by being Fascist but not a part of the Axis powers.
- Franco's alliance with Italian and German Fascists in the Spanish Civil War represented a testing ground for World War II and resulted in authoritarian rule in Spain from 1936 to the mid-1970s.

## Authoritarian Dictatorships in Central and Eastern Europe

After failing to establish functioning democracies, authoritarian dictatorships took power in Central and Eastern Europe during the interwar period. Poland, Hungary, and Romania all established authoritarian dictatorships that functioned poorly.

- In Poland, Jozef Piłsudski never claimed personal power, although he exercised extensive influence over Polish politics after the Sanation coup d'état in 1926 promised a restoration of political life.
- In Romania, the Iron Guard led by Ion Antonescu forced King Carol II to abdicate in 1940, allowing the Iron Guard's pro-Nazi regime to take power.
- In Hungary, a Fascist prime minister was appointed by 1932 and the Arrow Cross movement of Fascists there gained power.

## Prelude to War

The rise of nationalist, industrialist, and imperialist single-party states was a significant factor contributing to the outbreak of the Second World War. One political factor was the personal will of Adolf Hitler, which many historians credit with being a major cause of the war. Another was the weakness of the Treaty of Versailles, which did not fix the underlying economic and social pressures in Western Europe, leaving the Continent ripe for another war. The failure of the League of Nations to intervene in many instances when Hitler or Hideki Tojo (r. 1941–1945) of Japan broke the Treaty of Versailles made the dictators more brazen. Finally, the policy of appeasement led to more and more aggression from the Axis powers of Germany, Italy, and Japan.

> ### SPECIAL NOTE
>
> The Second World War is examined in chronological order. It is broken into different periods of the war, from aggression and appeasement to the aftermath.

## Aggression and Appeasement

### 1931

- Japan invaded Manchuria, and the League of Nations did not intervene in any meaningful way.
- Japan began to imperialize China.
- The Japanese occupation of Manchuria lasted until the end of the war.

### 1933

- Hitler pulled Germany out of the League of Nations.

### 1935

- Hitler began rebuilding the German armed forces in open violation of the Treaty of Versailles.
- The Western powers, immersed in the Great Depression, objected to Hitler's action but did not act.
- The Saar Plebiscite returned the Saar Valley to Germany.
- Mussolini attacked the independent kingdom of Ethiopia in East Africa.
- The League of Nations ordered *sanctions* (an embargo on trade in arms and raw materials) against Italy, but the sanctions were not enforced.

### 1936

- Hitler's troops occupied the *Rhineland*, which the Treaty of Versailles had made into a demilitarized zone between France and Germany.
- France and England failed to act, giving birth to the policy of *appeasement*.
- General *Francisco Franco* and his Spanish Falangists, who were Fascists, began an insurrection against the democratically chosen republican government of Spain.
  - The Fascist dictators Mussolini and Hitler supported Franco with men, arms, and money.
  - Stalin backed the Republicans, a significant number of whom were Communists.
  - The brutal and destructive *Spanish Civil War*, which lasted for over three years and claimed the lives of 600,000, became a testing ground for the war machines of the dictatorships.
  - The Fascists won the Spanish Civil War. Franco remained the longest-reigning Fascist dictator in history, his regime ending only when he died in 1975.

## 1937

- The second Sino-Japanese War began in earnest as the Japanese launched a full-scale attack, made significant territorial gains, and committed atrocities on the Chinese people, such as the Rape of Nanking.
  - The League of Nations again did not respond.

- Germany, Italy, and Japan signed the *Anti-Comintern Pact* to oppose international communism.
  - This marked the beginning of their alliance, the *Axis*.

- Japan invaded mainland China, quickly conquering the seacoast and driving *Chiang Kai-shek's Nationalists* deep into the interior. There they, along with their political opposition led by Mao Tse-tung, waged a guerrilla war that proved costly to the Japanese.

## 1938

- Hitler engineered the *Anschluss* (the forced union of Germany and Austria), again in violation of the Treaty of Versailles.
- Once again, the Western powers failed to act.
- Hitler prepared to annex the *Sudetenland* (a part of Czechoslovakia that before the First World War had been German territory).
  - France and England, at the urging of the U.S.S.R., issued warnings.
  - After tensions and talks, a conference was called at Mussolini's suggestion. *Neville Chamberlain*, prime minister of Britain, and *Édouard Daladier*, prime minister of France, met with Hitler and Mussolini.
  - The infamous *Munich Conference* ceded the Sudetenland to Germany and marked the pinnacle of appeasement.

## 1939

- Hitler seized the rest of Czechoslovakia, which was abandoned by the West, and the western part of Lithuania.
- Mussolini invaded Albania.
- Hitler and Stalin signed a *nonaggression pact*, which cleared the way for Hitler's *invasion of Poland*.

# Triumph of the Axis Powers (1939–1942)

Although Germany, Italy, and Japan were often referred to as Fascists, their dictatorships were significantly different.

- The German Nazis and, to a lesser degree, the Italian Fascists imposed totalitarian systems upon their people.
- The Japanese, whose constitutional government was loyal to the emperor (who was seen as a living god), had a military dictatorship imposed in the 1930s.
- The term *Axis* came from the Rome, Berlin, Tokyo Axis. This was a pledge of mutual cooperation between the three nations that, in the end, led to virtually no combined military ventures involving the two European powers and Japan.

## The War Against the Minorities

In addition to the military attacks on nations, wars against ethnic and other minorities were a separate front. These wars were waged more by Germany and Japan than by Italy.

- The Japanese economically and militarily dominated the areas they conquered.

- The Japanese turned the civilians into a slave-labor force, including hundreds of thousands of women forced into prostitution for Japanese soldiers and commonly referred to as *comfort women*.
- It is believed that almost 20 million Chinese were killed in the course of the Second World War.
- The Japanese performed medical experimentation with biological agents on Chinese civilians.
- The Nazis created a systematic method for enslaving the peoples they conquered.
  - The Nazis had a system for deciding a civilian's fate based on that person's ethnicity.
    - Germanic people held all positions of importance or power.
    - Slavs and Russians were sent to forced work camps and factories.
    - Jews, the Roma, Jehovah's Witnesses, LGBTQ+ people, people with disabilities, known Communists, and dissidents were sent to concentration camps to be exterminated.
  - The Jews were a special target for genocide.
    - Jews were first ostracized and forced from positions of authority by the racist Nuremberg Laws.
    - Then all Jewish people in Nazi-occupied territories were sent from their homes without their possessions to ghettos to live in squalid conditions.
    - After the secret Wannsee Conference of 1942, the Germans decided on a *final solution* in which the ghettos would be liquidated and all the Jews would be sent to death camps, such as Auschwitz and Majdanek.
    - Many Jewish people were saved by Christians and humanitarian networks.
- The stories of *Anne Frank* and *Elie Wiesel* testify to the brutality of the Nazi regime.
- One Christian response was to try to protect Jewish people and others as seen in the famous poem and actions of the Protestant minister *Martin Niemoller*.

## 1939

*September 1:* Hitler invaded Poland, ostensibly to get back the part of East Prussia, the *Polish Corridor*, that the Treaty of Versailles had ceded to Poland for access to the Baltic Sea.

- The Germans used the *blitzkrieg* technique for this invasion: a massive air strike at a specific area of the enemy lines, followed by a reinforced, rapid, and massive mechanized attack at the point of the air strike.
  - The Germans penetrated Polish lines and divided the enemy troops, who could then be eliminated in sections by the superior firepower of the German war machine.
  - Tanks and mechanized infantry swept in at lightning speed, giving the *blitzkrieg* its name, "lightning war."
  - The Germans also used their *Einsatzgruppen*, a special military force dedicated to killing leaders of Jews, Communists, and the Roma during the invasion.

*September 3:* England and France declared war against Germany to honor their treaty with Poland.

*October:* Poland fell, occupied by the Germans in the west and the Russians in the east as part of the 1938 *nonaggression pact* between the two dictatorships.

- Russia also annexed the Baltic states of *Latvia*, *Lithuania*, and *Estonia*, which had been granted autonomy by the Treaty of Versailles.

## 1940

The time period from the fall of Poland to April 1940 was called the *sitzkrieg* because the French sat behind their supposedly impregnable *Maginot Line*, a series of fortresses on the German border, and the *British Expeditionary Force* in France made no moves. Meanwhile, the Germans prepared for a spring offensive.

- During this time, German forces overran and occupied Denmark and Norway in a matter of days.
- In May 1940, the German army cut through neutral Belgium and Luxembourg to outflank the Maginot Line.

- Within six weeks, the Nazi tactics of *blitzkreig* caused France to fall.
- Isolated and surrounded, the 250,000-man British Expeditionary Force retreated to *Dunkirk* in Belgium, most of them to be evacuated to England along with about 100,000 French troops. The Allies lost their heavy equipment.
- Mussolini invaded southern France, an invasion that was ineffectual militarily but symbolic of Nazi-Fascist solidarity.
- France surrendered on June 22. Germany occupied the north and west. As in all the Nazi-occupied lands, terror and repression reigned there.
  - A puppet French government, known as the *Vichy Regime* and led by First World War hero *Marshal Philippe Petain*, controlled the south and the North African possessions.
  - General Charles de Gaulle (1880–1970), however, escaped to Britain, where he took command of the *Free French*.
    - The Free French continued to fight the Nazis.
    - They claimed the role of the provisional government of France.
    - The French Resistance undermined the Nazis from inside France.
- The *Battle of Britain* was an air war for supremacy of the skies over Britain.
  - It began in August 1940.
  - The battle targeted industrial cities of southern England, including London.
  - The population was subjected to nightly bombings called *the Blitz*, harking back to the "lightning" or *blitz*, in *blitzkrieg*.

## 1941

This was a pivotal year for the war. It looked like Great Britain was the last holdout at the beginning of the war when the war moved to Africa. However, that fall Germany invaded the U.S.S.R. In December, the Japanese attacked the United States at Pearl Harbor and in the Philippines. The U.S.S.R. and the United States joined the British as enemies of the Axis powers.

- The United States had been supporting the British through a *lend-lease program* that allowed the British to have the use of American-built ships and to purchase war materials.
- After Russia was invaded, it looked like it too might fall quickly. However, the Germans were soon caught in the Russian winter just as the Americans declared war on the Axis powers.
- President *Franklin D. Roosevelt*, Prime Minister *Winston Churchill*, and Soviet Premier *Joseph Stalin* became the *Big Three* who made policy for the Allied powers.

## 1942

By June, the Axis powers in Europe controlled virtually the entire continent from the Atlantic in the west to the gates of Moscow in the east, from Scandinavia in the north to a good part of North Africa in the south.

- The Nazis set up extermination camps in Poland, Austria, and Germany.
  - They transported millions of Jews, other minorities, Soviet prisoners of war, and political enemies to these extermination camps to be systematically murdered.
  - *Auschwitz* was the most infamous of these new extermination camps.
  - Almost 12 million people were slaughtered inside concentration camps in accord with Nazi racist doctrine; 6 million were European Jews (about 60 percent of the prewar Jewish population).
- The Asian Axis partner, Japan, seized the cities of coastal China and took Indochina from the French, Indonesia from the Dutch, Malaya and Burma from the British, and the Philippines from the United States.

- German General *Erwin Rommel*, the "Desert Fox," managed to push back the British in North Africa deep into Egypt, threatening the Suez Canal, which was a lifeline of the British Empire.

# The Tide of War Turns (Mid-1942–1943)

## 1942

- *June–November:* Rommel's Afrika Corps, the elite mechanized force that spearheaded the advance of Axis troops in this theater of war, was defeated at El Alamein in Egypt by the British under Field Marshall Bernard Montgomery.
- *June:* American aircraft carriers and their fighter planes won a stunning victory against a superior Japanese naval force at the *Battle of Midway* in the Pacific.
- *Summer to winter:* The Russian city of *Stalingrad* stood against German invaders and counterattacked.
  - The fierce battle there marked the end of Nazi advances in the Soviet Union and the eventual destruction of the German Sixth Army, with a loss of 600,000 troops.
- *November:* A joint Anglo-American force landed on the shores of Axis-held territory in North Africa.

## 1943

The Axis was cleared from North Africa.

- The Soviets began the advance that would ultimately lead them into Germany itself.
  - About 80 percent of German casualties in the Second World War were inflicted by the Soviets.
  - Between 25 and 30 million Soviets, both combatants and civilians, died during the war.
- Allied leaders Roosevelt and Churchill and representatives of Stalin met at *Casablanca* in North Africa. They agreed to settle on a strategy of stopping the war only when they had achieved the *unconditional surrender* of the Axis powers.

# Allied Victories (1943–1945)

## 1943

- American, British, and Canadian forces invaded the island of Sicily off the boot of Italy.
- Mussolini was overthrown.
- The Allies landed in Italy proper and fought against determined German resistance.
- At the *Tehran Conference*, the Big Three agreed that they would accept only unconditional surrender from all three of the Axis powers and that after the war was won, Germany would be occupied by the Allied powers and demilitarized.

## 1944

The *D-Day Invasion* of the French coast at *Normandy* marked the beginning of the end of Nazi domination of the Continent.

- Paris was liberated by August.
- The last German offensive took place at the *Battle of the Bulge* in Belgium that December.
- From that point on, the Germans were in retreat on all fronts.

## 1945

In February, a huge Allied air attack dropped 3,900 tons of high explosives and incendiary bombs on the old German city of Dresden, a cultural landmark, setting it ablaze and killing 25,000 civilians.

Meanwhile, the Soviet army smashed into East Prussia, Hungary, and Czechoslovakia while the Americans crossed the Rhine River. Hitler committed suicide. Encircled Berlin was seized by the Russians. Germany surrendered, unconditionally, on May 8.

- *August 6:* The United States dropped the *first atomic bomb* on the Japanese city of *Hiroshima.*
  - 70,000 people died immediately; tens of thousands suffered aftereffects.
- *August 9:* A second atomic bomb was dropped on the city of *Nagasaki*, and Japan surrendered.
- *September:* Japan signed an official surrender and agreed to occupation by U.S. forces.
  - Under the supervision of the commander of Allied forces in the Pacific theater, *General Douglas MacArthur*, the emperor denied his own divinity.
  - An antiwar constitution was imposed on Japan.
  - With American financial aid, some of Japan's wartime destruction was repaired.
  - Technical and financial assistance was given to Japan for further industrialization and modernization.
  - A democratic government was set up that still thrives today.

# Aftermath of the War

## Crucial Conferences for Postwar Europe

At the *Yalta Conference* in February of 1945, the Big Three drew up a plan for the postwar settlement in Europe.

- Eastern Europe (Bulgaria, Czechoslovakia, Hungary, Poland, and Romania) would be set up with coalition governments of Communists and non-Communists until free elections could be held.
- Germany would be partitioned into four zones of occupation: American, British, French, and Soviet.
- The Soviet Union would enter the war against Japan in return for territories in Asia and islands north of Japan.
- The *United Nations* was set up as a successor to the defunct League of Nations, with a *General Assembly* to represent all member nations in deliberations.
  - A separate *Security Council* was established. It has 15 members and was dominated by five permanent members: the "Great Powers" (the United States, the U.S.S.R., Britain, France, and China). Each permanent member was given veto rights over any proposal for involving the organization in preserving international peace.

The *Potsdam Conference*, in July 1945, was attended by Churchill, Stalin, and Harry S. Truman, who had become president after Roosevelt's sudden death in April. Already cracks were showing in the alliance between the Western democracies and the Communist U.S.S.R. when Truman and Churchill criticized Stalin for not allowing free elections in Soviet-occupied Eastern Europe.

- Millions of refugees from concentration camps and from the war itself attempted to return home or to make new lives for themselves.
  - Many tried to reconnect with families and friends with varying degrees of success.
  - Thousands of refugees from the Soviet Union and Yugoslavia were returned to those nations by the Western powers.
- The Marshall Plan offered U.S. financial aid to those European countries devastated by the Second World War.
  - The money came in the form of loans that had to be spent on American goods, helping to transition economies from wartime to peacetime.

○ The Marshall Plan also helped draw the lines between the capitalist countries that were tied together through the financial web of trade, symbolized by the Marshall Plan, and the Communist nations that rejected Marshall Plan aid.

○ This led to greater interconnectedness among the economies of Western Europe and the dissolution of trade barriers that had plagued prewar Europe.

## The Conflict for Control of Europe

At the end of the Second World War, only two great powers remained with the resources, land mass, population, industrial capacity, and military strength to affect world events. The United States, which was physically undamaged by the war, and the U.S.S.R., which was devastated but industrially and militarily powerful, became *superpowers.*

- Since the 17th century, there had been powerful single nations in Europe (Spain, France, England, or Austria). However, six or seven other great states had managed, through alliances, to maintain a balance of power.
- Soon after World War II, two competing blocs emerged. The *Soviet Bloc* had its *satellites* of puppet governments in Eastern and Central Europe. The *Western Bloc* or "Free World" was made up, primarily, of the democracies.
- With the collapse of the colonial empires (see chapter 9, "Imperialism"), a third bloc emerged. The *developing world* consisted of newly independent nations.
- In a speech in Fulton, Missouri, in 1946, former British Prime Minister Winston Churchill described Stalin's expansion of Communist totalitarianism as bringing down an *Iron Curtain* separating the captive peoples of Eastern and Central Europe from the rest of the world.
- A competition developed between the *superpowers* to win Europe. Even though Europe's cities were in ruins and its population was decimated and displaced, Europe was still a great industrial and population center of the world.

The *Cold War* had begun.

## Casualties of the Second World War by Nation

| Country | 1939 Population | Military Death Totals | Civilian Death Totals | Total Jewish Holocaust Deaths | Total Deaths | Deaths as Percentage of 1939 Population |
|---|---|---|---|---|---|---|
| Albania | 1,073,000 | 30,000 | | 200 | 30,200 | 2.63% |
| Australia | 6,998,000 | 40,500 | 700 | | 41,200 | 0.57% |
| Austria | 6,653,000 | | 40,500 | 65,000 | 105,500 | 5.5% |
| Belgium | 8,387,000 | 12,100 | 49,600 | 24,400 | 86,100 | 1.02% |
| Bulgaria | 6,458,000 | 22,000 | 3,000 | | 25,000 | 0.38% |
| China | 517,568,000 | 3,800,000 | 16,200,000 | | 20,000,000 | 3.86% |
| Czechoslovakia | 15,300,000 | 25,000 | 43,000 | 277,000 | 345,000 | 2.25% |
| Denmark | 3,795,000 | 2,100 | 1,000 | 100 | 3,200 | 0.08% |

| Country | 1939 Population | Military Death Totals | Civilian Death Totals | Total Jewish Holocaust Deaths | Total Deaths | Deaths as Percentage of 1939 Population |
|---|---|---|---|---|---|---|
| Dutch East Indies | 69,435,000 | 11,350 | 2,500,000–4,000,000 | | 2,511,350–4,011,350 | 3.75%–5.75% |
| Estonia | 1,134,000 | | 50,000 | 1,000 | 51,000 | 4.50% |
| Finland | 3,700,000 | 95,000 | 2,000 | | 97,000 | 2.62% |
| France | 41,700,000 | 217,600 | 267,000 | 83,000 | 567,600 | 1.35% |
| Germany | 69,623,000 | 5,533,000 | 1,540,000 | 160,000 | 7,233,000 | 8.6% |
| Greece | 7,222,000 | 20,000 | 220,000 | 71,300 | 311,300 | 4.31% |
| Hungary | 9,129,000 | 300,000 | 80,000 | 200,000 | 580,000 | 6.35% |
| Iceland | 119,000 | | 200 | | 200 | 0.17% |
| Italy | 44,394,000 | 301,400 | 145,100 | 8,000 | 454,500 | 1.02% |
| Japan | 71,380,000 | 2,120,000 | 580,000 | | 2,700,000 | 3.78% |
| Latvia | 1,995,000 | | 147,000 | 80,000 | 227,000 | 11.38% |
| Lithuania | 2,575,000 | | 212,000 | 141,000 | 353,000 | 13.71% |
| Luxembourg | 295,000 | | 1,300 | 700 | 2,000 | 0.68% |
| Netherlands | 8,729,000 | 21,000 | 176,000 | 104,000 | 301,000 | 3.44% |
| Norway | 2,945,000 | 3,000 | 5,800 | 700 | 9,500 | 0.32% |
| Poland | 34,849,000 | 240,000 | 2,760,000 | 3,000,000 | 6,000,000 | 17.2% |
| Romania | 19,934,000 | 300,000 | 64,000 | 469,000 | 833,000 | 4.22% |
| (Soviet Union) U.S.S.R. | 168,500,000 | 10,700,000 | 11,400,000 | 1,000,000 | 23,100,000 | 13.71% |
| United Kingdom | 47,760,000 | 382,700 | 67,100 | | 449,800 | 0.94% |
| United States | 131,028,000 | 416,800 | 1,700 | | 418,500 | 0.32% |
| Yugoslavia | 15,400,000 | 446,000 | 514,000 | 67,000 | 1,027,000 | 6.67% |
| World Totals | 1,963,205,000 | 25,282,100 | 42,168,400 | 5,752,400 | 73,169,900 | 3.71% |

## Practice Questions

### Long Essay

These questions are samples of the various types of thematic essays on the AP exam. See pages 27–28 for a detailed explanation of each type. Check over the generic rubric (see pages 28–29) before you begin any of these essays, and use that rubric to score your essay if you write one.

## Question 1

To what extent was Nazi totalitarianism a different breed from ordinary dictatorship?

### Comments on Question 1

This is a *compare* skill question. So be sure to describe the similarities and differences between Nazi totalitarianism and other forms of totalitarian dictatorship. Also account for or explain them by providing specific examples of Nazi totalitarianism and other dictators, such as Stalin, Mussolini, or Franco. You must consider the phrase "different breed." It implies that the Third Reich was far more encompassing and repressive than the usual military dictatorship. The task is to explain how. How did the Nazis use state-sponsored terrorism to gain and hold power? How did their racist theories lead to genocide? What was the structure of their police state? How did they use propaganda and education to inculcate their program? How was war an integral part of their ideology? This essay cannot be complete without comparing and contrasting Hitler's regime with that of Stalin, Mussolini, Franco, or other totalitarian rulers.

## Question 2

Explain how the Treaty of Versailles gave birth to the Nazis while the Great Depression gave them power.

### Comments on Question 2

This is a *causation* question. It requires you either to support or to refute the idea that two events, the Treaty of Versailles and the Great Depression, resulted in specific outcomes: the birth of the Nazi Party and its rise to power. Remember to describe the causes and/or effects of the Nazi party growth and rise to power. Support your analysis of those causes and effects through citing specific evidence. The essay must explain reasons that the Treaty of Versailles helped the Nazis be created while they increased their power through the Great Depression. The essay must also utilize specific evidence as a relevant support. A few crucial questions point the way when answered. How did the Nazis and other right-wing extremists grow in membership after Germany's defeat in the First World War? What part did the War Guilt Clause of the treaty play in their propaganda? How did the indemnity payments destabilize the German economy? How was racism involved? Why were the Nazis different from each other? What was happening to Nazi Party membership during the late 1920s, and how did the emergence of the Great Depression affect that trend?

## Question 3

Compare German Nazism with Italian fascism.

### Comments on Question 3

This is a *compare* skill question. So be sure to describe the similarities and differences between Nazism and Italian fascism as well as account for or explain them by providing specific examples of the similarities and differences between Nazism and Italian fascism. The similarities are easier to lay out: the means by which Hitler and Mussolini got into office, gained control of the state, and used propaganda, education, and force to subdue internal enemies; the ideology of war for the glorification of the state; and the subversion of the institutions of society to serve the state. The differences are of kind and degree. The Fascists in Italy never preached or practiced the poisonous racism that led to genocide. Their military never achieved the kind of power that enabled the Nazis to impose their murderous policies all over the Continent. Their program and ideology were never digested by the Italian people with the relish with which many Germans swallowed Nazism.

## Question 4

Assess the extent to which the Allied decision to demand "unconditional surrender" of the Axis powers lengthened the war needlessly.

### Comments on Question 4

This is a *causation* question because it requires you to explain how much the policy of "unconditional surrender" of the Axis powers resulted in a specific outcome, the lengthening of the Second World War. Remember to describe the causes and/or effects of the lengthening of the Second World War and to support your analysis of those causes and effects through citing specific evidence. The essay must also *explain* how the need for unconditional surrender did or did not lengthen the war needlessly by citing specific, relevant evidence as support. This has been an issue much argued, a hypothesis contrary to fact. Would the war have ended sooner if the Allies had negotiated with the Axis governments or even with antigovernment military factions? In framing your answer, consider that despite the saturation bombing of Germany's cities, the Nazis maintained an iron grip until the end. Despite assassination attempts, Hitler ruled until his suicide when the Russians were at the gates of Berlin. Despite being firebombed, the dropping of the first A-bomb, and running out of soldiers, the Japanese refused to surrender.

## Question 5

Compare the results of the Second World War on both the United States and the U.S.S.R.

### Comments on Question 5

This is a *compare* skill question. So be sure to describe the similarities and differences between the results of the Second World War on the Soviet Union and the United States. Account for or explain them by providing specific examples of how the United States and the U.S.S.R. experienced similar and different results from the war. Show the differences: What was the destruction to the homelands of each? What political, social, or economic changes took place for each? What were the human losses? What were the war gains? Examine the similarities: They were the only two powers, *superpowers*, with the strength left to influence European and world events; they established parallel spheres of influence; both were brought into the war through sneak attack; they simultaneously solidified their competing ideologies and launched the Cold War. This is an abstract question that requires crisp organization and thoughtful presentation.

## Question 6

Why did the wartime cooperation of the United States and the Soviet Union degenerate, within a few years after the end of the Second World War, into the Cold War?

### Comments on Question 6

This is a *causation* question because it requires you to explain what caused the degeneration of the alliance that had won the largest war in history into a virtual stalemate referred to as the Cold War. Remember to describe the causes and/or effects of the Cold War. Support your analysis of those causes and effects through citing specific evidence. The essay must also explain specific causes for the disintegration of the relationship between the United States and the Soviet Union, such as the Soviet actions in Eastern Europe and the American capture of Nazi scientists. The wartime alliance between the West and the Soviet Union was the cooperation of competing systems in order to defeat a common enemy. Strains showed early in the Russian push for opening a second front—strains seen in the tensions at Yalta and at Potsdam in the Soviet refusal to allow free elections in Russian-occupied Eastern Europe. The distrust between American and Soviet generals added fuel to the fire. The geographic expansion of communism because of the war frightened the West. The presence of massive American forces in Europe, American possession of atomic weapons, and personal distrust between Stalin and the new leaders of the other powers frightened the Soviets. The importance of the military propaganda, ideological differences, and huge profits for the American *military industrial complex* (which Eisenhower warned of in his farewell address) should also be examined.

## Short-Answer

1. Use the excerpt below and your knowledge of European history to answer all parts of the question that follows.

### The Decline of the West

The idealist of the early democracy regarded popular education as enlightenment pure and simple—but it is precisely this that smooths the path for the coming Caesars of the world. The last century [the nineteenth] was the winter of the West, the victory of materialism and skepticism, of socialism, parliamentarianism, and money. But in this century blood and instinct will regain their rights against the power of money and intellect. The era of individualism, liberalism and democracy, of humanitarianism and freedom, is nearing its end. The masses will accept with resignation the victory of the Caesars, the strong men, and will obey them. Life will descend to a level of general uniformity, a new kind of primitivism, and the world will be better for it.

—Oswald Spengler, 1922

(a) Briefly identify and explain ONE way that the source expresses the prevalent mood of Europeans in the period between the First World War and the Second World War.

(b) Briefly explain ONE assertion of the source that was proven to be correct over the last century.

(c) Briefly explain ONE assertion of the source that was proven to be incorrect over the last century.

2. Use the song below and your knowledge of European history to answer all parts of the question that follows.

### From Finland to the Black Sea

(German Marching Song from the Second World War)

The march of Horst Wessel began
In the brown robe of the SA
End completely the gray columns:
The great hour is here!
From Finland to the Black Sea:
Forward, forward!
Forward to the east, you stinging army!
Freedom the goal,
Victory the banner!
Leader, commanded!
We follow you!

Now the armies roar into the
Russian country.
Comrades, now to the rifles!
The victory will be ours!

From Finland to the Black Sea:

Forward, forward!

Forward to the east, you stinging army!

Freedom the goal,

Victory the banner!

Leader, commanded!

(a) Briefly identify and describe how the song supports the Nazi idea of *Lebensraum*.

(b) Briefly explain how the Soviet Union was brought into the Second World War.

(c) Briefly explain how the Nazi culture is expressed in the song.

## Multiple-Choice

**Questions 1–4 refer to the following excerpt from the introduction of *Economic Consequences of the Peace* by John Maynard Keynes.**

We assume some of the most peculiar and temporary of our late advantages as natural, permanent, and to be depended on, and we lay our plans accordingly. On this sandy and false foundation we scheme for social improvement and dress our political platforms, pursue our animosities and particular ambitions, and feel ourselves with enough margin in hand to foster, not assuage, civil conflict in the European family. Moved by insane delusion and reckless self-regard, the German people overturned the foundations on which we all lived and built. But the spokesmen of the French and British peoples have run the risk of completing the ruin, which Germany began, by a Peace which, if it is carried into effect, must impair yet further, when it might have restored, the delicate, complicated organization, already shaken and broken by war, through which alone the European peoples can employ themselves and live.

1. Which of the following peace settlements was Keynes criticizing in the passage?

   (A) The Treaty of Amiens
   (B) The Peace of Paris
   (C) The Treaty of Maastricht
   (D) The Treaty of Versailles

2. Which of the following conflicts disturbed the creation of the treaty discussed in the passage by making the negotiations more drawn out and arduous?

   (A) The conflict between Wilsonian idealism and the desire to punish Germany
   (B) The conflict between Russia and Prussia over the fate of Poland
   (C) The conflict between Great Britain and France over colonial empires
   (D) The conflict between nationalism and socialism

3. Which of the following was NOT a new nation created as a result of the treaty mentioned in the excerpt?

   (A) Czechoslovakia
   (B) Palestine
   (C) Hungary
   (D) Yugoslavia

4. Which of the following was correctly predicted by Keynes as a result of the peace treaty that he opposed?

   (A) Germany once again rose to be an economic powerhouse.
   (B) The Scandinavian economies did the best during this period.
   (C) A massive worldwide depression occurred as a long-term result of the treaty.
   (D) Great Britain rose to economic dominance of the world.

**Questions 5–7 refer to the following chart about Soviet farming.**

| Year | Number of Collective Farms in 1,000s | Sown Area of Collective Farms in Millions of Hectares | % of Collective Sown Area Serviced by Machine Tractor Stations (MTS) |
|------|------|------|------|
| 1929 | 57.0 | 4.2 | — |
| 1930 | 85.9 | 38.1 | 27.4 |
| 1931 | 211.1 | 79.0 | 37.1 |
| 1932 | 211.1 | 91.5 | 49.3 |
| 1933 | 224.6 | 93.6 | 58.7 |
| 1934 | 233.3 | 98.6 | 63.9 |
| 1935 | 245.4 | 104.5 | 72.4 |
| 1936 | 242.2 | 110.5 | 82.8 |
| 1937 | 243.7 | 116.0 | 91.2 |
| 1938 | 242.4 | 117.2 | 93.3 |
| 1939 | 241.1 | 114.9 | 94.0 |

5. Which of the following policies enacted by Stalin led to the growth in agriculture seen in the table?

   (A) Supporting the kulaks
   (B) Collectivization
   (C) Five-year plans
   (D) War communism

6. Which of the following is the best description of the major differences between the economic policies of Lenin and Stalin?

   (A) Lenin's five-year plans moved the country forward during the 1930s, while Stalin's New Economic Policy met with mixed results.
   (B) Stalin exerted much more state control over the economy with his five-year plans than Lenin did with his New Economic Policy.
   (C) Lenin exerted much more state control over the economy with his five-year plans than Stalin did with his New Economic Policy.
   (D) Stalin had more favorable policies toward the better-off peasants, or kulaks, than Lenin did.

7. Which of the following was the most likely fate for comrades who did not meet their economic targets under Stalin during the years cited in the table?

   (A) They were reeducated in Moscow.
   (B) They were sent to live as they pleased in Siberia.
   (C) They were imprisoned in gulags.
   (D) They were deported to capitalist countries.

**Questions 8–10 refer to the laws enacted in 1935 seen below.**

### Article 1

1. Marriages between Jews and subjects of the state of German or related blood are forbidden. Marriages nevertheless concluded are invalid, even if concluded abroad to circumvent this law.
2. Annulment proceedings can be initiated only by the state prosecutor.

### Article 2

Extramarital relations between Jews and subjects of the state of German or related blood are forbidden.

### Article 3

Jews may not employ in their households female subjects of the state of German or related blood who are under 45 years old.

8. The three articles were part of a series of laws that defined racial purity in Germany known as which of the following?

(A) The Wannsee Laws
(B) The Reichstag Laws
(C) The Nuremberg Laws
(D) The Nazi Code

9. Which of the following can be best supported by the actions of the Nazi government in Germany?

(A) Germany wanted to establish hegemony over the entire world.
(B) Germany wanted to create a new racial order in Europe.
(C) Germany wanted to rid Asia of Asians to make room for more Europeans.
(D) Germany wanted to destroy the national character of every European nationality.

10. Which of the following was the meeting at which the final solution was agreed upon by the Nazis?

(A) Wannsee Conference
(B) Berlin Conference
(C) Tehran Conference
(D) Potsdam Conference

# Answers and Explanations

## Short-Answer Explanations

1. (a) You should identify the period between the world wars as the age of anxiety. Explain the anxiety about the future of Europe that is expressed in the source by citing specific facts from the source that express that anxiety, such as the idea that Europe's dominance of the world was ending in 1922, the fear of the loss of individualism, the fear of losing democracy, the fear of losing freedom, the fear of losing humanitarianism, and the fear of the rise of strong leaders who would crush the will of the citizens.

   (b) You should explain the rise of dictators Lenin, Stalin, Hitler, and Mussolini as proof that strong men would rise and crush individual freedoms. An alternative is for you to cite the Second World War and the rise of blood and instinct in regaining power.

   (c) You should explain that the West continued to gain power almost until the end of the 20th century. Another option is for you to explain that individual rights and freedoms as well as humanitarianism continued to grow in Europe throughout the 20th century.

2. (a) You should explain that the idea of gaining land for the German people to expand into is the concept of *Lebensraum*. The song supports Germany expanding to reach from Finland to the Black Sea by conquering Soviet territory and annexing it into the German state.

   (b) You should start with the German-Soviet nonaggression pact of 1939, also known as the Molotov-Ribbentrop Pact. You should then explain Operation Barbarossa, the German invasion plan for the Soviet Union that aimed to gain land and oil resources for the German people.

   (c) You should explain that the song supports the ideals of the German "master race" and the growing militarism of the Nazi regime. The essay should also explain German reverence for their Nazi leaders, the idea of the Third Reich, and the idea that Germans would always be victorious in war.

## Practice Multiple-Choice Questions

1. (A) is wrong because Keynes was famously criticizing the Treaty of Versailles that ended the First World War.
   (B) is wrong because Keynes was famously criticizing the Treaty of Versailles that ended the First World War.
   (C) is wrong because Keynes was famously criticizing the Treaty of Versailles that ended the First World War.
   **(D) is CORRECT because Keynes was famously criticizing the Treaty of Versailles that ended the First World War.**

2. **(A) is CORRECT because the major problem at the conference table creating the Treaty of Versailles was the conflict between Wilson's idealistic Fourteen Points and the others' desire to punish Germany.**
   (B) is wrong because Prussia ceased to exist in 1871.
   (C) is wrong because France and the United Kingdom saw eye to eye at the conference table and did not squabble over possessions.
   (D) is wrong because nationalism and socialism began to work together in the 1880s after Bismarck joined them inextricably in Germany.

3. (A) is wrong because the Treaty of Versailles did create the official nation of Czechoslovakia.
   **(B) is CORRECT because the League of Nations made Palestine a British protectorate but did not create it as a separate nation.**
   (C) is wrong because the Treaty of Versailles did create the official nation of Hungary.
   (D) is wrong because the Treaty of Versailles did create the official nation of Yugoslavia.

4. (A) is wrong because Keynes predicted a worldwide depression, not the rise of Germany; rather, he predicted its fall.

(B) is wrong because Keynes predicted a worldwide depression, not the rise of Scandinavian economies that used his ideas.

**(C) is CORRECT because Keynes predicted a worldwide depression.**

(D) is wrong because Keynes predicted a worldwide depression, not the rise of Britain; rather, he predicted its fall.

5. (A) is wrong because Stalin eliminated the kulaks rather than supported them.

(B) is wrong because collectivization was a serious failure, and the output in agriculture increased only due to the mechanization provided by the five-year plans.

**(C) is CORRECT because the five-year plans allowed the increase of industry and the mechanization of agriculture, leading to higher output.**

(D) is wrong because war communism was used to fight the civil war but did not improve agriculture.

6. (A) is wrong because Lenin had a New Economic Policy while Stalin had his five-year plans.

**(B) is CORRECT because Stalin's five-year plans did exert much more state control than did Lenin's New Economic Policy.**

(C) is wrong because Lenin had a New Economic Policy, while Stalin had his five-year plans.

(D) is wrong because Stalin eliminated the better-off peasants as a class.

7. (A) is wrong because Moscow was the center of Soviet power and dissidents were sent away from there.

(B) is wrong because if they were sent to Siberia, they worked in prison camps and did not live as they pleased.

**(C) is CORRECT as the gulags were the prison camps for dissidents in the Soviet Union.**

(D) is wrong because the Soviets wanted to punish their wrong-minded citizens rather than reward their disobedience.

8. (A) is wrong because the Wannsee Conference was held to determine the fate of all Jewish people by deciding to exterminate all of them, as opposed to the Nuremberg Laws, which were Germany's racial purity laws and a step toward the dehumanization of Jewish people in Germany.

(B) is wrong because the Reichstag was the lower legislative branch in Germany, not a set of racist laws.

**(C) is CORRECT because the Nuremberg Laws were Germany's racial purity laws and a step toward the dehumanization of Jewish people in Germany.**

(D) is wrong because there was no Nazi Code relating to race called such.

9. (A) is wrong because Germany wanted hegemony only in Europe at first.

**(B) is CORRECT because the Nazis tried to create a new racial order in which Slavs would be servants to the superior Germans and Anglo-Saxons, while Jews, the Roma, and others would be exterminated.**

(C) is wrong because Germany was allied with Japan.

(D) is wrong because Germany was very nationalistic and wanted to preserve its own culture.

10. **(A) is CORRECT because the Wannsee Conference was held to determine the "final solution" of exterminating the Jewish people from the world.**

(B) is wrong because the Berlin Conference was held in 1885 to reorganize African colonies.

(C) is wrong because the Tehran Conference was among Allied leaders during the Second World War.

(D) is wrong because the Potsdam Conference was among Allied leaders during the Second World War.

# UNIT 9
# Cold War and Contemporary Europe

## Unit 9 Overview: Recovery from WWII, Ideological Conflict, European Unification, and Post-WWII Social Movements

**Unit description:** This unit covers everything that happened in Europe from 1945 to the present. The reconstruction of Europe after the devastation of World War II begins the unit with the *Marshall Plan* and the *Iron Curtain*. The 45-year-long Cold War; the changing social norms; the peak and decline of the welfare state; the increase in consumerism; increased individual, minority, and gender rights; increased implementation of and reliance on technology; and the creation and decline of the EU are all major ideas in this unit. This unit sees Europe transform from a divided squabbling continent into a more unified market that shares a common currency and set of legal codes with 22 European nations.

The consumer society that had been emerging since the height of the Dutch Empire began to take on a whole new gusto. Consumerism and the idea that we could all satisfy our wants via the market began to prevail. Marketing and advertising as well as the rise of corporate power increased the role of consumerism in society throughout this unit.

Europe's relationships with the rest of the world were deeply changed by decolonization after World War II. Different European nations' paths to decolonization impacted their relationships with the regions of the world that they formerly controlled. The rise in the rights of the individual and the fight against discrimination in Europe have led to many nationalist reactionary forces in places all over Europe as Europeans began to cope with a world that is no longer dominated by the Westerners who had centuries of technological advantage over the rest of the world.

After World War II, the world came together to form the United Nations and promote ethnic self-determination. The pursuant decolonization of former European colonies helped create the conflicts of the late-20th and early-21st centuries. This unit utilizes all seven of the themes in European history: Interaction of Europe and the World, Economic and Commercial Developments, Cultural and Intellectual Developments, States and Other Institutions of Power, Social Organization and Development, National and European Identity, and Technological and Scientific Innovation.

This unit is focused on the Cold War, its aftermath, the movement toward European unity, the rise of consumerism, and the creation of the contemporary world in Europe. The topics of study for this unit are: Contextualizing Cold War and Contemporary Europe; Rebuilding Europe; The Cold War; Two Superpowers Emerge; Postwar Nationalism, Ethnic Conflict, and Atrocities; Contemporary Western Democracies; The Fall of Communism; 20th-Century Feminism; Decolonization; The European Union; Migration and Immigration; Technology; Globalization; 20th- and 21st-Century Culture, Art, and Demographic Trends; and Continuity and Change in the 20th and 21st Centuries. All of this unit is discussed in this chapter. This last chapter of the historical information takes place completely in time period 4.

# 12

# Recovery, Cold War, and Contemporary Europe (1945 to Present)

## Overview

The destruction of Europe after the Second World War was far more extensive than that at the end of the First World War. The technology and tactics of the First World War had limited the worst damage to specific regions of Europe: Flanders—which consists of northeastern France and parts of Belgium, Poland, sections of European Russia, some provinces of northern Italy and southern Austria, and some areas of the Balkans. During the Second World War, the mass bombing of industrial and population centers severely damaged virtually all the cities of the European belligerents, and it left Germany in ruins. The German destruction and the scorched-earth policy of the Soviets leveled tens of thousands of villages, towns, and cities in the western Soviet Union. It ruined transport systems, factories, and housing. It shattered the economies of Western and Eastern Europe.

The economic recovery of Western Europe was so amazing that it was referred to as *the miracle*. Within a decade, productivity reached prewar levels; within two decades, unparalleled prosperity prevailed. West Germany, so recently defeated, demoralized, and divided from East Germany, was the key to recovery. The United States infused massive aid through the Marshall Plan to rebuild not only its former Allies but also its former enemies—West Germany and Italy. By the end of the 1950s, Western Europe had made the first moves toward economic and, eventually, political union. The United States also aided Japan and set up a viable democratic government there.

The rebuilding of the U.S.S.R. was no less spectacular. Under Stalin's five-year plans, most of the war damage was repaired within a decade. A vastly expanded Soviet empire, established by the successes of the Red Army against the Nazis, included most of the countries of Eastern Europe, which became satellites of the brutally repressive Stalinist Soviet Union. After the death of Stalin in 1953, new leaders redefined the role of Soviet communism but kept an iron grip on the U.S.S.R. and Eastern Europe. The emergence of the United States and the U.S.S.R. as superpowers at the end of the war created a new balance of power in Europe and in the world. Europe quickly became divided into the West and the Communist Bloc. The West was dedicated to the containment of Soviet expansionism. The Communists were intent on both spreading their philosophy and defending their gains against the *capitalist conspiracy*. The Cold War was the ideological, economic, and, at times, military rivalry between the two adversaries. It became all the more dangerous because of the development of nuclear weapons. Several hot spots in the Cold War—such as the Korean War, the Cuban Missile Crisis, the Vietnam War, the Yom Kippur War, and the Soviet invasion of Afghanistan—caused the world great concern. Peaks of tension, during which the superpower confrontations almost led to war or even nuclear holocaust, alternated with "thaws" until a policy of *peaceful coexistence* emerged.

In the 1970s, high energy prices resulting from instability in the Middle East and the disintegration of the American-dominated global monetary system brought about a worldwide recession. Western Europe suffered stagflation and huge government deficits.

During this decade, détente (a relaxation of tensions between East and West) was furthered by West Germany's attempts to reconcile with Eastern Europe and by the Helsinki Agreements. However, tensions were strained by U.S. involvement in Vietnam, the Soviet involvement in Afghanistan, and a massive American arms buildup.

The most important and dramatic developments of the 1980s and early 1990s were the largely peaceful anti-Communist revolutions in Eastern Europe and the collapse of Soviet communism that led to the dismantling of the Soviet Union. The Solidarity movement in Poland, liberalization in Hungary and Czechoslovakia, and the unification of East and West Germany marked the end of Soviet domination of Eastern Europe. The gradual decline of Soviet economic strength under Brezhnev and Andropov led Gorbachev to initiate profound political and social reform (*glasnost*) and economic restructuring (*perestroika*). In 1989, the first free elections were conducted since the 1917 Revolution. An attempted military coup against Gorbachev in the summer of 1991 faced popular opposition and failed. Many Soviet republics declared independence. With the promise of reform, Boris Yeltsin was elected president of the Russian Republic. Vladimir Putin replaced Yeltsin in 2000 and oversaw the privatization of the Soviet state possessions, such as oil companies and other industries. Dmitri Medvedev replaced Putin in 2008 as his handpicked successor, while Putin still held actual power as prime minister. Putin was reelected president in 2012 when he became constitutionally eligible to do so.

The entrance of great numbers of women into the workplace and the feminist movement altered the lives of women in Europe and the United States. The birth rate dropped, the divorce rate rose, and both sexual and social attitudes toward women changed. At the beginning of the 20th century, women could not vote. At the time of publication of this book, women have been elected as prime ministers in Great Britain, Germany, India, Portugal, Norway, Yugoslavia, Lithuania, Pakistan, France, Poland, Turkey, and many other nations. The 20th century was the century of the woman in many ways. Women in many countries gained intellectual and professional freedom and increased their earning power. Widespread use of contraception led to increased emancipation in industrialized nations, allowing women to participate more equally in society as their roles changed from caretakers to wage earners in many cases. By the 1990s, laws preventing wage and other forms of discrimination against women were prevalent in Western Europe as well as in the United States, Canada, and other industrially advanced countries. Women have risen to the highest positions of power in Europe and elsewhere as they have gained more legal, political, and economic freedom than at any previous time in European history.

Most recently, increasing nationalism in Europe has led to anti-immigration and right-wing parties gaining ground in elections. Financial crises as well as increasing sentiment against Muslim immigrants and others, who are changing the national cultures within Europe, threaten the once-growing European unity.

# Western European Recovery (1945–1957)

## The 1940s After the War: Setting the Stage for the Cold War

Since Germany's *Ruhr Basin* was the industrial center of a devastated Europe, the Western Allies decided that Germany would have to be rebuilt. The Soviets hoped to use German reparations for reconstruction of their own massive war damage. The *Morgenthau Plan* was developed by the U.S. secretary of the treasury to transform Germany back into an exclusively agricultural society. Led by the Americans, the British and French agreed that in order for Western Europe to recover, Germany would have to be rebuilt.

- The United Nations (U.N.), which replaced the defunct League of Nations and began with just 50 nations, now includes 193 nations and many nongovernmental organizations (NGOs) such as Amnesty International, which join in debate but do not vote.
  - The U.N. has a General Assembly and six main committees as well as a Human Rights Council and an Economic and Social Council. Its Security Council must approve any international military action.
  - The Security Council has five permanent members with veto power: France, Russia, China, the United Kingdom, and the United States.
  - The U.N. works to prevent human tragedy, preserve and promote human rights, improve health through the World Health Organization, improve education and economic development, and promote international peace and understanding.
- Joint administration of the *four occupation zones* in Germany broke down in 1946.
  - The American, British, and French sectors eventually became West Germany.
  - The Russian sector became East Germany.
- Agitation by Communist parties in France and Italy worsened relations between the democracies of Western Europe and the Soviet Union.
- In 1948, the Czech Communists seized power in Prague and set up a government.
- *The Marshall Plan*, developed by Secretary of State *George Marshall* (1880–1959), former U.S. military chief of staff, was put into operation. Marshall Plan funds from the United States financed an extensive reconstruction of industry and infrastructure and stimulated an extended period of growth in Western and Central Europe. This was often referred to as an *economic miracle*, which increased the economic and cultural importance of consumerism.
  - Billions of dollars in grants went to Western Europe to rebuild housing, transportation systems, and industrial plants.
  - The Western European nations created the Committee of European Economic Cooperation in 1948 as a result of the Marshall Plan as a way to coordinate economic efforts and get the most out of their aid dollars.
  - This eventually led to the creation of the Organization for European Economic Cooperation (OEEC), which was a primary tool of European integration until it was replaced by the Organization for Economic Co-operation and Development (OECD), which helped usher in the European Union.
- The Soviet response to the OEEC and the Marshall Plan was COMECON, the Council for Mutual Economic Assistance. It was set up in 1949 to facilitate and coordinate the economic activity of those countries in Eastern Europe in the Soviet sphere of influence known as the Eastern Bloc or Communist Bloc.
- Western Europe created new benefit systems for its citizens to reduce the peaks and valleys that capitalism creates in the human condition and to support basic necessities for all citizens. These were known as the *modern welfare state.*
  - Unemployment insurance became universal and lasted for long periods of time.
  - Housing subsidies were provided to low-income families.
  - Medical care was given to all for free, as a human right.
  - Pensions were created for all citizens.
  - Subsidies were given for large families.
  - Child care was provided in state-sponsored facilities.
  - Higher taxes on the wealthy paid for these benefits for the neediest.
- The rapid transformation of West Germany into an economic powerhouse that became the leading economy in Europe was labeled the *Wirtschaftswunder* or "West German miracle" due to the miraculous nature of economic growth there.

- The 1950s saw increasing standards of living, with a 73 percent rise in purchasing power for the average West German.
- The United States and 11 other nations formed the North Atlantic Treaty Organization (NATO) to rearm non-Communist Europe and safeguard it against invasion.
  - Soon after, West Germany (the Federal Republic of Germany), Greece, and Turkey joined.
  - Eventually, West Germany was encouraged to organize a national army under NATO command.
- The *Warsaw Pact* was formed as an alliance of the Soviet Union and its Eastern European satellite nations (East Germany, Poland, Czechoslovakia, Hungary, Romania, Bulgaria, and Albania) as an answer to the formation of NATO by Western Europe.

## Western Europe Begins Economic Integration

Productivity in those countries that received Marshall Plan aid exceeded prewar rates. The United States urged the Europeans to develop a European free-trade zone similar to that among the various American states.

- The Marshall Plan combined self-interest (communism in Europe would be contained and markets for U.S. goods would be opened) with altruism.
- The *General Agreement on Tariffs and Trade (GATT)* was completed in 1948. Its signatories agreed to reduce tariffs and negotiated during the United Nations Conference on Trade and Employment.
  - GATT resulted due to the failure of negotiating governments to create the International Trade Organization (ITO).
  - GATT was signed by 23 nations in Geneva on October 30, 1947, and took effect on January 1, 1948.
  - It lasted until the signing by 123 nations in *Marrakesh* on April 14, 1994, of the Uruguay Round Agreements. It established the *World Trade Organization (WTO)*, which took effect on January 1, 1995.
- Under the French-sponsored *Schuman and Monnet Plan*, six industrial countries on the Continent (Belgium, France, Holland, Italy, Luxembourg, and West Germany) formed the *European Coal and Steel Community* to pool their resources in 1952.
  - The *European Economic Community*, also known as the *Common Market*, was created by the same six nations that formed the European Coal and Steel Community.
  - It aimed at an end to internal tariffs and for the free exchange of money and workers among members.
  - By 1968, its plan would be in full effect.
  - In 1973, Britain, which was previously denied membership by France, joined as a full partner along with Ireland and Denmark.
- By 1960, many of the best scientists and engineers left Europe to go to the United States for higher salaries, creating the *brain drain*.

# Decolonization

France, Belgium, Great Britain, Italy, the Netherlands, and Portugal all gave up their colonial empires in the period after the Second World War. By 1975, most of Africa and Asia was back under African and Asian rule, with a few minor exceptions. The horrors of the world wars destroyed much of the confidence the Western powers previously had in thinking that they were better than those they ruled. These horrors also allowed Europeans to see that the rest of the world deserved self-rule.

- Britain gave up India first in 1947; much of Africa was then relinquished after 1960.
  - The British also gave up governing parts of the Middle East that now include Syria, Iraq, and Israel.
  - A Jewish homeland was created in Israel in 1948.

- Considerable bloodshed occurred during British decolonization. For example, approximately 12,000–20,000 Mau Mau rebels are estimated to have died fighting for independence in Kenya. Jewish rebels in Palestine fought fiercely against occupying British troops to force the United Kingdom to withdraw.
- The French gave up Indochina after their resounding defeat at Dien Bien Phu in 1954 but fought very hard to keep Algeria.
  - It was a long and brutal conflict that sapped France of resources and forced it to fight against guerrilla tactics and a native nationalist movement.
  - The conflict ended with a French commonwealth that included most of the African area France had fought to keep.
- Belgium used to rule a portion of Africa that was 75 times the size of Belgium itself.
  - The Democratic Republic of the Congo was formed in 1960, ending more than a century of Belgian rule in Africa.
- The Portuguese also decolonized slowly and reluctantly as their world power dissipated.
  - Angola was an example of their attempt to preserve rule that brutalized natives.
- Despite indigenous nationalist movements, independence for many African and Asian territories was delayed until the mid- and even late-20th century by the imperial powers' reluctance to relinquish control, threats of interference from other nations, unstable economic and political systems, and Cold War strategic alignments.
  - The *Indian National Congress* agitated for independence for almost half a century under the leadership of Mohandas K. Gandhi, before the British simply walked out of India in 1948.
  - In Vietnam, *Ho Chi Minh* organized the Viet Minh to fight for independence, first from France and then from American control, as he worked to establish Vietnam as a Communist state.
  - In Indonesia, Sukarno led his people to independence from the Netherlands, which had tried to restore its rule there after the Second World War.
- Some scholars argue that the proliferation of European languages in education and finance, as well as Cold War political pressures, led to an era of *neocolonialism* in which nations are still dominated financially and politically rather than militarily.

## May 1968 in France

The economy of France was brought to a standstill. President Charles de Gaulle was unable to solve the problems caused by a general strike and fled the country.

- The strikes began with student protests against the expulsion of a few students, the general poor quality of education in France, and the closure of major universities such as the Sorbonne.
- Workers joined the students, and a general strike brought the country to its knees. When de Gaulle returned in a landslide victory, dissolved the National Assembly, and promised to bring in the army, the strike lost momentum and the republic was saved.
- Questions plague historians as to whether or not these protests were part of a cultural diffusion from the United States, where riots over the shootings of Martin Luther King, Jr., and Bobby Kennedy led to general unrest and protests against the Vietnam War.

## Communism: The Soviet Union and Its Satellites (1945–1968)

### Immediately After the Second World War

Backed by the U.S.S.R. *Red Army*, local communist parties in Eastern Europe (Bulgaria, Czechoslovakia, Poland, and Romania) took over the coalition governments and fell under the Soviet orbit. East Germany, which was under Soviet occupation, also became a satellite.

*Albania* and *Yugoslavia*, under Communist Party rule, managed to maintain independence from Moscow since they had not been liberated from the Nazis by Soviet troops.

## The Soviets Consolidate Power (1945–1953)

Communist governments in the satellite nations carried out land distribution reforms and nationalization of industry.

- Forced *collectivization* of agriculture was only moderately successful. Soviet-type five-year plans helped reconstruction and built up heavy industry at the expense of consumer goods.
- Police state methods were used to silence opposition parties and to neutralize the influence of the Roman Catholic Church in newly Communist nations such as Poland. These methods included domestic spying, arbitrary imprisonment, censorship, and torture.
- Repression was tightened to the breaking point in the U.S.S.R. itself during the last years of Stalin.
  - His achievements (industrialization of Europe's backward giant, victory in the *Great Patriotic War* against the Nazis, postwar reconstruction accomplished in a decade, and the spread of a Soviet Communist empire to Eastern Europe) have to be measured against the brutal repression he imposed on the Soviet people.
  - Over the course of his totalitarian regime, Stalin was responsible for the slaughter of perhaps 30 million of his citizens, for denying basic civil rights, for establishing forced labor camps (gulags), and for repressing any and every form of free expression.
- Stalin died in 1953, and a power struggle occurred in the Soviet Union.
  - The party leadership executed Lavrenti Beria, head of the secret police, to prevent a coup. The leadership set up a figurehead premier.
  - Riots against Soviet domination broke out in East Berlin, a precursor of greater resistance from the satellites.

## The Era of Khrushchev (1956–1964)

*Nikita S. Khrushchev* (1894–1971), a former deputy of Stalin and by 1954 head of the Soviet Communist Party, gave a speech to the Central Committee on the *crimes of Stalin*. Stalin, he said, had built a *cult of personality*, had created terror among citizens and party leaders alike, and had even been responsible for the dismal failure of Soviet troops to stop the initial advances of the Nazi invaders in 1941.

- Khrushchev tried to find a middle road between the Western democracies and the old party hard-liners who had thrived under Stalin by defending communism while trying to fix the excesses of Stalin.
  - Khrushchev liberalized the arts, as typified by his allowing the publication of Soviet dissident Alexander Solzhenitsyn's *One Day in the Life of Ivan Denisovich*.
  - In a speech at the United Nations, he threatened to destroy the United States.
  - In 1962, in response to U.S. missiles being placed within range of Moscow, Khrushchev attempted to site nuclear missiles on the newly Communist Cuba and had a famous face-off with President John F. Kennedy in the *Cuban Missile Crisis*.
  - He also blockaded Berlin. This caused the United States under Kennedy to respond with a massive airlift to West Berlin in order to keep the people living the Western capitalist lifestyle.
  - After the Cuban Missile Crisis, Khrushchev softened his tone toward the United States; he signed a nuclear test-ban treaty in late 1963.
  - By backing down against Kennedy, he sealed his fate and lost power in the U.S.S.R.
- *De-Stalinization* encouraged resistance in the satellites; *revolts* broke out *in Poland and Hungary*.
  - After 1956, Soviet leader Nikita Khrushchev's de-Stalinization policies failed to meet their economic

goals within the Soviet Union. Combined with reactions to existing limitations on individual rights, this prompted revolts in Eastern Europe, which ended with a reimposition of Soviet rule and repressive totalitarian regimes.

- ○ In Poland, *Wladysaw Gomulka* (1905–1982) managed to win concessions from Soviet leaders to liberalize the government.
- ○ In Hungary, armed revolt in Budapest and other cities threatened the Communist regime. The Soviets brutally crushed all resistance.

- The launching of the first artificial Earth satellite, *Sputnik*, in 1957, pointed out the considerable technological achievements of the Soviets.
- In 1949, the Soviets tested *their first atomic bomb.*
- In 1953, they developed their first *hydrogen bomb.*
- Their work on rocketry, aided by German scientists captured after the Second World War, eventually enabled the Soviet Union to develop *intercontinental missiles* capable of striking the United States.
- *Centralized economic planning (Gosplan)* developed the five-year plans that reconstructed the U.S.S.R. after the Second World War and raised the Soviet gross national product from 30 percent of the American gross national product in 1950 to about 50 percent in the mid-1960s.
- Agriculture performed badly, though, partly because of the failure of collectivized farms to provide incentives for production and partly because of bad decisions by Khrushchev.
- Khrushchev was ousted in 1964. Party rivals resented his personal power, and they found an excuse to oust him in his alleged weakness with American presidents Kennedy and Johnson.

## The Conflicts of 1968

In August, Soviet leaders sent a massive military force to end the *liberalization of Czechoslovakia*, a threat to both the Warsaw Pact and Soviet domination.

- The *Brezhnev Doctrine,* formulated by head of the Soviet Communist Party and future premier Leonid Brezhnev (1906–1982), stated that the *U.S.S.R. had the right to intervene* in the internal affairs of any satellite nation if communism was threatened.
- This doctrine and the intervention in Czechoslovakia discredited Soviet leadership of the Communist world and its role as a model for Communist governments in the coming years of the Cold War.

# Recent European Economic History

Through the 1960s, Europe, led by the *Common Market*, accounted for a quarter of the world's industrial output. West Germany was third behind the United States and Japan in gross national product. In 1970, 25 years after the Second World War had ended, prosperity and democracy in Western Europe submerged centuries of national rivalry and promised peace and even greater economic progress and political cooperation.

- The United States exerted financial dominance in the capitalist Western democracies after the Second World War through the Marshall Plan and through control of vast amounts of gold.
- The Bretton-Woods Agreement set up rules for international financial exchange rates based on a set rate of gold for the dollar.
  - ○ Other currencies could exchange for dollars or gold at a set exchange rate.
  - ○ The International Monetary Fund (IMF) and the World Bank were created to finance nations in times of crisis.
  - ○ The IMF and the World Bank became tools in the Cold War and afterward for imposing austerity measures on nations, which almost always meant a loss of benefits to their citizens, by promising loans to debtor nations only supporting such austerity measures.

- Many liberal people across Europe and the United States protested against the intervention by the World Bank and the IMF in global economies because they thought that the policies of the IMF and World Bank would further impoverish those on the bottom rungs of the socioeconomic ladder.
- The United States was providing the capital that kick-started German, Japanese, and Western European economies as a way to create prosperity to fight communism.
- The *oil embargo of 1973* helped change this rosy picture.
  - The *Arab-Israeli War of 1973* incited Arab oil-producing nations to stop the flow of oil to those nations that supported Israel.
  - This stance was encouraged by the Soviet Union, which provided weapons and support to the Arab nations.
  - Since over 70 percent of Western Europe's petroleum came from the Middle East, the embargo and the resulting price rise threatened to destroy not only Europe's economy but the world's economy.
  - *Stagflation*, a combination of slowdown and inflation that developed into a worldwide recession, had already been a problem that the oil embargo only aggravated.
  - Western Europe's unparalleled economic growth and prosperity in the postwar period was threatened, as was that of the United States and the rest of the industrialized world.
  - Although the recession, the most severe since the Great Depression of the 1930s, improved by early 1976 and although unionism and welfare benefits enabled working people to cope with the recession more easily, economic growth rates slowed.
- The expansion of cradle-to-grave social welfare programs in the aftermath of World War II, accompanied by high taxes, became a contentious domestic political issue as the budgets of European nations came under pressure in the late-20th century.
- The 1980s saw Great Britain and the United States reduce spending on social programs under conservatives *Margaret Thatcher* and Ronald Reagan, respectively, which contrasted with the strong social programs in the rest of Europe.
  - Thatcher also led Britain during the last clear war for imperialism when she had the British navy defend the Falklands Islands off Argentina when the Argentines invaded.
  - Her brand of conservatism conflicted with the fact that she was a woman who led society forward on one social issue as she was cutting benefits to the poor in the U.K. on another social issue.

## The European Union

- By late 1991, the 12 members of the *European Community*, the Common Market, completed a plan to integrate economically and to consolidate politically. The *Maastricht Treaty* that went into force in November 1993 was the first major step toward European unification into the *European Union* (EU), which now shares a common currency, a central bank, and a set of trade regulations.
  - There are no tariffs or restrictions among the 28 member states that comprise the economic entity, which has one of the largest GDPs in the world at over $14 trillion.
  - The European Union has become a leading political as well as economic force on the world stage.
  - Eighteen of these nations use the *euro* (€) as their currency; all of them participate in a mixture of supranational and intergovernmental cooperation that holds this confederation of European states together.
  - The member states were Austria, Belgium, Bulgaria, Croatia, Cyprus, the Czech Republic, Denmark, Estonia, Finland, France, Germany, Greece, Hungary, Ireland, Italy, Latvia, Lithuania, Luxembourg, Malta, the Netherlands, Poland, Portugal, Romania, Slovakia, Slovenia, Spain, Sweden, and the United Kingdom. The United Kingdom voted to leave the EU in 2016 and also replaced their prime minister to do so. Boris Johnson was elected to complete the "Brexit" of the U.K. and completed it on January 31, 2020.
  - Member states are responsible for their own defense, but many belong to NATO.

- ○ The presidency of the European Union currently rotates, but there is some discussion about an elected president for the European Union.
- ○ This union has allowed cooperation on many fronts, from the financial sector, to the law enforcement sector, to planning common infrastructure and energy policy, to cooperation in engineering and science.
  - ■ The European Space Agency and Airbus, the world's second largest airplane manufacturer, are joint European projects demonstrating that the European Union is a study in international cooperation.
- ○ The expansion of the European Union into Eastern Europe and the Baltic states has caused tensions with Russia but has also modernized the economies of those areas.
  - ■ The Russian incursion into Ukraine in 2014 was caused in part by the citizens there protesting in favor of joining NATO.
- ○ EU member nations continue to balance questions of national sovereignty with the responsibilities of membership in an economic and political union.
- ○ Turkey has made gestures at joining the European Union, but so far that has not come to fruition.
- ○ This economic and political union has helped revive Europe as an economic powerhouse during the transition from the 20th to the 21st century.
- ○ In less than a decade, the euro became one of the most important currencies in the world, gaining value against other world currencies, such as the dollar.
- ○ Since 2013, the euro has been falling in value in large part due to the *Greek debt crisis*, which has threatened the strength of the European Union by testing the economic integration as well as the true independent sovereignty of member nations.
- ■ In 1994, the *World Trade Organization (WTO)* was created by the Marrakesh Agreement, which was signed by 123 nations on April 15.
  - ○ The WTO is an international trade-regulating body that enforces agreements on international trade. It includes a judicial body that has the power to impose penalties on member nations. By providing a framework for negotiating trade agreements and a dispute-resolution process aimed at enforcing participants' adherence to WTO agreements, which are signed by representatives of member governments, the WTO has become a powerful nongovernmental organization (NGO) globally.

## Cold War

The *Cold War* was the economic, cultural, ideological, political, diplomatic, and, under certain circumstances, military struggle between the Western nations and the Communist Bloc. This conflict took place over decades, in varying degrees of severity, after the end of the Second World War. The two superpowers (the United States and the U.S.S.R.) that led the opposing alliances allocated great portions of their productive output to increasing their military might for the aim of defeating the other in a projected war. However, the two superpowers never did *directly* confront each other in a military clash. The Cold War shaped the economic and political history of the second half of the 20th century in many ways, from the ideological conflict to exacerbating problems in the Middle East and Africa, using these regions in proxy battles in the Cold War.

- ■ The initial phase of the Cold War involved a struggle for control of war-devastated Europe.
  - ○ By the late 1940s, U.S. aid shored up the exhausted democracies of Western Europe against Soviet encroachment.
  - ○ The Soviets installed communist governments in Eastern Europe under Moscow's domination.
- ■ The next phase involved the *containment of communism* by the West in the *Less Economically Developed Countries* (LEDCs), those regions that emerged from colonialism after the Second World War.
  - ○ In 1946, former British Prime Minister Winston Churchill helped to define the Cold War (after he was dismissed by voters from office) when he spoke at Westminster College in Fulton, Missouri. He stated that "an iron curtain has descended upon the continent," describing the nations in the Soviet sphere of influence as prisoners in totalitarian regimes.

- Wars involving the European democracies or the United States against Marxist nationalists broke out in Asia, Africa, and Latin America.
  - When China's Communist revolution led by Mao Tse-tung (Mao Zedong) was triumphant in 1949, the United Nations refused to recognize the government of Mao and, instead, recognized the Nationalist Chinese government of Chiang Kai-shek in Taiwan.
  - The Soviet Union boycotted the United Nations as a result of the decision.
  - At this time, North Korea invaded South Korea with Soviet aid in 1950, attacking a United Nations force. Since the Soviets were boycotting the U.N., they could not prevent the body voting to oppose the North Koreans.
- The U.N. declared a police action to stop the North Korean invasion, and the Soviet Union was not in the Security Council to veto the action.
- Eventually the fighting was stopped at the 38th parallel, and a demilitarized zone (DMZ) was created between North and South Korea.
- With no official truce ever signed, the DMZ remains a military hot spot that instills fear around the world.
  - Foreign aid and regional alliances, primarily provided and engineered by the United States, countered the influence of Moscow.
  - A nuclear arms race created a *balance of terror* between the two superpowers, while cracks in their systems of alliances aggravated the overall conflict.
    - The world was saved from nuclear holocaust only by the fact that both sides knew that either side could literally destroy all life on Earth and, therefore, they could not afford to come into open conflict.
    - This balance of power, dubbed *mutually assured destruction* (MAD), is credited by many historians for preventing a nuclear conflict between the superpowers.
    - The role of the United Nations expanded as more newly independent nations joined, and the super-powers realized the limitations of their might.
- The first substantive reduction in Cold War tensions was realized in the *Helsinki Accords*, which were the final act of the Conference on Security and Cooperation held in 1975 in Helsinki, Finland.
  - Most of the European nations on both sides of the *Iron Curtain* signed these agreements.
    - The agreements codified respect for national sovereignty.
    - They acknowledged national borders.
    - Signatories promised to not use force against other nation signatories.
    - They promised nonintervention in the internal affairs of other nations.
    - Signatories agreed to show respect for human rights.
- Détente prevailed in the years that followed.
  - Splits in the ranks of both the Western alliance and Communist Bloc changed relations between the two superpowers, which through the late 1940s to the 1970s had faced off with the support of allies or satellite nations.
  - De Gaulle's France questioned the leadership of the United States in European affairs, just as Mao's China questioned that of the Soviet Union in the Communist world.
  - The military suppression of Czechoslovakia tarnished the Soviet image just as the Vietnam War tarnished the American image.
- A prosperous and independent Western Europe took more and more charge of its own affairs.
- Nationalist resistance in Eastern Europe diminished Soviet influence.
- The Cold War began to thaw.

## The Special Case of Turkey

Turkey poses a special problem in the early part of the 21st century; it lies partially in Europe but mostly in Asia. It has been the traditional and literal crossroads between Asia and Europe for millennia and has had both Asian and

European identities. Turkey must be examined as a political entity for this course because of its impact on the rest of Europe, but is Turkey a part of Europe? That is for the reader to decide as it is a current political question that the Turks themselves have not fully answered. It appears, though, that as their global trade increases, they may be attempting to create their own identity separate from Asia and Europe. The chart of ideas that follows may help you decide where to put Turkey in the camps of civilizations.

## Is Turkey Part of Europe or Not?

| Part of Europe | Not Part of Europe |
| --- | --- |
| Center of Christianity for a thousand years | Majority Muslim |
| Partially in Europe | Majority of nation in Asia |
| Some welfare systems | Many tribal and rural people |
| Modern economy | Crusades separated cultures |
| Industrialized | Ottoman Empire |
| Secular state | Muslim banking system |
| 50% of trade is with Europe | In 1999, 72% of trade was with Europe |
| Democracy | Current leadership most Islamic ever |
| Many centuries of trade with Europe | Thus far prevented from joining European Union |

# The Collapse of Communism and the End of the Cold War

In 1985, the election of *Mikhail Gorbachev* (1931–2022) by the Soviet Communist Party leadership to serve as party general secretary promised fresh blood to reform the ailing economy and to invigorate the party after the stagnation of the Brezhnev era. His policies of *glasnost*, or openness, and *perestroika*, or restructuring, gave the peoples of Eastern Europe hope for a better life. The facade of Soviet power crumbled, leaving the people ready for bigger changes. An intended reformer, Gorbachev became the agent of an unintended and unexpected revolution that led to the collapse of communism and the dissolution of the world order that had reigned since the end of the Second World War.

- In 1987, two years after he took office, Chairman Gorbachev and President Ronald Reagan signed the *INF Treaty*, which began the delicate and dangerous process of nuclear disarmament with the destruction of all short- and intermediate-range nuclear missiles.
- Two years after that, the U.S.S.R. withdrew from the *War in Afghanistan*.
- The Soviets were defeated by the local militias, the mujahidin, who were funded and armed by the American government through agents such as Osama bin Laden.
- Gorbachev's *perestroika*, or restructuring of the economy, and his policy of *glasnost*, or openness, seemed to be moving Soviet communism toward reform.
- The NATO nations engaged in a military buildup in the 1980s. In addition, massive television broadcasts were sent throughout Iron Curtain countries, implying American capitalist life was like that seen on the television shows *Dallas* and *The Jeffersons*. These acted as effective propaganda that destroyed the social belief in the Communist system.
  - Systemic corruption and party privilege also played huge roles in destroying faith in the Communist system.
  - Even the brutal suppression by the state police, such as the Stasi in East Germany or the KGB in the U.S.S.R., could not prevent the people in Warsaw Pact nations from revolting.
- The *collapse of the Soviet Union* in 1989 marked a very important change in the European balance of power.
  - With the collapse of the Eastern Bloc in the 1990s, the Cold War is said to have ended.

- The Soviet regime was overturned throughout Eastern Europe in mostly bloodless revolutions.
- The Supreme Soviet lost power to the *Congress of People's Deputies.*
  - The new body demanded greater reforms.
  - The Soviet Union was dissolved.
  - A bloody coup might have occurred if Moscow mayor *Boris Yeltsin* (1931–2007) had not intervened to ease tensions.
  - Many nations were formed from the former Soviet Union: Turkmenistan, Ukraine, and Georgia.
- Communism was rejected as a failure throughout the Continent.
- China was left as the only major Communist power.
- The United States, after the dissolution of the Soviet Union, became the sole superpower.
  - The Cold War gave a focus to the amorphous conflict and competition among Earth's peoples, and decades of waging this conflict seemed to establish some rational limitations to winning it.
  - The two main protagonists managed to keep the peace between themselves for nearly a half century.
  - Despite its repressiveness and creaky inefficiencies, Soviet communism helped to restrain the uglier expressions of narrow nationalism and ethnic rivalries.
- *Solidarity*, the Polish trade union movement led by Lech Walesa (1943–), opposed the rigid Communist government.
  - *Solidarity* was suppressed under martial law.
  - Walesa was swept into office by the first free elections in Poland since before the Second World War.
- Changes in the Communist governments of Hungary, Bulgaria, and Czechoslovakia took place over the next several months.
  - In November of 1989, the *Berlin Wall*, symbol of Communist oppression, was breached.
- The fall of the Berlin Wall marked the beginning of the downfall of the Communist East German government.
  - Violent revolution in Romania overthrew the longtime Communist dictatorship there.
  - Free elections established non-Communist governments in many of the old Eastern European satellites.
- In October of 1990, *Germany reunited.* Despite fears of a resurgent and aggressive united Germany, Gorbachev allowed the union of West and East Germany without the promise of its neutrality.
  - Germany joined NATO. Less than a year later, the Warsaw Pact, its Communist counterpart, was dissolved.

The *Cold War officially ended* in November 1990 when Soviet, U.S., and Western European leaders signed the *Paris Charter for a New Europe.*

## Timeline for the Start of the Cold War

What follows is a detailed timeline of the Cold War. The table provides more than enough information about the era to answer any questions that may appear on the AP exam.

| Year | Event |
|------|-------|
| 1945–1947 | ■ Communist-agitated strikes in Western Europe and takeovers of governments in Eastern Europe, contrary to Stalin's previous promises, worsened relations between the former Second World War Allies, the United States, and the U.S.S.R. |
| 1947 | ■ The *Truman Doctrine* was announced, pledging military aid to Greece, Turkey, and any other nation threatened with Communist aggression and expansion. |
| 1948 | ■ A Soviet *blockade of Berlin*—the former capital city administered by the four occupying powers but deep within the Russian zone—was countered by the *Berlin Airlift*.<br>■ The Soviets initiated the blockade to retaliate for the unification of the American, British, and French zones into West Germany. |
| 1948 | ■ The *European Recovery Plan* (Marshall Plan) went into effect; the Soviets, although invited, declined to participate and forbade their satellites to do so. |

| Year | Event |
|------|-------|
| 1949 | ▪ *NATO* was established along with regional military alliances in the Middle East, Southeast Asia, and the Southwest Pacific.<br>▪ After nearly two decades of civil war, the Chinese Communists, led by *Mao Tse-tung (Mao Zedong)* (1893–1976) and aided by the U.S.S.R., defeated the corrupt regime of *Chiang Kai-shek's Nationalists*, despite the Nationalists receiving massive U.S. military aid.<br>▪ Mao's forces drove Chiang Kai-shek's forces from the Chinese mainland to the island of *Formosa (Taiwan)*.<br>▪ The United States opposed the recognition of the Communist government of Mao and, instead, recognized the Nationalist Chinese government of Chiang Kai-shek in Taiwan. |
| 1950 | ▪ The Korean War (1950–1953) was the first major military conflict between the West and the Communists. After the Japanese withdrew from the Korean Peninsula, Korea was governed in the north by a government backed by the Soviets and Communist Chinese. South of the 38th parallel, the Korean government was backed by the United States and the United Nations.<br>▪ The Soviets rejected free elections for a unified Korea and, instead, supported a satellite regime under Kim Il Sung.<br>▪ In June 1950, a powerful North Korean army, supported by Soviet aid, invaded south of the 38th parallel and appeared to have won a quick victory.<br>▪ President Truman, determined not to repeat the pre–Second World War policy of appeasement, convinced the United Nations Security Council to condemn North Korean aggression and oppose North Korea militarily.<br>▪ Since the Russians were boycotting the United Nations for failing to recognize Communist China, they could not veto the proposal. A U.N. force led by General Douglas MacArthur (1880–1964) made up of mostly U.S. troops landed in South Korea. Mostly token contingents were provided by 15 other nations.<br>▪ The U.N. force advanced northward until hundreds of thousands of Chinese Communist troops counterattacked in November 1950, driving the U.N. forces back to the 38th parallel.<br>▪ General MacArthur insisted on attacking China itself.<br>▪ President Truman, fearful of involving the United States in an Asian land war, removed MacArthur from command. |
| 1951 | ▪ A cease-fire ended serious fighting in July 1951. |
| 1953 | ▪ The Korean War pitted United States forces against a Communist foe supported and aided by the Soviet Union. Despite the losses of 36,574 U.S. soldiers and almost 3 million Koreans and Chinese, the war convinced the United States that its military might could contain the spread of communism.<br>▪ Neither the European democracies, preoccupied with rebuilding their shattered nations, nor the large non-Communist Asian nations of India, Burma, and Indonesia, which were mistrustful of a new kind of Western imperialism, shared the enthusiasm of the United States.<br>▪ The death of Stalin thawed the Cold War.<br>▪ Tensions rose, relaxed, and then returned again. However, peaceful coexistence seemed possible.<br>▪ An armistice, returning the Koreas to the situation before the war, was signed in 1953. |
| 1955 | ▪ The Geneva Summit involving President Dwight Eisenhower, the British and French prime ministers, and Soviet leaders led to a conciliatory atmosphere. |
| 1956 | ▪ War in the Middle East, between Israel and its Arab neighbors, renewed tensions between the Soviets, who aided the Arab states, and the West, who supported Israel. (France, Britain, and Israel invaded Egypt for its nationalizing of the Suez Canal and captured the canal.)<br>▪ The Geneva Accords divided Vietnam into the Communist North Vietnam and the non-Communist South Vietnam. |
| 1959 | ▪ U.S. and Soviet relations soured further when Fidel Castro, an avowed Marxist, was openly aided by Soviet and Chinese Communists in his overthrow of Cuban dictator Fulgencio Batista. |
| 1960 | ▪ The Paris Summit ended when Khrushchev proved that the United States had been flying spy missions over the U.S.S.R. after a U-2 high-altitude reconnaissance plane was shot down over Soviet territory.<br>▪ The U.S.S.R. became capable of launching nuclear ICBM missiles. |
| 1961 | ▪ The Bay of Pigs invasion of Cuba by anti-Castro Cuban refugees was a total disaster and a humiliation for newly elected president John F. Kennedy, whose administration supported it.<br>▪ The infamous Berlin Wall, as powerful a symbol of Soviet tyranny as the Bastille had been of royal abuses, was erected. |

| Year | Event |
|------|-------|
| 1962 | ■ The first U.S. troops, called "military advisers," arrived in South Vietnam to shore up its anti-Communist government against attacks by Communist North Vietnamese infiltrators and South Vietnamese Vietcong guerrillas.<br>■ The Cuban Missile Crisis brought the world to the brink of nuclear war when President Kennedy demanded that Premier Khrushchev remove nuclear missiles the Soviets had installed in Cuba.<br>■ The "eyeball-to-eyeball" confrontation ended when the Russian bases were dismantled. |
| 1963 | ■ A nuclear test ban treaty to stop atmospheric explosions was signed by three of the world's four nuclear powers: the United States, the U.S.S.R., and Britain. France refused.<br>■ A hotline or direct communication phone was installed between the Kremlin and the White House to prevent accidental nuclear war.<br>■ A rift between the Soviets and Chinese Communists led to growing tensions and a parting of the ways between the two giants. |
| 1964 | ■ Communist China became the fifth member of the *nuclear bomb club*. |
| 1965 | ■ Lyndon Johnson, who succeeded to the presidency after the assassination of Kennedy, bolstered American involvement in the Vietnam conflict by continuing bombing raids against North Vietnam and by sending in a massive ground force.<br>■ The Soviets and Chinese Communists supplied great quantities of arms and other aid to help the North Vietnamese and Vietcong maintain the fight against an eventual U.S. force of well over 500,000 troops. |
| 1968 | ■ *Prague Spring* in Czechoslovakia occurred when the reformist Alexander Dubcek was elected and tried to give his people more civil and economic rights.<br>■ The other Warsaw Pact nations, led by the U.S.S.R., invaded Czechoslovakia with tanks and occupied the country until 1990. |
| 1969 | ■ President Richard Nixon was an avowed anti-Communist in his early political career. During his administration, Nixon and Secretary of State Henry Kissinger pursued a policy of détente, or peaceful coexistence, between the West and the Communist Bloc, although they widened the Vietnam War throughout Southeast Asia. Leaders exchanged visits, and the SALT negotiations (Strategic Arms Limitations Talks) began.<br>■ The United States landed a manned expedition on the moon. |
| 1970 | ■ A nonproliferation treaty to limit the spread of nuclear weapons was signed by the United States and the U.S.S.R.<br>■ Unfortunately, nations with nuclear power plants proved it was possible to reprocess spent fuel in order to make nuclear bombs.<br>■ India became the sixth member of the *nuclear bomb club* in this way in 1974. |
| 1972 | ■ Nixon's dramatic visit to Communist China, followed by scientific and cultural exchanges, established relations between the two former enemies. |

# Art

The period after the Second World War is often referred to as the postmodern period. *Postmodernist* ideas in philosophy and the analysis of culture have drastically influenced works of literature, architecture, and design. They have also reverberated in marketing/business and the interpretation of history, law, and culture. Postmodernism is typified by a reevaluation of the entire Western value system (love, marriage, popular culture, and the shift from an industrial to a service economy). This reevaluation began in the 1950s and 1960s and is reflected in the postmodernist movement. Although the term was popularized by Arnold Toynbee in the 1930s, it is a good way to define the reaction against the functionalism of the *age of anxiety*. Many new artistic forms emerged after the Second World War.

- *Modernism* eliminated ornamentation. It attempted to create clean, uncluttered lines for easy living, as typified by the Bauhaus movement.
- *Postmodernism* revived ornamentation and a personal relationship with art and life.
- *Pop art* emerged to poke fun at the art industry and to make art available and accessible to the common masses. This is typified by the soup cans painted by Andy Warhol.

- *Abstract expressionism*, typified by the works of Jackson Pollock, moved the center of the art world from Paris to New York City in the 1950s. Abstract expressionism was a successor to surrealism and focused on spontaneous or subconscious creation.

## Science

The Second World War changed the way scientists did their work, how they were funded, and where their research was directed. During the war, scientists the world over were employed by their various governments to aid the war effort. Their work led to technological advances, such as the use of atomic energy, the development of radar and jet aircraft, and the advent of computers. New discoveries, inventions, and industries spurred research after the war in both *pure and applied science*.

- New means of funding and organizing the increasingly specialized fields of research led to the advent of *big science*. It stressed teamwork, the combining of theoretical research with engineering techniques, and complex research facilities with professional managers and expensive, sophisticated equipment.
  - The United States took the lead in this area after the Second World War. By the mid-1960s, most scientific research (which doubled the sum of human knowledge every decade) was funded by the U.S. federal government, whose principal aim was defense.
- Many of the best scientists from Europe went to the United States for better wages and budgets in a phenomenon known as the *brain drain*.
- A *space race* between the United States and the U.S.S.R. led to Russia's development in 1957 of the first artificial satellite, *Sputnik*, and to a manned moon landing in 1969 by the United States.
- To stem the brain drain of their best scientists to the United States, European nations began funding their own research programs. The European Union, gaining prominence and focusing on cooperation, did much to stem the brain drain.
  - Cooperative endeavors drew scientists back to Europe in order to use the most advanced tools in the trade. For example, the international laboratory at CERN created the world's largest particle collider, the Large Hadron Collider.
    - Other international projects have led to Europe retaining many of the best minds in science.
    - Many scientists came from America and Asia to work on government-supported projects in Europe thanks, in large part, to the European Union.
- Medical theories and technologies extended life but posed social and moral questions that eluded consensus and crossed religious, political, and philosophical perspectives.
- Advances in genetics and medicine have raised many ethical questions in the last half century.
  - Fertility treatments have allowed couples who could not conceive to do so.
  - Scientific means of fertilization have led to people gaining much more control over when and how they will bear children.
  - Genetic engineering can already detect and sometimes alter genetic maladies in utero.
  - Parents may soon be able to alter their offspring genetically.
  - All of these advances raise a question: How will we use genetic information?

## Population and Poverty

Industrialization, urbanization, attitude changes, and modern contraception lowered the birthrate during this century in Europe and in other areas with developed economies. In the less economically developed countries (LEDCs), including newly independent nations that had been colonial possessions (mostly in Asia and Africa), the population exploded in the second half of the 20th century. Cultural and religious attitudes and economic dependence on large families maintained a high birthrate. Better food production and distribution plus modern medical and sanitation practices led to a decline in death rates. Investments that could have been made to improve the standard of living in these areas were instead used to support the burgeoning populations. Even with population-control programs and a growing women's movement, the problem has continued to get worse.

- The gap between the rich industrialized nations and the less economically developed countries widened.
- When the worldwide recession of the early 1970s caused the West to reduce its aid to the LEDCs, the less developed nations became more militant in demanding a more equitable share of the world's resources and industrial production.
- This was exploited by the Soviet Union. Many Communist movements gained strength and even power in former colonial possessions in Latin America, Africa, and especially Asia.
  - Women in the Soviet Union had a much bigger burden than men because the women were expected to be equal professionally but still had to do all of the traditional women's work at home, such as cooking, child care, elder care, and cleaning.
  - Asian nations China, Vietnam, North Korea, Cambodia, and to some extent Burma (Myanmar) all had or still have some form of Communist leadership.
- The result is a revolution of rising expectations that helps create worldwide political instability.
  - This can be seen in even the nations that still claim to be Communist, such as China and Vietnam.
  - The period after the Cold War saw rising incomes occur globally.

## After the Cold War

- In mid-1991, *Boris Yeltsin*, who was an outspoken and charismatic political rival of Gorbachev, was elected as president of the Soviet Republic of Russia.
  - He ran as an independent candidate on a platform of drastic economic and political reform.
- During that same month, June, *Croatia and Slovenia declared their independence from Yugoslavia*. A civil war, made more brutal by ancient ethnic rivalries, broke out.
- *START,* the Strategic Arms Reduction Treaty, was signed in July of 1991 by Gorbachev and President George H. W. Bush to reduce the number of long-range nuclear missiles of both nations.
  - One month later, old-line party and military leaders launched a coup against the vacationing Gorbachev by sending military units toward Moscow.
  - Within days, the coup collapsed in the face of massive public demonstrations against its leaders.
  - *Latvia, Lithuania,* and *Estonia* declared their independence from the Soviet Union.
  - By late 1991, Russia, Ukraine, and Belarus formed the *Commonwealth of Independent States*, and the Soviet Union effectively ceased to exist.
- By 1993, ethnic rivalries among the former Soviet-controlled republics resulted in a bloody war pitting Serbia and Croatia against their former Yugoslavian brothers Bosnia and Herzegovina.
  - Despite an initial reluctance to get involved in the Balkan crisis, the United States and Western European nations imposed a settlement on the warring factions and prosecuted war criminals in the World Court.
- The nations that comprise NATO all agreed to intervene. Serbian aggression was halted in Bosnia-Herzegovina and Kosovo, Europe's newest country.
- Former Yugoslavia was reorganized into several countries: Serbia, Bosnia-Herzegovina, Croatia, Macedonia, Slovenia, Montenegro, and Kosovo.
- The Yugoslav Wars can be divided into four smaller wars:
  - The Ten-Day War (1991)
  - The Croatian War of Independence (1991–1995)
  - The Bosnian War (1992–1995)
  - The Kosovo War (1998–1999)
- NATO was instrumental in preventing ethnic cleansing during the Yugoslav Wars of the 1990s as Croats, Muslims, and Serbs all tried to eliminate each other in these countries. Over 140,000 people were still killed.

- The collapse of communism in Europe created a *fluid political situation* globally similar to the disruptions of the old orders after the First and Second World Wars.
  - Power shifted; the rules changed. Asia is rising in importance in the 21st century. How will Europe meet that challenge?
- The end of the Cold War diminished the prospects of nuclear war but created new rivalries and unleashed bloody ethnic conflicts to test the resolve of NATO.
- Increasing nationalism combined with old conflicts, plus new wealth and power, made for disruptive situations.
- The allies of the Gulf War Coalition adopted varying policies in the Middle East that often reflected their own economic interests. At the same time, Russia gave tacit support to Iran as the rest of the world attempted to prevent Iran from attaining a nuclear weapon.
- The birth of a new international order also took into account the rising wealth in Asia and growing military power there.

## European Society at the End of the Twentieth Century

After the Second World War, European class distinctions blurred due to unprecedented economic growth in the West and the accompanying opportunities in jobs and in higher education. Western Europeans enjoyed a new social mobility and a greater democratization of their governments. Powerful social changes occurred after the Second World War.

- Education and ability outweighed family connections in reality for the first time ever.
- Health care and other social security programs alleviated traditional class conflicts and promoted greater economic equality.
- General prosperity promoted a *consumer culture*, making big businesses out of such products and services as food, leisure, entertainment, and travel.
- Mass production, new food technologies, and industrial efficiency increased disposable income. They also created a consumer culture in which greater domestic comforts, such as electricity, indoor plumbing, plastics, and synthetic fibers, became available. ·
- Prosperity and increased educational opportunities swelled the middle classes in both Europe and the United States.
- Government policies, such as subsidies for large families and government-run and government-funded child care facilities, encouraged population growth after the Second World War, resulting in a *baby boom*.
- With science and technology wedded by war, *big science*, which was funded by government and industry, created new products and new career opportunities.
  - With greater educational opportunities available to women, more females sought careers outside the home.
  - Cities grew as more agricultural workers left the farms in search of new, more lucrative, and exciting vocations.
- In the 1960s, a youth culture spread globally. This youth culture grew first in the United States from the great numbers of baby boomers, the unparalleled prosperity, and the increased enrollment in higher education.
  - Rebellion against the status quo manifested itself in rock music, the widespread use of illegal drugs, and less rigid sexual attitudes.
  - The materialism of the West encouraged a revolutionary idealism among young people, who participated in the antiwar movement in the United States and in the student radicalism of Europe.
  - Student revolts against rigid educational practices in universities broke out in France (1968) and in other European countries.
- Economic setbacks in the 1970s and 1980s spurred changes in family life.

- In order to maintain the family's standard of living, many women in Europe and the United States went into the workforce.
- Income independence enabled more women to get divorces.
- In Western Europe through the efforts of feminists and in Eastern Europe and the Soviet Union through government policy, women finally gained the vote, greater educational opportunities, and access to careers, even while continuing to face social inequalities.
- Birth control allowed people to plan their families and resulted in a decreased birthrate.
  - *Margaret Sanger*, an American who worked with poor immigrant women as a nurse and who was also a writer, championed the development and dissemination of birth control.
- This newfound independence and a number of gifted female writers, such as *Simone de Beauvoir* in France and *Betty Friedan* in the United States, helped launch a new feminism or a *second wave* of feminism. This new feminism attacked gender inequalities in all aspects of society and used political action and attitude alteration.
  - The dissolution of the Soviet Union and its Communist satellites also led many women, who had lived in those more gender-emancipated cultures, to encourage further emancipation of Western European women.
  - The increasing prevalence of scientific, business, and political leaders who were women, from Rosalind Franklin to Oprah Winfrey to Margaret Thatcher, also did much for the feminist cause.
    - *Margaret Thatcher* was prime minister of the United Kingdom from 1979–1990.
    - *Mary Robinson* was president of Ireland from 1990 to 1997.
    - *Edith Cresson* was prime minister of France for less than a year in 1991.
    - *Rosalind Franklin* was a scientist who is best known for her work in determining the structure of DNA.
    - *Oprah Winfrey* is a world-famous, self-made media executive and talk show host.
  - Moral questions arose about abortion, fertility treatments, and birth control—questions stimulated by the rise of feminism. Europeans generally answered that women should decide for themselves without government interference. These have become more divisive issues in America than in Europe.
  - New modes of marriage, partnership, motherhood, divorce, and reproduction gave women more options in their personal lives.
  - Europeans are more concerned about issues of genetic engineering than Americans are in general.
  - Women still face many social and professional inequalities, such as lower pay for the same work and underrepresentation in management.
  - The 21st century is witness to common bumper stickers that state that feminism is the radical notion that women are people.
- At the dawn of the 21st century, political parties such as the *Green Party* and the Pirate Party advocated for the desires of new generations of Europeans, who want a sustainable system and increased freedoms and social responsibility.
- Organized religion continued to play a role in European social and cultural life regardless of the challenges resulting from world war and ideological conflict, modern secularism, and rapid social changes.
  - Reform in the Catholic Church found expression in the *Second Vatican Council*, which redefined the Church's dogma and practices and started to redefine its relations with other religious communities.
    - It reshaped the Roman Catholic Church to the church it is today.
    - The Second Vatican Council engaged in modern dialogue.
    - It pardoned Galileo.
    - It made attempts at reconciliation with other world religions.
  - Pope John Paul II was originally from Poland, and his support for the Solidarity movement helped to topple communism.

- Increased immigration into Europe altered Europe's religious makeup. This caused debate and conflict over the role of religion in social and political life, particularly in regard to Islam as more Muslim immigrants arrived on the Continent.
  - Many non-Europeans came as *guest workers* after the Second World War and began to create ethnic enclaves in European countries.
  - These workers and their children were not citizens of the countries in which they lived.
  - The Turks in Germany are one example.
  - Because of the economic growth of the 1950s and 1960s, migrant workers from Southern Europe, Asia, and Africa immigrated to Western and Central Europe. However after the economic downturn of the 1970s, these workers and their families often became targets of anti-immigrant agitation and extreme nationalist political parties.
  - Many immigrants now come from Africa and the Middle East.
    - Increasing xenophobia in Europe has resulted in the emergence of modern nationalist parties in many European nations, such as the French National Front in France and the Austrian Freedom Party in Austria.
- Nationalism has remained a potent force in Europe. There has been a continuation and even an increase in the strength of various *separatist movements* in Europe, which have continued to exert pressure for independence or have increased such pressures.
  - Ireland has finally become a completely separate nation from the United Kingdom.
  - The Basque in the Pyrenees Mountains between Spain and France have continued to campaign for independence, both violently and peacefully.
  - The Chechen rebels in Chechnya have been trying to gain independence from Russia for almost two decades.
  - The Scottish held a referendum on separation from the United Kingdom in 2015 but decided to stay.
  - Some Flemish have been agitating for independence from Belgium as well.
  - Nationalism has also allowed some far-right parties to gain power in nations like Hungary and Austria in reaction to the increase in immigrants from Africa and the Muslim world.
  - Anti-immigrant political parties that use populist and nationalist messaging have gained power and prestige in the first decades of the 21st century.

# Recent Developments

The 1990s marked powerful political and economic changes in Europe, comparable in magnitude to those at the end of the two world wars. After the collapse of Communist governments in the former Soviet Union and its Cold War satellites, a new order emerged. The modern era saw a growth of European unity after the Second World War, which included the creation of a common market and the European Union.

## Rise of the European Union

From the modest start at the Treaty of Rome in 1957, the European Union (EU) has become a significant world player whose presidency has risen from a ceremonial role to a meaningful one with a significant budget. The establishment of the European Union in 1993 was met with some skepticism, and it has faced challenges such as the exit of Great Britain in the Brexit in 2020. However, the single currency, the *euro*, has been incredibly stable and the EU has continued to expand in the start of the 21st century.

The Maastricht Treaty introduced the euro as a single currency and outlined plans for a European political union. The Lisbon Treaty, signed in 2007 and entering into force in 2009, further streamlined EU decision-making processes and enhanced the role of the European Parliament.

The EU presidency is a rotating position held by a member state for six months. It involves coordinating and representing the EU at international summits and overseeing the Council of the European Union's legislative agenda. The presidency plays a crucial role in shaping the EU's agenda and ensuring the smooth functioning of its institutions.

The EU has evolved into a major global player, advocating for peace, democracy, and human rights. It has significantly contributed to economic growth, social progress, and environmental protection in Europe and beyond. With its expanding membership and deepening integration, the EU continues to shape the future of Europe and the world.

- Germany united completely and peacefully (although with unforeseen complications that came from the need to absorb the formerly Communist East Germany). Germany set up its capital in Berlin once again and became the most powerful economy in Europe, a status it had not held since the end of the Second World War.
    - There was some inequality between the former East Germany and West Germany as it took a long time to reindustrialize the antiquated systems and training of the former East Germans.
    - With Berlin once again named national capital, the houses of the Reichstag and the Bundesrat were moved there.
- Poland, Hungary, and the Czech Republic established democratic governments, instituted capitalist reforms of their economies, and joined NATO.
- Independence movements from the Serb-dominated Yugoslavian government in Belgrade degenerated into bitter and bloody struggles among various ethnic groups (Serbs, Croats, Bosnians, Kosovars, Montenegrins, and Albanians) and revived the specter of *genocide* in the form of *ethnic cleansing*.
    - The intervention of NATO resulted in a precarious peace and in the prosecution of Slobodan Milosevic, Serbian president, and other Serbian leaders for war crimes.
- Russia, the largest, richest, and most populous republic of the former Soviet Union, grappled with a faltering economy, a fitful start to democratization (widespread corruption during Boris Yeltsin's presidency tainted the effort), and a bloody ethnic war with Chechnya.
    - The replacement of Yeltsin by Vladimir Putin as president promised reform, a renewed *détente* with the West, and a more enlightened role for Russia in regional and world affairs.
    - Many promises were not kept.
        - Putin used power as a tool to enrich himself and his cronies.
        - *Oligarchs* became immensely rich businessmen with ties to the former Communist Party.
    - Putin is widely regarded as decreasing freedom and opportunity in Russia.
        - Putin and his former KGB connections enriched themselves through corruption.
    - Vladamir Putin was temporarily replaced as president in 2008 by Dmitri Medvedev but remained a key power holder.
    - Putin was reelected as president in 2012.
- The *9/11 Terrorist Attacks* against the United States in 2001 marked the beginning of a new international era more dangerous to world peace and stability than at any time since the height of the Cold War.
    - Widespread poverty in the less economically developed countries (LEDCs) and ethnic rivalries all over the globe have fostered religious fanaticism and conflict, such as that in the Middle East between Israelis and Palestinians.
    - Anti-Muslim xenophobia in Europe has resulted in laws like those that ban female face coverings in French public spaces.
- A huge financial crisis occurred in 2007–2008.
    - A housing bubble in the United States imploded in 2006 and caused a large global financial crisis.
    - Brought on by high-risk lending, the securitization of mortgages, and the irresponsibility of banks, this economic failure in the United States soon spread to Europe, where banks were heavily invested in the U.S. housing market through mortgages and securities.

- Banks in many European nations failed. Iceland, Ireland, Spain, Portugal, Greece, and Cyprus experienced deep economic crises due in large part to these bank failures, high national debt, and deficit spending.
- As credit became more expensive after the financial crisis, these national economies, the European Union, and the euro became vulnerable.
- In June of 2016, the United Kingdom voted to leave the European Union in an event commonly referred to as *Brexit*. This change in the ongoing trend toward European unity marks a drastic change in the political and financial momentum of unity that was observed in Europe from the 1980s until 2016. The negotiation process for the United Kingdom to leave the EU was long and protracted. It led to a change in prime ministers from Theresa May to Boris Johnson because the people of the U.K. thought he could get a better deal from the EU In the end the U.K. had a second snap election in 2019 that led to a conservative victory for Boris Johnson that ratified a Brexit deal.  This has weakened the EU with the departure of the second largest economy, net budget contributor, and third most populous nation. The trend of revival of European nationalism is one to watch in the coming years.

- In 2014, Russia invaded the Ukraine and annexed the Crimean Peninsula. The international community has been impotent in protecting the international sovereignty of Ukraine, emboldening Russia to act to influence the politics of other nations.
- Some sanctions have been put in place, but Russian forces exert more and more control over Ukraine each year.

Up to this point, the European landscape has changed a number of times. Wars were fought, and accords were signed. The next section is a quick summary of the important treaties and agreements that have molded the European continent.

## Important Treaties and Agreements in European History

### The Peace of Augsburg (1555)

This treaty ended the religious wars in the Holy Roman Empire and the surrounding area, including the Habsburg-Valois Wars. The Holy Roman Emperor (Charles V) lost the power of choosing the religion of the Germanic peoples as he allowed each German prince to choose the religion of his people (Catholicism or Lutheranism). It was a major victory for Lutherans, but Calvinism and other forms of Protestantism were not tolerated.

### The Peace of Westphalia (1648)

This treaty ended the Thirty Years' War, which began with the Defenestration of Prague in 1618. It was a treaty made among France, the Holy Roman Emperor (HRE), miscellaneous German principalities, Sweden, and Holland. France emerged as a powerful force in Germanic politics and took another step toward its longtime policy of keeping Germany divided. Ironically, the French regent, Cardinal Richelieu, had France fight with Protestant forces against Catholic Austria in the war, and the treaty gave freedom to more Protestants. In many ways, it was an extension of the Peace of Augsburg but allowed Calvinism in Germanic states. It was a checkmate to the Counter-Reformation. The HRE lost the Swiss cantons and the Dutch. France gained parts of Alsace and Lorraine. Over 300 German states attained the right to conduct their own diplomacy and make treaties with foreign powers. The Holy Roman Empire was badly weakened and was forbidden from making laws, levying taxes, and recruiting soldiers without consent of the imperial estates. Sweden got the bishoprics of Bremen and Verden and the west half of Pomerania, including Stettin. *The treaty weakened the Holy Roman Empire to the point that it became almost inconsequential.*

## The Peace (Treaty) of Utrecht (1714)

This treaty, which ended the War of Spanish Succession, was made between France on one side and Britain, Austria, miscellaneous German principalities, Sweden, and Holland on the other. Spain's colonial holdings were divided among the victors, and the thrones of Spain and France were never to be united. This treaty was a final loss for Louis XIV as his wars came to an end. The British got Gibraltar and Minorca as well as the right of the assiento (exclusive right to sell slaves to Spanish colonies in the New World). The Duke of Savoy (also known as Piedmont) attained Sardinia, which became the *Kingdom of Sardinia.* (Italy would eventually unite around the Kingdom of Sardinia.) Austria got Milan, Naples, Sicily, and the Spanish Netherlands (soon to be Belgium). Louis XIV's grandson was crowned Philip V of Spain but had to promise never to unite the kingdoms of Spain and France. Britain gained Newfoundland, Nova Scotia, and the Hudson Bay Territory from France. France kept Louis's gains in Franche-Comte and Alsace-Lorraine. The Grand Duchy of Brandenburg became the *Kingdom of Prussia.*

## Treaty of Aix-La-Chapelle (1748)

This treaty ended the eight-year-long War of the Austrian Succession. It was signed by France, Austria, and Prussia. The treaty recognized Frederick the Great's annexation of Silesia.

Austria kept Belgium for a buffer zone to protect the Dutch from the French. The treaty demonstrated the weakness of France under Louis XV.

## Peace of Paris (1763)

This treaty ended the Seven Years' War involving Britain, Spain, and France that began in 1756. (This war was called the French and Indian War in Colonial America.) The treaty ended the first war to be fought on three continents. In fact, the Seven Years' War has been termed the first truly global war. France gave all French territory in North America east of the Mississippi to Britain. Canada became a British possession. France gave all holdings west of the Mississippi to Spain. France was prohibited from building forts or negotiating with princes in India but could still trade there. France kept Guadeloupe and Martinique but did not want competition there anyway. This treaty resulted in British domination of international trade. At this point in history, Britain was undisputedly the most important naval power in the world. France realized that it could not simultaneously fight in Europe and overseas due to lack of resources and naval power.

## The Congress of Vienna (1815)

This treaty completely overhauled European borders and involved Castlereagh for Great Britain, Metternich for Austria, and Talleyrand for France. The Congress of Vienna ended the Napoleonic Wars and affected every nation in Europe. France, which was the belligerent power, was divided and penalized after European conquest. The Congress of Vienna occurred in three stages.

**The First Peace of Paris:** The Allies were lenient to France because they wanted to restore the Bourbons. France kept the borders of 1792, much of which had not been part of France in 1789. The Allies abandoned claims for indemnity. However, Napoleon capitalized on stalled talks at the Congress of Vienna, escaped from Elba, and began to raise an army. He took Paris for 100 days and was finally defeated at Waterloo.

**The second stage:** The Congress of Vienna was a meeting of the victors after the Battle of Nations, when Napoleon was exiled to Elba. The principles of settlement were legitimacy, compensation, and balance of power.

1. The Congress of Vienna established the German Confederation: 38 German provinces with Austria and Prussia.
2. Italy was reorganized.
3. Prussia and Russia were compensated. Alexander I wanted to restore the old kingdom of Poland; Prussia agreed if it could have a large German territory.

4. On January 3, 1815, Britain, Austria, and France made a secret alliance against Russia and Prussia to preserve the balance of power. Russia received a small part of Poland, and Prussia received a small part of the German province.

5. *Battle of Waterloo*, June 1815: Napoleon was defeated by an Anglo-Allied army led by the Duke of Wellington and by Prussians led by von Blücher.

6. Napoleon was exiled to St. Helena.

**The third stage:** This was the "Second" Treaty of Paris. It dealt more harshly with France, imposing a large indemnity, and loss of some minor territories.

1. France had to cede lots of land back to the Netherlands, Sardinia, Prussia, and the Germanic Confederation.
2. France was restricted to the boundaries of 1790.
3. Seventeen fortresses on the north and east frontiers were to be garrisoned for not more than five years by Allied troops. France had to pay their expenses.
4. France had to pay 700,000,000 francs for the cost of the war.
5. Art treasures that France had taken from all over Europe had to be returned to their rightful owners.

## Treaty of Frankfurt (1871)

This treaty ended the Franco-Prussian War. Alsace and Lorraine were ceded to Germany. German nationalism grew and prevailed, just as Bismarck had predicted. Germany became united as a result of this war, and Kaiser Wilhelm I was crowned emperor in the Hall of Mirrors at Versailles.

## Treaty of Nanking (1842)

This was a very unequal treaty forced upon China after the First Opium War. This treaty introduced China to the concept of *most favored nation status* because China was forced to grant that status to Great Britain.

1. The treaty abolished the trade system carried out in Canton.
2. Five ports were opened to the British: Nanking, Ningbo, Shanghai, Xiamen, and Fuzhou.
3. China paid $21 million in indemnities to Great Britain.
4. The British received Hong Kong until 1997, when it was given back to China.

## Treaty of Brest-Litovsk (1917)

This treaty took Russia out of the First World War. Lenin was forced to give up a quarter of Russian territory and a third of the Russian population in exchange for immediate peace in order to fulfill his promises to the Russian people and organize his new Socialist state.

## Treaty of Versailles (1919)

- The Paris Peace Conference of 1919 was set up to create a lasting peace after the First World War.
- The Big Three plus Italy's Vittorio Orlando, who was the president of the conference, participated. The members of the Big Three were David Lloyd George (Britain), George Clemenceau (France), and Woodrow Wilson (United States).

1. The Central Powers were excluded from the negotiations.
2. France was concerned mainly with its future security and reparations.
3. Wilson gave up his famous Fourteen Points for self-determination and the League of Nations.
4. The United States refused to ratify the treaty and did not participate in the League of Nations.
5. The Treaty of Versailles of 1919 mandated for former colonies and territories of the Central Powers to go to Allied countries.

6. Article 231 placed sole blame for the First World War on Germany. Germany would be severely punished:

   a. Germany was forced to pay huge reparations to Britain and France ($33 billion, which is over $500 billion in 2014 dollars).
   b. The German army and navy were severely reduced.
   c. The Rhineland would be demilitarized.
   d. The Saar coal mines were taken over by France.
   e. Germany lost all its colonies.

## Nazi-Soviet Nonaggression Pact (August 1939)

The world was shocked that Germany and the Soviet Union, which were two natural enemies, agreed not to attack each other. In this pact, they also agreed to a plan to divide Poland.

## Atlantic Charter (1941)

This was an agreement between FDR and Winston Churchill that an eventual peace to World War Two would be based on sovereign rights and self-government for countries deprived of them by the Nazis. Equal access to world trade and resources was also guaranteed.

## United Nations Created (1945)

All anti-Axis powers met in San Francisco to establish the United Nations, an international organization to promote peace and global well-being and to prevent another world war. The United States joined along with most countries in the world. The five most powerful nations (United States, United Kingdom, France, China, and U.S.S.R.) were made permanent members of the U.N. security council with veto powers on all security decisions.

## General Agreement on Tariffs and Trade (1948)

The United States convinced other countries to reduce trade restrictions on a bilateral basis, forming the General Agreement on Tariffs and Trade (GATT) in 1948. It began with 23 nations and expanded to 100 in the 1990s.

## North Atlantic Treaty Organization (1949)

The North Atlantic Treaty Organization (NATO) was created by the former Allies that were capitalist countries as a way to deter threats from the Soviet Union and her satellite states. NATO was a part of the Cold War and helped draw the lines between Communist and democratic nations. Some former Communist nations joined after the fall of the Berlin Wall in 1989.

## Warsaw Pact (1955)

This was a Soviet alliance created to counter NATO. It helped to continue the Cold War, included all Soviet satellite states, and saw a further ideological split between Eastern and Western Europe.

## Treaty of Rome (1957)

In 1957, this treaty created the European Economic Community (EEC), an international organization dedicated to creating a common market and the integration of European economies. The founding members were Belgium, France, Italy, Luxembourg, the Netherlands, and West Germany. Later, Spain, Denmark, Ireland, Greece, Portugal, and the United Kingdom joined. The admission of the United Kingdom was at first opposed by French president Charles de Gaulle, so the United Kingdom did not join the European Economic Community until 1973.

## Merger Treaty (1965)

The Merger Treaty (also known as the Brussels Treaty) combined the European Coal and Steel Community, the European Economic Community, and the European Atomic Energy Commission into a single institution called the European Economic Community. Some regard this as the beginning of the European Union that was formally created in 1993 after the Treaty of Maastricht came into effect.

## Treaty of Maastricht (1991)

This treaty created the European Union (EU) and established the rules for a single currency, the euro. A single currency (monetary union) was seen as a step toward political unity to come. Some Europeans opposed a monetary union, partly because of fears of a centralized bureaucracy and partly because of fears of cuts in social benefits.

# Practice Questions

## Long Essay

These questions are samples of the various types of thematic essays on the AP exam. See pages 27–28 for a detailed explanation of each type. Check over the generic rubric (see pages 28–29) before you begin any of these essays, and use that rubric to score your essay if you write one.

## Question 1

Evaluate the changing role of NATO in the defense of Western Europe from 1949–2019.

## Comments on Question 1

This question tests the *change and continuity over time* (CCOT) skill. Be sure to describe the level of historical continuity and change. For historical continuity, you can describe how the role of NATO stayed the same from its creation until the present. For change, you can describe how the role of NATO has changed over that same time period. Explain the reasons for the continuity and change by giving specific examples of what changed and what NATO did after the Cold War ended compared to NATO's role during the Cold War.

NATO seems to have averted an invasion of Western Europe after its inception. The stationing of hundreds of thousands of American troops as well as bases and nuclear weapons on European soil not only aided the Western Europeans in their defense but enabled them to invest in their economies the huge sums otherwise needed for defense. The United States also gave billions of dollars to other NATO powers to build up their military forces, and U.S. bases boosted their local economies. NATO needs to be evaluated not just for its success but for the threat of nuclear war that the ideological conflict between the United States and the Soviet Union held over the world. The changing role of NATO as the Cold War ended must be evaluated. The actions in former Yugoslavia as well as the changing political role of NATO should be assessed. The expansion of NATO to countries formerly in the Soviet sphere, such as Poland, should be examined for costs and benefits. Finally, the invasion of the Ukraine and the lack of any NATO support as Ukraine's people were clamoring to join the EU should be examined as well as the declining role of NATO as the military might of China rises and that of Europe wanes.

## Question 2

Analyze the movement toward economic union in Western Europe.

### Comments on Question 2

This question tests the *change and continuity over time* (CCOT) skill. Be sure to describe the level of historical continuity and change. For historical continuity, describe how the level of European unity stayed the same from 1945 until the present. For change, describe how Europe has become more unified in that same time period. Explain the continuity and change through specific examples, such as what changed from a time when Europe was united into two separate camps, the Warsaw Pact and NATO, and how the end of the Cold War and the creation of the European Union (EU) has affected European unity for the entire continent. Be sure to include a discussion of those states not included in the EU.

Recall that the Marshall Plan inspired the Organization for European Economic Cooperation. Did this set the tone for the Schuman and Monnet Plan? What was the European Coal and Steel Community? How did it evolve into the Common Market? Who were the Common Market's first members? What was the role of the French in delaying British membership? How has European consolidation gone beyond the economic sphere? How did all of this lead to the creation of the European Union and the euro? How did the Treaty of Maastricht come about? How has the development of the euro strengthened the European Union? How has the EU hurt unity? Who has been excluded? How has NATO been affected? What about the recent movement away from union with Brexit and growing nationalism in Europe again? Will nationalism once again trump internationalism?

## Question 3

Compare the status of the Eastern European satellites before and in the two decades after the death of Stalin.

### Comments on Question 3

This is clearly a *compare* skill question. Be sure to describe the similarities and differences between the Eastern European satellites both under Stalin and in the 20 years after his death, 1953–1974. Also account for or explain why they were so different by providing specific examples of how the nations were ruled differently. It is also important to evaluate the significance of these changes. This question could also be handled as a *change and continuity over time* (CCOT) question. In that case, you should describe what in the satellite states remained the same and what changed after Stalin died. Also account for why these changes occurred; include reasons other than the death of Stalin.

Either way, you must explain that Eastern Europe before the Soviet takeover after the Second World War was an agricultural, not an industrial, region. How did land redistribution and Soviet-type five-year plans change this? What was the political situation for the satellites? How did the East Berlin riots of 1953 set a new precedent in the relations between the Soviets and their satellites?

How did *de-Stalinization* help precipitate revolts in Poland and Hungary in 1956? How did these revolts affect the political and economic reform of Eastern Europe? How did the suppression of Czechoslovakia in 1968 diminish the Third World's opinion of the Soviet reputation as anti-imperialistic? What changed and what remained the same after Stalin's death?

## Question 4

Analyze how and why the Cold War gradually thawed.

### Comments on Question 4

This is a *causation* question because it requires you to explain *how* and *why* the Cold War generally thawed; it asks what *caused* the Cold War to thaw. Remember to describe the causes and effects of the thawing of the Cold War, indicating the degree to which it was caused by each factor by citing specific evidence. Remember to explain the reasons *why* the Cold War thawed over time.

The death of Stalin cannot be underestimated as an influence. Be aware, though, that while the *cult of personality* diminished in Soviet political life, the edifices of the totalitarian state remained. The so-called thaw involved a number of "quick-freeze" crises. The realization that any nuclear confrontation would destroy humanity (or at least reduce the global standard of living) and the mutually assured destruction (MAD) theory led both powers to be more conciliatory.

The summit meetings played an invaluable role in decreasing tensions between the superpowers. The Cuban Missile Crisis may have alerted the United States and the U.S.S.R. to the ultimate disaster that *brinksmanship* could lead to. The year 1963 was significant in that the Test Ban Treaty was signed and the monolithic Communist bloc cracked with the Soviet-Chinese rift. Nixon's policy of détente, despite the Vietnam War, was a giant step. The Nonproliferation Treaty and the SALT treaties were also significant.

The growing gap between the standard of living enjoyed by citizens of Western capitalist countries, compared to the standard of living endured by citizens of Communist nations, should be assessed as another cause of the thaw in the Cold War. The broadcast of the capitalist standard of living on television and radio around the world also helped persuade those living in Communist nations that capitalism was a better system of production.

## Question 5

To what extent and in what ways did Gorbachev's reforms bring about the dissolution of the U.S.S.R.?

### Comments on Question 5

This is another *causation* question because it requires you to decide to what extent Gorbachev's reforms *caused* the dissolution of the Soviet Union. Remember to describe the causes and effects of the thawing of the dissolution of the Soviet Union. By citing specific evidence to support your claims, indicate the degree to which the dissolution was caused by Gorbachev's reforms. Explain reasons why these changes took place. How important were his reforms in the process? Which ones affected it? Consider both *perestroika* and *glasnost*. Be sure to show how their degree of success or failure brought about the final breakdown. Consider Gorbachev's repudiation of the Brezhnev Doctrine. Would the U.S.S.R. have dissolved without Gorbachev's reforms?

## Question 6

Assess the causes of the economic crisis of the 1970s.

### Comments on Question 6

This is another *causation* question because it requires you to assess what *caused* the economic crisis of the 1970s. Remember to describe the causes and effects of the thawing of the crisis. Indicate the degree to which it was caused by each factor identified, citing specific evidence to support your claims. Explain the reasons why these changes took place or why they caused certain other effects. Trace the causes and determine the relationships of the world monetary crisis and the OPEC oil embargoes in bringing about the regional stagflation of the 1970s. The reasons for the embargoes, such as Western support for Israel, should be examined. This essay must examine the changing structures of the world economy and financial system seen in the 1970s—from Bretton-Woods to the end of the gold standard and the results of those changes.

## Question 7

How did the entrance of great numbers of women into the workplace alter European society?

### Comments on Question 7

This question tests the *change and continuity over time* (CCOT) skill. Be sure to describe the level of historical continuity (as in what did not change in society when women entered the workforce?) and change (as in what was different after women entered the workforce?). Analyze specific examples of what changed from a time (1850 until 1950) when Europe saw women work mostly in the home and how the entry of women into the workforce affected European society. Be sure to include a discussion of how women were integrated into the workforce and of the movement for women's rights. Relate the *big picture* and describe the specific effects of this powerful trend. How has life changed for the majority of European women? How has this affected the expectations placed on a modern woman? How has the trend affected family, birth rate, divorce, and marriage? How have wages and leisure time been affected? What are the trends in Europe concerning women getting the top positions of power in industry and government? How was the reaction in Iceland to the banking crisis of 2008 a landmark in the rise of female power?

### Short-Answer

1.  Use the excerpt from the speech below and your knowledge of European history to answer all parts of the question that follows.

    **Speech by Secretary of State George Marshall, 1947**

    The truth of the matter is that Europe's requirements for the next three or four years of foreign food and other essential products—principally from America—are so much greater than her present ability to pay that she must have substantial additional help or face economic, social, and political deterioration of a very grave character.

    The remedy lies in breaking the vicious circle and restoring the confidence of the European people in the economic future of their own countries and of Europe as a whole. The manufacturer and the farmer throughout wide areas must be able and willing to exchange their products for currencies the continuing value of which is not open to question.

    Aside from the demoralizing effect on the world at large and the possibilities of disturbances arising as a result of the desperation of the people concerned, the consequences to the economy of the United States should be apparent to all. It is logical that the United States should do whatever it is able to do to assist in the return of normal economic health in the world, without which there can be no political stability and no assured peace. Our policy is directed not against any country or doctrine but against hunger, poverty, desperation, and chaos.

    —George Marshall

    (a)  Briefly explain the plan authored by George Marshall to maintain peace and prosperity after the Second World War.
    (b)  Briefly explain TWO effects of the Marshall Plan discussed in the speech excerpt.

2. Use your knowledge of European history to answer all parts of the following question. Many historians believe that the second half of the 20th century saw increasing liberalism in much of Europe.

   (a) Identify TWO pieces of evidence that support this assertion.
   (b) Identify ONE piece of evidence to refute this assertion.

## Multiple-Choice

**Questions 1–3 refer to the following excerpt from *The Second Sex* by Simone de Beauvoir.**

But first we must ask: what is a woman? 'Tota mulier in utero', says one, 'woman is a womb.' But in speaking of certain women, connoisseurs declare that they are not women, although they are equipped with a uterus like the rest. All agree in recognizing the fact that females exist in the human species; today as always they make up about one half of humanity. And yet we are told that femininity is in danger; we are exhorted to be women, remain women, become women. It would appear, then, that every female human being is not necessarily a woman; to be so considered she must share in that mysterious and threatened reality known as femininity. Is this attribute something secreted by the ovaries? Or is it a Platonic essence, a product of the philosophic imagination? Is a rustling petticoat enough to bring it down to earth? Although some women try zealously to incarnate this essence, it is hardly patentable.

—*The Second Sex* by Simone de Beauvoir, 1949

1. Which of the following movements of the 20th century is being examined in the passage above?

   (A) Totalitarianism
   (B) Nihilism
   (C) Syllogism
   (D) Feminism

2. Which of the following was NOT a goal achieved by women in the 20th century in Europe?

   (A) Women earned equal pay for equal work.
   (B) Women gained suffrage rights.
   (C) Women gained access to higher education.
   (D) Women gained access to new professions.

3. Which of the following innovations was most liberating for women?

   (A) Electrical household appliances
   (B) Women gaining the right to own property
   (C) The example of Soviet women changing Western European women
   (D) Development of the birth control pill

**Questions 4–7 refer to the passage below by British novelist John le Carré.**

It was man who ended the Cold War in case you didn't notice. It wasn't weaponry, or technology, or armies or campaigns. It was just man. Not even Western man either, as it happened, but our sworn enemy in the East, who went into the streets, faced the bullets and the batons and said: we've had enough. It was their emperor, not ours, who had the nerve to mount the rostrum and declare he had no clothes. And the ideologies trailed after these impossible events like condemned prisoners, as ideologies do when they've had their day.

—John le Carré, British novelist, *The Secret Pilgrim*, 1990

4. Which of the following is the best explanation of what the passage has in common with other 20th-century Western European literature like that of Erich Remarque and Franz Kafka?

    (A) It is dark and foreboding, instilling fear.
    (B) It points out the strengths of Western society.
    (C) It questions the values of Western society.
    (D) It attacks Communists as morally weaker than capitalists.

5. The nations of Eastern Europe referred to in the passage were said to lie behind what imaginary structure during the Cold War?

    (A) The fortress of solitude
    (B) The Iron Curtain
    (C) The Berlin Wall
    (D) The red curtain

6. Which of the following is the best description of the end of the Cold War in Eastern Europe?

    (A) The transition from Communist to democratic rule was mostly peaceful but saw ethnic conflict in the Balkans and was violent in Romania.
    (B) The transition from Communist to democratic rule was brutally oppressive with the former Soviets being slaughtered by their new masters almost everywhere.
    (C) The transition from Communist to democratic rule was fought by the leadership of the Soviet Union and all other Communist nations.
    (D) The transition from Communist to democratic rule was never accomplished in much of Eastern Europe.

7. Which of the following policies by Mikhail Gorbachev encouraged public openness and accountability of the government to the people, helping to bring about the changes noted in the passage?

    (A) *Perestroika*
    (B) War communism
    (C) *Do svidaniya*
    (D) *Glasnost*

**Questions 8–10 refer to the following speech given by Fidel Castro.**

With what moral authority can [the U.S.] speak of human rights . . . the rulers of a nation in which the millionaire and beggar coexist; where the Indian is exterminated; the black man is discriminated against; the woman is prostituted; and the great masses of Chicanos, Puerto Ricans, and Latin Americans are scorned, exploited, and humiliated . . . Where the CIA organizes plans of global subversion and espionage, and the Pentagon creates neutron bombs capable of preserving material assets and wiping out human beings.

—Fidel Castro, speech, 1978

8. Which of the following nations would be most likely to support the views of Castro at the time he gave this speech?

(A) Poland
(B) France
(C) Chile
(D) Belgium

9. The Cuban Crisis that occurred 16 years before this speech heightened which of the following effects of the Cold War?

(A) Economic competition between developed and developing nations increased.
(B) The entire world became increasingly afraid of nuclear conflict.
(C) The Soviets fomented revolutions in many Caribbean nations.
(D) The U.S. and U.S.S.R. raced to put a man on the moon.

10. If true, which of the following political parties would agree with the American stance toward racial minorities as Castro describes it?

(A) The French National Front
(B) The Bolshevik Party
(C) The Austrian Green Party
(D) The French Popular Front

# Answers and Explanations

## Short-Answer Explanations

1. (a) You should explain that the United States created the Marshall Plan to offer funds to all participants in the Second World War, funds those nations could use to buy American goods. These goods ranged from agricultural products to heavy equipment and to the machines that run factories in order to prevent further economic turmoil as the world transitioned from a wartime economy to a consumer economy. The offer of funds to nations on both sides of the Iron Curtain should be mentioned. The answer should mention that the nations under the influence of the Soviet Union rejected this offer of funds from the United States.

   (b) You must fully explain *two* of the following: the divide between Eastern (Communist) and Western (free market) Europe after the plan, the rebuilding of Western Europe, the economic miracle in West Germany and/or Japan, the rise of American global power, the elevation of the dollar as the international currency of exchange, the Cold War, the creation of NATO and the Warsaw Pact, the rise of the European Union, and/or the continuation of democracy and the market system in Western Europe.

2. (a) You should identify *two* of the following: the rise of feminism, the end of the death penalty in much of Europe, the rise of socialized medicine, the growing welfare systems in Europe, the fall of the Berlin Wall and the Soviet Union, the spread of democracy, the rise of the Green Party, the rise of environmentalism, the growing acceptance of LGBTQ+ people, decolonization, the increase in protests by citizens of all beliefs being allowed by the rise of the European Union, reducing the criminalization of drug use, changing gender roles, and/or increased worker rights.

   (b) You should identify *one* of the following: growing nationalism at the end of the century, the rise of Vladimir Putin, the reduction of benefits in the United Kingdom under Margaret Thatcher, French actions in Algeria, Charles de Gaulle's putting down of the 1968 protests, the rise of neo-Nazis, the ethnic wars in the former Yugoslavia, the rise of nationalism in the last decade, anti-immigrant sentiment rising in much of Europe in the last decade, or decreasing contributions as a percentage of GDP from European nations to the United Nations.

## Practice Multiple-Choice Questions

1. (A) is wrong because the passage is about feminism as evidenced by the author and statements about femininity and women, not totalitarianism.

   (B) is wrong because the passage is about feminism as evidenced by the author and statements about femininity and women, not nihilism.

   (C) is wrong because the passage is about feminism as evidenced by the author and statements about femininity and women, not syllogism.

   **(D) is CORRECT because the passage is about feminism as evidenced by the author and statements about femininity and women.**

2. **(A) is CORRECT because women have achieved all other goals listed in the answer choices, but still have not attained equal pay for equal work.**

   (B) is wrong because women won the right to vote after the First World War.

   (C) is wrong because women were accepted equally at most universities in Europe after the Second World War.

   (D) is wrong because women did gain access to new professions, such as government, after the Second World War.

3. (A) is wrong because, although electrical household appliances did liberate women from some work, appliances did not change women's biology to give them greater freedom over their reproductive systems as did the birth control pill.

(B) is wrong because women gained the right to own property throughout most of Europe during the 19th century.

(C) is wrong because Western European women were not strongly affected by Soviet women for the most part.

**(D) is CORRECT because the birth control pill gave women greater freedom over their reproductive systems.**

4. (A) is wrong because the excerpt is hopeful rather than dark and foreboding.

(B) is wrong because the excerpt points out a failure of Western society to meet the challenge of the Cold War, while the Soviets are depicted as meeting that challenge.

**(C) is CORRECT because it challenges Western superiority and praises the Communist leader for his courage to speak out against the conflict.**

(D) is wrong because the excerpt praises the Communists.

5. (A) is wrong because the fortress of solitude exists only in Superman's world.

**(B) is CORRECT because the Iron Curtain was the metaphorical divider between the Communist and capitalist regions of Europe.**

(C) is wrong because the Berlin Wall was a real barrier constructed by the Soviets and East Germans to surround West Berlin.

(D) is wrong because the red curtain was made up for this question.

6. **(A) is CORRECT because the transition from Communist to democratic rule was mostly peaceful but saw massive ethnic conflict in the Balkans and was violent in Romania.**

(B) is wrong because there was no massive slaughter of Communists.

(C) is wrong because many Communist nations like Poland welcomed the fall of communism.

(D) is wrong because all of Europe transitioned out of Soviet communism.

7. (A) is wrong because *perestroika*, although a policy of Gorbachev, was not the openness of *glasnost*.

(B) is wrong because war communism played no role in the fall of communism in the Soviet Union.

(C) is wrong because *do svidaniya* means "goodbye" or "farewell" in Russian, and it was not a reform plan of Gorbachev.

**(D) is CORRECT because *glasnost* is a Russian word that means "openness," and Gorbachev's *glasnost* policy opened up the workings of the Soviet government to its people and made them aware of problems within their society and of ways to fix them.**

8. **(A) is CORRECT because Poland was in the Soviet sphere of influence behind the Iron Curtain and thus would support any criticism of the United States.**

(B) is wrong because France would not have openly criticized so much about America, which it valued as an ally.

(C) is wrong because Argentina was ruled by an arch-capitalist dictator, Augusto Pinochet, who was receiving CIA support and was thus in debt to the United States and in political conflict with Castro.

(D) is wrong because the Belgians are close NATO allies and would not publicly criticize the United States like that.

9. (A) is wrong because the Cuban Missile Crisis was about nuclear weapons in Cuba, not about economic conflict.

(B) **is CORRECT because the Cuban Missile Crisis was about nuclear weapons in Cuba and frightened the entire world into being on the brink of nuclear war.**

(C) is wrong because the only successful Soviet-style revolution in the Caribbean was in Cuba.

(D) is wrong because the Cuban Missile Crisis was about nuclear weapons in Cuba, not about putting a man on the moon.

10. (A) **is CORRECT because the French Nationalist Front is against immigrants and is widely seen as racist toward Muslims in France.**

(B) is wrong because, although the Bolsheviks did liquidate minorities under Stalin, it was never party policy to put any nationality above another.

(C) is wrong because the Green Party is antidiscriminatory.

(D) is wrong because the French Popular Front, a political party led by Leon Blum during the Depression, was socialist in nature but not discriminatory.

Visit Barron's Online Learning Hub to take the Time Period Four (1914 to Present) Practice Assessment

# PART 3
# Practice Exams

# ANSWER SHEET
## Practice Test 1

**Section 1**

1. Ⓐ Ⓑ Ⓒ Ⓓ
2. Ⓐ Ⓑ Ⓒ Ⓓ
3. Ⓐ Ⓑ Ⓒ Ⓓ
4. Ⓐ Ⓑ Ⓒ Ⓓ
5. Ⓐ Ⓑ Ⓒ Ⓓ
6. Ⓐ Ⓑ Ⓒ Ⓓ
7. Ⓐ Ⓑ Ⓒ Ⓓ
8. Ⓐ Ⓑ Ⓒ Ⓓ
9. Ⓐ Ⓑ Ⓒ Ⓓ
10. Ⓐ Ⓑ Ⓒ Ⓓ
11. Ⓐ Ⓑ Ⓒ Ⓓ
12. Ⓐ Ⓑ Ⓒ Ⓓ
13. Ⓐ Ⓑ Ⓒ Ⓓ
14. Ⓐ Ⓑ Ⓒ Ⓓ

15. Ⓐ Ⓑ Ⓒ Ⓓ
16. Ⓐ Ⓑ Ⓒ Ⓓ
17. Ⓐ Ⓑ Ⓒ Ⓓ
18. Ⓐ Ⓑ Ⓒ Ⓓ
19. Ⓐ Ⓑ Ⓒ Ⓓ
20. Ⓐ Ⓑ Ⓒ Ⓓ
21. Ⓐ Ⓑ Ⓒ Ⓓ
22. Ⓐ Ⓑ Ⓒ Ⓓ
23. Ⓐ Ⓑ Ⓒ Ⓓ
24. Ⓐ Ⓑ Ⓒ Ⓓ
25. Ⓐ Ⓑ Ⓒ Ⓓ
26. Ⓐ Ⓑ Ⓒ Ⓓ
27. Ⓐ Ⓑ Ⓒ Ⓓ
28. Ⓐ Ⓑ Ⓒ Ⓓ

29. Ⓐ Ⓑ Ⓒ Ⓓ
30. Ⓐ Ⓑ Ⓒ Ⓓ
31. Ⓐ Ⓑ Ⓒ Ⓓ
32. Ⓐ Ⓑ Ⓒ Ⓓ
33. Ⓐ Ⓑ Ⓒ Ⓓ
34. Ⓐ Ⓑ Ⓒ Ⓓ
35. Ⓐ Ⓑ Ⓒ Ⓓ
36. Ⓐ Ⓑ Ⓒ Ⓓ
37. Ⓐ Ⓑ Ⓒ Ⓓ
38. Ⓐ Ⓑ Ⓒ Ⓓ
39. Ⓐ Ⓑ Ⓒ Ⓓ
40. Ⓐ Ⓑ Ⓒ Ⓓ
41. Ⓐ Ⓑ Ⓒ Ⓓ
42. Ⓐ Ⓑ Ⓒ Ⓓ

43. Ⓐ Ⓑ Ⓒ Ⓓ
44. Ⓐ Ⓑ Ⓒ Ⓓ
45. Ⓐ Ⓑ Ⓒ Ⓓ
46. Ⓐ Ⓑ Ⓒ Ⓓ
47. Ⓐ Ⓑ Ⓒ Ⓓ
48. Ⓐ Ⓑ Ⓒ Ⓓ
49. Ⓐ Ⓑ Ⓒ Ⓓ
50. Ⓐ Ⓑ Ⓒ Ⓓ
51. Ⓐ Ⓑ Ⓒ Ⓓ
52. Ⓐ Ⓑ Ⓒ Ⓓ
53. Ⓐ Ⓑ Ⓒ Ⓓ
54. Ⓐ Ⓑ Ⓒ Ⓓ
55. Ⓐ Ⓑ Ⓒ Ⓓ

# Practice Test 1

## Section I

### Part A: Multiple-Choice Questions

TIME: 55 MINUTES

NUMBER OF QUESTIONS: 55

PERCENTAGE OF TOTAL AP EXAM SCORE: 40%

WRITING INSTRUMENT: PENCIL REQUIRED

---

**DIRECTIONS:** Section I, Part A of this exam contains 55 multiple-choice questions. Indicate all of your answers to the multiple-choice questions on the multiple-choice answer sheet. No credit will be given for anything written in the exam booklet, but you may write on the exam booklet to take notes and do scratch work.

Use your time efficiently, working as quickly as possible without losing accuracy. Do not spend too much time on any one question. Go on to other questions and come back to the ones that you have not answered if you have time. It is not expected that you will know the answers to all of the multiple-choice questions.

Your total score on the multiple-choice section is based only on the number of questions answered correctly. Points are not deducted for incorrect answers or unanswered questions.

**Questions 1–3 refer to the image below.**

Clergy torturing a layman.

1. The illustration illustrates the draconian tactics used at times during which of the following state actions to control religion and morality?

   (A) The ecclesiastical reforms of the Russian Church in the mid-17th century at the behest of the Patriarch Nikon and the czar

   (B) Persecution of the French Huguenots during the late 17th century after Louis XIV issued his Edict of Revocation

   (C) The initiation of Ferdinand and Isabella's Inquisition in 1478 to test the faith of those non-Catholics who converted to Catholicism

   (D) Religious turmoil in England, during the Tudor dynasty, between Catholics and Protestants

2. Religious trials, such as the one shown in the image, usually focused on the persecution of which of the following?

   (A) Recent converts to Christianity

   (B) Those accused of witchcraft

   (C) Christians in the Ottoman Empire

   (D) Calvinists found to have sinned

3. Which of the following is the best characterization of how much control the state has had over the religion and morality of its citizens in Europe from 1450 to the present?

   (A) There has been a steady gain in personal choice in morality and religion.

   (B) There was generally a rise in freedom of choice from 1517 until 1648, but after that, freedom of choice declined for two centuries until it rose recently.

   (C) There has been a general rise in personal freedom of religion and morality free of state control across Europe since the end of the Second World War.

   (D) Degrees of personal choice in morality and religion have gone up and down but have been at an all-time high in Europe since the 21st century began.

**Questions 4–7 refer to the excerpt below.**

I am of opinion that the principal and true profession of the Courtier ought to be that of arms; which I would have him follow actively above all else, and be known among others as bold and strong, and loyal to whomsoever he serves

I would have him well built and shapely of limb, and would have him show strength and lightness and suppleness, and know all bodily exercises that befit a man of war; whereof I think the first should be to handle every sort of weapon well on foot and on horse, to understand the advantages of each, and especially to be familiar with those weapons that are ordinarily used among gentlemen . . .

Our Courtier then will be esteemed excellent and will attain grace in everything, particularly in speaking . . .

I would have him more than passably accomplished in letters, at least in those studies that are called the humanities, and conversant not only with the Latin language but with the Greek, for the sake of the many different things that have been admirably written therein. Let him be well versed in the poets, and not less in the orators and historians, and also proficient in writing verse and prose, especially in this vulgar [vernacular] tongue of ours . . .

You must know that I am not content with the Courtier unless he be also a musician and unless, besides understanding and being able to read notes, he can play upon divers instruments . . .

I wish our Courtier to guard against getting the name of a liar or a boaster, which sometimes befalls even those who do not deserve it . . .

—From Baldassare Castiglione's *Book of the Courtier*, 1528

4. The excerpt was most likely seen as which of the following at the time it was written?

   (A) A guide for educating and training a "universal man"
   (B) A guide for how to be a good absolute ruler
   (C) A guide for how to meet a wife
   (D) A guide for how to be a troubadour

5. Which of the following themes of the Renaissance era is the excerpt most connected to?

   (A) Secularism
   (B) Individualism
   (C) Humanism
   (D) Perspective

6. Which of the following reforms would Castiglione most likely want to institute?

   (A) The creation of coeducational public high schools paid for by the state
   (B) The creation of male-only public high schools paid for by the state
   (C) The creation of public universities without tuition where all students of both genders could learn
   (D) The creation of private high schools for elite young men with many extracurricular activities

7. Which of the following skills that Castiglione recommends for a courtier would be valued LEAST by a European gentleman at the end of the 20th century?

   (A) Expertise with multiple languages
   (B) Being strong and attractive
   (C) Expertise with many kinds of weapons
   (D) The ability to write poetry and prose

**Questions 8–12 refer to the pair of excerpts below, written by explorer Christopher Columbus and the Dominican Bishop of Chiapas, Mexico, Bartolomé de las Casas.**

### Source 1

Indians would give whatever the seller required . . . Thus they bartered, like idiots, cotton and gold for fragments of bows, glasses, bottles, and jars; which I forbad as being unjust, and myself gave them many beautiful and acceptable articles which I had brought with me, taking nothing from them in return; I did this in order that I might the more easily conciliate them, that they might be led to become Christians, and be inclined to entertain a regard for the King and Queen, our Princes and all Spaniards, and that I might induce them to take an interest in seeking out, and collecting and delivering to us such things as they possessed in abundance, but which we greatly needed.

—Christopher Columbus: letter to Raphael Sanchez, 1493

### Source 2

It was upon these gentle lambs . . . that from the very first day they clapped eyes on them the Spanish fell like ravening wolves upon the fold, or like tigers and savage lions who have not eaten meat for days. The pattern established at the outset has remained unchanged to this day, and the Spaniards still do nothing save tear the natives to shreds, murder them and inflict upon them untold misery, suffering and distress, tormenting, harrying and persecuting them mercilessly. We shall in due course describe some of the many ingenious methods of torture they have invented and refined for this purpose, but one can get some idea of the effectiveness of their methods from the figures alone. When the Spanish first journeyed there, the indigenous population of the island of Hispaniola stood at some three million; today only two hundred survive. Their reason for killing and destroying such an infinite number of souls is that the Christians have an ultimate aim, which is to acquire gold, and to swell themselves with riches in a very brief time and thus rise to a high estate disproportionate to their merits.

—Bartolomé de las Casas: *A Short Account of the Destruction of the Indies*, 1542

8. Which of the following motives for exploration does de las Casas seem to be criticizing in **Source 2**?

    (A) Converting the natives to Christianity
    (B) Financial gain
    (C) Personal glory
    (D) Finding new mates

9. The free flow of plants and animals, as well as trade goods, between Europe and the Americas is referred to by historians as the Columbian Exchange and affected the natives in which of the following ways?

    (A) Economic opportunities were reduced.
    (B) They were subjugated and destroyed.
    (C) Economic opportunities were created.
    (D) They were enriched through trade in agricultural goods.

10. The free flow of plants and animals, as well as trade goods, between Europe and the Americas is referred to by historians as the Columbian Exchange and affected the Europeans in which of the following ways?

    (A) Economic opportunities were reduced.
    (B) They were subjugated and destroyed.
    (C) Economic opportunities were created.
    (D) They were enriched through trade in Native-American slaves.

11. Which of the following motives for exploration is de las Casas most likely to think is most important in **Source 2**?

    (A) Converting the natives to Christianity
    (B) Financial gain
    (C) Personal glory
    (D) Finding new mates

12. Which of the following would best account for the differences between the interactions of the Spaniards and the natives as described in the two accounts?

    (A) De las Casas was exaggerating to support the start of African slavery.
    (B) Columbus was biased in favor of himself in his writings.
    (C) Columbus's men were nicer to the natives than were later expeditions.
    (D) De las Casas wanted the Spanish to leave the Americas.

**Questions 13–14 refer to the sketch below of the circulatory and skeletal systems by Andreas Vesalius, c. 1546.**

13. This print clearly illustrates which of the following truths about scientific advances in this era?

    (A) They led to significant declines in mortality rates from disease during the 16th and 17th centuries.
    (B) They created the experimental proof for the theories of ancient Greeks such as Aristotle and Galen.
    (C) They occurred as a result of the rediscovery of ancient Greek and Roman texts.
    (D) They occurred as a result of the accumulation of information from dissection and led to conceptualizing the human being as a set of integrated systems.

14. The understanding of the human body that Vesalius drew is most similar to which of the following?

    (A) The mechanical universe explained by Sir Isaac Newton
    (B) The notion, espoused by astrology, that celestial bodies could affect events on Earth
    (C) The Enlightenment view that all problems can be solved through reason
    (D) The idea of subatomic quanta explained by Max Planck

**Questions 15–17 refer to the passage below by John Calvin.**

If we need to be recalled to the origin of election, to prove that we obtain salvation from no other source than the mere goodness of God, they who desire to extinguish this principle, do all they can to obscure what ought to be magnificently and loudly celebrated, and to pluck up humility by the roots. In ascribing the salvation of the remnant of the people to the election of grace, Paul clearly testifies, that it is then only known that God saves whom upon which there can be no claim. They who shut the gates to prevent anyone from presuming to approach and taste this doctrine, do no less injury to man than to God; for nothing else will be sufficient to produce in us suitable humility, or to impress us with a due sense of our great obligations to God. Nor is there any other basis for solid confidence, even according to the authority of Christ, who, to deliver us from all fear, and render us invincible amidst so many dangers, snares, and deadly conflicts, promises to preserve in safety all whom the Father has committed to His care.

—John Calvin, *Institutes of the Christian Religion*, 1559

15. Which of the following beliefs, supported first by Calvin, does this passage best seem to support?

    (A) Salvation
    (B) Predestination
    (C) Divinity of Jesus
    (D) Simony

16. Which of the following religions that started around the same time as Calvinism was destroyed for supporting adult baptism and pacifism?

    (A) Huguenots
    (B) Lutherans
    (C) Presbyterians
    (D) Anabaptists

17. Which of the following was NOT an abuse of the Catholic Church that Calvin and other religious leaders criticized?

    (A) Papal wealth
    (B) Pluralism
    (C) Nepotism
    (D) Indulgences

**Questions 18–20 refer to the excerpts below from the Navigation Acts of 1651.**

[A]fter the first day of December, one thousand six hundred fifty and one, and from thence forwards, no goods or commodities whatsoever of the growth, production or manufacture of Asia, Africa or America, or of any part thereof; or of any islands belonging to them, or which are described or laid down in the usual maps or cards of those places, as well of the English plantations as others, shall be imported or brought into this Commonwealth of England, or into Ireland, or any other lands, islands, plantations, or territories to this Commonwealth belonging, or in their possession, in any other ship or ships, vessel or vessels whatsoever, but only in such as do truly and without fraud belong only to the people of this Commonwealth, or the plantations thereof, as the proprietors or right owners thereof; and whereof the master and mariners are also of the people of this Commonwealth, under the penalty of the forfeiture and loss of all the goods that shall be imported contrary to this act . . .

[N]o goods or commodities of the growth, production, or manufacture of Europe, or of any part thereof, shall after the first day of December, one thousand six hundred fifty and one, be imported or brought into this Commonwealth of England, or any other lands or territories to this Commonwealth belonging, or in their possession, in any ship or ships, vessel or vessels whatsoever, but in such as do truly and without fraud belong only to the people of this Commonwealth, and in no other, except only such foreign ships and vessels as do truly and properly belong to the people of that country or place, of which the said goods are the growth, production or manufacture.

18. Which of the following was the desired outcome of the excerpted legislation by the Rump Parliament of England in 1651?

    (A) To prevent England's colonies from being bombarded with cheap goods manufactured by their mainland European competitors

    (B) To reclaim domination of the slave trade from Portugal in order to meet the growing need for slaves for sugar plantations in the English Caribbean colonies

    (C) To end Dutch domination of maritime trade by limiting their ability to move goods between England and her colonies as well as goods to and from England from other countries

    (D) To extricate the French from the Atlantic sea trade as well as the cod and whaling industries, which at this time were dominated by the French

19. The Navigation Acts of 1651 in the excerpt conflict with which of the following economic philosopher's theories and beliefs?

    (A) Thomas Malthus

    (B) Josiah Child

    (C) Adam Smith

    (D) Jean-Baptiste Colbert

20. Which of the following best describes the outcome of the Navigation Acts of 1651?

    (A) They served as a catalyst for the growth of English shipping and overseas trade but did little to limit the prospects of the Dutch in the 17th century.

    (B) They brought about almost immediate hardships for the Dutch economy as Dutch dominance of overseas trade quickly ended.

    (C) They were rescinded during the restoration of the Stuarts as the Stuarts sought normal diplomatic relations with the Dutch so as not to need Parliament's financial support for war.

    (D) They led to nearly a century of recurrent war between England and the Netherlands, which did not end until after American independence.

**Questions 21–23 refer to the map below.**

21. Which of the following is the best characterization of the impact of the land acquisitions of Peter I of Russia from 1682–1715?

    (A) They were of great strategic importance because Russia gained the ability to spy better on Prussia.
    (B) They were of great economic importance due to the vast mineral resources there.
    (C) They included many large cities and generally had a high population density.
    (D) They allowed Peter the Great to build a port and a new capital city.

22. Which of the following events allowed continued Russian territorial expansion after Peter left the throne?

    (A) The Ottoman Empire was weakened after the loss of the Battle of Vienna, leaving territory open to Russian expansion.
    (B) The Austrian Empire was weakened after the Napoleonic Wars, leaving territory open to Russian expansion.
    (C) The Spanish monarchy was weakened after the defeat of the Spanish Armada, leaving territory open to Russian expansion.
    (D) Poland and Russia made an alliance to divide the Germanic states.

23. Which of the following was a goal of Peter the Great that was continued by Catherine the Great but never realized under Romanov rule?

    (A) The complete subjugation of the boyar nobility through their taxation and service to the czar
    (B) The westernization of Russia as it embraced the culture and traditions of Western Europe
    (C) The creation of a strong navy that could fight against the other great navies of the world
    (D) The emancipation of the serfs in an equitable fashion in order to modernize Russia

**Questions 24–27 refer to the following quote from Voltaire in response to the 1755 Lisbon earthquake.**

My dear sir, nature is very cruel. One would find it hard to imagine how the laws of movement cause such frightful disasters in the best of possible worlds. A hundred thousand ants, our fellows, crushed all at once in our ant-hill, and half of them perishing, no doubt in unspeakable agony, beneath the wreckage from which they cannot be drawn. Families ruined all over Europe, the fortune of a hundred businessmen, your compatriots, swallowed up in the ruins of Lisbon. What a wretched gamble is the game of human life! What will the preachers say, especially if the palace of the Inquisition is still standing? I flatter myself that at least the reverend father inquisitors have been crushed like others. That ought to teach men not to persecute each other, for while a few holy scoundrels burn a few fanatics, the earth swallows up one and all.

—Voltaire, in a letter, 1755

24. Voltaire is best known for supporting which of the following demands of the Enlightenment *philosophes*?

    (A) Deism should be adopted by all as the only logical religion.
    (B) Religious toleration leads to the destruction of social unity.
    (C) Skepticism is not a reliable way of examining information.
    (D) Religious toleration should be given to all people of all religions.

25. Voltaire's statement in the last sentence, criticizing persecution, is most likely influenced by which of the following?

    (A) New concepts of legal equity and individual rights expressed by Locke and Rousseau
    (B) Europeans gaining a more thorough understanding of the rich cultural diversity to be found through trade and travel
    (C) New concepts of a deterministic mechanical universe based on the discovery of Newton's mathematical laws
    (D) Challenges on multiple fronts to the monopoly on truth held by the Roman Catholic Church

26. Which of the following Enlightenment *philosophes* questioned reliance on reason and began the Romantic movement for the rationale given?

    (A) Jean-Jacques Rousseau because he thought society corrupted noble souls
    (B) Baron Montesquieu because he thought that governments were not capable of being fair
    (C) Mary Wollstonecraft because she railed against the subjugation of women
    (D) Adam Smith because he stated that reason could not be used to understand how another feels

27. The ideas expressed by Voltaire in the quote best illustrate which of the following characteristics of Enlightenment intellectuals?

    (A) Many were accomplished scientists who added important pieces to human understanding of the universe.
    (B) They utilized new methods of communicating their ideas, such as salons and inexpensive printed pamphlets.
    (C) Most rejected religion altogether and adopted atheism as the only credo of a rational person.
    (D) Many believed that the new scientific discoveries justified a more tolerant and objective approach to social and cultural issues.

**Questions 28–30 refer to the following entries in the diary of Napoleon Bonaparte.**

Paris has a short memory. If I remain longer doing nothing, I am lost. In this great Babylon one reputation quickly succeeds another. After I have been seen three times at the theatre, I shall not be looked at again. I shall therefore not go very frequently. (diary, 1798)

If the press is not bridled, I shall not remain three days in power. (diary, 1799)

The presence of a general is necessary; he is the head, he is the all in all of an army. It was not the Roman army that conquered Gaul, it was Caesar, it was not the Carthaginians that made the armies of the Roman republic tremble at the very gates of Rome, it was Hannibal. (diary, 1801)

My power proceeds from my reputation, and my reputation from the victories I have won. My power would fall if I were not to support it with more glory and more victories. Conquest has made me what I am; only conquest can maintain me. (diary, 1802)

The revolution in France is over and now there is only one party in France and I shall never allow the newspapers to say anything contrary to my interests. They may publish a few little articles with just a bit of poison in them, but one fine day I shall shut their mouths forever. (diary, 1805)

28. Napoleon's entry from 1802 indicates that his conquest of most of Europe was due in part to which of the following?

    (A) Napoleon's fear that if he did not continue to win military victories, he would lose power
    (B) Napoleon's belief that he must conquer all of Europe to conquer the press
    (C) Napoleon's confidence that he would be the greatest leader Europe has ever seen
    (D) Napoleon's appreciation of his soldiers and their collective efforts

29. Although Napoleon was often praised for implementing his Napoleonic Code and a meritocracy in the army, the domestic issue that he was most often criticized for was which of the following?

    (A) Placing his relatives on foreign thrones
    (B) Changing the criminal code of France
    (C) Financial mismanagement
    (D) Curtailment of citizens' rights

30. Napoleon instituted the Continental System to accomplish which of the following?

    (A) Unify Italy with his brother as king
    (B) Punish Russia for his ill-fated invasion
    (C) Defeat England through economic war
    (D) Create a united Europe under the leadership of France

**Questions 31–33 refer to the following governmental regulation.**

### Press Law

So long as this decree shall remain in force no publication which appears in the form of daily issues, or as a serial not exceeding twenty sheets of printed matter, shall go to press in any state of the union without the previous knowledge and approval of the state officials. Writings which do not belong to one of the above-mentioned classes shall be treated according to the laws now in force, or which may be enacted, in the individual states of the union . . . Each state of the union is responsible, not only to the state against which the offense is directly committed, but to the whole Confederation, for every publication appearing under its supervision in which the honor or security of other states is infringed or their constitution or administration attacked . . .

—*Carlsbad Resolutions* adopted by the Germanic States, 1819

31. According to the resolutions, the German confederated states most feared which of the following?

    (A) The effect liberal young students would have on an impressionable faculty and the surrounding communities, where they would surely spread their message
    (B) The dissemination of liberal ideas by the media and the sharing of nationalist or liberal ideas at the university in the classroom or in secret
    (C) The dissolution of the union of German states that they had just created
    (D) Support of Bonapartism, which was growing in strength prior to the passage of these *Carlsbad Resolutions* and preceding Napoleon's invasion

32. The *Carlsbad Resolutions* were another of Metternich's schemes, like the Concert of Europe, that aimed to accomplish which of the following?

    (A) Establish control of European states by democracy in the tradition of the Enlightenment
    (B) Suppress all voices in government other than his own and control all aspects of his citizens' lives
    (C) Suppress all nationalist revolutions across the Continent
    (D) Suppress all speech but that of monarchs and the churches that they approve

33. Which of the following 19th-century figures would have been the LEAST likely to oppose those liberals described in the resolutions?

    (A) Pope Pius IX
    (B) Klemens von Metternich
    (C) Giuseppe Mazzini
    (D) William Frederick I

**Questions 34–36 refer to the text below.**

Under the name of Chartist well-meaning inconsiderate men and other misled men have in very many cases, all over the country from the extreme west to the extreme east and from Brighton in the south to nearly the extreme north of Scotland, denounced every man who is not a working man, applied to him, the grossest epithets and most atrocious intentions and conduct, have threatened them with vengeance and in some places, have proposed plans for the seizure and division of their property—numbers of misled men and others of bad character, under the self-denomination of Chartists have gone from place to place and in the most violent manner disturbed and dispersed meetings of various kinds. Your Committee object to the words Household Suffrage since under any honest definition of the words—they would exclude a large majority of the men of these kingdoms—and because they have become reasonably obnoxious to the political portion of the working people.

—Excerpt of a letter from British social reformer Francis Place, written in 1842

34.  Which of the following best characterizes the historical point of view of the excerpt?

(A)  The author must not be a radical reformer because he criticizes the Chartists.
(B)  The author must be a radical reformer because he criticizes the Chartists.
(C)  The author believes in universal male suffrage.
(D)  The author thinks the Chartists are the best part of the reform movement.

35.  The primary goal of the Chartist movement was which of the following?

(A)  Universal suffrage
(B)  Universal male suffrage
(C)  Universal health care
(D)  Social security and unemployment insurance

36.  Which of the following is the political reaction led by Klemens von Metternich that occurred as a result of the Chartists, the French Revolution, and other liberal movements?

(A)  Liberalism
(B)  Radicalism
(C)  Nationalism
(D)  Conservatism

**Questions 37–39 refer to the image below.**

*Scene at the Barricade*, Paris, June 1848.

37. The image suggests which of the following about the French Revolution of June 1848?

   (A) It was a multiethnic revolution in which many people of multiple races rose up in rebellion.
   (B) It was only a minor conflict when compared with the February Revolution of 1848.
   (C) It involved many Parisians, who had to be extricated from the narrow streets and barricades, resulting in high casualties.
   (D) It was particularly troublesome for Parisians, who had to battle the Prussians and then their own National Assembly's military force.

38. In which of the following ways was the experience of the Polish revolutionaries different from that of the French as seen in the image?

   (A) The Polish were successful in their revolt, and a constitutional government was formed.
   (B) The Polish were first encouraged by the Prussians, who had their own revolution going on; then Polish statehood aspirations were also crushed by the Prussians, resulting in a foreign military controlling them.
   (C) The military intervention of a coalition force of reactionary states Austria, Prussia, and Russia to quell the radical revolution occurred in Poland.
   (D) The Polish citizens in the cities took much heavier losses than the French citizens because more Polish citizens joined the revolution.

39. When compared with the other revolutions in the rest of Europe in 1848, the revolution in France can be characterized as which of the following?

   (A) It involved far more bloodshed but brought about many more positive, long-term changes for those involved.
   (B) It brought about change too swiftly, leading to an equally conservative backlash cancelling out any gains.
   (C) It mirrored the others where the revolutionaries failed to unite and were, therefore, played against one another, undermining the movement.
   (D) It was limited due to the threat of intervention by the old Congress System countries to the East.

**Questions 40–42 refer to the painting below.**

Jean Francois Millet, *Gleaners*, 1857.

40. Which of the following would be a suitable description of the painting?

   (A) Women of Western Europe during the height of the open-field system in Europe
   (B) Peasant farmers in France during the poor grain years immediately before the 1789 Revolution
   (C) Prussian serf women of the mid-19th century serving in the fields of Catholic Center Party members
   (D) British peasant farmers of the early Hanoverian years engaging in gleaning during lean farming years

41. Which of the following would have likely been the fate of women, such as those in the painting, in England as the enclosure movement moved forward?

   (A) The women would have likely been compelled to work on a communal farm, which they detested.
   (B) The women were likely destined to work in cottage industries, furthering protoindustrialization.
   (C) The corvée would have required that the women continued service at the behest of the state each year.
   (D) Emigration was likely, as the encomienda system was in a strong need of female workers in the New World.

42. Whose theories on population and inadequate food supply would the painting best support?

   (A) David Ricardo
   (B) Thomas Malthus
   (C) Karl Marx
   (D) Cornelius Vermuyden

**Questions 43–46 refer to the following excerpt from a speech by Vladimir I. Lenin.**

The independence of our country cannot be upheld unless we have an adequate industrial basis for defense. And such an industrial basis cannot be created if our industry is not more highly developed technically. That is why a fast rate of development of our industry is necessary and imperative. We cannot go on indefinitely, that is, for too long a period, basing the Soviet regime and socialist construction on two different foundations, the foundation of the most large-scale and united socialist industry and the foundation of the most scattered and backward, small commodity economy of the peasants. We must gradually, but systematically and persistently, place our agriculture on a new technical basis, the basis of large-scale production, and bring it up to the level of socialist industry. Either we accomplish this task—in which case the final victory of socialism in our country will be assured, or we turn away from it and do not accomplish it—in which case a return to capitalism may become inevitable.

—J. V. Stalin, *Industrialization of the Country and the Right Deviation in the C.P.S.U.*, November 19, 1928

43. Which of the following compromises of his New Economic Policy was Lenin saying needed to be fixed in the speech excerpt?

    (A) Compromising with free markets in rural areas after the civil war
    (B) Sharing power with the provisional government
    (C) Giving the government too much power to further communism
    (D) Freeing the peasants from their landlords in exchange for their support

44. Which of the following policies of Joseph Stalin was NOT used to correct the problem cited by Lenin in the excerpt?

    (A) Collectivization
    (B) Persecution of the better-off peasants
    (C) The Berlin blockade
    (D) The five-year plans

45. What was the result of Stalin's attempt to fix the problem cited by Lenin in the excerpt?

    (A) The Soviet Union saw steady growth in both industry and agriculture.
    (B) The Soviet Union saw steady growth in industry and a decline in agriculture.
    (C) The Soviet Union saw steady growth in agriculture, but industrial production fell behind.
    (D) The Soviet Union saw steady decline in both industry and agriculture.

46. Which of the following events was most likely the greatest influence on Lenin in his desire to industrialize his new nation?

    (A) His exile in Switzerland and other places led him to see how the industrialization of the West was needed in the Soviet Union.
    (B) Russia had a large percentage of its population working in factories before the revolution occurred, and he wanted to build on that.
    (C) Trotsky was able to lead the Bolshevik revolt in 1917 because he had control of the rail and telegraph stations.
    (D) The humiliating defeat of Russia during the First World War had led to his rise to power and he knew another defeat would spell his doom.

**Questions 47–48 refer to the following text.**

Addison's Act had been conceived in the belief that, unless working-class aspirations were quickly met after the war, Britain might experience a revolution similar to that in Russia. By 1920 that fear was beginning to recede and Addison's policy was being regarded as extravagant. An immediate victim of the new attitude was the Borough's Kingfield Street scheme, provisional plans for which were approved in September 1920. Much to the Council's surprise, the Government's Housing Board deferred the scheme, "having regard to the Council's present commitments and the money available at the present time, and in May 1921 the Government announced a drastic curtailment of the housing programme, cutting the housing target by half."

—Excerpt from a work by English historian Hermione Hobhouse,
*Public Housing in Poplar: The Inter-war Years*, 1994

47. Which of the following attitudes prevalent after the First World War is evident in the excerpt?

(A) Women's suffrage should increase.

(B) Society should become democratic.

(C) Disillusionment and cynicism increased.

(D) Communism rose as a world power.

48. Which of the following is the best description of the plans being changed in the excerpt?

(A) Welfare programs were questioned after the First World War.

(B) Housing was a large part of the British budget.

(C) Workers were threatening Communist revolution.

(D) The government Housing Board wanted to build more houses.

**Questions 49–51 refer to the charts below.**

### Table 1. Troops and Weapons Lost in the Battle of Stalingrad, August 1942 to February 1943

| Nation | Casualties | Lost Tanks | Lost Artillery | Lost Planes |
|---|---|---|---|---|
| U.S.S.R. | 1,129,619 | 4,341 | 15,728 | 2,769 |
| Axis Total | 850,000 | 500 | 6,000 | 900 |
| Germany | 400,000 | | | |
| Romania | 200,000 | | | |
| Italy | 130,000 | | | |
| Hungary | 120,000 | | | |

### Table 2. Total Casualties from the Second World War in Selected Nations

| Country | Total Population as of 1/1/1939 | Military Deaths | Civilian Deaths Due to Military Activity and Crimes Against Humanity | Total Deaths | Deaths by Percentage of Population |
|---|---|---|---|---|---|
| Soviet Union | 168,524,000 | 8,800,000 to 10,700,000 | 12,700,000 to 14,600,000 | 23,400,000 | 14.2% |
| Germany | 69,850,000 | 5,530,000 | 1,100,000 to 3,150,000 | 6,630,000 to 8,680,000 | 7.8% to 10% |
| Poland | 34,849,000 | 240,000 | 5,380,000 to 5,580,000 | 5,620,000 to 5,820,000 | 17.2% |

| Country | Total Population as of 1/1/1939 | Military Deaths | Civilian Deaths Due to Military Activity and Crimes Against Humanity | Total Deaths | Deaths by Percentage of Population |
|---|---|---|---|---|---|
| United Kingdom | 47,760,000 | 383,800 including overseas possessions | 67,100 | 450,900 | 0.94% |
| Belgium | 8,387,000 | 12,100 | 75,900 | 88,000 | 1.05% |
| Global totals | 1,995,537,400 | 22,426,600 to 25,487,500 | 37,585,300 to 54,594,000 | 62,171,600 to 78,041,700 | 3% to 4% |

49. Which of the following was the clearest result of the Battle of Stalingrad according to the data in Table 1?

   (A) The Axis powers saved their soldiers for future conquests, while the Soviets did everything they could to defend their city.

   (B) The Axis powers suffered greater losses on the Western Front than they did on the Eastern Front during 1943.

   (C) An entire generation of men was decimated.

   (D) The Germans won the battle and drove the Russians out of the territory surrounding Stalingrad.

50. Which of the following contributed most to the overall pattern shown in Table 2?

   (A) Greater populations in Russia and Poland were causing hunger problems there.

   (B) The German army was better trained, equipped, and fed than any other army.

   (C) The new Nazi racial order eliminated millions of people in Eastern Europe.

   (D) The Allies were unprepared for the Axis onslaught and took high casualties.

51. The data in both tables indicate which of the following about how total war affected the citizens' loyalty and respect for their nation-states?

   (A) Citizens lost all respect for their nation-states in many places during the Second World War.

   (B) The nation-state gained power over the people to the point where it could get them to treat other humans in ways that was previously inconceivable to most Europeans.

   (C) The citizens displayed greater respect for their nation-states and loyalty to them after the Second World War than they did during the war.

   (D) Nation-states found that they had lost the respect and loyalty of their citizens after the war.

**Questions 52–55 refer to the political platform below.**

To help heal the planet we will:

- Make achieving international agreement and action to limit climate change to below 2 degrees C of warming the major foreign policy priority.
- Invest in an £85 billion public programme of renewable electricity generation, flood defenses and building insulation.
- Support local sustainable agriculture, with respect for animals and wild places.

To become more equal and support our public services[,] we will:

- End privatization in the National Health Service.
- End tuition fees and cancel student debt.
- Provide 500,000 social homes for rent over the five-year Parliament.
- Control excessive rents and achieve house price stability.
- Increase public spending to almost half of national income.
- Make tax fair and crack down vigorously on tax avoidance and evasion.
- Ensure respect for everyone whatever their ethnicity, gender, age, religious belief or non-belief, sexual orientation, class, size, disability or other status.
- Make the highest wage in any organization no more than ten times the lowest wage.

To create a truly democratic central and local government and a common citizenship and to promote peace based on democratic principles[,] we will:

- Reform the benefits system. End workfare and sanctions. Double Child Benefit and pay a pension that people can live on in the longer term, unite tax and benefits in a Basic Income system covering everyone.
- Fund local government adequately and set democratically elected local authorities free to decide how to run education, public transport and other local services and to raise local taxes.
- Respect immigrants for the contribution they make and control immigration fairly.
- Decommission the Trident nuclear deterrent system and promote peacemaking.

—The 2015 Manifesto of the Green Party of England

52. Which of the following 20th-century events was the political platform outlined in the passage reacting to most?

(A) The failure of the European welfare state

(B) The expansion of women's rights

(C) The increasing political and economic integration of Europe

(D) The growing influence of consumerism

53. Which of the following trends in late-20th-century Europe is reflected in the platform's references to minorities and multicultural communities?

(A) The collapse of communism in Eastern Europe

(B) The increasing reliance on immigrant labor

(C) The reaction against the influence of American pop culture

(D) The effects of the postwar baby boom

54. Education and public services as a central plank in the Green Party's platform are most clearly evidence of which of the following?

(A) The emergence of nationalist political parties
(B) The requirements of membership in the European Union
(C) The influence of Catholic reforms after the Second Vatican Council
(D) The political debate over the cost of the welfare state

55. Based on its platform, the Green Party of England likely supported which of the following?

(A) Bans on immigration
(B) Expanded civil rights for LGBTQ+ people
(C) Free trade
(D) Expansionary foreign policy

**STOP**  If there is still time remaining, you may review your answers.

# Section I

## Part B: Short Answer

TIME: 40 MINUTES
NUMBER OF QUESTIONS: 3 OUT OF 4 CHOICES
PERCENTAGE OF TOTAL AP EXAM SCORE: 20%
WRITING INSTRUMENT: PEN WITH DARK BLUE OR BLACK INK

**DIRECTIONS:** Section I, Part B of this exam contains four short-answer questions. Write your responses in the corresponding boxes on the short-answer response sheets. You must answer Questions 1 and 2, but you choose to answer either Question 3 OR 4. Please indicate which question you answered on the answer sheet.

Answer all parts of every question. Use complete sentences; an outline or bulleted list alone is not acceptable. You may plan your answers in your exam booklet, but no credit will be given for what is written there. Sources have been edited for the purposes of this exercise.

**Answer all parts of the questions that follow.**

1. Historians have sometimes referred to the Renaissance era as the start of modern history.

    (a) Provide TWO pieces of evidence to support this characterization of this period and explain how they support it.

    (b) Provide ONE specific piece of evidence that undermines this characterization of this time period, and explain how it undermines it.

**Use the image below to answer both parts of the question that follows.**

*The Persistence of Memory*, by Spanish artist Salvador Dali, 1931.

2. (a) Briefly analyze how the artwork reflects artistic trends in the first part of the 20th century.
   (b) Based on the painting and your knowledge of European history, briefly analyze TWO aspects of change that affected Europeans' perceptions during the time between the First and Second World Wars.

**Please choose to answer either Question 3 or Question 4, and indicate which question you answer.**

**Use the passages below to answer all parts of the question that follows.**

### Source 1

The Cold War was a tragic conflict that was unnecessary and detrimental to people living on both sides of the Iron Curtain. The personal conflicts between the allied leaders, Winston Churchill and Joseph Stalin[, led] to increasing distrust and eventual hostility between two factions that emerged from the allied powers that had been victorious in World War II, the Warsaw pact or COMINTERN, and NATO. The United States was strongly influenced by Churchill to oppose Soviet foreign policy goals and thus created NATO to oppose all communist expansion. The cost of the military spending by both NATO and the COMINTERN nations was a huge loss of consumer goods and services. The costs of trying to supply consumer goods and services while continuing a military build-up eventually brought the Soviet Union to the point of collapse as the incredible consumer economies of the United States and other NATO nations out-produced them in almost every area. In the end, the Soviet Union fell and the Cold War ended because the NATO nations produced more goods and services including military goods and services which led the people of the COMINTERN nations to want a better life through capitalism, resulting in the fall of communism there.

—Historian Henokh Sharon, 2013

3.

### Source 2

Communism was a corrupt system that was bound to fail before the revolution ever began in Russia in 1917. The Cold War was an ideological battle based upon the moral superiority of the freedom associated with capitalism. The leadership of the Soviet Union believed in a fantasy of a classless society that their people knew would never be created due to the failings of human nature. The alliance of convenience with Joseph Stalin against the Nazi aggression was a necessary evil, but Western Europe realized the [S]oviet threat after World War II and met the threat of communist expansion everywhere with military force and economic aid, bringing communism to an end by the choice of its own leaders who saw the flaws in their system and chose to reform it.

—Historian Ruben van der Straaten, 1992

(a) Explain ONE major difference between Sharon's and van der Straaten's interpretations of the Cold War.
(b) Provide ONE piece of evidence from the Cold War that supports Sharon's interpretation (**Source 1**), and explain HOW it supports the interpretation.
(c) Provide ONE piece of evidence from the Cold War that supports van der Straaten's interpretation (**Source 2**), and explain HOW it supports the interpretation.

4.

## Source 1

Louis XIV was synonymous with the history of Europe for almost two decades. His influence on events was so immense that he was adored and feared by the people he ruled. He created the model for how to tame the nobility and become a true absolute monarch for all of Europe. France under Louis XIV was at its zenith of international power and has declined ever since his fall, with the exception of the Napoleonic Era. Louis XIV made the French court at Versailles the model of court life in Europe at the time. He influenced political and military events to make France the leading nation in Europe. He was a figure so grand and so spectacular that it was said that when Louis sneezed all of Europe caught cold.

—Historian Burke Arielle

## Source 2

Louis XIV may have been one of the most influential rulers of the time, but he was resented and resisted by the nobility in his realm, and he mismanaged the finances of the state so badly that the final result of his rule was the French Revolution, which occurred as a result of failed French finances. He was obsessed with his image and believed that appearances were the substance of ruling a nation. He was devoutly observant, but never lived by religious virtues. He may have been good for France for a short while, but his actions led to the bankruptcy of the French state by Louis's waging costly wars and building the palace of Versailles. That bankruptcy, although he did not live to see it, eventually caused the end of the Bourbon reign and monarchy in France.

—Historian Jessica Gillespie

(a) Based on **Source 1**, briefly analyze the positive aspects of the reign of Louis XIV for the European continent.
(b) Based upon **Source 2**, briefly analyze the negative aspects of the reign of Louis XIV for the European continent.
(c) What role did war play in the legacy of Louis XIV?

**STOP**    If there is still time remaining, you may review your answers.

## Section II

TOTAL TIME: 100 MINUTES

NUMBER OF QUESTIONS: 2

PERCENTAGE OF TOTAL AP EXAM SCORE: 40%

QUESTION 1: 25%

QUESTION 2: 15%

WRITING INSTRUMENT: PEN WITH DARK BLUE OR BLACK INK

**DIRECTIONS:** Section II of this exam contains three essay questions. You must respond to Question 1, the document-based question, but you must CHOOSE to answer Question 2, 3, or 4 for your long essay question. No credit is given for work written on the exam itself; all responses must be written in dark blue or black ink in essay format in the answer booklet. Be sure to indicate which long essay question you are answering on each page of the answer booklet.

## Question 1 (Document–Based Question—DBQ)

TIME: 60 MINUTES

SUGGESTED READING PERIOD: 15 MINUTES

SUGGESTED WRITING TIME: 45 MINUTES

**DIRECTIONS:** Question 1 is based on the accompanying documents. The documents have been edited for the purpose of the exercise.

In your response, you should do the following:

- State a relevant thesis that directly addresses all parts of the question.
- Support the thesis or a relevant argument with evidence from all, or all but one, of the documents.
- Incorporate analysis of all, or all but one, of the documents into your argument.
- Focus your analysis of each document on at least one of the following: intended audience, purpose, historical context, and/or point of view.
- Support your argument with analysis of historical examples outside the documents.
- Connect historical phenomena relevant to your argument to broader events or processes.
- Synthesize the elements above into a persuasive essay that extends your argument, connects it to a different historical context, or accounts for contradictory evidence on the topic.

1.  Analyze how changing reactions and responses to socialism reflected social, political, and economic changes in Europe from 1800 to 1949.

---

**DOCUMENT 1**

Source: *Letters from an Inhabitant of Geneva to His Contemporaries*, by Henri Saint-Simon, early French socialist, 1803.

Compared with those who own no property, you are not very many in number: how, then, does it come about that they consent to obey you? It is because the superiority of your intellect enables you to combine your forces (as they cannot), thus for the most part giving you an advantage over them in the struggle which, in the nature of things, must always exist between you and them.

Once this principle has been accepted, it is clearly in your interest to include those without property in your party; those who have proved the superiority of their intelligence with important discoveries; and it is equally clear that the interest being *general* for your class, each of the members who compose it should contribute.

Until you have adopted the measure which I propose to you, you will be exposed, each in your own country, to the sort of evils which some of your class have suffered in France. In order to convince yourselves of the truth of what I have said, you have only to think about the events that have occurred in that country since 1789. The first popular movement there was secretly fomented by scientists and artists. Once the success of the insurrection had lent it the appearance of legitimacy, they declared themselves its leaders. The resistance they encountered to the direction they gave to that insurrection's direction aimed at the destruction of all the institutions which had wounded their self-esteem, provoked them to inflame the passions of the ignorant and to burst all the bonds of subordination which, until then, had contained the rash passions of those without property. They succeeded in doing what they wanted. All the institutions which from the outset they had intended to overthrow were destroyed inevitably; in short, they won the battle and you lost it. This victory was to cost the victors dear; but you who were defeated have suffered even more.

## DOCUMENT 2

Source: *The People's Petition of 1838*, a document of the Chartist Movement.

It was the fond expectation of the people that a remedy for the greater part, if not for the whole, of their grievances, would be found in the Reform Act of 1832.

They were taught to regard that Act as a wise means to a worthy end; as the machinery of an improved legislation, when the will of the masses would be at length potential.

They have been bitterly and basely deceived.

The fruit which looked so fair to the eye has turned to dust and ashes when gathered.

The Reform Act has effected a transfer of power from one domineering faction to another, and left the people as helpless as before.

Our slavery has been exchanged for an apprenticeship to liberty, which has aggravated the painful feeling of our social degradation, by adding to it the sickening of still deferred hope.

We come before your Honourable House to tell you, with all humility, that this state of things must not be permitted to continue; that it cannot long continue without very seriously endangering the stability of the throne and the peace of the kingdom; and that if by God's help and all lawful and constitutional appliances, an end can be put to it, we are fully resolved that it shall speedily come to an end.

We tell your Honourable House that the capital of the master must no longer be deprived of its due reward; that the laws which make food dear, and those which by making money scarce, make labour cheap, must be abolished; that taxation must be made to fall on property, not on industry; that the good of the many, as it is the only legitimate end, so must it be the sole study of the Government.

**DOCUMENT 3**

Source: *Socialist Allegory*, an English illustration supporting the International Socialist and Trade Union Congress of 1896, showing the nations of Europe and America represented by workers.

English illustration by Walter Crane. The Granger Collection.

**DOCUMENT 4**

Source: *The War and the Workers*, by Rosa Luxemburg, a German socialist in the working class, 1916.

The fall of the socialist proletariat in the present world war is unprecedented. It is a misfortune for humanity. But socialism will be lost only if the international proletariat fails to measure the depth of this fall, if it refuses to learn from it.

The last forty-five year period in the development of the modern labor movement now stands in doubt.

The [Franco-Prussian] War and the defeat of the Paris Commune had shifted the center of gravity for the European workers' movement to Germany. As France was the classic site of the first phase of proletarian class struggle and Paris the beating, bleeding heart of the European laboring classes of those times, so the German workers became the vanguard of the second phase. By means of countless sacrifices and tireless attention to detail, they have built the strongest organization, the one most worthy of emulation; they created the biggest press, called the most effective means of education and enlightenment into being, gathered the most powerful masses of voters and attained the greatest number of parliamentary mandates. German Social Democracy was considered the purest embodiment of Marxist socialism.

And what did we in Germany experience when the great historical test came? The most precipitous fall, the most violent collapse. Nowhere has the organization of the proletariat been yoked so completely to the service of imperialism. Nowhere is the state of siege borne so docilely. Nowhere is the press so hobbled, public opinion so stifled, the economic and political class struggle of the working class so totally surrendered as in Germany.

But German Social Democracy was not merely the strongest vanguard troop, it was the thinking head of the International. For this reason, we must begin the analysis, the self-examination process, with its fall. It has the duty to begin the salvation of international socialism, [and] that means unsparing criticism of itself.

**DOCUMENT 5**

Source: Nazi propaganda poster from 1944.

Nazi propaganda poster from the Second World War. This anti-Semitic and anti-Soviet German poster, written in the Polish language, says: "Death to Jewish-Bolshevik plague of murdering!" Posted on the streets of Kraków, which was under German occupation, c. 1944.

## DOCUMENT 6

Source: *Conservative Party Principles*, by Winston Churchill, former British prime minister, 1946.

We oppose the establishment of a Socialist State, controlling the means of production, distribution and exchange. We are asked, "What is your alternative?" Our Conservative aim is to build a property-owning democracy, both independent and interdependent. In this I include profit-sharing schemes in suitable industries and intimate consultation between employers and wage-earners. In fact we seek so far as possible to make the status of the wage-earner that of a partner rather than of an irresponsible employee. It is in the interest of the wage-earner to have many other alternatives open to him than service under one all-powerful employer called the State. He will be in a better position to bargain collectively and production will be more abundant; there will be more for all and more freedom for all when the wage-earner is able, in the large majority of cases, to choose and change his work, and to deal with a private employer who, like himself, is subject to the ordinary pressures of life and, like himself, is dependent upon his personal thrift, ingenuity and good-housekeeping. In this way alone can the traditional virtues of the British character be preserved. We do not wish the people of this ancient island reduced to a mass of State-directed proletarians, thrown hither and thither, housed here and there, by an aristocracy of privileged officials or privileged Party, sectarian or Trade Union bosses. We are opposed to the tyranny and victimization of the closed shop [*Note: a unionized workplace where all workers must join the union*]. Our ideal is the consenting union of millions of free, independent families and homes to gain their livelihood and to serve true British glory and world peace.

## DOCUMENT 7

Source: *Why Socialism*, by Albert Einstein, 1949.

The profit motive, in conjunction with competition among capitalists, is responsible for an instability in the accumulation and utilization of capital which leads to increasingly severe depressions. Unlimited competition leads to a huge waste of labor, and to that crippling of the social consciousness of individuals which I mentioned before.

This crippling of individuals I consider the worst evil of capitalism. Our whole educational system suffers from this evil. An exaggerated competitive attitude is inculcated into the student, who is trained to worship acquisitive success as a preparation for his future career.

I am convinced there is only one way to eliminate these grave evils, namely through the establishment of a socialist economy, accompanied by an educational system which would be oriented toward social goals. In such an economy, the means of production are owned by society itself and are utilized in a planned fashion. A planned economy, which adjusts production to the needs of the community, would distribute the work to be done among all those able to work and would guarantee a livelihood to every man, woman, and child. The education of the individual, in addition to promoting his own innate abilities, would attempt to develop in him a sense of responsibility for his fellow men in place of the glorification of power and success in our present society.

Nevertheless, it is necessary to remember that a planned economy is not yet socialism. A planned economy as such may be accompanied by the complete enslavement of the individual. The achievement of socialism requires the solution of some extremely difficult socio-political problems: how is it possible, in view of the far-reaching centralization of political and economic power, to prevent bureaucracy from becoming all-powerful and overweening? How can the rights of the individual be protected and therewith a democratic counterweight to the power of bureaucracy be assured?

## Question 2, Question 3, or Question 4 (Long Essay Question)

SUGGESTED WRITING TIME: 35 MINUTES

> **DIRECTIONS:** Choose Question 2, Question 3, OR Question 4.
>
> In your response, you should do the following:
>
> - State a relevant thesis that directly addresses all parts of the question.
> - Support your argument with evidence, using specific examples.
> - Synthesize the elements above into a persuasive essay that extends your argument, connects it to a different historical context, or connects it to a different category of analysis.

2. Compare the impact of the printing press on the daily life and culture of the European people with that of the Columbian Exchange on the daily life and culture of the European people.

3. Compare the impact of the French Revolution of 1789 on the daily life and culture of the French people with that of the Russian Revolution of 1917 on the daily life and culture of the Russian people.

4. Compare the impact of the Scientific Revolution (1540–1700) on the daily life and culture of the European people with that of the Industrial Revolution (1780–1914) on the daily life and culture of the 19th-century Europeans.

**STOP**   If there is still time remaining, you may review your answers.

# Scoring and Answer Explanations

The AP European History exam is composed of four parts grouped into two sections. The multiple-choice test is scored with 1 point given for each correct answer.

- *There is no penalty for guessing*, so you should answer every question on the exam.
- Each of three short-answer questions is given a score of 0–3.
- The long essay question (LEQ) is given a score from 0–6.
- The document-based question (DBQ) is scored from 0–7.

To attain your final AP score on this exam, use the following method:

Multiple-Choice Score $\times$ 1.091 = _____

$+$

Short-Answer Score $\times$ 3.334 = _____

$+$

DBQ Score $\times$ 5.357 = _____

$+$

LEQ Score $\times$ 3.75 = _____

**Total of all above scores is composite score = _____ (round your score)**

## Composite Score Conversion Chart

| Score Range | AP Score |
|---|---|
| 104–150 | 5 |
| 91–103 | 4 |
| 79–91 | 3 |
| 69–78 | 2 |
| 0–69 | 1 |

**To get a final score for the exam, compare your composite score to the chart directly above.**

The following are four separate guides to scoring each section of this exam. Once you have scored each piece of the exam, place the score on the appropriate line above. When you are done, do the computations to get your final score. Remember that this test is designed to mimic the AP exam. However, you will not take it in the same conditions that you will during the real test, and it is not scored by professionals, who are reading 1,000 or more essays daily. Although this test is a good predictor of success, it is only as good as the student using it. So do not stop studying just because you earned a good score here.

## Scoring Guide for the Multiple-Choice Section

> ### SPECIAL NOTE
>
> There is a lot of valuable information in the explanations for the multiple-choice questions, so make certain to read the explanations for ALL responses for every question that gave you any trouble!

1. (A) is wrong because, despite roughshod treatment of nonconformists to Nikon's church by reformed church officials, most violence on Old Believers was self-inflicted.

   (B) is wrong because, in France, the Revocation of the Edict of Nantes mostly dealt with deportations, forced baptisms, and destruction of Huguenot churches.

   **(C) is CORRECT because, even though the amount of torture was less than originally thought, it was a common practice to force confessions from recent converts.**

   (D) is wrong because, although there were trials of nonconforming religious figures by Catholics and Protestants in England at this time, torture was mostly reserved for those accused of treason and other crimes.

2. **(A) is CORRECT because Jews (and some Muslims) not converting were deported, and as for those who did convert, the Spanish crown suspected they practiced their old religion in private.**

   (B) is wrong because witch trials were intermittent, occurred in more isolated areas of Europe, and the accused tended to be women.

   (C) is wrong because the Ottomans, provided a tax was paid, were generally more tolerant of Christians than Christians were tolerant of Jews and Muslims.

   (D) is wrong because Calvinists often dealt out swift and harsh punishments that did not usually necessitate the use of torture.

3. (A) is wrong because incidences such as the rise of the Nazis and the Communist ban on religion made the rise of personal choice in religion and morality see sporadic growth.

   (B) is wrong because after Napoleon spread his legal code across most of Europe in the early-19th century, freedom of choice rose significantly throughout the Continent.

   (C) is wrong because even though the amount of torture was less than originally thought, it was a common practice to force confessions from recent converts.

   **(D) is CORRECT because personal freedom is currently at an apex, in large part because of the end of communism in Europe and also the growing cultural relativism that has been trending upward slowly since the Enlightenment.**

4. **(A) is CORRECT because Castiglione's *Book of the Courtier* is about how to become the ideal "Renaissance man."**

   (B) is wrong because Castiglione's *Book of the Courtier* is not about how to become an ideal ruler but about how to serve one.

   (C) is wrong because Castiglione's *Book of the Courtier* is not about how to find a wife but about how to become a courtier.

   (D) is wrong because Castiglione's *Book of the Courtier* is not about how to become a troubadour (although it encourages musicianship) but about how to become a courtier.

5. (A) is wrong because, although the reading explains many ways to improve as an individual, it is also focuses on Greco-Roman texts and on perfection as an educational pursuit, making the excerpt more closely tied to humanism than to individualism.

   (B) is wrong because, although the reading does not mention any religious theme or goal, it is focused on Greco-Roman texts and on perfection as an educational pursuit, making it more closely tied to humanism than to secularism.

(C) **is CORRECT because the reading is focused on Greco-Roman texts and on perfection as an educational pursuit, making it more closely tied to humanism than to individualism or secularism.**

(D) is wrong because perspective is an artistic method not mentioned or alluded to in this reading.

6. (A) is wrong because the Renaissance was an elitist movement. Castiglione was against the noisy public being educated, and the idea of boys and girls being educated together would have been unacceptable to him.

(B) is wrong because the Renaissance was an elitist movement. Castiglione was against the noisy public being educated and would thus be against any kind of public schooling.

(C) is wrong because the Renaissance was an elitist movement. Castiglione was against the noisy public being educated, and the idea of boys and girls being educated together would have been unacceptable to him.

(D) **is CORRECT because the Renaissance was an elitist movement, and Castiglione wanted to get the best education in all pursuits for only the young men of the upper classes.**

7. (A) is wrong because gentlemen at the end of the 20th century in Europe were expected to know multiple languages but not how to fight with many weapons.

(B) is wrong because gentlemen at the end of the 20th century in Europe were still expected to be strong and attractive or "shapely of limb," as Castiglione puts it, but were not required to fight with multiple weapons.

(C) **is CORRECT because gentlemen at the end of the 20th century in Europe were no longer expected to know how to fight with multiple weapons.**

(D) is wrong because gentlemen at the end of the 20th century in Europe were expected to know how to write both prose and poetry but not how to fight with multiple weapons.

8. (A) is wrong because, as a bishop, de las Casas would not criticize the converting of natives.

(B) **is CORRECT because de las Casas is criticizing the greedy nature of the Europeans and how they have devastated the natives for profit.**

(C) is wrong because personal glory is not mentioned.

(D) is wrong because explorers did not cross the ocean to find new mates.

9. (A) is wrong because, although opportunities were reduced, the subjugation and destruction of all natives was a greater and clearer impact.

(B) **is CORRECT because the natives were wiped out by the Europeans.**

(C) is wrong because economic opportunities were not created for these enslaved peoples.

(D) is wrong because the agricultural wealth and produce of the natives were stolen from them.

10. (A) is wrong because economic opportunities increased for Europeans as many came to the New World to get rich.

(B) is wrong because the natives were wiped out by the Europeans.

(C) **is CORRECT because economic opportunities were created for the Europeans.**

(D) is wrong because the slave trade was not in Native Americans.

11. (A) **is CORRECT because, as a bishop, he would want to bring as many Christians into the faith as possible.**

(B) is wrong because de las Casas is criticizing the greedy nature of the Europeans and how they have devastated the natives for profit.

(C) is wrong because personal glory is not mentioned.

(D) is wrong because explorers did not cross the ocean to find new mates.

12. (A) is wrong because there is no evidence of de las Casas exaggerating.

(B) **is CORRECT because Columbus clearly wrote to make himself and his discovery look better.**

(C) is wrong because de las Casas stated that Columbus's men were cruel from the start.

(D) is wrong because there is no evidence of de las Casas wanting Spain to leave.

13. (A) is wrong because mortality rates did not decline as a result of science until the 18th century.

(B) is wrong because the ideas of Galen and Aristotle were discredited by experimental science.

(C) is wrong because these discoveries relied upon experimentation, not the revival of old ideas.

**(D) is CORRECT because Vesalius's idea that the circulatory system carried blood as but one system in the human body was supported by his dissections of corpses.**

14. **(A) is CORRECT because the image displays the human body as a set of systems much as the universe was a system according to Newton.**

(B) is wrong because astrology is based upon belief without proof, unlike Vesalius's work.

(C) is wrong because this image does not illustrate anything to support social problems being solved through reason.

(D) is wrong because subatomic quanta and both the circulatory and skeletal systems are not related in any way other than through this question, with one being about entropy and the other being about systems working—they could even be opposites.

15. (A) is wrong because, although the passage does discuss salvation, it is clearly more about the elect and predestination than about salvation alone.

**(B) is CORRECT because the passage describes the elect, who are predestined to go to heaven according to Calvin.**

(C) is wrong because the passage is not really about Jesus.

(D) is wrong because simony is paying someone else to perform one's church duties.

16. (A) is wrong because the Huguenots were French Calvinists, who did not believe in adult baptism.

(B) is wrong because Lutherans did not believe in adult baptism.

(C) is wrong because Presbyterians were Scottish Calvinists, who did not believe in adult baptism.

**(D) is CORRECT because the Anabaptists believed in adult baptism and in pacifism and were virtually wiped out.**

17. **(A) is CORRECT because Calvin and other reformers did not focus on the wealth of the popes but, instead, on the popes' alleged immorality and ignorance.**

(B) is wrong because reformers of the era did criticize pluralism.

(C) is wrong because reformers of the era did criticize nepotism.

(D) is wrong because reformers of the era did criticize indulgences.

18. (A) is wrong because, although many products did stream into the English colonies, much of the flow was not "cheap" but merely was done at a lower cost than the English could do it for and was carried almost exclusively by the Dutch.

(B) is wrong because the Portuguese were not the intended targets of this legislation and also did not have a monopoly on the Atlantic slave trade at this time.

**(C) is CORRECT because, after a failed attempt at an alliance, the British sought to simultaneously exert more financial control over their North American colonies as well as challenge Dutch maritime supremacy.**

(D) is wrong because the French did not dominate the cod or whaling industry nor were the French the main focus of this legislation.

19. (A) is wrong because Thomas Malthus did not specifically attribute inadequate food and capital to the acts of mercantilism.

(B) is wrong because Josiah Child was a major proponent of mercantilism and a supporter of the Navigation Acts.

**(C) is CORRECT because Adam Smith deliberated at length in his works condemning mercantilist practices carried out by many of the world's leading economic superpowers.**

(D) is wrong because Jean-Baptiste Colbert was a rigid proponent of mercantilist policies, many of which helped consolidate much wealth for Louis XIV to spend freely.

20. **(A) is CORRECT because, from the mid-17th century onward, the British overseas trade grew significantly but the Dutch were negatively affected in the years immediately after passage of the Navigation Acts.**

(B) is wrong because the Dutch continued their successful economic success well into the late-17th century, but wars and diplomacy led to their economic demise in the beginning of the 18th century.

(C) is wrong because the Navigation Acts were not rescinded by the Stuarts, and the British and Dutch in fact fought numerous times in the latter part of the 17th century.

(D) is wrong because, although the countries did engage in war several times, the British and Dutch did not continue to war late into the 18th century.

21. (A) is wrong because the lands gained were not of strategic importance other than gaining a port.

(B) is wrong because the territories gained had little economic importance.

(C) is wrong because the land was taken from Sweden and Poland.

**(D) is CORRECT because the result of the land acquisition was Peter I gaining his "window to the West" in the new capital of St. Petersburg, which had a port in the summer.**

22. **(A) is CORRECT because the Russians expanded southward and eastward under Catherine the Great, taking the Crimean Peninsula and the surrounding area.**

(B) is wrong because, after the Napoleonic Wars, Austria was the strongest empire in Europe, with its foreign minister, Klemens von Metternich, a central figure in the alliances of the time.

(C) is wrong because the Russians did not gain any meaningful territory from the decline of Spain.

(D) is wrong because Russia did not invade the Germanic states and did not have an alliance with Poland to do so.

23. (A) is wrong because the nobility was subjugated by Peter and by Ivan IV before him, leaving them docile and never a real threat to Catherine II.

**(B) is CORRECT because both Peter and Catherine were known for attempting to westernize Russia without really finding much success with the lower classes.**

(C) is wrong because Catherine did not pursue Peter's obsession with creating a Russian navy and did not show the zest he had for it.

(D) is wrong because Alexander II emancipated the serfs, and Peter I never had any intention of doing so.

24. (A) is wrong because the *philosophes*, and Voltaire in particular, believed in religious toleration, not imposing any religion on anyone.

(B) is wrong because Voltaire was a proponent of religious toleration.

(C) is wrong because the Enlightenment *philosophes* did support skepticism and believed it was a good way to analyze data.

**(D) is CORRECT because this passage clearly supports religious toleration.**

25. (A) is wrong because, although those concepts did influence this era, they are not referenced in that sentence.

**(B) is CORRECT because the concept that the Church should stop its discrimination against and conversion of peoples of different faiths around the world came from seeing the virtues of other cultures and methods of living in the world.**

(C) is wrong because, although those concepts did influence this era, they are not referenced in that sentence.

(D) is wrong because, although those concepts did influence this era, they are not directly referenced in that sentence.

26. **(A) is CORRECT because Rousseau did start the Romantic movement by questioning pure reason.**

    (B) is wrong because Montesquieu wrote about the separation of powers in government.

    (C) is wrong because Wollstonecraft was an early feminist who defended the French Revolution.

    (D) is wrong because Adam Smith wrote about economics, not religion.

27. (A) is wrong because, although many were accomplished scientists, that idea is not expressed in the quote.

    (B) is wrong because, although they did have new ways of communicating, that is not the thrust of this quote.

    (C) is wrong because only very few thinkers of this era were atheists; most were deists.

    **(D) is CORRECT because just as they were discovering the relative nature of the universe, they thought that humanity should also be viewed with a new sense of cultural relativism.**

28. **(A) is CORRECT because the passage makes clear that Napoleon believed his conquests kept him in power.**

    (B) is wrong because Napoleon did not need to conquer the Continent to destroy the press.

    (C) is wrong because Napoleon's diary showed more doubt than confidence.

    (D) is wrong because Napoleon credited commanders rather than soldiers with success in this passage.

29. (A) is wrong because placing relatives on foreign thrones is foreign, not domestic, policy.

    (B) is wrong because he was praised for his Napoleonic Code, which was both a criminal and civil code.

    (C) is wrong because the finances of the empire were well managed.

    **(D) is CORRECT because Napoleon was criticized for his secret police and censorship of the press at home.**

30. (A) is wrong because the Continental System was a form of economic warfare that banned British ships from continental trade and had nothing to do with Italian unification.

    (B) is wrong because the Continental System was a form of economic warfare that banned British ships from continental trade and was implemented *before* Napoleon invaded Russia.

    **(C) is CORRECT because the Continental System was a form of economic warfare that banned British ships from continental trade.**

    (D) is wrong because the Continental System was a form of economic warfare that banned British ships from continental trade and had nothing to do with a unified Europe.

31. (A) is wrong because, although they were concerned about liberal young men, the resolutions controlled the press.

    **(B) is CORRECT because the resolutions were clearly concerned with the press and the information disseminated.**

    (C) is wrong because the union of Germanic states was not strong, and Metternich wanted them weak so as to not threaten Austria.

    (D) is wrong because Napoleon was already on St. Helena when this was written.

32. (A) is wrong because Metternich opposed the ideas of nationalism, democracy, and self-determination that came from the Enlightenment.

    (B) is wrong because, although Metternich was oppressive, he did not have the tools to control his people as much as this answer would require.

    **(C) is CORRECT because Metternich, as Austria's foreign minister, was more concerned with nationalist revolts in his multiethnic empire than with any other threat to Austria.**

    (D) is wrong because Metternich knew that such suppression would stagnate his society.

33. (A) is wrong because Pope Pius IX was very conservative and supported a Metternichian view.

    (B) is wrong because Metternich helped to create the decrees.

    **(C) is CORRECT because Mazzini was a radical Italian nationalist republican.**

    (D) is wrong because the "Soldier King," as he was called, was very conservative and would support no changes.

34. **(A) is CORRECT because the Chartists were the most radical of the reformers who called for universal male suffrage.**

    (B) is wrong because, if he was more radical, he would support the Chartist Movement.

    (C) is wrong because the author makes it clear that he thinks some are not qualified to vote.

    (D) is wrong because the author is criticizing the Chartists.

35. (A) is wrong because the Chartists did not fight for women's right to vote.

    **(B) is CORRECT because the Chartists fought for universal male suffrage among other reforms, such as the end to the Corn Laws.**

    (C) is wrong because the Chartists just wanted the vote; government-supported health care was not even thought of as yet.

    (D) is wrong because the Chartists were focused on getting the right to vote first; the other reforms came much later in England.

36. (A) is wrong because liberalism was the movement that led to the Chartists.

    (B) is wrong because radicalism was extreme liberalism, and that was the opposite of what Metternich wanted.

    (C) is wrong because nationalism was a powerful force in the 19th century, but it was a part of liberalism and not supported by Metternich.

    **(D) is CORRECT because Metternich created conservatism in Europe.**

37. (A) is wrong because the revolutions in Prague and Vienna were actually multiethnic while France's was much more homogeneous.

    (B) is wrong because a small number of fatalities occurred in the February Revolution, but there were thousands of fatalities in the June Revolution.

    **(C) is CORRECT because General Cavaignac was forced to storm the barricades in the narrow Paris streets, and heavy casualties were the result.**

    (D) is wrong because the answer refers to events at the end of the Franco-Prussian War in 1871.

38. (A) is wrong because the Polish people were not successful in their revolt.

    **(B) is CORRECT because the Polish revolt began in Prussia and was ended by Prussia, resulting in animosity between the nations.**

    (C) is wrong because the coalition did not go into Poland.

    (D) is wrong because the Polish citizens did not join up in higher numbers or die in higher numbers, as most of the Polish revolutionary force was made of released Polish prisoners from Prussian jails.

39. **(A) is CORRECT because, although thousands died, an election for president immediately took place and domestic reforms improved civilian life immensely.**

    (B) is wrong because, although Cavaignac crushed the June uprising, the elections held thereafter included universal male suffrage and brought about at least a temporary republic.

    (C) is wrong because the violence and desperate economic situation and absence of overwhelming conservatism allowed the movement to succeed.

    (D) is wrong because Austria and Hungary, not France, felt the pressure of foreign troops to thwart the gains of the revolutionaries.

40. **(A) is CORRECT because women in Western Europe, prior to the Agricultural Revolution, practiced gleaning exclusively when the open-field system was popular.**

    (B) is wrong because France was utilizing crop rotation by the end of the 18th century, and rotation and the famine had little to do with one another.

(C) is wrong because serfdom was outlawed by 1807, during the wars of coalition against Napoleon, who enforced the emancipation of serfs.

(D) is wrong because the Hanoverian period in Britain did not begin until 1714, which was after crop rotation had been introduced and the open-field system had ended.

41. (A) is wrong because the answer here refers to the Russian Mir or, later, forced agriculture, which was compulsory in the Stalinist U.S.S.R.

(B) **is CORRECT because many farmers became landless cottagers who made their living in the putting-out system, producing textiles for entrepreneurial businessmen.**

(C) is wrong because the corvée had been around since antiquity and certainly did not arise due to the downfall of the open-field system.

(D) is wrong because the encomienda was a system of agriculture in the New World specific to the Spanish Empire, using labor of indigenous people at least a century before the end of the open-field system.

42. (A) is wrong because, although Ricardo did address food and labor with supply and demand, his studies did not focus specifically on population demographics and famine.

(B) **is CORRECT because the Malthusian dilemma addressed the likelihood that the world's food supply was not sufficient to keep up with population growth.**

(C) is wrong because Marx's writings delved into feudalism and the rise of capitalism, but he did not theorize specifically about population and food supply.

(D) is wrong because Cornelius Vermuyden was responsible for the reclamation of land from swamps and bogs, not for writing about population theories.

43. (A) **is CORRECT because Lenin's New Economic Policy allowed the peasants to own their property, sell produce, and make profits, which led to the creation of the kulaks, or better-off peasant class.**

(B) is wrong because Lenin did not share power with the provisional government.

(C) is wrong because the excerpt was not about that trade-off.

(D) is wrong because the passage was not about that trade-off.

44. (A) is wrong because collectivization was used by Stalin to end the kulak class, create huge farms, and increase agricultural production.

(B) is wrong because persecution of the better-off peasants, or kulaks, was a policy used to get the peasants to collectivize their farms and work together to feed the Soviet Union.

(C) **is CORRECT because the Berlin blockade was after the Second World War and was a part of the Cold War tensions in Germany, which have nothing to do with this passage.**

(D) is wrong because the five-year plans included Stalin's plans to collectivize farms and have the government run them.

45. (A) is wrong because, although industrial production rose incredibly as a result of the five-year plans, collective agriculture was a failure that resulted in the starving of millions of Soviet citizens.

(B) **is CORRECT because, although industrial production rose incredibly as a result of the five-year plans, collective agriculture was a failure that resulted in the starving of millions of Soviet citizens.**

(C) is wrong because agriculture was destroyed as a result of collectivization, resulting in the starving of millions.

(D) is wrong because the Soviet Union saw a rise in industrial production.

46. (A) is wrong because, although Lenin was in Switzerland and did see technology there, Russia's experience of losing two wars within 12 years—the 1905 Russo-Japanese War and the First World War—was ever present in his mind.

(B) is wrong because there was a relatively small percentage of Russians working in factories before the revolution.

(C) is wrong because, although Trotsky did facilitate the Bolshevik revolt through those means, Russia's experience with losing two wars within 12 years was ever present in his mind.

**(D) is CORRECT because Russia's experience with losing two wars within 12 years was ever present in Lenin's mind.**

47. (A) is wrong because there is nothing about women's suffrage in the passage.

(B) is wrong because the democratization of society is considered a good thing by the author of the excerpt.

**(C) is CORRECT because the passage indicates that the government is cynical about the creation of new housing and is disillusioned with the welfare system.**

(D) is wrong because communism's rise is not the main thrust of this reading.

48. **(A) is CORRECT because the public housing program, a form of welfare, is being questioned.**

(B) is wrong because the British budget is not examined in this piece.

(C) is wrong because, although the threat of a revolution is mentioned, it is not the workers who are driving it.

(D) is wrong because the Housing Board wanted to cut down on building houses.

49. (A) is wrong because the data do not indicate what was done with reserves, and the fact that both sides took huge losses is more evident.

(B) is wrong because the data do not indicate what was happening on the Western Front, and the fact that both sides took huge losses is more evident.

**(C) is CORRECT because such huge losses in one battle alone indicate much larger losses.**

(D) is wrong because the data do not indicate whether the Germans or Russians won, and the Russians in fact eventually won the battle.

50. (A) is wrong because there is no evidence of the hunger in Russia and Poland causing

the problems, and the pattern is that there were huge losses of civilian life in Eastern European countries conquered by the Nazis.

(B) is wrong because the better training of the German army does not explain lower Belgian and British casualties.

**(C) is CORRECT because the pattern is that there were huge losses of civilian life in Eastern European countries conquered by the Nazis, where the death camps were, and the Jewish people and other minorities were exterminated to make room for more Germans.**

(D) is wrong because the lack of preparation by the Allies does not explain the lower Belgian and British casualties.

51. (A) is wrong because fighting for your country, and perhaps killing or dying for it, are the ultimate signs of loyalty and respect for a government.

**(B) is CORRECT because the Nazis had convinced the vast majority of their citizens to support a Holocaust that included slavery, degradation of large populations, and genocide, which the overwhelming majority of the German people enthusiastically carried out because of their loyalty to the state and respect for it.**

(C) is wrong because fighting for your country and perhaps killing or dying for it are the ultimate signs of loyalty and respect for a government.

(D) is wrong because most veterans, meaning most men at the time, respected their nation and felt loyal to it.

52. (A) is wrong because the welfare state has not been deemed a failure or a success and that point is a matter of political debate in England and in other countries, but the Green Party seems to support the welfare state.

(B) is wrong because the Green Party supports women's rights, which has ceased to become a major plank in their platform.

(C) is wrong because the Green Party does not generally oppose economic integration and, in fact, wants to use it as a tool of foreign policy to encourage more environmental responsibility internationally.

(D) **is CORRECT because Green Parties were created in many nations as a reaction to growing consumerism and its effects on the environment.**

53. (A) is wrong because, although the Cold War ended with the collapse of the Communist regimes, the platform does not reflect that.

(B) **is CORRECT because many of the workers who came to Europe as invited guests in the 1950s and 1960s settled permanently but have been denied full citizenship rights, which the Green Party wants for them.**

(C) is wrong because members of the Green Party would react negatively to the consumerism of American pop culture.

(D) is wrong because the baby boom is no longer having a significant impact, and the European population is not growing rapidly or may even be shrinking.

54. (A) is wrong because there is no evidence of nationalism in this platform nor in the philosophy of members of the Green Party.

(B) is wrong because the EU does not make such requirements and the members of the Green Party want to expand their movement internationally to include more services to increase equality.

(C) is wrong because members of the Green Party are very secular and do not ally with any religion.

(D) **is CORRECT because members of the Green Party support the welfare state that has come under increasing scrutiny as conservatives and liberals argue over its efficacy and function.**

55. (A) is wrong because the Green Party supports immigrants.

(B) **is CORRECT because the Green Party supports equal rights for all.**

(C) is wrong because members of the Green Party think that fair trade is not fair to workers and has led to globalization and thus the eradication of culture and the promotion of consumerism.

(D) is wrong because most members of the Green Party condemn the idea of nations trying to expand their reach as being an increase in consumerism and conquest.

## Scoring Guide for the Short-Answer Section

Short answers are very straightforward. Either you did or did not get 1 point for each of the points available. Each question is worth up to 3 points for a total of 0–9 points available in this section, worth 20% of the exam score.

1. **0–3 points (2 points for a and 1 point for b)**

(a) 1 point will be given for *each* of *two* explanations of *how* pieces of evidence support the argument that the Italian Renaissance marked the start of modern history, such as: Italian intellectual hallmarks (individualism, humanism, and secularism), new methods of gathering information, increased interaction with the rest of the world, artistic achievement, reorganization of society and governments such as oligarchies and republics, the rise of the merchant elite, the rising importance of wealth, increased emphasis on perfection, and/or a revival of Greco-Roman political ideas.

(b) 1 point will be given for an explanation of *how* one piece of evidence undermines the argument that the Italian Renaissance marked the start of the modern world, such as: Europe was already increasing trade during the Crusades, these were not new ideas but a revival of old ideas from Greece and Rome, the Renaissance was primarily an artistic movement, the Renaissance affected only the upper classes, the Renaissance was still a mostly medieval time, religion was able to stop the advance of knowledge in Italy such as with Galileo, or Italy became the center of the Counter-Reformation.

2. **0–3 points (1 point for a and 2 points for b)**

(a) 1 point will be given for an analysis of how Salvador Dali's image is typical of the trends of the early 20th century, such as but not limited to: it questions perceptions of reality, it is typical of surrealism (with an explanation of surrealism), it places traditional objects into nontraditional formats or representations, it is dark in mood, it pokes fun at established rules and perceptions, and it displays a certain anxiety, all of which are characteristics of the interwar period in which it was created.

(b) 2 points will be awarded, *1 each* for an analysis of change that affected European thought during the period between world wars. A change must be more than mentioned but, instead, must be explored for causes and effects to be awarded a point for this question. Some changes to analyze include but are not limited to: loss of faith in reason and science or in religion to solve problems, increasing scientific knowledge without increasing moral knowledge, economic problems (the Great Depression or German hyperinflation), rise of dictators in most of Europe, rise of relative morality and existentialism, increase of pacifism, and governments and people becoming increasingly radical on both conservative and liberal sides.

3. **0–3 points (1 point for each letter: a, b, and c)**

(a) 1 point will be given for pointing out a significant difference between the historians' interpretations of the Cold War. Some examples of evidence include: Sharon argues more about economics while van der Straaten argues more about ethics, van der Straaten seems biased against the communists, they have different causes for the start of the Cold War, they have different causes for the end of the Cold War, and the sources were written almost a generation apart.

(b) 1 point will be given for a good answer that explains *how* one piece of evidence supports Sharon's argument that the Cold War was a wasteful, unnecessary struggle caused by personalities or his argument that the Cold

War was an economic struggle of production won by the NATO nations because they could produce more and have a higher standard of living. Evidence to support the first claim include: the Iron Curtain Speech, the Truman Doctrine, the Cuban Missile Crisis, the Korean War, missile tests, or peace dividend statistics. Evidence to support the second claim could include: the use of economic statistics, the Marshall Plan, the Comintern, the Common Market, the fall of the Soviet Union and the Berlin Wall, the rise of capitalism in Eastern Europe after 1990, the creation of the EU, or the Americanization of Europe after 1990.

(c) 1 point will be given for an explanation of *how* one piece of evidence supports van der Straaten's argument that the Cold War was an ideological battle of freedom versus tyranny or his second argument that the Cold War was ended by its own leaders. Evidence to support the first argument that it was an ideological battle can include: propaganda; the Red Scare; the Cuban Missile Crisis; the Prague Spring; the Afghan invasion of 1979; Soviet support of terrorism against NATO nations; the legacy of Cold War battles in Africa, Latin America, and the Middle East; or the brutal suppression of Soviet-style governments in all of Eastern Europe. Evidence to support the second claim that communism was brought down by its own leaders can include: Mikhail Gorbachev's *perestroika* and *glasnost*, the failed coup when Yeltsin was elected, Gorbachev's peaceful dissolution of the Soviet Union, the quick fall of the Berlin Wall, or communism all over Eastern Europe ending mostly bloodlessly.

4. **0–3 points (1 point for each letter: a, b, and c)**

(a) 1 point will be given for explaining the positive aspects of the rule of Louis XIV. The answer should explain how France rose to international esteem under the rule of Louis XIV. It should point out that other rulers, such as Peter I of Russia and the Habsburgs, copied his model of how to run a royal court.

Additionally, the response should point out Louis XIV's military victories and how he used his military to raise the power of his nation. It should also explain how he unified the French people under his rule because they were proud to be led by him.

(b) 1 point will be given for a good answer that explains the negative aspects of Louis XIV and his rule of France. It should indicate that his nation was at war for more than half of his rule. It should explain how his overuse of the military and the opulence of Versailles were responsible for eventually bankrupting the nation, leaving it open to revolution. Additionally, the essay should point out how the nobility detested Louis XIV. His use of clothes, wigs, and little ceremonies to enhance his image without any substance should be noted. His opulent lifestyle while his people suffered through war, enforced labor obligations, and turmoil should also be noted.

(c) 1 point will be given for an explanation of *how* war affected the legacy of Louis XIV, who said on his death bed that he had "gone to war too often and pursued it for vanity's sake." The resulting debts from the wars should be mentioned and placed into context. The might and reputation of the French army as a deterrent to any power attacking France should be mentioned. The winning of the Thirty Years' War should also be mentioned as having left Europe divided religiously, which allowed France to dominate the region for another century. The response should also explain the French role in the War of Spanish Succession and how the rest of Europe mostly teamed up against Louis XIV to prevent his armies from leaving France in control of the entire Iberian Peninsula.

## Scoring Guide for the Essay Section

### The Document-Based Question (DBQ)

The DBQ emphasizes your ability to analyze and synthesize historical evidence, including textual, quantitative, or visual materials. The question also requires you to formulate a thesis and support it with relevant evidence. The seven documents accompanying each DBQ may vary in length, type, and content, but they will allow you to illustrate complexities and interactions within the material and to utilize a broad spectrum of historical skills.

The document-based question will typically require you to relate the documents to a historical period or theme and, thus, to focus on major periods and issues. In this way, the DBQ assesses your ability to incorporate outside knowledge related to the question but beyond the specifics of the documents. This ability to place the documents in the historical context in which they were produced is essential for your success.

## Scoring Your DBQ

**Maximum Possible Points: 7**

### A. THESIS AND ARGUMENT DEVELOPMENT (0–1 total points)

**Targeted Skill—Argumentation**

**1 point:** Present a thesis that makes a historically defensible claim and responds to all parts of the question. The thesis must consist of one or more sentences located in one place, either in the introduction or the conclusion.

You must present a thesis that directly addresses all parts of the question and makes a historically defensible claim. The thesis must do more than restate the question.

> **Superb thesis:** "Socialism, which emerged as a response to the cruelties of pure capitalism, was at first an idea that was accepted only by radicals. However, as the workers gained economic and political power, the ideas became mainstream and were even utilized by conservatives. Socialist ideas then became an issue

of debate between conservatives and liberals after World War II." (This thesis is strong because it makes a historically defensible claim, responds to all parts of the question, and develops a cohesive argument that clearly recognizes historical complexity by explicitly illustrating relationships among historical evidence and including qualification. Some evidence of this is that the thesis is specific in its assessment of both political viewpoints—liberals, conservatives, and radicals—and political, social, or economic changes—workers gaining economic power, World War II, and conservatives gaining power.)

**Acceptable thesis:** "From 1800 to 1949, views on socialism changed as the world changed and opinions became more enlightened and focused on the plight of the common man." (This receives 1 point for directly addressing the question but does not account for historical complexity by illustrating any relationships.)

**Unacceptable theses:**

- "Those who were more radical or more liberal were always more in favor of socialism than those who were less radical, as can be seen through changes over time." (This is unacceptable because even though it states views, it does not state specific social, political, or economic changes.)
- "From the emergence of capitalism through the Industrial Revolution and the rise of nation-states, to the Great Depression, and through World War II, views on socialism have changed." (This is unacceptable because although it mentions specific social, economic, and political events, it mentions no specific views on socialism.)

## B. CONTEXTUALIZATION (0–1 total points)

**1 point:** The essay must describe a broader historical context immediately relevant to the question.

**Acceptable contextualization:**

- "After distrust as partners during World War II, Churchill came out publicly against Stalin in his speech in America in order to try to get the United States to be more active in challenging the growing power of the Soviet Union."
- "As the Cold War began, the opinions on socialism changed to a harder line from conservatives and were looked at more critically for flaws by intellectuals like Albert Einstein."

**Unacceptable contextualization:**

- "As the general who planned the Allied victory, Churchill was dedicated to keeping Europe free." (Churchill was not a general in World War II; he was the British political leader.)
- "As the inventor of the atomic bomb, Einstein was worried about a nuclear war." (There is no evidence to support that Einstein was worried in this document, and Einstein did not invent nuclear weapons.)

## C. EVIDENCE (0–3 total points)

**1 point:** The essay must utilize the content of at least THREE documents to address the topic of the question.
**Note:** This analysis may be in the topic sentence; the analysis must be connected to the argument.

OR

**2 points:** The essay must utilize the content of at least SIX documents to support an argument about the question.
**Note:** This analysis may be in the topic sentence; the analysis must be connected to the argument.

AND

## EVIDENCE BEYOND THE DOCUMENTS (0–1 total points)

**1 point:** The essay explains how at least one additional piece of specific evidence beyond those found in the documents relates to an argument about the question.

**Note:** This evidence must be DIFFERENT from the evidence used to earn the point for contextualization. This point is NOT awarded for a phrase or reference.

**Acceptable outside historical evidence:**

- "Bismarck's welfare reforms in Germany created the first modern welfare state there as a way to undermine the liberals and co-opt socialism into the conservative platform and thus convince voters to choose conservative leaders."
- "As the Fascists had come to power spreading hatred of communism across Europe, it made sense that one of the late propaganda posters in Germany would try to reignite that sentiment."

**Unacceptable outside historical evidence:**

- "The Nazis didn't like Communists, so it makes sense that their poster was against the Bolsheviks." (This is unacceptable because the evidence is pretty clear from the document, and no true outside evidence was presented.)

## D. ANALYSIS AND REASONING (0–2 total points)

**1 point:** For at least THREE documents, the essay explains how each document's point of view, purpose, historical situation, and/or audience are relevant to the argument.

**2 points:** The essay demonstrates a complex understanding of the historical development that is the focus of the prompt, using evidence to corroborate, qualify, or modify an argument that addresses the question.

**Guidance on awarding this point is given.**

**1 point:** For at least FOUR documents, explain how each document's point of view, purpose, historical situation, and/or audience is relevant to the argument.

**Example of acceptable analysis:** "Winston Churchill, after having been voted out of office as prime minister of England after winning World War II with the Allies, was mistrustful of socialism in general and of Stalin and his expansionary plans in particular, which is why he is asking the Conservative party to condemn socialism." (This correctly places Churchill in place, time, and importance, and specifically explains point of view and purpose as well as giving some context.)

**Example of unacceptable analysis:** "The Nazi propaganda poster seems to be supporting socialism instead of Bolshevism." (This is incorrect because this poster condemns Bolshevism, which was a specific type of socialism.)

**Intended Audience**

**Acceptable:** "The People's Petition was written to present to members of Parliament but also to convince workers and others to join the Chartist Movement."

**Unacceptable:** "The People's Charter was written for the people." (This is far too vague; specify which people in which place at which time?)

**Purpose**

**Acceptable:** "The Nazi propaganda poster was created and posted to encourage the German soldiers and citizens to continue to fight the advancing Soviet army."

**Unacceptable:** "Winston Churchill is writing to show how he supported socialism so everyone should." (This is a misinterpretation as Churchill was mostly writing against socialism.)

## Historical Context

**Acceptable:** "As the recently dismissed prime minister, Winston Churchill may be attempting to help his party get reorganized."

**Unacceptable:** "Because the Cold War was over, Einstein was writing that socialism was better than capitalism." (This is wrong because the Cold War was just beginning when Einstein wrote this.)

## Author's Point of View

**Acceptable:** "As an ardent Communist, Rosa Luxemburg would of course be disappointed that socialism was losing power in Germany during the First World War."

**Unacceptable:** "Because he was the king of England, Winston Churchill's statements should be considered as coming from the upper classes." (This is wrong because Churchill was prime minister rather than king, although he certainly was upper class as the Duke of Marlborough.)

## Document 1

### Key Points

- Pro-socialist
- Calls for those without property to share in profits
- Warns of revolution if things do not change
- Believes scientists and artists are leaders of change
- States proletariat won in France and bourgeoisie lost
- Asks scientists and artists

### Contextualization

- Napoleon ruling France in Empire period
- Industrial Revolution in England only
- French Revolution just ended
- Concert of Europe and Metternich alliance system in place against radical change

## Document 2

### Key Points

- Pro-socialist
- Calls for universal male suffrage, property tax, and more equality
- Part of political movement for suffrage and to repeal Corn Laws
- Believes equality is coming
- Pre-Communist ideas
- Asks scientists and artists

### Contextualization

- Part of political movement for suffrage and to repeal Corn Laws
- Industrial Revolution in England has spread to the Continent
- New class consciousness developing
- Huge gaps in wealth
- Urbanization
- Just after failed revolutions of 1830 but before 1848

## Document 3

### Key Points

- Pro-socialist
- Indicates international community of workers
- Appears peaceful and not radical through brotherhood
- Romantic era artistic themes and techniques
- Pro-Communist ideas
- Common man depicted
- Trade unions legal and powerful across Europe in 1896

*Contextualization*

- Part of political movement for suffrage and to repeal Corn Laws
- Industrial Revolution in England has spread to the European Continent
- New class consciousness developing
- Huge gaps in wealth
- Urbanization
- Just after failed revolutions of 1830 but before 1848

## Document 4

### Key Points

- Pro-socialist and written by a Jewish woman who was an immigrant and a Communist
- Indicates frustration at the setbacks socialism faced during the First World War
- Wanted to find problems in Socialist Party and fix them, and has a lamenting but angry and undeterred tone
- Examines Germany's history as a strong socialist economy
- Communist ideas and revolutionary outlook shared by Communists at the time
- Common man depicted
- Trade unions legal and powerful across Europe in 1896

*Contextualization*

- Rosa Luxemburg was murdered by the Freicorps in 1919.
- An ardent Communist, Luxemburg was a Polish Jew who grew up in Germany.
- The eras of self-criticism and criticism of others was to begin shortly.
- The First World War was going on with a *total war* effort in all countries, requiring rationing, price controls, and government institutions such as the German War Raw Materials Board and the British Ministry of Munitions.
- The war lasted much longer than anyone believed it would before it started.
- The First World War ended in 1918, and the age of anxiety began to question the belief that science and reason could create a better world.

## Document 5

### Key Points

- This poster was anti-Communist.
- This Nazi propaganda poster indicated that Bolsheviks create pain and suffering.
- It was meant to scare Polish citizens about what would happen if the Bolsheviks (Soviets) took over their region.

- Bolshevism is a specific type of socialism and the Nazi Party had "Socialist" in its name, but the Nazis hated Communists and claimed the Fascist mantle.
- The poster shows German racial prejudices at the time.
- It was just one of tens of thousands of pieces of German propaganda used on its people.

*Contextualization*

- Stalin and Hitler had created a nonaggression pact at the start of the Second World War in Europe in 1939, despite each hating the other's ideas and personality. However, Germany invaded the U.S.S.R. in 1941 and was not driven out until the end of 1944.
- The Soviets were very harsh on the people in the Polish and German areas they conquered at the end of the Second World War.
- Communism and Fascism were diametrically opposed ideas, but both systems ended up creating similar totalitarian dictatorships.
- The Second World War was going on with a *total war* effort in all countries, requiring rationing, price controls, and government institutions comparable to the German War Raw Materials Board and the British Ministry of Munitions during the First World War.
- The Second World War ended, leaving the Cold War in its wake.

## Document 6

### Key Points

- This document was anti-socialist.
- Winston Churchill was a conservative leader of the United Kingdom during the Second World War but was ejected from power. He is explaining what his party must do to regain power and send his country in the right direction.
- He was known for distrusting Stalin, communism, children, and pets as well as for being pompous, egotistical, and very conservative.
- He gave the speech that defined the Iron Curtain and helped get America more involved in the Cold War.
- This document shows his frustration at losing power, his plan for his party to regain it, and his thoughts that socialism has gone too far.
- He did support welfare and unemployment, just not the modern welfare state.
- The document shows Churchill's concern for a state that has grown too powerful and is too involved with the economic lives of its citizens.

*Contextualization*

- The Second World War has just ended, and the Cold War has not yet begun.
- The Soviets were taking over Eastern Europe and spreading their brand of communism.
- The United States was supporting much of the world through the Marshall Plan; the beauty of the plan was that it spread capitalism, reliance on American goods, and goodwill toward America all over the world.
- The Second World War had been a *total war* effort for all countries, requiring rationing, price controls, and government institutions to run the economy; the world was transitioning back to a peacetime consumer economy.

## Document 7

### Key Points

- The document was pro-socialist.

- Albert Einstein, one of the most brilliant theoretical physicists and of Jewish heritage, emigrated from Germany to the United States before the Second World War.
- Einstein was known for the theory of relativity and for urging Roosevelt to create an atom bomb before Hitler did.
- This document explains why raw capitalism is not a fair system and why society would be better served through a socialist system.
- It calls capitalism evil and blames it for economic depressions, stating it must be fixed or replaced.
- The document was written to show Americans and others that although there was a lot of propaganda starting up against socialism, it was a really good system if done right.

*Contextualization*

- With the Cold War starting, as well as the development of atomic weapons, Einstein felt guilty for suggesting the Allies build the bomb.
- The Soviets were taking over Eastern Europe and spreading their brand of communism.
- The United States was supporting much of the world through the Marshall Plan, and the beauty of the plan was that it spread capitalism, reliance on American goods, and goodwill toward America all over the world.
- The Second World War had devastated the world, and Einstein did not want another war over idealism.

## Scoring Guidelines for Long Essay Question 2

Compare the impact of the printing press on the daily life and culture of the European people with that of the Columbian Exchange on the daily lives and culture of the European people.

**Maximum possible points: 6**

## Comments on Question 2

This is clearly a *compare* skill question. So be sure to describe the similarities and differences between the ways that the daily lives and culture of people of all classes were affected by the advent of the printing press and the Columbian Exchange. Also account for or explain why they were so different by providing specific examples of how the two changes differed in human experiences, duration, impact on learning and knowledge, and societal changes. It is also important to tie the events that resulted from both the spread of the printing press and the Columbian Exchange to other historical trends politically, militarily, socially, economically, or scientifically.

The contrast is glaring. The printing press spread knowledge that people of Europe had been compartmentalizing for centuries and increased literacy as well as access to knowledge. The Columbian Exchange brought with it changes in the European balance of power, the foods people ate, the opportunities available to Europeans, and many other commodities and agricultural products.

**A detailed rubric for this specific question follows to help you score your long essay response.**

### A. THESIS (0–1 total points)

**1 point:** The essay presents a thesis that makes a historically defensible claim and responds to all parts of the question. The thesis must consist of one or more sentences located in one place, either in the introduction or the conclusion.

**Special note:** The thesis *must* consist of one or more sentences located in the introduction or the conclusion of the essay. However, neither the introduction nor the conclusion is strictly limited to one paragraph.

Acceptable thesis statements create an argument that responds to the task: identifying relevant impacts upon the social life and culture of the citizens of each nation caused by each revolution *and* explaining the similarities and differences between the ways each innovation changed the culture and lives of the people. For example, the printing press meant that killing a person with new ideas that challenged the status quo would no longer end those ideas; the printing press better spread knowledge to the lower classes as books became less expensive. The Columbian Exchange opened new lands for Europeans to own and new people for them to exploit as well as much new wealth and many new products, such as chocolate and vanilla.

You must present a thesis that directly addresses all parts of the question. Your thesis must do more than restate the question.

**Acceptable thesis:** "Although both the spread of the printing press from Asia to Europe and the Columbian Exchange affected the knowledge and lives of Europeans, they did so in different ways. The printing press made all information more accessible and easier to record and share; it spurred a reading revolution. The Columbian Exchange brought in knowledge from previously unknown parts of the world, opened up economic opportunities to colonize, and opened up entire new fields of knowledge because it involved another continent." (This thesis is acceptable because it is specific in its assessment of both innovations, and it gives specific comparisons and accounts for the similarities and differences between them.)

**Unacceptable theses:**

- "The printing press and Columbian Exchange had many effects on their peoples that were different and similar in a lot of ways." (This is unacceptable because it does not state any specific similarities or differences, much less account for them.)
- "Both the printing press and the Columbian Exchange changed the lives and culture of Europeans, with the printing press allowing Europeans better access to information they already had and the Columbian Exchange giving them access to new knowledge, organisms, and economic opportunities." (This is unacceptable because even though it compares and contrasts the Columbian Exchange with the printing press, there is nothing in the thesis about the daily lives of European citizens or their culture.)

## B. CONTEXTUALIZATION (0–1 total points)

**1 point:** The essay describes a broader historical context immediately relevant to the question.

## C. EVIDENCE (0–2 total points)

**1 point:** The essay develops and supports an argument that provides specific examples of evidence related to comparing the impact of the Columbian Exchange and the spread of the printing press.

OR

**2 points:** The essay adequately supports an argument about the comparison of the impact of the Columbian Exchange and the spread of the printing press.

## D. ANALYSIS AND REASONING (0–3 total points)

**1 point:** The essay uses historical reasoning (e.g., comparison, causation, CCOT) to frame or structure an argument that addresses the prompt.

OR

**2 points:** It demonstrates a complex understanding of the historical development that is the focus of the prompt, using evidence to corroborate, qualify, or modify an argument that addresses the question.

**Acceptable comparison:** The essay compares and contrasts the social, economic, and political impacts of the Columbian Exchange with that of the spread of the printing press throughout Europe and accounts for the different impacts of the two innovations through historical reasoning and presentation of evidence about how each changed culture and daily life in different European nations.

**Unacceptable comparison:**

- The essay is focused either solely on the printing press or the Columbian Exchange, but not both.
- The essay examines the events caused by each innovation but not the effects on the culture and daily lives of the citizens.
- The essay looks at similarities and differences in the culture and daily lives of the citizens but fails to account for them and/or provide detailed evidence for support.

## Scoring Guidelines for Long Essay Question 3

Compare the impact of the French Revolution of 1789 on the daily life and culture of the French people with that of the Russian Revolution of 1917 on the daily life and culture of the Russian people.

**Maximum possible points: 6**

## Comments on Question 3

This is clearly a *compare* skill question. So be sure to describe the similarities and differences between the ways that the French and Russian people were affected by their respective revolutions through their daily lives and cultural changes. Also account for or explain why they were so different by providing specific examples of how the two revolutions differed in human experiences, duration, control of the people, and societal changes. It is also important to tie the events of the revolutions to other historical trends politically, militarily, socially, economically, or scientifically.

The contrast is glaring. Although the French went through a relatively short period of terror and chaos, they ended up with a written constitution and a set of laws that created some degree of personal liberty. The Soviets, however, traded all freedom for the illusion of equality and lived under a totalitarian dictatorship for over 70 years.

**A detailed rubric for this specific question follows to help you score your long essay response.**

**A. THESIS (0–1 total points)**

**1 point:** The essay presents a thesis that makes a historically defensible claim and responds to all parts of the question. The thesis must consist of one or more sentences located in one place, either in the introduction or the conclusion.

**Special note:** The thesis *must* consist of one or more sentences located in the introduction or the conclusion of the essay. However, neither the introduction nor the conclusion is strictly limited to one paragraph.

Acceptable thesis statements create an argument that responds to both tasks: identifying relevant impacts upon the social life and culture of Europeans during each era caused by each revolution and explaining the similarities and differences between the ways the people of all classes were affected by each revolution. For example: The lives and cultures of both the French and Russian people were dramatically affected by the revolutions in each nation with revolutionary terror, shifting public norms, purges, and changes to class structure in both nations. These changes to class structure were short-lived in France compared to Russia, and thus had less impact shaping the people than in Russia.

You must present a thesis that directly addresses all parts of the question. Your thesis must do more than restate the question.

**Acceptable thesis:** "The French became more egalitarian and gained national pride as a result of their short-lived revolution, gaining many freedoms. In contrast, the Russian Revolution of 1917 left the Russian people as Soviet comrades who, due to totalitarian rule, had little freedom to make any important choices in their lives for over 70 years." (This thesis is acceptable because it is specific in its assessment of both revolutions, and it gives specific comparisons and accounts for the similarities and differences between the revolutions.)

**Unacceptable theses:**

- "The French Revolution and Russian Revolution had many effects on their peoples that were different and similar in a lot of ways." (This is unacceptable because it does not state any specific similarities or differences, much less account for them.)
- "Although both revolutions changed political beliefs, the French Revolution was much more about individual rights and political unity while the Russian Revolution was much more about economics and power." (This is unacceptable because even though it compares and contrasts the revolutions politically, there is nothing in the thesis about the daily lives of the citizens or their culture.)

## B. CONTEXTUALIZATION (0–1 total points)

**1 point:** The essay describes a broader historical context immediately relevant to the question.

## C. EVIDENCE (0–2 total points)

**1 point:** The essay provides specific examples of evidence related to comparing the French and Russian Revolutions.

**OR**

**2 points:** It adequately supports an argument about the comparison of the French and Russian Revolutions with specific and relevant evidence.

## D. ANALYSIS AND REASONING (0–3 total points)

**1 point:** The essay uses historical reasoning (e.g., comparison, causation, CCOT) to frame or structure an argument that addresses the prompt.

**OR**

**2 points:** It demonstrates a complex understanding of the historical development that is the focus of the prompt, using evidence to corroborate, qualify, or modify an argument that addresses the question.

**Acceptable comparison:** The essay compares and contrasts the political changes in each country to the changes in daily life and culture in that country. It also compares and contrasts the similarities and differences between those changes, citing specific facts in those arguments. The impact of one-party rule in the Soviet Union compared to many changes in French leadership over the same period can also be examined as factors that affected the freedoms and experiences of the citizens of each nation.

**Unacceptable comparison:**

- The essay is focused either solely on the French Revolution or the Russian Revolution but not on both.
- The essay examines the events of each revolution but not the effects on the culture and daily lives of the citizens.
- The essay looks at similarities and differences in the culture and daily lives of the citizens but fails to account for them and/or provide detailed evidence for support (1 point only).

## Scoring Guidelines for Long Essay Question 4

Compare the impact of the Scientific Revolution (1540–1700) on the daily life and culture of the European people with that of the Industrial Revolution (1780–1914) on the daily life and culture of the 19th-century Europeans.

**Maximum possible points: 6**

### Comments on Question 4

This is clearly a *compare* skill question. So be sure to describe the similarities and differences between the ways in which the European people were affected by their respective revolutions through their daily lives and cultural changes. Also account for or explain why they were so different by providing specific examples of how the two revolutions differed in level of impact on the common man, duration, effect on the economy, societal changes, intellectual changes, and artistic changes. It is also important to tie the events of the revolutions to other historical trends politically, militarily, socially, economically, or scientifically.

The contrast is glaring. While the Scientific Revolution changed the upper-class conception of the universe and led to the Enlightenment, there was little effect on the common man. The Industrial Revolution, however, changed not just the way the universe was conceived but the way people lived, worked, and learned.

**A detailed rubric for this specific question follows to help you score your long essay response.**

### A. THESIS (0–1 total points)

**1 point:** The essay presents a thesis that makes a historically defensible claim and responds to all parts of the question. The thesis must consist of one or more sentences located in one place, either in the introduction or the conclusion.

**Special note:** The thesis *must* consist of one or more sentences located in the introduction or the conclusion of the essay. However, neither the introduction nor the conclusion is strictly limited to one paragraph.

Acceptable thesis statements create an argument that responds to the task: identifying relevant impacts upon the social life and culture of the citizens of each nation caused by each revolution and explaining the similarities and differences between the ways that each innovation changed the culture and lives of the people. For example, the Scientific Revolution was short-lived and resulted mostly in upper-class changes and new discoveries that reshaped thinking that would later affect the lives of most people, while the Industrial Revolution is an ongoing process of industrialization that has reshaped almost every aspect of life for most people on Earth of all classes in different ways, from changing the tempo of their work to increasing their standard of living.

You must present a thesis that directly addresses all parts of the question. Your thesis must do more than restate the question.

**Acceptable thesis:** "The Scientific Revolution began to move Europeans toward new ways of thinking and investigating the universe by revealing truths about the way the universe worked. These truths eventually led to the Enlightenment and both political and economic freedoms, increasing first for the bourgeoisie and then for many others. However, they did not result in large cultural changes in the daily lives of most Europeans. In contrast, the Industrial Revolution drastically and rapidly changed the lives of all classes of society as soon as it reached their nation." (This thesis is acceptable because it is specific in its assessment of both revolutions. It also gives specific comparisons and accounts for the similarities and differences between the revolutions and their impacts on the culture and daily lives of those who lived through them.)

**Unacceptable theses:**

- "The Scientific Revolution and the Industrial Revolution had many effects on their peoples that were different and similar in a lot of ways." (This is unacceptable because it does not state any specific similarities or differences, much less account for them.)

- "Although both revolutions changed knowledge, the Industrial Revolution was much more about technology and profit, while the Scientific Revolution was much more about pure thought and learning." (This is unacceptable because even though it compares and contrasts the revolutions intellectually, there is nothing in the thesis about the daily lives of the people or their culture.)

## B. CONTEXTUALIZATION (0–1 total points)

**1 point:** The essay describes a broader historical context immediately relevant to the question.

## C. EVIDENCE (0–2 total points)

**1 point:** The essay develops and supports an argument that provides specific examples of evidence related to comparing the Scientific Revolution and the Industrial Revolution.

OR

**2 points:** The essay adequately supports an argument about the comparison of the Scientific Revolution and the Industrial Revolution with specific and relevant evidence.

## D. ANALYSIS AND REASONING (0–3 total points)

**1 point:** The essay uses historical reasoning (e.g., comparison, causation, CCOT) to frame or structure an argument that addresses the prompt.

OR

**2 points:** It demonstrates a complex understanding of the historical development that is the focus of the prompt, using evidence to corroborate, qualify, or modify an argument that addresses the question.

**Acceptable comparison:** The essay compares and contrasts how the intellectual and technological changes during each era led to different changes in daily life and culture. It compares and contrasts the similarities and differences between those changes citing specific facts to support those arguments. The lesser impact of the Scientific Revolution on the daily lives of most Europeans should be compared to the vast plethora of changes to every aspect of life, such as electricity, running water, urbanization, and increased production brought on by the Industrial Revolution.

**Unacceptable comparison:**

- The essay is solely focused on either the Industrial or the Scientific Revolutions, but not both.
- The essay examines the events of each revolution but not the effects on the culture and daily lives of the citizens.
- The essay looks at the similarities and differences in the culture and daily lives of the citizens but fails to account for them and/or provide detailed evidence for support (1 point only).

**This is the end of the scoring section. Once you have scored your answers, go back to the section on scoring the exam, plug your scores into the chart, and compute to get your score on your practice exam.**

# ANSWER SHEET
## Practice Test 2

**Section 1**

1. Ⓐ Ⓑ Ⓒ Ⓓ
2. Ⓐ Ⓑ Ⓒ Ⓓ
3. Ⓐ Ⓑ Ⓒ Ⓓ
4. Ⓐ Ⓑ Ⓒ Ⓓ
5. Ⓐ Ⓑ Ⓒ Ⓓ
6. Ⓐ Ⓑ Ⓒ Ⓓ
7. Ⓐ Ⓑ Ⓒ Ⓓ
8. Ⓐ Ⓑ Ⓒ Ⓓ
9. Ⓐ Ⓑ Ⓒ Ⓓ
10. Ⓐ Ⓑ Ⓒ Ⓓ
11. Ⓐ Ⓑ Ⓒ Ⓓ
12. Ⓐ Ⓑ Ⓒ Ⓓ
13. Ⓐ Ⓑ Ⓒ Ⓓ
14. Ⓐ Ⓑ Ⓒ Ⓓ

15. Ⓐ Ⓑ Ⓒ Ⓓ
16. Ⓐ Ⓑ Ⓒ Ⓓ
17. Ⓐ Ⓑ Ⓒ Ⓓ
18. Ⓐ Ⓑ Ⓒ Ⓓ
19. Ⓐ Ⓑ Ⓒ Ⓓ
20. Ⓐ Ⓑ Ⓒ Ⓓ
21. Ⓐ Ⓑ Ⓒ Ⓓ
22. Ⓐ Ⓑ Ⓒ Ⓓ
23. Ⓐ Ⓑ Ⓒ Ⓓ
24. Ⓐ Ⓑ Ⓒ Ⓓ
25. Ⓐ Ⓑ Ⓒ Ⓓ
26. Ⓐ Ⓑ Ⓒ Ⓓ
27. Ⓐ Ⓑ Ⓒ Ⓓ
28. Ⓐ Ⓑ Ⓒ Ⓓ

29. Ⓐ Ⓑ Ⓒ Ⓓ
30. Ⓐ Ⓑ Ⓒ Ⓓ
31. Ⓐ Ⓑ Ⓒ Ⓓ
32. Ⓐ Ⓑ Ⓒ Ⓓ
33. Ⓐ Ⓑ Ⓒ Ⓓ
34. Ⓐ Ⓑ Ⓒ Ⓓ
35. Ⓐ Ⓑ Ⓒ Ⓓ
36. Ⓐ Ⓑ Ⓒ Ⓓ
37. Ⓐ Ⓑ Ⓒ Ⓓ
38. Ⓐ Ⓑ Ⓒ Ⓓ
39. Ⓐ Ⓑ Ⓒ Ⓓ
40. Ⓐ Ⓑ Ⓒ Ⓓ
41. Ⓐ Ⓑ Ⓒ Ⓓ
42. Ⓐ Ⓑ Ⓒ Ⓓ

43. Ⓐ Ⓑ Ⓒ Ⓓ
44. Ⓐ Ⓑ Ⓒ Ⓓ
45. Ⓐ Ⓑ Ⓒ Ⓓ
46. Ⓐ Ⓑ Ⓒ Ⓓ
47. Ⓐ Ⓑ Ⓒ Ⓓ
48. Ⓐ Ⓑ Ⓒ Ⓓ
49. Ⓐ Ⓑ Ⓒ Ⓓ
50. Ⓐ Ⓑ Ⓒ Ⓓ
51. Ⓐ Ⓑ Ⓒ Ⓓ
52. Ⓐ Ⓑ Ⓒ Ⓓ
53. Ⓐ Ⓑ Ⓒ Ⓓ
54. Ⓐ Ⓑ Ⓒ Ⓓ
55. Ⓐ Ⓑ Ⓒ Ⓓ

# Practice Test 2

## Section I

### Part A: Multiple-Choice Questions

TIME: 55 MINUTES
NUMBER OF QUESTIONS: 55
PERCENTAGE OF TOTAL AP EXAM SCORE: 40%
WRITING INSTRUMENT: PENCIL REQUIRED

**DIRECTIONS:** Section I, Part A of this exam contains 55 multiple-choice questions. Indicate all of your answers to the multiple-choice questions on the multiple-choice answer sheet. No credit will be given for anything written in the exam booklet, but you may write on the exam booklet to take notes and do scratch work.

Use your time efficiently, working as quickly as possible without losing accuracy. Do not spend too much time on any one question. Go on to other questions and come back to the ones that you have not answered if you have time. It is not expected that you will know the answers to all of the multiple-choice questions.

Your total score on the multiple-choice section is based only on the number of questions answered correctly. Points are not deducted for incorrect answers or unanswered questions.

**Questions 1–3 refer to the fresco shown below.**

*School of Athens* by Raphael (1509–1511). This painting depicting the most famous Greek philosophers, such as Plato, Aristotle, Pythagoras, Euclid, and many others, was commissioned as one of four great masterpieces for the Papal Palace in Rome.

1.  The painting is often described as a Renaissance masterpiece that typifies the humanism that was which of the following?

    (A)  Just starting to emerge but would continue to spread uninterrupted throughout Europe over the course of the next 500 years as a central ideal

    (B)  Just coming to an end as the interaction with the Ottoman Turks in 1453 closed off trade routes and shut down communication between East and West

    (C)  In its prime, as the only major power in Europe that refused to employ humanist artists was the Catholic Church

    (D)  In its prime, as humanists such as Petrarch in Italy and Erasmus in Rotterdam were already writing major humanist works by the time this painting was finished

2.  What are three characteristics in the fresco that make it an Italian Renaissance painting?

    (A)  Perspective, sfumato, and scale

    (B)  Chiaroscuro, perspective, and the number of people depicted

    (C)  Perspective, humanist subject matter, and attention to anatomical detail

    (D)  Colors used, humanist subject matter, and the fact that it was a fresco

3.  Why would the patrons of this painting and its three companion paintings wish to pay huge sums of money for these works of art?

    (A)  They and the other people in their region believed that great public works of art demonstrated power and prestige to the people.

    (B)  They believed that it was their civic duty to pay people to paint in order to reduce unemployment in their towns.

    (C)  They simply wanted to be surrounded by beautiful objects and paintings because they loved beauty.

    (D)  They believed that if they surrounded themselves with pictures from ancient Greece, then they would be very wise and live for a long time, like Greek ideas did.

**Questions 4–6 refer to the following letter.**

It happened . . . that a Spaniard saw an Indian . . . eating a piece of flesh taken from the body of an Indian who had been killed . . . I had the culprit burned, explaining that the cause was his having killed that Indian and eaten him[,] which was prohibited by Your Majesty, and by me in Your Royal name. I further made the chief understand that all the people . . . must abstain from this custom . . . I came . . . to protect their lives as well as their property, and to teach them that they were to adore but one God . . . that they must turn from their idols, and the rites they had practiced until then, for these were lies and deceptions which the devil . . . had invented . . . I, likewise, had come to teach them that Your Majesty, by the will of Divine Providence, rules the universe, and that they also must submit themselves to the imperial yoke, and do all that we who are Your Majesty's ministers here might order them.

—Hernan Cortez, *Fifth Letter* to Holy Roman Emperor Charles V, 1521

4.  Which of the following motivations for exploration is most evident from the letter?

    (A) The rise of mercantilism gave the state a new role in promoting commercial development and the acquisition of colonies overseas.

    (B) European states sought direct access to gold, spices, and luxury goods as a means to enhance personal wealth and state power.

    (C) Individual captains sought great glory and wealth.

    (D) Christianity served as a stimulus for exploration as governments and religious authorities sought to spread the faith and to counter Islam and as a justification for the physical and cultural subjugation of indigenous civilizations.

5.  Which of the following was NOT a result of the European conquest of the Americas realized by the end of the 17th century?

    (A) Europeans established overseas colonies on the coasts of the Americas and throughout the continent of Africa.

    (B) Europe's colonial expansion led to a global exchange of goods, flora, fauna, cultural practices, and diseases.

    (C) Europeans created vast global trade networks that allowed them to gain large accumulations of wealth.

    (D) Europeans expanded the African slave trade in response to the establishment of a plantation economy in the Americas and to demographic catastrophes among indigenous peoples.

6.  Which of the following superior technologies was most crucial to the Europeans' success in the New World?

    (A) New sailing technologies like the compass and the astrolabe

    (B) New ships like the carrack and caravel

    (C) Weapons like cannons and war horses

    (D) Better educational systems that taught navigation and warfare

**Questions 7–8 refer to the excerpts below.**

This corruption is repeatedly designated by Paul by the term sin . . . such as adultery, fornication, theft, hatred, murder, revellings, he terms, in the same way, the fruits of sin, though in various passages of Scripture . . . we are, merely on account of such corruption, deservedly condemned by God, to whom nothing is acceptable but righteousness, innocence, and purity.

—John Calvin, from *The Institutes of Christian Religion*, Book 2: Chapter 1, 1545

The covenant of life is not preached equally to all, and among those to whom it is preached, does not always meet with the same reception. This diversity displays the unsearchable depth of the divine judgment, and is without doubt subordinate to God's purpose of eternal election. But if it is plainly owing to the mere pleasure of God that salvation is spontaneously offered to some, while others have no access to it, great and difficult questions immediately arise, questions which are inexplicable, when just views are not entertained concerning election and predestination . . . the grace of God being illustrated by the contrast, viz., that he does not adopt all promiscuously to the hope of salvation, but gives to some what he denies to others.

—John Calvin, from *The Institutes of Christian Religion*, Book 3: Chapter 21, 1545

7.  Which of the following justifications used by Protestant reformers such as Calvin is alluded to in the excerpts?

 (A)  Protestant reformers believed that their church should not be subordinate to the state.
 (B)  The corruption of the Roman Catholic Church and its leaders meant that reform was needed.
 (C)  Religion was used to challenge the authority of earthly monarchs.
 (D)  The concept that salvation comes from faith alone rather than through good works is supported.

8.  Which of the following is the biggest contrast between the ideas of Calvinists and their fellow Protestant Lutherans?

 (A)  Calvinists believed that the state is absolutely subordinate to the religious organization.
 (B)  Calvinists believed in consubstantiation, while Lutherans believed in transubstantiation.
 (C)  Lutherans used the reformed faith to their political advantage to break free from domination from the Pope and the Holy Roman Empire.
 (D)  Lutherans insisted upon maintaining all of the seven sacraments, while the Calvinists chose to honor only two of them.

**Questions 9–11 refer to the map below.**

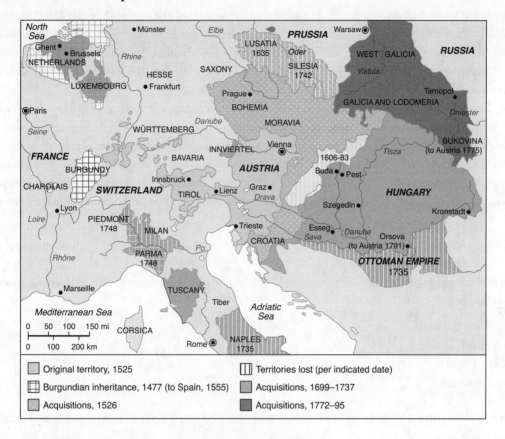

9. All of the shaded areas on the map represent which of the following?

   (A) Dynastic lands of the Habsburgs in the 16th century
   (B) Participants in the Thirty Years' War in the 17th century
   (C) Protestant regions in the 18th century
   (D) Members of the Holy Alliance in the 19th century

10. On the map, all of the shaded areas had in common which of the following during the 16th and 17th centuries?

   (A) They were regions that allowed religious pluralism during the 16th and 17th centuries.
   (B) They represent the areas that benefited most from transatlantic trade during the 16th and 17th centuries.
   (C) They represent areas where states took advantage of religious conflict to strengthen their own power during the 16th and 17th centuries.
   (D) They were areas that were mostly Roman Catholic by 1648.

11. Which of the following is the best description of how the map would change were it drawn to represent the same area 100 years after the first acquisitions were made?

   (A) The diverse German and Italian states would be unified into nations.
   (B) The Ottoman Empire would be significantly reduced as Russia and Austria began to take control of Eastern Europe.
   (C) France would become smaller as wars continually took little pieces of it away.
   (D) Greece would gain independence from the Ottoman Empire.

**Questions 12–15 refer to the following quote.**

I had now decided beyond all question that there existed in the heavens three stars wandering about Jupiter as do Venus and Mercury about the sun, and this became plainer than daylight from observations on similar occasions which followed. Nor were there just three such stars; four wanderers complete their revolutions about Jupiter, and of their alterations as observed more precisely later on we shall give a description here. Also I measured the distances between them by means of the telescope . . .

Such are the observations concerning the four Medicean planets recently first discovered by me, and although from this data their periods have not yet been reconstructed in numerical form, it is legitimate at least to put in evidence some facts worthy of note. Above all, since they sometimes follow and sometimes precede Jupiter by the same intervals, and they remain within very limited distances either to east or west of Jupiter, accompanying that planet in both its retrograde and direct movements in a constant manner, no one can doubt that they complete their revolutions about Jupiter and at the same time effect all together a twelve-year period about the center of the universe.

—Galileo Galilei, 1610

12. Which of the following Polish thinkers was most likely the person whose ideas convinced Galileo to have written the statement?

   (A) Nicolaus Copernicus
   (B) Johannes Kepler
   (C) Galileo Galilei
   (D) Josef Pilsudski

13. Which of the following conclusions drawn in part from the observations made in the quote was the most revolutionary over time?

   (A) There were four smaller stars that seemed to move around Jupiter.
   (B) Earth is not the center of the universe.
   (C) The heavens are occupied by bodies revolving around each other rather than by God alone.
   (D) Earth is but one tiny planet in an infinite universe or even multiverse.

14. Which of the following intellectual hallmarks of the Renaissance seem most in conflict with the questioning of the ancient philosophers, such as Aristotle, through experimentation in natural philosophy?

   (A) Humanism
   (B) Secularism
   (C) Individualism
   (D) Arête

15. Which of the following is best demonstrated by the passage about intellectual thought at the time?

   (A) It led to better scientific tools, which led to a rise in the standard of living during the 17th century across Europe.
   (B) The ideas of the ancient Greeks guided all of their ideas.
   (C) It used information obtained through experimentation to conceptualize the universe.
   (D) It provided experimental proof of the theories of ancient thinkers, such as Aristotle, on how the universe worked.

**Questions 16–18 refer to the following governmental report.**

Of the 450 sick persons whom the inhabitants were unable to relieve, 200 were turned out, and these we saw die one by one as they lay on the roadside. A large number still remain, and to each of them it is only possible to dole out the least scrap of bread. We only give bread to those who would otherwise die. The staple dish here consists of mice, which the inhabitants hunt, so desperate are they from hunger. They devour roots which the animals cannot eat; one can, in fact, not put into words the things one sees . . . This narrative, far from exaggerating, rather understates the horror of the case, for it does not record the hundredth part of the misery in this district. Those who have not witnessed it with their own eyes cannot imagine how great it is. Not a day passes but at least 200 people die of famine in the two provinces. We certify to having ourselves seen herds, not of cattle, but of men and women, wandering about the fields between Rheims and Rhétel, turning up the earth like pigs to find a few roots; and as they can only find rotten ones, and not half enough of them, they become so weak that they have not strength left to seek food. The parish priest at Boult, whose letter we enclose, tells us he has buried three of his parishioners who died of hunger. The rest subsisted on chopped straw mixed with earth, of which they composed a food which cannot be called bread. Other persons in the same place lived on the bodies of animals which had died of disease, and which the curé, otherwise unable to help his people, allowed them to roast at the presbytery fire.

—*Report of the Estates of Normandy*, 1651

16. Which of the following would be most responsible for ending the problems of hunger mentioned in the governmental report?

    (A) The elimination of the Black Plague in Europe during the 17th century
    (B) The elimination of fallow fields through the Agricultural Revolution during the 17th century
    (C) The creation of a strong putting-out system that allowed people to be paid for their work
    (D) A declining population during the 17th century that led to better food yields and less hunger as Europe urbanized

17. Which of the following contributed the LEAST to the health and hunger problems faced by the French people in the 17th century?

    (A) Low-productivity agricultural practices
    (B) Adverse weather
    (C) Low taxes on the peasants and middle class
    (D) Poor transportation

18. Which of the following intellectual movements was occurring in Europe at the time this document was created, which would help improve crop yields?

    (A) The Enlightenment
    (B) Divine right theory of rule
    (C) The rise of existentialism
    (D) The Scientific Revolution

**Questions 19–21 refer to the following memoir.**

Not only did he expect all persons of distinction to be in continual attendance at Court, but he was quick to notice the absence of those of inferior degree; at his lever, his couches, his meals, in the gardens of Versailles (the only place where the courtiers in general were allowed to follow him), he used to cast his eyes to right and left; nothing escaped him[;] he saw everybody. If anyone habitually living at Court absented himself he insisted on knowing the reason; those who came there only for flying visits had also to give a satisfactory explanation; anyone who seldom or never appeared there was certain to incur his displeasure. If asked to bestow a favor on such persons he would reply haughtily: "I do not know him"; of such as rarely presented themselves he would say, "He is a man I never see"; and from these judgments there was no appeal.

No one understood better than Louis XIV the art of enhancing the value of a favor by his manner of bestowing it; he knew how to make the most of a word, a smile, even of a glance.

He loved splendor, magnificence, and profusion in all things, and encouraged similar tastes in his Court; to spend money freely on equipages and buildings, on feasting and at cards, was a sure way to gain his favor, perhaps to obtain the honor of a word from him. Motives of policy had something to do with this; by making expensive habits the fashion, and, for people in a certain position, a necessity, he compelled his courtiers to live beyond their income, and gradually reduced them to depend on his bounty for the means of subsistence.

—Duke Saint-Simon, *Memoirs of Louis XIV and His Court and His Regency*, c. 1750

19. Which of the following is the best explanation of the bias found in the memoir?

    (A) The duke, as a member of the French nobility, is sympathetic to King Louis.
    (B) The duke, as a member of the French nobility, is biased against the king because of his suppression of the nobility.
    (C) The duke, as a member of the French nobility, supported the extension of the administrative, financial, military, and religious control of the central state over the French population.
    (D) The duke, as a member of the French nobility, supported King Louis's preservation of the aristocracy's social position and legal privileges while he removed their power.

20. Louis XIV was aided by many able advisers, but which of the following advisers helped him to reorganize France and make it into a world power?

    (A) Jean Martinet, his chief military adviser
    (B) Cardinal Mazarin, his regent and foreign policy adviser
    (C) Jean Baptiste Colbert, his finance minister
    (D) The Duke of Burgundy

21. Which of the following was the greatest weakness and regret of the rule of King Louis XIV?

    (A) His domination of the nobility left him without friends and allies.
    (B) He was so concerned with ceremonies and appearances that he did not rule his country well.
    (C) He left the administration of his kingdom to professional bureaucrats known as intendants.
    (D) He was at war for two-thirds of his reign and united the other major powers against him.

**Questions 22–24 refer to the list of complaints below.**

**Article 3:** Frenchmen should regard as laws of the kingdom those alone which have been prepared by the national assembly and sanctioned by the king.

**Article 11:** Personal liberty, proprietary rights and the security of citizens shall be established in a clear, precise and irrevocable manner. All *lettres de cachet* shall be abolished forever, subject to certain modifications which the States General may see fit to impose.

**Article 12:** And to remove forever the possibility of injury to the personal and proprietary rights of Frenchmen, the jury system shall be introduced in all criminal cases, and in civil cases for the determination of fact, in all the courts of the realm.

**Article 17:** All distinctions in penalties shall be abolished; and crimes committed by citizens of the different orders shall be punished irrespectively, according to the same forms of law and in the same manner. The States General shall seek to bring it about that the effects of transgression shall be confined to the individual and shall not be reflected upon the relatives of the transgressor, themselves innocent of all participation.

**Article 21:** No tax shall be legal unless accepted by the representatives of the people and sanctioned by the king.

—*Cahiers of the Third Estate of Versailles*, 1789

22. Which of the following was NOT one of the problems in France that caused the French Revolution referenced in the list of complaints?

    (A) Financial problems caused by debts and low revenues
    (B) The inequitable legal system of France
    (C) The proliferation of Enlightenment ideals
    (D) Social and political inequality in France in 1789

23. Which of the following changes brought on by the French Revolution was most approved of by the peasants of France?

    (A) Creation of a constitutional monarchy
    (B) The abolition of feudal dues and rents
    (C) Increased popular participation in politics
    (D) Nationalization of religion

24. During the radical phase of the Revolution, which of the following changes instituted by Robespierre was LEAST beneficial to the defense of France?

    (A) The conscription of huge armies
    (B) Fixing prices and wages
    (C) Pursuing a policy of de-Christianization
    (D) Promoting soldiers based upon their merits in the field

**Questions 25–28 refer to the following excerpt from a pamphlet.**

You will do me the justice to remember, that I have always strenuously supported the Right of every man to his own opinion, however different that opinion might be to mine. He who denies to another this right, makes a slave of himself to his present opinion, because he precludes himself the right of changing it.

The most formidable weapon against errors of every kind is Reason. I have never used any other, and I trust I never shall.

The circumstance that has now taken place in France of the total abolition of the whole national order of priest-hood, and of everything appertaining to compulsive systems of religion, and compulsive articles of faith, has not only precipitated my intention, but rendered a work of this kind exceedingly necessary, lest in the general wreck of super-stition, of false systems of government, and false theology, we lose sight of morality, of humanity, and of the theology that is true.

I believe in one God, and no more; and I hope for happiness beyond this life.

I believe in the equality of man; and I believe that religious duties consist in doing justice, loving mercy, and endeavoring to make our fellow-creatures happy.

I do not believe in the creed professed by the Jewish church, by the Roman church, by the Greek church, by the Turkish church, by the Protestant church, nor by any church that I know of. My own mind is my own church.

All national institutions of churches, whether Jewish, Christian or Turkish, appear to me no other than human inventions, set up to terrify and enslave mankind, and monopolize power and profit.

I do not mean by this declaration to condemn those who believe otherwise; they have the same right to their belief as I have to mine.

—Thomas Paine, *The Age of Reason*, 1794–1795

25. The document supports which of the following demands of the Enlightenment *philosophes*?

    (A) Deism should be adopted by all as the only logical religion.

    (B) Religious toleration leads to the destruction of social unity.

    (C) Skepticism is not a reliable way of examining information.

    (D) Religious toleration should be given to all people of all religions.

26. Paine's statement in the last sentence, criticizing persecution, was most likely influenced by which of the following?

    (A) New concepts of legal equity and individual rights expressed by Locke and Rousseau

    (B) Europeans gaining a more thorough under-standing of the rich cultural diversity through trade and travel

    (C) New concepts of a deterministic mechani-cal universe based upon the discovery of Newton's mathematical laws

    (D) Challenges to the monopoly on truth held by the Roman Catholic Church on multiple fronts

27. Which of the following Enlightenment *philosophes* designed a system of checks and balances for government to avoid abuses of power?

    (A) Jean-Jacques Rousseau

    (B) Baron Montesquieu

    (C) Mary Wollstonecraft

    (D) Adam Smith

28. The ideas expressed by Paine in the excerpt best illustrate which of the following characteristics of Enlightenment intellectuals?

    (A) Many were accomplished scientists who added important pieces to the human under-standing of the universe.

    (B) They utilized new methods of communicating their ideas, such as salons and inexpensive printed pamphlets.

    (C) Most rejected religion altogether and adopted atheism as the only credo of a rational person.

    (D) Many believed that the new scientific dis-coveries would allow humans to solve all problems.

**Questions 29–32 refer to the documents below.**

### Source 1

If then by the Use of Machines, the Manufacture of Cotton, an Article which we import, and are supplied with from other Countries, and which can everywhere be procured on equal Terms, has met with such amazing Success, may not greater Advantages be reasonably expected from cultivating to the utmost the Manufacture of Wool, the Produce of our own Island, an Article in Demand in all Countries, almost the universal Clothing of Mankind?

In the Manufacture of Woollens, the Scribbling Mill, the Spinning Frame, and the Fly Shuttle, have reduced manual Labour nearly One third, and each of them at its-first Introduction carried an Alarm to the Work People, yet each has contributed to advance the Wages and to increase the Trade, so that if an Attempt was now made to deprive us of the Use of them, there is no Doubt, but every Person engaged in the Business, would exert himself to defend them.

—*Statement by the Cloth Merchants of Leeds*, 1791

### Source 2

Come, cropper lads of high renown,
Who love to drink good ale that's brown,
And strike each haughty tyrant down,
With hatchet, pike, and gun!

Oh, the cropper lads for me,
The gallant lads for me,
Who with lusty stroke,
The shear frames broke,
The cropper lads for me!

What though the specials still advance,
And soldiers nightly round us prance;
The cropper lads still lead the dance,
With hatchet, pike, and gun!

Oh, the cropper lads for me,
The gallant lads for me,
Who with lusty stroke
The shear frames broke,
The cropper lads for me!

—*Luddite Song, The Cropper's Song*, c. 1812

29. Which of the following economic theories is **Source 1** referencing in support of the expansion and use of machines?

    (A) Laissez-faire capitalism
    (B) Mercantilism
    (C) Industrialization
    (D) Bullionism

30. **Source 2** was motivated most by which of the following changes brought on by industrialization?

    (A) The movement of many agricultural workers to the new industrial cities increased urbanization.
    (B) Industrialization promoted significant population growth as it was applied to many fields.
    (C) Parliament supported industrialization for its own interests.
    (D) Socioeconomic changes created divisions of labor that led to the development of self-conscious classes.

31. Which of the following best describes the governmental reactions to complaints such as those seen in **Source 2** before 1850?

    (A) Governments did little to address problems of industrialization before 1850.
    (B) Reform movements led to the creation of regulations on work hours and both ages and gender of workers.
    (C) The implementation of running water and sewers was begun in England.
    (D) The government created a national health care system.

32. Which of the following is NOT a result of the Industrial Revolution according to the documents and your knowledge of European history?

    (A) In some of the less industrialized areas of Europe, the dominance of agricultural elites persisted into the 20th century.
    (B) Cities experienced overcrowding, while affected rural areas suffered declines in available labor as well as weakened communities.
    (C) Class identity developed and was reinforced through daily life and participation in groups such as labor unions.
    (D) Greater social and economic equity emerged as the workers and their bosses saw their incomes become more equal.

**Questions 33–35 refer to the following excerpt.**

Never were talents of the highest genius of the most exalted kind, more profusely bestowed upon a human being. The genius of Napoleon is astounding. All branches of human knowledge seemed alike familiar to his gigantic mind. His conversations at St. Helena, scattered through the numerous and voluminous memorials of those who gleaned them, are replete with intensest interest. During the long agony of his imprisonment and his death, he conversed with perfect freedom upon the events of his marvelous career, and upon all those subjects or morals, politics, and religion, which most deeply concern the welfare of our race. There is no mind which will not be invigorated by familiarity with these profound thoughts, expressed with so much glow of feeling and energy of diction.

—John S. C. Abbott, historian, *Napoleon at St. Helena*, 1855

33. Which of the following features of the French Empire under Napoleon does Abbott seem most impressed with?

    (A) Napoleon's secret police
    (B) Napoleon's domestic reforms
    (C) Napoleon's suppression of women's rights
    (D) Napoleon's military tactics

34. How did Napoleon help make the French Revolution an international movement in the areas he conquered?

    (A) He imposed a universal currency based on the French franc.
    (B) He brutally suppressed guerrilla resistance.
    (C) He abolished feudalism and manorialism.
    (D) He encouraged the use of French as the universal language.

35. Which of the following actions of Napoleon does the author seem to be ignoring the hypocrisy of in his examination of the high-mindedness and praiseworthiness of Napoleon?

    (A) The invasion of Haiti to stop a slave revolt there
    (B) The creation of the Napoleonic Code
    (C) Promoting soldiers and government workers based upon their merits only
    (D) His conquest of Europe and use of the Continental System

**Questions 36–38 refer to the following excerpt.**

The revolutionary seed had penetrated into every country and spread more or less. It was greatly developed under the régime of the military despotism of Bonaparte. His conquests displaced a number of laws, institutions, and customs; broke through bonds sacred among all nations, strong enough to resist time itself; which is more than can be said of certain benefits conferred by these innovators.

The monarchs will fulfil the duties imposed upon them by Him who, by entrusting them with power, has charged them to watch over the maintenance of justice, and the rights of all, to avoid the paths of error, and tread firmly in the way of truth. Placed beyond the passions which agitate society, it is in days of trial chiefly that they are called upon to despoil realities of their false appearances, and to show themselves as they are, fathers invested with the authority belonging by right to the heads of families, to prove that, in days of mourning, they know how to be just, wise, and therefore strong, and that they will not abandon the people whom they ought to govern to be the sport of factions, to error and its consequences, which must involve the loss of society.

Union between the monarchs is the basis of the policy which must now be followed to save society from total ruin . . .

Let them not confound concessions made to parties with the good they ought to do for their people, in modifying, according to their recognized needs, such branches of the administration as require it.

Let them be just, but strong; beneficent, but strict.

Let them maintain religious principles in all their purity, and not allow the faith to be attacked and morality interpreted according to the social contract or the visions of foolish sectarians.

Let them suppress Secret Societies; that gangrene of society.

—Klemens von Metternich, *Political Confession of Faith*, 1820

36. Which of the following was the greatest cause of the fears expressed by Metternich in the excerpt?

    (A) The ideas of personal liberty and nationalism conceived during the Enlightenment resulted in radical revolutions that could spread throughout Europe.

    (B) The conquest of Europe by Napoleon led to the creation of new factions and shifted the European balance of power.

    (C) The power of monarchs had grown to the point where it needed to be checked by other powers within each nation or domination of civilians would occur.

    (D) The rising and falling economic cycle of the newly emerging capitalist economy could lead to civilian unrest that must be suppressed.

37. The final result of the negotiations led by Metternich during the Congress of Vienna is being referenced in the excerpt in which of the following ways?

    (A) Metternich's statement about the military despotism of Bonaparte led to the elimination of all empires in Europe.

    (B) Metternich's statement about fulfilling duties indicated his support for the Holy Alliance that controlled the fate of Europe.

    (C) Metternich's statement about the unity of monarchs alluded to the creation of the Concert of Europe.

    (D) Metternich's disgust for secret societies led to the creation of the Carlsbad Decrees.

38. Which of the following is the best description of the goals of the new ideology of conservatism as it was explained by Metternich?

    (A) The suppression of all new ideas in every field to prevent any changes to society

    (B) The suppression of nationalist and liberal revolutions that called for democratic and economic reforms

    (C) The suppression of secret societies in hopes of spreading democracy to the masses

    (D) The suppression of political change only while allowing economic and social change

**Questions 39–41 refer to the following excerpt.**

If civilized education developed in every child its natural inclinations, we should see nearly all rich children enamored of various very plebeian occupations, such as that of the mason, the carpenter, the smith, the saddler. I have instanced Louis the XVI, who loved the trade of locksmith; an Infanta of Spain preferred that of shoemaker; a certain king of Denmark gratified himself by manufacturing syringes; the former king of Naples loved to sell the fish he had caught in the market-place himself; the prince of Parma, whom Condillac had trained in metaphysical subtitles, in the understanding of intuition, of cognition, had no taste but for the occupation of church-warden and lay-brother.

The great majority of wealthy children would follow these plebeian tastes, if civilized education did not oppose the development of them; and if the filthiness of the workshops and the coarseness of the workmen did not arouse a repugnance stronger than the attraction. What child of a prince is there who has no taste for one of the four occupations I have just mentioned, that of mason, carpenter, smith, saddler, and who would not advance in them if he beheld from an early age the work carried on in blight workshops, by refined people, who would always arrange a miniature workshop for children, with little implements and light labor?

—Charles Fourier, *On Education*, 1838

39. Which of the following groups of intellectuals would Fourier belong to, according to the excerpt?

   (A) Utilitarians
   (B) Laissez-faire capitalists
   (C) Utopian socialists
   (D) Marxist communists

40. What nation experimented with utilizing the ideas of Fourier and others like him to create national workshops in 1848?

   (A) Germany
   (B) France
   (C) Great Britain
   (D) Austria

41. Many in Fourier's circles advocated for universal male suffrage, which was propagated most by which of the following groups?

   (A) Luddites
   (B) Liberals
   (C) Benthamites
   (D) Chartists

**Questions 42–44 refer to the images below.**

**Image 1**

*Dance Song*, portrait of a family at home
in Germany, by Hugo Bürkner, 1854.

**Image 2**

*"Some foolish people imagine our ladies will neglect their family
duties. Quite a mistake."* Cartoon from *Punch Magazine*, 1887.

42. To which of the following is the material prosperity evident in **Image 1** partially attributable?

    (A) The increasing standard of living of German industrial workers
    (B) The social welfare policies instituted by governments of the Germanic states
    (C) The adoption by the Frankfurt Parliament of a liberal constitution for Germany
    (D) The restoration of political stability in the aftermath of the Congress of Vienna

43. A historian of 19th-century European society is most likely to use **Image 2** as evidence of which of the following?

    (A) Many women used the Revolutions of 1848 as an opportunity to express their sexuality more freely.
    (B) Many men were becoming more involved in child rearing and household management.
    (C) Many men feared that women's participation in the public sphere would undermine the established social order.
    (D) Many women were increasingly taking on the role of decision maker in their families.

44. Which of the following transformations in the ideals of family life and gender roles during the late 19th century is expressed in the images?

    (A) The ideals were largely overcome by socialist notions of collective child rearing.
    (B) The ideals were increasingly adopted by working-class families.
    (C) The ideals were modified to accommodate the fact that most women had become part of the paid workforce.
    (D) The professional and academic journals of the time recommended fathers become less involved in child rearing.

**Questions 45–47 refer to the following government proclamation.**

On the basis of the above-mentioned new arrangements, the serfs will receive in time the full rights of free rural inhabitants.

The nobles, while retaining their property rights to all the lands belonging to them, grant the peasants perpetual use of their household plots in return for a specified obligation . . . [the nobles] grant them a portion of arable land fixed by the said arrangements as well as other property . . . While enjoying these land allotments, the peasants are obliged, in return, to fulfill obligations to the noblemen fixed by the same arrangements. In this status, which is temporary, the peasants are temporarily bound . . .

[T]hey are granted the right to purchase their household plots, and, with the consent of the nobles, they may acquire in full ownership the arable lands and other properties which are allotted them for permanent use. Following such acquisition of full ownership of land, the peasants will be freed from their obligations to the nobles for the land thus purchased and will become free peasant landowners.

WE have deemed it advisable:

3. To organize Peace Offices on the estates of the nobles, leaving the village communes as they are, and to open cantonal offices in the large villages and unite small village communes.

4. To formulate, verify, and confirm in each village commune or estate a charter which will specify, on the basis of local conditions, the amount of land allotted to the peasants for permanent use, and the scope of their obligations to the nobleman for the land.

6. Until that time, peasants and household serfs must be obedient towards their nobles, and scrupulously fulfill their former obligations.

7. The nobles will continue to keep order on their estates, with the right of jurisdiction and of police, until the organization of cantons and of cantonal courts.

—Alexander II, "The Abolition of Serfdom in Russia," Manifesto of February 19, 1861

45. Which of the following best articulates the new conditions for the recently emancipated serfs of Russia as stated in the government proclamation?

   (A) The czar's manifesto allowed for a heterogeneous class of farmers to emerge, with many former serfs becoming quite prosperous while others struggled.

   (B) The manifesto was mostly ineffective in improving the economic condition of former serfs but paved the way for local self-rule and, soon after, a national legislature.

   (C) The czar's insistence on cooperation between the nobility and recently emancipated people limited the financial potential of all impacted by the manifesto.

   (D) The manifesto, although emancipating the serfs, saddled them with financial responsibilities and other restrictions, while the aristocracy retained too many of its former rights.

46. Which of the following was a major impetus in convincing Czar Alexander II of the necessity of freeing the serfs?

   (A) Recent defeat in the Crimean War convinced the czar some domestic reforms were necessary.

   (B) Enlightened rulers in Prussia and Austria had recently done the same, which pressured Alexander II to act.

   (C) The Decembrist Revolt and its aftermath convinced the young czar to make reforms.

   (D) A labor force to complete the Trans-Siberian Railroad was needed as well as military recruits.

47. Which of the following best describes the long-term effects of Czar Alexander II's emancipation?

   (A) Food production soared, which allowed Russians to export agricultural goods while investing the profits into their industrial sector.

   (B) The program was a complete disaster as agricultural output plummeted until Pyotr Stolypin's reforms made privatized Russian farming profitable.

   (C) The emancipation terms relegated former serfs to communal farming, thus keeping them in perpetual poverty and making wealthy conservatives nervous.

   (D) No longer tied to the land, former serfs moved to the cities, thus spurning the commencement of an industrial revolution in Russia.

**Questions 48–49 refer to the treaty below.**

The leaders of Europe, deeply sensible of their solemn duty to promote the welfare of mankind;

Persuaded that the time has come when a frank renunciation of war as an instrument of national policy should be made to the end that the peaceful and friendly relations now existing between their peoples may be perpetuated;

**ARTICLE I**

The High Contracting Parties solemnly declare in the names of their respective peoples that they condemn recourse to war for the solution of international controversies, and renounce it, as an instrument of national policy in their relations with one another.

**ARTICLE II**

The High Contracting Parties agree that the settlement or solution of all disputes or conflicts of whatever nature or of whatever origin they may be, which may arise among them, shall never be sought except by pacific means.

—Kellogg-Briand Pact, 1928

48. Which of the following factors LEAST influenced the signatory nations to agree to this treaty?

    (A) The effects of military stalemate and total war led to protest and insurrection in belligerent nations during the First World War.
    (B) Wilsonian idealism was not adhered to in the Treaty of Versailles that created the weak League of Nations, and leaders were trying to create another tool to help prevent war.
    (C) The leadership of Germany was threatening expansion again, and the other nations wanted to be ready to meet the German threat.
    (D) The ideas of John Maynard Keynes in *Economic Consequences of the Peace* said that the Treaty of Versailles was too harsh on Germany.

49. Which of the following is the best characterization of the international movement to prevent war from 1928 through the modern era?

    (A) The movement has steadily gained speed as more and more nations in Europe have condemned war and have refused to support military action.
    (B) There was a period of pacifism until 1939, and since then there has been steadily increasing support for national military action.
    (C) The idea of pacifism has been adopted when threats to national sovereignty and personal liberty are less apparent, but Europeans choose violent options whenever they are threatened.
    (D) The concept of Europeans fighting wars has all but disappeared since the Second World War.

Questions 50–51 are based upon the following tables.

### Source 1

The movement toward European Union: The table below lists the years that each nation joined and shows the first three forming a customs union in 1944 to be replaced by the European Economic Community (EEC) or Common Market and then, finally, the European Union (EU).

| Nation | Year Joined | Organization |
|---|---|---|
| Belgium | 1944 | BENELUX |
| Netherlands | 1944 | BENELUX |
| Luxembourg | 1944 | BENELUX |
| France | 1951 | EEC |
| West Germany | 1951 | EEC |
| Italy | 1951 | EEC |
| Denmark | 1973 | EU |
| Ireland | 1973 | EU |
| United Kingdom | 1973 | EU |
| Greece | 1981 | EU |
| Spain | 1986 | EU |
| Portugal | 1986 | EU |
| Sweden | 1995 | EU |
| Finland | 1995 | EU |
| Austria | 1995 | EU |
| Czech Republic | 2004 | EU |
| Estonia | 2004 | EU |
| Latvia | 2004 | EU |
| Lithuania | 2004 | EU |
| Cyprus | 2004 | EU |
| Hungary | 2004 | EU |
| Poland | 2004 | EU |
| Slovakia | 2004 | EU |
| Slovenia | 2004 | EU |
| Malta | 2004 | EU |
| Romania | 2007 | EU |
| Bulgaria | 2007 | EU |
| Croatia | 2013 | EU |

## Source 2

Historic Real GDP Measured in $Billions (Dollar Value for Base Year 2010)

| Country | 1969 | 1974 | 1979 | 1984 | 1989 | 1994 | 1999 | 2004 | 2009 | 2014 | % Growth 1969–2014 |
|---|---|---|---|---|---|---|---|---|---|---|---|
| Belgium | 183.00 | 234.16 | 258.53 | 278.51 | 319.57 | 348.38 | 396.07 | 436.78 | 460.78 | 485.08 | 165% |
| France | 985.10 | 1,280.00 | 1,470.67 | 1,588.30 | 1,842.63 | 1,969.14 | 2,216.00 | 2,443.33 | 2,523.49 | 2,635.73 | 168% |
| Greece | 105.38 | 136.68 | 177.13 | 175.15 | 190.95 | 198.98 | 230.38 | 286.84 | 309.77 | 248.29 | 136% |
| Luxembourg | 11.61 | 14.60 | 15.13 | 16.78 | 23.49 | 29.60 | 37.28 | 45.78 | 50.52 | 55.64 | 379% |
| Netherlands | 278.29 | 346.93 | 387.30 | 412.19 | 478.51 | 541.50 | 655.03 | 712.40 | 766.05 | 774.06 | 178% |
| Poland | 119.79 | 139.50 | 162.45 | 189.17 | 220.29 | 229.95 | 307.03 | 359.59 | 452.29 | 523.83 | 337% |
| Russia | 823.71 | 959.21 | 1,117.01 | 1,300.76 | 1,457.58 | 916.23 | 865.03 | 1,204.49 | 1,459.27 | 1,670.38 | 103% |
| Ukraine | 116.58 | 135.75 | 158.09 | 184.09 | 219.83 | 112.56 | 84.47 | 126.02 | 130.60 | 137.37 | 18% |
| United Kingdom | 887.94 | 1,017.76 | 1,128.25 | 1,183.83 | 1,432.93 | 1,568.30 | 1,869.42 | 2,187.16 | 2,258.05 | 2,437.65 | 175% |

—All data from World Bank

50. Using the information in both sources, which of the following best characterizes the economic achievement of the nations listed in **Source 2**?

(A) A nation's level of economic success can be tied directly to when it joined forces with other European nations economically.

(B) Those nations that did join together to eventually form the European Union in general did better than those that did not join.

(C) Those nations that joined together to eventually form the European Union all did better than those that did not join.

(D) The nations that had been part of COMECON did more poorly than those that had not.

51. Which of the following has been the greatest effect of the overall economic growth that Europe has experienced over the past half century?

(A) The welfare state has increasingly cared for the people of Europe, giving greater and greater amounts of aid to the poor across the Continent.

(B) The society has become generally wealthier, which has resulted in decreased national identities and tensions.

(C) Rising wages have allowed the vast majority of Europeans to become property owners as the class structures have generally eroded.

(D) Rising consumerism has caused many to purchase goods from all over the world, leading to environmental issues.

**Questions 52–55 refer to the document below.**

## The Universal Declaration of Human Rights

Whereas the peoples of the United Nations have in the Charter reaffirmed their faith in fundamental human rights, in the dignity and worth of the human person and in the equal rights of men and women and have determined to promote social progress and better standards of life in larger freedom,

Now, Therefore THE GENERAL ASSEMBLY proclaims THIS UNIVERSAL DECLARATION OF HUMAN RIGHTS as a common standard of achievement for all peoples and all nations, to the end that every individual and every organ of society . . .

### Article 1
All human beings are born free and equal in dignity and rights. They are endowed with reason and conscience and should act towards one another in a spirit of brotherhood.

### Article 2
Everyone is entitled to all the rights and freedoms set forth in this Declaration, without distinction of any kind, such as race, colour, sex, language, religion, political or other opinion, national or social origin, property, birth or other status.

### Article 3
Everyone has the right to life, liberty and security of person.

### Article 6
Everyone has the right to recognition everywhere as a person before the law.

### Article 7
All are equal before the law and are entitled without any discrimination to equal protection of the law. All are entitled to equal protection against any discrimination in violation of this Declaration and against any incitement to such discrimination.

### Article 18
Everyone has the right to freedom of thought, conscience and religion; this right includes freedom to change his religion or belief, and freedom, either alone or in community with others and in public or private, to manifest his religion or belief in teaching, practice, worship and observance.

### Article 26
Everyone has the right to education. Education shall be free, at least in the elementary and fundamental stages. Elementary education shall be compulsory. Technical and professional education shall be made generally available and higher education shall be equally accessible to all on the basis of merit.

52. Which of the following is the best characterization of how the Universal Declaration of Human Rights was used by the different factions during the Cold War?

    (A) It was used by the NATO nations to illustrate the lack of rights for those living in the Warsaw Pact nations.
    (B) It was used by the Warsaw Pact nations to illustrate the lack of rights for those living in the NATO nations.
    (C) It was used by both sides during the Cold War to prove that their side was more ethical than the other.
    (D) Neither side used the Universal Declaration of Human Rights for propaganda purposes.

53. Which of the following trends in Europe in the late 20th century was affected most by the declaration's references to minorities and multicultural acceptance?

    (A) The collapse of communism in Eastern Europe
    (B) The increasing reliance on immigrant labor
    (C) The implementation of benefits in the growing welfare states
    (D) Growing consumerism

54. Which of the following is the best description of how education and public services described as a right in the declaration are treated politically in Europe at the start of the 21 century?

    (A) The emergence of nationalist political parties has increased spending on these programs.
    (B) The requirements of membership in the European Union compel higher spending on these programs.
    (C) The influence of Catholic reforms after the Second Vatican Council have reduced spending on these programs.
    (D) The political debate over the cost of the welfare state has threatened these programs in much of Europe.

55. Based on the Universal Declaration of Human Rights, the United Nations likely supports which of the following?

    (A) Bans on immigration to Europe
    (B) Expanded civil rights for LGBTQ+ people
    (C) Barriers to trade
    (D) Expanding European global power

PRACTICE TEST 2

**STOP**    If there is still time remaining, you may review your answers.

# Section I

## Part B: Short Answer

TIME: 40 MINUTES
NUMBER OF QUESTIONS: 3 OUT OF 4 CHOICES
PERCENTAGE OF TOTAL AP EXAM SCORE: 20%
WRITING INSTRUMENT: PEN WITH DARK BLUE OR BLACK INK

> **DIRECTIONS:** Section I, Part B of this exam contains four short-answer questions. Write your responses in the corresponding boxes on the short-answer response sheets. You must answer Questions 1 and 2, but you choose to answer either Question 3 OR 4. Please indicate which question you answered on the answer sheet.
>
> Answer all parts of every question. Use complete sentences; an outline or bulleted list alone is not acceptable. You may plan your answers in your exam booklet, but no credit will be given for what is written there. Sources have been edited for the purposes of this exercise.

**Use the passages below to answer all parts of the question that follows.**

### Source 1

Petrarch does not deserve to be praised for simply reviving the ideas of Greeks and Romans who were dead for centuries if not millennia. His idea of humanism was not his idea, but that of Socrates, Plato, and Aristotle, whose ideas were never lost, just ignored as they are in twenty-first century America. The only truly great humanist thinker of the Renaissance era was Erasmus. His Christian Humanism was a truly elegant new idea formed by combining the beauty of traditional Greco-Roman thought with Christian moral values. It this way, Erasmus was the greatest thinker of the Renaissance.

—Historian Jaw Switlick, 2008

### Source 2

The Northern Renaissance was a third-rate copy of the Italian Renaissance with few new ideas and no new artistic methods, just less grand subject matter. All of the great thinkers of the Renaissance were Italians. Rafael, Donatello, Masaccio, Da Vinci, Michelangelo, etc. were all the first great thinkers to achieve new ideas in centuries of European intellectual stagnation known as the Dark Ages. The Renaissance was perhaps the greatest blossoming of thought that has ever occurred in Europe, and it was due to the genius of the Italian individual. Another Italian genius would also begin the field of modern science through his experimentation and willingness to record his observations and share them: Galileo Galilei, who ushered in the modern world, is but one example of the superior nature of the Italian Renaissance.

—Historian Eugene Cho, 1992

1. (a) Explain ONE major difference between Cho's and Switlick's interpretations of the Renaissance.

   (b) Provide ONE piece of evidence from the Renaissance that supports Switlick's interpretation (**Source 1**) and explain HOW it supports the interpretation.

   (c) Provide ONE piece of evidence from the Renaissance that supports Cho's interpretation (**Source 2**) and explain HOW it supports the interpretation.

**Answer all parts of the question that follows.**

2. Historians have often depicted the Cold War as a conflict between communism on one side opposed by capitalism on the other side.

   (a) Provide TWO pieces of evidence to SUPPORT this characterization of this period and explain how they support it.

   (b) Provide ONE specific piece of evidence that UNDERMINES this characterization of this time period and explain how it undermines it.

**Please choose to answer either Question 3 or Question 4, and indicate which question you answer.**

**Use the image below to answer all parts of the question that follows.**

3. The image is a late 17th century engraving of the old observing room at the Greenwich Observatory, England, from The Granger Collection, New York.

   (a) Briefly explain ONE effect on the Protestant European economies during the 17th and 18th centuries due to their attitudes toward science and experimentation.

   (b) Briefly explain ONE effect on the Roman Catholic European economies during the 17th and 18th centuries due to their attitudes toward science and experimentation.

   (c) Briefly explain ONE effect on the ways approaches to knowledge in subjects outside of science changed as a result of the type of work done in the picture above.

**Use the document and image given below to answer all parts of the question that follows.**

### Source 1

The City of Mexico is luxuriously provided with fruit, both of Spanish and native varieties: they all yield abundantly. There are excellent olive groves from which they gather quantities of eating olives. Grapes are brought in from Queretaro, and there are a few vines in the city, as well as peaches, large and small, pippins, quinces, pomegranates, oranges, limes, grapefruit, citrons, and lemons; the gardens produce in abundance all varieties of Spanish garden stuff and vegetables; the lake provides delicious fish of different sorts. [In the surrounding countryside] there are fertile fields which yield an abundance of corn, wheat, and other cereals, both native and Spanish; there is plenty of pastureland, and in consequence large cattle ranches of sheep and cows.

—Antonio Vazquez, Carmelite Friar, *The Spread of European Plants and Animals*, 1620

### Source 2

Vincent van Gogh, Oil on Canvas, *The Potato Eaters*, 1885.

4. (a) Briefly analyze how the artwork above in **Source 2** reflects artistic trends at the end of the 19th century.
   (b) Based on **Source 1** and your knowledge of European history, briefly analyze ONE aspect of how interaction between Europe and the Americas changed the economic lives of Native Americans.
   (c) Based on **both sources** and your knowledge of European history, briefly analyze ONE aspect of how interaction between Europe and the Americas changed the economic lives of Europeans.

# Section II

TOTAL TIME: 100 MINUTES
NUMBER OF QUESTIONS: 2
PERCENTAGE OF TOTAL AP EXAM SCORE: 40%
QUESTION 1: 25%
QUESTION 2: 15%
WRITING INSTRUMENT: PEN WITH DARK BLUE OR BLACK INK

**DIRECTIONS:** Section II of this exam contains three essay questions. You must respond to Question 1, the document-based question, but you must CHOOSE to answer Question 2, 3, or 4 for your long essay question. No credit is given for work written on the exam itself; all responses must be written in dark blue or black ink in essay format in the answer booklet. Be sure to indicate which long essay question you are answering on each page of the answer booklet.

## Question 1 (Document–Based Question—DBQ)

TIME: 60 MINUTES
SUGGESTED READING PERIOD: 15 MINUTES
SUGGESTED WRITING TIME: 45 MINUTES

**DIRECTIONS:** Question 1 is based on the accompanying documents. The documents have been edited for the purpose of the exercise.

In your response you should do the following:

- State a relevant thesis that directly addresses all parts of the question.
- Support the thesis or a relevant argument with evidence from all, or all but one, of the documents.
- Incorporate analysis of all, or all but one, of the documents into your argument.
- Focus your analysis of each document on at least one of the following: intended audience, purpose, historical context, and/or point of view.
- Support your argument with analysis of historical examples outside the documents.
- Connect historical phenomena relevant to your argument to broader events or processes.
- Synthesize the elements above into a persuasive essay that extends your argument, connects it to a different historical context, or accounts for contradictory evidence on the topic.

1. Analyze how changing reactions and responses to "total war" reflected social, political, and economic changes in Europe during the first half of the 20th century.

---

### DOCUMENT 1

Source: V. Bourtzeff, Russian socialist leader, letter to the editor of the *London Times*, 1914.

Sir—May I be allowed to say a few words in connection with the excellent letter by my compatriot, Professor Vinogradov, which appeared in your paper today (September 14)? Professor Vinogradov is absolutely right when he says that not only is it desirable that complete unity of feeling should exist in Russian political circles, but that this unity is already an accomplished fact.

The representatives of all political parties and of all nationalities in Russia are now at one with the Government, and this war with Germany and Austria, both guided by the Kaiser, has already become a national war for Russia.

Even we, the adherents of the parties of the Extreme Left, and hitherto ardent anti militarists and pacifists, even we believe in the necessity of this war. This war is a war to protect justice and civilization. It will, we hope, be a decisive factor in our united war against war, and we hope that after it, it will at last be possible to consider seriously the question of disarmament and universal peace. There can be no doubt that victory, and decisive victory at that (personally I await this in the immediate future), will be on the side of the Allied nations—England, France, Belgium, Servia, and Russia.

The German peril, the curse which has hung over the whole world for so many decades, will be crushed, and crushed so that it will never again become a danger to the peace of the world. The peoples of the world desire peace.

To Russia this war will bring regeneration.

We are convinced that after this war there will no longer be any room for political reaction, and Russia will be associated with the existing group of cultured and civilized countries.

## DOCUMENT 2

Source: Official Statement by French Prime Minister Aristide Briand on *Deportations from Lille*, June 30, 1916.

Not content with subjecting our people in the North to every kind of oppression, the Germans have recently treated them in the most iniquitous way.

In contempt of rules universally recognized and of their own express promises not to molest the civil population, they have taken women and girls away from their families; they have sent them off, mixed up with men, to destinations unknown, to work unknown.

The Germans decided to have recourse to compulsion. A General and a large force arrived at Lille, among others the 64th Regiment from Verdun.

On April 19th and 20th, the public were warned by proclamation to be prepared for a compulsory evacuation.

About three in the morning, troops, with fixed bayonets, barred the streets, machine guns commanded the road, against unarmed people.

Soldiers made their way into the houses. The officer pointed out the people who were to go, and, half an hour later, everybody was marched pell-mell into an adjacent factory, and from there to the station, whence the departure took place.

The victims of this brutal act displayed the greatest courage. They were heard crying 'Vive la France', and singing the Marseillaise in the cattle-trucks in which they were carried off.

It is said that the men are employed in agriculture, road-mending, the making of munitions and trench digging.

The women are employed in cooking and laundry-work for the soldiers and as substitutes for officers' servants.

For this severe work, housemaids, domestic servants and factory women have been taken by preference.

The unfortunate people, thus requisitioned, have been scattered from Seclin and Templeuve, as far as the Ardennes.

Their number is estimated at about 25,000, from the towns of Lille, Roubaix, and Tourcoing.

## DOCUMENT 3

Source: Middle-class factory worker, Naomi Loughnan, *Munitions Work*, 1918.

We little thought when we first put on our overalls and caps and enlisted in the Munitions Army how much more inspiring our life was to be than we had dared to hope. Though we munitions workers sacrifice our ease we gain a life worth living. Our long days are filled with interest, and with the zest of doing work for our country in the grand cause of Freedom. As we handle the weapons of war we are learning great lessons of life. In the busy, noisy workshops we come face to face with every kind of class, and each one of these classes has something to learn from the others. Our muscles may be aching, and the brightness fading a little from our eyes, but our minds are expanding, our very souls are growing stronger. And excellent, too, is the discipline for our bodies, though we do not always recognize this . . .

The day is long, the atmosphere is breathed and rebreathed, and the oil smells. Our hands are black with warm, thick oozings from the machines, which coat the work and, incidentally, the workers. We regard our horrible, be-grimed members [limbs] with disgust and secret pride.

Whatever sacrifice we make of wearied bodies, brains dulled by interminable night-shifts, of roughened hands, and faces robbed of their soft curves, it is, after all, so small a thing. We live in safety, we have shelter, and food whenever necessary, and we are even earning quite a lot of money. What is ours beside the great sacrifice? Men in their prime, on the verge of ambition realized, surrounded by the benefits won by their earlier struggles, are offering up their very lives. And those boys with Life, all glorious and untried, spread before them at their feet, are turning a smiling face to Death.

## DOCUMENT 4

Source: Winston Churchill, British Prime Minister, *Letter to the Minister of Food*, July 4, 1941.

It is always difficult to hold the balance between the need for increasing total food supplies and the need to maintain a fair distribution. We should not be too hard on the private individual who increases his supplies by his own productive efforts.

It is satisfactory that the meat prospects are improving, and I hope that pressure on the United States to increase her pork output will soon enable us to raise the ration without risk of having subsequently to reduce it.

We do not wish to create a grievance among farmers by compelling them to slaughter beasts which they can fatten without imported feeding stuffs; on the other hand of course the country cannot go hungry because farmers do not choose to bring their beasts to market.

It will no doubt be possible to arrange with the Minister of Agriculture, perhaps by a carefully worked out price policy, a scheme which will keep the meat supply as constant as possible having regard to seasonal factors.

## DOCUMENT 5

Source: Soviet propaganda poster from 1942.

Second World War: Russian Poster, 1942.

СОРЕВНУЙТЕСЬ НА ЛУЧШУЮ ПОМОЩЬ ФРОНТУ!

"Follow This Worker's Example Produce More for the Front."

## DOCUMENT 6

Source: Joseph Stalin, Soviet Leader, *Order of the Day Number 55*, February 1942.

The enemy is still strong. He will exert his last forces in order to attain success. And the more he suffers defeat, the more brutal he will become. Therefore it is essential that in our country the training of reserves in aid of the front should not be relaxed for a moment. It is essential that ever-new military units should go to the front to forge victory over the bestial enemy. It is essential that our industry, particularly our war industry, should work with redoubled energy. It is essential that with every day the front should receive ever more tanks, planes, guns, mortars, machine-guns, rifles, automatic rifles, and ammunition.

Herein lies one of the basic sources of the strength and power of the Red Army.

But the strength of the Red Army does not consist only in this. The strength of the Red Army rests, above all, in the fact that it is waging, not a predatory, not an imperialist war, but a patriotic war, a war of liberation, a just war. The Red Army's task is to liberate our Soviet territory from the German invaders; to liberate from the yoke of the German invaders the citizens of our villages and towns who were free and lived like human beings before the war, but are now oppressed and suffer pillage, ruin and famine; and finally, to liberate our women from that disgrace and outrage to which they are subjected by the German-fascist monsters. What could be more noble, more lofty, than such a task? Not one German soldier can say that he is waging a just war, because he cannot fail to see that he is forced to fight for the despoliation and oppression of other peoples. The German soldier has no such lofty and noble aim in the war which could inspire him and of which he could be proud. But, in contrast, any Red Army man can say with pride that he is waging a just war, a war for liberation, a war for the freedom and independence of his Motherland. The Red Army does have a noble and lofty aim in the war which inspires it to great exploits. It is precisely this that explains why the patriotic war brings forth among us thousands of heroes and heroines ready to go to their death for the sake of the liberty of their Motherland.

## DOCUMENT 7

Source: Charter of the United Nations, 1945.

WE THE PEOPLES OF THE UNITED NATIONS DETERMINED

- to save succeeding generations from the scourge of war, which twice in our lifetime has brought untold sorrow to mankind, and
- to reaffirm faith in fundamental human rights, in the dignity and worth of the human person, in the equal rights of men and women and of nations large and small, and
- to establish conditions under which justice and respect for the obligations arising from treaties and other sources of international law can be maintained, and
- to promote social progress and better standards of life in larger freedom,

AND FOR THESE ENDS

- to practice tolerance and live together in peace with one another as good neighbors, and
- to unite our strength to maintain international peace and security, and
- to ensure, by the acceptance of principles and the institution of methods, that armed force shall not be used, save in the common interest, and
- to employ international machinery for the promotion of the economic and social advancement of all peoples,

HAVE RESOLVED TO COMBINE OUR EFFORTS TO ACCOMPLISH THESE AIMS:

- to maintain international peace and security, and to that end: to take effective collective measures for the prevention and removal of threats to the peace . . .
- to develop friendly relations among nations based upon respect,
- to achieve international co-operation in solving international problems of an economic, social, cultural, or humanitarian character, and in promoting and encouraging respect for human rights and for fundamental freedoms for all without distinction as to race, sex, language, or religion; and
- to be a center for harmonizing the actions of nations in the attainment of these common ends.

## Question 2, Question 3, or Question 4 (Long Essay Question)

SUGGESTED WRITING TIME: 35 MINUTES

---

**DIRECTIONS:** Choose Question 2, Question 3, OR Question 4.

In your response, you should do the following:

- State a relevant thesis that directly addresses all parts of the question.
- Support your argument with evidence, using specific examples.
- Synthesize the elements above into a persuasive essay that extends your argument, connects it to a different historical context, or connects it to a different category of analysis.

---

2. Analyze the ways in which the opening of Atlantic trade led to or resulted from a shift in social, economic, and political power from the Mediterranean Basin to Western Europe.

3. Analyze the ways in which the public health movement and urban planning led to or resulted from a shift in social, political, and economic power at the end of the 19th century.

4. Analyze the causes of the changing roles and rights of European women from 1900–2000.

# Scoring and Answer Explanations

The AP European History exam is composed of four parts grouped into two sections. The multiple-choice test is scored with 1 point given for each correct answer.

- *There is no penalty for guessing,* so you should answer every question on the exam.
- Each of three short-answer questions is given a score of 0–3.
- The long essay is given a score from 0–6.
- The document-based question (DBQ) is scored from 0–7.

To attain your final AP score on this exam, use the following method:

Multiple-Choice Score × 1.091 = _____

+

Short-Answer Score × 3.334 = _____

+

DBQ Score × 5.357 = _____

+

LEQ Score × 3.75 = _____

**Total of all above scores is composite score = _____ (round your score)**

## Composite Score Conversion Chart

| Score Range | AP Score |
| --- | --- |
| 104–150 | 5 |
| 91–103 | 4 |
| 79–91 | 3 |
| 69–78 | 2 |
| 0–69 | 1 |

**To get a final score for the exam, compare your composite score to the chart directly above.**

The following are four separate guides to scoring each section of this exam. Once you have scored each piece of the exam, place the score on the appropriate line above. When you are done, do the computations to get your final score. Remember that this test is designed to mimic the AP exam. However, you will not take it in the same conditions that you will during the real test, and it is not scored by professionals, who are reading 1,000 or more essays daily. Although this test is a good predictor of success, it is only as good as the student using it. So do not stop studying just because you earned a good score here.

## Scoring Guide for the Multiple-Choice Section

> **SPECIAL NOTE**
>
> There is a lot of valuable information in the explanations for the multiple-choice questions, so make certain to read the explanations for ALL responses for every question that gave you any trouble!

1.  (A)  is wrong because the spread of humanist ideas happened in bursts and stops throughout European history.
    (B)  is wrong because humanism was at its height in the early 1500s with Erasmus just reaching his most productive period.
    (C)  is wrong because the Roman Catholic Church's leaders embraced humanism as this painting in the papal residences illustrates.
    **(D)  is CORRECT because humanists, such as Petrarch in Italy and Erasmus in Rotterdam, were already writing major humanist works by the time this painting was finished.**

2.  (A)  is wrong because sfumato cannot be used on frescoes and is not present.
    (B)  is wrong because chiaroscuro cannot be used on frescoes and is not present.
    **(C)  is CORRECT because perspective, humanist subject matter, and attention to anatomical detail are all present characteristics of Renaissance art.**
    (D)  is wrong because frescoes have been used in European art since the Greek era.

3.  **(A)  is CORRECT because the Renaissance saw people believe that great public works of art demonstrated power and prestige.**
    (B)  is wrong because reducing unemployment was not seen as a civic duty at the time.
    (C)  is wrong because they had other motives concerned with power and prestige that overrode the desire for beauty.
    (D)  is wrong because the idea of getting wisdom from the Greeks was but a small part of what was going on and misses the bigger picture.

4.  (A)  is wrong because the document is more about religion than about mercantilism or profit.

(B)  is wrong because the document is more about religion than about gold and profit.
(C)  is wrong because the personal glory of captains is not mentioned in the document.
**(D)  is CORRECT because the document clearly displays religious motivations for exploration.**

5.  **(A)  is CORRECT because the Europeans did not create colonies in the interior of Africa until the 19th century.**
    (B)  is wrong because the Columbian Exchange was a result of European overseas exploration.
    (C)  is wrong because vast trade networks were created as a result of European overseas exploration.
    (D)  is wrong because the slave trade with Africa resulted from European overseas exploration.

6.  (A)  is wrong because those technologies got Europeans to the New World but did not help them once there.
    (B)  is wrong because those technologies got Europeans to the New World but did not help them once there.
    **(C)  is CORRECT because gunpowder and horses allowed the Europeans to conquer the natives with relative ease.**
    (D)  is wrong because those technologies got Europeans to the New World but did not help them once there.

7.  (A)  is wrong because, although Calvin and some other Protestants believed this, the document states nothing to support that idea.
    **(B)  is CORRECT because the part about corruption at the start of these excerpts alludes to the corruption of the Roman Catholic Church.**

(C) is wrong because, although Luther and some other Protestants practiced this, the documents state nothing to support that idea.

(D) is wrong because the idea of salvation through faith alone belongs to Martin Luther and is contradicted by the writings of Calvin in the excerpts.

8. **(A) is CORRECT because Calvinists indeed felt the religious organization supersedes all authority of the state.**

(B) is wrong because Lutherans believed in consubstantiation, while Calvinists believed the Eucharist was celebrated only to symbolize, not emulate, Christ.

(C) is wrong because Calvinists, or Huguenots, in France used the Reformation for their political advantage to gain power and influence in France.

(D) is wrong because Lutherans chose to keep only communion, baptism, and absolution as the sacraments.

9. **(A) is CORRECT because the shaded areas do represent the Habsburg lands during the 16th century, including Austria, the 17 provinces of the Netherlands as one nation, and parts of Italy.**

(B) is wrong because the Germanic states would all be included, as would all of northern Italy, if the map displayed the combatants of the Thirty Years' War.

(C) is wrong because most of the shaded area was Roman Catholic and still is.

(D) is wrong because Russia, Austria, and France would be shaded along with Prussia if this were a map of the Holy Alliance.

10. (A) is wrong because most of the areas shaded were Roman Catholic under the Habsburgs, who fought wars to preserve the religion there, such as the invasion of the Dutch and the Spanish Armada campaign.

(B) is wrong because Austria, Milan, and southern Italy would definitely not be shaded as they lost significant power as a result of transatlantic trade.

(C) is wrong because most of the areas shaded remained Catholic as Habsburg lands, with only the Dutch taking advantage of this religious conflict.

**(D) is CORRECT because most of the areas shaded remained Catholic as Habsburg lands and the Habsburgs fought numerous wars to ensure this, including the Thirty Years' War that re-Catholicized the Bohemians and other areas such as modern Belgium.**

11. (A) is wrong because this map depicts the mid- to late-16th century Germany and Italy, which would not be unified until 1871. The key to this question is the size of the huge Ottoman Empire and the United Provinces of the Netherlands that tell you the place in time.

**(B) is CORRECT because this map depicts the mid- to late-16th century. During the late-17th century, the Ottoman Empire began to decline as first the Austrians and then the Russians began to gain control in Eastern Europe. The key to this question is the size of the huge Ottoman Empire and the United Provinces of the Netherlands that tell you the place in time.**

(C) is wrong because France began to expand under Louis XIII and Richelieu and expanded further under Louis XIV by the time a century had passed from the time depicted on the map. The key to this question is the size of the huge Ottoman Empire and the United Provinces of the Netherlands that tell you the place in time.

(D) is wrong because Greece remained under Ottoman control until the start of the 19th century, more than a century after the time depicted on this map. The key to this question is the size of the huge Ottoman Empire and the United Provinces of the Netherlands that tell you the place in time.

12. **(A) is CORRECT because Copernicus wrote his *On the Revolutions of the Heavenly Spheres*, which opened up Europe to considering a heliocentric universe.**

(B) is wrong because Kepler wrote about the laws of planetary motion, but this quote seems to be more a reaction to Copernicus.

(C) is wrong because Galileo supported the Copernican theory in his *Dialogue Concerning the Two Chief World Systems*.

(D) is wrong because Pilsudski was important in Poland after the First World War.

13. (A) is wrong because the revolutions of Jupiter's moons was worldview changing but not nearly as much as its implication that Earth is but one tiny planet in an infinite universe or even multiverse.

(B) is wrong because Earth's removal from the center of the universe was worldview changing but not nearly as much as its implication that Earth is but one tiny planet in an infinite universe or even multiverse.

(C) is wrong because God's removal from the physical heavens above our heads to a metaphysical space did change Europe's worldview but not nearly as much as the fact that Earth is but one tiny planet in an infinite universe or even multiverse.

(D) **is CORRECT because the realization that Earth is but one tiny planet in an infinite universe or even multiverse is still affecting the development of all human society today.**

14. (A) **is CORRECT because humanism was an educational program based upon the ancient Greeks and Romans, such as Aristotle, and Galileo's observations and conclusions contradicted those of Aristotle and other Greeks.**

(B) is wrong because the idea of removing Earth from the center of the universe did not conflict with the movement away from religion.

(C) is wrong because the ideas of individualism and uniqueness and the pursuit of excellence did not conflict with the movement away from religion.

(D) is wrong because the idea of arête, or pursuit of excellence, did not conflict with the movement away from religion.

15. (A) is wrong because the standard of living did not rise across Europe at that time, and intellectual thought affected very few people for a long time.

(B) is wrong because Galileo actually went against ancient Greek thought in many areas in this writing.

(C) **is CORRECT because Galileo was clearly using experimentation to help shift the European worldview from the Aristotelian to the Copernican one.**

(D) is wrong because intellectual thought refuted Aristotle.

16. (A) is wrong because the Black Plague's elimination would lead to greater famine because there would be more mouths to feed.

(B) **is CORRECT because the Agricultural Revolution increased food production, decreased hunger, and increased health.**

(C) is wrong because the putting-out system did not improve agricultural production in and of itself.

(D) is wrong because populations rose during the 18th century.

17. (A) is wrong because low agricultural production added to the problems with hunger.

(B) is wrong because adverse weather hurt crop production during this era, contributing to hunger problems.

(C) **is CORRECT because low taxes would have stimulated the economy and increased food production, yet the French people paid relatively high taxes.**

(D) is wrong because poor transportation led to poor harvests and distributions of those harvests, further leading to hunger problems.

18. (A) is wrong because the Enlightenment occurred during the 18th century.

(B) is wrong because the divine right theory did not immediately improve crop yields.

(C) is wrong because existentialism was not conceived of until the late-19th century.

(D) **is CORRECT because the Scientific Revolution led to scientific experimentation in farming that led to crop rotation,** advanced breeding, fertilization of crops, and other innovations that improved agricultural production by the end of the 17th century.

19. (A) is wrong because the tone of this writing is critical of the king and, as a noble, the duke resents the subjugation of the nobility.

   **(B) is CORRECT because the duke is displaying his bias against the king for subjugating the nobility.**

   (C) is wrong because the duke clearly thinks that the king is overreaching his power.

   (D) is wrong because the duke seems to be criticizing the nobility's subjugation through diversion.

20. (A) is wrong because, although Martinet trained the military well, Colbert, the finance minister, redesigned the finances of France based upon mercantilist theories.

   (B) is wrong because, although Mazarin was his regent, Louis XIV dismissed him after the Fronde, and Colbert, the finance minister, redesigned the finances of France based upon mercantilist theories.

   **(C) is CORRECT because Colbert, the finance minister, redesigned the finances of France based upon mercantilist theories.**

   (D) is wrong because the Duke of Burgundy was not a major adviser to the king.

21. (A) is wrong because Louis XIV did not regret the subjugation of the nobility, and in fact, it made him a model for other monarchs.

   (B) is wrong because, although he delighted in ceremony, Louis XIV was a strong leader who led France into an era of prestige.

   (C) is wrong because the use of bureaucrats to perform the duties of state was beneficial to Louis XIV and France.

   **(D) is CORRECT because his wars were very costly, leaving the country in debt and detracting from his other successes.**

22. **(A) is CORRECT because the list of complaints does not address the debts of France.**

   (B) is wrong because the list of complaints explains the problems with the legal system.

(C) is wrong because the list of complaints refers to the ideals of the Enlightenment as the basis for what laws should be.

(D) is wrong because the list of complaints refers to problems with the equality.

23. (A) is wrong because the peasants cared more about their rents and dues than about the constitutional monarchy.

   **(B) is CORRECT because the peasants cared more about their rents and dues than about anything else.**

   (C) is wrong because the peasants cared more about their rents and dues than about their level of political participation.

   (D) is wrong because the peasants did not really approve of a change in religion.

24. (A) is wrong because huge armies were needed to fight against the monarchies of Europe.

   (B) is wrong because fixing wages and prices made it easier to plan for the defense of France.

   **(C) is CORRECT because this distracted many from their support of the revolution as they were torn between their faith and their nation.**

   (D) is wrong because the promotion of soldiers based upon merit supported revolutionary ideals.

25. (A) is wrong because the *philosophes*, and Voltaire in particular, believed in religious toleration, not imposing any religion on anyone.

   (B) is wrong because Voltaire was a proponent of religious toleration.

   (C) is wrong because the *philosophes* did support skepticism and believed it was a good way to analyze data.

   **(D) is CORRECT because this passage clearly supports religious toleration.**

26. (A) is wrong because, although those concepts did influence this era, they are not referenced in that sentence.

   **(B) is CORRECT because the concept that the Church should stop its discrimination against, and conversion of, peoples of different faiths around the world came from**

**seeing the virtues of other cultures and methods of living in the world.**

(C) is wrong because, although those concepts did influence this era, they are not referenced in that sentence.

(D) is wrong because, although those concepts did influence this era, they are not directly referenced in that sentence.

27. (A) is wrong because Rousseau wrote *The Social Contract* and began the Romantic movement by questioning pure reason.

   **(B) is CORRECT because Montesquieu wrote about the separation of powers in government.**

   (C) is wrong because Wollstonecraft was an early feminist who defended the French Revolution.

   (D) is wrong because Adam Smith wrote about economics, not government.

28. (A) is wrong because, although many were accomplished scientists, that idea is not being expressed here.

   **(B) is CORRECT because this excerpt is from a pamphlet.**

   (C) is wrong because only very few thinkers of this era were atheists; Paine clearly was not.

   (D) is wrong because, although many did believe this at the time, that idea is not being expressed here.

29. (A) is wrong because the document cites the idea of building the national economy by reducing imports, which is mercantilism, while the pursuit of capitalism would mean that they were not concerned with the government.

   **(B) is CORRECT because the document cites the idea of building the national economy by reducing imports, which is mercantilism.**

   (C) is wrong because industrialization is not an economic theory.

   (D) is wrong because bullionism was a form of mercantilism.

30. (A) is wrong because urbanization was an issue but not as much so as the growing class consciousness and changing way of life.

(B) is wrong because population growth is not discussed in this document and was not a part of the problems cited within it.

(C) is wrong because Parliament's support of industrialization was not as much a motivator for the lower classes as was their growing class consciousness brought on by socioeconomic changes.

**(D) is CORRECT because their growing class consciousness was brought on by socioeconomic changes that are evident in the document.**

31. (A) is wrong because the governments did pass reform bills like the Factory Act of 1833 and the Mines Act of 1842.

   **(B) is CORRECT because most of the reforms made before 1850 focused on work hours and separating genders at work.**

   (C) is wrong because the song does not mention or allude to Parliament.

   (D) is wrong because the national health systems were not created until the end of the 19th century or later in some places.

32. (A) is wrong because there was a domination of industry in Eastern Europe by nobility and aristocrats.

   (B) is wrong because urbanization of society was one of the most important results of the Industrial Revolution.

   (C) is wrong because class identity emerged and was supported by societal experiences.

   **(D) is CORRECT because social inequality emerged with wealthy factory owners contrasted with impoverished workers.**

33. (A) is wrong because Abbott is praising Napoleon for being a cultured genius, and secret police are not very enlightened.

   **(B) is CORRECT because Abbott is impressed with Napoleon's intelligence and worldliness, which were most evident in his domestic reforms such as the Napoleonic Code.**

   (C) is wrong because someone impressed by enlightened thinking would not be impressed by suppressing the rights of women.

(D) is wrong because, although there is much to praise in the genius of his military tactics, Abbott is more impressed by the wide breadth of Napoleon's knowledge, which is most evident in his domestic reforms.

34. (A) is wrong because a universal currency was not imposed.

(B) is wrong because the suppression of guerrilla factions hurt the reputation of Napoleon internationally.

**(C) is CORRECT because the old order (feudalism and manorialism) was dismantled by decree in all areas Napoleon conquered, inspiring a shift of power from the landowning aristocracy to the middle classes and promising all classes social and economic justice, which appealed to all Europeans.**

(D) is wrong because French was in decline as an international language because of the rise of English.

35. **(A) is CORRECT because the failed conquest of Haiti was in no way enlightened.**

(B) is wrong because the Code Napoleon was indeed an enlightened action.

(C) is wrong because promoting soldiers and government workers based upon their merits only was indeed an enlightened action.

(D) is wrong because, although they were not great ideas, they did show the particular genius of Napoleon, and the invasion of Haiti is much more hypocritical for someone spreading freedom in Europe.

36. **(A) is CORRECT because Metternich was displaying fears about the impact of spreading liberalism and revolution caused by those ideas, and he expressed plans to suppress the ideas of personal liberty and nationalism.**

(B) is wrong because Metternich had already addressed this issue at the Congress of Vienna five years earlier and was no longer in fear of Napoleon or his impact.

(C) is wrong because Metternich was in favor of increasing monarchical power and preserving it.

(D) is wrong because the economic cycle is not addressed in this document, and fear of economic cycles was not a major issue in Europe until later in the 19th century.

37. (A) is wrong because empires were strong in Europe until after the First World War, 1914–1918.

(B) is wrong because the Holy Alliance was more of a formality than a real alliance, and it had very little power over European affairs.

**(C) is CORRECT because the Concert of Europe was created as a way to promote unity and was the most important result of the Congress of Vienna.**

(D) is wrong because the Congress of Vienna did nothing to address secret societies.

38. (A) is wrong because Metternich did not want to stop all knowledge, just political and economic change.

**(B) is CORRECT because the overall goal of conservatism at that time was to prevent the political and economic revolutions from occurring on the Continent the way they had in England.**

(C) is wrong because suppressing secret societies harmed democracy rather than helped it.

(D) is wrong because, at the time, both political and economic change were considered by conservatives as worth stopping.

39. (A) is wrong because Fourier was not advocating the greatest good for the greatest number but for a perfect society, which makes him a utopian socialist.

(B) is wrong because Fourier was not advocating for the government to leave business alone but for a perfect society, which makes him a utopian socialist.

**(C) is CORRECT because Fourier argued in favor of creating a perfect society.**

(D) is wrong because Fourier did not wish to eliminate or nationalize all private property.

40. (A) is wrong because Germany did not get far in creating a government in 1848 before the revolution ended.

   **(B) is CORRECT because France was led for a short while by Louis Blanc, who created national workshops according to Fourier's ideas.**

   (C) is wrong because 1848 did not affect Great Britain as it was already an industrialized democracy.

   (D) is wrong because, from 1815–1848, Austria was run by Metternich, the prototype conservative, and he detested socialism in all forms.

41. (A) is wrong because Luddites wanted to smash machines and destroy the order, not join it by voting.

   (B) is wrong because liberals were more moderate at this time and did not believe in universal male suffrage.

   (C) is wrong because Benthamites wanted the greatest good for the greatest number while Chartists wanted universal male suffrage according to their People's Charter.

   **(D) is CORRECT because Benthamites wanted the greatest good for the greatest number.**

42. (A) is wrong because, as industrialization began in Germany, many skilled workers lost their positions as a result of mechanization and because the illustration depicts a middle-class family.

   (B) is wrong because states did not implement social welfare policies until the late-19th and early-20th centuries.

   (C) is wrong because, in the years 1848–1849, the deputies in the Frankfurt Parliament failed to create a constitution for a united Germany.

   **(D) is CORRECT because the quarter century of revolutionary and Napoleonic wars in central Europe gave economic development a setback, which was only reversed by the return of stability after the Congress of Vienna.**

43. (A) is wrong because the Revolutions of 1848 focused primarily on liberal and national political change; women participated, often

on behalf of their class, but did not organize specifically for the gender freedom warned against in the cartoon.

   (B) is wrong because the cartoon satirizes the notion that the proper place of men is a domestic one, suggesting that role reversal leads to social chaos.

   **(C) is CORRECT because, through its caption, the cartoon demonstrates a female reaction to male anxieties over the prospect of women becoming more engaged in political life.**

   (D) is wrong because, although companionate marriage patterns were developing in the 19th century, the primary decision-making role in families remained male dominated.

44. (A) is wrong because socialist notions of family and child rearing did not take strong hold in Europe, despite being briefly embraced by leaders of the Russian Revolution.

   **(B) is CORRECT because, as working-class families gained higher wages and had access to more leisure opportunities because of government reforms, they began to adopt similar child-rearing patterns and a more gendered division of labor.**

   (C) is wrong because women's entrance into the paid workforce in large numbers did not occur until the First World War.

   (D) is wrong because the professional and academic journals of the time recommended fathers become more involved in child rearing.

45. (A) is wrong because, although there were still prosperous farmers, the majority of those were the previously wealthy landowners, and nearly all former serfs struggled to work within the new communal system.

   (B) is wrong because the zemstvos' power was short-lived, and a national legislature did not come about until 1906, after the 1905 Revolution had forced the hand of Czar Nicholas II.

   (C) is wrong because the wealthy landowning elite, although suspicious of the recent liberal reforms, were left in an economic condition vastly superior to that of former serfs.

**(D) is CORRECT because the least-desired land was parceled to the serfs, and they owed large financial obligations, crippling them and often their children with debt.**

46. **(A) is CORRECT because Russian military and domestic ineptitude were exposed in this inglorious defeat, which convinced the new czar and his advisers that immediate, major reforms were needed.**

    (B) is wrong because serfdom was abolished by Napoleon in Prussia in 1807 and then in Austria as a result of the 1848 Revolution.

    (C) is wrong because the Decembrist Revolt occurred in 1825 and inaugurated the tenure of Nicholas I, one of Russia's most conservative czars.

    (D) is wrong because construction on the Trans-Siberian Railroad did not commence until 30 years later in 1891, which was ten years after the czar's assassination.

47. (A) is wrong because food production increased but was offset by population increase, while the agricultural sacrifice for industrial glory was part of Stalin's five-year plans in the 1930s.

    (B) is wrong because agricultural output did not plummet, and Stolypin's reforms improved the economic viability of only a fraction of peasant farmers.

    **(C) is CORRECT because the financial burden owed by former serfs limited their mobility and mostly kept them in debt, while conservative landowner elites felt the czar's administration had become overly radical.**

    (D) is wrong because many former serfs were financially limited, and their debts kept them from being able to seek employment in cities, thus preventing large numbers of them from relocating from their farms.

48. (A) is wrong because the fear of revolt encouraged leaders across the world to agree to this treaty.

(B) is wrong because another tool was sorely needed to prevent war as Germany rearmed and the rest of Europe practiced appeasement.

**(C) is CORRECT because German leadership was not trying to expand Germany until after Adolf Hitler took office in 1933.**

(D) is wrong because Keynes's work influenced many leaders and citizens to want to be easier on Germany, and, thus, appeasement was put into effect.

49. (A) is wrong because the Second World War made this choice impossible.

    (B) is wrong because this response ignores issues like Yugoslavia in the 1990s and Ukraine today.

    **(C) is CORRECT because, whenever "civilized" Europeans are threatened, they seem to turn quickly to violence as has happened recently in Ukraine.**

    (D) is wrong because there is still fighting in Europe, right now, in Ukraine.

50. (A) is wrong because Belgium did more poorly than Poland or the United Kingdom, while Poland did better than any other nation and joined later than most.

    **(B) is CORRECT because that trend is true, with Russia and Ukraine doing worse than the EU nations.**

    (C) is wrong because Greece did worse than Russia or the Ukraine.

    (D) is wrong because Poland did the second best of all and it was a COMECON nation.

51. (A) is wrong because, with the fall of communism and the rise of conservatism in more recent years, the welfare state has been reduced across Europe, leading to a greater gap between the rich and poor, especially in Eastern Europe.

    (B) is wrong because nationalism and national tensions have grown in Europe at the end of the 20th century and into the 21st century as evidenced by the breakup of the former Yugoslavia and the issues in Ukraine in 2014–2015.

(C) is wrong because most Europeans do not own property but rent their homes and have always done so.

**(D) is CORRECT because rising GDP is a clear indicator of higher consumption, which has occurred mostly as a result of the rising consumerism at the end of the 20th century.**

52. (A) is wrong because it was used by both sides to make their side look better during the Cold War.

(B) is wrong because it was used by both sides to make their side look better during the Cold War.

**(C) is CORRECT because it was used by both sides to make their side look better during the Cold War.**

(D) is wrong because it was used by both sides to make their side look better during the Cold War.

53. (A) is wrong because the fall of communism did not really affect the racial composition of the Continent.

**(B) is CORRECT because many of the guest workers who came to Europe as invited guests in the 1950s and 1960s settled permanently but have been denied full citizenship rights, which the Green Party wants for them.**

(C) is wrong because the benefits of the welfare state are not truly affected by racial discrimination.

(D) is wrong because, while the economic miracle shook Europe and consumerism rose, none of this was based upon race or immigrant status.

54. (A) is wrong because nationalist parties throughout Europe at the start of the 21st century were against education as a right.

(B) is wrong because the EU does not have such requirements.

(C) is wrong because the declaration was secular and did not ally with any religion, and the Catholic Church supported spending on such programs.

**(D) is CORRECT because the political debate over the welfare state is tearing Europe apart as disagreement over austerity measures for Greece and the proper level of welfare spending are dominated by a rising conflict between liberals and conservatives in the modern sense of the terms.**

55. (A) is wrong because the Declaration of Human Rights supports the rights of immigrants.

**(B) is CORRECT because the Declaration of Human Rights supports equal rights for all.**

(C) is wrong because the Declaration of Human Rights was issued by the United Nations, which supports free trade.

(D) is wrong because the Declaration of Human Rights is against any nation dominating another.

## Scoring Guide for the Short-Answer Section

Short answers are very straightforward. Either you did or did not get 1 point for each of the points available. Each question is worth up to 3 points for a total of 0–9 points available in this section, worth 20 percent of the exam score.

1. **0–3 points (1 point for each letter: a, b, and c)**

   (a) 1 point will be given for pointing out a significant difference between the historians' interpretations of the Renaissance. Some examples of evidence include: Cho is more impressed by the Italians and Switlick by the Northern Europeans, Switlick criticizes Petrarch and praises Erasmus, Cho praises the artists more, or Cho brings in science.

   (b) 1 point will be given for a good answer that explains *how* one piece of evidence supports Switlick's argument that the Northern Renaissance is superior to that of the Italian Renaissance. Evidence to support the claim include: the Dutch Golden Age, Dürer, Shakespeare, Vermeer, Rembrandt, Brueghel, van Eyck, or the rise in Western European economic and political dominance.

   (c) 1 point will be given for an explanation of *how* one piece of evidence supports Cho's argument that the Italian Renaissance was the height of the Renaissance. Evidence to support this can include: mastery of Italian artists in memory of the world (*Mona Lisa*, etc.), the spread of Italian Renaissance ideas all over the world, the success of humanism and secularism absent from the Northern Renaissance, or the importance of Galileo to Newton and others since.

2. **0–3 points (2 points for a and 1 point for b)**

   (a) 1 point will be given for *each* of *two* explanations of *how* pieces of evidence support the argument that the Cold War was a conflict between communism and capitalism, such as: Marxist propaganda from the Soviets and capitalist propaganda from NATO nations, examination of property in both systems or nations, a look at who was aided by which side around the world during the Cold War, Mao's *Little Red Book*, Brezhnev Doctrine, Truman Doctrine, Iron Curtain speech, Marshall Plan funds use, and/or IMF and World Bank rules.

   (b) 1 point will be given for an explanation of *how* one piece of evidence undermines the argument that the Cold War was a conflict between communism and capitalism, such as: it was a power struggle; NATO is not capitalist, and the U.S.S.R. is not really communist; Scandinavian Compromise; or still chilly relations 25 years after the Cold War ended.

3. **0–3 points (1 point for each letter: a, b, and c)**

   (a) 1 point will be given for explaining that the growth of science led to better machines and technology, particularly for exploration but eventually for weaponry and everything else. These better machines and technology were utilized by Protestant nations, giving them an advantage over the Catholic nations, such as Spain, that stayed away from science due to the Roman Catholic Church's conflict with Galileo and Copernicus.

   (b) 1 point will be given for explaining that the growth of science led to better machines and technology, particularly for exploration for Protestants only. These better machines

and technology gave Protestant nations an advantage over the Catholic nations, such as Spain, that stayed away from science due to the Roman Catholic Church's conflict with Galileo and Copernicus. Thus, Spain and other Catholic nations, such as Austria, saw an economic decline.

   (c) 1 point will be given for explaining that discoveries like those seen in the picture led to Newton's view of the universe, changing how all knowledge was approached and allowing Europeans to believe they could solve all social and legal problems through the use of reason and experimentation.

4. **0–3 points (1 point for each letter: a, b, and c)**

   (a) 1 point will be given for an analysis of how Vincent van Gogh's image is typical of the trends of the late 19th century. For example: it shows common people in daily pursuits, typifying realism; it shows the sympathy for the common man for the plight of the poor typical of the time; the artwork was a mass-produced lithograph indicating that more people consumed art at the time; and it has a somber mood that fits the time.

   (b) 1 point will be awarded for identifying one way Native Americans were affected by transatlantic trade, which includes: enslaved; depopulated; land stolen; Christianized; got horses, cows, goats, and many vegetables; ravaged by epidemics; or lost wealth and power.

   (c) 1 point will be awarded for explaining the impact on Europeans, including: new foods like the potato and corn, new place to emigrate to, vast income comes to Europe, inflation, new immigrants to and from Europe, tobacco, racism, ability to own land in the New World, or reinforcement of their racism.

## Scoring Guide for the Essay Section

### The Document-Based Question (DBQ)

The DBQ emphasizes your ability to analyze and synthesize historical evidence, including textual, quantitative, or visual materials. The question also requires you to formulate a thesis and support it with relevant evidence. The seven documents accompanying each DBQ may vary in length, type, and content, but they will allow you to illustrate complexities and interactions within the material and to utilize a broad spectrum of historical skills.

The document-based question will typically require you to relate the documents to a historical period or theme and, thus, to focus on major periods and issues, in this way assessing your ability to incorporate outside knowledge related to the question but beyond the specifics of the documents. This ability to place the documents in the historical context in which they were produced is essential for your success.

### Scoring Your DBQ

**Maximum Possible Points: 7**

### A. THESIS AND ARGUMENT DEVELOPMENT (0–1 total points)

**TARGETED SKILL—Argumentation**

**1 point:** Presents a thesis that makes a historically defensible claim and responds to all parts of the question. The thesis must consist of one or more sentences located in one place, either in the introduction or the conclusion.

The student presents a thesis that directly addresses all parts of the question and makes a historically defensible claim. The thesis must do more than restate the question.

> **Acceptable thesis:** "As the First World War began, rampant nationalism led many to embrace total war as the best means to forward their national agendas. Some, though, saw the dangers to civilians posed by total war as the concept gained governmental support through its success in both world wars. Yet when the United Nations was formed in 1945, the international conflict over appropriate levels of governmental involvement in the economic lives of their citizens emerged into the Cold War." (This thesis is acceptable because it is specific in its assessment of how the concept of total war was viewed. It also puts the topic of total war into historical perspective with some qualification and contradiction.)

> **Unacceptable theses:**

- "During the first half of the 20th century, views on total war changed as the world changed and people became more controlled by their governments." (This is unacceptable because it does not state any specific changes or any specific views on total war.)
- "Those who were more conservative or radical were always more in favor of total war than those who were less extreme as can be seen through changes over time." (This is unacceptable because even though it states views, it does not state specific social, political, or economic changes.)

### B. CONTEXTUALIZATION (0–1 total points)

**1 point:** The essay must describe a broader historical context immediately relevant to the question.

> **Acceptable contextualization:** "As the Cold War began, the concept of total war gave way to the use of more limited forms of war after nuclear weapons had been used in World War II."

> **Unacceptable contextualization:** "Because so many women continued in the workforce as full-time workers after the First World War, Lougnan should be seen as defending their new jobs." (Women did not remain in the workforce in large numbers until after World War II, so the context here is incorrect.)

## C. EVIDENCE (0–3 total points)

**1 point:** The essay must utilize the content of at least THREE documents to address the topic of the question. **Note:** This analysis may be in the topic sentence; the analysis must be connected to the argument.

**OR**

**2 points:** The essay must utilize the content of at least SIX documents to support an argument about the question. **Note:** This analysis may be in the topic sentence; the analysis must be connected to the argument.

**AND**

## EVIDENCE BEYOND THE DOCUMENTS (0–1 total points)

**1 point:** The essay explains how at least one additional piece of specific evidence beyond those found in the documents relates to an argument about the question.

**Note:** This evidence must be DIFFERENT from the evidence used to earn the point for contextualization. This point is NOT awarded for a phrase or reference.

### Acceptable outside historical evidence:

- "The Scandinavian model of a strong social welfare system combined with high taxation and cooperation while allowing free markets between the wars left them more ready for the total war market reforms than other nations."
- "While total war allowed the European nations to meet the challenges of world wars, the economic boom of Western Europe during the 1950s and 1960s illustrates how free markets generate better standards of living."

**Unacceptable outside historical evidence:** "Total war was supported by governments." (This response is unacceptable because the evidence is pretty clear from the document and no true outside evidence was presented.)

## D. ANALYSIS AND REASONING (0–2 total points)

**1 point:** For at least THREE documents, the essay explains how each document's point of view, purpose, historical situation, and/or audience is relevant to the argument.

**2 points:** The essay demonstrates a complex understanding of the historical development that is the focus of the prompt, using evidence to corroborate, qualify, or modify an argument that addresses the question.

**Guidance on awarding this point is given.**

**1 point:** For at least FOUR documents, explain how each document's point of view, purpose, historical situation, and/or audience is relevant to the argument.

**Example of acceptable analysis:** "Just as the Soviets were starting to push the Germans out after brutal sieges, Joseph Stalin, the general secretary of the Soviet Union, was urging his people to engage in total war in order to ensure victory and used propaganda to motivate them." (This correctly places Stalin in place, time, and importance. Specifically, it explains point of view and purpose as well as gives some context.)

**Example of unacceptable analysis:** "The United Nations Charter seems to be supporting total war." (This is incorrect because the charter explains that its goal is to prevent war.)

### Intended Audience

**Acceptable:** "Churchill is very specific with the Minister of Food to whom he is writing because he wants his intentions to be followed." (It is clear that the letter was written to the Minister of Food and even connects tone to audience.)

**Unacceptable:** "Loughnan was writing for anyone who cared about World War I women." (This is far too vague; specify which people in which place at which time.)

## Purpose

**Acceptable:** "The Soviet propaganda poster was created and posted to encourage people on the home front to support the soldiers by working harder."

**Unacceptable:** "Winston Churchill was writing to show how he believed that the government should control every decision." (This is a misinterpretation as Churchill seems to be trying to limit the reach of the Minister of Food by asking to give farmers more control.)

## Historical Context

**Acceptable:** "The Soviets were just beginning to push the Germans back from the sieges of their major cities."

**Unacceptable:** "Because the First World War was over, Aristide was making the Germans out to be evil to get France more from the peace treaty." (This is wrong because the First World War was in full force when Aristide wrote this.)

## Author's Point of View

**Acceptable:** "The Soviet leader, Stalin, wanted to uplift his people and praise them for what they had done but also encourage them to keep working to defeat Germany completely."

**Unacceptable:** "Because he was the king of England, Winston Churchill's statements should be considered as coming from the upper classes." (This is wrong because Churchill was prime minister rather than king, although he certainly was upper class as the Duke of Marlborough.)

**Special note:** This evidence must be DIFFERENT from the evidence used to earn the point for contextualization. This point is NOT awarded for a phrase or reference.

**Document summaries:** Each document's key points will be listed along with some information on how it may relate to concepts and themes or processes relevant to the document and the course.

**Document 1**

## Key Points

- Pro–total war
- Propaganda
- Anti-German but anti-nationalistic
- From a socialist leader
- Calls for support of the war from all fronts
- Believes Allies will win war
- Predicts Russian Revolution
- States proletariat won in France and bourgeoisie lost
- Asks scientists and artists

*Contextualization*

- First World War just began
- Allies—Russia, France, Belgium, Serbia, and the United Kingdom
- First time total war was employed in full
- Still very hopeful in tone, so definitely belongs to prewar intellectual period

## Document 2

**Key Points**

- Against total war
- Complains of German abuses of French and Belgian citizens being used for total war effort
- Shows brutality of enemy in Germans
- Official report, so needs to be evaluated for validity because of diplomatic effect and propaganda
- Illustrates German use of total war during the First World War and its efficiency

*Contextualization*

- Germany was starting to be outproduced by Allies.
- Both sides were dug in for trench warfare on the Western Front.
- The First World War became a war of attrition.
- French and German enmity went back centuries and, more recently, to the Franco-Prussian War.

## Document 3

**Key Points**

- Pro–total war
- Indicates value and pride of female workers
- Demonstrates efforts at total war on the home front
- Written by a woman in favor of women working
- Illustrates understanding of the loss felt by all who know/knew soldiers
- Middle-class perspective supplied

*Contextualization*

- The document was written in the last year of the war.
- Most of Europe won women's suffrage after the First World War.
- It displays the very early inklings of modern feminism and links to later rights to work at all jobs for equal pay.

## Document 4

**Key Points**

- Supports total war but wants some reasonable exceptions
- Indicates frustration at the lack of available food for his nation
- Alludes to rationing of food used by all nations during total war
- Illustrates alliance with the United States in trade before the United States joined the war
- Examines the best way to distribute and grow food
- Common man depicted
- Trade unions legal and powerful across Europe in 1896

*Contextualization*

- Churchill was prime minister of the United Kingdom at the time.
- He was a descendant of the Duke of Marlborough and dedicated his life to serving his country regardless of his wealth.

- The United Kingdom was the last major power in Europe either not to fall to or not to make a nonaggression agreement with the Nazis, who seemed to be winning the Second World War.
- Most nations involved in the war were attempting some form of total war.
- The war lasted much longer than anyone believed it would before it started.

## Document 5

**Key Points**

- Pro-total war
- Soviet propaganda poster indicating that working in a factory helps the military win the war
- Meant to encourage workers to work their hardest; even if not, soldiers are still helping win the war
- Propaganda displaying Soviet airplanes and factory as images of power and modernity
- Has Lenin and Stalin together on the flag
- Just one of tens of thousands of pieces of Soviet propaganda used on its people

*Contextualization*

- Stalin and Hitler created a nonaggression pact in 1939 at the start of the Second World War. This occurred despite each hating the other's ideas and personality. However, Germany invaded the U.S.S.R. in 1941 and was not driven out until 1944.
- The Soviets were trying to catch up to the Germans industrially.
- Communism was trying to show the world that it would not be defeated by fascism.
- The Second World War was going on with a total war effort in all countries, requiring rationing, price controls, and government institutions, comparable to the German War Raw Materials Board and the British Ministry of Munitions during the First World War.
- Communism used the tactics of total war as far as government management of the economy went; those countries that became the Warsaw Pact were more prepared for life under such conditions than they would have been without needing world wars and total war to be employed.

## Document 6

**Key Points**

- Pro-total war
- Soviet propaganda, telling his people what needs to be done to defeat the Germans and why
- Meant to encourage workers to work their hardest; even if not, soldiers are still helping win the war
- Uses ideology, morality, fear, and praise together
- Mentions heroines and also German abuse of women

*Contextualization*

- The Second World War was going on with a total war effort in all countries, requiring rationing, price controls, and government control of all aspects of society.
- The Germans invaded the Soviet Union, violating their nonaggression pact, and the Soviets were just starting to break free of a German siege.
- The Soviets were trying to catch up to the Germans industrially.
- Communism was trying to show the world that it would not be defeated by fascism.
- Communism used the tactics of total war as far as government management of the economy went; those countries that became the Warsaw Pact were more prepared for life under such conditions than they would have been without needing world wars and total war to be employed.

**Document 7**

**Key Points**

- Against total war and all war if possible
- Created after the Second World War and very hopeful in tone as it created the United Nations
- Preserves human rights and Enlightenment ideals of justice and tolerance
- Wants to improve the economic and social lives of *all* people
- All nations were to become members
- Tries to solve problems without war but can declare international *police actions* by limited military force
- Includes World Health Organization and UNESCO
- Shows concern for any state that has grown too powerful and is too involved with the lives of its citizens

*Contextualization*

- The League of Nations had failed to prevent the Second World War, and it needed to be replaced and strengthened.
- The Cold War was emerging, which was a contest between two superpowers armed with many nuclear weapons.
- The world economy needed to be rebuilt after years of warfare tore it apart.
- World war had devastated the world, and most people did not want another war that many feared could eliminate humanity.

## Scoring Guidelines for Long Essay Question 2

Analyze the ways in which the opening of Atlantic trade led to or resulted from a shift in social, economic, and political power from the Mediterranean Basin to Western Europe.

**Maximum possible points: 6**

## Comments on Question 2

This is a *causation* question because it requires you to explain how one event, the opening of transatlantic trade, resulted in or *caused* a specific outcome, the shift in social, political, and economic power from the Mediterranean Basin to Western Europe. Remember to describe causes of the shifts, indicating which shift was caused by each factor cited as a result of the Columbian Exchange. Also explain the reasons for the causes and effects of those shifts with specific facts.

Your essay should explain how and why exploration and colonization in the 15th and 16th centuries enabled the countries that bordered the Atlantic Ocean to achieve economic, social, political, and military dominance in Europe. For centuries, Italy dominated European trade with the Far East due to its strategic location on the Mediterranean. New trade routes with Asia established by Portuguese explorers and the discovery of the New World by Spanish and other explorers whose nations had Atlantic access offered new routes and new products. Explain how the Columbian Exchange gave Spain, and eventually England and the Netherlands, huge economic power. The importance of Northern European advances in naval technology and knowledge as factors in shifting power farther north can also be examined.

**A detailed rubric for this specific question follows to help you score your long essay response.**

### A. THESIS (0–1 total points)

**1 point:** The essay presents a thesis that makes a historically defensible claim and responds to all parts of the question. The thesis must consist of one or more sentences located in one place, either in the introduction or the conclusion.

**Special note:** The thesis *must* consist of one or more sentences located in the introduction or the conclusion of the essay. However, neither the introduction nor the conclusion is strictly limited to one paragraph.

Acceptable thesis statements create an argument that responds to the task. They describe the causes and/or explain the effects of the opening of transatlantic trade on the shift in political, social, and economic power from the Mediterranean Basin (Italy) to Western Europe and explain specific examples that illustrate those causes and effects.

You must present a thesis that directly addresses all parts of the question. The thesis must do more than restate the question.

**Acceptable thesis:** "When Western Europeans began to open transatlantic trade, vast wealth and resources poured into that region. It created the best opportunities to improve one's station in life that Europeans had had in centuries. It drew the best and brightest to Western Europe and shifted the social, political, and economic power center from Italy to first Spain and then to the rest of Western Europe." (This thesis is acceptable because it is specific in its assessment of the impact of the opening of trade across the Atlantic and provides specific reasons for the shifts in economic and political power.)

**Unacceptable theses:**

- "The beginning of the Columbian Exchange had many effects on Europe and shifted political, economic, and social power from the Mediterranean Basin to Western Europe." (This is unacceptable because it does not state any specific ways that the opening of transatlantic trade caused those shifts.)
- "The opening of transatlantic trade made those in Western Europe rich and opened opportunities for trade, shifting the center of Europe's trade economy from Italy to Western Europe." (This is unacceptable because even though it explains the causes for economic change, there is no cause for political or social change stated.)

## B. CONTEXTUALIZATION (0–1 total points)

**1 point:** The essay describes a broader historical context immediately relevant to the question.

## C. EVIDENCE (0–2 total points)

**1 point:** The essay develops and supports an argument that provides specific examples of evidence related to how the opening of Atlantic Trade affected Mediterranean trade.

OR

**2 points:** The essay develops and adequately supports an argument about how the opening of Atlantic Trade affected the Mediterranean basin.

## D. ANALYSIS AND REASONING (0–3 total points)

**1 point:** The essay uses historical reasoning (e.g., comparison, causation, or CCOT) to frame or structure an argument that addresses the prompt.

OR

**2 points:** The essay demonstrates a complex understanding of the historical development that is the focus of the prompt, using evidence to corroborate, qualify, or modify an argument that addresses the question.

**Special note:** Responses can only receive the second point if they also meet the criteria for the first contextualization point.

## Scoring Guidelines for Long Essay Question 3

Analyze the ways in which the public health movement and urban planning led to or resulted from a shift in social, political, and economic power at the end of the 19th century.

**Maximum possible points: 6**

### Comments on Question 3

This is a *causation* question because it requires you to explain how two events, the start of urban planning and the public health movement, resulted in or *caused* a specific outcome, the shift in social, political, and economic power at the end of the 19th century. Remember to describe causes of the shifts, indicating which factor was responsible for each shift—urban planning or the public health movement. Support your explanation of the reasons for the causes and effects of those shifts with specific supporting evidence.

Your essay must first explain that the first half of the century resulted in overcrowded cities full of people who, for the most part, lacked any political power. The conditions that led Marx and Engels to conceive of communism were rampant, with the workers oppressed and their conditions deplorable. From there you should explain how the implementation of public health laws and urban planning reduced overcrowding and unsanitary conditions but also helped the working classes develop a class consciousness as they lived and commuted together. These factors led the working classes to gain political power through the rise of republican forms of government, constitutional monarchies, and labor unions as a result of the urban planning and public health movements that made increased urbanization not only possible but desirable.

**A detailed rubric for this specific question follows to help you score your long essay response.**

### A. THESIS (0–1 total points)

**1 point:** The essay presents a thesis that makes a historically defensible claim and responds to all parts of the question. The thesis must consist of one or more sentences located in one place, either in the introduction or the conclusion.

**Special note:** The thesis *must* consist of one or more sentences located in the introduction or the conclusion of the essay. However, neither the introduction nor the conclusion is strictly limited to one paragraph.

Acceptable thesis statements create an argument that responds to the task. They describe the causes and/or explain the effects of the implementation of urban planning and the public health movement on the shift in political, social, and economic power during the second half of the 19th century and explain specific examples of reasons for those causes and effects.

The student must presents a thesis that directly addresses all parts of the question. The thesis must do more than restate the question.

**Acceptable thesis:** "Although most urban workers lived in filth and despair in 1850 Europe, the rise of the public health movement and the beginning of urban planning in Europe eventually resulted in increased sanitation and convenience of city life, a growing understanding of the plight of Europe's poor among other classes, as well as time spent in conversation during commutes on newly created public transportation. These factors all led to drastic changes in the social, political, and economic power structure of Europe by the end of the century, including moderate constitutional monarchies in Germany and Italy, a republic or two in France, a generally growing standard of living, and a growing social welfare system across the continent." (This thesis is acceptable because it is specific in its assessment of both causes, and it gives specific effects of the causes supported by specific evidence.)

**Unacceptable theses:**

- "The implementation of urban planning and public health movements resulted in many changes in the social, political, and economic structure of Europe by the end of the 19th century." (This is unacceptable because it does not state any specific social, political, or economic impacts.)
- "The implementation of public health laws and urban planning improved the lives of city dwellers in Europe by the end of the 19th century by giving them more sanitary lives, greater freedom of travel, and better incomes." (This is unacceptable because even though it gives specific social and possibly economic impacts, the political impacts are forgotten.)

## B. CONTEXTUALIZATION (0–1 total points)

**1 point:** The essay describes a broader historical context immediately relevant to the question.

## C. EVIDENCE (0–2 total points)

**1 point:** The essay develops and supports an argument that provides specific examples of evidence related to the topic of the question.

OR

**2 points:** The essay develops and adequately supports an argument about the question with specific and relevant evidence.

## D. ANALYSIS AND REASONING (0–3 total points)

**1 point:** The essay uses historical reasoning (e.g., comparison, causation, or CCOT) to frame or structure an argument that addresses the prompt.

OR

**2 points:** The essay demonstrates a complex understanding of the historical development that is the focus of the prompt, using evidence to corroborate, qualify, or modify an argument that addresses the question.

**Acceptable causation:**

- The essay explains how the public health movement led to more sanitary cities that drew more people to them.
- The essay explains how urban planning led to public transportation to relieve crowding, which then supported political movements and unionization as workers traveled together outside of work.
- The essay explains how better organized workers tried to gain political and economic power such as higher wages and voting rights.

**Unacceptable causation:**

- The essay is focused solely on either the public health movement or urban planning but not both.
- The essay is focused on a narrative and does not provide causation.
- The essay looks at causation of the changes to the social, political, and economic power structure of Europe during the second half of the 19th century but fails to account for them and/or provide detailed evidence for support.

Essays can earn the point(s) here without a stated thesis if a relevant argument that completes both tasks effectively emerges in the body of the essay. For example, an essay may be able to develop an argument that draws on the changes in the social, political, and economic power of Europeans, such as: growth of democratic power, rise of constitutions, nations unifying, rising standards of living, rising public education, healthier cities with low mortality rates, and rising wages. The essay must tie these changes to how they were caused by the implementation of urban planning and public health laws.

**Acceptable arguments:** The essay links the changes in social, political, and economic power in Europe at the end of the 19th century to the implementation of urban planning and public health laws, citing specific facts to support those arguments. The essay should tie these specific facts such as those stated above to the implementation of urban planning and public health laws.

**Unacceptable arguments:**

- The essay is focused solely on either the urban planning or public health laws but not on both.
- The essay examines the events of the end of the 19th century but does not specifically cite causation of evidence.

## Scoring Guidelines for Long Essay Question 4

Analyze the causes of the changing roles and rights of European women from 1900–2000.

**Maximum possible points: 6**

## Comments on Question 4

This is a *causation* question because it requires you to explain how changing gender perceptions, industrialization, the increase in individual rights, the world wars, and other factors resulted in or *caused* a specific outcome: the increased rights of women and a change in their roles in the family, the work world, the economy, and politics. Remember to describe causes of the shifts, indicating which was caused by each factor. Support your explanation of the reasons for the causes and effects of those shifts with specific supporting evidence.

The essay must first explain that women, who for the most part lacked any political and economic power at the start of the 20th century, gained power and individual rights. The causes of the increase in rights and the bending of gender roles must be examined. From there you should explain how those women of the 19th century, who were just starting to advocate for their rights and changing roles as suffragettes, later became feminists who advocated for rights and responsibilities equal to those of men; account for how and why society and governments granted them those rights. The impact of industrialization, the rise of communism, the efforts of women, the increase in individual rights in general, the world wars and women's role in them, the reduction of religiosity, the economic realities of the 20th century, and global geopolitics all helped women gain rights and equality. The strongest essays will also point out that women have not yet achieved full equality in the realms of pay and household responsibility in much of Europe today.

**A detailed rubric for this specific question follows to help you score your long essay response.**

### A. THESIS (0–1 total points)

**1 point:** The essay presents a thesis that makes a historically defensible claim and responds to all parts of the question. The thesis must consist of one or more sentences located in one place, either in the introduction or the conclusion.

**Special note:** The thesis *must* consist of one or more sentences located in the introduction or the conclusion of the essay. However, neither the introduction nor the conclusion is strictly limited to one paragraph.

Acceptable thesis statements create an argument that responds to the task. They describe the causes and/or explain the effects of changing gender roles and increased equality and rights for European women. They also explain specific examples that illustrate reasons for those causes and effects.

You must present a thesis that directly addresses all parts of the question. The thesis must do more than restate the question.

**Acceptable thesis:** "During the 20th century, women in Europe gained significant rights and were welcomed into spheres of influence that had eluded them for centuries. These included the armed forces, the working world, politics, and business. How females functioned in society, politics, and the economy drastically changed in large part due to the impact of industrialization, the rise of communism, the increase in individual rights in general, the world wars and women's role in them, the efforts of women, the reduction of religiosity, the economic realities of the 20th century, and global geopolitics. These all helped women gain rights and equality." (This thesis is acceptable because it is specific in its assessment of both causes, and it gives specific effects of the causes supported by specific evidence.)

**Unacceptable thesis:** "Women gained more rights and changed their gender roles during the 20th century because people became more open-minded." (This is unacceptable because it does not state any specific social, political, or economic causes of that change.)

## B. CONTEXTUALIZATION (0–1 total points)

**1 point:** The essay describes a broader historical context immediately relevant to the question.

## C. EVIDENCE (0–2 total points)

**1 point:** The essay develops and supports an argument that provides specific examples of evidence related to the topic of the question.

**OR**

**2 points:** The essay develops and adequately supports an argument about the question with specific and relevant evidence.

## D. ANALYSIS AND REASONING (0–3 total points)

**1 point:** Uses historical reasoning (e.g., comparison, causation, or CCOT) to frame or structure an argument that addresses the prompt.

**OR**

**2 points:** The essay demonstrates a complex understanding of the historical development that is the focus of the prompt, using evidence to corroborate, qualify, or modify an argument that addresses the question.

**Acceptable causation:**

- The essay explains how the First and Second World Wars required women to enter professions previously exclusive to men due to total war efforts on both sides.
- The essay explains how industrialization meant that most workers no longer needed brute strength, which left women on an equal basis with men in most professions.
- The essay explains how women organized themselves and their male allies to attain greater opportunities and voting rights.

**Unacceptable causation:**

- The essay is focused solely on either the public women's rights or women's roles but not on both.
- The essay is focused on a narrative and does not provide causation.
- The essay looks at causation of the changes to the social, political, and economic power structure of Europe during the 20th century but fails to account for them and/or to provide detailed evidence for support.

**Acceptable arguments:** The essay links the changes in social, political, and economic rights and power of women in Europe during the 20th century to the impact of industrialization, the rise of communism, the increase in individual rights in general, the world wars and women's role in them, the efforts of women, the reduction of religiosity, the economic realities of the 20th century, and/or global geopolitics.

**Unacceptable arguments:**

- The essay is focused solely on either women's rights or women's roles but not on both.
- The essay examines the events during the 20th century but does not specifically cite causation of evidence.

**This is the end of the scoring section. Once you have scored your answers, go back to the section on scoring the exam, plug your scores into the chart, and compute to get your score on your practice exam.**

# Index

Internal combustion engine, 204
International Monetary Fund (IMF), 351
International Trade Organization
    (ITO), 348
Interpretation, 12–13
Inventors, in Industrial
    Revolution, 212–213
Irish Question, 315
Iron Curtain, 332, 353–354
Iron Law of Wages (Ricardo), 210
Isolationism, 316
Israel, 348, 352
*Italia irredenta*, 293
Italian Renaissance, 60–64
    arts in, 62–63, 81
    banking, 61–62, 65
    city-states in, 60–61
    defined, 59–60
    humanism in, 63–64
    individualism in, 62
    Medici family in, 61–62
Italy
    fascism in, 313, 321–322
    First World War and, 293
    imperialism and, 267
    unification of, 243–244, 252
Ivan the Great, 136
Ivan the Terrible, 74, 136

**J**

Jacobins, 180
James I (King of Scotland), 128
James II (King of England), 130
Janissaries, 133
Jansenism, 135
Japan
    atom bombing of, 331
    First World War and, 292, 296
    militarism in, 242–243
    modernization in, 268–269
    in Second World War, 326–333
Jesuits, 104–105
Johnson, Boris, 352, 365
Joint-stock companies, 156
Joseph II (King of Austria), 161
Joyce, James, 317
July Revolution (France), 223, 227
June Days uprising (France), 223–224

**K**

Kafka, Franz, 317
Kant, Immanuel, 165
Kay, John, 203
Kellogg-Briand Pact (1928), 316, 323
Kempis, Thomas à, 66
Kennedy, Bobby, 349
Kennedy, Joseph, 350
Kepler, Johannes, 77, 162
Kerensky, Alexander, 299
Keynes, John Maynard, 295
Khrushchev, Nikita S., 251, 350–351
Kierkegaard, Soren, 271, 317
King, Martin Luther Jr., 349
King William's War, 135
Kipling, Rudyard, 272, 274
Kohl, Helmut, 249
Korean War, 354, 357

Kossuth, Louis, 230
*Kristallnacht*, 324
Kruger Telegram, 276
Kulak class, 301
*Kulturkampf*, 246

**L**

Labor
    industrialization and, 203–204
    Industrial Revolution and, 206–208
    slave-labor, 156
    union movement and, 222–223
Labour Party (Great Britain), 315
Lafayette, Marquis de, 223
La Fontaine, 134
*Laissez-faire*, 159, 209, 224, 253
*Last Supper* (Da Vinci), 63
Laud (Archbishop), 128
Lausanne Settlement, 316
Lawrence, T. E., 292, 295
League of Nations, 294, 315–316, 326
League of Schmalkalden, 103
*Lebensraum*, Nazi policy of, 323
Leeuwenhoek, Anton van, 161
Legislative Assembly (France), 179
Legislative Assembly (Prussia), 227
Leibniz, Gottfried Wilhelm, 163
Leisure time, 208
Leninist doctrine, 299
Lenin, Vladimir Ilyich, 251, 272, 274,
    297, 299
Leopold II (King of Belgium), 267
Leo X (Pope), 101, 103
Lespinasse, Julia de, 165
Less economically developed countries
    (LEDCs), 353, 359–360, 364
*Lettres de cachet*, 178
Liberal Empire (France), 224
Liberalism, 158, 210, 253
    Metternich and, 226
Liberal Party (Great Britain), 208, 315
*Liberty Leading the People*
    (Delacroix), 223
Lifestyles, demographic changes
    in, 201–202
List, Friedrich, 205
Literature, 127, 272–273, 317
Little Ice Age, 73, 75
Liturgy, 127
Livingstone, David, 267
Locarno Pact (1925), 316, 323
Locke, John, 151, 158, 166–167
Long essay questions (LEQs), 7, 28–32
    answers, 30
    interpretation, 26–28
    scoring, 28–29
Long Parliament, 128
Lorenzo the Magnificent. *See* Medici,
    Lorenzo the Magnificent
Lost generation, 316–317
Louis Napoleon Bonaparte (Napoleon
    III), 224, 242
Louis Philippe (King of France), 223
Louis XIII (King of France), 68, 123, 125
Louis XII (King of France), 67
Louis XI (King of France), 67

Louis XIV (King of France, Sun King),
    125, 133–135, 178
Louis XVI (King of France), 178, 180, 223
Louis XVIII (King of France), 223
L'Ouverture, Toussaint, 181, 185
Low countries
    Dutch revolt and, 131
    Renaissance in, 68
    war and conflict in, 74–75
Ludendorff, Erich, 323
*Lusitania*, sinking of, 293
Lutheranism, 101–102
Luther, Martin, 100–102
Lvov, Georgii (Prince), 299

**M**

Maastricht Treaty. *See* Treaty of
    Maastricht (1991)
MacArthur, Douglas, 331, 357
MacDonald, Ramsay, 315
Machiavelli, Niccolò, 64
Magellan, Ferdinand, 71
Maginot Line, 328
Magna Carta, 123
Maistre, Joseph de, 226
Malthus, Thomas, 209–210
Manchuria, Japanese invasion of, 326
Mandate system, 294, 296, 315
Manet, Eduard, 255
Mannerism (artistic movement), 82
Manorialism, 102
Manufacturing, Industrial Revolution
    and, 206
Many Faiths chart, 110
Mapmaking, 70
Marat, Jean Paul, 179
March Revolution (Russia), 298–299
Margaret (Princess), 131
Maria Theresa, 133, 161
Marie Antoinette, 180
Markets
    imperialism and expansion
        of, 265–266
    in Renaissance, 68
Marlowe, Christopher, 67, 127
Marshall, George, 347–348
Marshall Plan, 331–332, 347
Marston Moor, 129
Marxism, Russian Revolution and,
    297, 299
Marx, Karl, 209–212
Mary I, Queen of England, 104, 126
Masaccio, 63
Mass marketing, 204, 212
Mass production, 212
Mathematics, 65–66
Matisse, Henri, 255
Matthias (Bohemian king), 106
May, Theresa, 365
Mazarin (Cardinal), 125, 133–134
Mazzini, Giuseppe, 243
Media, in 20th century, 318
Medici, Catherine de', 68, 124, 133
Medici, Cosimo de', 62
Medici family, 61–62, 73
Medici, Giovanni de', 62